CRITICAL THINKING

JOHN HOAGLUND

FOURTH EDITION

VALE PRESS NEWPORT NEWS, VIRGINIA

7 6 5 4 3 2 1

Vale Press
P.O. Box 6519
Newport News VA 23606
valepres@erols.com

Cover Design by Chuck Haas

ISBN 0-916475-12-3

PREFACE TO THE FOURTH EDITION

This edition, like the previous, brings new material on statement relations and consistency analysis as well as argument analysis. At the same time we have attempted to honor requests of those using the text that we not make major changes.

The distinction of logical from hypothetical assumptions in Chapters Two—Four builds on earlier work. Chapter Two now has a treatment of what constitutes a statement relative to truth claims. Included are suggestions how to associate truth claims with material lacking them, e.g. phrases or questions, and an Exercise 2—3 dealing with this. New to Chapter Three is an emphasis on sources that prove consistent on analysis. Exercise 2—1 is now shorter with some new material. Exercise 3—1 now has two parts with many new problems. A number of new logical puzzles are added to the exercises in Chapter Four and the Critical Thinking Journal puzzles, including two truth-teller puzzles, which had been under-represented. There is new material on explanation in Chapter Five, and on the distinction of convergent from linked pertaining to evaluation in Chapter Seven. There is also new material on analyzing and evaluating compound arguments in Chapter Eight. This is accompanied by some new exercise material in Chapters Five—Seven and considerable material and a new progression from easier to more challenging in Exercise 8—1. One section in Chapter Nine that was not achieving its purpose was dropped, and this completes the important changes.

I am very grateful to a considerable number of Christopher Newport students whose Critical Thinking Journals yielded material for illustration and exercises. They are listed under "Sources" below. Colleagues and former students too have been generous in supplying me with ideas and material, with Stuart Smith being particularly helpful on logical puzzles. Among these are George Teschner, Kip Redick, Patrick Grace, Jeffrey Carr, Gary Sayre, Paul Gerder, Jessica Shumake, Scott Krasche, Lori Underwood, Alessandro Tomasi, and Steven Strehle. On matters of theory in critical thinking and informal logic

I have benefited greatly from discussions at meetings and conferences with James B. Freeman, Robert H. Ennis, Michael Scriven, Mark Weinstein, Ralph H. Johnson, J. Anthony Blair, Robert Pinto, Trudy Govier, Hans Hansen, Douglas Walton, Christian Plantin and Christopher Tindale. In particular, discussions with these Amsterdam School leaders have helped me better understand the social context in which argument and critical thinking occur: the late Rob Grootendorst, Frans van Eemeren, Franciska Snoeck Henkemans, and Peter Houtlosser. I am thankful for their help and encouragement.

PREFACE TO THE SECOND EDITION

Taking changes and added material into account, this is almost a wholly new textbook. Teaching critical thinking classes with Stephen N. Thomas' *Practical Reasoning in Natural Language* convinced me of the value of arrow diagramming for analyzing arguments in natural language. I have also adopted his basic argument patterns and his approach to teaching the difference of necessary and sufficient conditions. The influence of Thomas' work is evident from Chapter Six on, but it is also present on the concept of argument in Chapter Five. Teaching with Jack Meiland's *College Thinking*, particularly Chapters Three–Six, has similarly influenced the material on analyzing longer pieces of argumentative writing (Chapter Fifteen) and on the argumentative essay (Chapter Sixteen). Howard Kahane's pioneering work on analyzing extended arguments (Chapter Six of the current sixth edition of *Logic and Contemporary Rhetoric*) was also helpful with Chapter Fifteen.

On the conception of critical thinking, I owe much of the view taken here to writings, lectures, workshops and discussions with Robert H. Ennis, Richard Paul, Harvey Siegel, and Matthew Lipman. I have also learned from Stephen P. Norris, and from Mark Weinstein and John McPeck, especially when I did not agree with them.

On the enterprise of argument analysis and informal logic in its broader significance I owe most to Michael Scriven, though my debt to the work of and interaction with Ralph H. Johnson, J. Anthony Blair, and Trudy Govier is only marginally smaller. In recent years the books, articles, and discussions with James B. Freeman and Alec Fisher have been very helpful. On the informal logical fallacies, after the monograph of C. L. Hamblin, I have found most enlightenment in the prodigious group of writings by John Woods and Douglas N. Walton, which comprises articles singly and co-authored, textbooks, surveys, and monographs. The general dialogue background is explored and developed in the writings of Walton, Frans van Eemeren, Rob Grootendorst, and Nicholas Rescher. I have also consulted and benefited from fallacies-oriented textbooks by Johnson and Blair, Kahane, T. Edward Damer, Morris Engel, and Nicholas Capaldi.

I wish I could remember more specific contributions by my students, as I remember Mark Guzzi pressing me to distinguish assumptions from implications. Some stimuli like this are acknowledged in Sources and in the *Solutions Manual*, and sample work of these students is found in the two student argumentative essays as well as in the Sample Student Critical Thinking Journal.

Richard Raring contributed a detailed, helpful commentary on the first edition. Kip Redick produced a detailed critique of the entire second edition in typescript, as did Greg Rich of the first few chapters. I continue to benefit from discussions of both theoretical and teaching questions with my colleague George Teschner, and also with Kip Redick, formerly student and now my colleague at Christopher Newport University.

CONTENTS

CHAPTER THREE

Consistency and Assumptions 37

CHAPTER FOUR

Reasoning and Inference 59

PART TWO: A LOGIC OF ARGUMENTS 91

CHAPTER FIVE

Arguments 93

PART FOUR: CONTEXT 305

CHAPTER ELEVEN

CHAPTER TWELVE

PART FIVE: CONDITIONAL AND INDUCTIVE ARGUMENTS 391

CHAPTER THIRTEEN

CHAPTER SIXTEEN

Writing the Argumentative Essay 509

CHAPTER ONE

CRITICAL THINKING

Critical thinking is a practical reflective activity that has reasonable belief or action as its goal.
Robert H. Ennis

1. WHAT IS CRITICAL THINKING?

Critical thinking is a type of thinking. What is thinking? In the most general sense, anything that goes on in your mind is thinking. You may be fantasizing about winning the lottery or working a crossword puzzle; you may be saddened by the loss of a pet goldfish or watching a game show on TV; you may worry about paying the bills at the end of the month; you may be choosing among candidates in an election; or you may be elated at finally getting the promotion at work you have deserved for so long.

In the narrower sense—more closely allied to critical thinking—thinking is a goal-directed activity, one organized toward a certain goal or purpose. As a goal-directed mental activity, thinking might draw an inference from given information, such as that rain is approaching from the sound of thunder; it might detect an inconsistency between claim and fact, such as the claim that a certain toothpaste will enhance your sex appeal and the fact that you tried it without noticing any difference; it might assess an argument, such as that smoking cigarettes should be prohibited in federal buildings because even secondary smoke (that inhaled by non-smokers) kills 3,000 people a year; it may find an explanation, such as why the lamp doesn't turn on (not plugged in, bulb burned out); or it may solve a problem, such as using food coloring to brighten up a holiday punch that tastes fine but looks anemic. So this narrower range of thinking activities more closely related to critical thinking includes reasoning, inferring, creating and assessing arguments, finding explanations, and solving problems.

Critical thinking is reflective thinking. The critical thinker thinks (infers, reasons) reflectively. But what does it mean for thinking to be reflective in a way that tends to make it critical? Critical thinking is reflective in that it observes its own progress, evaluates each step to decide whether it is justified, and corrects its own errors. The critical thinker might originally have taken the thunderous sound for the sonic boom of a jet plane advancing beyond the speed of sound. But she ruled this out by the absence of the attending screeching sound of an accelerating jet, and also by being unable to see any plane in the sky. Then she confirmed the sound was thunder by spotting dark, menacing clouds on the horizon with heat lightning as well. Critical thinking is not perfect thinking because critical thinkers do make mistakes. But the self-observing and self-correcting nature of critical thinking means they make fewer mistakes than those who do not think critically.

Critical thinking is sometimes mistaken as negative thinking or destructive thinking. But look at the relation of critical thinking to belief. It is not the goal of critical thinking to destroy belief but to arrive at reasonable belief. Critical thinking is not a negative thinking as opposed to a positive or a creative thinking. It is a careful thinking as opposed to a sloppy or careless thinking. The critical thinker does ask questions, but she asks them in order to decide what is reasonable to believe. The critical thinker is obviously not so gullible that she believes everything she is told. But neither is she so skeptical that she believes nothing she is told. The critical thinker distinguishes reliable testimony from unreliable and weighs evidence to decide what is reasonable.

The critical thinker is self-reliant and aspires to a degree of independence or autonomy in her thinking. This does not mean that the critical thinker doesn't heed the opinions of others, or does not go beyond her own store of knowledge. She is not only open to new opinions and fresh evidence, the critical thinker actively seeks them out. Critical thinking is independent, autonomous thinking in the sense that it observes and improves itself. The critical thinker has already asked of her own position on a controversial topic the same questions a hostile critic would ask. She either improves her position to meet these objections, or relinquishes her position and searches for a better one. To hold a position critically is to have raised and responded to those objections that expose its weaknesses.

2. What Can Critical Thinking Do for Us?

Critical thinking can benefit us as persons, students, workers, consumers, and citizens. The first and foremost benefit we can anticipate from instruction in critical thinking is the discipline and improvement of our own minds. Our world is growing more rather than less complex, and it is becoming increasingly difficult to understand what is going on in it. Critical thinking helps us ask the important questions and seek answers to them. Before we can act rationally we need to know what we stand for in life, and for this it is essential that we know who we are. Self-knowledge can be the hardest knowledge to come by. The same reflective scrutiny that critical thinking teaches can be focused on our actions and values, and so help us attain self-knowledge. A disciplined mind can help put us in charge of our own lives.

Similarly a disciplined mind is of much value to us as students. The ability to draw out the implications of a given text and to detect inconsistencies is useful in any humanistic study, and in many other areas as well. An appreciation of the relevance of evidence to a claim is also valuable in every scholarly discipline. Critical thinking requires a versatile vocabulary, an appreciation of nuances of meaning, and some precision in the use of words. These features are again welcome in all disciplines. Critical thinkers also learn to state a thesis and advance arguments in support of it, and to consider and respond to objections to these arguments. This model critical thinking activity is especially valuable for pre-law and law students, debaters, and for students of philosophy and political science as well. These are some critical thinking abilities helpful to us as students.

Critical thinking and the communication skills that depend on it are increasingly in demand in the job market. After listening to one hundred Virginia employers tell of writing and speaking deficiencies in their newly hired employees, the authors of the study *Changing Job Skills in Virginia* ventured that "the whole business of interpersonal and technological skills really comes down to skills in logic and reasoning. If you can't reason, you can neither write nor speak." A fiercely competitive world market puts pressure on American business to get the most from its employees. Well paying jobs requiring modest skills are fewer and fewer in the American economy. Simple, repetitive manufacturing jobs are either being transferred to countries with labor costs substantially lower than ours, or they are being automated so that a high level of skill is demanded of the employee who carries them out. Thus a sound education in critical thinking helps both for the entry-level job, and in growing with the job to hold it securely. Further, many of today's jobs didn't exist ten or even five years ago, whereas many of today's workers were trained for jobs that are increasingly lost to technological advance, such as typesetting or stenography. Again a solid foundation in critical thinking contributes greatly to the flexibility needed to adapt and prepare for new careers.

As consumers, critical thinking helps us in at least two important ways. In our free market economy we are bombarded daily with hundreds of advertisements for products. Some of these products we may need, but others we surely don't. Critical thinking helps us evaluate the information we get about these products. Many ads give little or no factual information about their products that would allow a consumer to make an informed decision. Instead the advertisement makes an emotional or psychological appeal, which is often an attempt to escape the scrutiny of the thinking mind. Critical thinking helps us distinguish emotional appeals from useful information about a product. This leads to better decisions about whether we need the product, and whether this brand of the product is superior to other brands for our needs. Secondly, when we can't get the information about a product we need from ads, critical thinking helps us find sources of objective, factual information that will inform our decisions.

Finally, critical thinking is specially important in a nation with a democratic form of government where the welfare of the nation depends to a considerable extent on the ability of its citizens to understand complex issues, to articulate opinions on them, and to make decisions after having gathered and weighed the evidence. A basic principle of democracy is that the citizen who benefits from the protection and opportunities offered by the state shall share the burden of keeping the state functioning well. As Pericles, leader of Athenian democracy at its peak, recognized, it is not necessary for the success of a democracy that every citizen be capable of leadership in formulating public policy. Citizens have only to be able to judge policy and decide what lies in the public interest. For this, critical thinking attitudes and skills are of the utmost importance.

> *The very process of thinking is, of course, simply an inner conversation that goes on, but it is a conversation of gestures, which in its completion implies . . . [what] one thinks to an audience.*
> G. H. Mead

3. Critical Thinking—A Socratic Model

This book takes the Socratic method as a model critical thinking activity, a method named for the Athenian philosopher of the 5th century B.C. who invented it. Together with friends Socrates inquired into the nature of justice, friendship, beauty, courage, and other values important in our lives. When a friend explained courage as standing one's ground under attack, Socrates questioned whether standing one's ground against overwhelming odds would be courageous. He also questioned whether bearing a painful illness well is courageous. In this way he led others to reflect on inherited beliefs and to render them more clear and precise, or else abandon them and search for better ones. He served as a critic of their beliefs, for they learned from him what questions they had to ask and answer before they could hold their beliefs critically.

Once evidence or reasons are advanced in support of an opinion or belief, the result becomes an argument. The belief or opinion is the conclusion of the argument. The activity of analyzing whether the belief is actually supported by evidence or reasons is called argument analysis, and argument analysis is what this book is organized around. It is here conceived broadly to include recognizing an argument, clarifying it or establishing what is intended to support what, and evaluating it, deciding whether the claimed support is actually there.

Taking the Socratic method as a model critical thinking activity, you first learn to criticize the arguments and claims of others, then make the reflective twist of turning this criticism on your own arguments and claims. In a sense you learn to internalize the critic of your own position, or to ask of it the questions that would be asked by a penetrating critic like Socrates. You take the attitude toward your own position of someone who is considerably more skeptical of its merits than you may be initially. G. H. Mead refers to this internalizing the attitude of someone we're conversing with as a "conversation of gestures." Alternately, Richard Paul emphasizes the aspect of a dialogue between one and one's critic and calls it "dialogical thinking."

Writing the argumentative essay, the final project of the present text, clearly calls for this dialogue. In this essay you must raise and respond to serious objections to your own arguments. To write a good argumentative essay is to demonstrate that you can reflect on your own thinking, examine it closely, and improve it when needed. To do this is to think critically. So the argumentative essay is at the same time a challenge to the student to demonstrate what she has learned of critical thinking. It is the critical thinking activity in which the teaching techniques of this text culminate.

Many of the skills of critical thinking are taught here both in a more general sense and as they relate to argument analysis. The critical thinker must be able to distinguish fact from opinion. But this distinction also relates to recognizing argument and argument strategy because what people generally argue for are opinions rather than facts. We also need to distinguish reliable reports from erroneous ones in order to acquire sound information. But deciding how reliable a source is often helps us assess an argument by revealing how strong or weak is its foundation in fact. The critical thinker should also know the difference between necessary and sufficient conditions, and this knowledge promotes a better understanding of how some important conditional arguments succeed or fail.

> *The ideal critical thinker is habitually inquisitive, well informed, trustful of reason, open-minded, flexible, fair-minded in evaluation, honest in facing personal biases, prudent in making judgments, willing to reconsider, clear about issues, orderly in complex matters, diligent in seeking relevant information reasonable in the selection of criteria, focused in inquiry, and persistent in seeking results which are as precise as the subject and the circumstances of inquiry permit.*
>
> Consensus stated by Peter Facione

For the maximum benefit from this text, critical thinking dispositions as well as skills should be encouraged and exercised. The disposition to seek reasons can be exercised when you are challenged in class by another student or the instructor to give reasons for an interpretation or judgment. This disposition must be exercised in working on the Critical Thinking Journal where you must identify arguments in reading material of your own choosing. You must seek reasons in order to find arguments and also to support your choices. Dispositions to seek clear statements of questions and theses, as well as to remain relevant to the main point, are exercised in the longer and more independent writing projects, the analytical and argumentative essays. The instructor may break the class up into smaller groups for certain projects such as working logical puzzles, analyzing compound arguments, or assessing advertisements. Among the dispositions that can be encouraged this way are those to be sensitive to the feelings, level of knowledge, and degree of sophistication of others, and to consider seriously points of view other than one's own. This latter disposition is also exercised in writing the argumentative essay.

We start with some simple logical relations of statements. We need to learn when one statement implies another, or makes the other true, and also when one contradicts another, or makes it false. We will also learn to decide whether several statements can all be true together, in which case they are logically consistent, or whether they cannot and are inconsistent. Then we will study statements that are logically assumed by other statements, and also learn what it means to infer one statement from another. These logical and reasoning skills are introduced at a level to be accessible to all college students.

Study Questions

Section 1

1. Define critical thinking
2. Mention one variety of thinking as a goal-directed activity and illustrate it.
3. In what sense is critical thinking reflective?
4. How does critical thinking relate to negative thinking?
5. In what sense is critical thinking autonomous thinking?

Section 2

6. Name four ways in which critical thinking can benefit us.

Section 3

7. For what activity is Socrates best known?
8. What is an argument?
9. What is argument analysis?
10. Explain how the Socratic method is a model critical thinking activity.
11. State three traits of the ideal critical thinker.

Further Reading

Robert H. Ennis, "Critical Thinking: A Streamlined Conception," *Teaching Philosophy* Vol. XIV No. 1 (Mar. 1991), pp. 5–24. The latest version of the article most influential in defining critical thinking, lists and briefly explains the most important critical thinking dispositions and abilities.

Peter A. Facione, *Critical Thinking. A Statement of Expert Consensus for Purposes of Educational Assessment and Instruction* (Fullerton, CA 1990).

Alec Fisher and Michael Scriven, *Critical Thinking: Its Definition and Assessment* (Point Reyes 1997).

John Hoaglund, "Critical Thinking: A Socratic Model," *Argumentation* Vol VII (1993) pp. 291–311. Elaborates a Socratic model of critical thinking.

Matthew Lipman, *Thinking in Education* (Cambridge 1991). Stresses that critical thinking involves judgment, and that judgments are made according to criteria.

Stephen P. Norris and Robert H. Ennis, *Evaluating Critical Thinking* (Pacific Grove 1989).

Richard Paul, "Socratic Questioning," *Critical Thinking. What Every Person Needs to Survive in a Rapidly Changing World* (Rohnert Park 1990), pp. 1–6.

Harvey Siegel, *Educating Reason* (New York 1988). Equates critical thinking with rationality, and takes the critical thinker to be one appropriately moved by reasons.

PART ONE

A LOGIC OF STATEMENTS

CHAPTER TWO

SOME LOGICAL RELATIONS OF STATEMENTS

A foolish consistency is the hobgoblin of little minds
Ralph Waldo Emerson

1. INCONSISTENCY

Despite Emerson's comment we expect people to be consistent in their ideas and statements. His criticism appears directed at consistency pushed to an extreme, perhaps in insignificant details. But consistency is the norm for all of us—we value it and censure its opposite, inconsistency. For an illustration let's look in on a debate.

"But Melanie, that's an entirely different matter," urged Glenn. "Abortion is wrong because it is the destruction of human life. You can't respect human life and at the same time destroy it. The war in Vietnam is a completely separate and distinct issue. We're fighting that war to prevent the communists from dominating the whole earth. Our nation is committed to the war. Your friends and mine are sacrificing their blood and even their lives in it. You cannot be a loyal American and a patriot if you don't support the American position in Vietnam."

"Glenn, you can't be serious," Melanie rejoined. "You say one thing this minute and the opposite the next. What we are doing in Vietnam is destroying human life, at times with deadly efficiency. It would be idle to deny this, and it is to your credit that you don't even try. But here's the catch. If abortion is wrong because it destroys human life, then the war in Vietnam has got to be wrong also because it destroys human life too. It is logically inconsistent to say that abortion is wrong because it destroys human life, then turn around and say that the war in Vietnam—which also destroys human life—is right. If the destruction of human life is wrong in one case, then it has got to be wrong in the other too. You can't have it both ways."

Inconsistency—What is this fault Melanie accuses Glenn of? It is a logical fault of claiming that two or more statements are true which cannot be true together. Two statements are inconsistent if it is not possible for both of them to be true together. A person's beliefs are inconsistent when it is not possible for them all to be true together.

In our above glance at part of a debate at the time of the Vietnam War, Melanie accuses Glenn of inconsistency in his beliefs on the destruction of human life. Glenn believes that abortion is wrong because it is a case of destroying human life, and destroying human life is wrong. Its being a case of destroying human life is what makes abortion wrong. On the other hand he believes that U.S. participation in the Vietnam War is right. But the Vietnam War also destroys human life. So here is a case of destroying human life that is right (at least in his belief). Glenn's inconsistency can be stated in different ways. He is claiming that destroying human life is always wrong and that destroying human life is sometimes right. Or he is maintaining that destroying human life is both wrong and right.

Now let us look in on a murder trial. Raymond George has been charged with murder in the second degree for the stabbing death of his estranged wife Stella. Prosecution witnesses have testified that they heard Stella and a man shouting in her apartment on the night of the murder. One witness testified to seeing Raymond enter the building earlier in the evening. Other testimony indicates that Raymond and Stella argued a lot before separating, and that Raymond blamed Stella for the failure of their marriage. The coroner's report establishes that the woman's death occurred about 11:00 P.M. But now the defense produces a witness who positively identifies Raymond as the man he saw about 11:00 P.M. on the night of the murder at a nightclub over fifty miles away from Stella's apartment.

We sense in this case that an inconsistency has arisen. Where does it occur? And how? All of the evidence introduced by the prosecution (including the testimony) tends to place Raymond at the scene of the crime at an opportune time and with sufficient motive. It is all consistent. But then when the defense witness testifies to seeing Raymond fifty miles away at the time of the crime, the inconsistency arises. His testimony is inconsistent with the evidence previously introduced. This inconsistency should be perceived by any thinking person who is scrutinizing the evidence as it is introduced—the judge, members of the jury, and on-lookers like us.

The testimony has become inconsistent because it involves incompatible factual claims. Raymond cannot have been at the scene of the crime and fifty miles away at the same time. An inconsistency piques human curiosity—it needs explaining. In the present case as in many others there is more than one possible explanation. One or more of the witnesses may be lying. Or one of them may have made an honest mistake, thinking that she saw Raymond George enter the building when she actually saw someone who resembled him.

Although this second case of inconsistency is a fictitious one, you may judge for yourself whether it resembles those you encounter in real life. For our third case, which actually happened, we must travel to Schleswig, a city of 30,000 in north Germany. By the 1930s the Gothic wall paintings in the city's cathedral were in quite poor shape. In 1937, several painters who were acquiring a good reputation were hired to restore the medieval frescos. On completion their work was hailed by all as an outstanding success and documented by an expert art historian in a large art book. The original anonymous master of about 1280 A.D. was now reckoned among the great artists of the world.

Malskat's Turkey *Photo: Fred Ihrt*

Among the various animals depicted in the frescoes is one clearly identifiable by his prominent wattle and other features as a turkey gobbler. This immediately struck some observers as strange. The turkey is native to North America, and it is an accepted fact that it was unknown in Europe until specimens were brought back by Spanish navigators in the middle of the 16th century.

Now we encounter inconsistency in another guise. This time the inconsistency is neither in one person's statements expressing his beliefs, nor in the conflicting testimony of witnesses in a court of law. Our present case is the conflict of a claim with an accepted fact. The claim is that the restored frescos were all original works of an unknown 13th century master. The accepted fact is that turkeys are not native to Europe and were unknown there till the middle of the 16th century. This inconsistency will of course only be noticed by someone who is aware of the accepted fact. Some logicians think that inconsistencies involving incompatible facts should be classed as factual inconsistencies and distinguished from logical inconsistencies in a narrow, technical sense. But this will not be necessary for our purposes. All such inconsistencies have a logical component in that they become inconsistencies only for a mind that takes note of facts, compares them, and (sensing some incongruity) raises the question of consistency.

The inconsistency of the turkey in the 13th century German frescos was noticed as soon as the paintings were unveiled for the public. But the restored works were so greatly admired, and such was the authority of the art experts who praised them that for a number of years the inconsistency was addressed by adjusting the accepted fact. It was assumed that Viking voyagers to the New World had brought back turkeys so that the North German master could have become acquainted with them in the 13th century. But finally the frescos turned out to be forgeries. When the restorers cleaned away later overpainting, only the faintest traces of 13th century paint remained. Rather than disappoint their patron, the most technically gifted of the restorers, Lothar Malskat, painted new frescos in the medieval style. But his facility at painting in the medieval style exceeded his historical knowledge (as the turkey shows), and he eventually confessed to this and other forgeries.

Before we try our hand at detecting inconsistencies, we need to notice two cases that are sometimes mistaken for logical inconsistencies but really are not. Mrs. Bolden, a neighbor just returned from a stay at Nag's Head, is telling us of her vacation activities while her son Bill mows their lawn.

> "It was a wonderful week. There was only one overcast day with a few drops of rain. We spent a lot of time at the beach, and Bill went surfing every day. (shouts) Oh Bill, be careful near the flower beds! You've already ruined two marigolds. Now, where was I? Oh yes. Susan wanted to try hang gliding at Jockey Ridge. We let her, even though it seemed pretty dangerous. But we insisted on her taking lessons. She said it was scary but exciting."

Mrs. Bolden does indeed change the subject abruptly as she directs her words to her son instead of us. But this does not constitute a logical inconsistency because it is possible for all of her statements to be true together. Statements are logically inconsistent only when it is not possible for them all to be true together. If you were unaware of the context of her statements, you might allege that she was inconsistent because she didn't stick to the point. But statements that don't fit together very well are different from statements that cannot be true together. Only the latter are *logically* inconsistent.

The other case that is sometimes mistaken for logical inconsistency is that of an abrupt shift of style or tone of speech. Suppose you encounter the following directions in an auto maintenance manual:

> Remove the old battery from your car with caution. First loosen the nut on the clamp end of the negative cable. Then spread the clamp and remove it. Don't touch metal with your wrench or you'll get a shock. Remove the positive cable clamp the same way. Take the wing nuts off the long bolts holding the battery to its support plate. Lift the old battery up and out. Maintain the top battery surface on a horizontal plane as tilt toward the verticle releases acid whose caustic action produces severe skin inflammation and destroys apparel.

The language of these instructions is simple and straightforward but for the final sentence. It is scholarly and Latinate, and it seems labored and unnecessarily difficult. One way of describing this would be to say that it is inconsistent with the rest of the text. Something like "Don't tilt the battery or you'll spill acid and burn your skin" would be more appropriate. Again this can be described as an inconsistency or shift of style. But it is not a *logical* inconsistency because it is possible for all of the statements to be true together. Our interest here is in logical inconsistencies alone.

Any two or more statements are either logically consistent or logically inconsistent. There is no other possibility: these alternatives jointly exhaust the possibilities. Since any two statements are either related in meaning or not, there is an asymmetry of meaning and consistency. Statements must be related in meaning in order for them to be logically inconsistent.

A. Raymond George was at the scene of the crime at 11:00 PM.
B. Raymond George was fifty miles away from the scene when the crime was committed.
C. There is a MacDonalds on the corner of 3rd Avenue and Maple.

Statement A can be inconsistent with B—they are related in meaning. But neither A nor B can be inconsistent with C—they are not related in meaning.

Statements do not have to be related in meaning to be logically consistent with each other. For instance, Statement C is consistent with A and B, even though it is not related in meaning to them. Statements that are related in meaning can be consistent with each other as well as inconsistent.

D. Stella worked as a manicurist at Beulah's Hair Gallery.

Statement D is related in meaning to A and B (Stella is the crime victim) and consistent with both.

Now we will get some practice at detecting inconsistencies.

EXERCISE 2—1: DETECTING INCONSISTENCIES

Decide whether each of the following passages is logically consistent or inconsistent. For the inconsistent passages, point out which statements cannot be true together, and why. In explaining why, try to interpret the source as containing two statements that obviously cannot be true together. Inconsistencies should be rather obvious. Do not press your analysis to the point of finding inconsistencies in every case. Answers to starred problems are given at the end of the book.

1. The great French painter Camille Corot brought a certain ethereal naturalness to his landscapes. Over a long productive life (1796-1875)

his total output of somewhat fewer than 2000 canvases dwarfs the 30 or so meticulous genre pieces by Vermeer. The peculiar charm of his vision is appreciated particularly in the U.S. In fact, there are over 3000 Corots in American collections alone.

2. The speed of light is an absolute limit—nothing can move faster. Except that, on some occasions, light itself moves faster than the speed of light.

3. In the kitchen, he found Cathy, red-faced, drinking her second cocktail; wisps of hair protruded from the brown bun at the nape of her neck; there was a rich smell of burning from the oven, where the chocolate bread pudding had bubbled over.

Mary McCarthy, *The Groves of Academe* (New York 1963), p. 167.

*4. He sat down facing the scaffold erected for the leader of the insurgents. Already the hangman has drawn the sword and is preparing to strike the blow. "Stop," said the duke, "take the bandage from his eyes and help him up."

Johann Huizinga, *The Waning of the Middle Ages* (Harmondsworth 1968), p. 69.

5. A Mexican schoolteacher is suing Pepsico Inc. and a grocery chain after finding rat parts in a can of Diet Pepsi she was drinking. Maria Del Consuelo Lazaro . . . went to a hospital, complaining of abdominal pain, diarrhea and vomiting . . . Federal investigators confirmed rat parts were in the can, but found no health problems at the Orange County Pepsi-Cola distributor where it had originated.

Daily Press, Oct. 21, 1994.

6. With interest rates at historic lows, now is an excellent time to refinance your student loans. Everyone paying an annual rate of 5% or more should seize this opportunity. It will significantly reduce the total interest you pay over the lifetime of the loans. Under current regulations, if you have previously consolidated two or more student loans you are not allowed to refinance.

7. (Notice on an electricity pylon in Sussex, England)
Touching this pylon means instant death. Anyone doing so will be subject to prosecution.

Malcolm Acock, *Informal Logic. Examples and Exercises* (Belmont 1985), p. 207.

8. In nineteen hundred, when she was twenty-six, Florence walked out through the cabin door. She had thought to wait until her mother, who was so ill now that she no longer stirred out of bed, should be buried—but suddenly she knew that she would wait no longer, the time had come.

James Baldwin, *Go Tell It on the Mountain* (London 1954), p. 84.

9. Unlike the runes of prehistoric Scandinavia and the hieroglyphs of ancient Egypt, the writing of the early Indus valley civilization has never been deciphered by linguists. Much has been learned about the commerce of this latter civilization by archeologists reading seals in Indus script recovered from digging at sites like Harappa (in today's Pakistan).

10. The hot unlivable interior of the earth reveals itself to research submarines that descend a mile and a half to the edge of deep holes in the sea bottom, where open vents spew superheated seawater in plumes from chimneys in the earth's crust. This is extremely hot water under extremely high pressure, with temperatures near 600° Fahrenheit. In such heat life cannot exist. Proteins and DNA fall apart, enzymes melt away, anything alive dies instantly. The possibility of life on Venus has been ruled out because of its comparable temperatures. . . . Baross and Deming recently discovered thriving colonies of bacteria in water taken directly from these deep-sea vents. When sealed under pressure and heated to 480°F, these bacteria not only survive but reproduce themselves enthusiastically.

Adapted from an essay on new scientific discoveries.

11. (Benito Mussolini writes in the newspaper of the Italian Fascist party in early 1920.)

Down with the state in all its forms, the state of yesterday, today, tomorrow. The bourgeois state and the socialist state. For us, the last champions of individualism, there remains in the face of the gloomy present and an awful tomorrow nothing but an admittedly absurd but always consoling religion: anarchy.

(Mussolini writing in the same newspaper, *Il Popolo D'Italia*, later the same year.)

Everything for the state, nothing against the state, nothing outside the state.

Quoted in Evert Vedung, *Political Reasoning* (Beverly Hills 1982), p. 159.

12. (When Perkins, a London chemist, invented the first analine dye in 1856, its color mauve, a shade of purple, swiftly conquered fashions in Europe.)

Perkin discovered that his method of making mauve was being copied throughout Europe, and was being used to make other colours to meet new demands for the latest fashion trends, particularly the new lines of walking dresses and women's sports costumes for croquet and tennis. Mauve, and the other aniline dyes it inspired, combined with new directions in fashion in ways that even the most ambitious dyemaker could never have imagined. No wonder *Punch* [a London weekly] and traditionalists disapproved: for they were witnessing an early show of the female independent consumer.

Simon Garfield, *Mauve. How One Man Invented a Color that Changed the World* (New York 2001), p. 69.

13. Five motorcycle riders have been killed in traffic accidents during this year's Harley-Davidson rally, the most in seven years at the annual event.

The latest killed was Donald L. Ashford, 49, of Aberdeen, Md., who died at a hospital Friday after running off a road and striking his head on the pavement.

Law enforcement officials say there isn't a common thread among the wrecks this year. "It's just the crowd." said Highway Patrol Trooper 1st Class Ashley Mew. "And most of the ones who have been fatally injured were not wearing helmets."

Associated Press, Myrtle Beach, SC 2003.

14. From a distance, the White Stripes look like formalist, their music and overall style governed by a series of considered limitations. They're not only two, guitar and drums, they're both named White; they dress only in red, white and black; they proclaim affinity for blues, country, American roots music and pre-1965 recording technology.

. . . the best of Jack White's screaming guitar solos in the band's show at the Hammerstiem Ballroom . . . were done with a digital whammy pedal, which lets his guitar swoop up into higher octave with a needlelike, pitiless *whinggg*! Ditto for the solos on the band's fourth record, "elephant" . . . Pedals weren't made until the early 90's and are favored by certified guitar heroes like Steve Vai and Tom Morello, not antiheroes like Mr. White.

15. Most recent theories of the origin of the universe agree that it began with the explosion and rapid expansion of an extremely dense hot point, commonly referred to as the 'big bang.' Today's universe continues to expand. But how did such large structures as the galaxies—great batches of 100 billion stars—come to be created? This is a most perplexing question.

Astronomy tells us that such glowing galaxies are immersed in dark veils, and cosmologists theorize about just what this dark matter—known only by its gravitational effects—might be. According to one theory the dark matter is cold, moves far slower than the speed of light, and comprises theoretical entities known as axions and photinos. Computer models of the gravitational pull of cold dark matter on ordinary matter locate the formation of the first galaxies about 10 billion years ago. According to another theory the dark matter is hot and composed of neutrinos moving near the speed of light. Computer models of their gravitational force locate the formation of the galaxies even more recently.

2. IMPLICATION

Ken and Wally are discussing a proposed regulation that would make used-car dealers tell customers of any major defects of cars they were thinking of buying.

"Nobody could ever make a living selling used cars," complained Wally.

"Oh, I don't know," replied Ken. "People need wheels, and a lot of 'em can't afford to buy a new car."

"Would you buy a car you liked if the salesman told you that the compression was down and it would probably need a valve job in 10,000 miles?"

"I might, depending on the price, how much use I was likely to get out of it before the valve job had to be done, and the cost of the valve job."

"I still think it should be up to the buyer to fend for himself. In a free country the rule of the market is: Let the buyer beware. You shouldn't treat adults like children who need protecting all the time."

"Wally, there's some justice to what you say, and I don't object to it as much as I object to what it implies. For it clearly implies that the law should help the unscrupulous used-car dealer. Some used-car dealers are honest—maybe they hope to get you back as a customer, or maybe they hope you'll tell your friends you got a good deal. Whatever the reason, some of these dealers are honest. The effect of this regulation would be to force unscrupulous competitors to clean up their act. By opposing it, you're making it harder for the honest used-car dealer to stay in business."

. . . Implications take us beyond the literal meaning of a discourse to its broader meaning . . .

One thing we notice about this exchange right away is that Wally doesn't say that the unscrupulous dealer ought to be helped. He is accused of implying it. What does it mean to imply something? Implication is a logical relation of statements such that one being true makes the other true. Can a person fairly be held responsible not so much for what he says as for what his statements imply? The implications of a statement, when we know or assume it is true, are whatever other statements are made true by it.

A statement does not occur in a vacuum. It occurs in a context, in a situation comprising one or more persons, and it refers beyond itself to objects, people, actions, events, and other extra-linguistic things. Viewed in this context, in relation to what has gone before and what is to come, a statement sends forth suggestions about other statements. We say that it implies those other statements it makes true, and we refer to those other statements as its implications.

For example, let us take this statement:

A. The oven has been on five minutes.

Here are some statements in the area of our immediate interest that are made true or implied by Statement A:

B. The oven is hot.

C. The oven is ready for the pizza.

A number of other statements are made true also, statements that we could be interested in under special circumstances:

D. The electricity is still on. (It wasn't knocked out in the thunderstorm.)

E. That puzzling unpleasant odor must be burning grease remnants.

In the case where Statement A makes Statement B true, we say that Statement A implies Statement B, and that Statement B is an implication of Statement A.

In ordinary usage "imply" is often used to mean something that is hinted at or only suggested:

I realize you didn't *say* you'd attend, but you certainly did *imply* it.

A person who suggests or hints at something is often not putting forth a very strong truth claim for the statement:

I merely said I'd come if nothing more important came up, and an urgent matter arose.

In logic, the bond between the two statements is a strong one. If A implies B, then it is unusual (but not impossible) to find A true and B false. In most cases, where "The oven has been on five minutes" is true, "The oven is hot" will be true also. We might encounter a circumstance where A is true but B isn't. Perhaps the oven has been on for five minutes but the fuse is blown so the oven isn't hot. Of course someone could always object that because the fuse was blown, the oven was never really on in the first place.

Statements must be related in meaning for them to be related by implication. It is not the case (as some formal logics hold) that any given true statement implies any other. It is entirely possible for two statements to be true because they correspond to two different facts *without* there being a relation of implication between them. Take these two:

F. The star Sirius is 8.7 light years from the earth.

G. A misdemeanor is a less serious offense than a felony.

Both F and G are true, but they are about quite different matters, and there is no relation of implication between them.

Statements that are related by implication must be logically consistent with each other. When we say that Statement A implies Statement B, we are claiming that A's being true *makes* B true. In order for A to make B true (for A to imply B), it must be possible for them to be true together (A must be consistent with B).

How might a writer claim that a relation of logical implication does hold? In "How Many Species are There?" it is reported how scientists extrapolate from known species to species yet to be discovered. There are more small animals than large, and one can generalize about the ratios of species. If you count the number of species of animals down to a certain body length, there will be 100 times as many species averaging 1/10 of this body length. This ratio holds for creatures as small as one centimeter (about 2/5 of an inch) in body length.

> If the same relationship holds for the tiniest creatures visible to the naked eye—those about a millimeter long—then known numbers of animals such as mammals, reptiles, and amphibians imply a worldwide total of about 10 million species of all land-dwelling animals.

This claim of implication is based on the assumption that going to animals 1/10 the length yields 100 times as many species.

H. There are about 100,000 known species of land animals one centimeter in length or longer.

This implies:

I. [There is] "a worldwide total of about 10 million species of all land-dwelling animals."

The claim that A implies B can mean two different things, depending on two different senses of "imply."

Sense 1. Statement A being true makes Statement B true.
Sense 2. The meaning of B lies implicit in A.

A meaning lies implicit when it is there but at least partially concealed or hidden away. It is not stated outright or explicitly. The following case poses a problem for a logic of statement relations.

J. Yosemite is filled with natural wonders and beauties.

K. Yosemite is filled with natural wonders and beauties.

J implies K in Sense 1. It is not possible for J to be true and K false because both state the same thing. But J does not imply K in Sense 2. The meaning of K is stated explicitly in J rather than being implicit or hidden away. The question how a statement relates to itself forces us to choose Sense 1 and to set Sense 2 aside. J implies K when the two are identical, even though no hidden or implicit meaning is being drawn out.

3. CONTRADICTION

. . . Do I contradict myself? Very well then, I contradict myself.
(I am large, I contain multitudes.)
Walt Whitman

We ordinary mortals cannot be as cavalier about contradictions as the great American poet. An example may illustrate how serious a contradiction is.

"I agree," conceded Chris, "the latest news is not all that good. Housing starts are down, new car sales are down, and net tonnage at the port has dropped too. But I still don't think the local economy is in all that bad a shape."

"You must be kidding," Beth persisted. "The only thing up is unemployment."

"All right, retail sales are still sluggish, but the rate of decline has slowed. And even though motel and tourist attractions are down a lot from a year ago, the decline from last month is slight. To me, all the evidence indicates that we're beginning to bottom out. Basically we are talking about a healthy

> economy."
>
> "Let's face it, Chris, you're a hopeless optimist. How can you agree that all the indicators are down, then turn around and claim that the economy is doing well? Why that's a flat contradiction! These indicators are the only way we have of judging the performance of the economy. So what you're really saying is that the economy is down in all areas but it's up on the whole."

Beth accuses Chris of committing a contradiction. What is a contradiction? A contradiction is a logical relation between two statements such that when one of the statements is true, the other must be false. We say the one statement contradicts the other. Contradiction resembles inconsistency, and as we shall soon discover, the analysis of statements that seem inconsistent often turns up a contradiction. Inconsistency is often thought of as involving several statements, though we do say sometimes that two statements are inconsistent.

Why is it bad to commit a contradiction? A contradiction is a logical blunder in which you take away with one breath what you have just said with another. If your writing contains a contradiction, this means at least that you are careless or worse, that you understand only imperfectly what you are writing about. For example, a reviewer of a book on Winston Churchill's post-World-War II political activity charges author Klaus Larres with contradictions.

> On occasion . . . Larres contradicts himself, some times on the same page; he remarks upon "Churchill's vacillations about Europe," and a few lines later comments on Churchill's own deeply held convictions regarding the shape of post-war Europe. Churchill "needed to avoid American domination of Europe after the war," but his main worry was that after the war the Americans would take their troops home from Europe. There are other contradictory statements in this otherwise valuable and serious tome.
>
> Review by John Lukas of *Churchill's Cold War*
> in *The New Republic* (Jan. 13, 2003), p. 36.

It is often said that contradictions destroy the possibility of rational communication. But we are unlikely to encounter people uttering outright contradictions like "It is both raining and not raining" or "The cap is both red and not red." Far more often a person commits a contradiction because he doesn't fully understand what he is talking about, and the contradiction is sometimes concealed from both speaker and listeners until it is brought out by analysis.

In the case of a contradiction we start out with a statement we take to be true, then a second statement contradicts it:

> A. The keys are on the sideboard.
> B. No, I have them in my pocket.

The same keys cannot be both on the sideboard and in a pocket at the same time. So if A is true, B must be false, and vice versa.

We can recognize that two statements are contradictory without knowing which of them is true and which false:

> C. The earth's orbit around the sun is circular.
> D. The earth's orbit is elliptical.

In the early modern era Statement C was believed to be true. Today there is far more evidence to support Statement D, and its being true makes C false. As this example shows, we can determine that two statements are contradictory without knowing which is true and which false. We know they are contradictory when one being true makes the other false.

For there to be a contradiction in the logical sense, we must have two statements such that one's being true makes the other false. "Contradict" is sometimes used in a broader sense to mean "deny" or "oppose." This goes back to the Latin roots *contra* and *dicere*, meaning "to speak against." In this broader sense all three of the following statements mean roughly the same.

> I know how to make this business profitable, and I will not be contradicted.
> I know how to make this business profitable, and I will not be gainsaid.
> I know how to make this business profitable, and I will not be denied.

Such opposition does not constitute a logical contradiction, however. From the logical standpoint, it is only that special opposition of meanings where one statement's being true makes another false that constitutes a contradiction.

As with implication and inconsistency, statements must be related in meaning for them to be contradictory. So not every case of one statement being true and another false is a case of logical contradiction. For example:

> E. Warsaw is the capital of Poland.
> F. Gold dissolves in sulfuric acid.

Here E is true and F false. But it is not a case of contradiction because the statements are unrelated in meaning. The first is true because it corresponds to a fact, and the second is false because it does not correspond to one. Statements are only contradictory when one being true makes the other false.

4. Truth Claims and Assumptions

To seek inconsistent statements is to look for statements that cannot be true together, and similarly implication and contradiction involve relations of truth and falsity among statements. But what counts as a statement? And can only statements be related as implication or contradiction?

A statement is a piece of discourse claimed by someone to be true or false. This means that for the claim to be appropriate, the piece of discourse must be capable of being true or false. Logicians frequently refer to the truth value of a statement (true or false), or sometimes consider what types of discourse can be bearers of truth. Two candidates readily pass muster. A complete sentence can be a statement.

> Tiny air bubbles trapped in ice hundreds of feet below the Greenland surface can reveal to scientists the composition of the atmosphere thousands of years ago.

The only other possibility is for a statement to be an independent clause, of which the following sentence contains two:

> She has forgotten the key, but she was able to get the locked door open by using her VISA card.

A dependent clause by itself does not make a truth claim. So it is not a statement and cannot stand in logical relation to other statements. Consider this relative clause.

> A. After she waded across the rock-bottomed stream . . .

As stated, it is incomplete and cannot be true or false. But suppose we know the entire statement in which it functions as a temporal clause.

> B. After she waded across the rock-bottomed stream, she removed her boots and stockings to dry them in the sun.

We notice that this entire statement cannot be true unless the following statement is true.

> C. She waded across the rock-bottomed stream.

This statement is a *logical assumption* of statement B—it must be true for statement B to be true. We might say that C is what the dependent clause of B, minus the adverb of time *after* asserts. In a sense C is equivalent to part of B, the part that must be true if the main clause of B is to be true. A similar analysis can be given of the following participle phrase.

> D. Having waded across the rock-bottomed stream . . .

More than one statement is logically assumed by B. For example:

E. The stream has a rock bottom.
F. She can wade.

Sometimes a phrase is sufficiently detailed for us to determine what is logically assumed, even in the absence of context.

G. The porthole above the chest in the stateroom on the starboard side of the fifth deck

The phrase cannot become part of any true statement unless the following statement is true.

H. There is a porthole above the chest in the stateroom on the starboard side of the fifth deck.

In this sense H is an assumption of G.

Similarly "the old oaken bucket" cannot fit into a true statement without this statement being true.

I. There is an old bucket made of oak.

The model statement from the standpoint of truth claims is a declarative sentence.

J. Pop idols of the 1950s and 60s like Elvis and the Beatles are still listened to today.

It is clear that if people still play the works of these artists, J is true. If they do not, it is false. We are in no doubt about what the truth claim is.

But there are many uses of language that interest us where no similar clear truth claim is made. *Questions*, for example.

K. Are any votes still left uncounted?

K by itself is neither true nor false. But for K to be appropriately used in a context, each of the following statements is assumed.

L. People have voted in an election or referendum.
M. At least some of the votes have been counted.

They are rightly called logical assumptions of the appropriate use of the question.

The following *request* is another case.

N. Would you please save a seat for me?

The following are logical assumptions of the appropriate use of this request.

O. Speaker and addressee are attending an event or function.
P. The addressee will arrive before the speaker.

For a final example, notice the following *promise.*

Q. I won't disappoint you this time.

For this promise to be appropriate to the circumstances, the following is logically assumed.

R. I have disappointed you in the past.

Similarly much discourse that lacks truth claims logically assumes discourse that does make truth claims. This is important for us to know in itself as well as for the type of consistency analysis we will learn to carry out now. For it means that a logical assumption can take the place in an analysis of a piece of discourse that does not make a truth claim.

SUMMARY

Statements are inconsistent when it is not logically possible for them all to be true together.

Statements are consistent when it is possible for them all to be true together.

One statement implies another when it makes that other statement true. We may know that the first statement is true, or we may assume that it is true.

One statement contradicts another when it makes that other statement false. We can determine that statements are logically contradictory without knowing which statement is true and which false.

Statements must be related in meaning for them to be implications or contradictions. They must also be related in meaning to be inconsistent. It is not necessary for statements to be related in meaning for them to be consistent.

Implications must be consistent with one another. An implication is made true by another statement. In order for it to be made true by that statement, it must be possible for it to be true with that statement.

Only a statement in the indicative mood can participate in logical relations. Only it makes the needed truth claim, i.e., only it can be true or false. Although phrases, dependent clauses, questions and the like are ruled out, they may carry logical assumptions. A logical assumption is a statement that must be true for some other statement to be true, or for some sentence fragment or non-indicative language to find an appropriate use. The assumption is a statement that makes a truth claim.

Study Questions

Section 1: Inconsistency

1. When are two statements logically inconsistent?
2. How do Glenn's statements appear inconsistent?
3. In what way is the testimony at the murder trial inconsistent?
4. How does the cathedral wall painting involve inconsistent claims?
5. Give an example of two statements that are logically inconsistent.
6. Describe two kinds of inconsistency that are not logical inconsistency but might be mistaken for it.

Section 2: Implication

7. How are two statements related when one implies the other?
8. Give an example of one statement logically implying another.
9. How strong is the bond between two statements related by implication?
10. Explain the senses in which a statement does and does not imply itself.

Section 3: Contradiction

11. Explain what a logical contradiction is and give an example.
12. Can we know that two statements are logically contradictory without knowing which is true? Illustrate.

Section 4: Truth Claims and Assumptions

13. How does a statement make a truth claim?
14. What types of discourse make truth claims?
15. Give examples.
16. What types do not?
17. Give examples.
18. What is a logical assumption?
19. Give an example.

General

20. When one statement implies another, what other logical relation must hold between them?
21. Statements must be related in meaning for them to be logically related as ________?
22. In which of our four logical relations can statements stand to each other when they are not related in meaning

EXERCISE 2—2: IMPLICATIONS AND CONTRADICTIONS

Part A. Single Statements

For each of the following problems, assume that Statement A is true. When Statement A being true *makes* Statement B true, then A implies B. When Statement A being true *makes* B false, then A contradicts B. When Statement A being true does *not* make Statement B false, we say that A and B are consistent. Decide which pairs are contradictions and which are cases of implication. Identify those that are neither contradiction nor implication as consistent, but bear in mind that all pairs that are implications are consistent too.

1. A. Spain is a European country.
   B. Spaniards are Europeans.

*2. A. Much summer foliage is green
   B. The Japanese maple has purplish leaves in the summer.

3. A. Heavy cigarette smokers are more likely to die of heart disease or develop lung cancer than non-smokers.
   B. It is safe to smoke cigarettes.

4. A. Some cases of rabies are not fatal.
   B. It is possible to catch rabies and still survive.

5. A. Only authorized personnel can enter.
   B. Anyone is allowed to go in.

6. A. In soccer only the goalie is allowed to touch the ball with her hands.
   B. In basketball you're not allowed to kick the ball.

7. A. The violin can produce a beautiful sound.
   B. A violin will sound good no matter who plays it.

8. A. All Masons are members of a secret fraternal organization.
   B. Smith is a Mason, but he doesn't belong to any secret fraternal organization.

*9. A. Some aptitude tests are culturally biased.
   B. All aptitude tests are culturally neutral.

10. A. Only buses are permitted in the right lane.
    B. Buses are permitted only in the right lane.

11. A. Asbestos has been strongly linked to a fatal form of cancer.
    B. Exposure to asbestos can be dangerous to your health.

*12. A. The photo shows the Golden Gate bridge.
    B. The photo was taken in California.

13. A. The long drought has ruined the corn crop in the Southeast.
    B. It is likely the price of corn and corn products will rise.

14. A. Water is a colorless and odorless liquid.
    B. This well water looks dirty, and it leaves a rust-colored stain when it runs off or dries on concrete.

15. A. *Gone With the Wind* is one of the most popular movies of all time.
    B. Not many people have seen *Gone With the Wind.*

16. A. Rubber is a poor conductor of electricity.
    B. Rubber does not conduct electricity well.

17. A. Eskimos adapt to cold by burning more energy to raise body temperature and produce high blood flow in their limbs.
    B. Australian aborigines adapt to cold by burning less energy and allowing body temperature in their legs and feet to drop during sleep.

18. A. Today a computer smaller than a typewriter operates faster and stores more information than the room-sized UNIVAC, the first commercially available computer.
    B. Today's computers are more efficient than those of the 1950s.

19. A. The eye responds to bright light by contracting the pupil.
    B. Your pupils expand when you look at the camera in flash photography.

20. A. In early spring the young queen bumblebee flies from her winter hideaway in search of a place to start a new colony.
    B. It is aerodynamically impossible for an insect of the body weight and wing size of the bumblebee to fly.

Part B. Contexts

Assume that all of the statements in the quotation are true. Decide whether each of the following statements is implied (made true), contradicted (made false), or left undecided by (is consistent with) what is said in the quotation. Recall that statements that are implications must be consistent too.

A. When historians of a future age sift through 20th century archives in search of the great scientist-humanitarians of our time, the name Norman Borlaug will be high on the list. His work as a plant geneticist culminated in the development of sturdy, short-stemmed wheat varieties that have helped check the specter of starvation in many of the lesser developed countries. He was awarded the Nobel Peace Prize in 1970 for his leadership role in the "Green Revolution."

Reprinted from *Du Pont Context.*

1. The wheat strains produced by Borlaug survived and produced high yields where other wheat strains failed.
2. It's not possible for the same person to be both a great scientist and a great humanitarian..
3. Even though he has developed improved varieties of wheat, Borlaug himself doesn't care much for bread.
4. Borlaug's work has helped bring many people closer to starvation, especially in the lesser developed countries.
5. Borlaug has been recognized for a significant contribution to world peace."

B. In sundry of these storms the winds were so fierce and the seas so high, as they could not bear a knot of sail, but were forced to hull for divers days together. And in one of them, as they thus lay at hull in a mighty storm, a lusty young man called John Howland, coming upon some occasion above the gratings, was, with a roll of the ship, thrown into the sea; but it pleased God that he caught hold of the topsail halyards which hung overboard and ran out at length. Yet he held his hold (Though he was sundry fathoms under water) till he was hauled up by the same rope to the brim of the water, and then with a boat hook and other means got into the ship again and his life saved.

William Bradford, *Of Plymouth Plantation.*

1. John Howland was thrown overboard and drowned.
2. On some of the days at sea the winds were so strong that they couldn't run up any sail at all.
3. Howland came up from below during the storm because the air below was dank and stale.
4. He bobbed on the water's surface in his life-vest until he was hauled out with a fishhook.

*5. Howland experienced a storm on a ship at sea.

C. Copper wires are used almost everywhere in home wiring. For a brief period aluminum wires were popular because copper was in short supply. But aluminum has the disadvantage of tending to overheat in some conditions, so many local electrical codes have banned its use. You should check your local code before you install aluminum wire. Better yet, don't use it at all.

Adapted from a manual on installing and repairing electrical circuits.

1. In some conditions aluminum wire can overheat.
2. Aluminum wire has never been banned anywhere.
3. Silver is a good conductor of electricity.
4. Aluminum wire has always been more widely used than copper.
5. Many electricians prefer to work with aluminum wire because it is lighter and easier to handle.

D. There is no composition of Western music, no matter for what instruments or voices it has been written, that cannot be played on a piano. In the white and black keys of the piano keyboard we have at our disposal the full set of tones from which the musical compositions of our civilization have been constructed. Yet a cat walking across a keyboard does not necessarily produce a melody. The fact that the successively sounding tones all belong to the tonal order of our music does not guarantee that the tone sequence is a melody.

Victor Zuckerkandl, *The Sense of Music*, (Princeton 1959), p. 18.

1. Any Western musical composition whatever can be played on a piano.
2. The white keys and the black constitute all the keys there are on a piano.
3. Some good piano players prefer the Bechstein to the Baldwin.
4. If a computer were programmed so that piano keys were struck randomly, the result would not necessarily be a melody.

*5. Some important Western music cannot be played on a piano.

E. The two chief virtues of hyacinths in your garden are their wonderful fat spikes of bright flowers and their fragrance. Plant them near a door or a window, near a path where you can walk in early spring sunshine and enjoy their heavenly smell. In the coldest parts of the country they are practical only as forced plants for indoors: elsewhere they can be happily used to border a walk, as plantings through a border, or in the rock garden.

Lois Wilson, *The Complete Gardener*
(New York 1972), p. 265.

1. The hyacinth flowers on slender spikes.
2. Gardenias are more fragrant than hyacinths.
3. Hyacinths will flourish outdoors as far north as you want to go.
4. The hyacinth is characterized by an unpleasant odor.
5. Hyacinths can make an attractive border.

EXERCISE 2—3: TRUTH CLAIMS

Supply one logical assumption for each of the following. In the case of the sentence fragment, your statement will be a logical assumption of the truth of the complete statement of which the fragment is a part. In the case of a non-indicative statement, supply a logical assumption of its appropriate use.

1. Before Shiela could delete all the spam,
2. Tired of serving two customers at once,
3. the face on the barroom floor
4. to the left of the odometer on the instrument panel
5. Forcing her way into the closed meeting,
6. Is the red too bright for the room?
7. Would you please remove your hat?
8. I hope she finds a job she likes.
9. He doubts that the matter will even be investigated.
10. She wished that Kathy would finally succeed.
11. the dark olives, not the green ones
12. Did you clean the gun before firing it?
13. all his winnings on Twinkle Toes in the seventh
14. a painted ship on a painted ocean

15. She vows never to shop there again.

THE CRITICAL THINKING JOURNAL

The Critical Thinking Journal is your opportunity to apply critical thinking techniques outside the classroom to material of your own choosing. You decide which sources you will exercise the required critical thinking operations on. This Journal provides you the opportunity to develop the attitudes necessary for critical thinking as well as to further develop the skills.

An inexpensive binder for your sources and work will be needed. When placing materials or writing in your journal, please remember to leave an ample margin on the left for comments by the instructor. Comments right where you have done something especially well, or where you need to improve, can be very helpful.

Do not take sample arguments from textbooks on critical thinking or informal logic. For this Journal you are challenged to identify as well as to analyze arguments, but you cannot practice this if an author has already identified the arguments for you. Also remember that the statements whose logical relations we are studying are always complete sentences, with at least a subject and a predicate. So you must either complete sentence fragments, or use their assumptions, as you can use the assumptions of questions and other non-indicative language. Do not interpret comic strips or cartoons. There is much scope for critical thinking in interpreting imagery, but this is a different exercise from interpreting verbal statements. Your Journal should contain the following materials. You may cut materials from newspapers or periodicals that you own, Xerox them from those you don't own, or copy them. Please give the name, date and page number(s) for all your source materials.

Part A. Statement Relations and Inference

1. Logical Relations of Statements

You need two sources from print media, such as a newspaper or magazine. For each source, provide two statements that are implied, two that are contradictory, and two statements that are related in meaning and consistent with the passage but not implications of it.

Hint. Your implications, contradictions, and consistent statements must be different from any of the express statements in your source. So they cannot be taken directly from your source. You produce them outside of your source; you do not find them in your source.

Hint. Each implication, contradiction, or consistent statement can relate to your source as a whole, to some part of your source, or to some specific statement in your source. If it is unclear what the statement relates to, you may want to write a separate statement indicating what implies it and why, or what it contradicts and why.

Tip. Treat your implications, contradictions, and consistent statements as objects. Each originates as an idea in your mind. But now as you go public with them, put them there as objects with separate labels and explanations when needed. They are now objects for study and analysis.

Tip. Do not bury your implications etc. away in relative clauses with subordinate explanatory clauses where they must be dug out by your instructor. Write each implication etc. separately. Avoid syntax like "X (your source) implies Y (your implication) because Z (your explanation)." If your example needs explaining, write the explanation separate from the object statement that is being explained.

Wrong: The above paragraph implies that some examples may need explaining because it instructs you on the form the explanation should take.

Right: Implication of the above paragraph: Some examples may need explaining.

This is implied because the paragraph gives instruction on the form the explanation should take.

Further Reading

Consistency, inconsistency, implication, and contradiction are not usually treated in logic as relations to be mastered independent of their role in inference. The above material on recognizing and learning to work with these logical relations was developed in the author's critical thinking courses.

The following works contain clear and helpful treatments:

Michael Scriven, *Reasoning* (New York 1976), pp. 29–39.

P. F. Strawson, *Introduction to Logical Theory* (London 1952), pp. 1–9.

Various roles that inconsistency and contradiction can play in discourse are studied in the following:

Manfred Kienpointner, "Uses and Functions of Paradoxes in Natural Language," *International Society for the Study of Argumentation (ISSA) Newsletter*, No. 7 (1991), pp. 2–16.

Chaim Perelman and L. Olbrechts-Tyteca, *The New Rhetoric. A Treatise on Argumentation* (Notre Dame 1971), pp. 195–210.

CHAPTER THREE

CONSISTENCY AND ASSUMPTIONS

The avoidance of inconsistency is crucial simply because consistency is a requirement of communication
Michael Scriven

1. CONSISTENCY ANALYSIS

> Zeke succeeded in loosening the bonds on his arms, but he stayed in the tent where he was held prisoner as the enemy soldiers ate supper around the campfire. Under the cover of dusk he slipped unnoticed over to the edge of the deep forest. Breathing freer, he set his course due west toward friendly lines by the barely visible moss on the north side of the trees. Hobbled in places by the thick undergrowth, he had traveled half an hour before he heard the shots announcing that his escape had been discovered. Fearing pursuit, he redoubled his efforts, steering west by the stars. Hours later he fell exhausted under a rhododendron thicket and slept on a bed of pine needles. The crack of a dry branch under a man's boot awoke him with a start. Hugging the ground, he saw two men not fifty yards away exchange words as the new sentry took his post. Beyond them, he peered mortified into the very camp he had fled the night before.

When we read this passage we become aware that it doesn't all fit together well. We sense that something is wrong. It has aroused in us a suspicion of inconsistency. When we suspect a discourse of being inconsistent, we carry out a consistency analysis to confirm or disprove our suspicion. The point of the consistency analysis is to decide whether the discourse is consistent or not. If it turns out inconsistent, our suspicion is confirmed; if it turns out consistent, our suspicion is disproved. How do we set about analyzing such a narrative to establish whether it is consistent or not?

The first thing we need to notice is that not all of the information is of equal importance in testing the narrative for consistency. We must set aside whatever is irrelevant and focus on those statements or clauses that bear directly on the matter. Our suspicion was aroused on hearing that Zeke traveled straight away from the camp yet ended up at the camp. Let us focus now on the statements that bear on this.

A. . . . he set his course due west . . .
B. Hobbled . . . by thick undergrowth, he had traveled half an hour . . .
C. . . . he redoubled his efforts, steering west by the stars. Hours later he fell exhausted . . .
D. [on waking from his exhausted sleep] he peered mortified into the very camp he had fled the night before.

We letter each statement "A," "B," etc. for economy of reference in our analysis. It provides a convenient shorthand for referring to the statement without getting tangled or confused in its details. Comparing statements A, B, C, and D, we find no direct contradiction.

Our next step is to draw out implications of one or more of these statements to see whether we encounter a contradiction. When we take Statements A and B together, they put Zeke the distance he has traveled in half an hour west of the camp. We know that it takes a person on the average 15 to 20 minutes to walk a mile. It is likely that Zeke would have run considerably faster than this. But we cannot forget that he traveled at night in a forest with undergrowth, and in addition he had to move silently when he was still near the camp. Statement C puts Zeke an additional several hours west of the camp. So let us make the following assumptions.

E. Zeke averaged a mile each 20 minutes.
F. Zeke traveled a total of four hours.

Then when we take statements A, B, C, E and F together they imply

G. Zeke slept about 12 miles west of the enemy camp.

However, Statement D reveals that Zeke slept in sight of the enemy camp, which we can put this way:

H. Zeke slept at the enemy camp.

It is obvious that Zeke cannot be both at the enemy camp and 12 miles west of the camp at the same time. Statement H contradicts Statement G. If a set of statements either contains or implies a contradiction, then the statements are inconsistent. They cannot all be true together. Having found the contradiction, we have established that the narrative is indeed inconsistent. Finding the contradiction also reveals to us *why* the statements are inconsistent.

A contradiction needs explaining. In the present case, if Zeke is really staring at the same camp he left the night before, then the account of his flight cannot be accurate. What is the most likely explanation? In the dark, in haste and fearing pursuit, he may well have misread his directional signs along the way and circled back on himself. People lost in unfamiliar terrain have been known to do that.

When we look at a source from the standpoint of logical consistency, it falls into one of two categories. It either arouses suspicion of inconsistency, or it does not. We do not carry out a consistency analysis of the source that arouses no suspicion. Indeed since an analysis begins with statements that arouse suspicion of inconsistency, if there are no such statements there is no material for an analysis to begin with. Consider the following description.

> Through a jagged aperture in the dome of clouds the light of a few stars fell upon the black sea, rising and falling confusedly. Sometimes the head of a watery cone would topple on board and mingle with the rolling flurry of foam on the swamped deck; and the Nan-Shen wallowed heavily at the bottom of a circular cistern of clouds. This ring of dense vapor, gyrating madly around the calm of the center, encompassed the ship like a motionless and unbroken wall of an aspect inconceivably sinister. Within, the sea, as if agitated by an internal commotion, leaped in peaked mounds that jostled each other, slapping heavily against her sides; and a low moaning sound, the infinite plaint of the storm's fury, came from beyond the limits of the menacing calm. . . . Juke's ready ear caught suddenly the faint, long-drawn roar of some immense wave—rushing unseen under that thick blackness, which made the appalling boundary of his vision.
>
> Joseph Conrad, "Typhoon"

Nothing arouses suspicion here. We classify this source consistent.

For the source that arouses suspicion, we carry out an analysis. Its starting point is the statements that arouse suspicion, and its steps are the following.

1. **Write down separately the statements or clauses that seem suspicious.**
2. **Compare the statements to see whether any two of them are contradictory.**

(The analysis ends here if you turn up a direct contradiction. Often you will have to proceed to the next step.)

3. **Draw out those implications of the statements that seem promising for the analysis.**
4. **Compare the implications with the original statements and with each other to see whether there are any contradictions.**

Our goal is to reach one of two outcomes. If we find no contradiction, then it is possible for all of the statements to be true together, and our source is consistent on analysis. If we do find a contradiction (that is, if one statement being true makes another false), then it is not possible for all of the statements to be true together, and they are inconsistent. Further, finding the contradiction locates the source of the inconsistency. There may be cases that are difficult to decide one way or the other. In such a case it is better to give the speaker or writer the benefit of the doubt.

When we write down our suspicious statements, we quote them word-for-word from the source. We do not need to enclose these statements in quotation marks, since it is understood that we are quoting them verbatim. But frequently we need to delete material that is irrelevant to the question of consistency. It gets in our way and hinders our analysis. When we delete we employ scholarly technique, placing three dots (...) where the material was omitted.

Above we learned that truth claims must be made in order for statements to be either consistent or inconsistent with each other. This means that whatever we quote and use in a consistency analysis must be either a complete sentence or an independent clause. We may need to insert words to supplement or clarify what we have quoted. In some cases we may need to paraphrase as much as an entire sentence. Whatever we insert into quoted material goes in square brackets. The knowledgeable reader will recognize what we are quoting directly from the source, and what we have added.

There are three good reasons for the extra caution this small amount of scholarly technique provides.

1. Our quotes will be clearer and more precise, both of which are important critical thinking goals.
2. We are being fair to the writer we're quoting; we won't be accusing anyone of inconsistency until we complete a careful analysis.
3. We may have to defend our allegation of inconsistency, and the consistency analysis puts this defense right in our hands.

Note that when we state implications as we did in G and H above, we do not use dots or square brackets. We are not quoting any source. We choose the words to state the implication. Our choice is influenced by these two factors.

1. Our new statement must be a logical implication of one or more specified statements from the source.
2. It should be stated so that it brings out the suspected contradiction as starkly as possible.

The case is similar with assumptions, though not identical because assumptions differ from implications. We make assumptions here because the information needed for our consistency analysis is not available in our source. This type of assumption is like a hypothesis. It is a statement we take to be true in the absence of supporting evidence or facts because it furthers our analysis.

Accordingly, any hypothetical assumptions we make in our work on consistency should satisfy these guidelines.

1. The assumption should be compatible with the facts and probable, given these facts.
2. The assumption should enable us to progress with our consistency analysis.

2. Outcome: Consistent

The consistency analysis we carried out above resulted in the uncovering of a contradiction and the source proving inconsistent on analyses. But in some cases a source will arouse enough suspicion for us to carry out an analysis where, all factors considered, we still judge the source to be logically consistent.

This source about the clash of the Clinton administration with the GOP Congress arouses suspicion.

> Though still exchanging threats and harsh criticism, top GOP and Clinton administration officials began signaling Sunday some grounds for possible compromise on two major issues before Congress—welfare reform and funding government operations—to avert a collision.

Even in a source this brief we can narrow the focus to what arouses suspicion.

A. . . . [top GOP and Clinton administration officials are] still exchanging threats and harsh criticism.
B. . . . top GOP and Clinton administration officials began signaling Sunday some grounds for possible compromise . . .

Use of scholarly quotation technique allows us to focus more closely on an incongruity. It seems improbable that opposed government officials would be both threatening each other and seeking compromise at the same time. Statement A appears to imply:

C. There can be no basis for compromise.

B. clearly implies:

D. There might be a basis for compromise.

C and D are obviously contradictory.

A reporter defending this account might respond that A and B can be true together because both correspond to the facts. Politicians may threaten opponents in public to impress their supporters, yet still seek compromise behind the scenes to keep the government running. On this reasonable interpretation, A does not imply C, and it is possible for A and B to be true together. So the source is consistent on analysis.

A good analysis to justify the outcome "consistent on analysis" must address these two questions.

1. What aroused our suspicion?
2. Why is the source not inconsistent?

Since we were suspicious enough to carry out an analysis, we must treat the source as we learned to above. We need quoted statements and implications that if possible will lead to a contradiction. Then the reason for the source not actually being logically inconsistent can be explained by the contradiction turning out to be apparent rather than actual, or as in the above case, by one or more of the implications turning out apparent rather than actual.

Here is another example.

> On the surface there is nothing remarkable about the South African Breweries (SAB) plant in Tianjin, a city some 85 miles southeast of Beijing. Truck-size vats of water and hops gurgling as they ferment, beer scientists in white lab coats mixing steaming beakers in search of a new taste combo; 24,000 bottles per hour clattering along a conveyor belt to be filled with the factory's elixir. But the Tianjin brewery actually differs sharply from many foreign ventures producing for the Chinese market: It is successful.
>
> "Making It in China," *US News & World Report*, Oct 7, 2002, p. 44.

Suspicious statements:

A. On the surface, there is nothing remarkable about the South Arican Breweries (SAB) plant in Tianjin, a city some 85 miles southeast of Beijing.
B. But the Tianjin brewery actually differs sharply from many foreign ventures producing for the Chinese market:
C. It is successful.

Analysis:

A appears to imply:

D. The SAB plant does not differ from many other plants.

In such case D contradicts B, and the passage is inconsistent.

But A is introduced with the phrase "on the surface," which leaves open the possibility that on close examination under the surface there may be something remarkable about the SAB plant. Accepting this interpretation, A does not actually imply D, and the passage is consistent on analysis.

In the two above cases the contradiction that aroused suspicion was due to an apparent implication that on close examination was not an actual implication. There is also the possibility that what appears to be a contradiction may turn out after careful study not to be an actual contradiction.

Another factor we need to consider is whether we should seek inconsistencies in reported or indirect speech. Consider the following case of an income tax auditor reporting statements made on an IRS form by a sales executive for a Chicago manufacturer of machine tools.

> Mr. Gardner, according to the supplemental material to your business expense claims on Form 2106, you regularly entertain clients at the Lido, a popular local nightclub. Five times in March, six in April, five in May, six in June, and so on. But according to your information on travel expenses in foreign countries, you were in Europe from April 28 to June 2 contacting your firm's clients there. Are you asking us to believe that you returned from Europe to Chicago on five separate occasions in May just to entertain clients at the Lido? You haven't claimed any air travel deductions for such trips. Let's go over your Diner's Club receipts verifying those evenings at the Lido.

The statements of the auditor arouse no suspicion. He is simply reporting information stated by Mr. Gardner on his Form 2106. His statements are of the type "Mr. Gardner said this," "Mr. Gardner said that" etc. But Mr. Gardner's statements on the tax form definitely do arouse suspicion—he appears to claim to be at two widely separated places at the same time. Let us examine this more closely.

Suspicious statements:

A. Mr. Gardner [a Chicago manufacturer] . . . regularly entertain[s] clients at the Lido, a . . . local nightclub.
B. [He did so] . . . five [times] in May . . .
C. [Mr. Gardner was] in Europe from April 28 to June 2 . . .

A and B together imply:

D. Mr. Gardner was in Chicago in May.

Analysis: D contradicts C. Mr. Gardner cannot have been in both places simultaneously. As the auditor points out, if Gardner actually had flown back each time to entertain, he would certainly have claimed air travel, a substantial expense. The statements on Mr. Gardner's Form 2106 are inconsistent.

We suspect that in this case Mr. Gardner will end up paying more tax. But we would not know unless we carried out an analysis. So it is important to check reported statements as well as direct ones for consistency.

The case is no different with opinions, which are typically truth claims. There are opinions which can be true together.

Chicago is the best musical of 2002.
The Pianist is the best drama of 2002.

Opinions which can be true together are frequently referred to as compatible. The following opinions cannot be true together—they are incompatible.

Chicago is the best film of 2002.
The Pianist is the best film of 2002.

The fact that there are many incompatible opinions—cases where one being true makes the other false—signifies that some opinions are better than others. Since it is not the case that all opinions are equally good, we will need to discriminate carefully in those cases where it is important to know which is true and which false.

Similarly with theories, some are consistent in that it is possible for them to be true together.

Many diseases are caused by microorganisms
Many diseases are caused by an imbalance of bodily humors.

These theories are compatible, even though modern medicine rejects the second. Other theories are inconsistent or incompatible in that it is not possible for them to be true together.

The world was created by God in the year 4004 BC.
Dinosaurs ruled the earth for 160 million years.

Since a world containing the earth would be a little over 6000 years old in the early 21st century AD, the earth could not have been ruled by anything for 160 million years.

The role of a logic of statement relations is to help us determine which theories can be true together (are compatible) and which are not.

EXERCISE 3—1: ANALYZING FOR CONSISTENCY

Examine each of the following passages and decide whether or not the statements are consistent. If you suspect inconsistency, employ as many of the four steps needed to decide the question. Be sure to draw at least one implication for any consistency analysis.

Part A. Little Suspicion or Inconsistent

1. (To the question "Do you expect your new book on Vietnam, *Up Country*, to rekindle the debate about the war?" author Nelson DeMille responds:)

   Vietnam is almost a dead issue because of September 11. But you can't have a discussion about the gulf war or the current war without talking about Vietnam.

   "A Timely Return to Vietnam,"
   Newsweek (Feb. 4, 2002), p. 4.

2. Raleigh, NC, bankruptcy lawyer Mark Kirby was indicted on federal fraud charges in December. According to a prosecutor, while Kirby was working for the Brown, Kirby & Bunch law firm in 1990 and 1991, he billed clients an average of nearly 1,200 hours a month—from a low of 851 hours to a high of 1,547. [A 31-day month has only 744 hours.]

   Chuck Shepherd, *News of the Weird.*

3. There had never been such a June in Eagle County. Usually it was a month of moods, with abrupt alterations of belated frost and mid-summer heat; this year, day followed day in a sequence of temperate beauty. Every morning a breeze blew steadily from the hills. Toward noon it built up great canopies of white cloud that threw a cool shadow over fields and woods; then before sunset the clouds dissolved again . . .

   Edith Wharton, *Summer* (New York 1993), p. 33.

4. All dinosaurs are cold-blooded like lizards. They are unable to regulate their body temperatures except by choosing sun or shade. They had to be cold-blooded to cope with the sweltering heat of the Mesozoic era. Ninety-foot sauropods reared up on their hind legs to munch foliage from tree tops. A ten-ton triceratops was fast enough to gallop past a charging rhino. Warm-bloodedness is the only way to explain the dinosaur's evolutionary success. They could not have dominated the globe for 160 million years without being able to keep their bodies at the optimum temperatures regardless of surroundings.

   Adapted from an Aug. 18, 1997 science report.

5. (Insurance policy holder providing a brief description of the accident) My car was legally parked as it backed into the other vehicle.

   Permission granted by Ann Landers and Creators Syndicate

*6. Maryland law requires the state to educate students 6 to 16. In October 1987 a 16-year-old student was expelled for carrying a steak knife on a school bus. The strict expulsion policy of the Prince Georges County School Board prohibits teaching expelled students, so this student has received no tutoring or alternative instruction.

   From a report in *Insight* (May 30, 1988).

7. When electricity is transmitted through conventional copper wire, resistance causes a loss of about 20 percent in the form of heat. Certain substances like mercury have been known since 1911 to be able to conduct electricity wholly without resistance. Superconductivity, as this phenomenon is called, is of great practical importance for its energy efficiency. But it occurs only at temperatures of extreme cold—near absolute zero or –460° Fahrenheit—which are prohibitively expensive to maintain. Superconductivity occurs in some substances at temperatures you could experience in North Dakota or Minnesota in the winter

   Adapted from a 1987 news magazine account of superconductivity

8. At nine o'clock, one morning late in July, Gatsby's gorgeous car lurched up the rocky drive to my door and gave out a burst of melody from its three-noted horn. It was the first time he had called on me, though I had gone to two of his parties, mounted in his hydroplane, and, at his urgent invitation, made frequent use of his beach.

   F. Scott Fitzberald, *The Great Gatsby*
   (Harmondsworth 1950) p. 69f.

9. Montgomery County police say about 600 teens were at a dance hall disturbance on Rockville Pike Sunday night. . . . told to leave the club, some of the teens started throwing bottles and rocks, which broke a window. Rockville Pike was closed for a time as police in riot gear moved in with pepper spray to bring the crowd under control at the alcohol-free teen party. . . . "It wasn't that anybody was doing anything wrong . . . , said Montgomery County Police Spokeswoman Diane McCarthy.

10. Traveling? Visit your nearest participating American Express Representatives Travel Services location to purchase your FEE FREE American Express Travelers Cheques. Get them before you go.

    American Express promotional mailing, Jan. 2003.

11. Black holes are regions in space of extremely dense matter. Their gravitational pull is so strong that nothing, not even light, can escape. Physicists theorize that a black hole might be formed when a burned-out star implodes. The black hole may be surrounded by an event horizon, a sort of trap door through which matter can pass in but not out, which seals

the black hole off from the rest of the universe. Black holes were first theorized about in the 18th century, but there is no convincing physical evidence that they even exist. So we are constructing an optical telescope that should be powerful enough, when operated in space, to give us our first glimpse of a black hole.

12. Squeezed into the triangle where Pakistan, Iran, and Afghanistan meet, Balochistan is a rugged, lawless sort of place, riven by violence and rich in political intrigue; it has been a battleground for imperial armies and tribal warlords for centuries. Its ordered chaos is presided over by seventeen major tribes that make up two major ethnic groups, the Pathans, in the north, and the Baloch, in the south, led by irascible chiefs.

    Mary Anne Weaver, "The Stranger," *The New Yorker* (Nov 95) p. 62.

13. Two men on Colorado's death row were spared yesterday when the state's highest court ruled that their death sentences, imposed by three-judge panels, were unconstitutional. The Colorado Supreme Court ordered George Woldt and Francisco Martinez Jr. to be resentenced to life in prison without parole. The decision follows a ruling by the U.S. Supreme Court in June that held that juries, not judges, must determine whether the death penalty is appropriate. The court ruled in an Arizona case.

    washtimes.com Feb 25, 2003.

14. The explorer speaks apprehensively to a small band of natives encountered deep in the forest.

    "Is it true that there are still cannibals in these parts?"

    Their leader responds.

    "No, not now. There used to be. But we ate the last one a few weeks ago."

    Adapted from Kienpointner
    [see p. 35 above], p. 5f.

15. . . during the last year, politicians, pundits, and the media (including *The New Republic*) have used the phrase "weapons of mass destruction" as a constant shorthand for chemical, biological, and atomic arms. As of this writing, the phrase "weapons of mass destruction" had appeared in *The New York Times* in some 250 articles over the past month alone. And while I do not claim to have examined all of these citations, it is a safe bet that most referred collectively to chemical, biological, and atomic arms, implying equivalent power to inflict "death on a massive scale."

    Yet their lethal potential is emphatically not equivalent. Chemical weapons are dangerous, to be sure, but not "weapons of mass destruction" in any meaningful sense. In actual use, chemical arms have proven less deadly than regular bombs, bullets, and artillery shells.

    Gregg Easterbrook, "Term Limits. The Meaninglessness of WMD," *The New Republic*, (Oct. 7, 2002), p. 22.

Part B. Little Suspicion, Inconsistent or Consistent on Analysis

1. The second oldest college in the United States is the College of William and Mary at Williamsburg, Virginia. It was chartered in 1693, opened in 1694, and acquired university status in 1779. However, its antecedents were in the planned university at Henrico, Virginia (1619-22) which was postponed because of the Indian massacre of 1822.

   The Guiness Book of Records (1991), p. 219.

2. Social phobia hit Steve Fox so hard in high school that girls made a sport of saying "hello" just to watch him turn beet red. He refused to speak in class and never dated; even walking in front of other people left him with sweaty palms and gasping for air. By the time Fox was 19, his father was concerned enough to find a doctor. . . . Fox, now 23, recently gave a speech in front of 1700 people, and he is married to one of the cheerleaders who used to tease him.

   Adapted from a June 1999 news weekly report.

3. At an emergency summit in Rome in April [2002], Pope John Paul II told American cardinals that "there is no place in the priesthood or religious life for those who would harm the young." But he also affirmed the church teaching that even the worst sinner can repent and receive pardon.

4. On a warm May morning, the winter wheat is barely a foot tall. A slight wind teases the top of the grass, changing it from light green to dark and back again. Pin oaks and loblolly pines surround the 50 or so acres of open farmland. A footpath winds around the edge of the wheat fields and disappears into the woods. Pine needles soften the walk as the trail sinks into the earth where wagon wheels once carved ruts into the dirt road. A healthy black snake slithers across the path, curls himself under a decaying log and cocks his head to warn away hikers.

   HR Monthly (Sept. 2002), p. 79.

5. From 1881 to 1905 there occurred no less than thirty-seven thousand strikes, some of them brief and local, some of them prolonged and nationwide. The most spectacular strikes of this period were the railroad strike of 1877, which first introduced large-scale industrial violence to Americans, the strike at the McCormick-Harvester works in 1886, which culminated in the tragedy of the Haymarket riot; the Homestead strike of 1892, which was marked by a pitched battle on the banks of the Monongahela; the great Pullman strike of 1894, which tied up half the railroads of the nation; the terrible Cripple Creek war in the Colorado

coalfields; and the anthracite-coal strike of 1902, which threatened to paralyze industry throughout the country and which was finally settled only by the intervention of President Theodore Roosevelt.

Allan Nevins & Henry Steele Commager
A Pocket History of the United States,
New enlarged ed. (New York 1965), p. 296f.

6. The accident victim had been dead for over two hours when she began to moan and roll her head from side to side.

7. Writing in 1881, [former President of the Confederacy Jefferson Davis argued] that "slavery was in no wise the cause of the conflict, but only an incident." . . . Not all former Confederates bought into the rhetoric. "We went to war on account of the thing we quarreled with the North about. I never heard of any other cause of quarrel than slavery," wrote Confederate guerrilla John Mosby, the famous Gray Ghost.

"The Better Angels," *U.S. News & World Report*
(Sept. 30, 2002), p. 60.

8. They call it "minor surgery" but Nancy Greenly, Sean Berman, and a dozen others, all admitted to Memorial Hospital for routine procedures, are victims of the same inexplicable, hideous tragedy on the operating table. They never wake up again. Some traceless error in anesthesia has caused irreversible brain death, leaving each of them in a hopeless coma.

Blurb from Robin Cook, *Coma* (New York 1977).

9. The layoff parade got a little longer this week. Disney is axing 400 people as it shutters its Go.com portal. Amazon.com will cut 1300 jobs, and ailing Daimler-Chrysler plans to chop 26,000 jobs. But the current situation is far from dire. The unemployment rate is still low, and most economists don't expect it to exceed 5 percent this year.

"A Layoff Frenzy?" *U.S. News & World Report* (Feb. 12, 2001).

10. But even if you don't have a 20-car garage and a conference center in your home [like Bill Gates], wireless home networking may be in your league. Networking your computers allows you to send files from one computer to another—no more transferring files to a floppy disk and then shuttling them downstairs to the other computer. You can share peripherals, such as printers and scanners, and if you have a computer equipped with high-speed cable Internet access, your other computers will be able to tap into that high-speed connection without additional cables.

Michael J. Martinez, "No Strings Attached,"
Kiplinger's (April 2001), p. 112.

11. On January 3 [2002], Israel captured a ship, the *Katrine A*, headed to Gaza [in the Palestinian Authority] from Iran packed with 50 tons of rockets, guns, and mortars. . . . [Palestinian Authority Chairman Arafat's response included] a letter to [President] Bush in which he denied any knowledge of the ship or its mission. . . . Secretary of State Colin Powell . . . [insisted] that he had "not seen any information that yet links [the *Katrine A*] directly to Chairman Arafat." . . . on January 9, senior Israeli intelligence officials briefed their American counterparts on evidence of Arafat's involvement with the *Katrine A*—the use of Palestinian Authority funds for the arms purchases, the involvement of Arafat's deputies, and proof that the Palestinian leader himself authorized the transfer . . .

   Lawrence F. Kaplan, "Torpedo Boat," *The New Republic* (Feb. 18, 2002), p. 19.

12. Can getting a mammogram save your life? Most women wouldn't think twice before answering that question: years of popular opinion have left little doubt that a mammogram, uncomfortable and slightly embarrassing as it may be, is a lifesaving tool in the war against breast cancer. Research conducted in the 1970s and 80s found that mammograms reduce breast cancer deaths by 30 percent—a comforting statistic to the 30 million American women who undergo the procedure each year.

   ... a two-year-old Danish study . . . published in the British journal *The Lancet* . . . posits that numerous flaws in current mammography technique render the results virtually useless. It also suggests that while mammograms may mean earlier detection of breast cancer, earlier detection does not necessarily mean a lower mortality rate.

   Jessica Reaves, "Mammograms: Can We Live Without Them?" *TIME.com* (Jan. 25, 2002).

13. About 90% of the matter in the Universe is thought to be cold dark matter, not amenable to normal methods of detection. But that is not all that is missing. Almost two thirds of the 'normal' visible matter in the local Universe, made up of protons, electrons, and neutrons—known collectively as baryons—has yet to be accounted for. Simulations of galaxy formation predict that a large fraction of these baryons escape detection because of their high temperature and low density. But high-resolution spectroscopic data from the FUSE satellite and Chandra and XMM-Newton orbiting observatories allow this material to be detected as 'high velocity' absorption clouds against bright cosmological sources such as quasars. Using these techniques the 'missing' baryons are revealed in gas clouds associated with our Local Group of galaxies.

   "Lost and Found," *Nature* (Feb. 13, 2003), p. vii.

14. As Betty screwed the medicine dropper back inside its small brown bottle, I went to the microscope on a nearby counter, stared through the eyepiece and began moving the wetmount around on the stage. In the field of polarized light were several multicolored fibers, flat and ribbon-shaped with twists at irregular intervals. The fibers were neither animal hair nor man-made.

    Patricia Cornwell, *Postmortem* (New York 1990), p. 99.

15. (The preoccupied young lord of the manor dashed off with his friends to the tavern, leaving this note for his servant.)

    I am gone to the Boar's Head Tavern where you can find me and if you can't read this note, take it down to the Stationer's and he will red it for you.

    Adapted from Kienpointner [see p. 35 above], p. 6.

[An assumption is] something taken for granted by or underlying an assertion or position.
Johnson & Blair

3. More on Assumptions

We have been dealing with two different types of assumption that we now need to distinguish more carefully. In Chapter 2 we noticed that certain statements and other uses of language involve or carry logical assumptions. A *logical* assumption is a statement that must be true in order for some other statements to be true, or in order for some other discourse to be used appropriately. Here are examples.

Statement:	I notice you've switched from Virginia Slims to Salems.
Assumption:	You smoke cigarettes.
Statement:	Without high wind, storm, earthquake or other force, the roof of the building collapsed into the top floor.
Assumption:	Construction, maintenance, or inspection of the building was faulty.
Phrase:	the scrap of post-it note in the bird nest
Assumption:	There is a scrap of post-it note in the bird nest.

While our main interest from the vantage point of a logic of statement relations is in logical assumptions, we also note that in our initial consistency analysis above we used a different kind of assumption. We needed to know how far Zeke had traveled to carry out our consistency analysis. We know approximately how long he traveled, so to get the distance we made an assumption about his speed. We called this a *hypothetical* assumption, a statement we took for true in the absence of more reliable information.

Assumptions of the hypothetical variety are not uncommon. We make them because we are in situations that require us to act, and we don't have sufficient knowledge at our ready disposal to decide which of several mutually exclusive courses of action is most advisable. Cindy thinks she is coming down with flu, but all she has at home for her headache is aspirin. Should she take one or two? More than one hypothetical assumption may be needed to guide her action. How likely is it that she actually has influenza? Is aspirin the pain-killer that can trigger or be associated with a rare but serious disease in flu patients? Is there a risk great enough that she should drive to a pharmacy for a different pain-killer?

In any interpersonal communication a hypothetical assumption will usually be stated or explicit. This is necessarily the case when several such assumption are almost equally probable. Without a choice, not even the reasoner would have a specific assumption. On the other hand, logical assumptions are frequently unstated or implicit in discourse until they are made explicit by analysis. Like other logical relations, they exist whether or not attention is drawn to them and they are made explicit.

One and the same statement may be both a logical and a hypothetical assumption of some piece of discourse. Here is an example.

A. (Discourse): There are canals on the planet Mars.

B. (Assumption): There is or was intelligent life on Mars.

B is a logical assumption of A because a canal is a manmade waterway. If there had been no creatures resembling humans in intelligence on Mars, there would be no canals. But B is also a hypothetical assumption in that there is currently no good evidences to support it.

We note a subtle but important point that helps us further to distinguish the two types of assumption. Should a future Mars probe find convincing evidence of a civilization that could build canals, B would cease to be an assumption in the hypothetical sense. The evidence to back it up is now available, so it becomes a true statement, a statement of fact. However, B does not cease being a logical assumption of A. So long as the words of A retain their meaning, it is still the case that B must be true in order for A to be true.

Focusing now on the logical assumption, it must be related in meaning to the statement of which it is an assumption. So no statement unrelated in meaning to a discourse will be a logical assumption of it. Some statements related in meaning will not be logical assumptions of that discourse. Compare the following to A.

C. There are huge impact craters on Mars.

C is related in meaning but not a logical assumption of A.

This leads us to a type of statement that interests us. This type of statement *seems* to be an assumption of a given discourse, but actually isn't. Learning to deal with such statements helps us to achieve a more subtle understanding of our given discourse. For example.

C. He was arrested leaving the scene of the crime.

D. A police officer made the arrest.

D appears to be an assumption of C. But it is not actually an assumption because arrests can be made by citizens too.

In one of the exercises below we will seek statements that seem logically assumed in given statements but really are not.

Summary

When we confront discourse with an eye to its consistency, either it arouses suspicion of inconsistency or it does not. Only if it arouses suspicion do we carry out a consistency analysis. The point of a consistency analysis is to determine whether a discourse is consistent or inconsistent. The method of a consistency analysis is to attempt to find a contradiction.

In a consistency analysis we first write out the statements that give rise to our suspicion and compare them. If there is no contradiction, we draw out their implications, then compare them with each other and with the original statements. If at any point we find a contradiction, the statements are inconsistent. If not, they are consistent.

So from the vantage point of consistency, all discourse fits in one of three categories.

1. Consistent because it arouses no suspicion.
2. Proven consistent by analysis.
3. Proven inconsistent by analysis.

A hypothetical assumption is a statement we take for true in the absence of evidence that would support it. It is usually stated explicitly, whereas a logical assumption may remain implicit until brought out by analysis. A hypothetical assumption may convert to knowledge when evidence is produced. Logical assumptions remain that as long as the words of the discourse retain their meaning.

Study Questions

Section 1: Consistency Analysis

1. When do we carry out a consistency analysis?
2. What are the steps of a consistency analysis?
3. What are the two possible outcomes of a consistency analysis?
4. How do we classify a passage for which a consistency analysis is unnecessary?

Section 2: More on Assumptions

5. What is a hypothetical assumption?
6. State two ways in which it usually differs from a logical assumption.

EXERCISE 3—2: IDENTIFYING ASSUMPTIONS

Part A. Picking Assumptions Out

Read the initial statement or group of statements. Then decide which of the subsequent statements are assumed and which are not.

1. With cancer spreading like that, she will not live long unless she has surgery or radiation therapy.
   A. The patient has cancer.
   B. Surgery can cure the cancer.
   *C. The patient confronts the possibility of death.
   D. Cancer treatment is quite costly.

2. Time is important, so we'd better travel by plane.
   A. Plane service to this destination is available.
   B. It costs less to travel by air than by train.
   C. Air travel is faster than ground travel.
   D. Air travel is more comfortable than travel by car.

3. That college is not well run. They've never made a profit, and they haven't had a winning football season in the last seven years.
   A. Students will receive a good education at a well-run college.
   B. A well-run college will make a profit.
   C. No college has proper leadership unless it has an attractive campus.
   *D. You have to have winning football seasons at a well-run college.

4. Fibers are pliable hair-like substances that are very small in diameter in relation to their length. They are the fundamental units used in the making of textile yarns and fabrics. Until the twentieth century, all fibers were obtained from natural sources. Only four fibers—cotton, wool, flax, and silk—were commonly used. Because wool and flax were easy to spin, they were used more than the others when spinning and weaving were hand processes. But when the Industrial Revolution made spinning a machine process, cotton became most widely used.

   Adapted from a monograph on the textile industry.

   A. There are fibers obtained from natural sources that are not commonly used by man.
   B. Spider web is a very strong fiber.
   C. The diameter of some fiber is greater than the length.
   *D. Natural fibers must be spun before they are useful to man.
   E. Some manufacturing was no longer done by hand after the Industrial Revolution.

5. It would be wise to pay more attention to quality-of-life factors when deciding where to locate a new plant. Good schools should be convenient for the children of the employees. If the community is a small one, check the ages of the local physicians. Small communities have trouble attracting new physicians. There should be a hospital within a thirty-minute drive.

   Adapted from Kurt R. Student, "Cost vs. Human Values in Plant Location," *Business Horizons* (April 1976), pp. 5–14.

   A. Right now not much attention is paid to quality-of-life factors.
   *B. Small communities are pleasant to live in.
   C. You won't have energy shortages in communities with good schools.
   D. The location of a new plant can affect its success.
   E. People generally prefer to have their children attend good schools rather than poor ones.
   F. People don't care much about whether physicians are available or not.

Part B. Supplying Assumptions

In some or all of the problems below, at least one important assumption is left unstated. Supply the assumption. Note that there may be more than one important assumption for any given statement. Also supply for each a statement that is related in meaning but *not* assumed, even though someone might think it is. Be prepared to explain why someone might think it is assumed, and why it is not actually assumed.

1. Steelworker, before you hang girders on that tower you'd better pay up your insurance.
2. Shirley ran the marathon in less than five hours.
3. Jeb is suffering from black lung disease.
4. You'd better open that can of beans before you heat it at the campfire.
5. Even though Virginia Beach lies on the ocean, the city wants to import water from far inland.
6. Have you stopped beating your wife yet?

*7. That dinosaur is quite unusual because it didn't hatch from an egg.

8. Cigarette smoking has been strongly linked to lung cancer and heart disease.
9. Exporters are delighted at the dollar's decrease in value.
10. The government said civil liberties had been restored, but a 10:00 P.M. curfew was still in effect.
11. Haven't you resigned from the Communist Party yet?
12. No one bought any of Vincent Van Gogh's paintings when the artist was alive, but a single painting sold recently for over $50 million, and another for over $80 million.

*13. The city of Texarkana lies on the border of two states.

14. The Monterey Jack cheese in the refrigerator has white and greenish spots on it.
15. Several high-ranking officials of the Nixon administration were convicted and served prison terms.
16. Bungee jumping isn't recommended for those who have survived heart attacks.
17. Some bloodhounds can pick up and follow a scent over 100 hours old.
18. The trend for typewriter sales in the U.S. is downward.

19. The air is noticeably thinner in such high-altitude cities as Denver, Mexico City, and Nairobi.
20. Not many people die annually from hornet stings, so you can get right up close to spray that nest with the insecticide.

THE CRITICAL THINKING JOURNAL

Part A. Statement Relations and Inference

2. Consistency Analysis

For your Journal select three passages of about paragraph length from the standpoint of logical consistency. One passage should arouse little or no suspicion of inconsistency; one should arouse suspicion but prove consistent on analysis; the third should turn out inconsistent on analysis. The statements taken for analysis should be quoted verbatim from your source, using (...) for deletions and [ ] for insertions. The goal of analysis is to show an actual or apparent contradiction between statements from the source and/or their implications. Refer to p. 39 above for the steps a consistency analysis may need.

Hint. An analysis is not required of a passage that gives rise to little or no suspicion of inconsistency.

Hint. For the passage that arouses suspicion but proves consistent, you must clearly show what causes it to appear inconsistent. You must also establish by analysis that it is consistent and why it is consistent.

Hint. For your inconsistent passage you may have to adapt material. This means to state it in your own terms in order to stress those aspects that will exhibit the inconsistency. The reason why you may have to adapt material is that most writers try to avoid inconsistencies, so obvious ones are difficult to find. But state that you are adapting material.

3. Logical Assumptions

For a passage you have taken from some print medium, produce two statements that are assumed and explain why they are assumed. Produce two that some might think are assumed but really are not assumed. Explain why someone might think they are assumed, and explain also why they are not actually assumed.

No statement from your source should be quoted as an assumption. The assumptions you are producing are presupposed; they are statements that must be true in order for one or more statements in your source to be true. You are not here considering whether statements in your source are adequately supported by evidence.

Hint. The assumptions we are looking for are related to the substance of the discourse rather than to the author or other external factors.

Yes: The above paragraph assumes:

Assumptions can relate to substance or external factors.

No: The above paragraph assumes:

Its author can write English.

Tip. Use only a verbal statement for your source. Do not search for assumptions of cartoons or comic strips.

Use the same format recommended for implications in (1) and the other logical relations of statements. Write the assumption as a separate statement or independent clause. Its label as assumption or supposed assumption, and any explanation why it is or is not an assumption should be written separately.

Further Reading

The role of assumptions in reasoning is only recently coming to be studied. The following are useful accounts of how assumptions function in reasoning:

Ralph H. Johnson & J. Anthony Blair, *Logical Self-Defense*, 2nd ed. (Toronto: McGraw-Hill Ryerson 1983), pp. 180–182.

Michael Scriven, *Reasoning* (New York: McGraw-Hill 1976), pp. 81–88.

The following is a careful examination that draws distinctions important for a clearer understanding of assumptions.

Robert H. Ennis, "Identifying Implicit Assumptions," *Synthese*, Vol. 51 (1982), pp. 61–86.

CHAPTER FOUR

REASONING AND INFERENCE

The object of reasoning is to find out, from the consideration of what we already know, something else which we do not know.
C. S. Peirce

1. LOGICAL PUZZLES AS REASONING EXERCISES

Reasoning is needed for critical thinking, so sharpening some reasoning skills helps prepare us to be critical thinkers. We've already been doing some reasoning. It is by reasoning that we determine that one statement implies another, that two statements are contradictory, or that some discourse is consistent. Solving logical puzzles calls on all these skills. To solve such puzzles we are especially concerned with reasoning as inference, in which we draw out the implications of given information, compare them, uncover inconsistencies, then make further inferences till we reach a solution. Working logical puzzles allows us to exercise the reasoning skills we need for inference.

In a logical puzzle we are given a certain amount of information and one or more questions to answer. The puzzle or perplexity of the matter is that the answers are not at all obvious. We have to reason out the implications of the given material, then draw further inferences, often by trial and error, until we reach a solution that answers the questions. Here is an example.

The Footrace

At the annual spring picnic five youngsters vied for first place in a footrace. Tanya wasn't second. Doug came in right after the person who finished behind Tanya. John didn't finish first, but he didn't finish last either. Rosa had to watch from the sidelines because she turned her ankle in the three-leg race. Sheila didn't win either, and Bruce came in just behind her.

In what order did each finish the race?

Try solving the puzzle on your own before turning to the solution that follows.

How does one set about working such a puzzle? First we must focus on the question we are to answer: "In what order did each finish the race?" The goal of answering this question focuses our attention on the given information more narrowly. Now we know what we are looking for. We're not interested in whether Bruce wore Nikes or Reeboks, only in how he finished. Two things are noticed right away. First, we're not told directly how any of five racers finished, so we must reason all of it out for ourselves. Second, all of the information appears relevant to the question except Rosa's turned ankle.

Putting that aside, we are told of three persons where they didn't finish (Tanya, John, and Sheila), and of two that they finished behind others (Doug and Bruce). The first step toward a solution comes when we put this information together.

1. John wasn't first; Sheila wasn't first either.
2. Doug couldn't have finished first. He finished two persons behind Tanya, and you can't finish behind someone and still win. For the same reason Bruce didn't win. He was behind Sheila.
3. Since we now know of five contestants that four didn't win, we can infer that the remaining one—Tanya—was the winner. This is implied by the information we are given about the race.

At this point (if not earlier) we need a more efficient way of keeping track of the given information, the implications we are drawing from it, and our progress in solving the puzzle. For puzzles of the present type, where each of a number of persons or objects is characterized by one or more features, a grid (sometimes called a matrix) can be helpful. The names are in a column on the left, the places finished in a row at the top.

	1	2	3	4	5
Tanya					
Doug					
John					
Sheila					
Bruce					

First we look at the given information and then put an "O" everywhere we know someone didn't finish.

	1	2	3	4	5
Tanya		O			
Doug					
John	O				O
Sheila	O				
Bruce					

For example, Tanya wasn't second, so we put an "O" after Tanya under the 2, etc.

Now we can add the results of our inferences, which were, if you recall, that neither Doug nor Bruce was first. This allows us to put an "X" after Tanya under 1 to show that she won.

	1	2	3	4	5
Tanya	X	O			
Doug	O				
John	O				O
Sheila	O				
Bruce	O				

Since Tanya was first, she couldn't have finished anywhere else. This allows us to enter an "O" in every other spot after her name.

	1	2	3	4	5
Tanya	X	O	O	O	O
Doug	O				
John	O				O
Sheila	O				
Bruce	O				

But where do we go from here? We know that Doug finished two places behind Tanya. This puts him in third place. So we put an "O" in all the other places after his name, and also in all the other spaces below 3 (since no one else can finish third).

	1	2	3	4	5
Tanya	X	O	O	O	O
Doug	O	O	X	O	O
John	O		O		O
Sheila	O		O		
Bruce	O		O		

The information that Bruce finished behind Sheila helps us now. We already know that Sheila can't be first or third. This implies that she can't be second either, for Bruce would have to follow her. And he can't do this, since Doug is already in third place. Sheila can't be fifth either, because again there would be no place for Bruce to follow her. So Sheila must be in fourth place, with Bruce following her in fifth. Finally, by elimination John is in second place.

	1	2	3	4	5
Tanya	X	O	O	O	O
Doug	O	O	X	O	O
John	O	X	O	O	O
Sheila	O	O	O	X	O
Bruce	O	O	O	O	X

So the runners finish in this order:
First: Tanya; Second: John; Third: Doug; Fourth: Sheila; Fifth: Bruce.

Critical thinking is a practical reflective activity that has reasonable belief or action as its goal
Robert H. Ennis

2. The Logical Proof as a Critical Thinking Exercise

We now have a technique that helps us solve one kind of logical puzzle. Puzzles like the above are sometimes called combinatorial. To solve them you must combine a number of pieces of information in different ways.

Those who solved or attempted to solve the above puzzle are aware that thinking is required to do so. *Critical* thinking, however, goes beyond *just* thinking. In critical thinking the person doing the thinking is aware of the steps she is taking and can give an account of them. Or said another way, she is taking steps in reasoning and can justify each step she takes. By contrast an uncritical thinker is not a person who does not think; it is a person who thinks uncritically. The uncritical thinker may think logically. But she cannot exhibit the logical steps in her thought, so she is unable to demonstrate to anyone that she is thinking logically.

Solving logical puzzles falls short of being a model critical thinking activity. Critical thinking concerns what to believe and do, while logical puzzles are reasoning exercises with no connection to what we believe and do. But we can work these puzzles as critical thinking exercises in a way that leads us to reflect about our own reasoning, and this is a necessary part of critical thinking. This method focuses attention on the logical steps we are taking. It is not so much a different way of solving a puzzle as it as a way of showing or demonstrating at the same time that our solution is indeed a solution. We call it the logical proof or demonstration.

We develop this proof in the context of a dialogue between us and a sceptic or challenger, one who continually asks, "How do you know that?" or "Can you prove that?" There doesn't have to be an actual challenger or sceptic here pressing us with such questions. We simply must formulate our solution so that we can demonstrate to such a challenger that our solution is a good one.

First of all we must be clear just what it is that we are trying to find out, or what the puzzle is we're trying to solve. Then we must also be clear on what the given information is. We need to put this given information into a form where we can refer to parts of it clearly and unambiguously. This can be accomplished by giving each simple piece of information a separate statement. In our case we give each such statement a capital letter for the purpose of later reference. It then looks like this.

A. Tanya wasn't second.

B. Doug was two places behind Tanya.

C. John was neither first nor last.

D. Sheila wasn't first.

E. Bruce finished behind Sheila.

The goal of this procedure is to establish an unbroken chain of reasoning linking the given information to our solution. Each step in this solution is justified by reference to:

a. one or more given pieces of information;

or

b. one or more previous steps of reasoning;

or

c. some combination of (a) and (b);

and

d. some acceptable reasoning procedure.

When we establish this unbroken chain of reasoning linking the given information to the solution we have both solved our puzzle, and we have demonstrated that our solution is a solution by laying bare its logic. This is always more difficult to do than just solving the puzzle. But it is absolutely necessary if we are to think critically in the sense of being aware what steps we are taking and how they are justified.

Our present goal is to show that our solution is a solution, but we may notice certain ideals of logical demonstrations and keep them in the back of our mind where they might influence our decisions. Ideally we should not take any step that is not necessary to establish our solution. In other words, there should be no superfluous steps.

Nor should we make any assumptions that are not absolutely necessary. In the case of any puzzle we assume things because we think they're understood and that no normal person would question them. In the present case we tacitly assume that a footrace involves fleetness of foot, that all of the contenders start at the same time, and that they all cover the same distance. We don't comment on such points because they're involved in understanding what a footrace is. An illegitimate assumption is that Bruce probably finished first because his name precedes the others in alphabetical order. What would an assumption be in the present case that is not trivial? We are assuming that there were no ties, and this assumption is borne out by the solution. Perhaps we should have made this assumption explicit at the outset.

The specific steps we now take toward a solution follow closely the reasoning described above. Statements C and D tell us that neither John nor Sheila was first. So the first two steps in our proof establish on the basis of the given information that neither Doug nor Bruce was first either.

1. Doug wasn't first.	B, You can't finish behind someone and still be first

Note here that (B) refers to the statement "Doug was two places behind Tanya," and gives the reason why this means Doug couldn't have been first.

2. Bruce wasn't first	E, Same reason as for (1)

Our next step is to infer on the basis of statements (C), (D), (1), and (2) that Tanya finished first. The proof is that there are five people in the race, and we know of four that they didn't finish first. By elimination the remaining one is the winner.

*3. Tanya finished first	C, D, 1, 2—elimination: since 4 of 5 aren't first, the remaining one is the winner

We mark the (3) with an asterisk to denote that it forms part of the final solution. We can advance right away to another part of the final solution since (B) tells us that Doug finished two places behind Tanya.

*4. Doug was third	B, 3

At this point we start matching up the remaining contestants Sheila, Bruce, and John, with the remaining places second, fourth, and fifth, on the basis of the given information. We know from (E) that Sheila can't be last. If she were, Bruce couldn't finish behind her.

5. Sheila wasn't last	E, Bruce couldn't finish behind her if she were

But we also know that Sheila couldn't have been second. We established in (4) that Doug was third. If we assume Sheila is second, Bruce can't finish behind her because Doug is already in third place. The assumption isn't borne out, and Sheila can't be second.

6. Sheila wasn't second	E, Since Doug is in third place, Bruce couldn't finish behind her
7. Sheila wasn't third	4
*8. Sheila was fourth	D, 5, 6, 7—elimination

Here we establish that Sheila finished fourth since she couldn't have finished in any of the other four places. Some might question whether step (7) is necessary, since we just proved in step (4) that Doug is third. We supply it for reasons of clarity and completeness.

Finally we know that Bruce was fifth, since (E) tells us that he finished behind Sheila who was fourth. And we know that John was second since it is the only place left.

*9. Bruce was fifth	8, E
*10. John was second	3, 4, 8, 9—elimination

Now we will draw together in compact form our proof.

Given

A. Tanya wasn't second.

B. Doug was two places behind Tanya.

C. John was neither first nor last.

D. Sheila wasn't first.

E. Bruce finished behind Sheila.

Proof

1. Doug wasn't first	B, You can't finish behind someone and still be first
2. Bruce wasn't first	E, Same reason as (1)
*3. Tanya finished first	C, D, 1, 2—elimination: since 4 of 5 aren't first, the remaining one is the winner
*4. Doug was third	B, 3
5. Sheila wasn't last	E, Bruce couldn't finish behind her if she were
6. Sheila wasn't second	E, 4 Since Doug is in third place, Bruce couldn't finish behind her
7. Sheila wasn't third	4
*8. Sheila was fourth	D, 5, 6, 7—elimination
*9. Bruce was fifth	8, E
*10. John was second	3, 4, 8, 9—elimination

Inferring, drawing conclusions . . . Here you know some facts or truths already, and are concerned to see what further information can be derived from them; to find out their logical consequences.
P. F. Strawson

Implications and Inferences

We have used the terms "imply" and "infer" in our work on this puzzle. Before we can go on to work puzzles on our own, we should examine briefly the relation of the two. There is a considerable area where they overlap and the terms can be used interchangeably. But let us begin by examining each statement relation separately.

Implications are meanings or contents that lie embedded in a piece of discourse. Implications need to be drawn out and put in the form of statements if we are to work with them and form precise ideas of them. In the case of our logical puzzle, the given pieces of information *imply* some statements that may interest us in our effort to solve the puzzle. We call these implied statements "implications." It is the given information or discourse itself that does the implying, or to put this more conventionally, that has the implications. We, the would-be solvers of the puzzle, neither *have* the implications nor *do* the implying. We *draw* or *draw out* the implications of the given information or discourse.

Inferences are conclusions that are logically deduced or derived by reasoning from given facts or given information. To infer a statement from given facts is to draw it as a logical conclusion from those facts. The result that we infer from given information must of course be in that information to begin with, but its being there may not be obvious. The statement we infer is an *inference.*

This brings us to the one area where implication and inference cannot overlap. Given facts or information may *imply* a lot, or may have many implications. But given facts or information never *infers* anything. An inference is always a mental act (or a product of a mental act), and as such inference requires a mental agent or mind to carry it out. So only persons can infer. To infer a statement is to deduce it logically from given information.

Right:

> The given information that Sheila wasn't first or third *implies* that Sheila was second, fourth, or fifth.

Wrong:

> The given information that Sheila wasn't first or third *infers* that Sheila was second, fourth, or fifth.

Right:

> We *infer* that Sheila was second, fourth, or fifth from the given information that she wasn't first or third.

Wrong:

> We *imply* that Sheila was second, fourth, or fifth from the given information that she wasn't first or third.

Beyond this prohibition there are no hard and fast guidelines for distinguishing implications and inferences, so the area where the terms are used interchangeably is quite large. We do *see* implications where we do not similarly *see* inferences. So implications may be more straightforward or obvious, closer to the surface, or more obviously supported by the given information. An inference is always the product of a mental act. So inferences may involve several steps of reasoning, or may involve standard procedures of reasoning that can be codified as rules, or may refer to unstated generalizations or other unstated information.

We can briefly describe part of the reasoning we used to solve the above puzzle. In figuring out that Sheila had to be in fourth place, we worked mainly with these three pieces of information.

1. Sheila wasn't first or third
2. Bruce finished behind Sheila
3. Doug finished third

We *inferred* from this information that Sheila is fourth. From the fact that she's not first or third (1) and our knowledge that there are only five contestants, we *inferred* that she could only be second, fourth or fifth. The fact that Bruce finished behind her (2) *implies* she couldn't be last, because there is no place for someone to finish behind her. But it also *implies* she couldn't be second, since Doug is already in third place (3) and Bruce couldn't finish behind her (2). Our *inference* from this given information and reasoning is that Sheila is fourth, since she couldn't have finished in any of the other four places.

3. Advanced Puzzles

Now that we have had some practice working elementary logical puzzles, we can go on to more challenging ones. This one is a combinatorial where gathering information on a grid may help.

> Alice, Betty, Carol, and Dorothy were either a lifeguard, a lawyer, a pilot, or a professor. Each wore a white, yellow, pink, or blue dress.
>
> The lifeguard beat Betty at canasta, and Carol and the pilot often played bridge with the women in pink and blue dresses. Alice and the professor envied the woman in the blue dress, but this was not the lawyer, as she always wore a white dress.
>
> What was each woman's occupation and dress color?
>
> Irving M. Copi and Carl Cohen, *Introduction to Logic*, 9th ed., p. 76. Copyright © 1994 Paramount Publishing.

First we know that since the lifeguard beat Betty at canasta, Betty is not the lifeguard. Since Carol and the pilot played bridge with the women in pink and blue, Carol is not the pilot nor does she wear pink or blue, and the pilot wears neither pink nor blue. Alice and the professor envied the woman in blue, so Alice is not the professor, and neither Alice nor the professor wears blue. The lawyer wore white, so she didn't wear any of the other colors, and no one else wore white.

At this point let us introduce some abbreviations for economy of reference. Then we can sum up the results of our inferences from the given information on a grid as we did before.

A = Alice	lf = lifeguard	w = white
B = Betty	pl = pilot	y = yellow
C = Carol	pf = professor	pn = pink
D = Dorothy	lw = lawyer	b = blue

	lf	pl	pf	lw	w	y	pn	b
A			O					O
B	O							
C		O					O	O
D								
w	O	O	O	X				
y				O				
pn		O		O				
b		O	O	O				

Now we can see that the pilot is yellow by elimination, so no one else is yellow. And the professor is pink, so the only remaining color for the lifeguard is blue. Entering these results allows us to fill in the lower part of our grid and establish all the relations of professions and dress colors.

	lf	pl	pf	lw	w	y	pn	b
A			O					O
B	O							
C		O					O	O
D								
w	O	O	O	X				
y	O	X	O	O				
pn	O	O	X	O				
b	X	O	O	O				

But now we are stumped. Going back to the given, can we assume on the basis of the final statement that since the lawyer in white was mistaken for the woman envied by Alice and the professor, Alice can't be the lawyer in white? This assumption would be risky at this point, and we would like to get along without it if we could. Let us turn to our grid again instead to see whether we can make any more inferences there. We notice that Carol cannot be in pink or blue, and we now know that since she's not the pilot, who wears yellow, she can't be in yellow either. So Carol can only be in white, and no one else wears white. But we already know that the lawyer is in white, so Carol is the lawyer. This means Carol isn't anything else, and no one else is the lawyer.

We already know of Alice that she's neither professor nor lawyer. We also know that she's not in blue. Since the lifeguard is in blue, Alice can't be the lifeguard. So by elimination Alice is the pilot, and no one else is the pilot. Since the pilot is in yellow, Alice must be in yellow. No one else is in yellow, and Alice of course isn't in pink. But now the only thing left for Betty to be is the professor in pink, and by elimination Dorothy is the lifeguard in blue. Entering this information as we go along fills in our grid.

	lf	pl	pf	lw	w	y	pn	b
A	O	X	O	O	O	X	O	O
B	O	O	X	O	O	O	X	O
C	O	O	O	X	X	O	O	O
D	X	O	O	O	O	O	O	X
w	O	O	O	X				
y	O	X	O	O				
pn	O	O	X	O				
b	X	O	O	O				

So our final result looks like this.

Carol is the lawyer in white.
Alice is the pilot in yellow.
Betty is the professor in pink.
Dorothy is the lifeguard in blue.

Before going further you may want to attempt a proof for this puzzle. It isn't easy, but if you persevere you can probably get it. Compare yours with the one below.

Given

A. lf beat B
B. C and pl played against pn and b
C. A and pf envied b
D. lw is w

Proof

1.	B is not lf	A
2.	C is not pl	B
3.	C is not pn	B
4.	C is not b	B
5.	pl is not pn	B
6.	pl is not b	B
7.	A is not pf	C
8.	A is not b	C
9.	pf is not b	C

10.	lw is not b	D
11.	lf is b	6, 9, 10, elim.
12.	A is not lf	8, 11
13.	lw is not y	D
14.	lw is not pn	D
15.	pl is not w	D
16.	pl is y	5, 6, 15, elim.
17.	pf is pn	D, 11, 16, elim.
18.	C is not y	2, 16
*19.	C is lw and w	3, 4, 18, D, elim.
*20.	D is lf and b	1, 12, 19, 11, elim.
*21.	A is pl and y	7, 19, 20, 16, elim.
*22.	B is pf and pn	19, 20, 21, elim.

Grouping

Sometimes our inference from given information suffices for us to assert something outright about a specific person. For example, in Step 2 we assert that Carol is not the pilot because B states something about Carol and the pilot. This implies that they are two different people.

At other times we infer some information but not enough to support a claim so forthright as that in Step 2. Our inference narrows the possibilities, but not down to a specific individual or item. In such a case we must *group* the remaining possibilities together until further information allows us a more specific reference. We didn't need to use grouping to solve the above puzzle. But we need to be familiar with its use. Some puzzles cannot be solved without it, and others are much easier to solve with it.

In Step 3 we learn that Carol doesn't wear the pink dress, and in Step 4 that she doesn't wear the blue. At this point we can state that she wears either the yellow or the white dress. Since the reference is not to a specific item, we group these two possibilities in parentheses.

4a. C is (y or w) 2, 3, elim.

This grouping means we know Carol wears one of these two colors, but we aren't sure which. We must await further information to determine which. The further information comes in Step 18 where we learn that Carol doesn't wear yellow. Now that yellow is eliminated, we know she wears white.

We can group persons as well as things. Step 1 shows that Betty is not the lifeguard, and Step 12 eliminates Alice too. At this point we can show by grouping that the possibilities for lifeguard are narrowed to Carol and Dorothy.

12a. (C or D) is lf 1, 12, elim.

Again we must await the information that allows us to decide between the two. It comes in Step 19 where we learn that Carol is the lawyer. Since she is eliminated, Dorothy is the lifeguard.

Truth-teller and Liar Puzzles

Our next puzzle is the type where you know that one or more of the speakers are lying. So you have to figure out who is lying and who is telling the truth, but this also helps you find your solution. A grid is usually of little or no help with such puzzles.

Whodunnit?

The TV show *Lie Detector* has now been changed to allow the audience to participate in solving crimes. Assume that the lie detector is infallible. Sandwell, the gifted but caustic stand-up comedian, has been murdered by one of the four suspects now appearing on *Lie Detector*. Below are the responses of each to the question "Who killed Sandwell?" According to the lie detector, three of the responses are lies. But we aren't told which three.

Who killed Sandwell? Who is telling the truth?

Glass: "I am not the murderer."
Dinwiddie: "Sandwell was killed by Adorno. Adorno was the butt of some of his most cutting jokes."
Barchester: "Dinwiddie murdered him. He hated him."
Adorno: "I didn't kill him."

Now try your hand at solving it before looking at the solution that follows.

Where do we start? What method do we use? We start by focusing on the questions to be answered. We are to find out who killed Sandwell, and which of the suspects is telling the truth. What we have to go on are the statements of the four suspects, plus the information supplied by the lie detector that three of these are false. It looks like we must begin by assuming that one of the statements is true, then draw out the implications of this assumption. If this doesn't yield a solution, we simply go on to the next statement and assume that it is true. We will work our way systematically through the statements until we get a solution.

We assume to begin with that Glass is telling the truth. This implies that he is not the killer (his statement "I'm not the murderer" is true). But it also implies that the other three statements are false. Since Dinwiddie's statement "Sandwell was killed by Adorno" is false, this implies Adorno isn't the killer. The falsity of Barchester's statement "Dinwiddie murdered him" implies Dinwiddie isn't the murderer. And Adorno's "I didn't kill him" being false implies Adorno did kill him.

We notice now that our assumption has led to a contradiction. The falsity of Dinwiddie's statement implies Adorno isn't the killer, whereas the falsity of Adorno's own statement implies that he is the killer. It is a contradiction to say that Adorno both is and isn't the killer. For this reason we must reject our first assumption and go on to the next.

At this point it is advisable to abbreviate our steps for the sake of clarity in working toward a solution. Shown below are shortened versions of not only our first assumption, but the others we must make to arrive at a solution.

S = Sandwell
G = Glass
D = Dinwiddie
B = Barchester
A = Adorno

Assumption #1: G—"I am not the murderer" is true.

D—"S was killed by A" is false; implies A isn't killer.
B—"D murdered him" is false; implies D isn't killer.
A—"I didn't kill him" is false; implies A is killer.

The falsity of the statements of D and A implies a contradiction, that A both is and isn't the killer. So this assumption fails.

Assumption #2: D—"S was killed by A" is true.

G—"I'm not the murderer" is false; implies G is the killer.
B—"D murdered him" is false; implies D isn't killer.
A—"I didn't kill him" is false; implies A is killer.

On this assumption there is not one but two killers: G and A. So it too must be rejected.

Assumption #3: B—"D murdered him" is true.

G—"I'm not the murderer" is false; implies G is killer.
D—"S was killed by A" is false; implies A isn't killer.
A—"I didn't kill him" is false; implies A is killer.

As in Assumption #1, the falsity of statements D and A implies a contradiction. This assumption fails also.

Assumption #4:—A "I didn't kill him" is true.

G—"I am not the murderer" is false; implies G is the killer.
D—"S was murdered by A" is false; implies A isn't killer.
B—"D murdered him" is false; implies D isn't killer.

On this assumption, all of the implications are consistent. The murderer is Glass. The truth-teller is Adorno.

Depending on how good you are at solving such puzzles and how well you start with this one, you might find a solution much quicker. Here is an example of a well reasoned but quite rapid solution.

Once you have established that Glass's statement is false (as a result of our first assumption), you know that he must be the killer. The falsity of "I am not the murderer" implies "I am the murderer." The falsity of Glass's statement is compatible with the falsity of the statements by Dinwiddie and Barchester. They claim that someone else is the murderer, and the falsity of these claims is compatible with Glass being the murderer. But it is not compatible with the falsity of Adorno's statement.

The falsity of "I didn't kill him" implies that Adorno is the killer, whereas we know we already have our killer in Glass. So Adorno must be the one telling the truth.

Logical Assumptions and Implications

To ask for the implications of Statement A is to ask what other statements it makes true, or what other statements must be true if it is true. To ask for the logical assumptions of Statement A is to ask what statements must be true in order for it to be true. These may also be called its presuppositions. When we ask for its logical assumptions we may be indirectly calling Statement A into question. Its truth remains questionable until we establish that its assumptions (the statements that must be true for it to be true) are true also. So to inquire after logical assumptions is to seek the wider context in which the statement is located to gain more information about it.

Summary

Solving logical puzzles involves reasoning or inference, where we draw out implications of given information and proceed toward solutions by avoiding inconsistencies. Using a grid helps us keep track of what we learn as we work toward solving the puzzle.

When we demonstrate in a logical proof that our solution to a puzzle is a good solution, this makes us think critically about our reasoning. In such a proof we respond every step of the way to a skeptic who asks us for our reasons. We must reflect on our reasoning and justify it, which is critical thinking.

Inferences and implications agree in that both may be drawn from given information. But implications are viewed more from the vantage point of the information they are drawn from, while inferences are viewed more from the standpoint of the reasoning mind that carries them out.

An implication is a statement that is made true, or logically implied, by some other statement or statements. A logical assumption is a statement that must be true for some other statement or statements to be true.

Study Questions

Section 1: Logical Puzzles as Reasoning Exercises

1. What is the object of reasoning? (Peirce)
2. What is a logical puzzle?

Section 2: The Logical Proof as a Critical Thinking Exercise

3. Why isn't solving logical puzzles a model critical thinking activity?
4. What is the goal of a logical proof?
5. What are the ways of justifying steps in a logical proof?
6. What is an inference?
7. How is *implying* something different from *inferring* something?

Section 3: Advanced Puzzles

8. Distinguish a logical assumption from an implication.

EXERCISE 4—1: ELEMENTARY LOGICAL PUZZLES

Provide solutions and proofs for the following elementary logical puzzles. Use the techniques you have just learned. Almost all of these puzzles have some combinatorial aspect, so a grid may help. In general each succeeding puzzle is a bit more challenging. Give a proof for each puzzle you work.

1. Software Associates

Software Associates is a small computer services firm. Its employees are a technician, a mainframe programmer, and a PC programmer: Lee, Oswald, and Cantrell, though not necessarily in that order. The mainframe programmer likes bowling. But Cantrell's only sport is poker, which he sometimes plays with the technician and Lee. What does each person do?

2. The Picnic

At the picnic Mike went for soft drinks for Wendy, Brian, Janet, and Sean, as well as for himself. He brought back iced tea, grape juice, Diet Coke, Pepsi, and 7-Up. What drink did he bring for each person?

A. Mike couldn't tolerate carbonated drinks.
B. Janet would drink either 7-Up or Pepsi.
C. Wendy only liked sodas.
D. Brian preferred the drink he would put lemon and sugar into.
E. Sean only liked clear drinks.

3. Paintball

During a crazy weekend of paintball, four friends were having great fun. The paint came in blue, green, yellow and red. Coincidentally, the four friends had T-shirts in those same colors. Brenda used blue paint balls. The person in the green T-shirt used yellow paint balls. James was not wearing a red T-shirt. Diane used green paint balls and wore a blue T-shirt. Simon was the only person who used paint which was the same color as his T-shirt.

Match the players with the color of paint used and T-shirt color.

4. Family Reunions

Five families decide to hold family reunions at a large hotel. Each family occupies a suite on a different floor. On which floor is each family?

A. The Carley family is on the floor directly under the Wright family.
B. The Malloy family is on a floor below all the others.
C. There is one floor between the Brown and the Malloy families.
D. The Brown children have to ride the elevator up 17 floors to visit the Snows.
E. The Wright children are not on the 16th floor, but their friends the Carleys are. These same friends are 10 floors above the Malloys.

Logic, Anyone by Beverly Post &Sandra Eads.

5. Gossip

Talkative Mrs. Bambola was very well informed and had a good memory for what went on in her neighborhood. But she had trouble with numbers and a poor memory for addresses. She told us the following about her neighbors on Hubbard Lane, each individual or couple living in a separate house.

A. Coach, at 23, 25 or 27 had a high-stakes poker game in his den every Friday night.
B. The widow at 23 or 27 had pizza delivered by the same good-looking

boy several times a week.

C. The ageing hippie at 27 or 29 grew marijuana in his sun room.

D. The couple at 23, 25 or 29 had shouting matches that could be heard several houses away.

E. The hippie lives next door to the couple.

At which Hubbard Lane address does each live?

6. The Dinner Party

Smith, Brown, Jones, and Williams had dinner together the other night, washed down with good wine and followed by cognac and cigars. When they parted, each of them, by mistake, was wearing the hat belonging to one other member of the party, and the coat belonging to another. The man who took Williams' hat took Jones' coat. The hat taken by Jones belonged to the owner of the coat taken by Williams. Smith took Brown's hat.

Who wore what away from the party?

7. Artists and Dwellings

Chung, Gardner, and Russo are an editor, a fashion designer, and an interior decorator, though not necessarily in that order. The fashion designer is trying to get the interior decorator to do her new loft, but she has to finish the editor's townhouse first. She also plans some renovations on her own bungalow.

Gardner knows nothing of Russo. Russo earns more than Chung. The inhabitant of the townhouse earns least. Match up each woman with her profession.

8. Research Assistantship

Professor Throckmorton had two equally well-trained applicants for her one-year research assistantship. Not wanting luck to decide, she devised a simple reasoning test. She asked the two to sit at one side of a table, each with a pencil and steno pad. On the other she placed one 9-by-12 brown clasp envelope, a similar sized white Tyvec envelope, and a slightly larger red-white-and-blue priority mail envelope.

"Inside one envelope," she stated, "is a research-assistant employment contract for $9,000 which I have already signed. The successful applicant will be the first to reason out which envelope the contract is in, based on one sentence written on each envelope. At least one of the three sentences is false, and at least one is true."

Which envelope contained the contract? How did the successful applicant reason?

Brown clasp: The contract is in this envelope.
White Tyvec: The contract is not in this envelope.
Red white and blue: The contract is not in the white envelope.

9. Smith, Jones, and Robinson

Mr. Smith, Mr. Jones, and Mr. Robinson live in Chicago, Omaha, and Detroit, but not necessarily respectively. They are passengers on a train run by a three-man crew. The men on the crew are named Smith, Jones, and Robinson, and they are engineer, fireman, and brakeman, but not necessarily respectively. Mr. Robinson lives in Detroit. Mr. Jones never studied algebra. Smith beat the fireman at billiards. The passenger whose name is the same as the brakeman's lives in Chicago. The brakeman lives in Omaha. The brakeman's nearest neighbor, one of the passengers, is a mathematician. What positions do Smith, Jones, and Robinson hold on the crew?

Ronald Munson, *The Way of Words*
(Atlanta, 1976), p. 406.

EXERCISE 4□2: CHALLENGING LOGICAL PUZZLES

Part A. Moderately Difficult

Try to solve the following puzzles. Be able to give a reason for each step you take.

1. The Artists

Boronoff, Pavlow, Revitsky, and Sukarek are four talented artists, one a dancer, one a painter, one a singer, and one a writer (though not necessarily respectively).

A. Boronoff and Revitsky were in the audience the night the singer made his debut on the concert stage.
B. Both Pavlow and the writer have sat for portraits by the painter.
C. The writer, whose biography of Sukarek was a best-seller, is planning to write a biography of Boronoff.
D. Boronoff has never heard of Revitsky.

What is each man's artistic field?

C. R. Wylie, Jr., *101 Puzzles in Thought and Logic*,
"Introduction." Copyright © 1957 Dover Publications.

2. The Hot Tub

Heather, Rob, Cheryl, and David get out of the hot tub and towel off. Going into the next room, they discover the dog has played with their footwear and bags, mixing them up. In the pile are canvas deck shoes, tan leather shoes, and bags of suede, canvas, and tan leather. The one with suede shoes has a khaki bag. Cheryl finds leather too stiff and prefers cloth for both. Only David uses shoe polish to buff his shoes. Heather's bag is the same material as David's shoes, but she doesn't wear the wool foot-warmers. Can you match bags and shoes with their owners?

3. Kathy's Mr. Right

Kathy's Mr. Right is attractive, warm, and fun-loving. Four men are interested in her: Aaron, Buddy, Charlie, and Don. About them we know the following.

A. Only one of the men has all three traits.
B. Each man has at least one of the traits.
C. Only three of the men are attractive, only two are warm, and only one is fun-loving.
D. Aaron and Charlie are either equally warm or equally uptight.
E. Charlie and Don have modeled clothes.
F. Don and Aaron aren't both photogenic.

Which of the four is Kathy's Mr. Right?

4. Music Lover

In my collection of classical music there are several pieces where one plays just a minute longer than the other. Each is on a different format. Given the following information, can you match the music, the format, and the playing time?

A. The pieces last 6, 7, 8 and 9 minutes.
B. The Bach lasts 8 minutes.
C. The CD lasts longer than the Haydn.
D. The piece on tape lasts longer than the Vivaldi.
E. The single takes 7 minutes to play.
F. The album contains no Haydn.
G. The Rossini is on tape.

5. Sir Christopher

Christopher rode through the world searching for adventure when he came upon an ugly old woman trying to cross a stream. Christopher gallantly let her ride upon his horse and when they reached the other side, the old woman took Christopher to her hut and revealed to him four magnificent swords. Two had hilts of gold, the other two of silver; and one hilt of each metal was inlaid with pearl, the other with opal. Then the hag offered Christopher his choice of the swords in gratitude for his chivalry.

Christopher's interest was roused when he heard that one of the swords had been forged by his ancestor Taliessin and bore powerful enchantments. The other three were made by the swordsmiths Regin, Siegfried, and Weland; but as to which was which, all the woman would tell him was the following:

A. The sword Taliessin made is older than the opal-and-gold sword.
B. The sword of Regin is the same age as the pearl-and-silver sword.
C. Siegfried's sword is older than either pearl-inlaid sword.
D. The sword of Weland has a gold hilt.

Sir Christopher immediately knew which blade was forged by which swordsmith, and he chose his ancestor's weapon. How quickly can you match swords with swordsmiths?

Games (November 1986), p.10.

6. The Jellybeans

Marge had hidden several small bags of jellybeans bought as favors for an office party. But when she looked in the covered crock in the kitchen cabinet, they were missing. Her children Sara, Tom, Jessica, and Dawn all liked jelly beans. She knew the one who found them wouldn't share, so she examined them for sticky fingers, signs of upset stomach, or guilty conscience. Finding none, she determined to get to the bottom of the matter and punish the culprit. When she asked who took the jellybeans, each child responded as follows. Moral education had been somewhat slighted in Marge's family, so that on any given occasion only one child told the truth consistently. The others all lied consistently. Who was the culprit, and how did Marge figure it out?

Jessica: "I didn't take them. I like M&Ms better.
Sara: "Dawn found them. She is such a snoop."
Dawn: "Tom took them. I saw him eating them."
Tom: "I did not take them. I was eating chocolate covered peanuts I bought with money from my allowance."

7. Lunch

Six women meet bi-weekly for salad, brie, and chardonnay at the Ritz Hotel. When it is sunny they gather on the terrace overlooking the park, where they all sit today at a circular table. They are Uma, Vanessa, Wendy, Xena, Yvonne, and Zelda. One admires Wendy's jade pantsuit, one is a financial analyst, one has dandruff flakes, one picks up the tab, one drives a BMW, and one wears a turban.

The woman who admires Wendy's jade pantsuit sits directly across from Yvonne. The financial analyst sits opposite Xena, who is seated between the woman with dandruff flakes and the one admiring Wendy's jade pantsuit. The turbaned woman sits directly across from Zelda, next to the financial analyst and to the left of the pantsuit admirer. The one with dandruff flakes sits between Zena and the one opposite the woman who admires Wendy's jade pantsuit. Uma, who is colorblind, sits next to the one wearing a turban and opposite the woman who picks up the tab.

Match the women with the features (drives BMW etc.).

8. Resort in Europe

In one of the famous resort towns of Europe, where tourists from a dozen countries may always be encountered, four travelers once struck up an acquaintance. They were of different nationalities and although each man could speak two of the four languages, English, French, German, and Italian, there was still no common tongue in which they could all converse. In fact only one of the languages was spoken by more than two of the men.

Nobody spoke both French and German. Although John couldn't speak English he could still act as interpreter when Peter and Jacob wanted to speak to each other. Jacob spoke German and could also talk to William although the latter knew not a word of German. John, Peter, and William could not all converse in the same language.

What two languages did each man speak?

C. R. Wylie, Jr., *101 Puzzles in Thought and Logic*, No. 35.
Copyright © 1957 Dover Publications.

Part B. Difficult Puzzles

1. Speaking of Tennis

Four people played a tennis game: Winifred, her father, her husband, and their daughter. After the game, one of them spoke truthfully about one time during the game:

"I was directly across the net from the server's daughter. My partner (on the same side of the net as I) was directly across the net from the receiver's father. The server was diagonally across the net from the receiver."

Who spoke?

George J. Summers, *Mind Puzzlers*
(New York 1984), p. 13.

2. Mordred's Daughter

King Mordred didn't want his only child, the princess, to marry a dullard. The chap might have some work to do in the kingdom. And of course he had to be a prince and bring some land to the union. Mordred's wealth was great and his kingdom extended far and wide, but not far enough.

Several princes had already failed the test you now have to pass to win the princess' hand. Two court ladies of height and figure similar to the princess speak like the princess behind veils concealing their eyes, all disguising their voices. The duchess and the chatelaine have eyes different from the princess, but we don't know which is blue, brown, or green. You must match Aspasia, Rowena and Gwendolyn with their positions and eye color to win the princess. When they state the following, you know that one always lies, and the other two, even though they too are courtiers, lie only once.

Aspasia:

1. Rowena is the chatelaine.
2. The blue-eyed one is the chatelaine.
3. The duchess has brown eyes.

Rowena:

4. I am the princess.
5. The duchess has blue eyes.
6. The chatelaine doesn't have brown eyes.

Gwen:

7. Rowena is the duchess.
8. The blue-eyed one is the princess.
9. Aspasia is the chatelaine.
10. The duchess has green eyes.

Can you win the princess?

2. Cabbies and Their Fares

Five cabbies have been summoned to pick up five fares at the Belaire Business Club. On arrival, they find that their passengers are slightly intoxicated. Each man has a different first and last name, a different profession, a different destination; and each man's wife has a different first name. Unable to determine who's who and who's going where, the cabbies ask you, the central dispatcher, to find out. Match the fares' first and last names, spouses, jobs, cab number, and streets. You collect these facts from the intoxicated passengers.

A. Brad is married to Betty.
B. Barbara's husband gets in the third cab.
C. Bart is a banker.
D. The last cab goes to Barton St.
E. Beatrice lives on Burton St.
F. The butcher gets in the fourth cab.
G. Bret gets into the second cab.
H. Bernice is married to the broker.
I. Mr. Barker lives on Burton St.
J. Mr. Burger gets in the cab in front of Brenda's husband.
K. Mr. Bunger gets in the first cab.
L. Mr. Baker lives on Bourbon St.
M. The barber lives on Baker St.
N. Mr. Baker gets in the cab in front of Mr. Burke.
O. The barber is three cabs in front of Brian.
P. Mr. Burger is in the cab in front of the butcher.

3. Bank Employees

In a certain bank there were eleven distinct positions, namely, in decreasing rank, President, First Vice-President, Second Vice-President, Third Vice-President, Cashier, Teller, Assistant Teller, Bookkeeper, First Stenographer, Second Stenographer, and Janitor. These eleven positions are occupied by the following, here listed alphabetically: Mr. Adams, Mrs. Brown, Mr. Camp, Miss Dale, Mr. Evans, Mrs. Ford, Mr. Grant, Miss Hill, Mr. Jones, Mrs. Kane, and Mr. Long. Concerning them, only the following facts are known.

A. The Third Vice-President is the pampered grandson of the President but is disliked by both Mrs. Brown and the Assistant Teller.
B. The Assistant Teller and the Second Stenographer shared equally in their father's estate.
C. The Second Vice-President and the Assistant Teller wear the same style of hats.
D. Mr. Grant told Miss Hill to send him a stenographer at once.
E. The President's nearest neighbors are Mrs. Kane, Mr. Grant, and Mr. Long.
F. The First Vice-President and the Cashier live at the exclusive Bachelor's Club.
G. The Janitor, a miser, has occupied the same garret room since boyhood.
H. Mr. Adams and the Second Stenographer are leaders in the social life of the younger unmarried set.
I. The Second Vice-President and the Bookkeeper were once engaged to be married to each other.

J. The fashionable Teller is the son-in-law of the First Stenographer.
K. Mr. Jones regularly gives Mr. Evans his discarded clothing to wear, without the elderly Bookkeeper knowing about the gift.

Show how to match correctly the eleven names against the eleven positions occupied.

Irving M. Copi and Carl Cohen, *Introduction to Logic*, 9th ed., p. 75f. Copyright © 1994 Paramount Publishing.

THE CRITICAL THINKING JOURNAL

Part A. Statement Relations and Inference

4. Logical Puzzles

Work one of the following puzzles with a proof for your journal. B puzzles are more challenging than A, C more yet, and D most.

1. Tastes in Music (A)

There's no guessing what a person's taste in music is from their choice of wheels or dwelling, as the following puzzle shows. Match the people with their dwellings, wheels, and favorite music groups.

*A. Michelle likes the Beatles.
*B. Jan is a fan of the Grateful Dead.
C. The person who rides the Kawasaki lives in the townhouse.
D. Greg doesn't live in the colonial.
E. Vic doesn't drive the Buick.
F. The Nirvana fan lives in the apartment and drives the pick-up.
G. Michelle doesn't live in the rancher or colonial.
H. The person who likes the Beach Boys drives the Buick.
I. Someone drives a Geo.

2. The Teachers (D)

In the Stillwater High School the economics, English, French, history, Latin, and mathematics classes are taught, though not necessarily respectively, by Mrs. Arthur, Miss Bascomb, Mrs. Conroy, Mr. Duval, Mr. Eggleston, and Mr. Furness.

A. The mathematics teacher and the Latin teacher were roommates in college.
B. Eggleston is older than Furness but has not taught as long as the economics teacher.
C. As students, Mrs. Arthur and Miss Bascomb attended one high school while the others attended a different high school.
D. Furness is the French teacher's father.
E. The English teacher is the oldest of the six both in age and in years of service. In fact, he had the mathematics teacher and the history teacher in class when they were students in the Stillwater High School.
F. Mrs. Arthur is older than the Latin teacher.

What subject does each person teach?

C. R. Wylie, Jr., *101 Puzzles in Thought and Logic*, No. 12. Copyright © 1957 Dover Publications.

3. The Conference (B)

Mumford, Ephor, Klich, Billups, Ho, and Jaskowski had breakfast together in the cafe in the lobby of a resort hotel. They were attending a conference of the American Society of Mechanical Engineers. They all headed for the elevator when they finished, and each had one matter to attend to. The matters were visiting the equipment display, going by the newsstand, listening to an address, swimming laps, attending a committee meeting, and stopping off at the travel office. Match the men with their matters and floors. (You may need to find out where the mezzanine is located.)

A. All of the men except Jaskowski entered the elevator in the lobby.
B. Three children also got in, making the elevator crowded.
C. Ho exited on the mezzanine.
D. The address was scheduled in the main ballroom on the 2nd floor, while the committee meeting was on the mezzanine.
E. The three children rushed out on the 3rd floor.
F. The man who wanted to swim laps got out on the 4th floor.
G. Billups exited the elevator last, on the 5th floor.
H. The travel office is in the lobby.
I. Klich was the seventh person to get out of the elevator.
J. Ho was given a newspaper by the man who bought it on the mezzanine.
K. Mumford was briefed on the address by the man who attended it.

4. Jobs (B)

Gargaro, Hong, Dwyer, and Slocumb are lathe operator, sales associate, chef, and sports reporter, though not necessarily in that order. About these four men we have the following information. Who does what?

A. Hong plays tennis frequently with Gargaro, and usually wins.
B. Dwyer and Hong ride in the same car pool to get to work.
C. Slocumb earns less than Dwyer.
D. The lathe operator rides his Harley to work.
E. Neither the sales associate nor the sports reporter earns as much as the chef.
F. The chef lives on the opposite side of the city from the sales associate.
G. The sports reporter knows the chef only from the latter's second place finish in the Cedars Hospital 10K Benefit Run.

5. Daniel's Law Partner (C)

Daniel has a new law partner.

A. His partner is either Melissa, Kimberly, Rhonda, or Lynette.
B. Daniel and each of these women either always tells the truth or always lies.
C. Melissa says: "Exactly one of us four women always tells the truth."
D. Kimberly says: "Exactly one of us four women always lies."
E. Rhonda says: "Melissa or Kimberly is Daniel's new law partner."
F. Lynette says nothing.
G. Daniel says: "I won't have a liar for my new law partner."
H. Daniel says: "Either I always tell the truth or I always lie."

Who is Daniel's new law partner?

6. The City Officials (D)

Anderson, Bristow, Risher, and Weintraub serve their community as city architect, waterworks director, prosecuting attorney, and assistant city manager, though not necessarily respectively.

Give each man's position.

A. Anderson is more conservative than Risher but more liberal than Weintraub.
B. Anderson earns more than the man younger than Bristow.
C. The waterworks director is neither the oldest nor the youngest.
D. The waterworks director earns more than the assistant city manager.
E. The assistant city manager is more conservative than the city architect.

F. Risher earns more than the city architect.
G. The oldest earns most and is the most conservative.

7. Talent Contest (C)

Ten people are finalists in a talent contest. For the final judging, they are lined up in order of the tallest to the shortest. Where does each person stand? Number the people from the tallest (#1) to the shortest (#10).

A. Maria is standing next to Bill.
B. Ray is taller than Josh, who is standing next to Kim, who is shorter.
C. Bill is the tallest person.
D. Perin is taller than Kim, and they are both taller than Ruth.
E. No one is standing between Perin (the taller) and Abby.
F. No one is standing between Frances and Maria.
G. Abby is shorter than Abe, who is also shorter than Frances.
H. Abe is taller than Perin, who is taller than Ray; they are all taller than Kim.

Logic, Anyone by Beverly Post and Sandra Eads, p. 37.

8. A Week in Burmingham (B)

The town of Burmingham has a supermarket, a department store, and a bank. On the day I went into Burmingham, the bank was open.

A. The supermarket, the department store, and the bank are not open together on any day of the week.
B. The department store is open four days a week.
C. The supermarket is open five days a week.
D. All three places are closed on Sunday and Wednesday.
E. On three consecutive days:
the department store was closed on the first day
the bank was closed on the second day
the supermarket was closed on the third day
F. On three consecutive days:
the bank was closed on the first day
the supermarket was closed on the second day
the department store was closed on the third day

On which of the seven days did I go into the town of Burmingham?

George J. Summers, *New Puzzles in Logical Deduction*, p. 29.

9. Pizza Party (A)

Six friends go out for a pizza. They soon find out that they can't share a large pizza because each person likes a different type. The friends end up ordering six individual pizzas: plain cheese; cheese and pepperoni; cheese, pepperoni, and sausage; cheese and anchovies; The Works; and cheese and bacon. Who orders what?

A. Kent likes only one item other than cheese, and that is not pepperoni.
B. Tom sits next to the person who orders cheese and bacon.
C. Fred hates any kind of fish.
D. The person who orders two items and cheese sits directly across from Betty.
E. Trina orders The Works.
F. Willie won't eat sausage or bacon.
G. Betty and Tom sit next to each other.
H. Fred and Tom both like pepperoni.

Logic, Anyone by Beverly Post and Sandra Eads, p. 38.

10. At the Bank (A)

At the bank the positions of loan officer, teller, trust administrator, cashier, and mortgage officer are held by Mr. FitzPatrick, Miss Bailey, Mr. Perez, Miss Weber, and Mr. Tucker, though not necessarily in that order. What position does each person fill?

A. The trust administrator borrowed clear nail polish from the loan officer.
B. The mortgage officer never found the right girl to marry.
C. Miss Weber and Mr. FitzPatrick once dated, but that romance died.
D. Mr. Tucker reported happily to his wife that the loan officer had approved their auto loan.
E. Mr. Perez will sing at the wedding of the cashier and the trust administrator.

Further Reading

Douglas N. Walton, "What Is Reasoning? What Is an Argument?" *Journal of Philosophy*, Vol. 87 (1990), pp. 399–419. Discusses reasoning from logical and psychological standpoints and considers both theoretical and practical reasoning.

You will find more logical puzzles to test your skills in the following works.

Irving M. Copi and Carl Cohen, *Introduction to Logic*, 9th ed. (New York 1994), pp. 76–77. Fifteen puzzles, some quite challenging.

Marvin Grosswirth and Abbie Salney, *The Mensa Genius Quiz Book* (Reading 1981). Chapter Four on "Mathematics, Reasoning, and Logic" contains some good puzzles.

Ronald Munson, *The Way of Words* (Boston 1976). See Chapter 11 "The Logic of Puzzles" for more puzzles and help on how to work them.

Beverly Post and Sandra Eads, *Logic, Anyone?* (Belmont 1982). Several types of fairly elementary puzzles.

George J. Summers, *Mind Puzzlers* (New York 1984). A number of these puzzles are deceptively simple. You don't realize how challenging they are until you attempt them.

George J. Summers, *New Puzzles in Logical Deduction* (New York 1968). These puzzles range from moderately to rather challenging.

C. R. Wylie, Jr., *101 Puzzles in Thought & Logic* (New York 1957). Begins with relatively simple and proceeds to fairly complex puzzles.

Part Two

A Logic of Arguments

CHAPTER FIVE

ARGUMENTS

What is a question of fact?—Quite simply,
it's deciding what really happened in a case.
The Answer Book for Jury Service

1. FACTS AND OPINIONS

"Where did you put the postage stamps? I have to get this check in the mail today."

"They're in the desk drawer," replied Doug.

"No they're not," Sally rejoined. "I already looked there."

"Oh, I remember. They're probably on the end table by the front door. Mrs. Sims needed to borrow a couple of stamps in a hurry, and I probably forgot to put them back."

Sally walked over to the end table. The stamps were there.

The question of the whereabouts of the postage stamps is a question of fact. It can be answered by going to a certain place and looking. Many questions of fact can be answered by someone going to a certain place at a certain time and observing. But it is not always possible for someone to actually be there. We do accept some historical facts even in the absence of eyewitness testimony, and of course it is impossible for any contemporary to go back and witness what happened long ago. And we do accept some facts about distant regions of the universe, even though no earthling has traveled farther than the moon, our nearest celestial neighbor.

Many factual questions are answerable in a relatively straightforward manner, even when we don't actually have the answers. We don't know, for instance, whether the land masses of Africa and South America were ever joined together. But we know where we would have had to be, and we have a pretty good idea when, in order to find out. Often when we are dealing with facts we do not expect people to disagree about them. If three people stand looking at an end table, we do not expect two of them to affirm that there are postage stamps on it and the third to deny it.

> "See how Mt. Shasta rises majestically out of the plain?"
> "Yes. Isn't it the tallest mountain in California?"
> "No. According to *Hammond's Road Atlas*, Mt. Whitney in southern California is 14,494 feet high, but Mt. Shasta is only 14,162 feet."

For numerous facts we rely on the observations and measurements of others. Anyone can travel from Mt. Shasta to Mt. Whitney and observe them both. But far fewer people would know how to go about measuring them to settle the question. Those who possess this specialized knowledge and have mastered the use of the appropriate measuring instruments are experts, and in accepting facts like this we depend on the work of such experts. In cases where the experts agree, their determinations are usually accepted as facts. When they disagree, we realize that they are dealing with a matter of fact that they haven't quite got right yet.

But there are other areas where people (even knowledgeable people) disagree, areas where we do not really expect people to agree.

> "Don't you think it was wrong of David to just take the money from that wallet he found lying in the parking lot, then throw it back down?"
> "Oh, I don't know. We've all lost money or things of value like watches or rings without ever having them returned. Maybe it all balances out in the end."
> "Well I sure don't agree with you on that. That money could easily belong to someone who needs it desperately, and is even now searching for it frantically."

> "In my opinion, *Despair* is the best of Nabokov's novels. It is innovative in form, slyly humorous, and its interpretation of character has a solid psychological foundation."
> "I much prefer *Pnin*. It treats the slightly ridiculous and vulnerable Russian professor with great tenderness. It glows with a warm humanity you seek in vain in much of Nabokov's other writing."

On such matters as these, where reasonable people can disagree, we hold and advance opinions. There are certain areas of experience where we are more likely to encounter opinions. All normal people hold opinions similar to those in our first example about right and wrong, or what is morally good and bad. And most people also have opinions about whether one painting is more beautiful (or less beautiful) than another, or as in our second example, whether one novel is better or worse than another.

It is often said that aesthetic questions such as these latter ones are matters of taste, and that it makes no sense to dispute matters of taste.[1] But this view is mistaken, or at least short-sighted. Matters of taste *can* be disputed, and sometimes it makes very good sense to dispute them. Just think—if they couldn't, adults would still appreciate best the same bright colors and soothing sounds that pleased them most as infants. Of course, there is expertise in aesthetic matters too. But it exists not so much to establish and communicate facts as to provide the information and perspectives we need to form our own taste.

Is there expertise on what is morally good or bad? Most people would say: No. Yet some people get turned to more often than others for advice on such matters. But here even more than in aesthetic matters, advice remains advice, and people must make up their own minds. Many people are strongly committed to certain moral values (often conjoined with religious convictions), and these fundamental values then form the basis of their opinions.

In some cases, however, we hold opinions on matters that are instrumental rather than basic or fundamental. We may agree with someone on a fundamental value—say that of human life or health—yet differ on the instrumental question of how to achieve or maintain it.

> "I recommend an immediate operation, Mrs. Rader. We don't need to know whether that lump in your breast is malignant. It certainly isn't doing you any good, and it might eventually turn malignant if we leave it in."
>
> "Don't take this wrong, Doctor, but I want a second opinion before I undergo surgery. If I don't have cancer, I'd rather avoid the risk—however slight—as well as the pain and inconvenience of surgery."

Two different physicians, confronted with the same facts, can evaluate them differently and reach different opinions.

To judge from the above examples, the distinction of fact from opinion is relatively straightforward and clear-cut. This is deceptive. Not everything one likes, for instance, forms the basis of an opinion. An opinion always solicits the assent of at least a few other people.

> "I just love sundaes with slices of dill and pickle juice on vanilla ice cream."

This may express an individual quirk. The person confessing this could well be expressing her individuality rather than soliciting the assent or even the approval of others.

As important as it is for us to make the distinction of fact from opinion, the distinction is sharp and clear only at one level. When you press on, it grows complex and less clear. Not seldom we discover that an odd assortment of assumptions and tacit understandings or conventions plays an important role in

---

[1] The Latin *de gustibus non est disputandum* is sometimes cited in this connection.

what we all agree is a fact. Usually we don't become aware of this until some unforseen development—such as an advance in science, technology, or medicine—brings it starkly before us.

Forty or fifty years ago, for instance, there was little question about when a person was dead. It was accepted as a fact that when the heart stopped beating, life was at an end. Then a series of advances in biomedical techniques culminated in the blood pump, an apparatus that can oxygenate and circulate a person's blood indefinitely after his own heart has ceased to function. What was once a fact now became an obsolete view. We do not say that a person is dead when his heart has stopped beating for several hours. Many such patients recover from extensive open-heart surgery and go on to lead normal lives.

Now, after thirty or more years of discussion and debate, we are agreed that a person is dead when his brain has totally ceased to function for good. But many of us are too aware of the deliberations and conscious decisions that led to this agreement to feel that it is appropriate to label the result "fact." One such decision, for example, was that we would not say of such a person that he had died and returned to life.

It is true that values, deliberations, and decisions are at play in matters we all agree are factual. It is equally true that facts bear importantly on matters that are primarily questions of value. Look at this example.

> "Much of the choral music in *The Magic Flute* is in Mozart's Masonic key," volunteered Tanya.
>
> "What do you mean by 'Masonic key'? And which key is it?" Kyle asked incredulously.
>
> "Gosh, I've forgotten which key it is. But it was apparently associated in Mozart's mind with the Masons, or with his lodge and its ceremonies. Schikaneder, who wrote the libretto for *The Magic Flute*, was a member of the same Vienna Masonic lodge as Mozart."
>
> "I find that awfully hard to believe. The Masons don't even use music in their ceremonies, at least not in the U.S."
>
> Tanya strides briskly over to the bookshelf, pulls out and thumbs the pages of a paperbound volume by Alfred Einstein[2] entitled *Mozart: His Character, His Work*. She reads:
>
> "Mozart wrote a whole series of significant works for Masonic ceremonies, and the consciousness of his membership in the order permeates his entire work. Not only [*The Magic Flute*] but many others of his works are Masonic, even though they reveal nothing of this quality to the uninitiated. . . .[of *The Magic Flute*] He began and ended the work in E-flat major, the Masonic key."

On the level where Tanya addresses it, the question here is a factual one. Is

[2] Not to be confused with Albert Einstein, the physicist

citing an authority, and Kyle accepts her answer. You might still question whether music is at all appropriate for Masonic ceremonies. Unlike the question of fact, these are questions of value, judgement, or preference, where different people may have different opinions.

As the writings by Perry Weddle and Carl Becker cited at the end of this chapter suggest, there are many more complexities to the distinction of fact from opinion than are treated above. But we need to sharpen our appreciation of the distinction itself before we can benefit from more advanced work on its complexities.

Now we will get some practice in distinguishing factual statements from statements of opinion.

EXERCISE 5—1: DISTINGUISHING FACTS FROM OPINIONS

Decide which state facts and which state opinions. You may give reasons for your answers, but don't pursue questions to great subtlety.

1. Most Americans still measure longer distances in miles rather than kilometers.
2. Thelma plays the piano better than Ralph.
3. Bradley, who has predicted the stock market quite accurately in the recent past, seems to me a wiser investment counselor than Warrenton.
4. The upper atmosphere, called the stratosphere, is thinner than the lower.
5. Mt. McKinley is the tallest mountain in North America.
6. Even though a lot of people do it, I still think it's wrong to get paid in cash so you can avoid the income tax.
7. At blossoming time no tree is lovelier than the crabapple.
8. Water boils at 212 degrees on a Fahrenheit scale, but at 100 on a centigrade.

*9. Charleston is the capital of West Virginia.

10. Rubies are far more beautiful than diamonds.
11. It ought to be forbidden to administer physical punishment to children in public schools.
12. California is the most populous state.

13. It isn't right for federal economic policy to so favor the wealthy few when a vast number of people are struggling with unemployment, poverty, and hardship.
14. The Japanese attacked Pearl Harbor on December 7, 1941.
15. Saffron is much better than cinnamon for adding color and flavor to breakfast rolls.
16. *Julius Caesar* is a better tragedy than *Timon of Athens.*

*17. Chocolate ice cream is more flavorful than vanilla.

18. Horses were unknown to the Indians of North America until Spanish conquerors brought them here early in the 16th century.
19. The Treaty of Versailles concluded the First World War.
20. Marigolds make a much more attractive border than petunias.

In argument, evidence or reasons are advanced in support of a claim or opinion.

2. Recognizing Arguments

Socrates was one of the earliest thinkers to distinguish opinion from fact. He pointed out that it makes little sense to dispute matters that can be rapidly settled by measurement, counting, or arithmetic. These count as facts. This leaves open the possibility, of course, that it could make sense to dispute matters that cannot be settled like this, which would include matters of opinion. Indeed we have just finished examining several such disputes.

What we need to do now is to refine our idea of what constitutes a dispute or argument. Let's begin with this example.

> "Watcha got there?" demanded Midge.
> "Nothin'," said Connie.
> "You're a one legged liar!" said Midge.
> He strode over to his brother's chair and grasped the hand that concealed the coin.
> "Let loose!" he ordered.
> Connie began to cry.
> "Let loose and shut your noise," said the elder, and jerked his brother's hand from the chair arm.
>
> Ring Lardner, "Champion," The Best Short Stories of *Ring Lardner* (New York 1957), p.109.

The difference of opinion or clash of wills we call "argument" often involves excitement, racing pulses, flushed faces, voices raised or shouting, agitated gestures, and physical violence, or at least the threat of it. This way of treating an issue is often called emotional, and contrasted unfavorably with a cool, dispassionate, objective, rational approach. To adopt this latter approach you must keep your emotions in check. What you are doing is still called "argument." But instead of shouting and shaking your fist, you advance evidence or reasons in support of your claim or opinion.

> "For me *The Magic Flute* is by far the best of Mozart's operas," said Tanya. "Much of the music is as beautiful as anything Mozart ever composed, it contains several of his loveliest arias like 'O loveliness beyond compare,' and a great rhythmic vitality pulses through it from beginning to end."
>
> "Frankly I just don't find fairy-tale kingdoms of light and darkness visited by bird-people credible," rejoined Kyle. "*Don Giovanni* is a much better work. The music is in no way inferior, the characters are credible and their delineation far more subtle, and the work has a taut dramatic unity as well."

Let us examine more closely how this exchange breaks down into clashing claims and evidence advanced to back them up.

Tany's claim:	*The Magic Flute* is Mozart's best opera.
Reasons or evidence:	1. Much of its music is as beautiful as any of Mozart's. 2. It contains several of his loveliest arias. 3. It pulses with great rhythmic vitality.

This is a matter on which reasonable people can hold different opinions. First Kyle cites a reason for not accepting the claim.

Evidence against:	An opera containing kingdoms of light and Darkness and bird-people is incredible.

Then he advances his own differing view, along with the evidence for it.

Kyle's claim:	*Don Giovanni* is a better work.
Reasons or evidence:	1. The music is equally good. 2. The characters are credible. 3. Their delineation is more subtle. 4. The opera has a taut dramatic unity.

Tanya does not have to accept this, of course. If she is unconvinced, she can cite her reasons for not accepting *Don Giovanni* as Mozart's best opera.

Evidence against: An opera containing a stone statue that speaks, knocks on doors, strides across a room, and drags the hero into the pit of Hell is scarcely more credible.

When you support a claim by advancing reasons or evidence to back it up, or by citing evidence against some competing claim, you are arguing in a narrower sense of the term "argument." In this narrower sense, argument is a special concern of logic. What we as logicians are most interested in is whether the evidence or reasons advanced actually do support the claim. When your claim is challenged, you give your reasons for holding it, or cite evidence in support of it. Your claim is now advanced as a conclusion logically supported by these reasons or this evidence. Logic focuses particularly on the relation of the evidence or reasons to the conclusion, and helps us decide whether the claim is adequately supported.

Inferring, drawing conclusions . . . Here you know some facts or truths already, and are concerned to see what further information can be derived from them; to find out their logical consequences.

P. F. Strawson

Inference and Argument

Here is an example of a preoccupied teacher attempting to locate her textbook.

> Either I put the book on my desk, or I left it in the car. But I can't find it on the desk. So it must be in the car.

The teacher reasons from what she knows (book is on the desk or in the car) and can readily find out (book isn't on the desk) to what she wanted to know (book is in the car). Reasoning from what we know to what we didn't know is commonly called "inference." We infer the new bit of information from what we already know.

Is inference different from argument? Inference and argument do differ, but the differences are subtle and difficult to appreciate. The same group of statements can be more argument in one context, inference in another. It is difficult to find a group of statements that constitute an argument but could never be inference in any context, or a group that constitutes inference and could never be argument.

How does context function to indicate argument or inference? The context of argument is that of providing evidence, reasons, or support for some claim we want to uphold, defend, or convince others of. So we come forward with an argument when a claim we have advanced is challenged, and the purpose of our argument is to meet and blunt the challenge. It is not necessary for our claim to actually be challenged for us to have an argument. We may come forward with the argument if we anticipate a challenge, or think that our claim might be challenged.

Suppose for instance that we are convinced that welfare payments to persons able to work ought to be stopped. The topic is controversial, and our claim might be challenged. So we advance reasons to support it.

> Welfare robs people able to work of initiative.
> People without initiative may become permanently dependent.
> So we should stop welfare payments to people able to work to prevent them from becoming permanently dependent.

In an argument the claim we want to establish is our first priority, and the evidence is brought in to buttress it.

In inference, by contrast, one begins with a body of evidence or group of facts and the need or desire to get some new piece of information from them. For instance, I notice a mark on a blouse and wonder whether it will come out in the wash. Facts are summoned to answer this question.

> The mark on the blouse was made by a ball-point pen.
> Ball-point inks don't usually wash out.
> So the mark on the blouse probably won't wash out.

The inference we draw from these facts is that the mark will probably not come out.

The startling results of great fictional detectives like Sherlock Holmes are generally inferences from observations, known facts, and general or specific bits of knowledge. For example, one day Holmes surprises his companion Watson by informing him that his bedroom window is on the right hand side. This he has inferred from Watson's military neatness, his shaving every morning by sunlight, and Holmes' own observation that the left side of Watson's face is much less cleanly shaven than the right. Then at the crime scene in "The Boscombe Valley Mystery," from a close study of footprints, cigar ashes, and the angle from which the mortal blow was struck, Holmes infers that the murderer "is a tall man, left-handed, limps with the right leg, wears thick-soled shooting boots, . . . smokes Indian cigars, uses a cigar holder, and carries a blunt penknife in his pocket."

So when the context is one of drawing new information or results from given facts or information, what we have is inference.

> These footprints approaching the victim from behind are those of the murderer.
> They are farther apart than those made by the stride of a man of average height.

So the murderer is a tall man.

But when the context is one of establishing a claim against actual or possible opposition, we have an argument.

> We must protect the American economy from a flood of cheap imported wares because if we don't hundreds of thousands of American workers could lose their jobs.

The distinction of argument from inference is not exclusive in that if a piece of discourse is argument, it can't be inference. When we say the ashtray is made either of glass or of metal, we mean it can't be both. The distinction we are dealing with is non-exclusive in that the same piece of discourse can be both argument and inference, depending on the context. As argument, it is evidence supporting a conclusion; as inference, it is new information drawn from what is already given. Sometimes it is quite difficult to view the same piece of discourse as both argument and inference simultaneously. If we see the inference, we don't see the argument. In this respect the distinction resembles the famous figure-ground shifts of the gestalt psychologists. In the one given here, you see either the head of the young woman or that of the old. It is very difficult to see both simultaneously.

Young Woman/Old Woman

Argument: because one or more statements are true, some other statement must be true.

Argument as a Use of Language

At the moment our chief concern is learning how to recognize arguments. For this purpose we will avail ourselves of another perspective of contemporary logic, that which regards argument as a use of language. When we use language in argument or inference, we always maintain that because one or more statements are true, some other statement must be true. In inference our contention is that what we know establishes what we didn't know but wanted to know. In argument it is that the evidence or reasons cited establish our claim.

It will be easier for us to learn how to recognize arguments or inferences if we compare and contrast the use of language to establish conclusions with some other common uses of language. Language is frequently used to convey information about the world around us. Such a use is descriptive when, as in the following examples, features of a scene are described.

> Wingfield Hall lies on the right as you drive into the college from Shoe Lane. It's a two-story building with a low hip roof set against a grove of pine trees.

The use of language to describe an action or a process is narrative.

> Spade lagged a little . . . leaned sideways suddenly and grasped the boy from behind by both arms, just beneath the boy's elbows. He forced the boy's arms forward so that the boy's hands, in his overcoat-pockets, lifted the overcoat up before him. The boy struggled . . . .
>
> Dashiell Hammett, *The Maltese Falcon*, in *Five Complete Novels* (New York 1980), p. 374.

Language is also used to express feelings or emotions.

> Ugh, the spaghetti sauce makes me nauseous.

It is used to command or give orders.

> Put the new shipment in the empty space on the left side of the storeroom.

Language is used to find things out by asking questions.

> How do I get to the nearest post office?

By uttering a promise you use language to commit yourself to performing some act.

> I promise to return your compressor as soon as I finish painting the fence.

These are only a few of the many uses of language that are different from its use in argument or inference.

We distinguish arguments and inferences from other uses of language because we want to evaluate them to decide whether they are strong or weak. This is the same as to decide whether we should accept or be convinced by them, and add their results or conclusions to our beliefs.

"If . . . then . . ." statements look like arguments but they are not. No "if . . . then . . ." statement is an argument by itself. It does not contend that one or more statements being true make some other statement true. It is a conditional or hypothetical statement, because it states what will or can follow if a certain condition is met.

> If you allow gasoline to evaporate into the air of a closed room, then you have the potential for an explosion.

Even though the "if . . . then . . ." statement by itself does not constitute an argument, it can join with other statements to form one. We will examine this more closely later.[3]

Explanations clarify or elucidate; arguments attempt to prove.

Arguments and Explanations

Another difficult but important distinction to be made is that between argument and explanation. We recall that an argument always comprises the contention that some statement must be true because certain other statements are true. The conclusion, as the statement made true is called, is supported by evidence or reasons, which are advanced to justify it.

An explanation, on the other hand, attempts to clarify something we don't understand, something perhaps that puzzles or baffles us.

> Upstairs is warmer than downstairs because warm air rises.

> She shops for groceries on Thursdays to avoid the weekend rush.

The difficulty distinguishing argument from explanation arises because there are a number of cases that appear to be both. So it may be helpful to begin by noting that some arguments are not likely to be taken for explanations. Inductive generalizations are an example.

> Item a is a male cardinal and red.
> Item b is a male cardinal and red.
> .
> .
> .
> *Item n is a male cardinal and red.*
> So all male cardinals are red.

---

[3] See below, Chapter 13.

And fortunately there are explanations that are not likely to be mistaken for arguments. Here are several whose functions are commented on by John Passmore.

1. "As I got into the street-car, I noticed a large brown cylinder which was emitting a continuous clicking noise. The driver explained that I was to put my fare into it."

In this instance, I am confronted by an object which I do not know how to use. The explanation tells me how to use it, what it is for.

2. "On the menu there was something called 'scrod.' The waitress explained that this is young cod."

As in case (1), I am now being taught how to use something—a word. But the explanation now takes the form of a definition.

3. "I found one passage in his essay very obscure. I asked him about it, and he explained what he was getting at."

To explain is, in this case, to elucidate, to paraphrase, to make clear how something fits into a general context.

4. "I asked him how he had got home, and he explained that he first caught a subway, then a street-car, then a taxi."

This explanation fills in detail. I already knew that he got home; the explanation tells me by what stages he did so.

5. "I thought Mary was winking at me, but they explained that she had a tic."

In this case, to explain is to reclassify, or reinterpret.

We can see that explanations serve many purposes. They can tell us what something is for, and how to use it; they can define, resolve puzzlement, elucidate, paraphrase, make clear, fill in detail, supply stages, reclassify, or reinterpret.

One important fact to notice about all of the above explanations is that they have no conclusions. In an argument, the conclusion is what receives or is intended to receive the support. So we have discovered one important way in which at least some explanations differ importantly from arguments: they have no conclusions.

As we learned earlier, an explanation is called for when we confront something we do not understand, something that puzzles or baffles us. For example, Frank Gendron worked in a nearby hospital as a clinical engineer. He was responsible for the maintenance and safe use of the medical equipment. Once over a period of a few weeks three patients were found in post-op to have serious burns after cardiac surgery. This situation calls for explanation. We want enlightenment. We seek the cause of these burns so future patients can avoid them. A good explanation will enlighten us where an argument need not do so. An argument does not have to explain anything.

An argument is advanced in support of or against a claim or proposition. In any strong argument the choice of the evidence or premises is suggested by the claim or proposition to be proved. So one starts with the claim, then seeks ways of supporting or proving it. Against the claim, for example, that our current medical malpractice system is adequate (where an injured patient sues for compensation), Eugene R. Anderson advances an argument. He urges that of the $68 billion that we spend annually for liability insurance, 75 cents of every premium dollar goes to insurance companies and lawyers, while only 25 cents goes to victims. When defenders of the present system respond that it punishes wrongdoers and deters negligent conduct, Anderson rejoins that if this were true, after two decades of increasing medical malpractice cases, one would have expected them to decline. But on the contrary they are still rising.

Our focus in this book is on analyzing and evaluating arguments. But as critical thinkers, once we have identified an explanation, there are some questions we can ask to determine its adequacy.

1. Is the explanation initially plausible?
2. Does the explanation overlook some obvious factor?
3. Does it explain in terms of important factors rather than simply repeat what needs explaining?
4. Is it the simplest explanation that will do the job?
5. Is there some way of testing it to determine its validity?

These steps are well suited for evaluating explanations that operate by giving the cause of some phenomenon or state of affairs. In fact, such explanations can easily be taken for arguments by the unsuspecting. Here are examples of causal explanation—explaining physical effects by physical causes—that we frequently find in science, technology, and in our interactions with objects, tools, materials, and utensils. The first is about a 1985 earthquake that killed several thousands in Mexico City. Among the survivors dug out of the rubble days later were 19 newborn infants.

> How did these babies, completely helpless and vulnerable, survive without milk or water? . . . the most popular theory is that the babies—deprived of sound, light, or other stimuli—went into a sort of hibernation. They moved

little, conserved energy and used less glucose and oxygen than would normally be expected, allowing them to live longer.

David Wallechinsky, "How Infants Lived Through an Earthquake," *Parade* (Nov. 15, 1995), p. 15.

This is not an attempt to establish the claim *that* they survived, which was already attested to by eye witnesses. It sets out to explain *how* they survived by providing a cause—a sort of hibernation.

The following example from natural science explains why (what causes) meteorites to appear black, and then explains the cause of this fusion crust.

[Meteorites] often look black because of the presence of a fusion crust, the result of surface melting caused by friction as they plunge through our atmosphere.

Jim Phillips, "Ask Astro," *Astronomy* (May 1998), p. 84

Causal explanations are quite different from arguments , and must be tested by different techniques. Our focus on argument means that we will be little occupied with them here—many belong in the area of scientific explanation.

A type of explanation that does interest us very much is the explanation offered to justify some action or avoid some action. Conclusions are typically couched in language that claims we should not perform some act, or we must perform some other act. The words "should" and "should not" alert us to look for an explanation attempting to justify a claim. We call these *explanations as justifications*, and they may be advice to us personally, or advice in general; they may report results of scientific or other research to support urging us to act or not, or they may conclude with advice on what public policy to carry out or avoid. The following explanations as justifications illustrate some of these possibilities.

When you're navigating city streets . . . [you should be] on the lookout for parked cars with people inside. A door could open into traffic, or the vehicle could pull out in front of you.

Gina Powell, "The Lay of the Land—More City Driving Tips," *GEICO Direct* (Fall 2000), p. 8.

The National Institute on Aging says consumers should avoid taking human growth hormone, melatonin, and DHEA because there's no evidence they work.

Richard Falken, "Since You Asked..." *U.S. News and World Report* (May 1998), p. 75

Childhood allergies are on the rise, but research suggests raising children in a home with pets may be a good way to keep kids healthy. In a study following 474 children from birth to age six or seven, allergist Dennis

> Ownby, of the Medical College of Georgia, found that those who had been exposed to two or more household cats or dogs since birth were less likely to react to allergens than those born to animal-free homes.
>
> "For a Sneeze-Free Future, Get a Kitty,"
> *Reader's Digest* (Dec. 2002), p. 48.

In the first case, open doors or pulling out are cited to justify the admonition to be on the lookout. In the second and third we are advised what or what not to do based on explanations that justify.

The reason for our interest in explanations as justifications is that they both explain and justify, i.e. recommend for or against actions, and in this sense constitute arguments. We consider them arguments because we can analyze and evaluate them as arguments. We do this by ascertaining the relations of the evidence to the advice or injunction to act or not to act, and deciding whether the evidence is sufficient to support this.

To sum up, we can now separate and treat accordingly the following four cases.

1. Arguments like inductive generalizations that are not explanations.
2. Explanations such as the functional that are not arguments.
3. Causal explanations whose cause-effect structure resembles the premise-conclusion structure of arguments but which are best analyzed as explanations.
4. Explanations that are justifications (or justifications posing as explanations) that are best treated as arguments.

EXERCISE 5—2: RECOGNIZING ARGUMENTS AND INFERENCES

Examine each of these groups of statements and decide which are arguments or inferences. If one does not seem to be an argument or inference, try to identify it as some other use of language such as descriptive or narrative. If it is an argument or inference, try to distinguish the conclusion from reasons or evidence, or the new information that is inferred from the given. Give an estimate whether it is strong or weak, and why. Note that it is far more important to distinguish argument and inference from other uses of language than to distinguish them from each other. You may want to support your identification as argument or inference by supplying more information about the context.

Part A. Arguments and Inferences

1. No natural grass can maintain its deep green color in these persistent sub-zero temperatures. Thus that patch over in front of the fast-food place must be artificial grass.

2. Get to work over there! If you get any lazier, your blood will stop circulating.

3. Interplanetary probes have revealed that the so-called "canals" of Mars do not contain water, and so they are not really canals at all. In fact, no free water has been found on Mars. That means there cannot be any animal life on Mars, since animals need water to survive.

4. Are the green ones over there on sale too? Or is it only the red ones?

5. Edinburgh stands on seven hills between the waters of the Firth of Forth and the 2000-foot summits of the Pentlands. Until 200 years ago this great center of culture and learning was little more than a cluster of houses along the Royal Mile, a cobbled slope that followed a windy ridge from Castle Hill to the Palace of Holyrood.

   Touring Guide to Britain (Basingstoke 1978), p. 218.

6. Rain makes the streets slippery, and slippery streets are harder to stop on. So when it is raining, you should drive more slowly and carefully.

7. He threaded his way back to the ferry landing, found nobody at large there, and walked boldly on board the boat, for he knew she was tenantless except that there was a watchman, who always turned in and slept like a graven image. He untied the skiff at the stern, slipped into it, and was soon rowing cautiously upstream.

   Mark Twain, *Adventures of Tom Sawyer*, in *Illustrated Works of Mark Twain* (New York 1979), p. 128.

*8. Let me borrow your bicycle. I have to go down to the store. I'll give it back to you as soon as I return.

9. The face is the best means of identifying a person; thus, the most important factor in apprehending a criminal is to get an accurate facial description.

   Carin Rubenstein, "The Face," *Psychology Today* (January, 1983), p. 54.

10. Take the question of size of a city. While one cannot judge these things with precision, I think it is fairly safe to say that the upper limit of what is desirable for the size of a city is probably something of the order of half a million inhabitants.

   E. F. Schumacher, *Small Is Beautiful* (New York 1973), p. 63.

B: Arguments, Inferences, and Explanations

The instructions for Part B are the same as for Part A, except that you should also identify any explanations you encounter and comment on whether they are causal explanations, as well as whether they are good or poor explanations.

1. Unopened eggs shouldn't be cooked in a microwave oven. They explode and spatter the oven.

2. Eggs in the shell explode in a microwave oven because the increasingly hotter yoke and white expand but the shell doesn't.

3. The musket was the principal military firearm of the Wars of the French Revolution and Napoleonic Wars. A smoothbore, muzzleloading piece, the musket had been introduced in the early part of the 16th century . . .

   Albert A. Nofi, *The Waterloo Campaign June 1815* (Conshohocken PA 1998), p. 93.

4. A retractor is a surgical instrument that holds back the edges of a wound.

5. When you buy a ticket for a bus, plane, or train, you put your life in the hands of another. You wouldn't trust another person with your life if you knew that person was incapacitated by narcotics. The public has a right to know that drivers, engineers, pilots and other essential crew members are not impaired by drugs. So drug testing of such personnel should be mandatory.

6. The tire went flat because it naturally tends to flatness.

7. Amphibians never drink water, because they absorb the water they need through their skin.

   Kary Steele, "Closer Look at 'Cold-Blooded' Crawly Critters," *Daily Press* (Feb. 10, 2002), p. J3.

8. We are dealing here with two kinds of long-range vision. The democracies' is based in law and relies chiefly for respect of that law on the parties' sincerity and pragmatic restraint. The Communists consider nothing but the balance of power and see treaties merely as one of the many ways to lull their adversaries' already somnolent vigilance for a while.

   Jean Francoise Revel, *How Democracies Perish*, (New York 1985), p. 107.

9. Thirty years after Congress passed the Clean Water Act, lots of communities are having trouble paying the escalating tab for safe drinking water. The cost of repairing and replacing long-neglected

water mains and treatment plants in thousands of towns nationwide is estimated to be as much as $1 trillion. So, local leaders are increasingly turning to private companies.

U.S. News & World Report (Nov. 18, 2002).

10. Buildings in areas threatened by hurricanes are typically built to withstand 100 mph winds. But they are readily demolished by powerful storms like hurricane Andrew of September 1992, with sustained winds of 145 mph.

E

11. Biodegradable disposable diapers are a plus for the environment because disposable diapers constitute a bulky waste that consumes much space in landfills.

A

E

12. Midge said her daughter was going to break a leg if she continued to play field hockey so aggressively.

13. Redheads have that color hair because they have what scientists call a dysfunctional melanocortin 1 receptor on certain cells that give pigment to skin and hair. This dysfunctional receptor may interfere with the release of a hormone that stimulates the pigment cells, but it may also stimulate a related brain chemical that increases pain sensitivity.

Washington Post (Oct. 21, 2002) p. A9.

14. The unlined cardigan jacket has shoulder pads, front and neckbands, patch pockets with bands and long two-piece sleeves with bands.

15. We can tell by the red warning light that the engine oil is getting low, and we know that the engine will be ruined if we try to drive the car without oil. So we'd better stop at the next station and fill up on oil.

*16. Perhaps his boldness was built upon the belief that his old friend Winwood could check the king. Yet Ralegh, even before he sailed, knew the plans for the Spanish Match had changed the king's views and altered the power and influence of his faction. Knew, or should have known, that Winwood's influence was waning. Knew, before deciding to return, that his actions would have sorely tested Winwood at the least, at most have diminished his powers. And therefore could not, in reason, expect Winwood to risk becoming his advocate.

George Garrett, *Death of the Fox*
(New York 1971), p. 99.

17. We were told there were bats in the area. We looked everywhere for an entire day, using binoculars too, and we didn't see a single bat. Those who said there were bats must be mistaken.

18. [Arbitrageurs speculate in stocks of companies they think might be taken over, gambling that they will be able to sell at a profit.]

The stocks of companies controlled by family interests are often depressed by an expectation that they can't be taken over, so any news of difficulties in a powerful family is eagerly sought by arbitrageurs.

James B. Stewart, *Den of Thieves*
(New York 1992), p. 165.

19. A good lullaby puts an infant to sleep because it has a soporific quality.
20. Mosquitoes are more of a nuisance this year because it has been a damp summer and because dwindling tax revenues forced the local authorities to stop aerial spraying for them.

An argument is just one or more sentences. . . . called premises . . . , offered in support of another sentence . . . , called the conclusion.
Howard Kahane

3. Premises and Conclusions

This practice at picking out arguments helps us better appreciate what is common to all arguments and inferences but lacking in other uses of language. The distinction of evidence or reasons from claim or conclusion yields a structure found in every argument. Every argument falls into two separate parts. The part containing what the writer or speaker wants to prove is called the conclusion. The part containing the evidence or reasons is called the premises, or if there is only one, the premise. Anyone who advances an argument is urging that the premises establish the conclusion, or that the conclusion must be true because the premises are true.

In one of the inferences we looked at in the previous section, there are two premises which together present the evidence that is supposed to make the conclusion true.

Premise:	Either I put the book on my desk, or I left it in the car.
Premise:	But I can't find it on the desk.
Conclusion:	So it must be in the car.

Even though the first sentence in this inference contains two separate clauses that are of equal weight grammatically, it counts as only one premise.

Many arguments have two or more premises. Still it is not unusual for an argument to have only one premise. Here is an example.

Premise:	All of the windows and doors were locked and untouched.
Conclusion:	So the theft must have been an inside job.

This new distinction of premises from conclusion may prove helpful to us for the practical problem of recognizing an argument. Suppose we are confronted with a piece of writing we think might be an argument, but we aren't sure. What is our first step? What do we look for? The first thing we look for is the claim or conclusion. Often the conclusion will be stressed or displayed prominently, since it is what the writer is attempting to prove. Say now that we have found a statement that appears to be a conclusion. What is our next step? Now we ask whether any of the other statements advance evidence or reasons that tend to support it. If so, what we have is an argument. If not, then it isn't. For an example we can examine a problem from the exercise we have just completed working.

> Rain makes the streets slippery, and slippery streets are harder to stop on. So when it is raining, you should drive more slowly and carefully.

When we look for a conclusion, a claim the writer is trying to convince us of, our attention is drawn to this.

> So when it is raining, you should drive more slowly and carefully.

This is our candidate for conclusion of an argument. Do any of the other statements offer reasons or evidence in support of it?

> Rain makes the streets slippery, and slippery streets are harder to stop on.

The answer appears to be: Yes. The writer seems to be offering the connection of rain, slippery streets, and difficulty in stopping as reasons supporting this conclusion. We might rearrange the statements slightly to better exhibit the structure of this argument.

Premise:	Rain makes the streets slippery.
Premise:	Slippery streets are harder to stop on.
Conclusion:	So when it is raining, you should drive more slowly and carefully.

Note that it isn't necessary for these premises to actually prove the conclusion in order for this to be an argument. All that is needed is that they be advanced in support of it. Not all arguments are good arguments or sound arguments. Suppose we have an argument where the premises rather obviously fall short of proving the conclusion.

> You cannot prove conclusively that an accident caused by a drunk driver would not have happened if the driver had been sober. So there is no justification for the stiff legal penalties for driving while intoxicated.

Everyone might agree that this premise does not prove this conclusion, yet the two do not for this shortcoming fail to constitute an argument. Weak arguments and unsound arguments are still arguments. What is necessary to an argument is that a premise or premises be advanced in support of a conclusion, not that they prove the conclusion true.

Fortunately for us in our endeavor to recognize arguments, there are frequently verbal cues to help us. Our first step is to locate what we take to be the conclusion. Here are some words and phrases that can be used to introduce conclusions of arguments. The most commonly used ones are italicized.

Conclusion Cues

Therefore
Thus
So
proves that
shows that
I conclude that
It follows that
Hence . . .
entails that
implies that
demonstrates that
leads to the conclusion that

The above are *conclusion cues.* Words that are often used to introduce premises. are called *premise cues.*

Premise Cues

Since
For
Because
follows from
as shown by
for the reason that
in view of the fact that
as indicated by
may be deduced from
may be inferred from

Let us see now how such cues can help us recognize arguments.

> It is not permitted for someone to practice law in our state unless he has taken the bar exam. So Tom Marston isn't permitted to practice law here, since he didn't take the bar exam.

The conclusion cue *so* helps us locate the conclusion that assures us that this is an argument.

So Tom Marston isn't permitted to practice law here.

The premise cue *since* helps us identify a premise.

since he didn't take the bar exam.

Taken together with the first statement, which is also a premise, it constitutes evidence for the conclusion. This argument has the following structure.

Premise:	It is not permitted for someone to practice law in our state unless he has taken the bar exam.
Premise:	since he didn't take the bar exam.
Conclusion:	Tom Marston isn't permitted to practice law here.

Let us look at another example.

Kim Walters missed the meeting yesterday afternoon. It is likely she was ill, because she's only missed meetings in the past when she was ill.

Here the premise cue *because* helps us identify its clause as a premise of an argument.

because she's only missed meetings in the past when she was ill.

What is the conclusion of the argument of which this is a premise? Could it be this?

Kim Walters missed the meeting yesterday afternoon.

This isn't a promising candidate. Neither of the other two statements tend to prove it or to provide evidence for it. It is a statement of fact, attested to by those who did attend the meeting. This is our conclusion:

It is likely she was ill.

Taken together, the other two statements constitute evidence for it. The argument has this structure.

Premise:	Kim Walters missed the meeting yesterday afternoon.
Premise:	Because she's only missed meetings in the past when she was ill.
Conclusion:	it is likely she was ill.

The above words and phrases are not the only ones that can serve as conclusion cues or premise cues. But it would not be a wise step to memorize these and others as infallible guides to conclusions or premises. They are not infallible guides because they have other functions too, and serve not only to introduce parts of arguments. Here are some examples.

> She has detested asparagus *since* she was a little child.

> *Thus* began the most fateful day in the history of the Holy Roman Empire.

> *For* over three years she had steadily embezzled funds with computer manipulations without being detected.

These cues are most helpful to us while we are learning to recognize arguments and appreciate their structures.

But there is no guarantee that any given argument will contain either conclusion cues or premise cues. And not containing them doesn't make it any the less an argument, as the following example illustrates.

> Subjects are bound to obey their king only so long as he retains the power to protect them. Men have a natural right to protect themselves, when no one else can protect them. This natural right cannot be bargained away in any agreement to obey a king.
>
> Adapted from Thomas Hobbes, *Leviathan*, Chapter 21.

In the absence of cue words, how do we go about deciding whether this is an argument or not? Obviously Hobbes is advancing a claim here, namely that:

> Subjects are bound to obey their king only so long as he retains the power to protect them.

But is this the conclusion of an argument? Perhaps this is best answered by asking another question. Do any of the other statements provide evidence or reasons in support of it? The answer is: Yes. One states that men have a right to protect themselves when no one else can protect them. The other states that this right is inalienable. You cannot even give it away of your own free will, as when you would take an oath of loyalty always to obey a king.

So the statements from Hobbes are an argument. It has this structure.

Premise:	Men have a natural right to protect themselves when no one else can protect them.
Premise:	This natural right cannot be bargained away in any agreement to obey a king.
Conclusion:	Subjects are bound to obey a king only so long as he retains the power to protect them.

When we structure an argument for analysis and evaluation, we always put the premises first and the conclusion last. This is a convention that makes it easier for us to appreciate and assess the relations of premises to conclusion and of premises to each other.

Typically the person who advances an argument is most interested in convincing us and others of the conclusion. This is why it is not unusual to find an argument with the conclusion stated first, followed then by the premises. This is the case in the above argument from Hobbes. There will be other cases where the conclusion is stated first, then repeated (sometimes with different words) after the premises are given.

These are the steps we can take to identify an argument.

1. **Search for conclusion cues or premises cues.**
2. **If you find one or more, organize the material as an argument with premises first and conclusion last.**
3. **If there are no cues, search for a conclusion.**
4. **If you find a likely candidate, see whether the other material can be structured as premises.**
5. **If you can find no conclusion, see whether you can identify the material as descriptive, narrative, or anything other than argument.**

Summary

We expect people to agree on facts—they are what is the case. Where the facts aren't known, or aren't in yet, people hold opinions. Their opinions may also express their beliefs about right and wrong, or what is aesthetically superior or mediocre. Questions about these cannot be settled, as can questions about what is the case, by going and looking, or speaking with a witness.

Claims or opinions backed up by reasons or evidence constitute arguments. Every claim for which reasons or evidence is advanced counts as argument. In inference, new information is logically deduced from given facts or evidence. Inference and argument overlap considerably. In argument the context is a social one of debate or dispute. We back up a claim because someone has challenged it, or because we expect a challenge. Inference is logically deducing new information from what is given.

We use language in many different ways, such as to tell stories, describe things, ask questions, or give orders. In every argument, language is used to urge that because one or more statements are true, some other statement must be true. It must be maintained *that* some statements are true. The "if . . . then . . ." statement does not count as argument. In argument, the statement supposed to be made true is the conclusion, the statements with the evidence are the premises.

Explanations, unlike arguments, do not typically seek to establish or prove something. They clarify the obscure, simplify the complicated, or resolve puzzlement. Explanations of natural events by cause and effect look like arguments, but they are not. Explanations that attempt to justify some statement or claim do count as arguments.

In learning to recognize arguments, we first look for cue words that introduce conclusions or premises. Finding none, we look for a conclusion, a statement others are advanced in support of.

Study Questions

Section 1: Facts and Opinions

1. Give a statement of fact.
2. A statement of opinion.
3. How is a typical question of fact answered?

Section 2: Recognizing Arguments

4. What is argument from a critical thinking standpoint?
5. What is inference?
6. How do argument and inference differ?
7. Describe argument as a use of language.
8. How do argument and explanation differ?
9. Give an explanation that is not an argument.
10. How do we classify explanation as justification? Why?

Section 3: Premises and Conclusions

11. Into what two parts does every argument divide?
12. Must the conclusion be proved for the discourse to count as argument?
13. Name four conclusion cues.
14. Three premise cues.
15. What are the steps in identifying an argument?

EXERCISE 5—3: ORGANIZING ARGUMENTS AND INFERENCES

Follow the above steps to decide which are arguments or inferences and which aren't. Organize arguments so that premises come first and conclusion last, and order inferences so that the given information is first, the new information last.

Decide whether the argument or inference is weak or strong, and for what reasons. If the passage does not appear to be inference or argument, try to identify it as some other use of language.

1. Your Honor, a blood test will not be needed to establish that the accused man cannot be the father of the child. Simple genetics of inheritance will suffice. The child has blue eyes, yet the accused man has brown eyes, just like the child's mother. Every blue-eyed child must have at least one blue-eyed parent.

2. Mr. Braxton was asleep at once as usual, but was awakened by the beating of a blind which had slipped its moorings. Reluctantly he got out of bed and went to fix it. As he was doing so he became conscious of the frenzied hysterical barking of a dog.

   H. R. Wakefield, *The Clock Strikes 12* (New York 1961), p. 99.

3. Wherefore, security being the true design and end of government, it unanswerably follows that whatever form thereof appears most likely to ensure it to us, with the least expense and greatest benefit, is preferable to all others.

   Thomas Paine, *Common Sense,* ed. by Thomas Wendel (New York 1975), p. 50.

4. It turns blue litmus red, so it must be acid.

5. If it uses the heat of the sun to dry clothes, then it's a solar dryer.

6. From the beginning of his malady, from the time when Ivan Ilyich for the first time went to see the doctor, his life was divided into two conflicting tendencies, alternately succeeding each other. Now it was despair, and the expectation of an incomprehensible and frightful death; now it was hope, and the observation of the functional activity of his body, so full of interest for him.

   Leo Tolstoy, *Death of Ivan Ilyich.*

*7. Up to the age of seven or eight, children make no effort to stick to one opinion on any given subject. They do not indeed believe what is self-contradictory, but they adopt successively opinions, which if they were compared would contradict one another. . . . in passing from one point of view to another they always forget the point of view which they had first adopted.

   Jean Piaget, *The Language and Thought of the Child,* 3rd ed. (London 1959), p. 74.

8. In a gasoline-powered, four-cycle piston engine, each piston travels the length of the cylinder and stops four times for each power stroke delivered to the shaft. In a comparable gasoline-powered rotary engine, the rotor has one power stroke each rotation of the shaft. So

a rotary engine can produce as much power as a considerably larger piston engine.

9. During a relaxed moment I asked the Chief why he promoted Rowsterson over Filbert to VP for marketing.
   "It occurred to me that I had lunched with Filbert several times, and he always salted his food before tasting it. He tends to make snap decisions without first investigating thoroughly."

10. The thief or swindler who has gained great wealth by his delinquency has a better chance than the small thief of escaping the rigorous penalty of the law; and some good repute accrues to him from his increased wealth and from his spending the irregularly acquired possessions in a seemly manner. A well-bred expenditure of his booty especially appeals with great effect to persons of a cultivated sense of the proprieties, and goes far to mitigate the sense of moral turpitude with which his dereliction is viewed by them.

    Thorstein Veblen, *Theory of the Leisure Class.* (Boston 1973), p. 89.

11. No one has a right to use a relatively unreliable procedure in order to decide whether to punish another. Using such a system, he is in no position to know that the other deserves punishment; hence he has no right to punish him.

    Robert Nozick, *Anarchy, State, and Utopia* (New York: Basic, 1974), p. 106.

*12. (Tom Canty, serving as king in ancient England, judges a trial where a woman and her young daughter are accused of selling themselves to the devil. There were no witnesses to the event, and since the accused have not confessed, Tom inquires after the evidence. The sheriff replies that with their wicked power they caused a storm that wasted the entire region and was witnessed by forty thousand people.)
   "Certes this is a serious matter." Tom turned this dark piece of scoundrelism over in his mind a while, then asked,
   "Suffered the woman, also, by the storm?"
   Several old heads among the assemblage nodded their recognition of the wisdom of this question. The sheriff, however, saw nothing consequential in the inquiry; he answered, with simple directness,
   "Indeed, did she, your majesty, and most righteously, as all aver. Her habitation was swept away, and herself and child left shelterless."
   "Methinks the power to do herself so ill a turn was dearly bought. She had been cheated, had she paid but a farthing for it; that she paid her soul, and her child's, argueth that she is mad; if she is mad she knoweth not what she doth, therefore sinneth not."

    Mark Twain, *The Prince and the Pauper; Illustrated Works of Mark Twain* (New York 1979), p. 768.

13. (Junk bond king Michael Milken, under federal investigation for suspected securities fraud, appears at an annual celebration of bond brokers.)
. . . everything about Milken—his energy, his demeanor, his constant presence—conveyed reassurance. Milken "hasn't been hampered by any guilty conscience that I can see," one participant told *The Washington Post*. "I figure that means he's either not guilty or he doesn't have a conscience."
James B. Stewart, *Den of Thieves* (New York 1992), p. 415.

14. The process of articulating and refining commitments in an open, but rational discourse will not eliminate all differences between the positions taken. Any such unanimity should rightly lead us to suspect that some subtle coercion, rather than persuasion, has been at work in the dialogue. The discourse should, however, lead us to a point at which choices can be made on the basis of a clear awareness of what the choice implies, rather than on the basis of a visceral reaction or a quick tally of existing majority opinion on the issue.
Robin W. Lovin, "The Public Purposes of Liberal Education," *Perspectives*, Vol. 17, No. 1 (Spring 1987), p. 11.

15. It's the law: Teachers in all 50 states are required to report suspected cases of child abuse to child protective-service agencies. But a nationwide survey shows that in most cases, it doesn't work that way.
The National Committee for Prevention of Child Abuse questioned nearly 500 K-6 teachers in 39 school districts about their experiences with suspected cases of abuse. More than 70 percent said they had encountered at least one child they felt was being abused or neglected; 90 percent of them reported their suspicions.
But of those teachers, only 20 percent notified the appropriate social agency as required by law. The balance reported their observation to other school personnel.
"Abused Responsibility," *Teacher Magazine* (Nov. 1989), p. 69.

16. The town, when I drove back, had settled down to its own night life. At night now, in the increasingly crowded main streets, there was the atmosphere of the village, with unsteady groups around the little drinking stalls in the shanty areas, the cooking fires on the pavements, the barring off of sleeping places, the lunatic or drunken old men in rags, ready to snarl like dogs, taking their food to dark corners, to eat out of the sight of others. The windows of some shops—especially clothing shops, with their expensive imported goods—were brightly lit, as a precaution against theft.
V. S. Naipaul, *A Bend in the River* (New York 1989), p. 177.

17. (Machiavelli weighs whether a prince is better off loved or feared if he cannot be both.)

It is much safer to be feared than to be loved when one of the two must be lacking. For one can generally say this about men: that they are ungrateful, fickle, simulators and deceivers, avoiders of danger, greedy for gain; and while you work for their good they are completely yours, offering you their blood, their property, their lives, and their sons . . . when danger is far away; but when it comes nearer to you they turn away. And that prince who bases his power entirely on their words, finding himself completely without other preparations, comes to ruin; for friendships that are acquired and not by greatness and nobility of character are purchased but not owned, and at the proper moment they cannot be spent. And men are less hesitant about harming someone who makes himself loved than one who makes himself feared because love is held together by a chain of obligation which, since men are such wretched creatures, is broken on every occasion in which their own interests are concerned; but fear is sustained by a dread of punishment which will never abandon you.

Machiavelli, *The Prince*, Chapter 17; in *The Italian Renaissance Reader*, ed. by J. C. Bondanella and M. Musa (New York 1987), p. 277.

18. (Through the dark, Edmund discerns the shadowy figure of a woman on the lawn.)

My first mad thought was that it was Lydia coming back to the house. Then I thought it must be Flora, Flora despairing, Flora running mad. But hazy as the form was, scarcely assembled in the dawn light, I knew that it was not Flora. It was someone else, someone unknown. I heard the sigh again, born clearly on the damp, silent air, a little higher, a little louder, "Aaah." . . . Who was standing there alone and lamenting in front of the dark house like a little figure in a dreadful picture?

Iris Murdoch, *The Italian Girl* (Harmondsworth 1967), p. 56.

19. A fluorescent lamp produces light because ultraviolet rays, themselves invisible, hit the phosphor coating of the inside of the tube, energizing the phosphor atoms to release white light.

20. (Concentration camp inmates were paid for forced labor by coupons they could exchange for cigarettes. A cigarette might be exchanged for a bowl of soup that could stave off starvation. A Capo was a prisoner serving as a trustee, carrying out the orders of guards, SS officers, and the warden.)

The privilege of actually smoking cigarettes was reserved for the

Capo, who had his assured quota of weekly coupons; or possibly for a prisoner who worked as a foreman in a warehouse or workshop and received a few cigarettes in exchange for doing dangerous jobs. The only exceptions to this were those who had lost the will to live and wanted to "enjoy" their last days. Thus, when we saw a comrade smoking his own cigarettes, we knew he had given up faith in his strength to carry on, and, once lost, the will to live seldom returned.

Viktor Frankl, *Man's Search for Meaning*
(New York 1984), p. 26.

THE CRITICAL THINKING JOURNAL

Part B. The Logic of Arguments and Inferences

5. Facts and Opinions

Quote from print media two statements of fact and two statements of opinion, giving the name, date, and pages of your source. Since we are contrasting opinion with argument, the opinions you select should not be backed up with reasons so that they constitute arguments.

6. Distinguishing Argument and Inference

Quote the following from print media:

A. one passage of narrative and one of descriptive writing, neither of which is argumentative.

Hint. Since one point of the exercise is to identify discourse that contrasts with argument, these passages should contain neither arguments nor inferences.

Tip. Since you are asked for both narrative and descriptive, your selections should attempt to distinguish them. The narrative should tell a story or convey action, while the descriptive would be better to describe an object or person rather than an action.

B. two examples of argument, one with one or more premise or conclusion cues, the other with none; encircle all such cues.

Tip. If the answers to the following questions are not obvious, write out answers to them.

1. What is the conclusion?
2. What are the premises?

C. two examples of inference, one with one or more premise or conclusion cues, the other with none; encircle all such cues.

Tip. If the answers to the following questions are not obvious, write out answers to them.

1. What are the facts?
2. What is inferred from them?

D. two examples of explanation, one used as a justification, the other not. The non-justifying one should clear up some perplexity or puzzlement that is stated in the source.

Tip. If the answers to the following questions are not obvious, write out answers to them.

1. What is being explained?
2. What is the explanation?

For the case of justification:

3. What is being justified?
4. What is the justification?

Further Reading

Some of the issues and complexities of distinguishing fact from opinion are treated in the following sources.

Carl Becker, "What Are Historical Facts?" *Detachment and the Writing of History: Essays and Letters of Carl Becker*, ed. by P. L. Snyder (Ithaca: Cornell University Press, 1958), pp. 41–64.

Perry Weddle, "Fact from Opinion," *Informal Logic*, Vol. 7 No. 1 (1985/86), pp. 19–26. Cites eight different ways of distinguishing fact from opinion; reduces the legitimate distinction to the quality of evidence supporting a statement.

The following accounts of argument also distinguish it from explanation. They tend to stress its function of persuading where the above account interprets it as marshalling evidence.

Trudy Govier, *A Practical Study of Argument*, 3rd ed. (Belmont 1992), pp. 1–19.

R. H. Johnson and J. A. Blair, *Logical Self-Defense*, (New York 1994), pp. 5–16.

This work has helpful comments on the distinction of argument from conditional statements and inference as well as from explanation.

Michael Scriven, *Reasoning* (New York 1976), pp. 55f., 60f., 65f., 219–223.

Helpful treatments of scientific reasoning are found in these textbooks.

Robert H. Ennis, *Critical Thinking*, (Upper Saddle River NJ 1996) chs. 4, 8, 9, and 10.

Ronald N. Giere, *Understanding Scientific Reasoning*, 4th ed. (Fort Worth 1997).

CHAPTER SIX

ARGUMENT ANALYSIS BY DIAGRAMING

We analyze an argument to understand how the evidence is advanced in support of the conclusion.

1. SIMPLE, SERIAL, AND DIVERGENT ARGUMENTS

In the case of each of the arguments we identified in the last chapter, we attempted to assess the overall strength of the argument and decide whether it was weak or strong. To decide whether an argument is weak or strong is the goal of argument analysis in a broad sense. This is to evaluate the argument, and we will learn more about this in the next chapter.

But now we focus on argument analysis in a narrow sense, which aims to clarify the relation of the premises to each other and to the conclusion. At the same time we may need to clarify the meaning of the premises, and also to ask what evidence supports the premises. Answering this question should enable us to attempt a preliminary evaluation of the argument.

Our technique of argument analysis uses arrows to show relations of support of premises for conclusions. We draw these arrows, not from one statement to another, but between the numbers that we assign to the statements of the argument. This allows us a better view of the pattern of the argument, which may be one of five basic argument patterns. Or the argument may prove to be a compound of two or more basic patterns, but we won't work with such arguments until Chapter Eight.

We recall that we recognize a piece of discourse as argument when we find the relation of evidence or premises to a conclusion. The first step in analyzing an argument is to mark up all the statements of the argument in angle brackets and assign numbers to them consecutively. It is not necessary that each sentence in our discourse be either a premise or a conclusion of an argument. One sentence may contain two premises, or a premise and a conclusion. In such cases we divide the sentence into two parts in the process of marking it up. At the same time we mark up with angle brackets we look for premise or conclusion cues, and encircle any that we find. We also underline the conclusion of the argument. An example will illustrate.

> Alcohol and safe driving go together like oil and water. So when you drive, don't drink.

First we use brackets to enclose the separate statements and number the statements consecutively or as they occur. Then we encircle "so" as a conclusion cue and underline the statement following it as the conclusion.

①
<Alcohol and safe driving go together like oil and water.> [So] <when you drive, don't drink.>
②

Now the pattern of this argument is easier to make out. It is a *simple* argument, or an argument in which one premise is advanced in support of a conclusion. Simple arguments are represented by the following diagram.

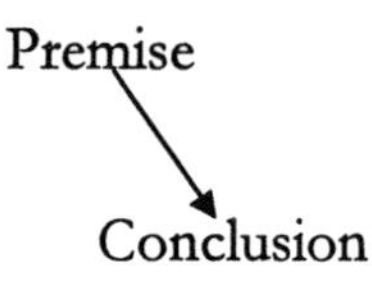

We have identified ② as the conclusion, and ① as the premise advanced to support it. So we draw an arrow from ① down to ② to represent this support relation. Our diagram of the argument looks like this:

Is it a strong argument or a weak one? The premise is an analogy or comparison, and may be ironic in intent. While it is common knowledge that oil and water do not mix, it is not at all clear what the basis for the comparison with alcohol and safe driving is. In the absence of some basis for the analogy, and of any other evidence, we must judge this argument weak. The conclusion seems true or at least quite plausible. But it is not supported by this evidence.

In the above argument the premise occurs first and the conclusion second, so we diagram it as ① supporting ②. We will encounter simple arguments and other types where the conclusion comes first and the support second. How do we show this in a diagram? We always number our statements consecutively, so when we construct our diagram we show by the use of these numbers which statement is supported (the conclusion) and which does the supporting (the premise). The following example is part of a claim about what medical students are taught.

> ... diagnosis starts as the patient walks through the door. His gait, for example, may reveal a previous stroke or Parkinson's disease.
>
> Theodore Dalrymple, "My Face or Yours," *The Spectator* (May 22, 1999), p. 12.

We identify two statements in the argument. First comes the conclusion, then the supporting statement. We mark it up and diagram it accordingly.

①
<...diagnosis starts as the patient walks through the door.> <His gait, for
②
example, may reveal a previous stroke or Parkinson's disease.>

②
↓
①

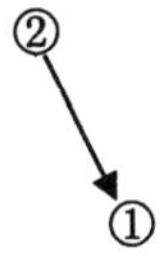

Here ① makes a claim for which ② is offered in at least partial justification. So the diagram of this simple argument shows the conclusion first and the premise second. Is it a strong or weak argument? The question is tougher to answer than in the case of our first argument because we really need to know more about the claim. If it means "diagnosis should start" or "diagnosis must start," more evidence is needed and the argument is weak. On the other hand, if it means "diagnosis can start," the evidence supports this more modest claim and we have a strong argument.

Not infrequently we find a pattern of support in natural-language argument that was never captured well nor treated effectively in formal logic. Here is an example.[1]

> In writing a collection letter, keep in mind that 95 percent of all the people who use credit pay their bills on time, 4 percent are slow payers, and only 1 percent never pay. Thus, most of the collection letters you will ever write are to people who will eventually pay. So it is extremely important that you not only persuade these readers to pay but keep their goodwill and perhaps obtain new business from them as well.

---

[1] James M. Reid, Jr. and Robert M. Wendlinger, *Effective Letters* (New York 1978), p. 244.

When we start to work on this argument, we are confronted with two conclusion cues: "thus" introduces the second statement, and "so" introduces the third. We circle them accordingly. Since we have two conclusions here, we must await analysis to decide which is the final conclusion, the one we will underline. In breaking the material down into statements for marking up, we have the option of interpreting it as three separate statements, two of which are compound, or of interpreting it as a greater number of statements. We exercise our first option because it is simpler, and the more involved one does not contribute to a better understanding of the argument.

①
<In writing a collection letter, keep in mind that 95 percent of all the people who use credit pay their bills on time, 4 percent are slow payers, and only 1 percent never pay.> [Thus,] <most of the collection letters ② you will ever write are to people who will eventually pay.>
③
[So] <it is extremely important that you not only persuade these readers to pay but keep their goodwill and perhaps obtain new business from them as well.>

Here we appear to discern the following pattern of support: The facts advanced in ① support the conclusion in ②, but this in turn provides evidence in support of ③. Now we go back and underline ③ as the final conclusion. This is the *serial* argument pattern. In this argument form, we have one or more premises supporting an intermediate conclusion, while the intermediate conclusion in turn provides support for a final conclusion.

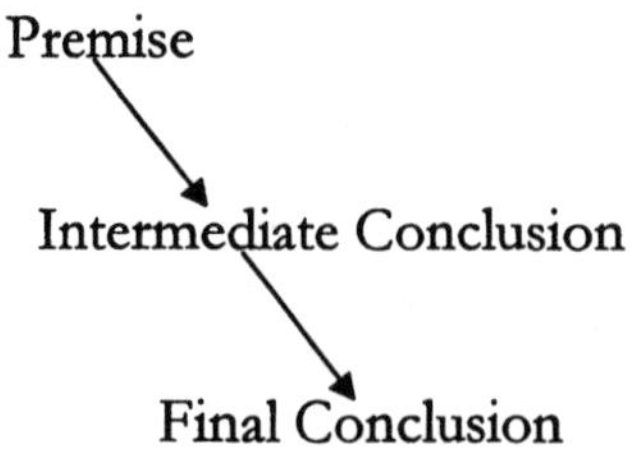

Premise
↓
Intermediate Conclusion
↓
Final Conclusion

In our case we have the following specific pattern.

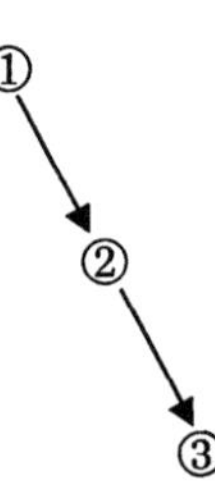

Is this a weak or strong argument? Let us assume that the premise states facts and that the context is that of merchants wanting to collect overdue bills yet retain the goodwill of their customers. In this context it is a strong argument.

As with the simple argument, we cannot assume that the order of occurrence of the statements is the same as the pattern of support. The following explanation as justification concerns aquarium occupants filmed for educational purposes at the Eames Office (famed for its modern chair designs).

> "The octopus got to be a ham," says Barbara Charles ... "Whenever the lights were turned on, it started swimming for the camera and getting in the way." The animal had to be given its own tank.
>
> Doug Stewart, "Eames. The Best Seat in the House," *Smithsonian* (May 1999), p. 80.

We need to break the source into its parts and mark them up.

①
<"The octopus got to be a ham,"> says Barbara Charles . . . > <"Whenever the
②
lights were turned on, it started swimming for the camera and getting in the

③
way."> <The animal had to be given its own tank. >

We recognize ② as an observation statement offered in support of a claim. It appears to more specifically support the claim in ①. ③ definitely does not support ②, and it is quite unlikely to support ①. It was not because the animal had to be given its own tank that it got to be a ham. It is far more likely that ① is advanced in support of ③. So ③ is our final conclusion.

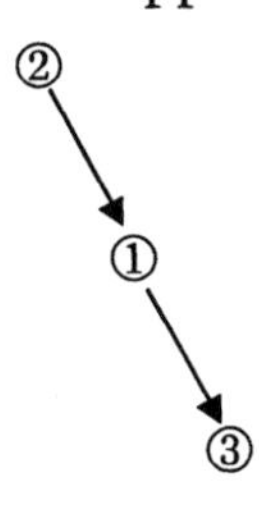

Is the argument strong or weak? The combination of (2) supporting (1) adequately explains and justifies (3). It is reasonable to assume that filming the other aquatic residents of the tank was a goal that was frustrated by the octopus hogging the camera. The argument is strong.

Another argument pattern not so common as the simple or the serial often shares with some serial arguments the feature of a single premise supporting two conclusions. But the nature of the support is different. Here is an example.[2]

> Two important points have been clearly identified by the Soviet attack on KAL Flight 007:
> 1. The Soviets do not recognize individual rights;
> 2. The Soviets cannot be trusted.

In this argument both statements 1 and 2 (as they are numbered) are conclusions supported by a single premise. The phrase "Two important points have been clearly identified by" introduces the two conclusions. The premise is better interpreted as the factual statement "The Soviets attacked KAL Flight 007." It is always preferable to deal with complete clauses or sentences as premises. Sometimes we need to paraphrase to get them. Let us mark up what we have so far.

①<Two important points have been clearly identified ~~by~~ ②<the Soviet[s] attack[ed] ~~on~~ KAL Flight 007.> 1. ③<The Soviets do not recognize individual rights.> 2. <The Soviets cannot be trusted.>

To determine whether this is a serial argument, we ask whether the writer is claiming that the Soviets cannot be trusted because they do not recognize individual rights (whether ② supports ③), or whether the Soviets do not recognize individual rights because they cannot be trusted (whether ③ supports ②). The answer appears to be neither. The claim in this case is that both ② and ③ as conclusions receive direct support from ① as premise. This yields an argument pattern we have not yet encountered:

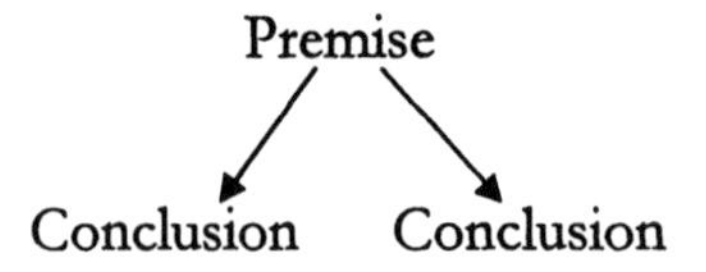

When one premise supports two or more separate conclusions, we have a *divergent* argument. Our diagram of the argument is the following:

---

[2] From a letter by Wayne Morgan Caverly to *U.S. News & World Report*, (Sept. 26, 1983), p.7.

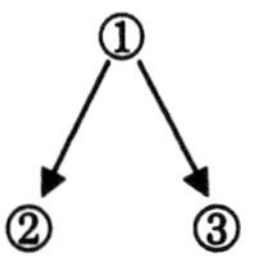

Is it a strong or weak argument? First of all, we need to add the information that the airliner was recognized as such and was intentionally shot down by a Russian fighter plane in Russian airspace. The connection between ① and ② does not seem very strong. At best it provides some corroboration for stronger evidence such as the imprisonment of dissenters, the denial of the right of assembly, or the denial of exit visas to citizens desiring to emigrate or travel abroad. But ① provides stronger support for ③. We could not trust a country that had a policy of shooting down unarmed commercial airliners on scheduled flights. On the other hand, a country that did this once and recognized it as unacceptable might still be trusted. Since it is only in connection with other factors that the argument has strength, on balance we may judge it a comparatively weak argument.

Let us now sum up what we have learned of argument patterns.

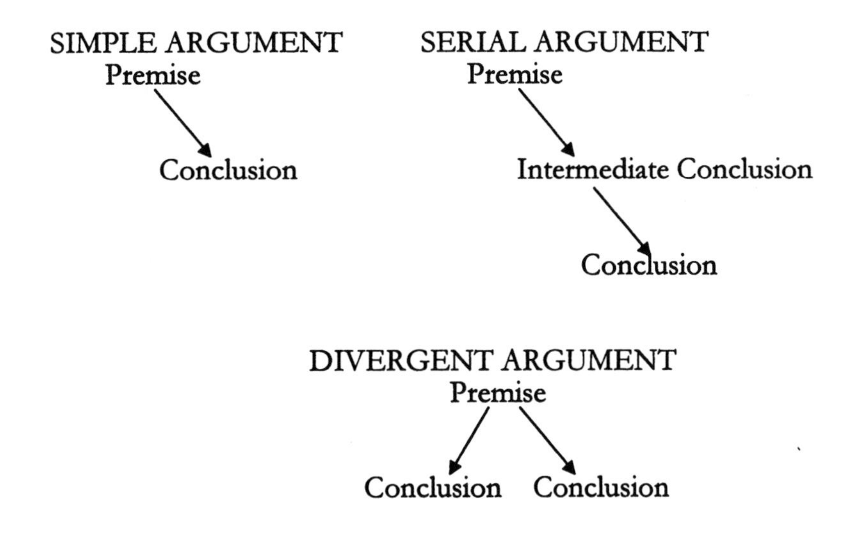

2. CONVERGENT AND LINKED ARGUMENTS

In a linked argument the premises depend on each other for the support they give the conclusion; in a convergent argument each premise provides a measure of separate, independent support.

We now turn our attention to two argument patterns different from those we've just worked with. Both are very useful in analyzing arguments in natural language to discover patterns of support. One occurs in the following argument.

> The cost of raising the Titanic would be prohibitive; hence the Titanic should not be raised. Another reason for this is that it would be wrong to disturb the graves of those who died on board.

To begin our analysis, the "hence" in the second clause of the first sentence gives a cue to the conclusion. Does the other clause along with the second statement tend to provide support? It seems they do, so they are both premises.

①
<The cost of raising the Titanic would be prohibitive;> [hence]
②
<the Titanic should not be raised.> [Another reason for this is that]
③
<it would be wrong to disturb the graves of those who died on board.>

Do the premises support the conclusion jointly, or does each provide a measure of separate support? The sources of the support are quite distinct in this case, since ① cites financial factors while ③ asserts the moral wrong of disturbing graves. So each premise appears to offer a measure of separate support for the conclusion. If this analysis is correct, then what we have here is a *convergent* argument, one in which each of two or more premises provides separate support for the conclusion.

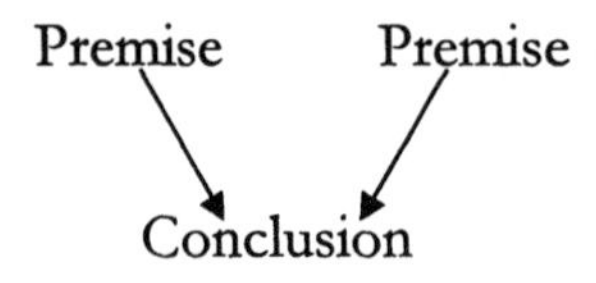

In the present argument the support looks like this.

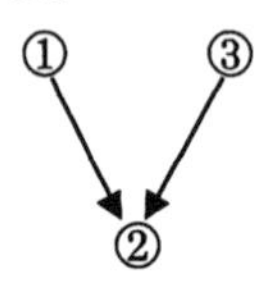

Again we notice that the order in which the statements occur does not determine what supports what. The conclusion can occur initially, finally, or anywhere between.

Is this a strong or weak argument? ③ is a weak premise, although it does have some force. Ancient and recent vessels, military or commercial, are routinely salvaged for a variety of reasons. Mel Fisher has salvaged hundreds of millions of dollars worth of gold, silver, emeralds, and other valuables from the wrecks of the *Atocha* and the *Margarita* off the Florida Keys in recent years. Disturbing graves has not been an important factor in the discussion of this or similar work. The same holds for the case of a sunken naval vessel, which might be salvaged to keep a secret code from falling into the wrong hands.

But ① is a strong premise. If it is true that by today's methods raising the *Titanic* involves unacceptable costs, then this provides strong support for the conclusion. Overall it is a strong argument.

As in the cases of serial and divergent arguments, the order of occurrence of the statements has no bearing on their role in the argument. In the above convergent argument comprising three statements, the middle one was the conclusion and the outer ones the premises. The following argument also appears convergent.

> By itself solar energy is not a solution to our energy problem, for solar energy is too expensive as it is produced today, and on cloudy days it is hard to get.

Here the first statement looks like a conclusion of an argument. The "for" introducing the two subsequent clauses indicates that they are premises. When we mark this up, underline our conclusion, and number the statements, we get the following analysis and pattern.

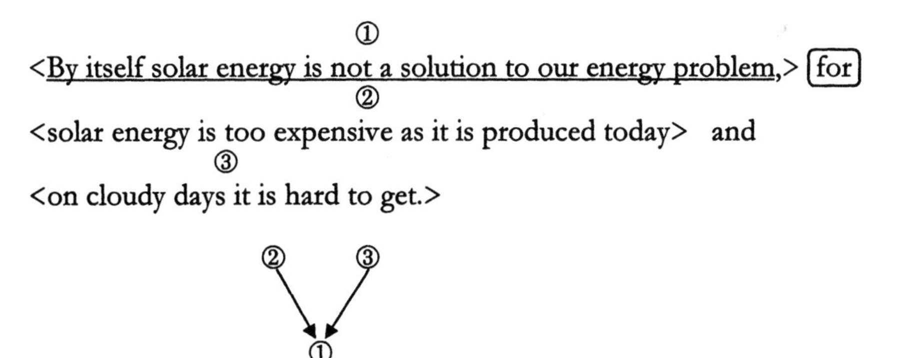

Is the argument strong or weak? Both premises appear to be true and also to provide substantial support for the conclusion, so this is a strong argument.

The final argument form we will work with is very similar to the convergent in several respects, but it also differs in one important way. Here is an example.

> Since Gloria has good hand-eye coordination, she will do well in this class because students with good hand-eye coordination usually do well in it.

The premise cues "since" introducing the first clause and "because" introducing the third help us identify these as the premises, and the second clause is the conclusion they are advanced in support of. We can mark our statements off and number them.

Since ① <Gloria has good hand-eye coordination,> ② < she will do well in this class> because ③ <students with good hand-eye coordination usually do well in it.>

In the case of our first convergent argument above (the one about raising the Titanic), we asked of its two premises whether they supported the conclusion jointly, or whether each provided a measure of separate support. We decided that the support was separate. This question is one we must ask of the above argument also. Do ① and ③ provide joint or separate support for ②? In this case the two premises are linked by the idea of manual dexterity: ① identifies Gloria as having good hand-eye coordination, and ③ states that students who have good hand-eye coordination tend to do well in the class referred to. By itself ③ provides no support for ①. Knowing that well coordinated students prosper in a certain class tells us nothing about how Gloria will do in it unless we also know that Gloria has good hand-eye coordination. This we are told in ①. So the support that ② receives is the joint or linked support of ① and ③. We call the argument pattern that shows this type of support *linked.*

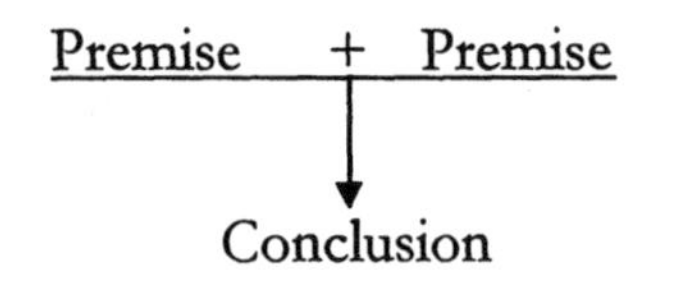

The diagram of the argument is the following:

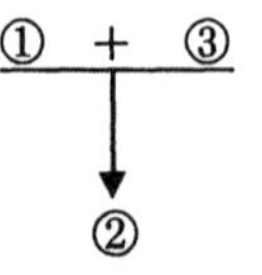

Is it a strong or a weak argument? Assuming the truth of the premises, it is a moderately strong argument. Why only moderately strong? Because the conclusion makes a claim that reaches beyond the evidence of statement ③. The latter states that students *usually* do well in the course, whereas the conclusion states that Gloria *will* do well in it. The argument would be stronger if the conclusion were hedged or stated more cautiously, such as that Gloria will *probably* do well in it.

Let us now examine another argument whose pattern seems either convergent or linked.

> Sometimes nations have a right to fight a war, for sometimes the only way a nation can continue to exist is to engage in warfare, and a nation that has a right to exist has a right to use the means absolutely necessary to preserve that existence.

The "for" introducing the second and third clauses is a premise cue, so the first clause is a conclusion which these two clauses are advanced to support. We can mark up the parts as follows.

①
<Sometimes nations have a right to fight a war,> [for] <sometimes the
②
only way a nation can continue to exist is to engage in warfare> and
③
<a nation that has a right to exist has a right to use the means absolutely

necessary to preserve that existence.>

As in the Gloria argument the two supporting clauses are linked to provide joint support. The link in this case is the idea of continuing existence of a nation. So the following diagram represents this linked argument.

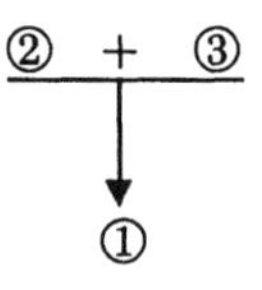

Is the argument strong or weak? It seems a fairly strong argument. The type of warfare it attempts to justify appears to be a war of defense against an attempt to attack and conquer. Most people would regard self-defense as a valid reason for fighting. But the notion of a nation having a right to exist is somewhat problematic. There is no agreed on procedure for determining whether a nation has a right to exist or not. Often this question is itself decided by warfare, and the ability to gain official recognition by other nations.

Soon we will confront the task of analyzing arguments by diagraming them and then deciding whether they are weak or strong. A natural question arises concerning the convergent and linked arguments. Since we have already indicated that in some cases it is quite difficult to decide whether the given argument is convergent or linked, how are we to master this skill? There are two quite different responses to this legitimate question.

The first response is that pinning a pattern label on a given argument is not the ultimate goal of argument analysis. That goal is to learn enough about the argument by analysis, diagraming, and evaluation to decide whether it is strong or weak. To put this another way, argument diagraming is not an end in itself but a tool in the service of argument analysis and evaluation. So it is the questions you must ask and attempt to answer that are more important than the decision on convergent or linked itself. For you must ask how each premise relates separately to the conclusion, how each relates to the other relative to the conclusion, and whether this makes their support for the conclusion stronger or weaker. These questions would have to be asked and answered for the purpose of evaluating an argument even if we did no diagraming of arguments. So one purpose of diagraming is to provide an effective way of raising these questions.

The second response is that there is an operation we can perform—suggested by Stephen N. Thomas—to determine whether a given argument is convergent or linked. The operation is the removal of a premise. If the argument is greatly weakened by this, it is linked. If its strength is not affected, it is convergent.

Let us examine a pair of arguments to see how the operation works. Here is the first.

> You shouldn't smoke marijuana. It causes blindness, and possession of it is illegal. Moreover, it's bad for your health in general.

We recognize the first sentence as the conclusion right away. So we mark the argument up.

① ②
<<u>You shouldn't smoke marijuana</u>.> <It causes blindness,> and

③ ④
<possession of it is illegal.> Moreover, <it's bad for your health in general.>

With ① as our conclusion, we see that ②, ③, and ④ are all advanced in support of it. Is it linked or convergent? Let's begin by asking whether it is linked.

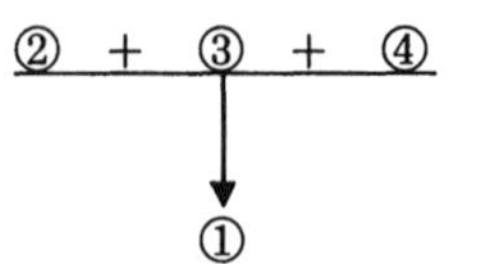

What happens now if we cancel out ②, the first premise, and consider the argument without it? Does this greatly diminish support for the conclusion? If smoking marijuana did cause blindness, this by itself would provide strong support for the conclusion. However the statement is false. Marijuana does not in fact cause blindness. Are either of the other two premises related to the claim of blindness in such a way that when it turns out false, the amount of support they provide for the conclusion is greatly diminished too? ③ has nothing to do with ②, so whatever support it yields is quite undiminished. ④ is related to ②, but distantly, since it is a general claim of which ② is only one part. When ② disappears, ④ still offers substantial support for the conclusion. So it is not the premises combined or interrelated that provide strong support for the conclusion. Each premise provides a certain amount of separate support. When ② vanishes from the argument, ③ and ④ each provide a considerable amount of separate support. So we judge this a strong argument. The separate nature of the support means it should be diagramed as convergent.

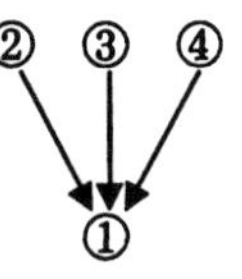

We also learn from this technique and example that it is possible for a convergent argument to have one (or more) false premise(s) yet still be a strong argument.

Now to a final example.

> Those fresh, dirty handprints on the wall came from one of you children. Let me look at your hands. Johnny, you're the one with dirty hands, so the handprints are yours.

We can restate this example to better exhibit its inference aspects (drawing something new out of what we already know).

① <The dirty handprints were caused by one of the children.> ② <Only Johnny has dirty hands.> [So] ③ <the handprints are Johnny's.>

The conclusion cue helps us identify ③ as the conclusion of the inference, and we recognize ① and ② as the support statements. Again we begin by considering them together.

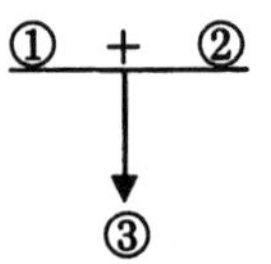

We can remove ① and ask what support ② separately and by itself provides for ③. Very little, it seems. The fact that Johnny has dirty hands yields small evidence for the handprints on the wall being his unless we know what ① tells us, namely that the handprints on the wall are dirty. Similarly, if we get rid of ②, ① gives us little basis for inferring ③. What links the dirty handprints on the wall to Johnny is Johnny's dirty hands, so ① alone provides weak support for ③. However, ① and ② together, linking up Johnny via the dirty hands to the handprints, provide strong support for ③. So our initial diagram of the inference as linked is correct, and we have a strong inference. We assume in this analysis and evaluation that Johnny is the only one of the children with dirty hands.

Let us now gather together what we have learned of argument patterns in our diagraming.

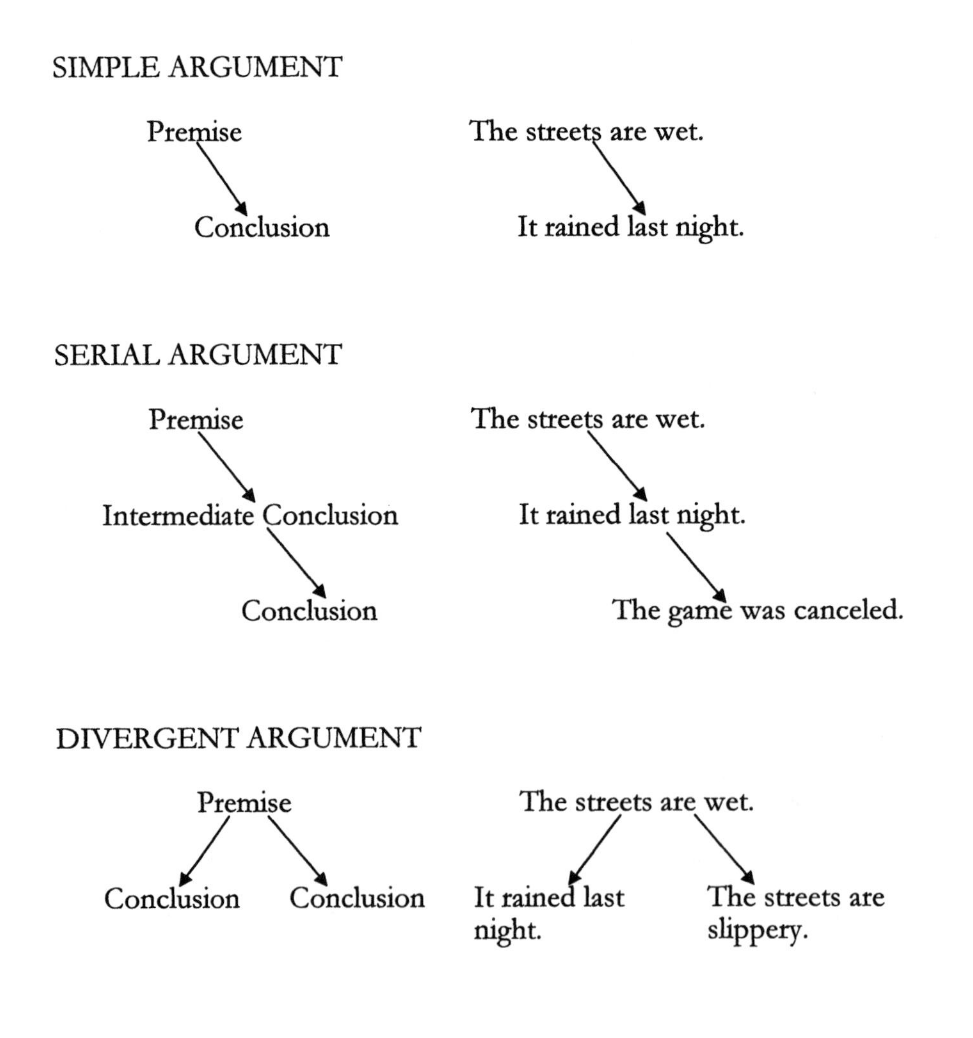
SIMPLE ARGUMENT
Premise
Conclusion
The streets are wet.
It rained last night.
SERIAL ARGUMENT
Premise
Intermediate Conclusion
Conclusion
The streets are wet.
It rained last night.
The game was canceled.
DIVERGENT ARGUMENT
Premise
Conclusion
Conclusion
The streets are wet.
It rained last night.
The streets are slippery.

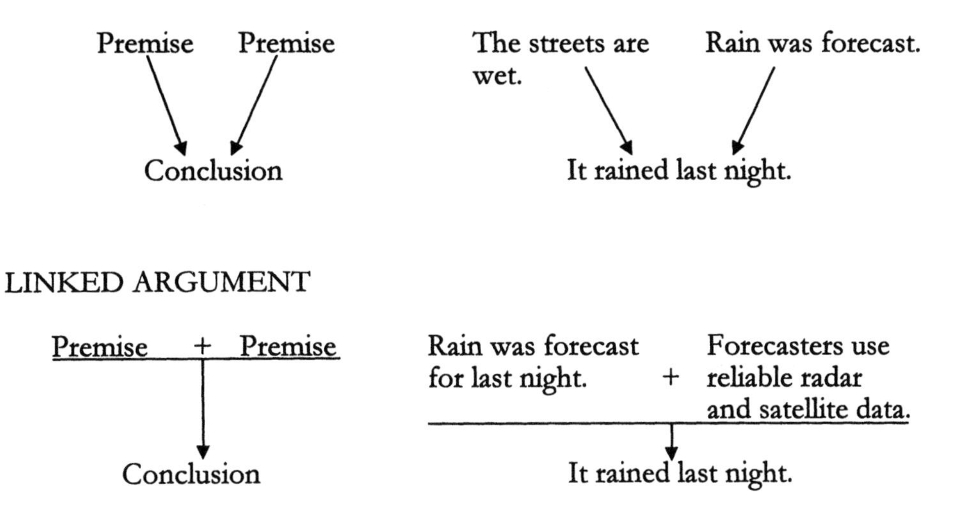

To decide whether an argument is weak or strong after an analysis is to evaluate or assess the argument. It frequently involves going beyond the argument itself for information, e.g. about how far we can depend on the premises. We have evaluated all the arguments we have worked with, even though we won't benefit from a treatment of evaluation until Chapter Seven below. We evaluate them to remind ourselves that evaluating an argument is the goal of argument analysis, and to avoid the temptation of thinking that our work as critical thinkers is done once we have discerned the type of argument. In evaluating arguments it is best to work with three broad categories:

strong: substantial support for the conclusion

moderately strong: evidence for outweighs evidence against

weak: little or no support for the conclusion.

EXERCISE 6—1: ELEMENTARY ARGUMENT DIAGRAMING

Following the procedure used on the examples in the text, mark up, number, and diagram each of these arguments or inferences. Identify the argument pattern. Decide whether the argument is strong, moderately strong or weak. Be prepared to explain how you located the conclusion, how you identified the argument pattern, and why the argument is strong or weak.

1. Some pesticides damage more plant or animal life than they are intended to because they don't break down readily into harmless ingredients.

2. We'll keep the old car another year. So let's pay up the insurance premium. And we'll have to get the clutch repaired.

*3. A home is more than a house. A home has to be lived in, and a home is where your family is.

4. It's a mistake to be over-eager to conclude a deal when you're shopping for a used car. The customer for a used car can end up paying a lot of money for an inferior product. You should get satisfactory answers to all the important questions *before* you sign the sales contract.

5. Currently 43,000,000 Americans have no health insurance at all. So a vast number of Americans are unable to pay the market price for medical care for serious injuries or illnesses.

6. When running a grocery store, if you charge customers for bags to carry home the groceries they've bought, they'll shop at a competing store that doesn't charge them. You don't want that to happen. So provide your customers with free bags.

7. You should buy the Aston Martin. It uses more gasoline per mile than any other road car. And it also costs more than any other make, including the Bentley.

8. Spiders aren't insects. All insects have six legs. But spiders have eight.

9. The world is suffering from an AIDS epidemic. It follows that modern medical science cannot protect us from all lethal sexually transmitted diseases. This also shows that careless casual sex has become Russian roulette.

10. When a hurricane strikes, electrical power is quickly lost. The hurricane warning just broadcast means the electrical pumps at the gasoline station will likely soon cease to operate. So fill your tank immediately before the hurricane arrives.

3. Argument Strategy and Diagraming Aids

There are cases where we suspect we are dealing with an argument because we sense that one statement is being advanced in support of another. But we aren't clear which statement is being advanced in support of which. One way of dealing with this question is to ask what could reasonably be advanced in support of what. The answer to this question reveals to us something about the informed use of argument.

A. It makes little sense to argue for a proposition that can be confirmed or disconfirmed by going and looking, or by some other direct perception such as listening.

①
<We didn't leave the map in the trunk of the car.> <There it is, over on
②
the end table.>

When we ask in this case whether ① supports ② or vice versa, we notice that ② is based on direct perception, an observation statement. The observation statement ② is more likely to be advanced in support of the claim in ① than vice versa. Usually there is no stronger evidence for the truth of a statement than its being based on direct perception.

B. We reason or draw inferences from what we know to what we do not yet know or are uncertain about.

There are cases of reasoning with hypotheses where we assume or postulate a statement to see where it leads. We worked with cases like this when we were dealing with logical puzzles. But we only made assumptions and reasoned from them because we reached a point where we had no further facts to go on. Whenever we have facts, we start reasoning with them and try to reach what we want to know. Suppose for example we notice a curious angular and unsightly pattern of fade on a curtain. We would like to know what caused it. Since the pattern is not curved or mottled, we infer that it is not caused by mistakenly spilling bleach on it in the wash. We have known such patterns to have been caused by this in the past. We also infer that sunlight striking the curtain from a certain angle over a period of time could be the cause. Further observation of how sunlight strikes the curtain establishes this as the cause. In this example we start out with something we know by direct perception—that the curtain is faded—and infer from it and further facts something of interest to us—information about the cause of the fading. Before we replace or dye the curtain, knowing the sort of wear it will get, we will want to get a curtain or dye that doesn't fade easily in sunlight.

C. When we construct our own arguments, we argue from what others will agree to (or at least concede) to some more controversial proposition. If the purpose of our argument is to establish the truth of some proposition and convince others of its truth, two practical guidelines can steer us away from ill-conceived arguments.

1. There is no point in attempting to convince people of what they already concede or are already convinced of. Since the matter at hand is either not

controversial or not doubted by a certain group, convincing them of what they are already convinced is both impossible and a waste of time.

① <Next year Easter will fall on a Sunday.> ② <It always comes two days after Good Friday,> and ③ <the day following the day after Good Friday is always a Sunday.>

This is a clever enough argument. But there is little point to it. Anyone who knows what Good Friday is also knows already that Easter falls on a Sunday, and consequently needs no convincing of it. If our arguments are to serve some purpose, we must attempt to convince people of what they doubt or dispute.

For example, many people sympathetic to Kenneth Starr's investigation of President Clinton agree with Starr's claim that the president is not above the law, and that he should be treated like everyone else. Jonathan Lear employs the following among other arguments to convince these people of what they doubt:

> . . . that, in the name of treating him like everybody else, he is treating the president like nobody else. No prosecutor, after all, would pursue an ordinary citizen in similar circumstances or with such zeal. Perjury is a serious crime because it is only prosecuted in serious cases. If every citizen had his or her own prosecutor who actually prosecuted every lie about every sexual liaison, perjury would be about as serious as speeding. The president is in the unique position of being accused of a serious crime—but one that wouldn't be serious if everyone were treated just like him.
>
> Jonathan Lear, "Freudian Slip," *The New Republic* (Sept. 28, 1998), p. 25

We should remember this in judging the arguments of others, and also in deciding whether they are arguments. We can always ask the question of some possible conclusion of an argument whether the proposition is one some dispute and the writer wants to prove.

2. You cannot convince others of a proposition if you base it on premises they do not accept. Since they do not accept the premises, the fact that you establish a strong connection between the premises and the conclusion (assuming you can do this) has no weight for them. What this means is that you will search for the more obvious or more reliable or more likely to be conceded statements for your premises, and argue from them to what is more controversial or doubtful.

① <In the year 1572 A.D. Pope Gregory XIII decreed that October 4 would be followed by October 15.> And ② <it came to pass.> [So] ③ <Wednesday follows Tuesday every week of the year.>

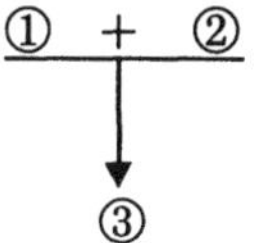

The premises are true enough, but their facts are obscure and known to few. Also they are sufficiently strange that many people would be unwilling to concede them. So the argument is weaker than it need be because it argues from what is obscure or doubtful. It is weakened further by the fact that Wednesday followed Tuesday even before Pope Gregory reformed the calendar, so this sequence of days did not result from that. Moreover, the conclusion is so obviously true that no one would doubt it, so as in the above case the argument serves no purpose and is superfluous.

This raises a question. When you construct an argument, are you always obliged to search for new premises when someone rejects those you want to start with? Not always. There will always be some people who just don't want to change their ideas and will stubbornly reject even obviously true premises. You can't force such people to be reasonable. In many cases you can ignore people who won't accept obvious truths. In some cases your need to convince others may be great. So it is well to note that sometimes a proposition may be established by more than one set of true premises. So if it is very important to convince others of a proposition, you might put aside premises they reject and search for premises acceptable to them that will also accomplish the task.

① <The Bible prohibits work on the Sabbath.> [So] ② <you shouldn't work on Sunday.>

①
↓
②

A religious skeptic might reject this argument yet be open to persuasion by the following one based on different premises.

① <People feel better when they break up their workweek with a day off.> ② <They stay healthier> and ③ < [they] are also more productive.> So ④ <you shouldn't work on Sunday.>

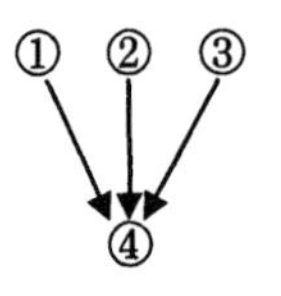

Could we construct out of this material an argument of potential appeal to both believers and skeptics? Why not just combine the premises in an overall convergent argument?

① <The Bible prohibits work on the Sabbath.> ② <People feel better when they break up their workweek with a day off.> ③ <They stay healthier≈ and ④ <[they] are also more productive.> So ⑤ <you shouldn't work on Sunday.>

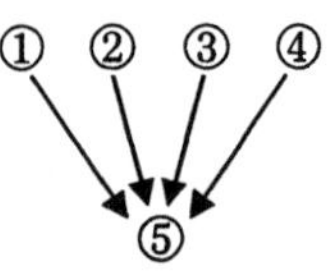

This argument now appears to be stronger than it was before. The different premises have no tendency to cancel each other out, and the conclusion might now be accepted by a wider group than before.

D. Another technique useful in helping us decide what supports what is inserting inference indicators (conclusion cues or premise cues) into the discourse to see whether they can help us discern relations of support. Earlier we dealt with the problem of deciding in the absence of inference indicators which of the following statements was claimed to support the other.

> Kim Walters missed the meeting yesterday afternoon. It is likely she was ill.

Even though there are actually no inference indicators, we can supply them in order to study the relation of the two statements. Our first hypothesis is that the writer aims to establish that because Kim Walters was ill, she missed the meeting. Let's add first a premise cue then a conclusion cue and make the necessary adjustments.

[Because] <it is likely [that Kim Walters] was ill,> ② <she missed the meeting yesterday afternoon.> ①

Another variation would be like this.

<It is likely [that Kim Walters] was ill.> ② [Thus] <she missed the meeting yesterday afternoon.> ①

This doesn't seem a very plausible interpretation. The writer would be arguing that because she was ill, Kim missed this meeting. But he doesn't make the claim he would have to make for this interpretation to work, namely that he knows Kim Walters was ill. Notice how he qualifies this assertion with "it is likely that." The other hypothesis is that instead of ② supporting ① we have ① supporting ②.

[Since] <Kim Walters missed the meeting yesterday afternoon,> ① <it is likely she was ill.> ②

Or another variation would be this.

<Kim Walters missed the meeting yesterday afternoon,≈ ① [so] <it is likely she was ill.> ②

This interpretation seems more likely. The writer may have the evidence to support ①, perhaps by attending the meeting himself and noticing Kim's absence. At least it is not qualified like the assertion in ②.

E. What we have just done raises another question. Are we at liberty to rephrase, re-cast, or re-state material in order to make an argumentative structure clearer? Yes, not only are we at liberty, we are strongly advised to do so. In fact, we have already applied this technique. We recall that it is always good to have complete sentences or complete independent clauses for premises or conclusions in our arguments. In the argument we just examined above about not working on Sunday, the following was one of the premises.

They stay healthier and are also more productive.

In analyzing and diagraming the argument, we decided to consider each of the independent clauses in this sentence as a separate premise. Doing so allowed us to focus more clearly on the nature of the support, which we decided was convergent. To make it easier to consider the clauses separately, we made the grammatical subject of the second clause explicit in square brackets [ ], which we always use as distinct from our normal angle brackets <...> when inserting material into an argument.

They stay healthier and [they] are also more productive.

<They stay healthier.> and <[they] are also more productive..>

Separating the two clauses and clarifying their structure and relation in this way enabled us to focus more effectively on the question whether their support for the conclusion was linked, convergent, or serial.

Another case where we had to alter a statement and add something in order to clarify its role in an argument was the above one concerning the Soviet shooting down of Korean Airline Flight 007 over Russian territory. The first statement was this.

Two important points are clearly indicated by the Soviet attack on KAL Flight 007:

When we examined this statement relative to the other two, it seemed to provide support for them but it wasn't clear how. When we separated off the long premise cue, we were left with two phrases.

Two important points are clearly indicated by

the Soviet attack on KAL Flight 007:

Then we had to convert the two phrases into an independent clause to clarify this supporting statement.

<[The Soviets attacked] KAL Flight 007.>

This helped us to identify the argument as divergent with two conclusions, each deriving separate support from this statement.

In general we must re-phrase or add material any time this is necessary to clarify the structure of the argument.

SUMMARY

We analyze an argument to find out how the premises are advanced to support the conclusion, and how they relate to each other in this support. Analysis can also involve clarifying the meaning of the premises or conclusion. Our technique of analysis is to mark up the statements of the argument in angle brackets and number them, encircle premise and conclusion cues, and underline final conclusions. Then we represent the structure of the argument in a diagram where arrows indicate relations of support of premises for conclusion. Finally we identify the brief arguments we work with here as fitting one of five basic argument patterns: simple, serial, divergent, convergent, or linked. For each argument we analyze we also give a rough estimate of its strength.

With some arguments we may need to insert a word or phrase to clarify meaning or to complete a sentence or clause. Any words we add to the argument are enclosed in *square* brackets. This distinguishes our words from those of the argument in angle brackets. In cases where we think we are dealing with an argument but have difficulty identifying the conclusion, we can insert (again in square brackets) a conclusion or premise cue before any of the statements. Often this helps clarify the argument's structure.

It may also help us identify conclusions to note that we seldom find observation statements as conclusions of arguments. The intelligent use of argument is to argue from premises that are generally accepted to a conclusion that is doubted or disputed. To argue for what everyone agrees on is pointless. Similarly the intelligent use of inference is to infer what we now do not know but want to know from what we already know. These rules of thumb may help us analyze and clarify the arguments of others, and to construct arguments of our own.

Study Questions

Section 1: Simple, Serial, and Divergent Arguments

1. What is the aim of argument analysis in the narrow sense?
2. What is the goal of argument analysis in the broad sense?
3. How do you mark up an argument?
4. How are numbers assigned to statements?
5. The number of which part of an argument is always at the bottom of an arrow diagram?
6. Draw sample diagrams for simple, divergent, and serial arguments.

Section 2: Convergent and Linked Arguments

7. How does support in a convergent argument differ from that in a linked?
8. What questions must you ask and answer to decide whether a given argument is linked or convergent?
9. What operation can we perform to determine whether a given argument is convergent or linked?
10. Draw sample diagrams for convergent and linked arguments.

Section 3: Argument strategy and diagraming aids

11. What role do observation statements commonly play in arguments?
12. For an inference to make sense, where must it start and where end up?
13. Where does the well conceived argument start and end up?
14. State two cases where an argument will not convince people.
15. Is it always the case that a given conclusion can be proved with only one set of premises?
16. What further help aside from identifying cue words or a conclusion do we have in distinguishing parts of an argument?
17. Are we allowed to re-phrase an argument in order to make its structure clearer?

EXERCISE 6—2: INTERMEDIATE ARGUMENT DIAGRAMING

Following the procedure used on the examples in the text, mark up, number, and diagram each of these arguments or inferences. Identify the argument pattern. Decide whether the argument is strong, moderately strong, or weak. Be prepared to explain how you identified the conclusion, why you chose one argument pattern over another, and why the argument is strong or weak.

1. Sassafras tea is sold in health food stores. Sassafras tea must be good for your health.

2. James Wolfe has two problems—his health and his health insurance. He needs $1,644 worth of prescription medicines to stay alive from month to month but [he] has only $613 in income to pay for them.

"Benefit Shift Puts Man on Brink for Lifesaving Drugs,"
Daily Press (Apr. 2, 1999), p. C2.

3. ... most [savants] are incapable of abstract thought. Lacking a filter on their experience, they're powerless to make sense of it.

G. Cowley & A. Underwood, "Memory,"
Newsweek (June 15, 1998), p. 51.

*4. We totally oppose topless dancing. The Bible admonishes that nakedness of women is very enticing to the male.

Adapted from Rev. Eugene C. Knautz,
Seattle Times, (Oct. 20, 1974).

5. Water is an excellent conductor of electricity. So your hands should be dry when you plug in a lamp or appliance, since you don't want to get a shock.

6. The cake didn't rise like it should. Maybe we put in too little baking powder.

7. In a telephone conversation with *The Washington Post*, John W. Hinckley Jr. said he likes being in St. Elizabeth's Hospital for the mentally ill: Nobody bothers him, they call him Mr. Hinckley and people began asking for his autograph as soon as he arrived.

Birmingham Post–Herald, July 5, 1982.

8. One headlight isn't working. The lamp may be burned out. Another possibility is a short-circuit.

9. You should buy Barcardi dark rum. It tastes good mixed because it tastes good unmixed.

Adapted from a Barcardi rum ad in *Newsweek* (March 16, 1981).

10. It's late but the video rental store still seems to be open. The lights are on.

11. A powerful wind can hurl objects through windows. Flying glass fragments can be lethal. When a hurricane approaches, tape your windows diagonally to hinder shattering.

12. Buick Park Avenue. An automobile with the substance and solidity to command the great American road.

Ad in *Newsweek*. (Oct. 30, 1989), p. 87.

13. "There are three reasons to purchase a new car," suggests Jack Gilles … "You'll get the best safety features, there is a likelihood that you'll be purchasing a more reliable vehicle, and you'll get what are generally very good warranties.

Suzanne Carmichael, "Getting Deals on Wheels," *Modern Maturity* (Mar./Apr. 1996), p. 64.

14. . Late Sunday, when they [Cody and Luke] returned, Ruth came out to the driveway. The night was chilly, and she wore no sweater but hugged herself as she walked towards the car, her white, freckled face oddly set and her faded red hair standing up in the wind. This was how Cody guessed something was wrong. Ruth hated cold weather, and ordinarily would have waited inside the house.

Anne Tyler, *Dinner at the Homesick Restaurant* (New York 1982) p. 316.

15. You should wear vertically striped pants if you have shorter legs. The vertical lines give the illusion of height because they draw the eyes up and down.

YM (July 2002), p. 96.

Further Reading

Michael Scriven, *Reasoning* (New York 1976). The best guide to the rationale and techniques of argument analysis, and also good on the importance of reasoning and argument analysis for education in general. The seven steps of argument analysis, given on p. 39, are elaborated and illustrated in the sequel.

Stephen N. Thomas, *Practical Reasoning in Natural Language*, 3rd ed. (Englewood Cliffs 1986). The pioneering work in the arrow diagram technique for the analysis of natural-language arguments, and also for the distinction and rationale of the resulting argument patterns. The material on pp. 37-82 corresponds roughly to that treated in the above chapter. Thomas also has a wealth of problems for analysis and diagraming.

Malcolm Acock, *Informal Logic Examples and Exercises* (Belmont 1985). Good examples of arguments in natural language for analysis and diagraming are hard to come by. This makes Acock's full collection of argument examples all the more valuable. Examples of arguments corresponding to the five basic patterns used above are found on pp. 61-94.

CHAPTER SEVEN

EVALUATING ARGUMENTS

To decide for reasons that an argument is strong or weak is to evaluate or assess the argument.

1. RELIABILITY AND RELEVANCE OF PREMISES

The evaluation of argument is by now not something completely new to us. Since we learned to identify arguments we have been asking whether they are strong or weak, and to decide for reasons that an argument is strong or weak is to evaluate that argument. In the chapter on argument analysis just completed, one of the most important things we learned is that the analysis of argument is not carried out for its own sake but for the sake of evaluating the argument. Deciding whether an argument is strong or weak also helps us decide whether to add its conclusion to the store of beliefs we are prepared to act on. We now turn our attention to the factors involved in evaluating arguments.

A. Premise Reliability

Analyzing the argument reveals how the premises relate to each other and to the conclusion they are advanced in support of. In most cases we need to go beyond the argument itself for information that will help us assess its strength. Our prime objective is to determine how reliable the premises are in any case where one or more of them is in doubt or questionable. This is the most important single question information from beyond the argument can answer for us. Ideally we would like to decide of each premise whether it is true or false, but very many premises in real-world arguments fall somewhere in between. A premise is reliable when it provides adequate evidence or good reasons in support of the conclusion.

The information useful for establishing whether a premise is reliable can be of different types.

i. The premise itself may be *general or common knowledge*, or it may depend on or be implied by common knowledge. For example, it is common knowledge that there are two major political parties in the U.S. Many statements of fact are common knowledge. It is a fact that winters are colder than summers. A premise that is a statement of fact or based on fact is a reliable premise. This textbook is written for students in North America who are qualified to work at college level. The general knowledge of twelve years of education is presupposed, as well as of a minimum of two decades of coping with life's challenges as a family member, worker, consumer, and citizen, as well as in other roles.

ii. The premise may be a piece of *specific information*, or may be based on specific information. At some point baking a good carrot cake from basic ingredients involves specific information. The same holds for trouble-shooting a stalled auto, estimating whether a stock will rise or fall, or appreciating how Vermeer's use of color differs from that of contemporaries like de Hooch or Fabritius. The dividing line between general or common knowledge and specific information is fuzzy, but that is not a burdensome problem for us. It is common knowledge, for example, that a mouse is a device for operating a computer; but that a cookie is a file on your computer storing data about how you use your computer is information specific to computer buffs. Many facts count as specific pieces of information, but they are known to few or to specialists. Most of what we get from advanced academic disciplines, from research in the natural and social sciences, from developments in technology, for examples, counts as specific information.

It is a challenge for us as critical thinkers to decide how far we need to go in search of specific information in a given case. If the conclusion of the argument is a matter of little consequence to us, we probably won't search very far. When deciding the strength of an argument is important for us—say that it bears on personal health or safety—we go as far as we need to for the necessary information.

iii. Some premises will be *observation statements*, or based on observation statements. An observation statement is considered more reliable than any statement inferred from it. In assessing the reliability of an observation statement we need to consider the conditions where the observations were made, as well as whether the observer has normal faculties and is trustworthy.

iv. The *testimony* of people about their own experiences—what they have witnessed, undergone, or suffered—is also a source of information. Some factors that make testimony more or less trustworthy are examined below (Chapter Twelve).

We also make an initial assessment of the conclusion of an argument by comparing it with general knowledge on the topic, or whatever specific information we can readily obtain. In some cases, as soon as we confront an argument we form a first impression of its strength. Not infrequently we must revise this estimate because of further study, but in cases like the following the first impression stands up rather well.

① <You cannot prove conclusively that an accident caused by a drunk driver would not have happened if the driver had been sober.> [So] ② <there is no justification for the stiff legal penalties for driving while intoxicated.>

Simple
Weak

Here our initial impression is that we have a weak argument.

But if someone asks why it is weak, how do we respond? We could respond in quite general terms and cite either an unsound premise or a failure of the premise to support the conclusion. This is a good step as far as it goes, but we need to get down to specifics before it will support our estimate of a weak argument. To allege that an argument is weak because a premise is unsound, unless you specify which premise and explain why it is unsound, is to allege little more than that an argument is weak because it is weak. A good assessment of an argument deals with specifics, and frequently it is the information we gather that enables us to deal accurately with specifics.

In the present case our claim is indeed that the premise ① is unsound, and since there is only one premise, that the conclusion ② receives no support. ① is stated so sweepingly as to be made factually false. There are cases where you can offer strong evidence that an accident caused by a drunk driver would not have happened if the driver had been sober. In such a case you might for example show that a sober driver would have been able to stop in time to avoid the collision, whereas the drunk driver could not react fast enough. Studies have been made of the reaction times to various stimuli of people who have consumed certain amounts of alcohol, and these studies are part of the basis for states setting limits on the amount of alcohol one can consume and still legally operate a motor vehicle. The pertinent information here is that reaction times are relevant to auto accidents, slower reactions are more likely to cause accidents, and alcohol slows reaction times.

Another point to be made about ① concerns the term "conclusively." If this term means "with absolute certainty" the premise itself gains in plausibility. However this makes it much less applicable to human actions, as any number of analogous arguments show. For example, you can argue that a man should not be convicted of murder because there is no conclusive proof that the man he killed wouldn't have been killed anyway by a bolt of lightning five minutes later. If on the other hand "conclusively" means "beyond reasonable doubt," this is the appropriate standard of evidence for felony cases in the criminal courts. You can prove beyond reasonable doubt that the man would not have been killed by lightning five minutes later by noting that no lightning struck anywhere near the murder scene. Bringing information to bear on the premise and clarifying its claim substantiate our initial impression of the argument's weakness. But now we have a reasoned evaluation of the argument, not just an impression.

B. Premise Relevance

Although a false or unreliable premise cannot support a conclusion, it isn't automatically the case that a reliable premise does support it. To decide whether this is the case, we must return from the external factors bearing on reliability to an internal assessment of the relevance of the premise to the conclusion. The specific type of relevance that interests us here is *probative* relevance.

A premise is *probatively* relevant when either by itself or linked with other premises it can contribute to establishing the conclusion. "Probative" is a modifier related to "prove," and we say that a premise has probative force when it contributes to proving the conclusion.

An argument we diagramed earlier[1] is instructive from the standpoint of premise relevance. We diagramed it as divergent.

Two important points have clearly been identified ~~by~~
① ②
<the Soviet[s] attack[ed] ~~on~~ KAL Flight 007.> 1. <The Soviets do not
③
recognize individual rights.> 2. <The Soviets cannot be trusted.>

Divergent
Weak

Let us focus our attention on the support it is alleged that ① provides for ②. First we note that the premise is true, a statement of fact. Then and now it was disputed by no one including the Soviets that a Russian fighter plane attacked and shot down this unarmed commercial passenger jet. The question we must consider to evaluate this argument is whether the undisputed fact supports the contention that the Soviets do not recognize individual rights. What does it mean for a nation to support individual rights? This is the information we need to evaluate the support of ① for ②. Usually when we consider whether a nation

[1] Chapter Six, p. 132f.

observes individual rights we focus on how it treats its own citizens rather than those of other nations. We ask whether they have the right to speak in public on controversial matters without being restrained or taken away by force, or whether when they are arrested they have the right to be informed of the charges against them and to consult a lawyer. Generally a nation that grants its citizens considerable individual or civil rights also extends these rights to resident aliens and visiting foreigners. But the crux of the question of individual rights is whether they are enjoyed by the nation's citizens.

Viewed in the light of this information, we notice a considerable discrepancy between the premise and the conclusion. The premise cites the shooting down of a commercial plane that violated Russian air space, an act that is dastardly but also lacks direct bearing on the question of individual rights in the Soviet Union. What we have here is a sound premise that fails to support the conclusion. It is not probatively relevant. As we concluded earlier, ① provides no support for ② and only moderate support for ③.

So our second argument is weak for a different reason. The first was weak because a false premise provided no support. This one is weak despite having a true premise because the premise is irrelevant to the conclusion. Again further information was needed to assess the argument, this time about what it meant for a nation to recognize individual rights.

2. Phrasing of the Conclusion and Context

C. Phrasing of the Conclusion

When we have gathered and applied the information for an at least initial estimate of premise reliability and relevance, we turn our attention to the phrasing of the conclusion. By its nature the conclusion of an argument is a claim, and the claim may be a bold one or a modest one. Useful for us here is the idea of a *modal qualifier*. The modality of an argument is the boldness of its conclusion's claim, and modal qualifiers are words or phrases occurring in the conclusion that influence the strength of this claim. The words "can" or "might" are modal qualifiers, as are such phrases as "must be" or "might be." All other factors being equal, a conclusion with the modal qualifier "must be" makes a bolder claim than one with "might be."

The boldness or modesty of a conclusion's claim relates inversely to the strength of the argument. The bolder the claim in the conclusion (relative to the same body of evidence), the weaker the argument. The more modest the claim, the stronger the argument. A bold claim claims more, and it takes correspondingly more evidence or better reasons to support it. The modest claim claims less, so it is better supported by the existing evidence, and this yields a stronger argument. This means that an argument can be made stronger or weaker by varying the strength of the claim of its conclusion while the premises remain the same. Here is an example.

①
<The leading cause of AIDS is sexual contact with an infected person.>
②
[So] <by avoiding sexual contact with infected persons you won't get AIDS.>

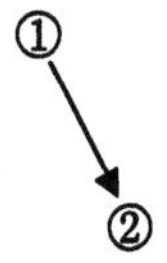

①
↓
②

Simple
Weak

The conclusion makes a bold claim relative to the evidence, giving us a weak argument. Now let us alter the conclusion to make the claim even bolder.

> . . . by avoiding sexual contact with infected persons, you *can be absolutely certain of* not getting AIDS.

This makes the argument weaker yet. To make the argument stronger (again relative to the same body of evidence, which means we have made no changes in the premise), we can alter the conclusion to make a more modest claim.

> . . . by avoiding sexual contact with infected persons you *can decrease your chances of* getting AIDS.

As it stands, without either of the variations we carried out, the argument is weak. Of AIDS cases in adults reported to mid-1993, 23.7% were injecting drug users (sharing contaminated needles), and 1.8% received blood transfusions. So you cannot be sure of escaping AIDS by avoiding sexual contact with infected persons.

This raises an interesting question about argument strategy. Why would anyone aware that a modest claim in the conclusion makes for a stronger argument still want to make a bold claim in the conclusion? She would want to do this because the bold claim is frequently what interests us most and is more valuable to us. In the above case we would like to know what we could do to be sure of avoiding AIDS, since it is a fatal disease with no known cure. Here the motive for desiring the bold claim is our interest in our own survival. We appreciate of course any information that will decrease our likelihood of contracting AIDS. But what we would like most is information on how to be sure of not getting it.

D. Context (Scenario)

A quite different type of information about the argument is helpful for assessing strength in many cases: information about the context of the argument. The context is the setting or situation in which the argument is created or produced by the person who originates it. Some of the contextual factors that may be of importance are the person who originates the argument and the time and place of its origin. Many of the arguments we work with here are chosen for learning purposes, and this frequently means that they are brief and taken from their actual context. Our information about that context may be too scant to support an evaluation.

In such cases we can work with *scenarios*, where a scenario is a possible context for the argument, or a filling out of important details of an actual context. For example, our information about the context of the following argument is scant indeed. We are told only that the speaker[2] is George Meany, president of the American Federation of Labor.

①

<<u>There is something basically wrong with our economy</u>> [because]

②

<a man working full time can't support his family above the poverty level.>

Simple

Meany could have spoken this any time between 1952, the year he became president of the AFL, and 1979, the year he retired as president of the combined AFL-CIO. Let's take 1979 because it is closer and more interesting to us. We can use scenarios here to clarify the meaning. Filling out a scenario sends us after the information we need to evaluate the argument. On one scenario, the average salary at the time Meany spoke was below poverty level. In 1979, poverty level for the U.S. non-farm family of four was $6,700. Poverty level income is the income a family must have to cover its basic needs. We take a family of four (poverty level differs with the size of the family) because that was the size of the average American family at that time. We chose the non-farm family because Meany, as a union leader, is considering the question relative to organized labor. Few farm workers were organized in unions at that time, although some are now. The average weekly wage in 1978 was $249.27, which amounts to an annual income of $12,962.04. This is almost double the poverty level. So

[2] Quoted in Thomas, *Practical Reasoning in Natural Language*, p. 50.

on this scenario, Meany's premise is false and his argument weak.

Another scenario would take the wage, not of the average worker, but of the worker getting the minimum wage. In 1978 this was $2.65 per hour. This adds up to an annual income of $5,512, nearly $1,200 below the poverty level. On this scenario Meany's premise is true in the sense that it is *possible* for a man who heads a family of four to work full time at minimum wage and still have annual earnings more than $1,200 below poverty level. When we turn to assess the argument, however, the question is whether this supports the claim that there is something basically wrong with our economy.

In the present case Meany as a union leader would apparently adjust the minimum wage upward until someone earning this minimum wage would be above the poverty level, i.e. able to provide for the basic needs of a family of four. The simplest and most straightforward way of doing this would be to simply raise the minimum wage to about $3.25 per hour. But we should consider some possible consequences of adopting a sizable hike in the minimum wage.

1. Employers who could not pass the increase on to consumers by raising prices might absorb it by laying off workers, making some of them exist on unemployment benefits and welfare, and thereby driving them even further below the poverty line.

2. Those who could raise prices would contribute to a higher rate of inflation, so the same amount of money would buy less.

3. Those who raised prices could lose their market share to foreign manufacturers with cheaper labor costs, forcing them to close down and lay off all employees.

The objective of Meany's argument is to better the lot of the working man. Increasing unemployment and inflation tend to the opposite effect, worsening the lot of the working man. So in this scenario, where we hypothetically raise the minimum wage, this objective eludes us. Another perspective concedes that it is possible for a man to work full time etc. yet questions the probative relevance of this sole premise to the conclusion. If we assume that this state of affairs is not a secret, that is, people realize that they can't support a family well with a minimum-wage job, the same premise supports a different and opposed conclusion. We might conclude that someone who starts a family when his marketable skills are at minimum-wage level exercises poor judgment. He should have waited until his education and skills improved to the point of securing an income adequate to support his family. This argument turns out weak in both of the scenarios we considered.

It is possible for an argument, however, to be weak on one scenario and strong on another. Suppose for example we need to analyze and evaluate the following argument.

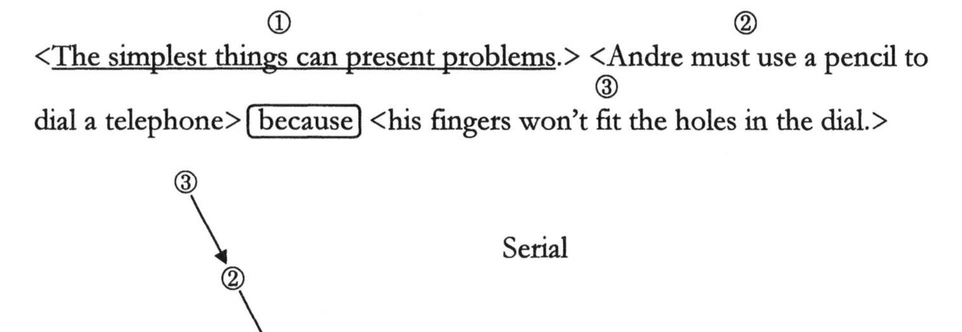

The conclusion of the argument is paradoxical and in need of clarification. Problems are in a sense complications, and things are rightly considered simple when they are relatively free of complications. So we need a *scenario* or situation that makes sense of the argument. Perhaps Andre, like Gulliver in *Gulliver's Travels*, is visiting a country where the people are small, which is why his fingers won't fit in their telephone dials. This scenario would give us a strong argument. Another scenario would be in the present day United States with Andre being a person of average size. This scenario gives us a weak argument. A person of average size has no difficulty dialing a phone with his index finger. A third scenario would have the same locale as the second but make Andre a giant with fingers too large for the dial. In this scenario the conclusion would be made more specific: "The simplest things can present problems [for a giant]." This is a strong argument. The title of the piece the argument was taken from, "A Giant Among Us,"[3] points to the third scenario. There will be cases where our information about the context is too slender for us to decide among scenarios. In such cases we evaluate the argument using the most plausible scenario.

Note too that the phrasing of the conclusion is of importance in the scenario that refers to the giant. The conclusion contains the modal qualifier "can," and it does not take a great amount of evidence to establish that the simplest things *can* present problems. A few, like dialing the phone, are sufficient. Suppose however the conclusion claimed "The simplest things always present problems." With the modal qualifier "always" in the conclusion the argument is weak. Some simple things, like getting something down from the top shelf, are much easier for a giant than for a person of average height.

Before we attempt to solve problems of evaluating arguments, let's sum up briefly the techniques we will employ.

---

[3] By Terry Todd, *Reader's Digest* (May 1982), p. 117.

1. **Seek out information bearing on the reliability of the premises.**
2. **Examine whether the premises are probatively relevant, or contribute to establishing the conclusion.**
3. **Examine the phrasing of the conclusion, being alert for modal qualifiers.**
4. **Place the argument in context, and/or devise scenarios for the specific details important for evaluation.**

EXERCISE 7—1: ARGUMENTS TO EVALUATE

Mark up, diagram, and identify the pattern of each of these arguments. Evaluate each argument, and be prepared to support your evaluation with reasons.

*1. Chiffon is superior to taffeta for flounces. Of course it does depend on the type of garment you're making. For a party dress it is lighter in weight and livelier in appearance.

2. According to a new report, miniscule amount of over-the-counter weed killers impair reproduction in mice and therefore might also affect other animals, people included.

Science News (Oct. 12, 2002), p. 228.

3. Since age-related memory loss is a chemical problem, there is at least the possibility that drugs might be developed that could ameliorate it. ....age-related memory loss may be preventable, through lifestyle changes that might keep the brain's chemistry from going awry in the first place.

Wray Herbert, "Losing Your Mind?" *U.S. News & World Report* (July 26, 1999), p. 49.

4. The microwave oven is a godsend for people who schedule too much work, school, and activities in their lives. Not only does it save big chunks of cooking time. It also leaves some foods like vegetables more nutritious by preserving vitamins that would be boiled away in cooking.

5. Ultraviolet rays like those from the sun kill germs and are used for example in the pasteurization of milk. So it is surprising that people aren't told by their doctors to spend more time in the sun.

6. The process of automation hasn't been carried far enough yet in the automobile. On many new models you open windows by pushing a button instead of cranking a handle. But you ought to be able to open the doors electrically too by pushing a button instead of pulling a handle.

7. (At Standard Oil of Indiana in 1909, William Burton experimented with putting oil at high temperatures under high pressure, and the resulting process, called thermal cracking, more than doubled the amount of gasoline refined from oil.)

The scientists were cautious, and rightly so, for danger was ever present. There was precious little knowledge about how oil behaved under such conditions.

Daniel Yeargin, *The Prize* (New York 1992), p. 111.

8. Dogs are definitely more intelligent than people. They don't pay taxes, they don't cause automobile accidents, and they don't do drugs or get drunk.

*9. The tax policy of the federal government is anti-marriage. A spouse pays more tax on the same income than she would as a single person. She also pays more than she would if she lived with a man without being married to him. The federal government opposes marriage so it will have more activities to run in the area of social services, like food stamps.

10. Cases of food poisoning, some fatal, from salmonella bacteria are on the rise. Eggs are often the source. Heat destroys these bacteria. So you should eat only fully cooked eggs.

11. (From a review of *The Ninth Gate* by Stanley Kauffmann)
It all comes out ridiculous and boring, because [Depp slouches around in private-eye clichés], because [the Gothic settings are corny], because [the screenplay is ill-jointed.]

The New Republic (Apr. 3, 2000), p. 25.

12. "The pit bull was becoming a nightmare," said Morris. "Whenever we let him out of his cage, he would attack the guards." The dog had to be put to sleep.

Farmville Herald (Sept. 5, 2002)

3. Counter-examples and Counter-arguments

Finding counter-examples and constructing counter-arguments are both ways of going beyond the argument in search of information to test its strength.

A. Counter-examples

A counter-example is one of the items or entities referred to in the conclusion that lacks the feature the argument attributes to it. A search for a counter-example is a quest for an item contrary to the conclusion that indicates weakness in the argument. As above we sought information that would test the reliability of premises, so here we seek one or more individual items to test the conclusion

Counter-examples are of limited usefulness, but quite valuable in their restricted area. They apply only to arguments that have generalizations for their conclusions. Many such arguments are arguments by inductive generalization, which are examined more closely in Chapter Fourteen below. A generalization is a statement that makes a claim about many or all members of a group or class, on the basis of a sample. "Most tomatoes are larger than grapes" is an example of the first type of generalization; "All lemons are yellow" is an example of the second. Counter-examples are usually only effective for the second kind, sometimes called universal generalizations, that refer to all members of a class or group. In such cases we search for a counter-instance or counter-example to the universal generalization. In some cases finding such a counter-example destroys an argument.

The following exchange occurs in Eugene Ionesco's drama *The Rhinocerous.*

Logician: "Here's an example of a syllogism. Cats have four paws. Isidore and Fricot each have four paws. So Isidore and Fricot are cats."

Old Man: "My dog also has four paws."

The Logician concludes that the dog is a cat. Unfortunately the Old Man defers to him. He shouldn't have because his criticism of the syllogism[4] is valid. What he does is offer a counter-example to test the conclusion and the validity of the argument that purports to establish it. We can rephrase the argument to better gauge the impact of the counter-example.

Logician: "All animals with four paws are cats. Isidore and Fricot are animals with four paws. So Isidore and Fricot are cats."
Old Man: "Wait a minute. My dog has four paws. Does that make him a cat?"

Of course his dog is not a cat. The impact of his counter-example is to call the first premise into question.

All animals with four paws are cats.

We realize that we could add numerous counter-examples to that of the Old Man. Bears, wolves, foxes, etc. are all animals with four paws that are not cats. So the first premise is obviously false. This linked argument is destroyed by the impact of these counter-examples. It proves nothing.

Does a successful counter-example always destroy an argument? To address this question, let us look at some early evidence gathered to address the debate whether cigarette smoking is dangerous to your health. We are presented with the following conclusion.

Cigarette smoking is dangerous to your health.

Among the evidence supporting this conclusion is the research conducted by Dr. Hammond and his group. They examined and followed up nearly 188,000 American men for over three and a half years, and were able to establish the following statistical correlation between cigarette smoking and deaths from lung cancer.

---

[4] A syllogism is a special type of argument with two premises that relates items in three different groups or classes.

Cigarettes smoked per day	Lung cancer death rate (per 100,000 annually)
nonsmoker	3.4
less than half a pack	51.4
one-half to one pack	59.3
one to two packs	143.9
more than two packs	217.3

What these data mean is that about 3 of every 100,000 nonsmokers die a year of lung cancer, whereas from 51 to 217 of every 100,000 smokers die of the same cause. And the more they smoke, up to more than two packs a day, the more they die.

Now let us consider the following counter-examples.

> I don't care what the authorities say. My Uncle George smoked two and a half packs a day and lived to be 84, and my grandfather smokes one and a half packs a day, and he is close to 90. Then too, I read somewhere that Golda Meir, once Prime Minister of Israel, smoked two packs a day. And she lived to be about 80.

What is the bearing of these counter-examples on the argument cited above? It is indeed true that a small number of people smoke cigarettes and smoke heavily, yet live to a ripe old age. And when they do die, they die of something other than lung cancer. But the evidence is too massive in this case for the argument to be dented by a few counter-examples. The argument that cigarette smoking is dangerous to your health is a strong argument. The counter-examples show only that cigarette smoking doesn't shorten lives in every case.

The general tendency of a counter-example is to weaken an argument. But each case must be decided individually. On the other hand, if we search with determination for a counter-example and cannot find one, this suggests we may be dealing with a strong argument.

B. Counter-Arguments

A counter-argument is an argument with a conclusion opposed to or in some cases the contradictory opposite of the conclusion of the original argument. It is an attempt to disprove the conclusion of the original argument and thereby show that this argument is weak. Sometimes we can find counter-arguments in print media on a topic that is being hotly debated. Far more frequently we must construct counter-arguments ourselves. We do that by first stating a conclusion opposite that of the original argument, then seeking evidence or reasons to back up this new conclusion. This search for counter-arguments or evidence takes us to the context of an argument in a different way. It takes us into the context of debate where different factors have been cited for and against a controversial conclusion. We need to familiarize ourselves with some of these factors in order to construct good counter-arguments Ralph H. Johnson refers to this arena of debate as the dialectical tier of evaluation, and it is examined more closely in connection with writing the argumentative essay in Chapter Sixteen below.

Let us look at an example.

Argument:	The 23 chromosome pairs constituted at conception create a human being. A heartbeat is discernable at 3 to 4 weeks. Brain-wave activity can be monitored at 8 weeks. So the fetus is a human being.
Counter-argument:	The law has never treated the fetus as a human being. The 1973 Roe v. Wade decision of the U.S. Supreme Court only protects the fetus at viability, or from the seventh month. Thus the fetus is not yet a human being.

Here the argument marshals evidence to establish that the fetus is a human being, whereas the counter-argument gathers evidence that points in the opposite direction. Notice that a counter-argument functions differently from a counter-example. It does not present several fetuses for examination and then say, "Look, examine them! These, at least, are not human beings." To oppose the claim that science establishes fetuses to be humans, it cites evidence from the law that fetuses are not humans.

After we have constructed a counter-argument we still need to assess its impact on the original. Its impact may be near negligible, it may somewhat weaken or greatly weaken the original, or it may destroy the force of the original argument. In the present case the counter-argument in this case reduces the force of the argument but doesn't reduce it to zero. A defender of the original could contend that the law is mistaken in this case.

Some counter-arguments are complex and may include counter-examples in their scope. It is not a matter of great importance for us to distinguish counter-example neatly from counter-argument. It is important for us to understand how each affects an original argument so that we can assess its strength or weakness.

Another example suggests some of the complexity of the counter-argument technique. Primitive humans were able to make a precarious existence slightly more secure when over a great period of time they established connections between the positions of heavenly bodies and events vital to their survival. The position of the sun decided the season of the year, whether it was warm or cold, the migration of the animals they hunted, and the best times to plant and harvest their crops. The moon governed the tides, and the stars provided navigational aid for seafaring peoples.

For these primitive humans this knowledge extended also to the positions of the sun, moon, and planets exerting a powerful influence over the events of people's lives. As it finally became codified in the pseudo-science of astrology, the belief was that the positions of the planets in the astral constellations at the time of one's birth determined one's future life.

In his *Confessions*, St. Augustine develops a counter-argument against the argument of the astrologers. He proposes the following hypothesis, then sets out to test it.

Hypothesis:	If the thesis of the astrologers is true, then people born at the same time under the same constellations should have the same fate.

Augustine's friend Firminius reported that his father had an opportunity to test this hypothesis on the occasion of his own birth. A maid in his father's household gave birth to a son at the same time Firminius was born. The constellations were observed carefully and found to be exactly the same. Yet Firminius got a good education, prospered, and reaped honors, whereas the slave led an abject existence.

Augustine puts himself in the position of an astrologer consulted about Firminius at his birth. He would have examined the constellations and predicted prosperity. Then he puts himself as an astrologer consulted at the slave's birth. To predict accurately, he would have had to examine the exact same constellation and predict a quite different fate. Augustine concludes that astrological prediction on the basis of the constellations is worthless. As further evidence he cites the case of twins such as Jacob and Esau who are born at the same time yet meet quite different fates.

We can state the argument and counter-argument thus.

Argument:	The position of the heavenly bodies determines seasons, harvests, animal migrations, and other events of import to man. So the position of the heavenly bodies determines man's fate.
Counter-argument:	If the position of the heavenly bodies determines man's fate, then men born at the same time should have the same fate. But men born at the same time have different fates. So the position of the heavenly bodies doesn't determine the fate of man.

The counter-argument seems rather strong in this case. You would think that few people would seek to learn their fate from the stars. Yet we know that millions of people read astrology columns in newspapers every day. Are they unaware of this counter-argument? Or is their desire to know something about the future stronger than their skeptical doubts?

EXERCISE 7—2: COUNTER-ARGUMENTS

To get some practice in the use of this argument evaluation technique, we will deal with argumentative contexts more complex than those we have diagramed, analyzed, and evaluated. We will attempt to carry out this exercise *without* diagramming the material.

Part A: Counter-Arguments Given

In each problem you are given an argument and then a counter-example or counter-argument. In the case of a counter-argument you need to locate and state the conclusion of both the original and the counter-argument. Examine the bearing of the counter-argument on the original. Decide whether the original argument is weakened or not, and if so why.

1. "Let's get asbestos insulation for the heating ducts," urged Mel. "It's fireproof, corrosion resistant, less expensive than other insulation of comparable quality, and it can be easily obtained locally."

   "I agree it's everything you say, but fiberglass is still preferable," rejoined Betty. "Getting asbestos fibers in the air is just too dangerous to your health. They can cause asbestosis, a lung disease that makes it hard for you to breathe, cancer of the bronchial tubes, and a fatal cancer of the chest lining."

2. " Of course that film is obscene! It shows couples naked and performing sexual acts in three different scenes. It ought to be banned from public showing."

   "It is not the least bit obscene. If sexual acts were obscene, people wouldn't perform them, and the human race would have become extinct a long time ago."

3. ". . . many of the nations represented in the UN find political reality an uncomfortable matter they prefer to ignore. A former State Department official tells of a representative from Ghana who gave a moving speech to the General Assembly on the importance of free elections and full franchise. When he had finished, he was asked, 'How long has it been since you've had a free election in Ghana? Don't you feel strange faulting another country for a situation that exists in your own?' The reply was unhesitating: 'Can't a man admire flowers if he has no garden?'"

   Mary Schwarz, "Jean Kirkpatrick: Our Macho UN Ambassador," *National Review* (Jan. 21, 1983), p. 42.

*4. The economist Milton Friedman is addressing a claim that business corporations have social responsibilities.

"Only people can have responsibilities. A corporation is an artificial person and in this sense may have artificial responsibilities . . . ."

Milton Friedman, "The Social Responsibility of Business Is To Increase Its Profits," *New York Times Magazine* (Sept. 13, 1970), p. 33.

A counter-argument to this is:

"What do you mean when you say a corporation has a right to manufacture and market a product? That's a real right, and only persons can have real rights. A corporation is an artificial person, so it can only have artificial rights."

5. "What would I do if I discovered someone taking bribes to buy inferior products in my section of Purchasing? I'd report it to the supervisor, and then up the chain of command right to the top, if necessary. Then if the bribes still continued, I'd find a hungry newspaper or TV reporter and blow the whistle. After all, we are a government agency. It's my duty as a conscientious citizen to keep taxpayers' money from being squandered on bribes and inferior products purchased as a result of bribes."

"I disagree with you completely. Your course of action would probably cost you your job. If the supervisor doesn't do anything about it, that means he's probably on the take too. So he'll try to protect himself by getting you fired. I'd either shut up about it and mind my own business, or look for a job elsewhere."

6. "Have you seen recent reports on the effects of mandatory sentencing for using a gun while committing a crime? Now many experts are saying that such laws do not deter criminals from using guns. Most criminals, they say, don't even consider the penalty before committing a crime. They commit the crime because they're convinced they can get away with it. In 1975 Florida passed a law mandating a three year sentence for using a gun while committing a crime. In 1977 University of Michigan criminologists Loftin and McDowall surveyed 277 Florida inmates, and 73 percent reported that the law would not deter them from carrying a gun.'

Adapted from reports in the Newport News-Hampton *Daily Press* (Sept. 11, 1983).

"I'm not convinced that these laws don't have some deterrent effect, and I don't think that all of the evidence is in. A sample of convicted felons, many of whom used guns in committing their crimes, may not be representative. Some criminals may have been deterred from committing felonies by the thought that a gun was needed but would bring mandatory sentencing. And some people leaning toward crime may have been deterred altogether. Yet few or none of these would show up in a prison sample. Virginia passed a similar law with a mandatory one-year sentence in 1975, when guns were used in 55 percent of all reported robberies. Since then, guns have been used in 45 percent of all reported robberies."

Part B: Counter-Arguments Needed

Examine each argument closely. See whether you can find a counter-example or construct a counter-argument to test its strength. Remember to begin constructing your counter-argument with a conclusion opposed to that of the original. Decide in each case whether the argument is strong or weak, and why.

1. All oak trees are deciduous, and all deciduous trees lose their leaves in the winter. So all oak trees lose their leaves in the winter.

2. You can't trust a person who doesn't believe in God. Atheists shouldn't be allowed to testify in court because you can't count on them to tell the truth. No atheist can place his hand upon the Bible and swear to tell the truth, the whole truth, and nothing but the truth.

   Adapted from John Locke, "A Letter Concerning Toleration."

*3. "What makes you think that east lies in that direction?"

   "See those people kneeling on their prayer rugs in the corner of the square? They look like Muslims saying their noon prayers. Muslims always pray facing Mecca, which lies east of here."

4. "I've seen hundreds of cardinals, and they were all either red in the case of males, or brown in the case of females. There's no such thing as a cardinal that isn't either red or brown."

5. John Fishwick, former President of Norfolk & Virginia Railway and a critic of Political Action Committees (PACs), says this about the corporate rush to form PACs.

   "If steroids were made legal in the Olympics, any participant would have to take steroids to not be at a disadvantage. The business community has accepted PACs to such a wide extent that there's pressure on any company that doesn't have a PAC to start one□it's mass psychology."

   Quoted in *Common Cause*, Vol. 9 (Sept.-Oct. 1983), p. 15.

6. Lie detectors or polygraphs are based on the principle that a person who lies undergoes stress and will exhibit physical symptoms of stress. Of course they are accurate, because they work scientifically and objec-

tively. They measure such bodily symptoms of stress as blood pressure, breathing at the chest and at the stomach, and perspiration.

4. Argument Types and Strength

Premises are advanced in support of conclusions in different ways, and our identification of five different basic argument types captures some of these differences. In an important sense these types are different ways in which premises can be relevant to their conclusions. One advantage of argument diagraming is that it provides a graphic representation of the argument. When an argument is well diagramed, showing how each premise relates to other premises and to the conclusion, simply inspecting the diagram reveals the claimed relations of logical support. Our current task is to exploit these relations for what they can reveal to us about an argument's strength.

In the case of the simple argument, the reliability and relevance of the premise are the main determinants of the strength of the argument. Some strong simple arguments are rightly classed as cases of logical implication.

In the divergent argument, one premise is advanced as directly supporting two or more conclusions. The support received by each conclusion is calculated separately, so that one may receive strong support and another weak. We always attempt, however, to arrive at an assessment of the divergent argument as a whole. Some strong divergent arguments are cases of inferring or deducing consequences from a general principle.

When one or more premises provide *indirect* support for a conclusion, as in the serial argument, we first assess the strength of each support relation separately. Then on the basis of this we calculate the strength of the argument as a whole.

Let's see how this works.

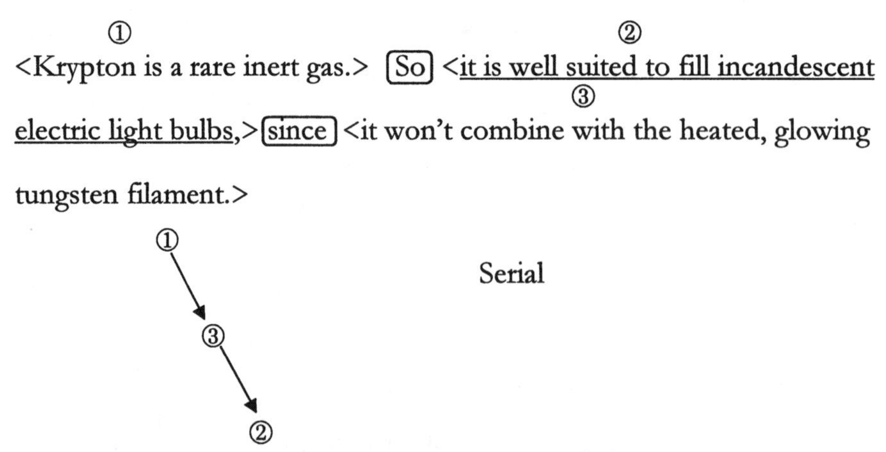

①
②
<Krypton is a rare inert gas.> So <it is well suited to fill incandescent
③
electric light bulbs,> since <it won't combine with the heated, glowing
tungsten filament.>
①
Serial
③
②

In this serial argument there are two support relations.

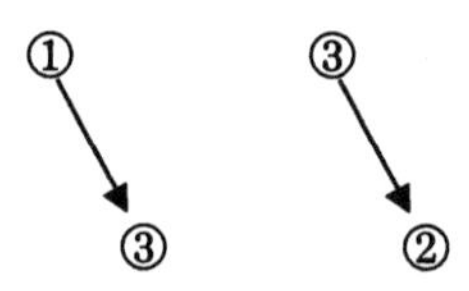

First, what support does ① provide for ③? It is true that krypton is an inert gas. An inert gas combines either not at all or only with great difficulty with other elements. Such a gas is needed inside the incandescent light bulb. If the gas were like oxygen, the very thin tungsten filament heated to 4,500° Fahrenheit would combine with it rapidly and burn out. So ① provides strong support for ③.

What support does ③ provide for ②? We would need to know more about krypton than we do to find this relation strong. We need to know, for instance, that when heated to this temperature it doesn't turn some color that would prevent the bulb from emitting white light. We also need to know, since it is a rare element, that it could be obtained in commercial quantities at a fairly modest cost. Otherwise people wouldn't be able to afford light bulbs. So as ② is stated, ③ provides weak support for it. Since ② is the final conclusion, the overall strength of the argument is weak. On the other hand, if we were to replace the modal qualifier "well-suited" in ② with "of possible use," the conclusion would make a more modest claim and the argument would be stronger.

The distinction of convergent from linked arguments can help us evaluate an argument more effectively. As we learned above (Chapter Six), the distinction is drawn based on different ways in which premises are advanced in support of a conclusion. When we advance converging premises in support of a conclusion, our claim is that each premise provides a measure of separate, independent support. We also learned above (Chapter Six) that because of this independence and separateness of premises, a convergent argument may have one or more premises turn out unreliable or false yet still be a strong argument. This is possible because the conclusion might still receive strong support from the remaining premises.

We note that this is only possible in informal logic, the logic associated with critical thinking. In formal logic a premise is usually thought of as a statement absolutely necessary to prove a conclusion. So when a premise is false, the argument must be weak. In informal logic a premise is a statement advanced in support of a conclusion. Whether a premise actually supports a conclusion in informal logic is decided by evaluating the reliability and relevance of each premise, one by one. And in the convergent argument, supposing we have found a premise to be unreliable or irrelevant, we still must decide how this affects the strength of the argument.

It was suggested above that part of the outcome of each argument evaluation should be to fit the argument in one of three broad categories: strong, moderately strong, or weak. The moderately strong argument has at least stronger reasons supporting the conclusion than there are reasons against it. It may also be thought of as an argument where the conclusion receives support on balancing the evidence for and the evidence against the conclusion, or where the conclusion is supported by the preponderance of the evidence. Some writers use the category "moderate" for argument strength, but this practice is not adopted here. "Moderate" equivocates on whether or not the burden of proof has been met (more on the burden of proof in Chapter Ten below), i.e. on whether the conclusion is at least minimally established (our "moderately strong"). To evaluate an argument and leave undecided whether the argument is weak or strong leaves us little or no better off than not evaluating the argument at all.

In the sense in which inference is *reasoning* and argument is backing up a claim on a controversial matter, convergent arguments tend more to resemble the latter. This is particularly true of the somewhat more complex ones we deal with in the next chapter. What this means for evaluation is that the actually stated convergent argument sometimes seems part of a larger debate lying unstated in the background. So we frequently need to do more than check the context to test the premise for reliability. Ralph Johnson has called the larger debate (the unstated pros and cons of the conclusion) of which the stated argument is only a part, the "dialectical tier." We consulted this dialectical tier for material for our counter-arguments in the last section, and evaluating a convergent argument well can also involve visiting the dialectical tier for objections to the conclusion and defenses of it against such objections. A convergent argument like the following, paraphrased from a lawyer arguing that some attempts to apply the law uniformly violate common sense, can seem more part of an on-going process than a finished product.

①
<Precision that makes the law the same for everyone does not ensure fairness.>

②
<Uniform sentencing guidelines (by weight of drug) yield the same sentence for a seller of 1.5 grams of LSD impregnated in 100 grams of blotter paper as for the supplier apprehended with 20,000 doses on his person.>

③
<Fire codes requiring enclosed fire escapes in transient lodging threaten to close many bed and breakfasts in old Upper New York State farmhouses.>

④
<EPA rules requiring scrubbers in all coal-burning power plants cost $4 billion and leave eastern plants that burn dirty black coal with higher pollution levels than western plants using clean brown coal had before they installed scrubbers.>

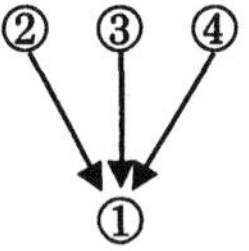

We can well imagine the dialectical tier for this argument containing horror stories about a defendant in one jurisdiction being sentenced 3-5 years for a crime very similar to the one for which a defendant in another jurisdiction received a 15-25-year sentence. Still the modality of the conclusion "Precision . . . does not ensure fairness" makes this a strong argument. All that is needed to establish the conclusion is one case where precision does not ensure fairness, and the writer gives several.

Many linked arguments, on the other hand, behave more like inference where inference differs from argument. In inference we are logically deducing some new information from given information, so the important given information must be there before the idea of inferring can be entertained. What this means for evaluation is that, like inference, linked arguments tend to be more self-contained, i.e. less dependent on a dialectical tier. We do of course attend to the context of the argument and general knowledge to decide whether the premises are reliable. But for linked arguments, deciding whether the premises are reliable and relevant constitutes the major part of the evaluation.

Calculating the strength of a linked argument is done differently from a convergent. Where in the convergent we add up the total of what each premise contributes, the strong linked argument involves a "leap of support"—the argument is typically far stronger than the sum total of separate premise contributions. To illustrate the difference we can analyze an inference we encountered above twice, first as convergent, then as linked.

① ② ③

<Spiders aren't insects.> <All insects have six legs.> But <spiders have eight.>

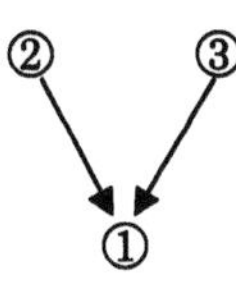

Convergent

When we analyze this as convergent we claim that each premise provides a measure of separate and independent support for the conclusion. But neither premise by itself has any tendency to establish the conclusion. Without the information in ③, ② by itself provides no support. As long as the possibility is open that spiders too have six legs (supposing we have not counted the legs on any spider), ② could count as supporting evidence for the exact opposite conclusion, that spiders are insects. So by itself, we can't even assign a degree of support to ② because it provides no support. The case is similar with ③ by itself.

Now we analyze the same argument as linked.

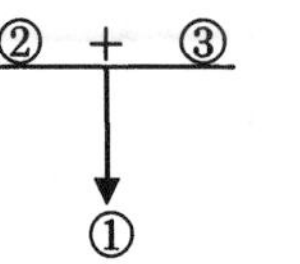

Linked

In this case ② and ③ jointly provide near certain support for the conclusion. It is true in general of linked arguments that the support of linked premises leaps beyond the summative support of the premises considered separately. This could well be due to the way the premises are linked conceptually. Of course this is only the case when the premises are both reliable and relevant. Failing one of these, the linked argument is usually quite weak. So the basic linked arguments we examine here tend to be either quite strong or quite weak.

Many educated people have at least an idea what inference is, while "linked argument" is recent terminology. So we do need to note an important difference in the use of the two terms. "Inference" is a success word. To infer ① from ② and ③ is to succeed in logically deducing it. If we cannot deduce it, there is no inference. "Linked argument" is by contrast a descriptive term. It describes premises as dependent on each other for whatever support they may provide a conclusion. So while there is no such thing as an inference where the conclusion cannot be inferred from the premises, there are very weak linked arguments where premises provide little or no support for the conclusion.

Summary

To evaluate or assess an argument is to decide for reasons that it is strong or weak. We go beyond the argument for information bearing on the reliability of the premises, availing ourselves of common knowledge, specific information, and other sources. We examine the argument internally to decide whether the premises are probatively relevant—whether they contribute to establishing the conclusion.

Our attention turns to the phrasing of the conclusion—the bolder its claim, the more evidence it require, and the more likely the argument is weak. We are especially alert for modal qualifiers that influence the boldness of the claim. Then we recur to the context of the argument—the situation where it is advanced—for factors bearing on its strength. Where specific information is needed but absent, we devise scenarios filling in that information to facilitate assessment.

At any point in this evaluation process we may need to clarify the specific meaning of a premise or the claim of the conclusion. The strength of any argument (such as an inductive one) that has a generalization for its conclusion, can be tested with a counter-example. The generalization attributes some property to most or all members of a group or class, and the counter-example is a member of the group that does not have the property. The argument can be destroyed, greatly or somewhat weakened, or little affected by the counter-example—depending in part on how the conclusion is stated.

Arguments of all types can be tested by constructing counter-arguments, arguments which attempt to establish the opposite of the original conclusion. To find premise material for this opposed conclusion, we search in the dialectical tier, the area of controversy to which the argument belongs. A counter-argument can reveal that the original argument is weak. Our inability to construct a good counter-argument is evidence for the strength of the original argument.

In the simple argument, the strength and relevance of the premise mainly determine the strength of the argument. The divergent argument has the strength of each conclusion calculated separately, and one conclusion may be strongly supported whereas the other receives only weak support. Serial arguments also have each support relation assessed separately, and in most cases the argument will not be strong if the intermediate conclusion receives only weak support from its premise. The convergent argument has the strength of each premise calculated separately to begin with, then the strength of the argument as a whole is the sum of what each premise contributes individually. In a linked argument the support provided by the combined premises is greater than the sum of the contributions of each.

Study Questions

Section 1. Reliability and relevance of premises

1. What is it to evaluate an argument?
2. When is a premise reliable?
3. What different types of information can influence a premise's reliability?
4. When is a premise topically relevant?
5. Probatively?

Section 2. Phrasing of the conclusion and context

6. What is the modality of an argument?
7. What is a modal qualifier?
8. Cite a word as an example. A phrase.
9. How does the boldness of a conclusion's claim relate to the strength of the argument?
10. What is the context of the argument?
11. What contextual factors can be important for evaluation?
12. What is a scenario?

Section 3. Counter-examples and counter-arguments

13. What is a counter-example?
14. What is a generalization?
15. How can a counter-example affect the strength of an argument?
16. How does a counter-argument's conclusion relate to that of the original argument?
17. Where do we seek premise material for a counter-argument?
18. After constructing the counter-argument, how do we apply it?

Section 4. Relevance and Argument Types

19. What mainly determines the strength of the simple argument?
20. How do we calculate the strength of a divergent argument?
21. How does the strength of a serial argument differ?
22. How is the strength of the linked argument calculated differently from that of the convergent?

EXERCISE 7–3: ARGUMENT TYPES AND EVALUATION

Mark up and diagram the arguments. Identify the type and explain why you chose this rather than some other type. Evaluate the argument as weak, moderately strong, or strong, and justify your evaluation with reasons.

1. Teachers have as much right to strike as any workers. Their salaries are low relative to their training and workload. They battle an oft hostile employer interested in keeping their salaries low. No other group will struggle to get higher salaries for them.

2. You should hire me ....because I am loyal to my employer at all costs, and you can easily respond to my application on my office voice mail.

Adapted from an actual application reported in *Fortune*

3. Since the band has lost their second guitar player, they will probably cancel the remainder of the tour, because most of the songs the band is playing live require the second guitar parts.

"Cave In Loses Guitarist" www.decapolis.com/news (Mar. 2003).

4. Every court decision risks setting a bad precedent, and bad precedents cause much harm in our legal system. So judges and jurors should avoid reaching decisions in their court cases.

5. (In directly observed therapy a health care provider or other responsible person watches the patient swallow the drugs.)

Because TB drugs cause side effects—most prominently, liver injury—[you should] prepare the patient for the fact that he'll need periodic blood draws for lab testing. [You should also] let the patient know that DOT [directly observed therapy] is standard practice today.

RN, Vol. 62, No. 6 (June 1999), p. 30.

6. *Playboy's* popularity cannot be wholly the result of its sexual content. Other magazines feature more nude photography, and they also contain more explicitly sexual stories and humor.

7. ("George wants to get married, but I'm not sure. I think I love him, but I don't feel ready for that kind of commitment. It's scary. What do you think?")

"Why don't you ask Myra about it? She's good at giving advice. And she's had lots of experience. She's been married four times already."

8. From the pathogen's point of view, a neonate is very different from a nurse. Neonates are highly susceptible to infection because they lack the acquired immunity of adults, the protective bacteria inhabiting the gut and skin, and strongly acidic stomach contents, which can kill many pathogens before they enter the intestine.

Paul W. Ewald, *Evolution of Infectious Disease* (Oxford & New York 1994), p. 87.

9. Everyone who applies for a job at Penn Starr Enterprises has to take a lie detector test. We want our employees to be honest so that we can work together fruitfully in an atmosphere of trust. You can't trust anyone who refuses to take a lie detector test about the information on their job application.

10. Exchanging tales over the backyard fence . . . helps a community of people establish moral boundaries. We gossip when people go astray as a way of delineating what's right and wrong. . . . Critical gossip helps us to discover, negotiate, transmit, and reinforce those [moral] rules.

Reader's Digest (July 2002), p. 189.

11. (From an article on a resurgence of diners in the U.S.; in the 1950s there were about 5,000 diners in the U.S.; at the time of the article, about 2,500.)

Diners represent both food and mobility. Americans love food and mobility. Americans love diners.

Newsweek (Mar 3, 1986), p. 54.

12. [dependency] is not love . . . It seeks to receive rather than to give. It nourishes infantilism rather than growth. It works to trap and constrict rather than to liberate. Ultimately it destroys rather than builds relationships, and it destroys rather than builds people.

M. Scott Peck, *The Road Less Traveled* (1978), p. 105.

THE CRITICAL THINKING JOURNAL

Part B. The Logic of Arguments and Inferences

7. Diagramming and Analyzing Arguments

Find in print media, diagram, analyze, and evaluate one example of each of these argument types: simple, convergent, divergent, linked, and serial.

FURTHER READING

Michael Scriven, *Reasoning* (New York 1976), specially pp. 39–45, 180, 185–187. Evaluation is the summing up of the critique of the argument.

Trudy Govier, *A Practical Study of Argument*, 3rd ed. (Belmont 1992), pp. 61–86. Stresses that for an argument to be strong, the premises must yield sufficient grounds for the conclusion.

Leo A. Groarke, Christopher W. Tindale, and Linda Fisher, *Good Reasoning Matters!* 2nd ed. (Toronto 1997). Chapter 10 "Assessing the Basics" is good on argument evaluation.

The following two influential informal logic texts stress fallacies for purposes of evaluation, the ways in which arguments can go wrong.

R. H. Johnson & J. A. Blair, *Logical Self-Defense,* (New York 1994), pp. 65–190; the examples and general observations on evaluation on pp. 49–57 are helpful.

Howard Kahane, *Logic and Contemporary Rhetoric,* 6th ed. (Belmont 1992), pp. 17–19, 27–117.

On modalities and modal qualifiers

Derek Allen, "Assessing Inferences," in *New Essays in Informal Logic,* ed. By R. H. Johnson and J. A. Blair (Windsor 1994), pp. 53–57. Does not refer to modal qualifiers by that name, but recognizes that some traditional criteria of inferential soundness ill apply to conclusions with modest claims.

James B. Freeman, *Dialectics and the Macrostructure of Arguments* (Berlin 1991). Chapter 5 is the best exploration of theoretical questions raised by modalities.

Stephen Toulmin, Richard Rieke, and Allan Janik, *An Introduction to Reasoning* (New York 1979). Chapter 6 is the pioneering treatment of modalities.

On the dialectical tier

Trudy Govier, *The Philosophy of Argument* (Newport News 1999). Chapters 12 and 13 give close scrutiny to the proposed dialectical tier of evaluation.

Ralph H. Johnson, *The Rise of Informal Logic* (Newport News 1996). The need for a dialectical tier is argued on pp. 262–266.

CHAPTER EIGHT

COMPOUND ARGUMENTS

1. CLASSIFYING COMPOUND ARGUMENTS

The arguments we have analyzed and evaluated up to now have almost all been identifiable as one of our five basic argument types: simple, divergent, serial, convergent, or linked. Knowing these basic types well gives us a solid foundation to build on now as we turn to the more challenging arguments that we often encounter in various situations. Many of the arguments we deal with in this chapter are compound. A compound argument contains arguments of two or more different basic types as its parts. Here is an example from a discussion of the economics of public education in the United States a century and a half ago.

① <The process of uniting two or more adjacent [school] districts . . . ought to be commenced at once. . . .> . . . ② <The number of teachers in demand would thus be reduced,> while ③ <the rate of compensation might be increased without adding to the burdens of the people> and thus ④ <the facilities for obtaining good instructors would be multiplied in a two-fold ratio.>

When we mark up this material we notice that "thus" in ② is not a conclusion cue, unlike the cue introducing ④. In ② "thus" means "thereby" or "in this way." Should we distinguish ② and ③? We should. Even though both are parts of one compound sentence, each presents a different factor. The conclusion cue enables us to identify ④ as a conclusion, as well as ② and ③ as evidence advanced in support of it. We can interpret the support as convergent, linked, or serial. Linked is preferable since the reduced number in ② links up with the increased compensation in ③. But how does all of this relate to ①? In ① we find that an education policy of uniting adjacent school districts is being advocated. The benefits anticipated from this policy are cited in ②, ③, and ④ as reasons for adopting the policy. So ① is the final conclusion supported by a linked argument comprising the other three statements.

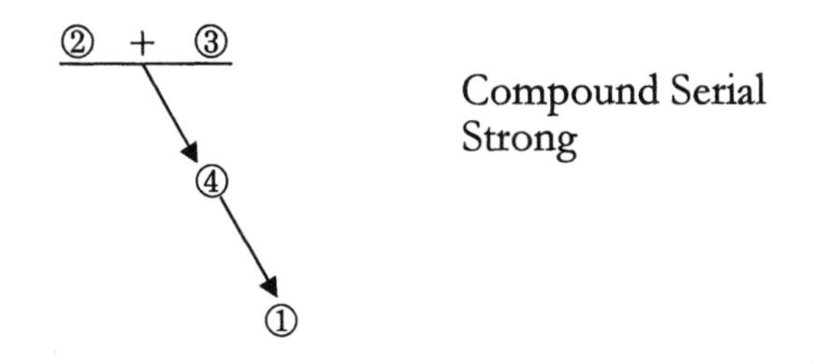

One matter we must address here is the question how to classify this compound argument. In classifying an argument, the most important part is the support for the final conclusion. In the present case, we have linked premises supporting an intermediate conclusion, which then itself becomes a premise supporting the final conclusion. From the vantage point of the final conclusion, ①, the argument most resembles a serial one. So we classify it as a compound serial.

A scenario may be helpful in assessing the strength of the argument. In the scenario, a town or county is attempting to provide a free public education for its school-age children without burdening its taxpayers with too great a cost. Combining adjacent school districts is advanced as a cost-cutting measure, with the savings to go to increase teacher pay. In ④ the purpose of increasing teacher pay is given as that of attracting better teachers to the profession and retaining them. If we make one assumption, we can judge this a strong argument. We have to assume that the question of transportation has been resolved, so that by combining school districts no children are left too distant from the school to make the trip daily, or else that provision is made to board them.

Now we can turn to an inference from one of the very first detective stories, Edgar Allen Poe's "The Murders in the Rue Morgue."

①
<The murderers *did* escape from one of these windows.> [Therefore,]
②
<they could not have re-fastened the sashes from the inside.> <Yet the
③ ④
sashes *were* fastened.> <<u>They must, then, have the power of fastening</u>
⑤
<u>themselves</u>.> <There was no escape from this conclusion.>

In searching for relations of support, we notice the conclusion cue preceding ②. Which of the other statements might be advanced in support of it? ③ states something almost contrary to it, making it a poor candidate for a premise. ④ looks more like a statement that ② would be advanced in support of rather than vice versa. ⑤ doesn't appear to figure in the inference in any substantial way. So ①, which in some other context might be the conclusion of reasoning, is here asserted as a fact supporting ②. As we noticed, ② is advanced to support ④. ② needs to be linked with ③. The following diagram results.

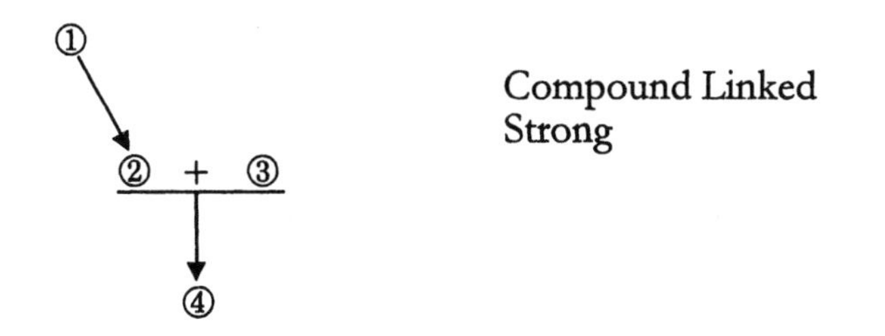

We classify this argument as compound linked because the final conclusion is supported by linked premises. It is compound because it combines linked and simple arguments.

What about its strength? Using the scenario of the actual story by Poe, which makes the premises true, it is a strong inference.

For a look at another type of compound argument, we can examine part of a comparison of rural with city driving.

① <Rural roads are definitely the most dangerous> ② <these lesser classified roads are two-lane.> ③ <Rights-of-way are narrow,> and ④ <the roads are full of fixed objects, like culvert walls and utility poles.> ⑤ <These create significant problems for people who inadvertently drive off the road.>

No cues guide us here, but ②, ③, and ④ appear to be observation statements and are thus more likely premises. ① is a bold claim definitely in need of support, while the role of ⑤ isn't quite clear. It could link with ④ in support of ①, but we will interpret ④ as supporting it in the sense "because the roads have numerous fixed objects, there are problems for those who drive off the road." But ⑤ cannot serve as intermediate conclusion for ② or ③, which present problems for drivers who stay on the road. We can sum this up in the following diagram.

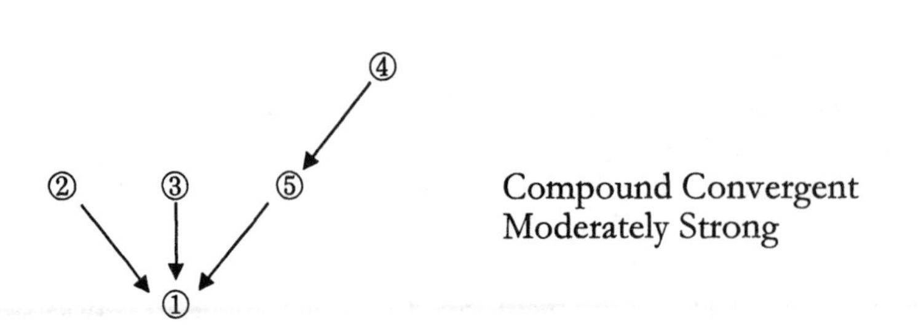

This a compound convergent argument because support for the final conclusion is convergent. It does offer considerable evidence for the claim in ①. The article we have quoted the argument from does provide information on some hazards of city driving which would enable us to make the comparison with rural. But it is not quoted as part of this argument, so considering the boldness of the conclusion, this argument is only moderately strong.

2. Analyzing and Evaluating Compound Arguments

How does analyzing a compound argument differ from analyzing one with a basic pattern? First we notice that compound arguments usually have more statements than basic ones. Every compound argument comprises at least four statements (most have more) whereas many basic arguments have only two or three. Any basic argument but the simple can consist of four or more statements, but no compound argument can consist of fewer than four.

Second and more important, every compound argument is more complex than any basic argument except the serial. The compound argument must have at least one intermediate conclusion. This leads to a somewhat different technique in analysis. Instead of first seeking a final conclusion, we simply look for and jot down support relations. A support relation is a relation of premise or premises to a conclusion, and jotting down means depicting their relations with arrow diagrams. A support relation will be a basic argument type, so in identifying them we avail ourselves of conclusion and premise cues, as well as our knowledge of good argument strategy.

In compound arguments we need to distinguish basic support from intermediate support. This is similar to the distinction of the basic premise of a serial argument from its intermediate conclusion. The basic support of a compound argument is those statements that function as premises by supporting other statements in the argument but are not themselves supported by any other statements in the argument. In diagraming, arrows go from them to other statements but not from other statements to them. Such basic support statements provide support for the conclusion of the argument either directly or indirectly. The person advancing the compound argument may believe that these basic support statements are not themselves in need of further support, or that such further support can readily be given if it is asked for. And indeed some statements must be accepted as basic support if there are to be arguments, because every argument must start with some evidence or reasons. Basic support may itself be based on common knowledge, specific information, observation, or testimony. One part of our task in evaluating any compound argument is to decide whether the basic support is strong enough to support intermediate and final conclusions.

Using this method, we may identify the final conclusion early in the analysis. But the important thing is that in the many cases when we cannot, we have a starting point for our analysis. The following example illustrates.

① <The Japanese should be able to put automobiles on the U.S. market at a very competitive price.> [Basic reason:] ② <it costs the Japanese about $1,500 less than it costs Detroit to manufacture a comparable vehicle.> ③ <According to *Business Week*, the Japanese worker is paid $10 an hour in wages and benefits to do what the American worker is supposed to do for $18.50 an hour.> Moreover, ④ <it takes twice as many executives and laborers to produce a car here.> ⑤ <In short, we are top-heavy in wages and manpower.>

The premises cue [Basic reason] identifies ② as providing support for ①.

③, ④, and ⑤ may fit together as a group. ③ cites much higher autoworker wages in the U.S., and ④ a manpower-per-unit requirement in the U.S. double that of Japan. If we consider them together, they support ⑤, which in a sense sums them up.

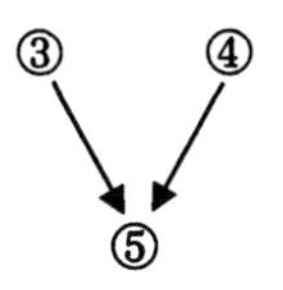

All of the statements in the argument are now fit into two separate support relations. The question remaining is how these two combine to form one argument. To answer this question we employ the jigsaw puzzle technique, and trial-and-error. We attempt to fit the pieces together, then use cue words and our knowledge of argument strategy to decide whether or not pieces fit together. First we ask whether ① can support ③.

Is it because the Japanese should be able to put autos on the U.S. market at a competitive price that the Japanese worker is paid $10 per hour versus the U.S. worker's $18.50 per hour? Very unlikely. How about ① supporting ④?

Again the question: Is it because the Japanese should be competitive in the U.S. auto market that it takes twice as many executives and workers to produce a car here? This is also quite unlikely.

The remaining obvious connecting point would be this.

Is it because we are top-heavy in wages and manpower that the Japanese can manufacture a comparable unit at substantially less cost? This seems far more probable than either of the above alternatives. Using this support relation to combine the other two yields the following diagram of the whole compound argument.

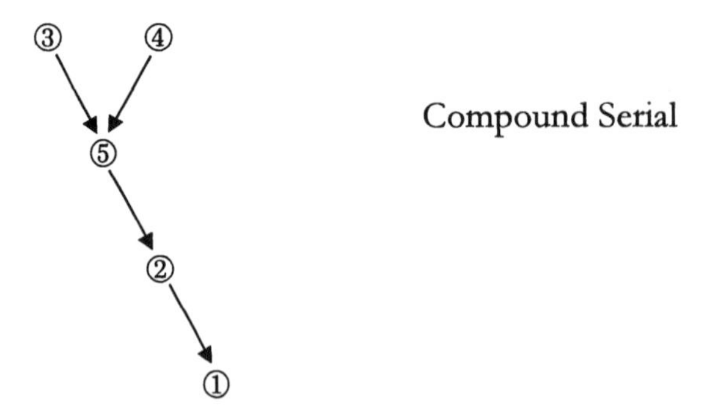

The argument turns out to be compound serial, like the first one we analyzed in this chapter. The information comes from a source that is both respected and reliable for its business reporting, and it provides much support for the conclusion. So at the time it was advanced (in its context: 1981) it was a strong argument. But we need a scenario nearer the present to assess it also. In 2003 the premises were no longer accurate. Labor costs had risen in Japan and U.S. production had become more efficient per unit, making Japanese cars more expensive in the U.S. So the $1,500 advantage in the American market had vanished, making the argument weak.

Another example introduces some interesting challenges for analysis.

① <Another area of the body which can particularly benefit from arthroscopy is the shoulder.> ② <"Compared to conventional surgery there is a lot less pain involved,> noted Dr. Thomas M. Stiles, "because ③ <no big incision is made.> ④ <You don't have to disturb the muscles to look inside.> ⑤ <In the shoulder, arthroscopy can be applied to repair ligaments, bursitis and cuff tears, which are partial tendon tears in the shoulder.">

First there is the question whether this is an argument. It might simply be an explanation why the shoulder can benefit from arthroscopy, a type of joint surgery using slender instruments and an image of the joint interior on a video screen. If we encountered this passage in a surgery textbook we would rightly classify it as explanation. But in the context of a bulletin advertising a hospital's services and specialties, its function is argumentative. It is less a scientific explanation of what is possible than an argument that these services are available and should be used by us on appropriate occasions.

When we interpret it more directly as an assertion, ① is a claim: "The shoulder can particularly benefit from arthroscopy." It is supported directly by ②, the absence of pain being a benefit. The premise cue "because" helps us see that ② is supported by ③. Together ② and ③ provide serial support for ①.

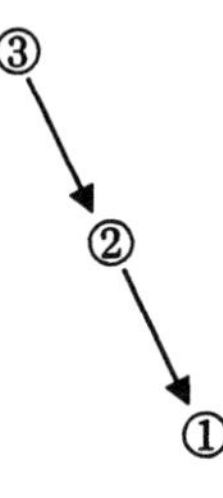

No doubt ④ supports ① also, but it isn't clear whether it does so directly or indirectly. Is there less pain because the muscles are not disturbed? In this case ④ would support ②. Or (which seems more likely) is it the case that not having to disturb muscles simplifies the surgical procedure? We adopt this latter interpretation here, and accordingly take ④ as providing direct support for ①. ⑤ also provides direct support for ①. It spells out the various ways a shoulder can benefit by citing specific defects that arthroscopy can remedy, whereas ② characterizes the benefit instrumentally as the absence of pain. So ④ and ⑤ taken together provide convergent support for ①.

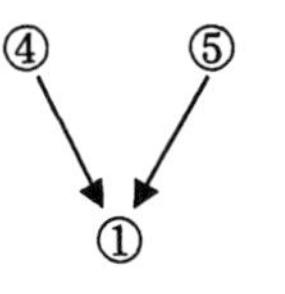

Now we can readily combine these two support relations into a compound argument with ③, ④, and ⑤ providing basic support and ② intermediate support for ① as the final conclusion. This is the diagram that results.

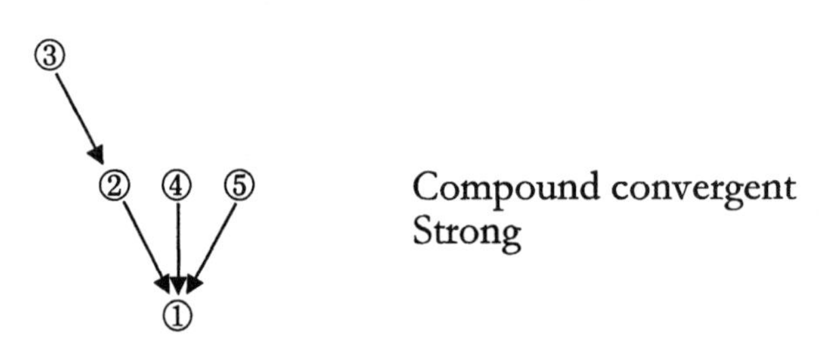

This time we get a compound convergent argument. It is convergent because the final conclusion ① is supported by the converging premises ②, ④, and ⑤. It is compound because ② is itself supported by ③ to form a serial argument together with ①, so that the overall convergent argument contains a serial argument as one of its parts.

Is this compound convergent argument strong or weak? Again we look closely at the conclusion and ask whether the premises are sufficient to establish it. That the shoulder *can* benefit from arthroscopy appears well established by the evidence. But how is it supposed to benefit particularly? The information does little to establish that arthroscopy is of particular benefit to the shoulder compared with other joints like the knee or ankle. But perhaps it is not intended to. Maybe "particular" is intended to refer instead to the specific ailments cited in ⑤ that arthroscopy can alleviate. If we accept this interpretation, then the evidence establishes the conclusion to yield a strong argument.

The evidence here is drawn from the context of medicine and surgery. It could be supplemented by evidence from sports showing how much more rapidly athletes recover from surgery on injured joints now that arthroscopic surgery is widely used in sports medicine. A baseball player, for instance, who a few years ago would have been out an entire season for shoulder surgery now returns to the active roster in three to six weeks. The same goes for the football player with a knee injury. So here we have a strong argument that could be made even stronger.

3. Diagraming Techniques for Compound Arguments

The question is raised with special reference to the longer arguments we often encounter when dealing with compound arguments whether all the statements we number when we mark up the material must actually occur in the argument as premises or conclusions. The answer is no. In our initial scrutiny of the material we may mark off and number a statement because it occurs among others that clearly exhibit the support relations of arguments. A conclusion, we recall, receives support, or is intended to receive support, from one or more other statements. Premises can only rightly be identified as such on the basis of being advanced in support of some other statement (the conclusion). Suppose now that we find among the statements numbered as part of the argument one or more that functions neither as conclusion nor as premise. No such statement, however interesting or informative it may be, is part of the argument. The statement that neither receives nor gives support is not part of the argument, and so should not be diagramed. Let's look at an example.

① <Gail left on the red-eye from Los Angeles International Airport.> ② <The red-eye is an overnight flight.> ③ <She may have flown with Continental, and she probably sat in an aisle seat, which she usually prefers.> ④ <She should have arrived in Newark about mid-morning.>

① and ② clearly tend to support ④, but ③ though informative does not appear to carry any weight or provide support in this argument at all. So rather than trying to fit it in the diagram of the argument somewhere, we simply leave it out. By leaving it out we signal our judgment that it does not belong in the argument proper.

Assuming the truth of the two premises, we have a relatively strong argument. The conclusion is not, of course, established with certainty. We can readily picture a scenario that would make the premises true and the conclusion false. The plane could have made an emergency landing, and Gail could have slept in a hotel in Omaha rather than arrived in Newark. But the conclusion is stated cautiously. It doesn't say Gail *had to have* arrived, only that she *should have* arrived. The fact that the conclusion is stated cautiously makes for a stronger argument.

Another example will help to illustrate the kind of information that might be unessential or parenthetical in the context of a given argument.

①
<Brenda is the one to go to for help with *Paradox*.> <She can show
②
you the most efficient way of entering your data> and <[she can show
③
you] all of the options you have for sorting it.> <She can also
④
demonstrate different ways of printing out the information.> <Her office
⑤
is just down the hall on your left.> Another thing is that <she can point
⑥
out the most common glitches and how to avoid them.>

We readily identify ① as the conclusion, then ②, ③, ④, and ⑥ as supporting statements. ⑤ is parenthetical in that it contributes nothing to support the claim in ① that Brenda should be consulted on *Paradox*. It provides information useful to the person who is convinced by the argument and seeks Brenda out by telling her where Brenda can be found. But when we diagram the argument, we signify its lack of probative relation to the conclusion by just leaving it out.

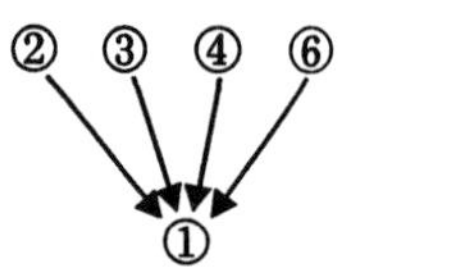

Convergent
Strong

Given the context and assuming the truth of the premises, this seems a fairly strong argument. Note that another interpretation of the argument is possible that would make ⑤ an important support statement. In this interpretation Brenda is being compared with other similarly qualified people who are located in some distant part of the building or perhaps at a different site. In this context Brenda's proximity would be a reason consulting her rather than the others.

Another question arises when we analyze longer or compound arguments by diagram: What do we do when a statement that is part of an argument is repeated at a later stage of the argument? The repetition may not reproduce the original statement word for word. It may instead say essentially the same thing with somewhat different words. When this happens, we simply give the repetition of the statement the same number we assigned to the original. The statement then occurs in the diagram only once. Here is an example.

① ②
<April is the prettiest month.> <Warm sunshine drives away winter
③
clouds,> and <trees shoot out their tender golden leaves.> <Green
④
overtakes the blossoming forsythia and redbud, and azaleas are bursting
①
into bloom.> <Truly no month is prettier than April.>

We recognize right away that ① is the conclusion, receiving support from ②, ③, and ④. The final statement simply says the same as ① with different words, so we will also number it ①. But then when we diagram the argument, ① will occur only once as the conclusion. Although it occurs twice in the discourse we are working with, it only occurs once in the argument whose structure we are diagraming.

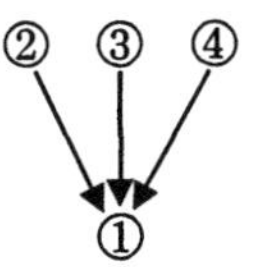

Convergent
Moderately Weak

Is the argument weak or strong? The evidence advanced does tend to support the conclusion. But before we could judge the argument strong, we would also have to consider any evidence against April as the prettiest month. Then too, someone might advance evidence in support of some other competing months, and this would have to be considered also. So on balance we would have to say it's a moderately weak argument. No account has been taken of the dialectical tier.

A somewhat more challenging example, this time a compound argument, also illustrates the repetition of material germane to the argument.

① ②
<The lipstick on his collar was Passionfruit,> so <it couldn't have been
③
Marge's.> This indicates that <he lied.> Moreover, <he claimed to
④
have driven to Raleigh on business, which is 60 miles distant.> <But the
⑤
odometer showed him only driving 14 miles after leaving home.>

This too indicates that ③ <he was lying.> So ⑥ <many of the nights he claimed to be working late may not have been spent at the office at all,> and hence ⑦ <he probably was having an affair.>

As we mark up the statements we note that ③ 'he lied' is repeated after ⑤ "he was lying," so we number the repeat statement ③ also. We also notice the abundance of conclusion cues. "So" introduces both ② and ⑥, "hence" introduces ⑦, and "this indicates that" serves as a conclusion cue for ③ on both of its appearances. ① and ② provide serial support for ③, while ④ and ⑤ give linked support for ③. We can combine these two support relations in the following diagram of a compound convergent argument.

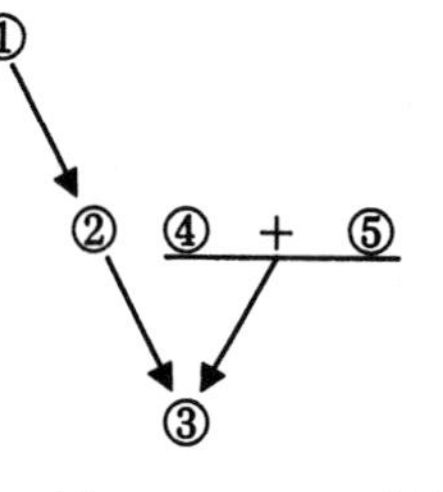

Compound
Convergent

⑥ is offered in support of ⑦.

How do the two support groups fit together? On its second appearance, ③ is followed by a conclusion cue introducing ⑥, so ③ is most likely advanced in support of that statement. This allows us to combine the two groups into an argument with the following pattern.

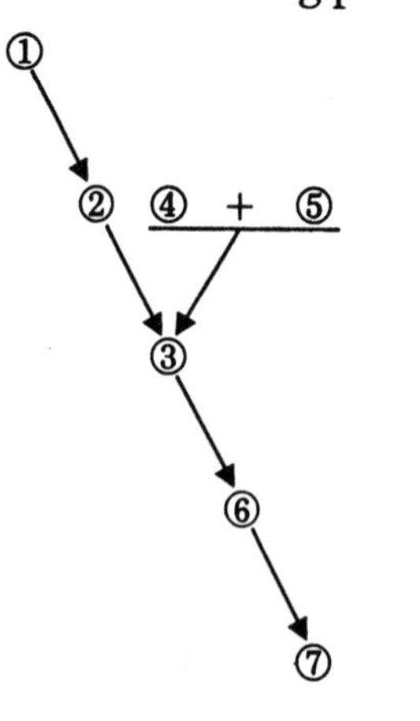

Compound Serial
Strong

What are we to make of the strength of the argument? Assuming that ①, ④, and ⑤ are facts, the support for ③ is strong. The inferences drawn from these facts are reasonable. One obviously inaccurate statement might be due to carelessness, but two such statements indicate deliberate untruth. The behavior pattern implied by the lipstick mark and fake trip lends support to ⑥, which is also supported by the propensity to lie summed up in ③. On balance a strong inference, specially since the conclusion is cautiously worded.

Another interesting problem in the analysis and evaluation of compound arguments arises less frequently but can be vexing nonetheless. An intermediate conclusion may seem to receive one kind of support whereas the final conclusion may require a quite different interpretation of this same support.

For an illustration, let us note the argument based on the following information.

> In 1988 ABC paid $309 million to televise the winter games in Calgary; all of Western Europe, with an economy of the same size and 25% more population, paid $5.7 million; the Soviet Union and Eastern Europe paid $1.2 million; Canada, whose economy is 1/10th the size of ours, paid $5.7 million. This is not the exception but the rule. For the 1988 summer games NBC paid $300 million, while Europe paid $28 million. For this, U.S. viewers see less. All nations get the same feed, but our networks run scads of commercials to recover this massive investment. Commercials clutter the broadcasts, and sometimes preempt significant live action. U.S. athletes, coaching programs, training facilities, and junior development programs are all under-funded. Eastern Europe and the Soviet Union have elaborate programs for their athletes, but paid together only $3 million for the 1988 summer games.

①<. . . the funding setup for the Olympics is a travesty.> ②<Americans get bilked in three ways.> ③<We pay more than our fair share for the games,> ④<we have to put up with an excessive number of commercials to see them,> and ⑤<our athletes receive little of the money we do pay.>

Robert Z. Lawrence with Jeffrey D. Pellegrom,
"Fool's Gold: How America Pays to Lose in the Olympics,"
The Brookings Review (Fall 1989), p. 5.

Here ② is supported by ③, ④, and ⑤ as basic support statements, while ① is a broader claim receiving support from ②. The problem arises when we note that ② specifies *three* ways in which Americans are bilked, with ③, ④, and ⑤ each specifying one of the three. This suggests that we should interpret the support as linked, on the principle that if there were only two ways, or if one of the three statements turned out false, ② would not be supported and our argument would have to be weak. Against this we note that we have identified ① as the final conclusion, the claim our writers are most keen to establish. If two of our basic support statements could establish that the funding is a travesty, then the total support provided for ① would make the argument strong.

How do we decide this question, since the overall argument cannot be both weak and strong? First we must assume that the writers are more concerned to establish ① rather than ② if they cannot establish both. In a sense we already made this assumption when we classified ② as an intermediate conclusion and ① as the final. The Principle of Charity enjoins us to adopt the interpretation more favorable to the arguers. This means that we will interpret the basic support as accumulative (each premise contributes a certain amount) or convergent rather than linked. The diagram is then the following.

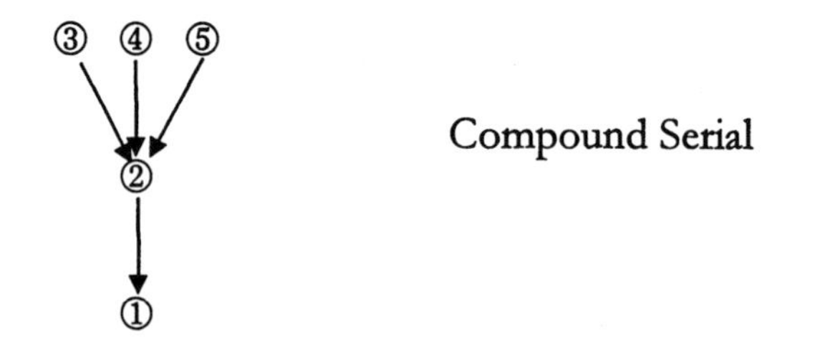

Analyzed this way, "travesty" means more to the authors than "three ways."

The argument is at least moderately strong. In 1989 when it was advanced, ③,④, and ⑤ were all reliable. What has changed in the interim is ⑤. U.S. athletes in recent Olympics have been much better funded, mainly due to better organized corporate sponsorship and private contributions. ③ and ④ still hold true, however, and provide at least enough for ① to have moderately strong support. Other areas of the world lack the fierce media competition that leads to bidding wars for the rights, and also to the excessive commercials the networks need to recover these massive investments.

SUMMARY

A compound argument comprises arguments of two more basic types as its parts. We classify and label compound arguments based on their final conclusion or conclusions. So if the support for the final conclusion is linked, the argument is compound linked, no matter what other material it may contain. There is no compound simple argument, and an argument with two or more final conclusions may be a hybrid like compound divergent-convergent.

The analysis of a compound argument begins with a provisional idea of the final conclusion for guidance. Premise cues, conclusion cues, and support claims help us identify individual support relations and basic argument types, which we then diagram. Then we fit these single support relations and basic patterns together by trial and error until a picture of the whole emerges. In the course of this analysis we may discover that some other statement is in fact the final conclusion.

The diagram of the whole allows us to distinguish basic support statements from intermediate and final conclusions. Basic support statements must be sound or capable of being backed up with evidence themselves if the argument is to be strong. We then estimate the strength of the parts of the argument before reaching a judgment of its strength as a whole.

One or more of the statements we initially mark up and number may turn out not to be advanced in support or to be a conclusion of the argument. We show this by omitting the statement's number from our diagram. In longer compound arguments the conclusion may be repeated. We assign it the same number on its second appearance, and use this number only once in our diagram. In distinguishing convergent and linked support in compound arguments we must interpret the conclusion carefully to capture the most important aspects of its meaning.

Study Questions

Section 1. What is a compound argument?

1. What is a compound argument?
2. What is decisive for classifying a compound argument?

Section 2. Analyzing and evaluating compound arguments

3. What must we find first in identifying a compound argument?
4. For what do we search after locating it?
5. What is a basic support statement in a compound argument?
6. How do we represent basic support statements in our diagrams?

Section 3. Diagraming techniques for compound arguments

7. How do we show in our diagram that a numbered statement functions neither as premise nor as conclusion in an argument?
8. In marking up an argument, how do we treat a statement that is part of the argument (e.g. conclusion) but is repeated?
9. How do we treat this same statement in the diagram?
10. When the conclusion of a compound argument makes quite specific claims, how do we decide whether the immediate support for it is convergent or linked?

EXERCISE 8—1: COMPOUND ARGUMENTS

Mark up, diagram, and identify the pattern of each of the following arguments. Some of them will be compound arguments, requiring you to employ the techniques we have just learned. State why you diagramed the argument as you did. Evaluate each argument. Give reasons for your evaluation.

1. This [2001 recession] . . . was unusual, first, because it seemed to happen so quickly. Normally, recessions creep up on America. Also, it was led by a sharp falloff in capital investment rather than a slump in consumer spending, and it came at a time of tame inflation and falling interest rates.

U. S. News & World Report, (Apr. 15, 2002), p. 30-31.

2. (Hindu nationalists smash offices to protest the Miss World contest eroding Indian values.)

But Michael Jackson isn't rash scheduling a rock concert in Bombay. He has struck a deal to give 85% of the net profit from the concert to a charity run by Bal Thackery, head of the Shiv Sena, a local political party. You cannot buy a better insurance policy. The Shiv Sena is thought to run not merely the local government, but part of the Mumbai mafia too, and few dare to tangle with it

The Economist (Nov. 2-8, 1996), p. 36.

3. Canadian retailers [hesitate to go online]. Generally conservative executives . . . balk at the time and expense involved in opening an online store, and [there is] a lack of sizeable and immediate profits. But the pace of change, driven by the falling costs of computing power and the rise in Internet use, is so rapid that waiting for the full picture to come into focus may not be an option.

Warren Caragata, "Net Gain," *Maclean's* (July 22, 1999), p. 34.

4. . . . in New York, people are inundated with business entertaining, and they're exhausted by it. Still, that doesn't excuse poor behavior. If you commit to going to someone's dinner, make an effort. Comb your hair. Look pretty. Talk to someone you don't know.

"Who Killed Entertainment?" *New York Times Magazine* (Nov. 5, 2000), p. 62.

5. The topic of this Roundtable [educational reform] is particularly timely because education is more closely linked to economic development now than at any time in our history. Nearly every industrialized nation is undertaking a serious assessment of its educational system. Being competitive in a world economy is now an essential ingredient in a state or national policy for economic survival, and education is going to have a significant role to play in providing the competitive edge.

Wallace G. Wilkinson, "Education Reform and Economic Competition," *Vital Speeches of the Day*, Vol. LVI, No. 2 (Nov. 1, 1989), p. 40.

6\. . . . the exercise of faith is [not] always an act of wisdom. We can be mistaken in the trust that we put in objects, ideas, and people. The information we have about them may be incorrect or we may be over-generous in our display of good will toward them. We can have too high a degree of faith in an unworthy object, idea, or person and we can have too low a degree of faith in a worthy object, idea, or person.

Baine Harris, "Faith and Reason in the Early Neoplatonists," *Dialogue and Alliance*, Vol. 1, No. 1 (Spring 1987), p. 8.

7. The [American Lung Association] . . . pointed out another reason to choose a gas fireplace: Storing firewood inside the house, where it's more convenient, can lead to nasty mold spores. The Lung Association's survey found that despite the danger, more than 1 in 3 wood burners still store their firewood inside the house—probably because the words 'mold spore' aren't as frightening as 'Go out and get some more wood, will you?'

Datadog: "Are fake fireplaces more popular than real ones nowadays?" *American Demographics* (Nov. 2000), p. 29.

*8. (The Canadian scientific ship Richardson was charting the basin of the Beaufort Sea in 1970. The geology of the area suggested oil in commercial quantities, and one question of interest was how it could be transported.)

The first pictures showed the bottom criss-crossed with deep gashes. The clear conclusion was that the ice pack was so thick and subject to such enormous pressures that "keels" of ice formed below it, extending to the bottom. The moving keels meant that oil from off-shore fields could not be brought ashore by pipelines since the passing keels would cut them, sooner or later. Some keels had slashed gullies in the bottom sixty miles from shore, where the water was three hundred feet deep.

Canada Today/ d'aujourd'hui, Vol. 18, No. 1 (1987), p. 12.

9. Even now, the vision of a hydrogen economy sounds too good to be true. Hydrogen occurs naturally in water, so the supply is as close to endless as the ocean. And pure hydrogen is a harmless gas, not a toxic liquid, so spills would dissipate in the air. Hydrogen-fuel cells emit only water vapor, and the electric motors make nary a sound.

Newsweek (April 2002)

10. (From an article on the dwindling greater one-horned rhinoceros. The writer mentions carrying out blood tests to assess the assumption of less genetic variability mentioned in the final clause. But the results were incomplete at publication time. Hint for analysis: regard the statement qualified as an assumption as one that evidence may provide support for.)

The absence of genetic variability can put a population in jeopardy of extinction since animals which are nearly identical are less likely to survive an epidemic or a sudden change to their environment. Moreover, large mammals are assumed to be more vulnerable to extinction because they are thought to carry less genetic variability than smaller animals.

Eric *Dinerstein*, "King of the Marsh,"
International Wildlife (Mar.-Apr. 1989), p. 6.

11. . . . the disadvantages of [mutual fund] supermarkets are apparent . . . Funds available at supermarkets without transaction fees typically carry higher expense ratios than other funds. Online brokerages that also serve as fund supermarkets are so overwhelmed with stock traders that they can be difficult to contact by phone. Incidental fees are a nuisance at many supermarkets, and infuriating at a few. Many supermarkets still don't tell you the cost basis of investments you make with them. That's vital information when it comes time to sell and pay taxes . . . In sum, you may end up wishing you'd never opted for one-stop shopping.

Steven T. Goldberg, "Supermarket Blues," *Kiplinger's* (August 1999), pp. 82-83.

12. (In a large leveraged buyout, in 1989 Kohlberg-Kravits-Roberts bought out RJR-Nabisco for $26 billion. The 35 syndicate members who provided the primary financing coordinated the effort to sell to secondary investors so they wouldn't compete with each other for the same capital. In the sell down, large loan exposures were reduced faster than smaller, which benefited most those syndicate members with larger commitments.)

The favoritism for the big over the small permeated the RJR deal. For example, secondary investors didn't receive some of the front-end fees that the syndicate members took home. And the fees for both secondary and syndicate members were paid by the borrower, KKR. This meant that the syndicate banks got to keep their entire early-bird and other front-end fees for their commitments, even as they sold down these commitments. So, as the size of their commitments shrunk, their yields went even higher.

Mark Feinberg, "The Anatomy of a Bank Syndication Deal," *Bankers Monthly* (Nov. 1989), p. 32.

13. The free exercise [of religion] clause [of the First Amendment to the Constitution] prohibits the government from directly prohibiting or requiring any sort of activity for purely religious reasons. Thus the courts have held that there can be no compulsion of religious belief and no imposition of penalties for religious belief. Moreover, they have held that the state may not "condition the receipt of an important benefit upon conduct prescribed by a religious faith," nor may it "deny such a benefit because of conduct mandated by religious belief."
It is for this reason that ministers and priests cannot be required to give up their professions in order to run for and hold public office.

Stephen Griffith, "Prayer in Public School,"
Public Affairs Quarterly, Vol 1, No. 2 (1978), p. 100.

14. (A West German engineer brought technology secrets to the communist East German government as a secret agent code-named Gorbachev.)

. . . Agent Gorbachev used less gadgetry in his spycraft than one would expect. He never even used a radio transmitter or receiver to communicate with his case officers, although he was an expert ham radio operator . . . Instead, future meetings were usually arranged at the meetings themselves or by telephone . . . . Gorbachev also was not trained in any other operational techniques, such as invisible ink or photography, until very late, when he learned microdot photography. In this respect, he differed greatly from East Germans who were groomed to become agents in the West.

Kristie Macrakie, "The Case of Agent Gorbachev," *American Scientist*, Vol. 88, p. 538.

15. Most Americans (60%) no longer break sweat on a daily basis. While no one wants to go back to hard manual labor, we need to *activate* our days by moving more intentionally and more often to maintain the basic fitness needed for good health. So, whether training for triathlons or just walking the dog, just do something—stay active.

The Compass, p. 2.

*16. The real estate market of the Nineties is unique, preceded by economic and demographic changes that were not present in earlier cycles and subject to forces in the future that may prevent a turnaround from occurring. In the Eighties, changes in the tax and banking laws unleashed a torrent of money looking for real estate deals. When the tax breaks vanished, the Japanese appeared, cash in hand, ready to build and buy. Supply found demand in good form as the baby boom filled the job market, women to the fore, and the service economy embraced them all. But these were all one-time events.

There are no similar demographic or economic shifts coming to re-float real estate in the Nineties. The growth rate for white-collar employment is slowing, and women aren't moving into the work force at the rate they once were. . . . [Moreover] The recession . . . is eviscerating the very industries financial, insurance, and retail that drive demand for commercial space.

Bill Saporito, "Real Estate's Low-Rise Future,"
Fortune (Jan. 28, 1991), p. 41.

17. The main advantage of hinting over more direct forms of communication is the protection it affords the speaker by enabling him to communicate without committing himself to what he says. Should the message be ill received, hinting leaves an escape route open. Indirect communications ensure the speaker that he will be held responsible only for the explicit meaning of his message. The overt message is thus a sort of vehicle for the covert message whose effect is feared.

Thomas S. Szasz, *The Myth of Mental Illness*, rev. ed. (New York 1974), p. 142.

18. (The author presents the results of interviewing 1200 European males at 40 locales in twenty-five countries about their interpretations of 20 common gestures, including the finger-tip kiss.)

In becoming informal [the finger-tip kiss] has split into two. It is either a salutation or an act of praise. In its earlier existence, it was transmitting both messages simultaneously, since it was only ever used as a salutation to a praised individual (or religious symbol). To kiss the fingertips to someone was both to salute *and* to praise them. Since then, the double message has divided and the gesture now transmits one or the other signal.

Desmond Morris et al., *Gestures*
(New York 1979), p. 78.

19. (President Truman was defeated in his effort to introduce national health insurance, which led supporters of comprehensive health care reform to change their strategy.)

. . . emphasis was shifted to protecting only the aged. In a way, this made more sense because the elderly were the ones in greatest need. Since Social Security beneficiaries were older they had greater medical needs; since they were retired they lacked the advantages of group enrollment through employment. As their health insurance costs rose, more of them lost their private coverage.

Rashi Fein, "Prescription for Change,"
Modern Maturity (Aug.-Sept. 1992), p. 25.

20. Japan is overtaking America as the world's No. 1 technological power. In 1970, the United States produced 100 percent of the world's consumer electronics. Today, our electronic production has plunged to less than five percent. In 1970, the United States produced 90 percent of the color television sets that were sold. Today, this has skidded to barely 10 percent. In 1970, the United States manufactured 99 percent of the world's telephones. Today—25 percent.

TIES Magazine (Oct. 1988), p. 1.

THE CRITICAL THINKING JOURNAL

Part C. Compound Arguments and Context

8. Assessing Compound Arguments

Find in print media, diagram, analyze, and evaluate one example of each of these argument types: compound linked, compound convergent, compound serial, and compound divergent.

Further Reading

Malcom Acock, *Informal Logic Examples and Exercises* (Belmont 1985). Several compound arguments are analyzed and a wealth of exercises for students are given on pp. 115–144.

James B. Freeman, *Thinking Logically* (Englewood Cliffs 1988). Analyzes compound arguments and provides exercises for students on pp. 203–224.

Trudy Govier, *A Practical Study of Argument*, 2nd ed. (Belmont 1988). Model analyses of compound arguments and problems for students to work are given on pp. 132–155.

Stephen N. Thomas, *Practical Reasoning in Natural Language*, 3rd ed. (Englewood Cliffs 1986). A good treatment of compound arguments with many exercises to work is found on pp. 65–108.

Part Three

Clarity

CHAPTER NINE

CLARITY IN MEANING

1. VERBAL DISPUTES, AMBIGUITY, AND WORD MISUSE

> Mary: "Jeff is an animal. His clothes are always wrinkled, his hair unkempt and greasy, and the only thing that smells worse then his unwashed body is his bad breath."
>
> Jeanie: "He is not an animal. He plays the violin beautifully, he is the best chess player in the area, and he speaks French fluently."

Mary and Jeanie disagree on whether or not Jeff is an animal. Because they disagree on what it is to be an "animal" this kind of dispute is often called a verbal dispute. Frequently a verbal dispute is thought of as a mere matter of words, not worthy of serious attention. Verbal disputes are then contrasted with substantial disputes or disputes of substance, which deal with real differences and can be quite important. Here is an example of such a substantial dispute.

> George: "I realize the economy is down. That's why we have to cut taxes more. This step will free up more funds for investment in the private sector, and this in turn will revitalize the economy."
>
> Sam: "That's not going to help unless you cut government spending at the same time. If you don't, the government will take in less money in taxes to finance its activities, so it will have to borrow large amounts on the money market. This will drive interest rates way up. Then the high cost of borrowing will deter firms from investing in new production facilities, so the economy will slump down even further."

Both George and Sam agree the economy is down. Their dispute concerns what ought to be done about it. George thinks taxes ought to be cut; Sam thinks it is more important to cut government spending. They are not using words misleadingly, nor do they misunderstand one another. They assess the situation differently, and this is why we call their dispute one of substance rather than words.

Yet many verbal disputes are not *merely* disputes about the meaning of one or more words. We know this because even when the disputants come to agree on the meaning of the words, important differences of opinion still remain. So we call a dispute a verbal one when it involves confusion or disagreement about the meaning of words, even when complete agreement on meanings would not settle the dispute.

In the above case Mary obviously thinks that a person is an "animal" who is careless about personal appearance and hygiene. On the other hand Jeanie thinks that in assessing a person the cultivation of intellectual and artistic skills is more important. So their dispute is at bottom not so much whether "animal" as an adjective applies correctly to Jeff as it is whether appearance and hygiene or cultural and intellectual attainments should rank higher in judging a person.

The following example exhibits another important feature of verbal disputes.[1]

> Dear Ann Landers: Will you please clear something up before I physically attack someone?
>
> A certain person told my son that when you lose you actually win. You and I both know that when you lose, you lose, and there is no way you can turn a defeat into a victory or a loss into a gain or a minus into a plus.
>
> This person has tried to make my son believe that by learning from the loss you actually become a winner. Isn't this the damndest piece of nonsense you ever heard of?
>
> I am so angry I am ready to punch somebody in the nose. Please print this letter and straighten the fool out.
>
> Not Crazy in Arkansas. Or Am I?
>
> Dear Ark.: The "fool" is trying to teach your son a valuable lesson. It is this: When things don't turn out as you would like them to, or if you make a mistake and suffer a loss because of it, it need not be a total loss if you learn from it. In other words, the experience gained from a defeat can be valuable. It can make us wiser, more compassionate, more experienced and better than we were before. It also makes the loss easier to bear.

The dispute here is obviously whether a defeat is a total loss or not. Yet there is also a verbal element because the two parties differ in their understanding of "defeat." The letter-writer interprets defeat to mean "total loss," and is aghast that anyone thinks a defeat in this sense can be beneficial. The disputant understands defeat to mean "setback," and stresses that one can learn and hence profit from adversity.

---

[1] Permission granted by Ann Landers and Creators Syndicate.

The fact that this dispute is referred to Ann Landers for arbitration suggests that the different meanings attached to "defeat" do more than keep the parties from reaching agreement. This ambiguity prevents them from ever seeing clearly what it is they disagree about. It is not seldom the case that parties to a verbal dispute utterly fail to make progress because they are unable to see clearly where their opinions differ. This obscurity is the most harmful aspect of a verbal dispute. In some cases there is a difference of substance, but it is concealed by verbal confusion and the parties are unable to locate the source of their disagreement. In either case the verbal confusion must be cleared up before any progress can be made either reaching agreement, or agreeing to disagree.

What is ambiguity, which lies behind the two above cases of verbal confusion? A given word is *ambiguous* when it has two or more meanings and the context does not allow us to decide readily which is the appropriate one. For the moment we are interested in unintentional ambiguity, ambiguity that causes undesired confusion. Words are ambiguous only in a context, not by themselves. Any word with two or more different meanings has a potential for ambiguity. But it cannot be ambiguous until it is used in a context that allows two or more of the meanings to be possible. Usually the person using the word is aware of only one of the meanings. Mary and Jeanie each attach a different meaning to "animal," and the confusion contributing to their verbal dispute arises in large part because each is unable to appreciate the meaning intended by the other. Ann Landers' letter writer sees only one meaning of "defeat," but probably the disputant and certainly Ann herself see both.

When we encounter unintentional ambiguity in a piece of writing it is usually because the writer was aware of only one of the meanings of the ambiguous word whereas we the readers are aware of both. For examples we can glance at some captions or headlines for news items from periodical literature. Writing good captions is especially tricky because an attempt must be made to capture the gist of the item in a very compressed space.

> Jerk Injures Neck, Wins Award
>
> *The Buffalo News*, 4/6/83.

Was the man really a bad sort, or did he suffer whiplash?

> U's food service feeds thousands, grosses millions
>
> *The Minnesota Daily*, 5/6/83.

Is the reputation or the smell of the food affecting an entire city, or is the food service taking in a lot of money?

> Woman to drop suit for sperm
>
> *Today* (Cocoa, FL), 9/17/82.

Is the woman eager to be inseminated, or is she withdrawing a legal action?

Shot Off Woman's Leg Helps Nicklaus To 66

St. Louis Post-Dispatch, 5/13/83.

Was Nicklaus using an unorthodox club, or did an important shot ricochet off a woman's leg into a good lie?

Some ambiguity on the other hand is intentional. People sometimes create ambiguity intentionally when they want to suggest or insinuate something to us without actually saying it (or more important without anyone being able to hold them responsible for saying it). Such intentional ambiguity occurs frequently in the marketing and advertising of consumer products. Intentional ambiguity is also frequently found in the public statements on policy by government officials, in the statements of candidates for public office, and in the announcements of public relations officials for large organizations.

Some intentional ambiguity is humorous in intent. A sex and security scandal rocked the Conservative government of Prime Minister Harold Macmillan in Great Britain when it was discovered in 1963 that his Minister of War John Profumo was having sexual relations with callgirl Christine Keeler at the same time as she was sharing her favors with the Russian military attache. Macmillan responded in the negative when asked by reporters if he would resign over the scandal, and the *London Times* headlined:

Government Won't Fall
Minister Says Tartly

To respond tartly is to respond sharply, and "tart" is a term commonly used for "prostitute" in England.

The Oracle of Delphi in ancient Greece maintained a reputation for accuracy for many centuries. We moderns are more inclined than the ancient Greeks to doubt that the accuracy came from the god Apollo, and to attribute it instead to the extremely well informed priests of the Temple of Apollo, as well as to their cleverness. They always communicated Apollo's pronouncements in polished hexameter couplets that were sometimes phrased carefully to allow for more than one interpretation. Kings and princes regularly consulted the Oracle before an important voyage, marriage, or military campaign. For example Kroesus, King of Lydia in Asia Minor, consulted the Oracle about his planned war against the Persians. We know the priests of Apollo sympathized with this venture against the Persians and wanted to encourage it. Their response was:

If you attack the Persians, you will destroy a mighty empire.

The army of the Lydians was routed by the Persians. When Kroesus reproached the Oracle, the priests responded that their prophecy had come true. Kroesus, they said, failed to interpret its proper meaning, namely that the kingdom that would fall was his own.

A second source of verbal confusion is the misuse of words. Some cases of incorrect usage give us pause, until we realize that we are dealing with someone inexperienced in the use of the English language, like a child or foreigner.

In New York I have seen many cloud-scratchers.

You may hear this from a foreign visitor in whose native German language very tall buildings are called *Wolkenkratzer.*

Above we learned that English has many words with two or more different meanings, which gives rise to ambiguity. Paradoxically enough, English also has an extraordinarily rich vocabulary, due in part to its peculiar historical development (about which more will be said shortly). One consequence is that it has a considerable number of word pairs (in some cases triplets) where the words are similar in spelling and often identical in pronunciation but different in meaning. This creates a potential for word misuse that even the most highly educated speakers of English never escape completely. The well educated person continues to grow in knowledge, to add to her vocabulary by trying out new words and appropriating the useful ones. It is in the trial period that misuse is most likely to occur.

Where even the most highly educated persons sometimes go astray, the potential for us more ordinary mortals to misstep is even greater. A glance at examples will help.

She was prosecuted for her unorthodox religious beliefs.

To prosecute someone is to initiate and carry out a legal action against them. So this statement as it stands can hardly rightly apply to anyone in the United States at present. The First Amendment to the Constitution forbids Congress from passing laws prohibiting the free exercise of a religion. And in the American criminal justice system people are prosecuted for allegedly illegal acts: there are no illegal thoughts or beliefs. The writer probably intended to use "persecuted," which means "harassed," or "treated ill."

He hit on an ingenuous solution to the problem.

This writer has probably chosen the wrong modifier for "solution." "Ingenuous" means "simple, artless, without sophistication." The correct modifier is "ingenious," which means "clever."

In fact, being able to use polysyllabic words correctly has traditionally been an important mark of an educated person in English-speaking countries like Great Britain, Canada, and the United States. The social climber with little education and less vocabulary has been a stock figure for ridicule and satire at least since Mrs. Malaprop in Sheridan's 1775 drama *The Rivals.* America's humorists have feasted on this topic. Here for example are Mrs. Partington's (a pen name for newspaper editor B. P. Shillaber) comments on the new math of her day, the mid-nineteenth century.

> When I was young, if a girl only understood the rules of distraction, provision, multiplying, replenishing, and the common denunciator, and knew all about rivers and obituaries, the convents and dormitories, the provinces and the umpires, they had eddication enough. But now they have to study

> bottomy, algebery, and have to demonstrate supposition about the sychophants of circuses, tangents, and Diogenese of parallelogromy, to say nothing about the oxhides, corostics, and the abstruse triangles.

A third source of verbal confusion is vagueness of word or phrase. A word or phrase is *vague* when it is too fuzzy or imprecise to convey the information appropriate to the situation. Words are vague only in a context, never by themselves. Vagueness occurs when the context requires more detail, specificity, or precision than the word or phrase in question supplies.

Suppose you are planning a tight daily schedule down to the minute in order to accomplish much on a brief visit to your customers in Topeka. You inquire of your associate,

> "What time was our meeting with the ATSF's representatives?"
> "Some time in the afternoon."

This phrase is too vague to be of help to you. You need an exact time like 2:15 p.m. so you can coordinate this meeting with other demands on your time.

Or picture yourself on the lot of a used car dealer admiring a late model Honda Accord. You wonder about what condition it's in and whether you can afford it. A salesman approaches.

> "Can I do anything for you?"
> "How much mileage does this Accord have on it?"
> "41,000."
> "How much are you asking for it?"
> "How much do you think it's worth?"
> "Just give me a ballpark figure."
> "How much would you be willing to pay for it?"

These responses are too vague to be of any help to you. You think they're probably asking more for the car than you can afford. You don't need completely specific information to answer your question. If the salesman would only say "Around $6,000" that would suffice. But what he actually says is too vague. We will learn more about vagueness from a different perspective below.

Many cases of vagueness, ambiguity, and mistaken word use are due to shortcomings on the part of the writer or speaker. For the most part we want to avoid them as much as we possibly can. We will soon turn to some steps we can take to reduce our chances of being unintentionally ambiguous or vague, or of using words mistakenly. But in some such cases people are neither utterly misguided about a word's meaning nor guilty of some especially reprehensible word misuse. Times change and put new demands on language; people grow, encounter new situations, and put a strain on their language resources in experiencing, describing, and assimilating them. Sometimes we take a word that is perfectly serviceable in several contexts and put it into a new context that gives rise to ambiguity. Often too we have not given careful thought to the precise meaning of a word, and we are able to get by on a number of occasions by using the word in a vague sense. Then there arises an occasion where much depends on the exact meaning of just this word (for example the word "justifiable" in a homicide trial), and we confront the need to clarify the meaning of the word to make it serviceable in this context.

One cause of ambiguity and vagueness is common to the languages of the developed nations and to those of many developing ones also. Medicine, science, and technology bring us new discoveries and inventions; institutions change, and customs shift, with old ones waning and new ones developing. Language itself, and specially its vocabulary, must adapt to these changes. Languages are often conservative in changing, and likely to resist neologisms or the introduction of completely new words. As a result existing words are often stretched by being given new but related meanings. For example, notice what "memory" means in computer use. It is most commonly used to designate the working space available, such as 32 megabytes. This RAM or random access memory is distinguished from ROM or read only memory, where small amounts of permanent data are stored. Neither sense is especially close to "memory" as the totality of what we remember, which corresponds more closely perhaps to "disk storage" in computer terminology.

A hypothetical case may help exhibit the process of change. Suppose we encounter a creature that looks like a human being, speaks like a human being, and behaves like a human being, but when fully grown is only nine inches tall. Would we be correct in applying "human being" to it? Or would it be better to find a new name for it? The fact that existing words are called on to deal with such new situations creates what Friedrich Waismann calls the possibility of vagueness. Such a question can only be answered when the situation arises, because only then can the advantages and disadvantages of each alternative be fully appreciated.

2. Some Characteristics of the English Language

While the challenge of coping with new situations and products is common to most living languages, English has an especially rich vocabulary and also a special potential for ambiguity. A glance at its development may help us understand why. English began as dialects of German spoken by the Anglo-Saxon invaders of the island they wrested from the indigenous Celtic peoples in the 5th century A.D., after the Roman rulers had left to defend Rome from invading Teutonic tribes. From the late 8th century bands of Danish and Norwegian Vikings raided and pillaged coastal areas of England until in 878 King Alfred ceded them a great tract of England north of the Thames called the Danelaw.

The Scandinavian settlers mingled with the native Angles, and their similar languages competed with each other. For a considerable period there were pairs of words designating the same object. In some cases of these struggling pairs, the Old English word is the one that survived.

Old English	Old Norse
gray	gro
few	fo
fish	fisk

But it wasn't of course always the Old English word that prevailed. William Caxton, printer of the first book in English about 1474, reports the struggle of Old English *ey* with Old Norse *egg*. Some merchants sailing the Thames went ashore to buy provisions.

> And one of theym named sheffelde, a mercer, cam in-to an hows and axed for mete; and specyally he axyd after eggys. And the goode wyf answerde, that she coude speke no frenshe. And the marchaunt was angry, for he also coude speke no frenshe, but wolde have hadde egges, and she understode hym not. And thenne at laste a nother sayd that he wolde have eyren. Then the good wyf sayd that she understod hym wel.

Not long after, the Old English *ey* disappeared from the language. Another interesting Old Norse survivor is *skyrta*, which reinforced the Old English *scyrte* to give us the modern *shirt*, but then in some unexplained manner also gave us the quite different modern *skirt*.

Even more decisive was the influence on the English language that followed from the defeat of England by William of Normandy at the Battle of Hastings in 1066. All of the great estates of the realm went to Norman noblemen, and the important positions in the church to Norman ecclesiastics. So England came to be ruled by French-speaking Normans. Perhaps 20,000 French settled among the 1.5 million natives in the century following the Norman Conquest. But they exercised an influence all out of proportion to their numbers because they comprised the entire ruling class in state and church.

The early Norman rulers never bothered to learn English. Anyone who expected to deal with them had to learn French, their language. Many of these Norman nobles continued to hold large estates in Normandy, and intermarriage with French from the Continent also sustained their use of French. By 1200 a knowledge of English was fairly common in the Norman upper class, while the native English lower nobility such as knights, and burgesses or middle-class merchants, knew some French. The common people, however, continued to speak English.

In Sir Walter Scott's famous historical romance *Ivanhoe*, which turns in large part on Saxon resentment of and rebellion against Norman over-lordship, the following conversation occurs between two Saxon serfs, Wamba the jester and Gurth the swineherd.

> ". . . how do you call those grunting brutes running about on their four legs?" demanded Wamba.
> "Swine, fool—swine," said the herd; "every fool knows that."
> "And swine is good Saxon," said the jester; "but how call you the sow when she is flayed, and drawn, and quartered, and hung by the heels, like a traitor?"
> "Pork," answered the swineherd.
> "I am very glad every fool knows that too," said Wamba, "and pork, I think, is good Norman-French; and so when the brute lives, and is in the charge of a Saxon slave, she goes by her Saxon name; but becomes a Norman, and is called pork, when she is carried to the castle hall to feast among the nobles."

There is considerably more linguistic evidence to support the claim that meat on the hoof, herded or hunted by Saxon serfs, has a Saxon name, but a Norman-French one when served on the table of Norman rulers.

on the hoof	on the table (modern French)
ox/cow	beef (boeuf)
calf	veal (veau)
sheep	mutton (mouton)
swine	pork (porc)/bacon (bacon)
boar	brawn
deer	venison

Early in the 13th century England lost Normandy to rising French power, and constant struggles against France caused the Anglo-Norman rulers to identify themselves more with England and the English language. The invigorating influences on French in England had waned, and by 1400 English was the spoken language of all classes in England. But the English language underwent tremendous changes in the Middle English period from 1150 to 1500. It lost about 85% of its Old English word stock, and took about 10,000 words from the French, about 75% of which are still in use. The appropriation of French words was especially intense from 1250 to 1400. The English of 1150 is unintelligible to today's reader; that of 1500 is like modern English (though as the quote from Caxton shows, spelling was yet to be standardized).

The net result of these developments was the creation of a modern English with a great wealth of word resources. Old English had already borrowed some words from Latin when St. Augustine brought Christianity to the isle in 597. Borrowings from Latin increased greatly with the arrival of the Renaissance in the 16th century, when the confluence of Humanism, science, and early technology brought an entire, new, learned and scientific Latin vocabulary into English.

Many languages resist borrowing words or word stock from other tongues, tending instead to meet the need for new terms by adapting native materials. For example, where most modern languages have a word similar to our "telephone" (a combination of the Greek words for distance and sound = distant sound), German constructed out of native materials "Fernsprecher" (distant speaker). The tendency of English to resist borrowing from other languages was softened by the Danish incursions and Old Norse, then battered by the Norman Conquest. Today's English has a vocabulary of some 500,000 words, more than half of which are of Latin origin (this includes of course words that came in through Norman-French which were themselves of Latin origin). Not only is it the native tongue of several hundred million people around the globe, it is the language most widely used as a second tongue. English, for instance, is the international language of airline flight control and of computer use. It is the lingua franca or common language of such multilingual nations as India and Singapore, and is used by river-boat traders in Africa as the language of their commerce.

The extraordinarily rich vocabulary resources of English provide us an important opportunity to express ourselves with precision in a number of ways on a variety of topics. The availability of a number of related words for the same object affords us a chance to choose words carefully to convey delicate shades of meaning. But the same circumstance presents a problem too. Every opportunity to use a word precisely is also an occasion to use a word vaguely or ambiguously, or simply to misuse it. This we would like to avoid.

It will help for us to sharpen our ability to distinguish the meanings of words that are often confused, not only because their meanings are similar or related, but often also because they sound the same. Unlike some of our earlier examples of word pairs, the ones in our exercise are all words of Latin origin. This exercise includes some of the most frequently confused words in English. We will also practice distinguishing substantial disputes from verbal ones, and will analyze several of the latter to establish the different meanings of the words or phrases that produce the confusion.

Critical thinking involves more than just a modicum of awareness of our tools of thought and communication. In the present case those are the words and syntax of the English language.

EXERCISE 9—1: CHOOSING WORDS CAREFULLY

Part A. Frequently Confused Words

For each word pair, one word fits the context and the other does not. Choose the right word for the context. Explain why you chose as you did.

1. He had several reasons for not wanting to go, but the desire not to see Effie again was the principle / principal one.

2. Many of Amanda's decisions were based on expediency, but her refusal to take advantage of her opponent's adversity was based on principle. / principal.

3. Rothbart's rage had no effect / affect whatever on Eagleton, who coolly mended the ruptured fishing net.

4. Many players would have gotten rattled under that pressure, but Southey didn't let it effect / affect him.

5. Sandy saw the egg come out of the performer's ear, but Gail explained to her that it was just an allusion. / illusion.

6. Was that an allusion / illusion to Pickett's charge or to the charge of the light brigade?

7. If you steal something valuable when the opportunity arises, you infer / imply that others have a right to do the same.

8. From his reluctance to testify Jill inferred / implied that he had something to hide.

9. In order to escape detection Wellston adapted / adopted a new identity complete with forged driver's license and Social Security card.

10. One way to adapt / adopt Mexican cuisine to Anglo-American taste is to go easy on the jalipeno peppers.

council
11. Cardill Construction had to await a decision of the on
counsel

their request to get the 6.4 acre parcel rezoned for commercial and light industrial use.

12. When the auditor produced evidence that a substantial amount was

council.
missing from the account, we advised Stanhall to retain
counsel.

13. They debated whether a novel where the narrator needed thirty pages to describe how he tossed and turned in bed before falling

legible.
asleep was
readable.

legible,
14. Jones' handwriting was scarcely so he hired the old
readable,

woman to write his essay for him. Thus he was surprised when this handwriting was analyzed as that of a vigorous, aggressive person of high executive potential.

15. The burglar / robber stepped from the dark alleyway and shoved the barrel of his .38 in the hapless pedestrian's ribs.

16. The burglar / robber undid the latch through the small hole he had poked in the screen, then opened the door and entered the unoccupied dwelling.

17. The Committee on Science and Technology debated the best site / cite for the huge new particle accelerator.

18. When you site / cite someone as an authority, be sure that her area of expertise includes the topic you are dealing with.

19. The Biology Club wants to know whether you'll except / accept the nomination for Vice-President.

20. All of the disciples were astonished and dismayed at Christ's statement except / accept Judas, who feigned surprise.

Part B. Ambiguity

Many of the following statements contain ambiguity. When you encounter ambiguity, identify the ambiguous word or phrase and point out how it can mislead. Then modify the original statement to remove the ambiguity.

1. He poured the wine from the bottle which was heavy and aromatic.
2. Utah Girl Does Well in Dog Shows.
   Salt Lake Tribune 12/30/81.
3. Kontakis is found guilty of murdering wife after brief deliberation.
   Somerset (NJ) *Spectator* 10/17/85.
4. As your Governor I assure you we've suffered no greater disaster since I took office than this flood.
5. Retired priest may marry Springstein
   Bloomington, IN *Herald-Times* 5/12/85.
6. Doreen scratched a leg when moving the coffee table.

*7. Ancestors of apes, humans may have originated in Asia.
   The Atlanta Constitution 8/16/85.

8. He felt a pain in his head which was sharp and penetrating.
9. Woman inherits antique lust from mother-in-law she never met.
   Kingston NY *Freeman* 4/21/85.
10. Orioles beat Rangers as pitcher relieves himself.
    Las Vegas Review-Journal 7/30/83.
11. FLC professor was intimate with wolves.
    Today (Durango, CO) 3/20/85.
12. Their backs were to the walls, arched and defiant.

*13. Short police officer loses sex appeal.
   The Louisville Times 12/13/83.

14. Park ends spraying Dutch for elm disease.
    Grosse Pointe, MI *News* 4/11/85.
15. He approves hunting dogs.
16. Woman survives period trapped in car in river.
    East Oregonian (Pendleton, OR) 2/5/85.
17. His hand gripped the handle so tight it turned white.
18. Man minus ear waives hearing.
    Jackson TN *Sun* 5/26/85.

19. Feet support the legs, the trunk, and the podiatrists.

20. Here's How You Can Lick Doberman's Leg Sores.
Reading (PA) *Eagle* 5/23/82.

Part C. Word Misuse

In each case identify the misused word, explain why it is a case of misuse, and substitute a better word in its place.

1. Her psychologist prescribed thorazine to help level out her mood swings.

2. Gorillas vow to kill Khomeini.
The Valley Independent (Monessen PA) 9/28/81.

3. She pushed ahead with plans to take over her competitor irregardless of the consequences.

4. Morality rates lower than normal at Mobil.
Woodbury NJ *Gloucester County Times* 6/10/85.

5. Though both were difficult, she didn't have as much trouble with the conjugation of the Russian verb as she did with the condescension of the noun and adjective.

6. He boiled the T-bone steaks 5 minutes in the oven until they were nicely browned.

7. When the leaves on the cucumber vines wilted in the cool of the morning and evening too, she realized the vines were struck by plight.

8. Even though many of her friends went into careers in law, commerce, or banking, Jane was at heart a homely person who put husband and children first.

9. The second witness corrugated the testimony of Mrs. Stepanski.

*10. When the federal agents had enough evidence for an indictment, instead of appraising Wheelwright they continued surveillance in the hope of implicating others in the espionage.

Part D. Verbal Disputes

Decide which are verbal disputes and which are substantial. In the case of a verbal dispute, locate the word or phrase at fault, and attempt to discern the different meanings assigned to it. Attempt to remove the verbal confusion. Does this leave a substantial dispute? What is it about?

1. Alice: "Jim's old Pinto conked out on him one time too many, so he traded it in on a new car. He's driving a Toyota now."

   Sally: "It's not really a new car though. It's a 1993 model."

2. Tricia: "Red is the best color for a warning light for motorists. For most people, red means danger."

   Jim: "No, amber is a better choice. You can see it from farther away, giving you more time to react to the danger."

3. Laches: "A brave man is one who stands his ground when the enemy attacks, fights back, and does not run away."

   Socrates: "A brave man is one who retreats when hopelessly outnumbered in order to survive and fight again when he has a chance to prevail."

   Adapted from Plato, *Laches*.

4. Jeff: "Natalie is a true saint. She spends all of her waking hours helping to feed and find shelter for the earthquake victims. And she continually risks her life helping doctors treat victims of typhus and other contagious diseases."

   Angie: "She is certainly compassionate, but she is not a saint. She never attends Mass, nor does she pray or even kneel and cross herself when passing a shrine."

5. First Mechanic: "That knock could mean real trouble, ma'm. Sounds to me like you've got a bearing going out. That could mean a complete overhaul."

   Second Mechanic (different repair shop): "Yes, I hear it lady, but I don't think it's anything serious. Most likely it's timing knock. Re-setting the points carefully ought to take care of it."

6. First Board Member: "Building a new production facility in South Carolina is the option that appeals most to me. Not only would we have our product closer to its strongest market, the labor costs are lower, and the city will give us a real break on taxes."

   Second Board Member: "Even with government-backed bonds to help us with the investment in a plant, I'm not sure a new facility is the solution to our problems at this time. Given today's economy, any marketing projections that justify a new plant may be over-optimistic. Do you think we've given enough consideration to expanding the existing facility?"

7. "Here are the binoculars. You can see the bird sitting in the nest." "I see it. It's a sparrow. You can tell by its size, shape, the streaked brown back, and the white line just above the eye."

"It could be. But its beak seems thicker and shorter than a sparrow's. The nest is rounder and more neatly woven than is usual with a sparrow's. One day when she was away I peeked at the eggs. They are pale blue. Most sparrow's eggs I've seen are white. I think it's a finch."

*8. Linda: "That man is a real teacher. When the textbook says something stupid, he points that out and tells us to ignore it. When the classroom gets too stuffy, he leads us out and holds class under one of the trees. And when you give him the trite, conventional response that has been expected of you so far, he throws it back at you and urges you to be yourself and think for yourself."

Sandra: "He's the furthest removed from being a teacher of anyone in the school. You can turn in an essay in perfect English with no misspellings and get it back with an 'F' on the grounds that your research was lacking, or your thought superficial. How is he supposed to know? Aside from that, he never even asks you to memorize any important lines. I just don't call that teaching."

9. Yvonne: "Smoking, which has proved to be harmful in a variety of laboratory tests, is sinful, I believe, because it deprives the smoker of 1) health; 2) eventually, life itself. Moreover, it deprives others of comfort, security, health and sometimes, in the case of stillborn infants and deaths of newborn babies, of their lives."

Charles: "Smoking is no more a sin than wearing high heel, spike-type shoes. These also are dangerous to your health and they destroy the property of others. Have you seen hardwood floors after a woman has walked over them in spike high heels?"

U.S. Catholic, June 1973, p. 221.

10. Arthur: "Why all this pother about the Supreme Court's decision to allow the burning of the U.S. flag under the First Amendment freedom of expression? After all, it's nothing more than a piece of colored cloth. I don't see that it's significantly different from a bandana you wear on your head on a sunny day out in the field, or from the pink cloth you wipe your hands on after working on the lawnmower motor."

Arjay: "That view is absurd. The flag is the object of some of the most noble and least selfish sentiments of a people often occupied with self-indulgence and self-aggrandizement. Many fine and brave men have bled on battlefields from Belleau Wood to Iwo Jima and the Chosin Reservoir for that flag, and too many of the best never returned home. Grease rag my foot!"

3. The Meaning of Words—Definitions

The types of question we must answer about the meaning of a given word like "effect" all arise in a specific context. This context must yield us some guidance on what meaning of the word fits. There is a sense in which words don't really *mean* in isolation, but only have a specific meaning in a context. By itself, a word has a range of possible meanings—the context decides which of them is appropriate.

Thus it is not so much by reading in dictionaries and memorizing definitions that we enhance our command of a language's verbal resources. This happens more when we are driven by a real need, such as encountering a puzzling word in a context, or writing something ourselves and feeling the need of a word we cannot find. In such cases a good dictionary is an invaluable resource we should know how to use. But the dictionary won't aid us directly in the search for a word we cannot find. One useful tactic here is to look up a word close to it in meaning, then examine the synonyms of this word. Another is to look in a thesaurus, which lists synonyms. If we can't find it here, then possibly we're searching for a word that doesn't exist. Professional translators occasionally encounter a similar difficulty. What for example is a good English equivalent for the Italian *dolce far niente*? Or German *Schadenfreude*? Or French *savoir faire*? We can also type the word in a search engine.

A good dictionary is our first recourse in tracking down the exact meaning of a word. Some sensitive users of a language can peruse such a dictionary for hours and benefit from what they learn about words.

But how can we help someone understand the meaning of an unfamiliar word when there is no dictionary handy, or when that person's command of our language is too meager to benefit from the dictionary? In such cases of a child or foreigner, for instance, one tactic that will work for a number of words is to say the word while pointing to the thing it applies to. If a foreigner hears the word "saucer" in a conversation and isn't familiar with it, we can help by pointing at a saucer and saying "saucer." If a child doesn't know what part of her anatomy "digit" applies to, we can say the word while pointing to the jointed sections of the finger. Such explanations are sometimes called ostensive definitions, from the Latin *ostendere* = to show or point.

Ostensive definitions can be useful in other situations also. One effective method of teaching a foreign language rapidly is to wholly avoid the learners' native tongue, forcing them to communicate only in the target foreign language. Sometimes called the "immersion" method, this technique makes extensive use of explanations by pointing or ostensive definitions. Then too there are some words that are best defined ostensively for adults as well as children. In such cases there is no better way than looking, hearing, tasting, or smelling to gather the essential information. For instance, is there a better way to convey to someone what "chartreuse" means than to point to some object that has this yellow-green color? Or is there a better way to convey "chocolate flavor" than to have someone taste chocolate candy (or ice cream or pudding)?

In some cases we can help explain a word by giving examples even when there is no object handy that we can point to. Suppose someone is puzzled by the word "vertebrate." We explain that it refers to a class of animals that have backbones like snakes, dogs, or humans, as distinguished from animals that don't, like earthworms or jellyfish. In this case we explain by naming and describing examples rather than by pointing to them.

Depending on the situation, the meaning of a word or phrase might be most effectively conveyed by giving the function of an object in its reference group.

> "What is that pin for?"
>
> "It's called a cotter pin. When you drive it through that hole in the axle and spread its split ends, it keeps the bearing from sliding off."

When we define a word by stating the main function of the object it refers to, we are giving a *functional* definition of that word.

Occasionally a word is explained by giving an *operational* definition. A term is defined operationally by giving a test or procedure to determine whether the term applies in a given case or not.

> Acid—A solution is acid when a piece of blue litmus paper inserted into it turns red.
>
> Allergy—A person has an allergy to a substance when placing the substance on his skin causes a rash to appear.

Operational definitions are frequently used in science, medicine, and technology.

Many words can be explained by analytical definitions. We examine the objects that the word refers to, analyze them, and attempt to locate features that are common to all or most of them. The analytical definition sums up the most important of the features common to all these objects.

> A book is a collection of printed pages bound together at one side and protected by covers.

Citing such features is sometimes called giving the *meaning* of the word in a narrow sense, whereas indicating the objects it applies to is called giving its *reference*.[2] Most words have both a meaning and a reference. Some words may have a meaning but no reference, such as words for hypothetical or imaginary

---

[2] John Stuart Mill calls meaning "connotation" and reference "denotation." Today "denotation" is sometimes used for reference, but "connotation" is used for what a word suggests beyond its literal meaning. Some writers call meaning "intensional meaning" and reference "extensional meaning."

objects like unicorns.

One method of defining developed by the Greek philosopher Aristotle works especially well for natural phenomena such as birds, trees, fish, and flowers. He noticed that many such objects tend to fall into natural groups or kinds. So he suggested that a word should be defined by first mentioning the larger group its objects fall into (the "genus"), then citing the features which distinguish these objects from others in the same genus. The smaller group then constitutes a species. Here are two examples (avoiding the Latin terminology needed by scientists for greater precision).

> Kingbirds are "aggressive, usually gray-headed fly-catchers of open or semi-open country."
>
> *Birds of North America* (Golden Field Guide), p. 192.

> Pokeweed is "a tall, large-leafed, branching plant with reddish stems and long clusters of small, white flowers."
>
> *Field Guide to North American Wild Flowers, Eastern Region* (Audubon Society), p. 679.

The first definition locates kingbirds in the genus flycatchers, then distinguishes them from other flycatchers. The second, though it does not use a technical genus of the botanist, fits pokeweed in with tall, large-leaf, branching plants, then distinguishes it from similar species.

Definitions similar to this can also be helpful in areas where we do not have natural groups or kinds. In some cases we can identify groups or kinds created as a result of human agency.

> A chair is a piece of furniture with a seat for one person raised from the floor and with a backrest.

Here the genus is furniture. The features cited in the definition distinguish the chair from other objects of furniture which resemble it and with which it could be confused. "For one person" distinguishes the chair from furniture pieces that seat more than one person, such as the sofa. "Raised from the floor" separates it from seats for one person on the floor, such as the cushion.

There are cases where the person we are explaining the word to isn't enlightened by an analytical definition. In such cases mentioning an example from the word's reference group may help.

> A reptile is a cold-blooded, egg-laying vertebrate.

Someone who listens blankly to this definition might perk up if you added "such as a snake or lizard."

All of the above approaches to defining are attempts to give standard definitions. A *standard* definition gives the meaning of a word as the word is currently used. This type of definition is sometimes called a lexical definition because it is the type given in a dictionary or lexicon. Often questions about a word's meaning can be settled by looking the word up in a good dictionary. This is not always the case, however, as we will see below.

But not all of the definitions we encounter are standard definitions. A *stipulative* definition occurs when a person or group stipulates that a word, phrase, or symbol is to have a certain meaning. Sometimes the purpose of a stipulative definition is economy. A writer will be using a certain idea quite frequently and so needs a shorthand way of referring to it.

The letter "v" shall mean "either. . . or. . ."

Modern symbolic logic, for instance, makes frequent use of "either . . . or . . ." as a sentence connector, so logicians stipulate that "v" shall stand for it. Sometimes a writer coins a word for an idea or object he thinks unduly neglected.

> A wog is a piece of food on the face.

Invented by Gelett Burgess and featured in a 1981 Russell Baker column in the *New York Times*, "wog" has not yet made the dictionaries.

There are also cases where a stipulative definition is intended to serve a specific, limited purpose.

> The term "mortgage" used herein shall include deed of trust, trust deed, or other security instrument.

Here "mortgage" is not given a meaning at variance with current use. It is only given a more precise meaning in the context of a legal document.

What begins as a stipulative definition may prove sufficiently useful to enter the language and its dictionaries. The American mathematician Edward Kasner invented a word and gave it this meaning.

> A googol is 10^{100}.

The word is now found in dictionaries of current American English, such as the *American Heritage Dictionary*. Other stipulative definitions may serve a limited purpose without entering the language. This happened to the following one advanced by the American philosopher Walter Kaufmann.

> Decidophobia is a dread of making decisions.

Once we recognize a definition as stipulative, our only further concern is whether it avoids confusion and serves its purpose. Acquaintance with the context is needed to decide this.

Another kind of definition different from the standard is the persuasive definition. Sometimes called a "loaded" definition, the *persuasive* definition does not attempt to give the meaning of a word so much as it attempts to influence attitudes of readers or listeners in a calculated way. The words selected to do the defining are chosen not to achieve precision of meaning but for their capacity to influence people's attitudes.

Democracy is the best form of government ever discovered.

Communism is government by gangsters through terror.

The first definition attempts to effect a positive attitude toward democracy, while the second aims at a negative attitude toward communism. We should be on guard against such persuasive definitions. In many cases our attitudes are too important for us to let them be dragged around by such verbal trickery.

4. Honing Definitions

It is sometimes thought that all questions about meanings of words can be settled by turning to a dictionary. Many of them can, of course, and most of us would profit from spending more time with a dictionary than we do. But on occasion questions arise when there is no dictionary around. In such a case we are forced to define a word as best we can, or leave the question hanging in the air.

Also it is a mistake to think that the purpose of a dictionary is to set down once and for all—carved in stone as it were—authoritative meanings for words. A good dictionary is indeed authoritative, but in a limited rather than an absolute sense. Language is a living entity that grows and changes as we confront different situations and respond to different challenges. Lexicographers first attend to how a word functions in the living language, then analyze and criticize before finally setting down as precise and useful a definition as they can. Dictionaries cannot settle all questions about how words are to be used, nor are they intended to. If they were, then such a heated debate as the current one about abortion could be settled by looking up definitions for "human being" or "person."

Language is extremely important in so many ways. It enables us to describe, analyze, and understand our natural and cultural surroundings (and ourselves as well). It can also further our efforts to act intelligently in the various situations we find ourselves in. An important part of learning to think critically is achieving more precision in our use of language. We have already learned some of the factors to be taken account of in defining a word. Now we are going to turn our attention to how we can test standard definitions for precision and so render them more adequate to their purpose.

1. Avoid *negative* terms. Generally—there are exceptions—the precision we desire in a definition is better achieved by stating the definition in affirmative rather than negative terms.

A just person is one who avoids being unjust.

A chair is a piece of furniture that is neither a table nor a sideboard.

A natural note is a musical note that is neither a flat nor a sharp.

The reason for avoiding definitions of this type is obvious. They appear to be detailed and precise whereas in fact they are vague and misleading. A chair is also not a lamp and not a bookshelf, but learning this does not bring us a whole lot closer to what it *is.*

2. Avoid *unnecessarily difficult* terms. One important function of a definition is to convey the meaning of a word to someone unfamiliar with it. If the words chosen to do the defining are unnecessarily difficult or comparatively rare of occurrence, then the definition will serve this purpose poorly. So whenever possible, the definition should be in terms simpler and more readily understandable than the word being defined.

A network is anything reticulated or decussated, at equal distances, with interstices between the intersections.

This definition fails by this criterion, even though it is from the first great dictionary of the English language, Samuel Johnson's.

At times a synonym or short equivalent phrase is the most effective definition. In such cases too the synonym or phrase should be simpler or better known than the word being defined.

Indefatigable—tireless.

Bachelor—an unmarried man.

3. Another fault that can prevent a definition from being adequate occurs when the word being defined turns up in the defining clause or phrase. This is called a *circular* definition.

A scallywag is one who acts like a scallywag.

A fidgeltick is one who ticks fidgels.

These examples reveal the fault of the circular definition. In most cases it fails to convey the meaning to someone who doesn't already know what the word means. If someone already understands what the word means, there is little point troubling him with a definition.

4. The definition should not be *too broad.* Our goal in framing a definition is to get it as accurate as we can. Special care should be exercised to assure that the reference group contains only those items it is supposed to contain, no more.

We say that a definition is too broad when it allows objects into the reference group that shouldn't be there.

> A chair is a piece of furniture with a seat for one person raised from the floor.

If we define "chair" like this, we allow into our reference group raised seats for one person like stools which shouldn't be there. So our definition fails by being too broad. We can exclude these items and make our definition more precise by adding the phrase "with a backrest."

4. The definition should not be *too narrow*. Similar to the above fault, this one occurs when items are excluded from the reference group that ought to be there.

> A chair is a piece of furniture made of wood with a seat for one person raised from the floor and with a backrest.

In this case we improperly exclude from our reference group items of furniture made of synthetics or metal that are chairs and ought to be included. So this definition is too narrow. We can remedy this by removing the phrase "made of wood."

It is possible for a definition to be too broad and too narrow at the same time. It is too broad relative to some objects and too narrow relative to others.

> A chair is a piece of furniture made of wood with a seat for one person raised from the floor.

This definition is too narrow for excluding chairs of metal or synthetics, and too broad for including stools.

Summary

A verbal dispute involves confusion or disagreement about the meanings of words. It contrasts with a substantial dispute, a dispute about the substance of some matter. Some disputes can be resolved when the parties agree on the meaning of words. Some verbal disputes resolve into substantial disputes.

A word is used ambiguously when it has two or more meanings and the context doesn't make clear which is appropriate. A word is vague in a context when it isn't precise enough to perform its function. Ambiguity and vagueness contribute to verbal confusion, so the critical thinker usually tries to avoid them. A special challenge for speakers of English is its rich vocabulary. Even diligent students continue to add to their vocabularies and try to make their contents more precise. Clear and effective command of language is an important goal for critical thinking.

One way of escaping verbal confusion is by defining words carefully. A word's meaning can be conveyed by pointing to an object it applies to (ostensive definition), or by citing examples of these objects. The objects a word applies to are its reference or denotation, which is distinguished from its meaning in a narrower sense. This narrower meaning is sometimes given by citing the genus or family the objects fall under, then listing features that distinguish this particular species from others of the same genus.

Words can also be defined functionally by stating the function their objects perform. An operational definition provides a test that decides whether the word applies in a given case or not. All of these kinds of definitions are standard, analytic, or lexical in that they define words as they are currently used. By contrast, a stipulative definition gives a word a special meaning for a certain use or occasion. Persuasive definitions attempt to influence attitudes by using words for their emotional effect.

Some common weaknesses of definitions are that they are:

1. **Negative—they tell what a word doesn't apply to rather than what it does.**
2. **Unnecessarily difficult—for many purposes like that of teaching someone a new word the language of the definition should aspire to be simpler than the word defined.**
3. **Circular—the word to be defined is used in the defining phrase or clause.**
4. **Too broad—items are allowed in the reference group that shouldn't be there.**
5. **Too narrow—items are excluded from the reference group that should be there.**

Study Questions

Section 1. Verbal disputes, ambiguity, and word misuse

1. Distinguish a verbal dispute from a substantial.
2. Cite three sources of verbal confusion.
3. When is a word ambiguous?
4. When is a word or phrase vague?

Section 2. Some characteristics of the English language

5. As what did the English language get its start?
6. What historical event most influenced modern English?
7. From what ancient language is more than half the vocabulary of modern English descended?

Section 3. Definitions

12. What is it to define a word ostensively? Give an example.
13. Explain and give an example of a functional definition. A definition by genus and species.
14. Distinguish a standard from a stipulative definition. Give an example of each.
15. What is a persuasive definition? Give an example.

Section 4. Honing definitions

16. State one of the five important defects of definitions. Illustrate it with a defective definition, then provide an improved definition that eliminates the defect.

EXERCISE 9—2: WORD MEANING

Part A: Ostensive Definitions

Define ostensively as many of the following as you can.

1. shoe	6. electric light
2. tree	7. ball-point pen
3. blue	8. doorknob
4. table	9. time
5. wall	10. jeans

Part B: Classifying Definitions

In each case decide whether the definition is standard, stipulative, or persuasive. For standard definitions, identify the type of definition and comment on its adequacy. For persuasive definitions, state how the definer is attempting to influence our attitudes.

1. A triangle is a closed, three-sided, plane figure.
2. An allibosh is a glaringly obvious falsehood.
3. A policeman is a killer charged by society with protecting the lives and property of the well-to-do.

*4. A pawdle is a person of mediocre ability raised to undeserved prominence.

5. A cure is a medical treatment that restores health.
6. An abortion is the murder of a fetus.
7. Money is a medium of exchange.
8. A pan is a shallow, wide, open container, usually of metal, used in cooking and holding liquids.
9. A liberal is a wild-eyed terror bent on uprooting all valuable tradition and totally destroying decency.
10. A mooble is a mildly amusing affair.

Part C: Recognizing Defects

Each of the definitions below is negative, unnecessarily difficult, circular, too broad, or too narrow. Study each definition and decide why it fails. Attempt to improve the definition so it avoids the defect or defects you identify.

1. A poem is a piece of writing by a poet.
2. A kiss is the anatomical juxtaposition of two orbicular oris muscles in a state of contraction.
3. A grandmother is a parent whose children have children.
4. Salvation is the state enjoyed by someone who is not condemned.
5. A pericoddler is one who coddles perries.
6. A lie is a prevarication.

7. An essay is a short, handwritten literary composition on one topic.
8. Iron is a metal that is hard, tough, and durable.
9. A floor is the wooden surface of a room that people stand on.
*10. Night is the condition that occurs when day is finished.

Part D: Improving Definitions

Some of the definitions below are adequate, and some suffer defects we are familiar with. If a definition is not adequate, identify its faults and attempt to improve it or substitute a better definition in its place.

1. Logic is the art of thinking logically.
2. Cuisse is plate armor worn to protect the thigh.
3. An automobile is a vehicle with a gasoline-powered internal combustion engine for transporting a few persons.
*4. A singletree is a whiffletree.
5. Mercury is a silvery white, poisonous metallic element that is liquid at room temperature.
6. Depth is distance the opposite direction from height.
7. A taxi is an automobile that carries passengers for a fee.
8. Language is a means of communication.
9. A photo is a reproduction of an object's superficial traits by exposing thin plastic treated with silver bromide and silver iodide to a controlled quantity of light emitted from the subject.
10. To lie is to say something untrue.
11. An allele is one of several possible mutational forms of a gene.
*12. Nitrogen is a gas that is neither oxygen nor hydrogen.
13. A pipe is a hollow tube made of metal.
14. To eat is to perform successively the functions of mastication, humectation, and deglutition.
15. To unlace is to loosen or untie a lace or laces.

Further Reading

The following are useful guides to definitions, synonyms, and usage.

The American Heritage Dictionary of the English Language, Second College Edition (Boston 1991).

Roget's II. The New Thesaurus (Boston 1980).

This rhetoric is laced with helpful points on usage and syntax, stressing clearness, simplicity, and precision.

William W. Watt, *An American Rhetoric*, 3rd ed. (New York 1964).

Of these histories of the English language, Jespersen is an older but concise and very readable work, Baugh a fuller history with a chapter on English in America, and the McCrum a lively, well-illustrated account based on a PBS TV series on the English language.

A. C. Baugh, *A History of the English Language*, 2nd ed. (London 1959).

Otto Jesperson, *Growth and Structure of the English Language*, 10th ed. (Chicago 1982).

Robert McCrum et al., *The Story of English* (New York 1987).

CHAPTER TEN

CLARITY IN ARGUMENTS

1. BURDEN OF PROOF

"Joe Ralston, your candidate for governor," said Daryl to his Republican friend, "often cuts corners on his real estate deals, and has crossed the border into illegality on a number of occasions."

"That's vicious slander," responded Teri heatedly. "He has done nothing of the sort."

"Prove it!" challenged Daryl.

Is Teri obligated to respond to Daryl's challenge? To answer this question we must consider in general who bears the responsibility for substantiating or providing evidence for a claim. But we can learn a bit more from this case. In it, Daryl advances a claim about a gubernatorial candidate. When challenged by Teri, he does not respond by supplying evidence for his claim. To so respond would be to advance one or more arguments in support of that claim.

Instead Daryl responds with a demand that Teri, his challenger, substantiate her claim that Ralston is not guilty of sharp practices or illegal acts. To substantiate a claim is to show that it has substance and is not empty by providing evidence for it. You can say that this is to prove the claim. But often this does not mean to prove with certainty, and in many cases it does not mean to prove beyond reasonable doubt. To substantiate a claim is to offer evidence for it that clearly outweighs evidence against it. The necessity of substantiating a claim to get it accepted is called the burden of proof. To accept the challenge of substantiating a claim is to shoulder or accept the burden of proof. To succeed is to discharge the burden of proof.

To illustrate the importance of the burden of proof, let's adopt for a moment the hypothesis that Teri should assume the burden of proof. This has several disadvantages.

1. It is unfair to Teri in her exchange with Daryl. He is permitted to advance a proposition without producing any evidence to support it whereas she is forced to produce evidence for hers.
2. It is also unfair to Joe Ralston. Daryl is permitted to accuse him of sharp practices and illegal activities without producing any evidence for these charges. In reprehensibility this advances quite beyond innuendo toward character assassination.
3. The listener who wants to think critically about the situation and evaluate it is ill served. He confronts a proposition advanced by Daryl that he wants to take seriously, yet the evidence that would allow him to take it seriously is withheld. The debate may be important to him even though he is not a participant. Perhaps he is trying to decide whether he should vote for Ralston in the upcoming election.
4. Teri's obligation to discharge the burden of proof is made unnecessarily, even unreasonably difficult. As in U.S. law the accused is considered innocent until proven guilty, so we generally assume that a person is honest until evidence to the contrary emerges. Given this presumption of honesty, in general the way to prove that a person is honest is to refute or disprove charges of dishonesty or illegality. But Teri cannot do this because she confronts only general accusations—no specific charges have been made. This is what we mean when we say that no evidence has been advanced. For instance, Daryl has not charged Ralston with conflict of interest in representing the seller of a 30.5-acre tract of farmland on Oct. 14, 1989 because Ralston concealed his ownership of 6.3% of the stock of Hayes-Wright Development Inc., which bought the land to develop a shopping center. In the absence of such evidence and specific charges, for all we know there are no such specific charges at all and Daryl's accusations are completely empty.

Though Teri's task has been made more difficult, it is not impossible. She can begin with the crime part, and check court and police records where Ralston has lived. These records can establish that in those places he has not been convicted of any offenses, and that he has not been indicted for any either. Advancing to the claim of sharp practices, she can check with the local and state bar associations as well as with the local real estate board to establish that he has not been censured or reprimanded by any of these professional organizations. Further inquiry could establish that the number of complaints received about Ralston are no greater than average, or that no complaints have been received about him at all.

Daryl can always respond that Ralston is so clever that his criminal activities have not yet been detected. But without evidence, at this point scarcely anyone would believe him. Sharp practices have victims, and in time some of the victims would discover that they had been cheated and blow the whistle on Ralston.

Teri has been handed a Herculean task without there being any need for it, and the other difficulties cited above are also serious ones. We can avoid them, and we do so, by insisting that the person who advances a claim should assume the burden of proving it. He ought to be in a good position to produce evidence for it, since this same evidence is presumably what convinced him of it in the first place. What is gained for critical thinking is that the evidence supporting the claim is brought out into the open. This is no small benefit. We must be able to inspect this evidence, decide whether it is complete, and test it in the manner we have learned to use to evaluate arguments in order to decide whether the writer has successfully discharged the burden of proof.

The demand that Daryl makes in the above example is an illegitimate one. We call what he did *illegitimately shifting the burden of proof.* When the asserter of a proposition refuses to assume the burden of proving it and instead insists that he be proven false, this is an illegitimate shift in the burden of proof. Illegitimately shifting the burden of proof is sometimes called the *fallacy of appeal to ignorance*, or *ad ignorantiam*. A weak or invalid argument that appears to establish its conclusion, or fools at least some of us into thinking it has established its conclusion, is called a *fallacy*. In general, fallacious reasoning is unsound reasoning masquerading as sound. Some fallacies occur over and over again. We need to detect them so that we won't be fooled by them, and we need to understand what makes them fallacious so that we can avoid them in our own reasoning. We label those that occur frequently to facilitate learning about them and detecting them. Illegitimately shifting the burden of proof is called the appeal to ignorance because the asserter of the proposition claims that it is made true by the absence (ignorance) of evidence against it. This is fallacious because a thesis cannot be proved by the absence of evidence against it. It can only be proved by positive evidence supporting it.

Suppose I want to establish this proposition: The U.S. ought to invest more of its taxpayer dollars in education programs that benefit economically and socially disadvantaged young people. But I advance no evidence in support of it. Instead I claim that it is true because no one has proved it false. In this case I am illegitimately shifting the burden of proof.

We should pay close attention to the context any time the question of burden of proof arises. What at first glance appears an illegitimate shift may on closer study turn out to be unobjectionable. For example, we can take a writer who desires to prove the immortality of the soul. He argues as follows.

> We may believe in immortality because there is no reason for *not* believing in it. In discussions of this kind we are constantly reminded that immortality has never been proved. To which there is the immediate and inevitable reply that immortality has never been disproved! As there is no positive testimony to prove it true, so is there no negative testimony to prove it untrue.

For purposes of argument analysis we focus on this:

① ②

<<u>We may believe in immortality</u>> [because] <there is no reason for not believing in it.>

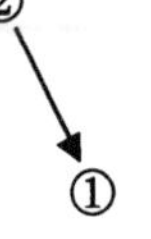

Simple

We may question the premise here. For instance, when our friends and loved ones die, they cease to be with us and communicate with us. If they were immortal, or if they continued to exist in some form, it is reasonable to assume that they would communicate with us. But our interest in the example is that it obviously shifts the burden of proof. Is the shift illegitimate (an appeal to ignorance)? On the basis of what we have seen, we would have to respond yes. But when we turn to the context of the passage, we get a different result. For this argument occurs in a sermon entitled "Ten Reasons for Believing in Immortality" in which John Haynes Holmes, drawing heavily on evidence from evolutionary processes, advances nine other arguments for immortality. Since he has assumed the burden of proof in this larger context, we cannot accuse him of illegitimately shifting it. An adequate response from an opponent has to deal with this evidence as well.

In a formal debate it can be stipulated from the start where the burden of proof lies and what the roles of the participants are relative to it. The debate that interests us most from the standpoint of critical thinking is sometimes referred to as a dialectic, or dialectical exchange. In this the initial speaker defends a thesis while a respondent has the task of testing the defense by raising objections to it. The overall burden of proof lies on the speaker. As the advocate of the position, he must produce the evidence that will establish it. This overall or primary burden of proof remains with the speaker throughout the discussion. But there is also a secondary burden, a duty to advance the dialectic or discussion, that shifts legitimately from speaker to respondent and back. In fact, there are two different cases of common occurrence where this secondary burden or duty to advance the discussion shifts.

1. Suppose that we are the respondent in a dialectic where Holmes is defending the thesis that the human soul is immortal. Our task is to question and test the evidence he advances in support of this thesis. He has presented his ten reasons. We respond as follows.

> But when are you going to prove your case?

This response indicates our failure to assume this secondary burden of proof. Holmes' arguments now occupy the field, so to speak, and in order to uphold our position that he has not proven his, we must deal with each of these arguments in turn and show that it does not establish the thesis. Once his evidence is presented, it is our duty to deal with it. We cannot escape this responsibility.

2. Suppose this time that in the course of dealing with Holmes' ten reasons we advance a positive thesis of our own.

> Several of Holmes' arguments depend on the theory of evolution. But this is a false account of the origin of the species. All the animals were created by God to serve his purposes.

Now Holmes calls on us to substantiate this new thesis. We are obliged to do so. At this point we have gone beyond questioning the relation of his reasons to his thesis to advance our own thesis about creation. Since we have advanced it, the secondary burden of advancing the dialectic now falls on us. The primary burden of proving immortality still rests with Holmes. This hasn't changed. But once we have advanced a thesis and are challenged, we must present our evidence for it.

The above comments on the burden of proof should not be taken as hard and fast rules of how debates or disputes should be conducted. But they are good guidelines for dialectical exchanges. They may be useful for those who participate in such exchanges as speaker or respondent. And they may also help those attempting to judge the course and outcome of such exchanges.

Many disputes arise more or less impromptu. You join a group of friends, for instance, and someone is advancing and defending a view you cannot accept. When you get an opportunity to speak, you advance your objections. Many debates begin in this fashion, with no agreed on rules. The above factors are worth bearing in mind for such occasions. They make such good sense they can help you guide the discussion in a fruitful direction. They may be stated explicitly if needed, and the parties to the discussion may agree to abide by them.

Such impromptu discussions as well as dialectical exchanges always take place against a background of (not necessarily true or proven but) accepted beliefs, and these also can constitute a factor in determining who is to bear the burden of proof. In general, the person who challenges accepted beliefs bears the burden of proving her position. For instance, in Massachusetts Bay Colony, which became in the 1630s the most populous of the English colonies in North America, one had to be a member in good standing of the puritan Congregationalist Church, the only church in the Colony, in order to vote or hold office. Consequently when Roger Williams disputes this union of church and state, and calls for religious tolerance, he properly assumes the burden of proof because he is challenging what is accepted in the Colony.

For another example, many students of nature during the scientific advance of the Renaissance held that the cause of an event produced its effect by a sort of necessity. If you only studied the cause closely enough, you might infer the effect without ever having experienced the event itself. So when the skeptical 18th century Scottish philosopher David Hume calls this interpretation of the cause-effect relation into question, he assumes the burden of proof for his dissenting position.

> In a word, then, every effect is a distinct event from its cause. It could not, therefore, be discovered in the cause, and the first invention or conception of it, *a priori*, must be entirely arbitrary. And even after it is suggested, the conjunction of it with the cause must appear equally arbitrary; since there are always many other effects, which, to reason, must seem fully as consistent and natural. In vain, therefore, should we pretend to determine any single event, or infer any cause or effect, without the assistance of observation and experience.

It is not always as easy to discern—as it is in Hume's case here—where the burden of proof lies and whether it has been assumed by the advancer of the thesis.

A fallacious argument . . . is one that seems to be valid *but* is not so.
C. L. Hamblin

2. Begging the Question

Let us turn our attention now from debate and the question of burden of proof to the relation of evidence and conclusion. We do need to recall at this point one important thing we have already learned about argument strategy.[1] We argue from premises that are reliable to something that is doubted or controversial. For an argument to be strong, the conclusion must in a sense advance beyond the premises to claim something different from what they explicitly state. Perhaps the best way for us to appreciate this is by looking at an argument that fails to satisfy this condition.

> "Emerald Bay is the most beautiful part of Lake Tahoe," said Cindy.
> "Why do you think that?" asked Steve.
> "Because it is the most beautiful part of Lake Tahoe," Cindy asserted.

Would you be convinced by this argument? Not unless you already believed that

[1] In Chapter Six, p. 145f.

Emerald Bay was the most beautiful part of Lake Tahoe. And in that case the argument would be pointless. If Steve is already convinced that Emerald Bay is the most beautiful part of Lake Tahoe, then it doesn't make any sense for Cindy to attempt to convince him of it.

Let us suppose now that Steve isn't convinced. As an argument, what Cindy claims looks like this.

①

<Emerald Bay is the most beautiful part of Lake Tahoe.> <Emerald Bay

②

is the most beautiful part of Lake Tahoe.>

Simple

The conclusion simply repeats the premise. If Steve were not already convinced of the conclusion, then he would scarcely concede the premise. And we know that if an argument has only one premise and that premise is doubtful (at least Steve won't concede it), the argument does not provide strong support for its conclusion. Such an argument suffers from a structural defect we call circularity. The premise already asserts as true what the argument is intended to prove, namely the conclusion.

In that the conclusion only repeats the premise, this argument is circular, but it is circular in a way we need to attend to carefully. Many arguments, including the quite strong ones, may be thought of as circular in that the conclusion states something that lies implicit in the premises. There is nothing wrong with this circularity—we may think of it as benign or virtuous. But the circularity we encounter in the above example greatly weakens an argument or renders it worthless. We call this a vicious circularity. A viciously circular argument does not establish its conclusion and this reveals to us something of importance about arguments. If an argument is to be strong, the conclusion cannot merely repeat the premise or premises. The premise or premises must present facts or information to some extent different from the conclusion. Good premises say something different from the conclusion, but something that tends to establish the conclusion.

Seldom is an argument as perfectly circular as our Lake Tahoe example above. You wonder whether it is really an argument at all. But you don't have to get very far away from strict circularity before you encounter positions that have a familiar sound.

> "How can you be so sure that God exists?" asked Daryl.
> "The Bible says he does," replied Susie.
> "But how do you know that what the Bible says is true?" rejoined Daryl.
> "The Bible has to be true. It is the word of God," stated Susie.

On analysis, this material breaks down into two separate arguments.

Argument #1: <The Bible is the word of God.>① [So] <what the Bible says is true.>②

Argument #2: <The Bible says God exists.>③ [Thus] <God exists.>④

① → ② Simple

③ → ④ Simple

When the argumentative material is analyzed in this manner, we again find a vicious circle, though not so tight a one as in the Tahoe case. The conclusion of Argument #2, "God exists," is already assumed in the premise of Argument #1, "The Bible is the word of God." To affirm that the Bible is the word of God and deny that God exists is to contradict oneself. So we see that ④, the conclusion of Argument #2, must be true in order for ①, the premise of Argument #1, to be true. In other words, the conclusion of the second argument is assumed in the premise of the first, rather than being proved by premises independent of it.

Arguments in vicious circles are called *fallacies of begging the question.* This label originated in argumentative debates in Greece at the time of Socrates and Plato.[2] The point of such a contest was for one speaker to establish a thesis by argument and defend it against a respondent. The thesis the speaker set out to establish was called the *question.* In our case "God exists" is the question. The respondent had to concede the speaker one or more premises to work with in his argument. The speaker could then *beg* for more and more until the opponent finally conceded (perhaps in somewhat different words) the very thesis in question. This explains the descriptive phrase *begging the question.* If in our case he conceded "The Bible is the word of God," he would in effect be conceding the thesis in question, since the step from this to the existence of God is a very short one. A fair challenge might be to concede "There exists an ordered universe." An argument for the existence of God could then be constructed on this as a premise. It would attempt to establish that order as distinct from chaos must be contributed by a mind, and that a mind powerful enough to conceive and bestow order in the universe would have to be a divine mind.

The fallacy of begging the question is an argument because it is an attempt to prove a conclusion. It is a fallacy because it fails to do so. It fails because the premise or premises are not significantly different from the conclusion. Suppose

[2] See C. L. Hamblin, *Fallacies* (Newport News 1998), pp. 32–35, for an excellent historical and analytical account.

you read some extraordinary item in a newspaper—say that a human infant is born with two heads. You find this incredible and want to either disprove or confirm it. You could go out and buy another copy of the same paper. This parallels begging the question because your evidence is just the same as in the first paper. Or you could visit the hospital and speak to someone who had first-hand knowledge of the case. Thus you would get new and independent evidence. Begging the question is a structural defect of an argument such that the argument can be complete and have strong premises yet fail to prove its conclusion.

3. Fallacies of Equivocation

For a mistake in reasoning to count as a logical fallacy it must occur in an inference or argument. In the case of an argument, one or more premises must be advanced in support of a conclusion. But in the fallacious argument these premises do not establish that conclusion. Also in the logical fallacy the premises must *seem to* establish the conclusion. That is, they must fool some of us, at least some of the time, into thinking that they do actually establish the conclusion. Similarly in the fallacious inference the conclusion does not actually follow from the premises, though it must appear to do so. The fallacies we will examine here tend to recur and fool people often enough to get recognized and named. One group of fallacies that turn on ambiguous use of language or misleading sentence structure is called *fallacies of equivocation* (some writers call them fallacies of ambiguity).

Composition and Division

> Feathers are very light in weight.
> Therefore a child can lift a ton of feathers.

This inference has a superficial plausibility to it, until we realize that a ton of anything weighs 2000 pounds. No child can lift 2000 pounds. The mistake in this inference lies in transferring a quality that rightly belongs to each member of the group—lightness to a feather—erroneously to the whole group itself—lightness to a ton. Here we first view the group distributively, or as its individual members. On this view we rightly call the feathers light. Then we advance to view the group collectively. And it is in this sense that we wrongly ascribe lightness to the ton of feathers. Such a case of erroneous reasoning from individual members to group as a whole is called the *fallacy of composition.*

Another form of the fallacy of composition involves fallacious reasoning from part to whole.

All the slices of blueberry pie are wedge shaped.
So the blueberry pie itself is wedge shaped.

In this instance a quality—being wedge shaped—that rightly belongs to the part or single slice of pie is wrongly transferred to the whole pie, which is of course not wedge shaped but circular.

Is all reasoning from part to whole fallacious? Not in the least. If there were not some sound reasoning from part to whole—and a considerable amount at that—we would never be fooled by the unsound. Here is an example of a rather strong inference from part to whole.

The shelves, back, and sides of that bookcase are all wooden.
So the bookcase itself is wooden.

There are also strong inferences, and many of them, from members of a group individually to the group collectively.

Rattlesnakes are poisonous and dangerous to humans.
Water moccasins are poisonous and dangerous to humans.
Copperheads are poisonous and dangerous to humans.
So all poisonous snakes are dangerous to humans.

In this case the individuals themselves are kinds of snakes, and the collective group is that of all poisonous snakes.

A related kind of equivocal inference occurs when we reason in the opposite direction, from whole to part. Here is an example from a fledgling chemistry student.

Salt is tasty and, in moderate quantities, good for your health.
Salt is composed of sodium and chlorine.
So chlorine must be tasty and, in moderate quantities, good for your health too.

This reasoning wouldn't survive one whiff of chlorine gas produced in a lab experiment. Chlorine gas is poisonous in itself, and chlorine also forms part of compounds that are poisonous to humans. Phosgene is an example, a poisonous gas used in World War I before the Geneva Convention outlawed such warfare. We go wrong here by taking two qualities that rightly belong to the whole or compound, salt (in moderate quantities) and transfer them illegitimately to the part or ingredient, chlorine. This time the flaw in the reasoning is the *fallacy of division*, fallacious reasoning from whole to part.

Similar to the fallacy of composition, the fallacy of division also occurs in reasoning from a group taken collectively to the individual members.

The 1989 San Francisco 49ers were a great team.
So all the players on the 1989 49ers were great players.

Few would question the greatness of this team, which dominated many of its opponents—including very tough ones—up to and including its lopsided victory in Superbowl XXII. Yet we cannot legitimately infer the greatness of all the players from the greatness of the team. In fact, "great" seems to mean somewhat different things when applied to a team and when applied to individual players. A great player contributes a clearly superior performance, especially in those clutch situations that decide games, over several seasons. Several of the 1989 49ers such as its starting quarterback qualify clearly. But not all. So our fallacy here is in transferring a quality—greatness—that rightly belongs to the group or team as a whole illegitimately to the individual members of the group, the players.

Again, not all reasoning from whole to part is fallacious. Here is an example of a strong inference from whole to part.

The carpet is acrylic.
So all of the parts of the carpet are acrylic.

In this case the quality of being acrylic applies both to the whole carpet and to the separate parts of it. There is also much legitimate reasoning from a group to the individual members of that group.

The combat troops of the U.S. Army are all male.
So Corporal Jones of the Panama strike force is male.

In this example the fact that combat troops as a group are all male ensures that any given combat soldier will be male also. The question whether female soldiers should be given combat roles is a matter of considerable debate.

Some cases of equivocal reasoning resemble one or the other of these two fallacies but do not analyze straightforwardly as either. Here is an example.

Eagles are birds.
Thus a small eagle is a small bird.

We know from the conclusion that this inference is unsound. No U.S. eagles are small eagles, but the smaller ones that occur in Africa are still the size of hawks. And a hawk, compared with a small bird like the sparrow, is still a large bird. Where the inference goes wrong is in the assumption that a division of eagles into small and large will parallel a division of the class of birds (which contains eagles as one of its parts) into small and large.

Fallacies of composition and division do not occur as frequently as some other fallacies. When we encounter one we are as likely to be puzzled as fooled by it. We may be lulled into accepting a conclusion occasionally, but usually when we focus on the inference and think a bit we recognize the conclusion as counter to fact. So one important reason why we study these two fallacies is that it enables us to resolve puzzlement and clear up equivocation.

Complex Question

A different fallacy of equivocation is illustrated in this courtroom example.

> Bailey, the prosecutor, turned to the defendant.
> "Mr. Jacobs, people are murdered either with premeditation, which is murder in the first degree, or they are killed in passion, which is second degree murder. Now you were frothing with rage when you bludgeoned Caroline Wallace to death, weren't you?"
> "No I was not."
> Bailey turns and gestures to the jury.
> "There you have it, ladies and gentlemen of the jury. Jacobs denies that he killed the victim in a rage, thereby conceding that he deliberately plotted her murder beforehand in cold blood."

The question posed by the prosecutor is a loaded question in that, whichever way he answers it, Jacobs concedes that he murdered Caroline Wallace. For if he answers yes, he concedes murder in the second degree.

From the legal vantage point of trial procedure this question falls into the general category of leading questions. Counsel for the defense should not allow Jacobs to respond to this question. She should object that the prosecutor is leading the defendant, and her objection should be sustained.

But from the standpoint of critical thinking, the question constitutes an argument because it attempts to establish the proposition that Jacobs is a murderer. We can bring out its argumentative character more clearly by paraphrasing the exchange to put the question in the indicative mood and incorporate Jacob's response to it.

① <Jacobs murdered either with premeditation or in a passion.> But ② <he did not murder in a passion.> [Therefore] ③ <he murdered with premeditation.> [So] ④ <Jacobs is guilty of murder.>

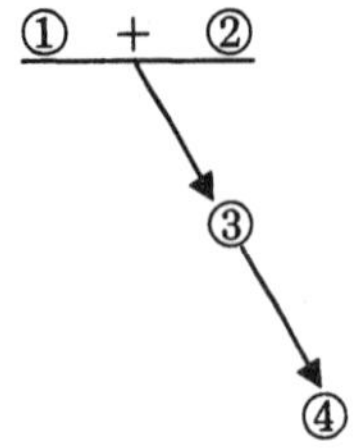

① + ②
↓
③
↓
④

Compound Serial

When we examine the argument we see that the prosecutor has not advanced evidence to support the final conclusion that Jacobs is a murderer. This final conclusion, that Jacobs is a murderer, is already assumed in the initial premise. In the example, the prosecutor smuggles this assumption into his initial question. So this fallacious argument resembles the fallacy of begging the question in that what the argument is intended to establish is already smuggled in as an assumption of one of the premises. The prosecutor has not discharged the burden of proof by bringing positive evidence to support his claim that Jacobs is guilty of murder. Instead he attempts to win his case with verbal trickery.

This verbal trickery is why we have a case of fallacy of equivocation. It is called the *fallacy of complex question*, though some writers call it the fallacy of many questions. The question is complex because the defendant is asked at least two questions: Did you kill Caroline Wallace? Did you kill her with premeditation or out of passion? The defendant does not directly address the first question because he isn't asked it explicitly. But his simply answering yes or no to the second question presupposes an affirmative answer to the first. Indirectly, perhaps without being aware of it, he confesses to being a murderer.

If such a complex question is directed to us, how should we confront it? The best tactic is to first divide the question into its separate parts, as we did with the example above. Then we can decide whether to answer any of the questions, and how to answer those we decide to address (or are instructed to answer as in a court of law). For instance in the above example, the judge can ask to have the question rephrased. Then when Jacobs is asked whether he killed Caroline Wallace, he can respond no, or he can invoke his Fifth Amendment right and refuse to answer on the grounds that he might incriminate himself.

Another situation that tends to engender complex questions is encounters of the media with public figures. This is particularly true of press conferences or interviews with public officials or candidates for public office, and has had an unfortunate focus on the sex lives of political candidates since Gary Hart's mishandling of his affair with Donna Rice removed him as a presidential contender in the democratic primaries in 1988. Officials or candidates may face questions like the following.

> Mr. Green, have you finally put an end to your extra-marital sexual flings?

> Ms. Denby, did you ever stop accepting illegal campaign contributions?

Both questions call for yes or no answers, which force the candidates to concede something against their interest and possibly untrue. Unless concrete evidence of misdeeds or questionable behavior has been made public, candidates may be best off following the advice of editorial writer Paul Greenberg: "Political candidates should ignore the prying personal questions." Some may choose to respond in kind, as did Illinois Representative Gus Savage to reporters questioning him about sex.

> Have you stopped wearing your wife's lingerie? Have you stopped messing around with little boys?

The further issue here is whether reporters are serving the public interest with such questions. In most cases the only thing served beyond idle curiosity appears to be mild prurience. The public would be better served by reporters digging away on matters of substance.

EXERCISE 10—1: FALLACIES OF ARGUMENT STRUCTURE AND LANGUAGE

Part A. Fallacies of Equivocation and Begging the Question

First decide whether the problem is an argument. If so, diagram and evaluate the argument. Decide whether it is strong or weak, and for what reason. Identify any cases of begging the question, and point out in each case what makes the argument viciously circular.

Also identify any fallacies of composition or division. In the case of a part-whole fallacy, show clearly which is the part and which the whole, and why the inference is unsound. Do the same for any group-member fallacy. Remember that some of the problems may have sound reasoning involving part-whole or group-members. Some fallacies of equivocation may resemble part-whole or group-members fallacies without fitting the pattern exactly.

Include as argument any fallacy of complex question. Analyze this fallacy by dividing the questions and stating them separately. Then paraphrase the questions in the indicative mood and show what the premise (or premises) and conclusion are. Diagram and evaluate the argument. Explain why it presents a conclusion one might be reluctant to accept.

1. A good physician cures most of his patients because he has a sound medical education, for a man with a sound medical education is a good physician who cures most of his patients.

2. It is impossible for poverty to be a problem in the United States. The United States is the wealthiest nation the world has ever known.

*3. Every contractor is free to submit whatever bid he pleases on state construction work. So there can be nothing wrong with contractors getting together and deciding what bid each shall submit on a state construction project.

4. Have you turned in your Communist Party card yet?

5. "Certainly Cowper's insane."

"But how do you know?"

"Well, he's admitted killing the innkeeper in an argument over the bill, and anyone who kills a fellow human being is insane."

6. Was it sheer incompetence that caused the administration to bungle domestic policy, or have they sold the electorate out in brazen dishonesty? Unless you favor incompetent bungling or brazen dishonesty, you should vote the incumbents out of office.

7. Foods that contain a lot of protein are nutritious. So soybeans must be nutritious, because they contain a lot of protein.

*8. If we want to know whether a state is brave we must look at its army, not because the soldiers are the only brave people in the community, but because it is only through their conduct that the courage or cowardice of the community can be manifested.

R. L. Nettleship, *Lectures on the Republic of Plato* (London 1962), p. 148.

9. Of course she loves me. She told me that she loved me, and I believe her. Would she lie to someone she loved?

10. The prime responsibility of a businessman is to make a profit. If he fails to do so for a long period, his business will collapse. Along with his employees he will join the ranks of the unemployed. So he is justified in setting ethics or even (within reason) the law aside if he must in order to make a profit.

11. Do you get a special thrill out of cheating at cards?

12. The governor must be a solid friend of the working man in this state. He said he was in a campaign speech in Union Hall last night, and a man wouldn't lie to his friends.

13. Each part of that heat pump can be lifted by a single man. So the whole heat pump can be lifted by a single man.

14. Is the year 2000 AD a leap year or not?

15. This is an iron chain. So the links of this chain are made of iron.

16. The cells of an elephant are the same size as the cells of a mouse. So an elephant is the same size as a mouse.

17. Has anyone ever committed more crimes without being convicted than you?

18. Each of the rails is only 39 feet long. So that railroad doesn't go very far.

19. A good quick test to find out whether a piece of furniture is a solid valuable wood or a veneer is to try to lift it. Most valuable woods like walnut or mahogany are much heavier than the plywood or composite board a veneer usually covers.

20. All the parts of the sheath dress are made of silk. Thus the sheath dress is made of silk.

Part B. Burden of Proof

Write an analysis of each of the following dialectics or partial dialectics. State the issue as a question that can be answered yes or no. Establish where the primary burden of proof lies and explain why it lies there. Identify and explain any failure to assume the primary burden of proof, or any attempt to shift it illegitimately. Identify and explain those cases where the primary burden of proof is assumed. In those cases where there is a respondent, explain whether the secondary burden of proof has been assumed and discharged. Identify and explain any legitimate shift in the secondary burden of proof. Identify and explain any case where a secondary burden of proof arises because a respondent advances a positive thesis, and explain whether this burden is discharged. Identify and explain any case of a burden of proof arising because a thesis challenges accepted beliefs, and explain whether this burden is discharged. Identify any fallacy of appealing to ignorance.

1. The question is raised whether capital punishment should be retained. My stand is that we should keep it. Opponents argue that capital punishment does not deter criminals. This cannot be. It stands to reason that a person will be deterred more by threat of loss of life than by threat of loss of freedom. It is always possible for you to get your freedom back, but no one gets their life back. Some argue that it is morally wrong or even savage for society to put criminals to death. But it isn't nearly as savage as allowing potential killers to prey on innocent victims secure in the knowledge that they will never have to forfeit their lives for their crimes. Still others object that we might mistakenly execute an innocent person. This is indeed a horrifying possibility, but has almost never occurred.

2. "Sandy, in my view T. R. Pearson's *Off for the Sweet Hereafter* is a better novel than his *A Short History of a Small Place.* In both, Pearson obviously delights in the sheer joy of story-telling. But Benton Lynch and Jane Elizabeth Firesheets are more rounded, more fully developed, and more

interesting characters than any in *Small Place*."

"They are both good and entertaining but quite different novels, George, and I dispute that *Sweet Hereafter* is clearly the better. Benton and Jane Elizabeth are more developed because the author devotes so much space to them and we learn of their motives and characters from their acts and conversations. But they are certainly not more interesting than Miss Pettigrew. On the other side, it takes a long time for *Sweet Hereafter* to get its story going, and it is excessively wordy in places."

3. "The constitution of the League of Concerned Citizens, adopted June 6, 1966, permits us to organize boycotts against firms we find crassly insensitive to environmental concerns. Each prospective member is given a copy of this document, which also gives the reasons for the positions taken, and specifically assents to and accepts them on becoming a member. Yet Mr. Legrand, as a new and quite welcome member, you want this specific policy changed. Why?"

   "It's just a bad policy. It never should have been adopted. It's just harmful all around. It would never be adopted by right thinking people. In fact, it's a surprisingly stupid policy for this organization to have. I want it changed because it badly needs changing."

4. "My position is that censorship is justified on many more occasions than some of my fellow Americans would accept. Smut peddlers, for instance, should not be protected by the First Amendment. They poison the veins of the body of society with the filth they purvey. If it were up to me, I'd clap them all in chains."

   "Your position on censorship is far too broad for me to accept. If your contention were sound, then nations that allow freedom of expression in sexual matters would be ailing or near collapse. Denmark, Sweden, and the U.S. are among those nations with the greatest freedom of expression, and they are also among the healthiest and most prosperous in the world. Moreover, censoring a movie or book in the U.S. has often had the unintended effect of calling the public's attention to some inferior work that otherwise would have gone mostly unnoticed."

5. "Now is the opportune time for us to address the question of serious cuts in the defense budget. The Russians are less of a military threat than at any time in recent decades. They are trying desperately to get a market economy functioning in their land rather than to challenge us militarily at various spots on the globe. So the amount we invest in exotic weaponry like Star Wars and the Stealth bomber to counter their first-strike capability can be much reduced to reflect the decreasing likelihood of such a first strike. We can also cut army personnel considerably now that it is no longer necessary to station 300,000 troops in West Europe. The Russians are already pulling their troops out of East

Europe. As the factors making it advisable for us to station troops in West Europe change, so should our policy."

"On the contrary, the Russians are nearly as much of a threat as they ever have been. The fragmentation of the nation and attempt to establish a free market economy are creating widespread economic hardship. Right wing forces are waiting to re-establish a centralized despotism."

6. "When you narrow your view to Arthur Miller's best drama, his most satisfying tragic hero is John Proctor in *The Crucible*. He does succumb to the temptation of adultery with Abigail Williams, but he struggles and masters that passion. He sees right through the nonsense of the witchcraft accusations while also recognizing their danger. So much does he love life that he is sorely tempted to sign the bogus confession to save himself from the hangman's noose. But finally he decides that life is not worth signing your name to a lie."

   "You make a strong case indeed for Proctor. But by the very same criterion you cite, the strength of the temptation to do evil and the power needed to resist it, Willy Loman in *Death of a Salesman* counts as a more satisfying tragic hero. He is seduced by a false vision of success in money terms and he cheats on his wife Linda. He influences his older son Biff to become an ineffectual drifter, and the younger Happy to become a mindless skirt-chaser. Willy sacrifices his life so that his family will get the insurance money, wealth being the supreme good from the vantage point of his limited vision of the world."

4. Paraphrase

What is paraphrase? To paraphrase a statement is to put it into other words. Frequently when we encounter an obscure statement we paraphrase it in an attempt to make it clear. Since getting clear about meaning is an important critical thinking goal, paraphrasing in order to clarify meaning is a valuable critical thinking technique. Brevity is another important goal of some paraphrase. Usually when we summarize a longer piece of discourse we use paraphrase. Paraphrasing to summarize serves another critical thinking goal of helping us get a view of the whole.

Stuart Chase relates the following case of language so obscure it deserves to be called gobbledygook.

> A New York plumber wrote the Bureau [of Standards in Washington] that he had found hydrochloric acid fine for cleaning drains, and was it harmless?

> Washington replied: "The efficacy of hydrochloric acid is indisputable, but the chlorine residue is incompatible with metallic permanence."
> The plumber wrote back that he was mighty glad the Bureau agreed with him. The Bureau replied with a note of alarm: "We cannot assume responsibility for the production of toxic and noxious residues with hydrochloric acid, and suggest that you use an alternate procedure." The plumber was happy to learn that the Bureau still agreed with him.
> Whereupon Washington exploded: "Don't use hydrochloric acid; it eats hell out of the pipes!"

Clarity and brevity are by no means the only goals of paraphrase. You can paraphrase for any number of reasons. Suppose for example the following statement seems to us too prosaic.

> Life flows on everywhere the same.

We might prefer the following more poetic and colorful paraphrase.

> The force that through the green fuse drives the flower
> Drives my green age;

Clarity and affording a view of the whole just happen to be the most important critical thinking goals paraphrase can serve, which is why we concentrate on them here.

Not all obscure prose lends itself easily to simplification and clarification. The following example of bureaucratese is a single sentence from a memo of the Santa Clara County Transportation Agency.

> A final and balancing change order resulting from monetary adjustments in bid items as provided for in the Contract Documents under the sections dealing with "measurement and payment" requires a simple majority vote by the Board if the contract amount is not being exceeded or if such adjustments are made pursuant to the supplemental work allowance item of the Contract Documents.

The deputy director who approved the memo explained it thus.

> The Board is being asked to agree to the amount of work done on a project and the appropriate payment.

It is very difficult for the outsider to see this in the original.

There are at least three different ways in which paraphrase can make an obscure text clearer for you.

1. You may find a text difficult that others have little trouble understanding. This is not something to be ashamed of. Part of being a student is having many

things to learn. Some of the most knowledgeable people are students in most areas much of their lives. The purpose of paraphrase in this case is to facilitate your understanding of the text by putting it in your own words. You may clarify the meanings of some of the words with techniques we worked with in Chapter Eight, or read some introductory literature on the topic, or seek advice from someone conversant with the topic. However you acquire it, you must gain some understanding of the text before you can put it in your own words. In this case you will be clarifying a text for yourself that is already clear to many others.

Suppose for example you are skimming your zoology textbook in preparation for a quiz. You encounter these statements.

> The first steps leading toward life on earth happened when simple organic molecules were generated in the earth's reducing atmosphere by the action of lightning, ultraviolet radiation, and perhaps other kinds of available energy. These simple molecules were washed into lakes and oceans where they formed a "primordial soup."

The meaning is clear to you except that you have forgotten what "reducing" means when applied to the earth's atmosphere. You check back and are reminded that a reducing agent contains no oxygen but is rich in hydrogen. So to clarify the passage for yourself you substitute "oxygen-free and hydrogen-rich" for "reducing." You clarified this only for yourself in skimming the text for your exam because those who read the text one page after another remember what "reducing" means when they encounter it.

2. The text that is obscure to you may also be obscure to others because it is technical, or contains difficult words, or is awkwardly written. In this case the goal of paraphrase is to simplify and clarify the text for yourself and others. Some prose uses so many uncommon words that its meaning is quite dense. Our challenge in this case is to clarify the meaning of the prose by paraphrase.

Some of us struggled with the following prose by the American economist Thorstein Veblen when we analyzed it as explanation rather than argument in Chapter Five above.[3]

> The thief or swindler who has gained great wealth by his delinquency has a better chance than the small thief of escaping the rigorous penalty of the law; and some good repute accrues to him from his increased wealth and from his spending the irregularly acquired possessions in a seemly manner. A well-bred expenditure of his booty especially appeals with great effect to persons of a cultivated sense of the proprieties, and goes far to mitigate the sense of moral turpitude with which his dereliction is viewed by them.

---

[3] Exercise 5–3, no. 10, p. 120.

We can divide this text into four statements and attempt to simplify each of them, then rejoin them and decide whether we have captured the gist of the original.

1. The thief or swindler who has gained great wealth by his delinquency has a better chance than the small thief of escaping the rigorous penalty of the law;

We can simplify "who has gained great wealth by his delinquency" by substituting "crimes" for "delinquency," a word that has acquired a more specialized meaning since Veblen wrote, and streamlining the syntax. The result is "whose crimes have made him rich." "has a better chance of escaping the rigorous penalty of the law" can be converted with some loss of nuance to "is more likely to escape punishment." This is how (1) looks with modifications.

1. The thief or swindler whose crimes have made him rich is more likely to escape punishment than the petty thief;

2. and some good repute accrues to him from his increased wealth and from his spending the irregularly acquired possessions in a seemly manner.

We can eliminate the phrase "some good repute accrues to him" and substitute the near equivalent "his reputation improves." The phrase with the gerund "spending" as object of the preposition "from" can be slimmed down considerably. We can substitute "loot" for "irregularly acquired possessions," and "properly" for "in a seemly manner." We can ignore "from his increased wealth" and cast the clause in the form of a conditional statement, thus simplifying while retaining most of the original meaning.

2. if he spends his loot properly, his reputation improves.

3. A well-bred expenditure of his booty especially appeals with great effect to persons of a cultivated sense of the proprieties,

"A well-bred expenditure of his booty" repeats the phrase in (2) that means "spending his loot properly," and "especially appeals with great effect" again repeats "improves his reputation." The phrase "to persons of a cultivated sense of the proprieties" is ironic and difficult to simplify. Probably the best we can do, preserving a hint of the irony, is "to proper, upright citizens." Thus transformed, (3) looks like this.

3. Spending his loot properly improves his reputation among proper, upright citizens.

4. and goes far to mitigate the sense of moral turpitude with which his dereliction is viewed by them.

Getting rid of some seldom used terms, we can substitute "crimes" for "dereliction," and "lessen the condemnation" for "mitigate the sense of moral turpitude." "Their" will serve for "with which . . . is viewed by them." The result is:

4. and lessens their condemnation of his crimes.

When we draw our paraphrases together, this is the result.

> The thief or swindler whose crimes have made him rich is more likely to escape punishment than the petty thief; if he spends his loot properly, his reputation improves. Spending his loot properly improves his reputation among proper, upright citizens, and lessens their condemnation of his crimes.

By eliminating the repetition noted above and making some minor adjustments in syntax, we get this paraphrase of the whole, which we can compare directly with the original.

> The thief or swindler whose crimes have made him rich is more likely to escape punishment than the petty thief. If he spends his loot properly, his reputation improves among proper, upright citizens, and lessens their condemnation of his crimes.

> The thief or swindler who has gained great wealth by his delinquency has a better chance than the small thief of escaping the rigorous penalty of the law; and some good repute accrues to him from his increased wealth and from his spending the irregularly acquired possessions in a seemly manner. A well-bred expenditure of his booty especially appeals with great effect to persons of a cultivated sense of the proprieties, and goes far to mitigate the sense of moral turpitude with which his dereliction is viewed by them.

You may be the judge of the effectiveness of the paraphrase by estimating whether someone who had difficulty understanding the original would be able to get the meaning of the new version, and whether the paraphrase captures the gist of the original. Any paraphrase of a good writer like Veblen will sacrifice something of the original. In this case Veblen's delicacy of expression and nuance of meaning suffers. For example, his phrase "irregularly acquired possessions" for "stolen goods," suggests that "persons of a cultivated sense of the proprieties" or "proper, upright citizens" are so morally obtuse that they welcome a thief in their society so long as he steals large amounts and spends it the way they spend their own money.

There are many cases where paraphrasing a piece of discourse serves both of the above purposes. In part you clarify the original for others, and in part you put the original into your own words. The goal of clarity remains the same. Perplexity over the original has diminished, either for you alone, or for others as well.

3. Paraphrase is also frequently used to produce a shortened or condensed version or a summary of a longer text. If you are asked to summarize the main points of a chapter in a textbook, chances are you will use some paraphrase. This is not necessarily the case. If you choose very carefully and if the text permits, you can give such a summary with direct quotations. But when you do paraphrase, you must have a good understanding of the text in order to paraphrase and condense it well. In this way paraphrasing to condense serves the goal of critical thinking by producing clarity. It enhances comprehension by giving a view of the whole in relation to the parts.

For example, we may condense the Veblen excerpt like this.

> The thief of large amounts is less likely to be punished than the petty because spending his riches intelligently wins the approval of proper, upright citizens.

We have spoken so far of paraphrasing a written text. It is also possible to paraphrase spoken discourse. Most students who take notes on lectures they attend employ some paraphrase. So when you take such notes, unless you capture all the words with shorthand or write down only the exact words of the lecturer, you are using paraphrase.

From the standpoint of critical thinking, the following factors are important in distinguishing good paraphrase from poor.

1. **The paraphrase should be simpler and more intelligible than the original.**
2. **The paraphrase should give the meaning of the original accurately.**
3. **In most cases the paraphrase should be briefer than the original.**
4. **When the paraphrase is of a long and complex piece it should convey a sense of the whole and its relation to the parts.**

5. The Dense Argument

Now we turn to a more specialized use of paraphrase. Up to now we have used it to achieve clarity, brevity, and sometimes an overview of difficult or obscure pieces of discourse. Now we will learn to apply it to argumentative discourse and inferences. Basically there are two types of argument that paraphrase can help us with.

1. The dense argument, an argument in difficult prose whose meaning is tightly packed.
2. The longer argument, an argument of considerable length.

In the case of the longer argument, paraphrase can help us summarize it and get a grip on its structure so that we see the relation of the whole to its parts. We will return to this type of argument in Chapter Fifteen. For now we will focus on the dense argument, where paraphrase can help us clarify the argument by unpacking and simplifying the meaning. This puts us in a much better position to analyze and evaluate the argument.

The example we deal with here has already been identified as argument before we begin with the paraphrase. In other cases, we may have to paraphrase a dense text before we can discover an argument in it. But in the present case our paraphrasing is guided by the knowledge that we are dealing with argument, and this rightly affects the way we go about our work. We want to confirm if possible our initial identification of the conclusion and the supporting statements. The following example will illustrate.

> A struggle for existence inevitably follows from the high rate at which all organic beings tend to increase. Every being, which during its natural lifetime produces several eggs or seeds, must suffer destruction during some period of its life, and during some season or occasional year, otherwise, on the principle of geometrical increase, its numbers would quickly become so inordinately great that no country could support the product. Hence, as more individuals are produced than can possibly survive, there must in every case be a struggle for existence, either one individual with another of the same species, or with the individuals of distinct species, or with the physical conditions of life.

Here as in so many cases of argument in natural language the conclusion is stated first, then repeated at the end. The first statement also refers to part of the evidence supporting this conclusion. We do not need to paraphrase it since it is relatively clear.

We can divide the second statement into two parts because it presents two pieces of evidence. The first part we can simplify somewhat as follows.

> Every being that produces several eggs or seeds must at some time be destroyed.

We can simplify the second part considerably as follows.

> If not, there would soon be too many for any country to provide sustenance for.

The first part of the third statement provides the final piece of evidence that links up directly with the conclusion. It is already stated clearly.

> Since more are produced than can possibly survive,

We can simplify the conclusion for purposes of argument analysis by omitting the details of how the struggle for existence may occur.

> there must be a struggle for existence.

Our paraphrase to this point can be summed up as follows.

> A struggle for existence inevitably follows from the high rate at which all organic beings tend to increase. Every being that produces several eggs or seeds must at some time be destroyed. If not, there would soon be too many for any country to provide sustenance for. Since more are produced than can possibly survive, there must be a struggle for existence.

In diagraming this argument, we can paraphrase further to simplify and exhibit the relation of the evidence to the conclusion. First of all, we will state the conclusion only once, at the end.

①
<Organic life reproduces at a rapid rate.> <Every being that produces
②
several eggs or seeds must at some time be destroyed.> <No country has
③
the substance to support this much organic life.> Since <more is
④ ⑤
produced than can possibly survive,> <a struggle for existence necessarily follows.>

When we mark up the argument and number the statements, we have already established that ⑤ is a conclusion. So ④, introduced by the premise cue "since," is advanced in support of it. The questions we must answer now are:

1. How do the first three statements relate to each other?
2. How do they relate to ④ and ⑤?

First of all, ① appears to provide basic support for other statements. It is based on numerous observations as they are reported earlier. ③ also appears to provide basic support. It is based partly on observations of how much food or nourishment it takes to sustain various animals and plants, as well as of how much food or nourishment a given area produces. It is also based on calculations of how much food or nourishment a given area could produce, and how much food or nourishment would be required to sustain a plant and animal population at various stages of its rapid increase.

At first glance ② seems to be a factual statement like ① and ③, based on observations of death and destruction in plant and animal life. But it is not an observation statement. Because it claims, not that beings *are* destroyed, which would make it an observation statement, but that beings *must be* destroyed. Instead it is an inference from ① and ③. It infers that beings must be destroyed from their rapid rate of reproduction and the supply of nourishment being inadequate to sustain them. Let us now draw up in diagram form the results of our analysis so far.

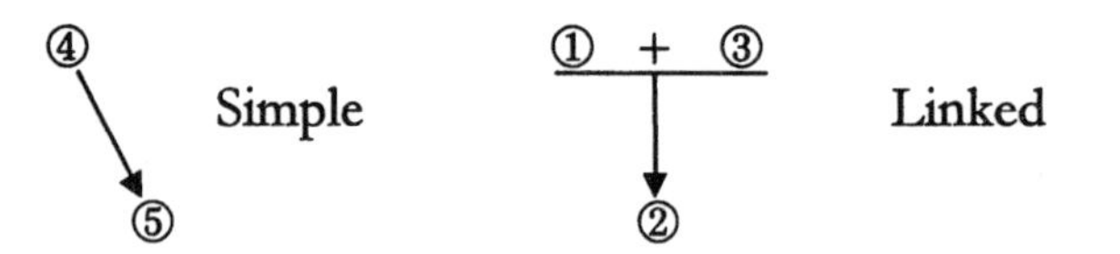

This brings us to our second question: How do these two groups relate to each other? One possibility is that ② supports ④. We can test this as we have learned to test for support relations by inserting an inference cue and combining the statements.

②
[Because] <Every being that produces several eggs or seeds must at
④
some time be destroyed,> <more is produced than can possibly survive.>

This doesn't work, however. Instead of following from ②, ④ just repeats ② in more general, briefer form. We confirm this result when we turn them around and attempt to infer ② from ④. Again we see that the two statements say virtually the same thing with different words.

Now we need to re-number the statements to reflect our discovery that ② and ④ are identical.

① <Organic life reproduces at a rapid rate.> ② <Every being that produces several eggs or seeds must at some time be destroyed.> ③ <No country has the substance to support this much organic life.> Since ② <more is produced than can possibly survive,> ④ <a struggle for existence necessarily follows.>

We are now in a better position to identify the structure of the argument. ② continues to receive support from ① and ③, but now in turn provides support for ④. This yields a compound serial argument.

Does ④ receive adequate support from ①, ②, and ③? This does seem to give the gist of Darwin's argument, but the argument is difficult to evaluate without more reference to the detailed observations supporting the premises. Some comment will be offered on this below.[4] Here we note that the argument with its supporting evidence has been accepted by natural scientists and much of the public. It is disputed mainly by those defending the Biblical account of creation.

There is a difference between paraphrasing argument and paraphrasing expository prose. In the argument we must identify a conclusion and state it carefully. We are not as free to omit material as we simplify, because we cannot omit any evidence or reasons important enough to count as premises of the argument. If we simplified the conclusion to the point that it claimed more, or omitted an important premise, we would be both inaccurately representing the argument and weakening it. Otherwise the goals of paraphrase are the same for both kinds of prose.

---

[4] Chapter Eleven, pp. 327f.

SUMMARY

The burden of proving (offering evidence or reasons in support of) a claim or proposition rests with the person who advances that claim or proposition. In the absence of any reasons or evidence, a thesis cannot count as established. An opponent of the thesis need only point out that it is backed up by no evidence or reasons. The asserter who offers no evidence for his thesis but challenges an opponent to disprove it attempts to illegitimately shift this burden of proof.

A fallacy is an unsound argument masquerading as a sound one. Illegitimately attempting to shift the burden of proof is the fallacy of appeal to ignorance, or *ad ignorantium*, an unacceptable claim that a thesis is established because there is no evidence advanced against it.

In a dialectical exchange, a speaker defends a thesis by offering evidence for it, while a respondent tests it by raising objections to the evidence. A secondary burden arises of advancing the dialectic or discussion. This means that when the speaker has advanced evidence, the respondent is obliged to address it.

The person who challenges widely held beliefs or accepted knowledge also bears the burden of proving them wrong.

The speaker who acknowledges and responds to his duty to produce evidence *assumes* the burden of proof. The speaker who advances substantial evidence for his thesis and defends this evidence from objections *discharges* the burden of proof.

The fallacy of begging the question is a circular argument in which the conclusion of the argument is already assumed to be true in the premises.

One group of fallacies that turn on ambiguous or equivocal use of language is the fallacies of equivocation. It includes the fallacy of composition, fallacious reasoning from part to whole or from member to group. There is also the fallacy of division, fallacious reasoning from whole to part or from a group to its members. In the fallacy of complex question a question is phrased equivocally to elicit, beyond a simple yes or no answer, a significant implication or concession the respondent probably doesn't want to make.

To paraphrase a passage is to put it in other words. For critical thinking we paraphrase to get a shorter and clearer version of the original. Paraphrase can be especially useful for prose that is technical, awkward, or sprinkled with difficult vocabulary. Paraphrase helps in argument analysis when we encounter a dense argument, one in difficult prose whose meaning is tightly packed. Paraphrase unpacks and clarifies this meaning.

Now we will practice to develop our skills of paraphrasing. Then we will put them to use to simplify dense arguments for the purposes of analysis and evaluation.

Study Questions

Section 1: Burden of Proof

1. What is it to substantiate a claim?
2. What is the burden of proof?
3. What is it to assume or shoulder the burden of proof?
4. What is it to discharge the burden of proof?
5. What is the gain for critical thinking in stipulating that the person who advances a claim should assume the burden of proof?
6. What is an illegitimate shift in the burden of proof?
7. What is a fallacy?
8. What is the fallacy ad ignorantiam or appeal to ignorance?
9. What is a dialectic or dialectical exchange?
10. Where does the primary or overall burden of proof lie in a dialectical exchange?
11. What is the secondary burden of proof?
12. Does the secondary burden of proof ever shift legitimately? If so, how?
13. Give two instances.
14. Who should shoulder the burden of proof relative to accepted beliefs?

Section 2: Begging the Question

15. In what sense are many good arguments circular?
16. What is wrong with an argument that is viciously circular?
17. What is the fallacy of begging the question?

Section 3: Fallacies of Equivocation

18. What is a fallacy of equivocation?
19. What is the fallacy of composition?
20. Distinguish its two different types.
21. Is all reasoning from part to whole fallacious?
22. What is the fallacy of division?
23. Distinguish its two different types.
24. Is all reasoning from whole to part fallacious?
25. What is the fallacy of complex question?
26. In what sense is this question complex?
27. Why is it a fallacy?
28. How should we confront a complex question directed to us?

Section 4: Paraphrase

29. What is paraphrase?
30. What are the two most important critical thinking goals paraphrase can serve?
31. State three different ways paraphrase can clarify an obscure text.
32. For what sort of prose can paraphrase be especially useful?
33. What four factors help distinguish good paraphrase?

Section 5: The Dense Argument

34. What is a dense argument?
35. How can paraphrase help with a dense argument?
36. Must we know that a difficult text is argument before we begin with paraphrase?
37. What do we do differently in paraphrasing *argumen*?

EXERCISE 10—2: PARAPHRASING FOR CLARITY

Part A. Paraphrasing Texts for Clarity and Brevity

Clarity: Paraphrase each of the following passages. Try to simplify any difficult vocabulary or grammar so that the meaning is clear for a high school senior. Your paraphrase should be no longer than the original—shorter is desirable. Check your paraphrase carefully for faithfulness to the original.

Brevity: Summarize each passage in one sentence.

Your instructor may want you to work on this project in groups of two to four. Each group has a primary responsibility for one or more of the passages. Each member produces a draft of a paraphrase, the drafts are exchanged with the other members who comment on them, then the group decides on its best paraphrase to present to the class. The group may present two versions, giving the class the pros and cons of each. The class then critiques the paraphrase and attempts to improve it.

1. Puritanism may be described empirically as that point of view, that code of values, carried to New England by the first settlers. These were English Protestants, and in their fundamental convictions were at one with the Protestants, or at least with the Calvinistic Protestants, of all Europe. But the peculiar isolation of the New England colonies—the homogeneous people, the sparse soil, the climate, the economic struggle—quickly made these Protestants a peculiar people. Because their societies were tightly organized, and above all because they were a highly articulate people, the New Englanders established Puritanism—for better or for worse—as one of the continuous factors in American life and thought. It has played so dominant a role because descendants of the Puritans have carried traits of the Puritan mind into a variety of pursuits and all the way across the continent. Many of these qualities have persisted even though the original creed is lost. Without some understanding of Puritanism, and that at its source, there is no understanding of America.

   Perry Miller, ed., *The American Puritans* (Garden City 1956), p. ix.

2. Wealth is not without its advantages and the case to the contrary, although it has often been made, has never proved widely persuasive. But, beyond doubt, wealth is the relentless enemy of the understanding. The poor man has always a precise view of his problem and its remedy: he hasn't enough and he needs more. The rich man can assume or imagine a much greater variety of ills and he will be correspondingly less certain of their remedy. Also, until he learns to live with his wealth, he will have a well-observed tendency to put it to the wrong purposes or otherwise to make himself foolish.

   As with individuals so with nations. And the experience of nations with well-being is exceedingly brief. Nearly all throughout all history have been very poor. The exception, almost insignificant in the whole span of human existence, has been the last few generations in the comparatively small corner of the world populated by Europeans. Here, and especially in the United States, there has been great and quite unprecedented affluence. But the ideas by which the people of this favored part of the world interpret their existence, and in measure guide their behavior, were not forged in a world of wealth. These ideas were the product of a world in which poverty had always been man's normal lot, and any other state was in degree unimaginable.

   J. K.Galbraith, *The Affluent Society* (Harmondsworth 1958), p. 13.

3. Co-payment Amount. This means the percentage of a Reasonable Charge or an Allowable Charge which you must pay for a Covered Service. Some services in your Schedules of Benefits are listed as paid at less than 100%. Your Co-payment Amount for a service which is listed as paid at less than 100% of the Reasonable Charge is the difference between 100% of the Reasonable Charge and the percentage listed. Your co-payment Amount for a service which is listed as paid at less than 100% of the Allowable Charge is the difference between 100% of the Allowable Charge and the percentage listed. In some cases, you will be required to pay amounts in excess of 100% of the Plan's Reasonable Charge or Allowable Charge. These amounts are not part of your Co-payment Amount. The following example will explain. Your Major Medical Service coverage pays 80% of the Allowable Charge for a Major Medical Service. Your Co-payment Amount is the other 20% of the Allowable Charge for that service. Facilities and health care professionals that do not "participate" or "contract" with the Plan may bill you for more than 100% of the Allowable Charge. Your Co-payment Amounts for Major Medical Services do not include the amounts these facilities or professionals may charge in excess of 100% of the Allowable Charge.

   "Commonwealth of Virginia Health Care Benefits"
   (Blue Cross & Blue Shield of Virginia, July 1, 1986), p. 10f.

4. (Transcendental philosophy stressed spiritual over material values.)
   New England furnished the only plot of ground on the planet where the transcendental philosophy had a chance to show what it was and what it proposed. The forms of life there were, in a measure, plastic. There were no immovable prejudices, no fixed and unalterable traditions. Laws and usages were fluent, malleable at all events. The sentiment of individual freedom was active; the truth was practically acknowledged that it takes all sorts of people to make a world, and the many minds of the many men were respected. No orders of men, no aristocracies of intellect, no privileged classes of thought were established. The old world supplied such literature as there was, in science, law, philosophy, ethics, theology; but an astonishing intellectual activity seized upon it, dealt with it in genuine democratic fashion, classified it, accepted it, dismissed it, paying no undue regard to its foreign reputation. Experiments in thought and life, of even audacious description, were made, not in defiance of precedent—for precedent was hardly respected enough to be defied—but in innocent unconsciousness of precedent. A feeling was abroad that all things must be new in the New World. There was call for immediate application of ideas to life. In the Old World, thoughts remained cloistered a generation before any questioned their bearing on public or private affairs. In the New World, the thinker was called on to justify himself on the spot by building an engine, and setting something in motion. The test of a truth was its availability. The popular faith in the capacities of men to make states, laws, religions for themselves, supplied a groundwork for the new philosophy.

   O. B. Frothingham, *Transcendalism in New England* (New York 1959), p. 105f.

5. (Clara Middleton discovers that a suitor she does not favor has gained her father's good will.)
   She was in a fever, lying like a stone, with her brain burning. Quick natures run out to calamity in any little shadow of it flung out before. Terrors of apprehension drive them. They stop not short of the uttermost when they are on the wings of dread. A frown means tempest, a wind wreck; to see fire is to be seized by it. When it is the approach of their loathing that they fear, they are in the tragedy of the embrace at a breath; and then is the wrestle between themselves and horror; between themselves and evil, which promises aid; themselves and weakness, which calls on evil; themselves and the better part of them, which whispers no beguilement.

   George Meredith, The *Egoist* (Moscow 1962), p. 239.

6. (The war referred to is the Second World War.)
   Whatever fervours, beliefs, and awful necessities the war created in other parts of the world, it was characterized in ours, right from the

start, by double-feeling. It was immediately evident that for us war was going to be a very fine thing. This wasn't a complicated thing that needed to be explained by experts. Material prosperity hit Central and South Africa tangibly; there was suddenly a great deal more money for everyone, and this was true even of the Africans, even in an economy designed to see that they had the minimum necessary to keep them alive and working. Nor were there any serious shortages of commodities to buy with the money. Not serious enough at least to interfere with the enjoyment of life. . . .

There was another reason for cynicism—because people began to be cynical, when they were tired of being ashamed, as they were, to start with. This war was presented to us as a crusade against the evil doctrines of Hitler, against racialism, etc., yet the whole of that enormous land-mass, about half the total area of Africa, was conducted on precisely Hitler's assumption—that some human beings are better than others because of their race. The mass of the Africans up and down the continent were sardonically amused at the sight of their white masters crusading off to fight the racialist devil—those Africans with any education at all. They enjoyed the sight of the white baases so eager to go off and fight on any available battle-front against a creed they would all die to defend on their own soil. Right through the war, the correspondence columns of the paper were crammed with arguments about whether it was safe to put so much as a pop-gun into the hands of any African soldier since he was likely to turn it against his white masters, or to use this useful knowledge later. It was decided, quite rightly, that it was not safe.

Doris Lessing, *The Golden Notebook* (Toronto 1981), p. 64f.

7. Finance Charge. Cash Advances. The Finance Charge for cash advances begins on the date the transaction is posted to your Account. Whenever you get a cash advance, you agree to pay a Finance Charge consisting of a one-time service charge equal to 2% of the cash advance. In addition, we also figure a Finance Charge on cash advances by applying a monthly periodic rate to the "highest daily balance" of cash advances (including current transactions). To get the "highest daily balance," we take the beginning balance of cash advances each day, add any new cash advances and unpaid Finance Charge on cash advances, and subtract any payments or credits applied to cash advances or applied to Finance Charge on cash advances. This gives us the daily balance. We then figure the highest daily balance for the Billing Period. We multiply this number by a monthly periodic rate of 1% (12% Annual Percentage Rate).

Bank of Virginia *MasterCard / Charge Plan Customer Agreement and Truth in Lending Disclosure.*

8. (The Tarasoffs sued psychologists when their daughter was not warned that a patient intended to kill her. The patient did in fact murder her.)

   We recognize the difficulty that a therapist encounters in attempting to forecast whether a patient presents a serious danger of violence. . .

   In the instant case, however, the pleadings do not raise any question as to failure of defendant therapists to predict that Poddar presented a serious danger of violence. On the contrary, the present complaints allege that defendant therapists did in fact predict that Poddar would kill, but were negligent in failing to warn.

   Amicus[5] contends, however, that even when a therapist does in fact predict that a patient poses a serious danger of violence to others, the therapist should be absolved of any responsibility for failing to act to protect the potential victim. In our view, however, once a therapist does in fact determine, or under applicable professional standards reasonably should have determined, that a patient poses a serious danger of violence to others, he bears a duty to exercise reasonable care to protect the foreseeable victim of that danger. While the discharge of this duty of due care will necessarily vary with the facts, in each instance the adequacy of the therapist's conduct must be measured against the traditional negligence standard of the rendition of reasonable care under the circumstances.

   Tarasoff v Regents, quoted in J. Arras & N. Rhoden, *Ethical Issues in Modern Medicine*, 3rd ed. (Mountain View 1989), p. 119f.

9. Even though other methods of acquiring equipment may cost less than leasing (cash purchases without financing costs least) they represent money savings on the financing of the purchase only. Loss of opportunity to make a profit on the additional capital that leasing avails may offset the savings of purchase. This is particularly true when the firm is making a good-to-excellent return on its investment. For instance, a company with an investment of $200,000 averaging annual sales of $1,000,000 with a net profit of 5 percent ($50,000) is earning 25% each year on its investment. If growth of this type of company merely requires the use of more capital, any money freed by leasing instead of purchasing, theoretically, could return 25% per annum to the company.

   The money freed by leasing instead of purchasing usually represents the difference in the down payment that a firm would make if they were financing, and the rental deposits that would be required for leasing. Down payments are characteristically more than deposits; therefore, for the firm mentioned above with a 25 percent return on investment, its return would represent 25 percent of the difference between

[5] Amicus (friend of the court) is a third party submitting information or arguments relevant to the case.

the cost of the down payment and the cost of the lease deposits.

C. R. Baker & R. S. Hayes, *Accounting, Finance, and Taxation* (Boston 1980), p. 282.

*10. In the course of the preceding papers I have endeavored, my fellow citizens, to place before you in a clear and convincing light the importance of Union to your political safety and happiness. I have unfolded to you a complication of dangers to which you would be exposed, should you permit that sacred knot which binds the people of America together to be severed or dissolved by ambition or by avarice, by jealousy or by misrepresentation. In the sequel of the inquiry through which I propose to accompany you, the truths intended to be inculcated will receive further complication from facts and arguments hitherto unnoticed. If the road over which you will still have to pass should in some places appear to you tedious or irksome, you will recollect that you are in quest of information on a subject the most momentous which can engage the attention of a free people, that the field through which you have to travel is in itself spacious, and that the difficulties of the journey have been unnecessarily increased by the mazes with which sophistry has beset the way. It will be my aim to remove the obstacles to your progress in as compendious a manner as it can be done, without sacrificing utility to dispatch.

John Hamilton, *Federalist Paper* No. 15, ed. by Clinton Rossiter (New York 1961), p. 105.

Part B. Paraphrasing Arguments for Analysis

Analyze and evaluate each of the following arguments, some of which are dense. Use paraphrase to clarify obscurity and to get an overview. You cannot evaluate an argument well if you weaken it by not stating the conclusion accurately, or by omitting important evidence or reasons. So you may not be able to simplify or omit as much as with expository prose. And you may need to aim beyond high school for your target reader.

1. [Sumner takes issue with those who hold that money is the root of all evil.]

   Money, properly speaking, has no more character than axes of stone, bronze, iron, or steel. It only does its own work impersonally and mechanically. The ethical functions and character ascribed to it are entirely false. There can be no such thing as "tainted money." Money bears no taint. It serves the murderer and the saint with equal indifference. It is a tool. It can be used one day for a crime, the next day for the most beneficient purpose. No use leaves any mark on it. The Solomon Islanders are expert merchants and "are fully the equal of white men in cheating." They do it with shell money as whites do it with gold, silver, and banknotes. That is to say, the "money" is indifferent because it has no ethical function at all and absolutely no character.

W. G. Sumner, *Folkways* (New York 1960), p.144f.

2. When the first mathematical, logical, and natural uniformities, the first *laws*, were discovered, men were so carried away by the clearness, beauty and simplification that resulted, that they believed themselves to have deciphered authentically the eternal thoughts of the Almighty. . . . He thought the archetypes of all things, and devised their variations; and when we rediscover any one of these his wondrous institutions, we seize his mind in its very literal intention.

   But as the sciences have developed further, the notion has gained ground that most, perhaps all, of our laws are only approximations. The laws themselves, moreover, have grown so numerous that there is no counting them; and so many rival formulations are proposed in all the branches of science that investigators have become accustomed to the notion that no theory is absolutely a transcript of reality, but that any one of them may from some point of view be useful. Their great use is to summarize old facts and to lead to new ones. They are only a man-made language, a conceptual shorthand, as someone calls them, in which we write our reports of nature; and languages, as is well known, tolerate much choice of expression and many dialects.

   Thus human arbitrariness has driven divine necessity from scientific logic.

   William James, "What Pragmatism Means," *The Writings of William James*, ed. and introd. by John J. McDermott(New York *1967*), p. 381.

3. Labor cannot exert itself without land. No labor-saving inventions can enable us to make something out of nothing, or in any wise lessen our dependence upon land. They can merely add to the efficiency of labor in working up the raw materials drawn from land. Therefore, wherever land has been subjected to private ownership, the ultimate effect of labor-saving inventions, and of all improved processes and discoveries, is to enable landowners to demand, and labor to pay, more for the use of land. Land becomes more valuable, but the wages of labor do not increase; on the contrary, if there is any margin for possible reductions, they may be absolutely reduced.

   Henry George, *Social Problems*, quoted in Perry Miller, ed., *American Thought* (New York 1954), p. 65f.

4. If Cezanne is among the last major 19th-century artists to be "revised," this lag is probably due to the special place that he holds in relation to 20th-century modernism as well as to the inherent difficulty of his work—especially the complex relationships between form and subject matter, which make easy sociological readings of his paintings difficult.

In fact, given the complexity of the relationship between form and subject in Cezanne's work, one would expect that a new kind of methodology might have to be devised for dealing with it.

Jack Flam, "Early Cezanne" (review of books on Cezanne by S. Geist and M. Tompkins), *Art in America* (Nov. 1989), p. 47.

*5. Only communism renders the state absolutely unnecessary, for there is *nobody* to be suppressed—"nobody"—in the sense of a *class,* in the sense of a systematic struggle against a definite section of the population. We are not utopians, and do not in the least deny the possibility and inevitability of excesses on the part of individual persons, or the need to suppress such excesses. In the first place, however, no special machine, no special apparatus of repression is needed for this; this will be done by the armed people themselves, as simply and as readily as any crowd of civilised people, even in modern society, interferes to put a stop to a scuffle or to prevent a woman from being assaulted. And secondly, we know that the fundamental social cause of excesses, which consist in the violation of the rules of social intercourse, is the exploitation of the people, their want and their poverty. With the removal of this chief cause, excesses will inevitably begin to "*wither away.*" We do not know how quickly and in what succession, but we do know they will wither away. With their withering away, the state will also *wither away.*

V. I. Lenin, *The State and Revolution,* in *Selected Works in Three Volumes,* Vol. 2 (Moscow/New York 1967), p. 336.

6. But to tear down a factory or to revolt against a government or to avoid repair of a motorcycle because it is a system is to attack effects rather than causes; and as long as the attack is upon effects only, no change is possible. The true system, the real system, is our present construction of systematic thought itself, rationality itself, and if a factory is torn down but the rationality which produced it is left standing, then that rationality will simply produce another factory. If a revolution destroys a systematic government, but the systematic patterns of thought that produced that government are left intact, then those patterns will repeat themselves in the succeeding government. There's so much talk about the system. And so little understanding.

Robert M. Pirsig, *Zen and the Art of Motorcycle Maintenance* (Toronto 1974), p. 88.

7. (The theory of dependency traces the social ills of Latin America to its countries being exporters of raw materials exploited by wealthy capitalist nations, specially the U.S.)

There are serious factual problems with the theory of dependency, whence socialism in Latin America seeks to derive its legitimacy. First, countries such as Canada and the U.S. have become far larger exporters of raw materials—grain, lumber, coal, etc.—than all of Latin America put together. As John Galbraith puts it, "If to be part of the Third World is to be a hewer of wood and a supplier of food and natural produce, the United States and Canada are, by a wide margin, the first of the Third World countries."

Second, other regions of the world, specifically on the East Asia rim, are far poorer in natural resources than Latin America, and yet have in recent years been far more successful in conducting land reform, building highly intelligent and dynamic free economies, overcoming poverty worse in 1945 than that of Latin America today, providing literacy and opportunity to rapidly growing (and more densely crowded) populations, and inspiring industriousness, ambition, and drive among their peoples. Dependency theory ill explains why Latin America is poor; poverty existed long before capitalism was a blight in Adam Smith's eye. Even more inadequately does it explain why Latin America has done so much worse with its own vast resources than such stellar performers as Japan, South Korea, Taiwan, Singapore, Hong Kong, and others have done with infinitely less.

Michael Novak, *Will It Liberate? Questions About Liberation Theology.* ©1986 Michael Novak (Lanham, MD: University Press of America), p. 25f.

8. (Mills argues against the view that being self-made confers special merit on members of America's managerial elite.)

More important than the proportions of the sons of wage workers among these higher circles is the criteria of admission to them, and the question of who applies these criteria. We cannot from upward mobility infer higher merit. Even if the rough figures that now generally hold were reversed, and 90 per cent of the elite were sons of wage workers—but the criteria of co-optation by the elite remained what they are now—we could not from that mobility necessarily infer merit. Only if the criteria of the top positions were meritorious, and only if they were self-applied, as in a purely entrepreneurial manner, could we smuggle merit into such statistics—from any statistics—of mobility. The idea that the self-made man is somehow "good" and that the family-made man is not good makes moral sense only when the career is independent, when one is on one's own as an entrepreneur. It would also make sense in a strict bureaucracy where examinations control advancement. It makes little sense in the system of corporate co-optation.

C. Wright Mills, *The Power Elite* (New York 1959), p. 348f.

9. (Mannheim describes two shifts in our understanding of mind or consciousness. The first in the late eighteenth century is from the mind as mirror of external reality to consciousness as determining the form in which the world appears to us. The second in the early nineteenth century is from this abstract consciousness to the mind as the spirit of a people influenced by historical factors like the rise of national states.)

Two consequences flow from this conception of consciousness: first we clearly perceive that human affairs cannot be understood by an isolation of their elements. Every fact and event in a historical period is only explicable in terms of meaning, and meaning in its turn always refers to another meaning. Thus the conception of the unity and interdependence of meaning in a period always underlies the interpretation of that period. Secondly, this interdependent system of meanings varies both in all its parts and in its totality from one historical period to another. Thus the re-interpretation of that continuous and coherent change in meaning becomes the main concern of our modern historical sciences. Although Hegel has probably done more than anyone else in emphasizing the need for integrating the various elements of meaning in a given historical experience, he proceeded in a speculative manner, while we have arrived at a stage of development where we are able to translate this constructive notion, given us by the philosophers, into empirical research.

Karl Mannheim, *Ideology and Utopia* (London 1966), p. 61.

10. It is self-evident that the definition of tyranny would be entirely empty unless natural rights could somehow be defined. It can be shown, I think, that we must specify a process by which specific natural rights can be defined in the context of some political society. To specify this process creates some dilemmas for the Madisonian.

If a natural right were defined, rather absurdly, to mean the right of every individual to do what he wishes to do, then every form of government must be tyrannical; for every government restrains at least some individuals from doing what they wish to do. For example, in this sense every government tyrannizes over criminals, whether these are defined by our own government or that of the U.S.S.R. A non-tyrannical republic would therefore be impossible. So this meaning of tyranny must be excluded.

It follows that tyranny must be defined to mean that severe penalties are inflicted only on some kinds of behavior.

Robert A. Dahl, *A Preface To Democratic Theory* (Chicago 1956), p. 23.

THE CRITICAL THINKING JOURNAL

Part C. Compound Arguments and Context

9. Dense Arguments

Find in some print medium one dense argument that needs considerable paraphrasing and clarification before it can be fully grasped and assessed. Then diagram, analyze, and evaluate this argument.

Further Reading

C. L. Hamblin, *Fallacies* (Newport News 1998). This may be the best single study of fallacies—a historical and analytical account. Treats begging the question, fallacy of the complex question, composition, division, and the appeal to ignorance.

Nicholas Rescher, *Dialectics* (Albany 1977). Chapter Two has a valuable treatment of the burden of proof.

William L. Rowe, "The Fallacy of Composition," *Mind*, Vol. 71 (1962), pp. 87–92. There are both sound and unsound inferences from part to whole. Some unsound cases are due to ambiguous use of relative terms like "heavy" or "small." But other unsound cases use no relative terms at all.

Douglas N. Walton, *Informal Fallacies* (Amsterdam/Philadelphia 1987). Examines informal fallacies in relation to logical dialogue games. Fallacies treated include the complex question, composition, division, and the appeal to ignorance.

John Woods & Douglas Walton, "Composition and Division," *Studia Logica*, Vol. 36 (1977), pp. 381–406. Distinguishes an earlier version of these fallacies from the current one, which turns on the collective and distributive use of descriptive terms. The fallacy of composition attributes a property that *rightly* belongs to a part *wrongly* to the whole, as when we argue that since the aluminum parts of a jetliner are light, the jetliner itself is also light.

PART FOUR

CONTEXT

CHAPTER ELEVEN

CONTEXT

Ordinary discourse is full of . . . presuppositions: what is explicitly stated in a linguistic utterance is as a rule embedded in a matrix of unformulated knowledge shared by speaker and listener.
Gabriël Nuchelmans

1. THE CONTEXT AND THE ARGUMENT

Many arguments are more readily identified, clarified and evaluated when we have information about the context in which they occur. The context we pursue here reveals the speaker, time, place, and some circumstances of the utterance. For example, let's look at the following statement in two contexts.

I bought them on sale at Macy's for $49.95.

Context I: Fran meets Jennifer at the mall and comments how stylishly she is clad.

"How much did you have to part with for those elegant pumps?"
"I bought them on sale at Macy's for $49.95."

Here Jennifer responds to her friend's request for information by explaining how much the pumps cost. The statement is explanation but does not serve as an argument or as part of one.

Context II: Husband Joe greets Jennifer as she comes in the front door, then comments somewhat warily as he sees her new shoes.

"The new shoes are very nice, but they do look expensive."
"They are $75 pumps."

"But honey, how can you spend that kind of money on shoes when we have to scrimp and save to meet the mortgage note?"

"I bought them on sale at Leggett's for $49.95."

Though Joe phrases his response as a question, the question may imply this argument.

① ②
<You shouldn't buy expensive shoes> because <we badly need money to pay the mortgage note> [and (perhaps) having a roof over our heads is more important than your getting expensive shoes.] [3]

In this context Jennifer's statement functions also as an explanation. But here its further function is to justify her action, and so being explanation as justification it constitutes an argument.

① ②
<I bought them> because <they were on sale at Macy's for $49.95>
[3]
[and this saves us $25.]

② + [3]
↓
①

Linked

Our main interest in this example is that the context decides whether Jennifer's statement functions as an argument (or part of an argument). We would need to know more of the context in order to comment effectively on the merit of her argument. If she needed the elegant pumps for her job where she met the public and was expected to be expensively and well clad, or if she and her husband were Yuppies whose total income and mortgage note made $50 insignificant, her argument would be strong. If $50 was a considerable amount measured with their note and income, or if she bought the pumps on impulse when the money was needed for a higher priority, her argument would be weaker.

There are also cases where the context provides what we need to know to decide what supports what, or to clearly distinguish the support from the conclusion. Such a case came up when we examined the relation of the following two statements.[1]

> Kim Walters missed the meeting yesterday afternoon. It is likely she was ill.

In the absence of premise or conclusion cues, we had to decide which statement was advanced in support of which. We decided this by considering the context and that the speaker was more likely to know of Kim's missing the meeting than her illness.

Arguments differ in the degree to which they are more or less dependent on a context. The ideal of formal logics is an argument that is not at all dependent on a context. Such an argument is self-contained in the sense that if you understand the language in which it is stated and are familiar with the rules governing its particular type, you know all you need to know to evaluate it. Sometimes such arguments are called deductive. Here is an example.

> All Greeks are humans.
> All Athenians are Greeks
> Therefore all Athenians are humans.

Since the premises are obviously true, you can be assured that you have a true conclusion if this argument passes the appropriate test of validity. It does pass the test of formal validity. But it suffers a weakness too common in arguments of formal logic. It establishes a conclusion so obvious no one would ever doubt it, and thus serves no purpose.

Many of the arguments we encounter are dependent on context to a much greater degree than this. Here is an example.

> Beware, for I am fearless, and therefore powerful.

To decide whether this argument is weak or strong we need to know whether the claim advanced as evidence is sound. And to know that we must know enough of the context to know who the utterer of these words is. If the speaker is a small child (perhaps one should add: unarmed), the argument is weak. If it is a large, menacing person, the argument is strong. We will return to this example in the next section.

Here is another case where context can decide whether we confront an inference, and if so, what is the conclusion and what the support.

①　　　　　　　　②
<The parking lot is full.> <Classes are in session.>

---

[1] Above, Chapter Five, p. 115.

These could both be simple statements of observation, made by someone perhaps looking over the campus from a third- or fourth-story window. But in specific contexts they can also constitute an inference.

Context I: It is about mid-January. We are driving along Warwick Boulevard past Christopher Newport University, and we wonder whether classes for the spring semester have started up yet. From Warwick the parking lot is visible, but not the quad or the walkways between the buildings. Out of the above material we construct the following inference.

② ①
<Classes are in session> because <the parking lot is full.>

In this context we have the following inference:

①
↓
② Simple
Strong

Is it a strong inference? To decide this, we need even more knowledge of the context. In particular we need to know in what circumstances other than classes being in session this parking lot could be full. We also need to know how likely such an event would be in mid-January. At Christopher Newport there are no such circumstances, so we have a strong inference.

Context II: We have to deliver bulky packages to an office in a lecture hall at Christopher Newport. We would like to know whether we can park close enough to the lecture hall to hand-carry the packages, or whether we have to wait until the other delivery truck returns from its run so we can take the dolly along with us. On the basis of our knowledge of the university calendar, we construct the following inference.

① ②
<The parking lot is full> because <classes are in session.>

We may want to add the final conclusion to this.

① ②
<The parking lot is full> because <classes are in session.>
[3]
[So we must wait for the other truck to return.]

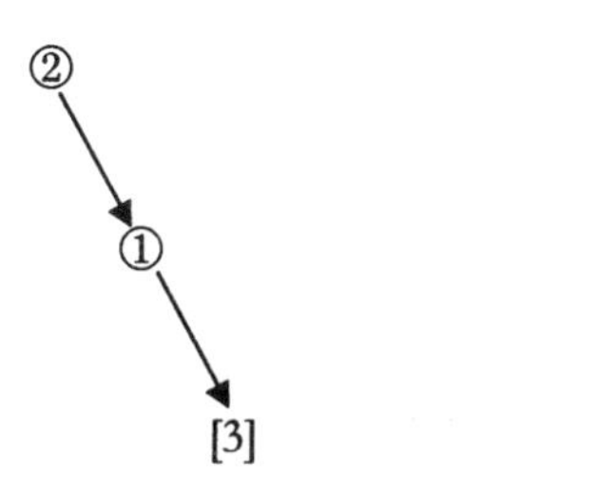

Serial
Strong

In this inference the direction of support is the exact opposite. So the context decides what is advanced in support of what. Is the inference strong or weak? Again knowledge helps. We know from past experience that when classes are in session, the parking lot is full at the time we want to make our delivery. And we know that classes are in session now. So it is a strong inference.

Knowledge of context can be as helpful for evaluating an argument as it is for identifying it, or for clarifying the support relations and the meaning. We examined the following argument[2] and found it to be convergent and strong.

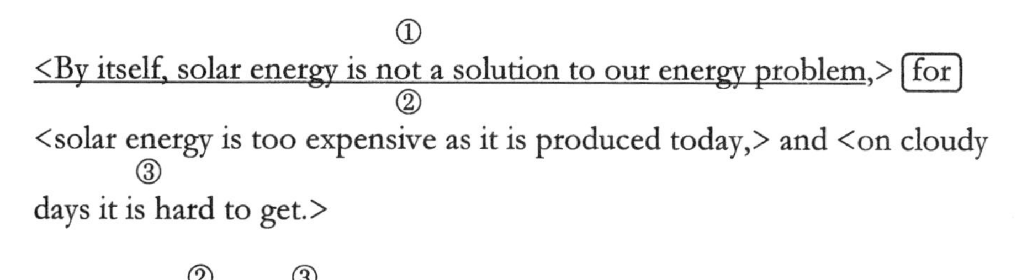
① <By itself, solar energy is not a solution to our energy problem,> [for] ② <solar energy is too expensive as it is produced today,> and ③ <on cloudy days it is hard to get.>

② ③ → ①

Convergent

In a specific context this argument could be considerably weaker. For example, suppose we are considering it in the Southwest, where the climate is dry and sunny. Here ③ would carry little weight because there would be so few cloudy days. Also in such a dry climate there may be little or no hydroelectric power, which is the least expensive method of generating energy. If we calculated in the environmental cost of burning fossil fuel and releasing hydrocarbons and sulphates into the atmosphere (acid rain), the cost differential could grow appreciably smaller.

Here's another argument which knowledge of context helps us evaluate.

① <We should eat heartily.> ② <It will be a long time before we enjoy another repast such as this.>

---

[2] Above Chapter Six, p. 135.

②
↓
①

Simple

If this is spoken, perhaps with irony, at a banquet table where even as she speaks the wealthy dowager is pondering what she will wear to tomorrow's feast, the argument is weak. On the other hand if it is spoken by backpackers at their last meal before a four-day trek where they will subsist on food from their packs, it's a strong argument.

Knowledge of the context of an argument, which amounts to knowledge of the situation in which it occurs, can be important in several different ways. Here are some important ways illustrated by the above examples.

1. It can help us decide whether what we confront is an argument or not. (Jennifer's pumps, parking lot)
2. It can help us decide what is the conclusion and what the support. (Kim Walters' meeting, parking lot)
3. It can help us get the meaning of the argument clearer. This is illustrated by all of the above arguments. It can be seen clearly in the terse arguments we are now turning to.
4. It can help us decide whether the argument is strong or weak. (solar energy, eating heartily)

How do we get enough knowledge of the context to make these decisions? In many cases we can draw on our general knowledge and its implications. In some cases we will have to dig the information we need out of literary or personal sources. In the classroom, the teacher can supply us with what we need to know about context.

2. Terse Arguments

A terse argument is a brief argument which leaves one or more important factors assumed but unstated. Our challenge in analyzing the terse argument is to fill in the missing places until we clearly understand and can then evaluate the argument. Terse arguments differ from dense arguments. In dense arguments the meaning is so tightly packed we must unravel it. Quite frequently we must clarify it with paraphrase. Dense arguments can be lengthy as well as brief, and they may not have open spaces to fill in, as terse arguments always do. Though density and terseness are distinct features of arguments, one argument may be both dense and terse. The dense part may need simplifying in paraphrase while the terse part needs elaborating.

Many terse arguments are one of the basic types rather than compound. An argument isn't compound unless it contains two or more arguments of basic types. Again, however, one or more parts or sub-arguments of a compound argument may themselves be terse arguments. Often the terse argument seems somehow incomplete, and must be fleshed out with material in order to constitute a complete argument. We do this fleshing out or filling in along with our process of analysis and evaluation. Some arguments are terse in that a single word represents an entire statement that may itself be a premise or a conclusion of an argument.

The argument we glanced at above[3] is just such a case. We can now examine it more closely.

> Beware, for I am fearless, and therefore powerful.

Is there an argument here? If so, what is it? What we notice first is that the speaker's fearlessness is being advanced to support the claim that he is powerful. The conclusion cue "therefore" helps us spot this. So initially we can mark off the statement like this.

<Beware, for I am fearless> and [therefore] <powerful.>

As we have already learned, when we analyze the structure of an argument we identify its parts as separate statements—they are either complete sentences or independent clauses. For a conclusion to an argument in the present case, however, we have only the single word "powerful." So we supply it with what is necessary to make it an independent clause. Then we can number the statements and show their relation.

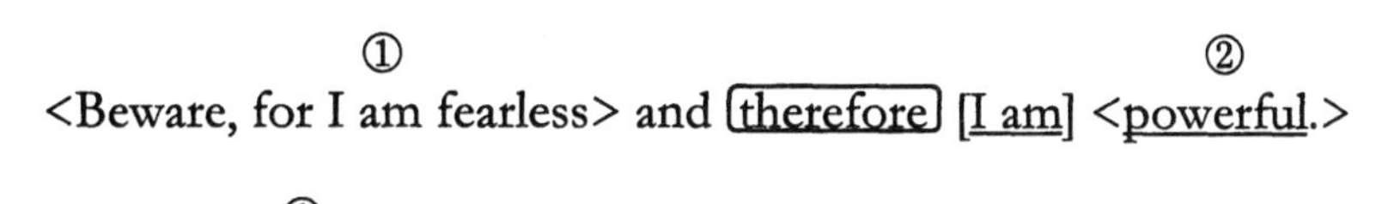
①
②
<Beware, for I am fearless> and therefore [I am] <powerful.>

① → ②   Simple

Our analysis is good as far as it goes, but does it go far enough? There appears to be more to the argumentative content of the statement. We have not yet taken account of the initial admonition "Beware" nor of the premise cue "for." How if at all do they fit into the argument? The admonition that we should beware is supported by the claim to be powerful. So we need to re-

[3] Page 309.

number to include "Beware" while at the same time we make its implied subject explicit. Then we can display the support relations among the three statements.

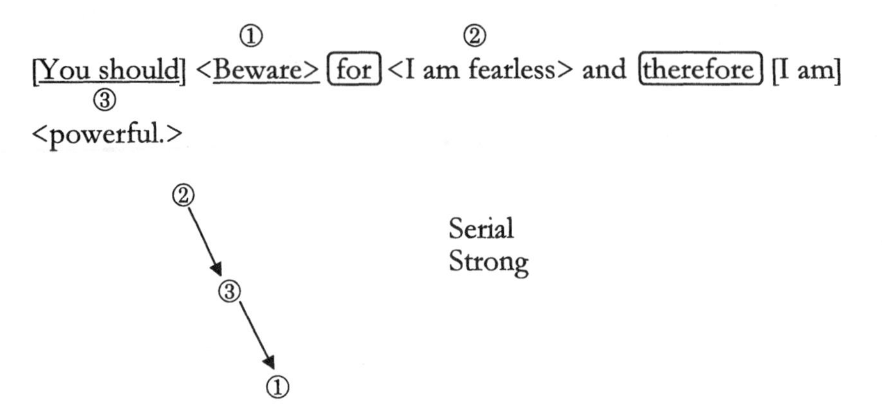

Is this a strong argument? Should one really beware? This depends on who the speaker is and the circumstances in which the statement is uttered. In the gothic horror tale by Mary Shelly, the words are spoken by the science-fiction creature to Dr. Frankenstein, who stitched him together from parts of dead bodies and brought him to life. We know of the creature's gigantic size, supernatural strength, bitterness at being rejected by humans, and fury at Dr. Frankenstein's aborting the project that was to provide him a bride as companion. In this context (adopting the conventions of the novel) Dr. Frankenstein should heed the creature's threat. So it is a strong argument. However, spoken by someone else in a different context, it could easily be a weak argument.

Complexities of a different kind occur in the following example, which needs clarification in more than one way.

> I watch laundromat washers the way other people watch television. It's soothing because you always know what to expect and you don't have to think about it.

First we mark up the argument guided by the premise cue "because." We note that it is not the first sentence that receives direct support from the two clauses following the "because." Instead it is the initial independent clause of the statement, "It's soothing." To clarify this we make its subject explicit.

①
<I watch laundromat washers the way other people watch television.>
②
[Watching laundromat washers is] <~~It's~~ soothing,> because <you
③ ④
always know what to expect> and <you don't have to think about it.>

The first question we must deal with here is the nature of the support that ③ and ④ provide for ②. Is it convergent in that each provides a measure of separate support? Or is it linked, meaning that ③ and ④ must be taken together for any chance of strong support? The two seem related but separate, so we show the support as convergent.

Another question we must address is whether the argument as we have interpreted and diagramed it captures everything of importance in the argumentative intent of the case. In other words, is it possible that the speaker offers the soothing quality of the experience as an explanation qua justification for his claim that he watches washers the way others watch TV? It seems quite likely. When we incorporate this into our diagram we get the following result.

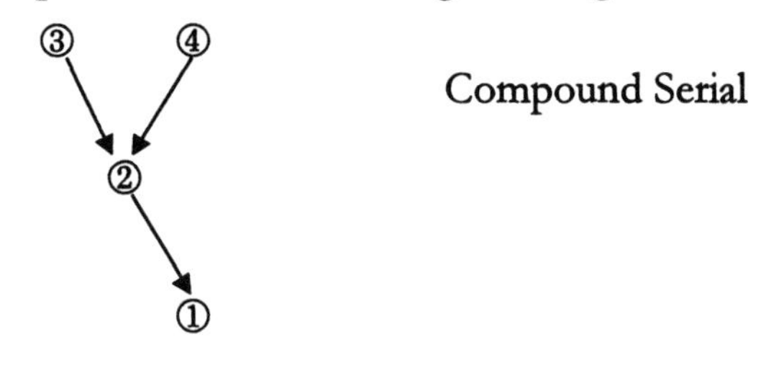

Now when we come to consider the strength of the argument, even more clarification is needed. It could well be the case that the most important aspect of the speaker's claim is not even stated outright. In so far as he is attempting to establish something of general interest, it is not that he watches laundromat washers because it's soothing. This would be an explanation for a bit of idiosyncratic behavior, and the natural response to it would be: "Fine and good—to each his own pleasure." The most important but unstated part of his claim is that people watch TV because it is soothing. We might want to flesh this out a bit and call it mindless and soothing, because this is the sense of "soothing" supported specially by premise ④. We must now make this explicit and so supply the unstated conclusion.

①
<I watch laundromat washers the way other people watch television.>

②
[Watching laundromat washers is] <~~It's~~ soothing,> because <you
③ ④
always know what to expect> and <you don't have to think about it.>

[5]
[People watch television because it's mindless and soothing.]

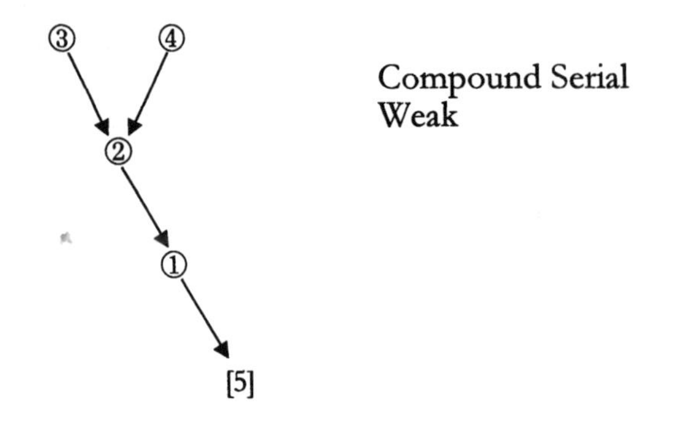

What are we to say of the strength of this argument? On balance probably that it is relatively weak. It is a clever and indirect way of suggesting the conclusion and so ironically claiming that TV is mindless. But its claim is very broad. If the conclusion claimed "Some people" the argument would be stronger. Also both premises ③ and ④ are stated too broadly to be literally true. Much TV programming may warrant that description, but not all. There are good dramatic productions where you do not know what to expect, for instance, and there are documentaries, specials, and news analyses like *The Lehrer Report* that provoke viewers to thought. So on balance, a weak argument.

3. Arguments with Unstated Conclusions

When we learned earlier to identify arguments we found help partly in the contrast with other uses of discourse and partly in the structural feature of locating a conclusion in support of which evidence or reasons were being advanced. It is sometimes the case, however, that the material advanced is of such subtlety that the conclusion is implied rather than stated outright. Rather than simply say that because we find no conclusion, we have no argument, it is preferable to analyze such cases as arguments with unstated conclusions. Often we can tell in such a case when we supply a conclusion that we are indeed confronting an argument.

We frequently find such arguments with unstated conclusions in print and electronic media advertising. In fact, few advertisers in the present age come right out and baldly urge us to buy their products. Special sales by retailers, for example automobiles or consumer electronic products, are the exception. More often the ad presents some claimed virtues or favorable comparisons of the product with the implied conclusion that we should purchase it.

This ad for Northwest Mutual Life Insurance appeared in *Newsweek*.

①

↔Life at its Best.≈

②

<For the last 50 years Northwest Mutual Life has ranked first in dividend performance for its policyowners more times than any other company.>

The implied conclusion is obviously:

Thus you should buy Northwest Mutual Life Insurance.

The context helps us decide that we are reading an advertisement and not a news item. Our general knowledge of media teaches us that a firm that pays tens of thousands of dollars for a full-page ad is attempting to get us to buy something. Here we encounter little difficulty figuring out what the sales pitch is for.

Before we begin with diagramming we need to consider what technique we will use to mark off material that we interpret as implied by a given piece of discourse, but which is not stated outright by the writer or speaker. It is important for us to make this distinction so that anyone examining our work will be able to distinguish between what is actually stated verbatim by a writer and what we have added in interpretation. We simply extend the technique we have already adopted[4] to designate material we have added in interpretation, which is to enclose it in square brackets:

[ ]

We already learned how to supply what is needed to make complete sentences or independent clauses out of sentence fragments or phrases, and to enclose the added material in square brackets. Now we employ the same square brackets to mark off any implicit conclusion that we supply for a piece of discourse, and we will soon apply it also for any assumed or missing premise or premises. Any such statements we supply will be numbered in sequence with the given statements. But when the numbers are used in a diagram to display the pattern of the argument, those for the added statements will be enclosed by square brackets here too, rather than by circles. This allows us a quick view of how the added statement or statements function in the pattern of the argument.

Adopting this technique, we mark off the conclusion and diagram this argument this way.

[3]

[Thus you should buy Northwest Mutual Life Insurance.]

[4] See above Chapter Six, p. 150.

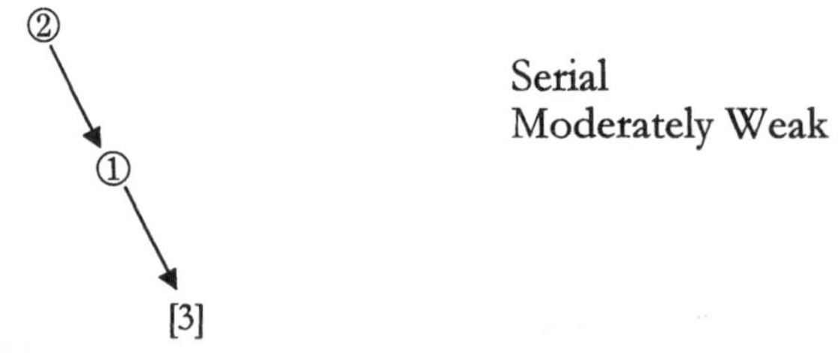

In assessing the argument, we first ask with what strength (if any) does ② support ①? Right away we must raise a question about ②. By whose count has Northwest Mutual ranked first most frequently? If the count was carried out by some independent agency, we should have been told that. But we were not. Was the count carried out by Northwest Mutual itself? If so, we would have to question its reliability. The likelihood of data biased in favor of Northwest Mutual is considerable if the firm is carrying out a study on itself. One suspects that if the data were not favorable or could not be made to appear favorable, we would never even get a report on the study. So this part of the serial argument is weak.

Given that ① may or may not be little more than Northwest Mutual patting itself on the back, what support does it provide for [3]? Normally you buy life insurance to protect those financially dependent on you so that they will receive the amount of the policy (e.g. $100,000) if you die while it is in force. The advantages one insurer might claim over another would be a lower premium for the same amount of coverage, or rapid, no-hassle payoff in the event of death.

But this is not what Northwest Mutual is claiming. It extols the dividend performance of its policies, which is the amount of money you get back on your policy without making any claim. So the superiority they claim for their product is that of an investment instrument more than that of an instrument of financial protection. As such, you have to compare it with other possible investment instruments such as certificates of deposit, bonds, stocks, mutual funds, and so forth. Investment counselors often advise against purchasing life insurance for investment purposes. Other investments offer higher returns at comparable risks, and financial protection for dependents can be provided with term insurance, for which premiums are significantly lower. Term insurance, as distinct from full-life insurance, is in force for a previously agreed on period of time such as five years or ten years. Your beneficiaries collect the value of the policy if you die during this period. When we assess the ad in connection with these factors, we judge it a moderately weak argument.

This example also illustrates one of the ways in which knowledge of a rather specialized type is useful in assessing the worth of an argument. We need to know something about life insurance to distinguish a lifetime from a term policy. And we need to know something about the potential of other investments to compare them with a full-life policy from a mutual insurance company.

There are cases where a terse argument may need to be supplied with even more than just a conclusion.

①
<C & P Yellow Pages ads mean business.>

The conclusion is obviously:

[2]
[(So) advertise in the C & P Yellow Pages.]

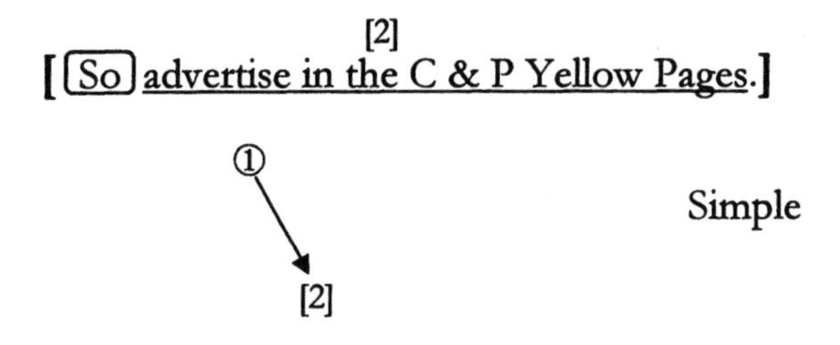

We can clarify the relation of the premise to the conclusion by making explicit the following implicit premise:

[3]
[You want business.]

Possibly we can better appreciate how [3] supplies a missing link (or fills a gap) between the premise and conclusion if we arrange the material in the following order.

①
<C & P Yellow Pages ads mean business.>
[3]
[You want business.]
[2]
[(So) advertise in the C & P Yellow Pages.]

[3] by itself provides no support for the conclusion. But linked with ① it could provide considerable support. So we diagram the argument linked.

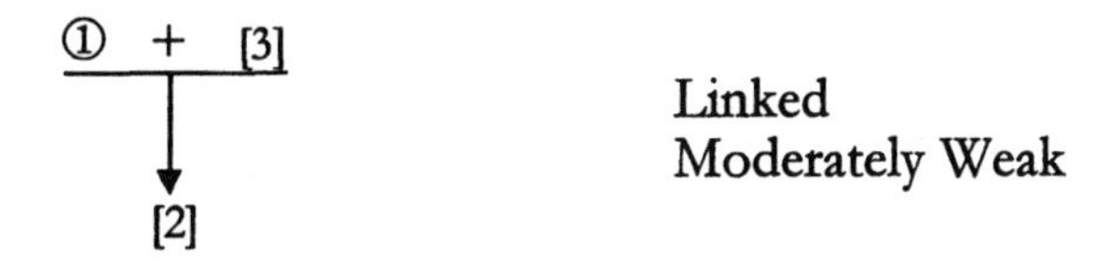

[3] is addressed to retailers or wholesalers who need to reach customers. The claim that they want business is quite plausible. That's why they're in business. It is difficult to regard the whole argument as strong, however, without more information to back up ①. The retailer who buys an ad in the Yellow Pages will

get more business than the one who doesn't, if all other factors are equal. But this claim has to be evaluated not in that context, but in the context of other means of advertising available to the merchants. So the conclusion of the argument [3] must be understood to mean:

> You should advertise in the C & P Yellow Pages rather than on the radio or the TV, or in the newspaper or magazine, or by direct mail, etc.

We have no information to convince us that $500 spent on advertising in the Yellow Pages will bring us more business than $500 spent on direct mailing of a flyer, for example. It is possible that a personal call by a C & P Yellow Pages representative could supply this information. But until we see it, we must regard the argument as moderately weak.

Are there cases of arguments with unstated conclusions other than in advertisements? At times the conclusion of an argument or inference may appear to be too obvious to need stating outright. Suppose we have just washed a load of clothes, and as we are hanging them out to dry we notice that a blue blouse has become discolored. We remember no discoloration when we put it in the washer, and we would like to know what caused it so we can prevent it from happening to other garments in the future. We reason as follows.

> Either the color of the blouse was not fast, or some other garment bled onto it in the wash. But the other garments in the machine were lighter, and lighter garments seldom bleed noticeably onto darker.

Despite its not being expressed, these statements appear to permit the following inference.

> The color of the blouse was not fast.

How do we analyze and evaluate such an inference? As soon as we realize that we confront an inference or argument with an unstated conclusion, we first supply the conclusion by stating it as much in the language of the evidence as we can. Then we treat the inference as we would any other. We mark it up, identify its pattern, and assess its strength.

①
<Either the color of the blouse was not fast, or some other garment bled onto it in the wash.> But ② <the other garments in the machine were lighter,> and ③ <lighter garments seldom bleed noticeably onto darker.>

[4]
[<u>The color of the garment was not fast</u>.]

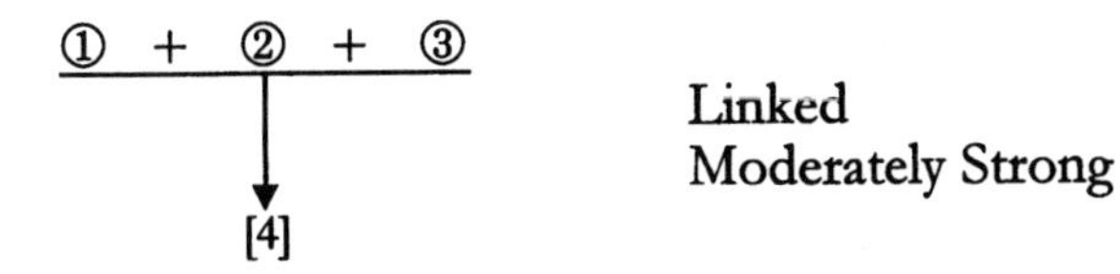

It must be linked because the premises depend on one another for any possibility of providing strong support.

Is the inference strong or weak? This depends rather heavily on whether ① exhausts all the important possibilities. For example, we might have carelessly poured bleach onto the blouse as we started the cycle. But if we assume that ① does exhaust the important possibilities, it is a strong inference.

There are also cases where someone wants to suggest or strongly hint something (almost always bad) about someone else or about something without bearing responsibility for having asserted it outright. There are cases of *innuendo* (which is what we call this) where the intended statement (even though it is oblique) can be clearly identified. In the following case, the speaker just discovered that Barlow scalped tickets for the big football game.

> No honest person would do that. But I'm not in the least surprised to hear that Barlow did it.

The intended conclusion is obviously:

> Barlow is not an honest person.

If we regard it as an argument, we can mark it up and identify its pattern.

① ②
<No honest person would do that.> But <I'm not in the least surprised
[3]
to hear that Barlow did it.> **[**<u>Barlow is not an honest person</u>.**]**

Two advantages accrue to us from considering it an argument.[5]

1. Making the intended conclusion explicit allows us to confront the speaker with it. She must then either accept it or disown it. In our present case, she must

[5] Many texts on critical thinking and informal logic do not consider innuendo; Moore and Parker do consider it (*Critical Thinking* 3rd ed. [Mountain View, CA, 1991], p. 128f.), but not as an argument.

now explicitly affirm that in her opinion Barlow is dishonest, or she must disavow it. If she disavows it, she should be able to interpret or change her words if she pleases so that they do not imply it.

2. If she affirms this conclusion, it now becomes worthwhile to inquire about the evidence supporting it. The context reveals that scalping tickets (selling them at a price higher than their cost) is being regarded as dishonest. But is this really dishonest? All retail and wholesale merchants, for example, buy items and sell them for more than they cost. In fact, this is in part what it means to be a retailer or wholesaler. Is this dishonest? And if not, how is it different from scalping?

Also, when the speaker says that learning of Barlow's questionable activity doesn't surprise her, this implies she already suspected his dishonesty. What evidence does she have to support this? If she can provide evidence, we may add it to the present argument and evaluate it accordingly. But on the basis of what the context provides by itself, we must judge the argument weak.

4. Arguments with Unstated Premises

How does one correctly formulate the missing premises of an argument?
. . . imagination *and* originality *are often required in this basic part of the critical process. . . . a process of careful trial and error will often work.*
Michael Scriven

We have already seen above that an argument can have an unstated premise as well as an unstated conclusion. The search for one or more unstated premises differs from that for an unstated conclusion in one important respect. We search for an unstated conclusion when we *suspect* we confront an argument. Without a conclusion we can't be sure that what we're dealing with is an argument. When we search for a missing premise we must already know that we have an argument. Otherwise the term "premise" would be quite out of place. We never search for an unstated premise of a statement or proposition, for these have no premises. Only arguments have premises.

When one statement must be true for another to be true, we call the first statement a *logical assumption* of the second. We have already learned to look for assumptions. An unstated premise is an assumption in the context of an argument. It can be called an assumed premise.

When do we search for an assumed premise or premises? Of course we can search for missing premises any time curiosity strikes us. Unfortunately we can be certain of finding at least a few for almost any argument. Just as almost any statement has assumptions, so does almost any argument. It is very seldom the case that a person advancing an argument states explicitly every proposition that bears on establishing the conclusion. Any argument constructed on this basis would be cumbersome and lack perspicuity, and so it would communicate poorly.

Let us rephrase the question. When should we search for missing premises? In general, any time something puzzles us about an argument, and particularly when the argument seems unclear or incomplete. Sometimes it is worthwhile to regard an argument as a type of form or gestalt, something requiring a certain number of parts to add up to a whole. We are given a conclusion and one or more premises, so we know we are dealing with an argument. But its gestalt is incomplete—something more is needed to make it whole. That something can be one or more missing premises.

Our first example is a statement familiar to most of us from cigarette advertising or cigarette packages.

> The Surgeon General has determined that smoking is dangerous to your health.

The conclusion that should be drawn from this is:

> You shouldn't smoke cigarettes.

We could add the following premise to contribute to the clarity of the argument.

> Health is valuable and shouldn't be unnecessarily sacrificed.

There is no doubt that the supplied premise is indeed assumed. We can mark this up and identify the pattern.

①
<The Surgeon General has determined that smoking is dangerous to your health.> [2] [<u>You shouldn't smoke cigarettes</u>.] [3] [Health is valuable and shouldn't be unnecessarily sacrificed.]

This argument is on the borderline of those where one should and those where one shouldn't seek an unstated premise. The person advancing the argument may have thought that the assumed premise was so patently true that nobody would ever doubt it. In this case, it was perhaps not necessary to state it outright. On the other hand, stating the missing premise may help clarify the argument. Searching for an assumed premise to help clarify an argument is a legitimate goal. Is this a strong argument? For anyone interested in good health, as well as quality and length of life, very strong.

Some writers cite as the goal of seeking unstated premises to turn informal arguments into formal deductive ones, which can then be checked by standard logical tests of validity. This view is not adopted in the present text. The deductive argument is not here taken as the model for the analysis and evaluation of arguments in natural language.

We have seen that we search for an unstated premise when finding one promises to clarify the argument being examined. We also search for one when we notice a gap between the stated premise (or premises) and conclusion, a gap that an assumed premise might fill. An example can be got from the following conversation of two children exploring the sea shore.

> "Look at that big jelly egg floating in the water."
> "It's big enough to be a whale egg."
> "Do whales lay eggs?"
> "Of course they do. All fish lay eggs."

Further attempts to satisfy by touch curiosity on this point soon teaches these youngsters a painful lesson about the jellyfish.

Our attention, however, is drawn to the argument being advanced.

① ②
<Whales do lay eggs.> <All fish lay eggs.>

②
↓
①

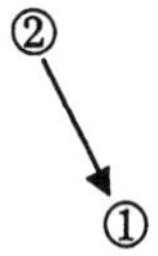

Simple

We notice an obvious gap between the premise and conclusion. We can close the gap by supplying the following assumed premise.

> All whales are fish.

Now we can state, mark up, diagram, and evaluate the whole argument.

① ② [3]
<Whales do lay eggs.> <All fish lay eggs.> [All whales are fish.]

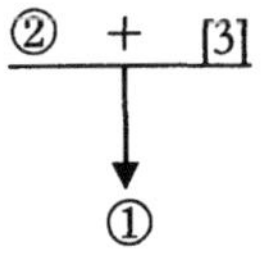

② + [3]
↓
①

Linked
Weak

What about the strength of this argument? Once we examine the assumed premise we become aware that it isn't true. Whales are warm-blooded mammals, not fish, and they give birth to their young like other mammals rather than lay eggs. We have identified this argument as linked, which means that the conclusion receives its support from combining ② and [3]. The falsity of [3] knocks away this support and gives us a weak argument.

The advantage we gained from supplying an unstated premise in this case is considerable. Though children might not know it, the average adult should know that whales are mammals and not fish. However, when a premise is only assumed rather than stated outright, the fact of its falsity might slip by an incautious adult. This reveals the mischief an assumed premise can cause. In order to evaluate an argument, we must evaluate all of its premises. But we can't evaluate all of the premises without knowing what all of the premises are.

There are also somewhat more challenging cases where we suspect that something is wrong with an argument. Listening in on the following conversation, for instance, we notice that an argument is being advanced.

> "Dr. Lessing is an unethical gynecologist in my book," asserted Carol.
> "Why do you say that?" Sandra inquired.
> "Well, everyone knows he performs abortions. But he told me once that he is a member of the American Medical Association. I happen to know that the AMA has an ethical code. So Dr. Lessing is unethical because he performs abortions."

Carol's statements constitute the argument here, so let us mark them up.

① <Dr. Lessing is an unethical gynecologist> in my book. Well, everyone knows ② <he performs abortions.> But he told me once that ③ <he is a member of the American Medical Association.> I happen to know that ④ <the AMA has an ethical code.> [So] ① <Dr. Lessing is unethical> [because] ② <he performs abortions.>

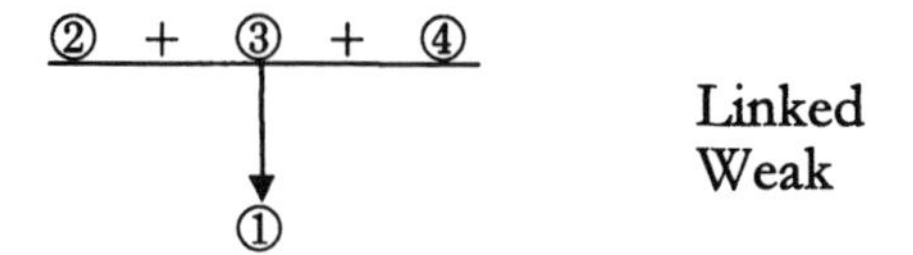

Again we notice a gap between the premises and the conclusion. The premises link up Dr. Lessing with performing abortions and with the AMA and its ethical code, whereas the conclusion links up Dr. Lessing with being unethical. The gap exists between performing abortions as an AMA member and being unethical. It can be closed by the following unstated premise.

[5]
[The Ethical Code of the AMA prohibits abortion.]

Without [5] the premises provide only very weak support for the conclusion. So let us add [5] and see how it fits in the diagram.

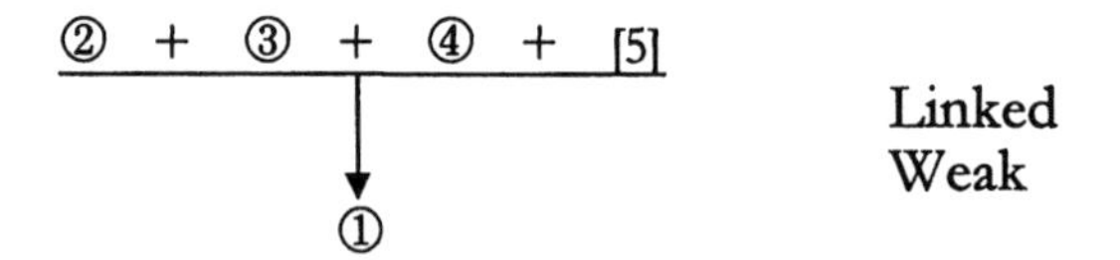

Now we can pose the question again whether the argument is weak or strong. This time we notice that the strength of the argument depends heavily on [5]. Is this added premise true? We know that abortion is legal in some cases in the United States. About 1.5 million are performed annually, many by physicians who are members of the AMA. What does the American Medical Association's Ethical Code say on abortions? When we go to the trouble of looking it up, we find that it doesn't even mention abortion. So the assumed premise is false, and the linked argument that depends heavily on it is quite weak. Carol may have confused the AMA Ethical Code with the Hippocratic Oath, which does prohibit abortion. Or she may be convinced herself that abortions are unethical, so she simply assumed that the AMA Ethical Code prohibited them

How do we tell whether the premises of an argument or inference are reliable or not? We follow the guidelines for establishing premise reliability.[6] In the above case, Carol's evidence that Dr. Lessing is an AMA member is direct observation, since he told her. Her evidence that he performs abortions is indirect, based ultimately on the testimony of those who have helped or participated.

How far should we look for assumptions? How persistent should we be in our search? This will vary from one argument or inference to the next. What we need to know is whether, in order to prove the conclusion, something of im-

---

[6] See above Chapter Seven, pp. 159–162.

portance is being assumed to be true which might be false. In some cases like the following quite complex argument of Darwin,[7] the question can arise whether or not a hidden assumption lies in the background and should be brought to the fore and asserted as an assumed premise.

> A struggle for existence inevitably follows from the high rate at which all organic beings tend to increase. Every being, which during its natural lifetime produces several eggs or seeds, must suffer destruction during some period of its life, and during some season or occasional year, otherwise, on the principle of geometrical increase, its numbers would quickly become so inordinately great that no country could support the product. Hence, as more individuals are produced than can possibly survive, there must in every case be a struggle for existence, either one individual with another of the same species, or with the individuals of distinct species, or with the physical conditions of life.

Here as in so many cases of argument in natural language the conclusion is stated first, then repeated at the end. The intervening argument is formidably complex, not least because Darwin is arguing for a causal interpretation or understanding of factors previously observed but not interpreted in terms of cause-effect relations. In our analysis above we adopted the following paraphrase of it.

① <Organic life reproduces at a rapid rate.> ② <Every being that produces several eggs or seeds must at some time be destroyed.> ③ <No country has the substance to support this much organic life.> Since ② <more is produced than can possibly survive,> ④ <a struggle for existence necessarily follows.>

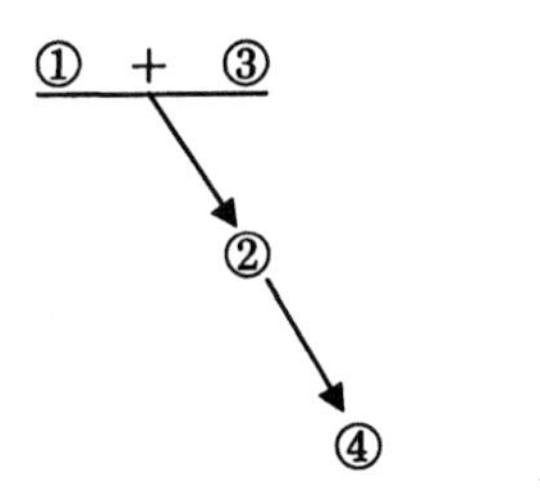

Compound
Serial

[7] Which we analyzed and paraphrased above, Chapter Ten, pp. 288–291.

Does the conclusion follow, or could the premises be true without it following? It is possible at least, though it seems to happen quite rarely in nature, that creatures confronted with a crushing shortage of food would simply become weak, give up, lie down, and die. The periodic marches of the curious Norwegian rodents called lemmings into the sea may be a response to some such shortage. And what about those occasional pods of whales that beach themselves to die, and when they are pulled back into the water by humans, swim right back and beach themselves again? It is not necessary that these phenomena be interpreted exactly as they are here; all we need to establish is that such behavior is possible. Once such a possibility is granted, it seems that the above argument establishes its conclusion at least partly on the basis of this background assumption.

[5]
[Organic beings have a will to survive.]

Is this assumption needed to close a gap in Darwin's argument?

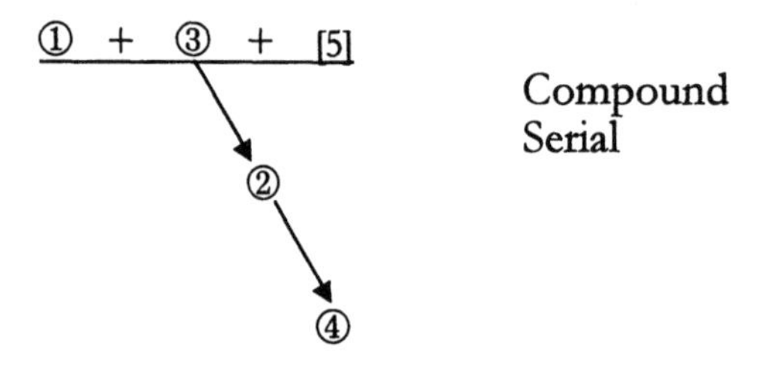

Probably not. At least not in the form we have stated it here. In one sense it appears to clarify Darwin's argument by closing a gap. But there are two good reasons for not bringing it in.

1. The real strength of the argument lies in the wealth of observations Darwin brings to support it. A will cannot be observed in the same way as the pollination of clover or cattle grazing away fir seedlings. So it is a different type of evidence and probably beyond the scope of Darwin's intent.

2. Much of Darwin's evidence derives from observations of plants, and a will is something we are reluctant to ascribe to plants, despite Aristotle ascribing them a soul.

What are we to say of the strength of the argument minus the assumption? Admittedly Darwin does not offer us the only possible interpretation of the evidence. But it is a good interpretation, one that is novel in a very insightful way. And it is solidly based on scores and scores of specific cases of observation, so the empirical evidence supporting the premise is very great. On balance we must call it a strong argument.

Now we have dealt with several arguments where we had to decide whether to supply an unstated premise. Once we decide to do so, as we did in several above cases, we must still decide just how that premise should be stated. The context will help us with this decision, as it helps us decide whether we have an argument or not. We can get further guidance from the *principle of charity.* The basic principle of charity enjoins us to put a favorable or charitable interpretation on a piece of discourse. Suppose we confront a piece of discourse that can be taken as an argument, but when we do so, it turns out to be a very weak argument. Suppose further that there is little or no evidence (like premise or conclusion cues) that the writer or speaker intended it to be an argument. In this case, instead of attributing a weak argument, we follow the principle of charity by not interpreting the discourse as argument at all.

Together with context, the principle of charity can help supply an assumed premise, or render explicit a premise that lies implicit in the given discourse. Context, as we have seen, is most helpful in deciding whether one or more premises are assumed. On this question the principle of charity has little bearing. Where it helps is on the decision how an assumed premise is to be stated. Suppose the assumed premise could be stated in two different ways, one of which would make the argument stronger, the other weaker. Following the principle of charity, we choose the version that makes the argument stronger. There are two reasons for adopting the principle of charity, a moral one and a practical one.

1. By putting the most favorable interpretation on a piece of discourse we treat the writer or speaker fairly.

2. Interpreting a piece of discourse at its strongest keeps our attention focused on matters of importance.

While the first reason needs no commentary, the second is illustrated by a case where you go against the principle of charity and intentionally add a premise that weakens an argument. You now find yourself engaged in the curious and self-defeating activity of analyzing and evaluating an argument you have purposely made weaker. This is like wrestling with a creature you brought into existence and made weak enough so you could win the match and claim victory, a childish activity. Doing this obscures the merits of the case being made by the writer or speaker, and it may well obscure the issue itself. In the context of arguing the merits of a case, setting up an opponent weak enough for you to defeat is an instance of the straw man fallacy.[8]

So when we choose between alternate ways of stating an assumed premise, we choose the way that makes the stronger contribution to the argument.

Context: Two physicians are consulting on treatment options for a patient with a prostate problem.

[8] See Chapter Twelve, p. 376ff.

① <It's very unlikely that Mr. Carlson will sign the operative consent form.>

② <The operation requires blood transfusion,> and ③ <Mr. Carlson is a Christian Scientist.>

There are two main options for stating the missing premise.

A. Christian Scientists never consent to blood transfusions.

B. Christian Scientists seldom consent to blood transfusions.

At first glance we might want to exercise option A. But it is so strongly stated that it is less likely to be true. It leaves no room for the possibility of Christian Scientists accepting blood transfusions, which some have actually done. Adding a premise that would have to be rejected as inaccurate obviously weakens the argument. So we follow the principle of charity and exercise option B. It is carefully enough stated to be supported by the facts, yet strong enough to contribute to support for the conclusion. The following argument results:

① <It's very unlikely that Mr. Carlson will sign the operative consent form.>

② <The operation requires blood transfusion,> and ③ <Mr. Carlson is a Christian Scientist.> [4] [Christian Scientists seldom consent to blood transfusions.]

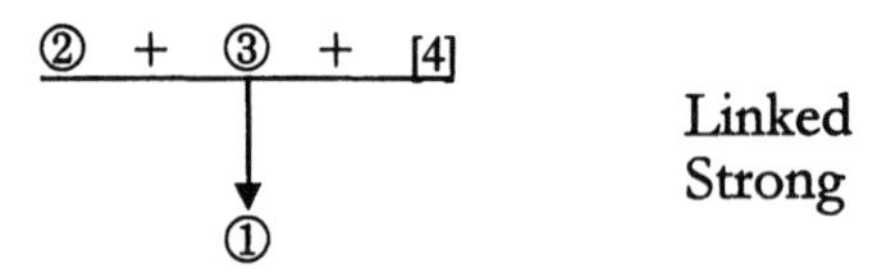

With the hidden premise added, the question arises whether it is true. It is accurate, because Christian Scientists believe that faith heals. So we see that we have a relatively strong argument. It leaves open the possibility of consent, but impels the physicians to seek other types of treatment.

Summary

The context of an argument is the situation in which it occurs. Context can decide whether a discourse constitutes an argument or not; it can also decide what is the conclusion of an argument and what are the premises. Information gleaned from the context can help us clarify an argument, and it can help us evaluate the argument.

Some knowledge of context is especially important for terse arguments—brief, succinct arguments in which one or more important factors are left implicit rather than stated outright. Any important implications or other significant material must be supplied in the form of complete sentences or independent clauses to clarify the argument.

In some arguments the conclusion is not stated outright. Many advertisements function as arguments whose conclusions urge you to purchase some product or patronize some facility. In other arguments with unstated conclusions, evidence points strongly toward this unstated conclusion. In those cases called innuendo, the unstated conclusion is derogatory or unfavorable. In all of the above cases the unstated conclusion must be supplied so that the argument can be analyzed and evaluated.

There are also arguments with one or more unstated premises. In some cases we notice a gap between the stated premises and the conclusion, a gap that could be filled in with one or more hitherto unstated premises. Some arguments depend on one or more important but unstated assumptions. These assumptions must be stated outright so that they can be tested along with the rest of the argument. If the assumptions prove doubtful, the argument is weaker; if they prove reliable, stronger. Following the principle of charity we state the missing premise as strong as needs be to serve the purpose, but no stronger. We want to test this argument at its strongest, not in some version we have weakened by the way we state it.

Study Questions

Section1: The Context and the Argument

1. What is the context of an argument?
2. Name three ways knowledge of context can help our work with arguments.

Section 2: Terse Arguments

3. What is a terse argument?
4. What challenge does a terse argument present us?
5. State two different ways an argument can be terse.
6. How does a dense argument differ from a terse?
7. How does a terse argument relate to a compound?
8. When do we fill in the missing parts of a terse argument?

Section 3: Arguments with Unstated Conclusions

9. Given that recognizing a conclusion is the key to identifying an argument, how can discourse be an argument without stating a conclusion?
10. Where do we commonly find such arguments?
11. How do we mark off and represent in a diagram a conclusion we have added?
12. In what case other than advertising do we encounter an unstated conclusion?
13. What is innuendo?

Section 4: Arguments with Unstated Premises

14. What is an unstated premise?
15. When does it make sense to search for a missing premise?
16. How can supplying an unstated premise help with evaluating an argument?
17. What type of unstated premise might we encounter when we delve more deeply into the argument?
18. How does the Principle of Charity both not help and help us with unstated premises?
19. How do we state an assumed premise according to the Principle of Charity?
20. For what two reasons?
21. How do we treat discourse that might be an argument according to the Principle of Charity?

EXERCISE 11—1: CONTEXT, ARGUMENT, AND MISSING ELEMENTS

Part A. Terse Arguments with Conclusion or Premises Unstated.

Mark up the argument and number the statements. Identify the unstated elements or element, state it briefly and number it. Then represent the argument with a diagram, and identify the pattern. Frequently in shorter arguments the unstated element is a conclusion. Often you need two or more premises to decide that another premise is missing. The linked pattern is common in arguments with unstated elements. Comment briefly on the strength of the argument. Identify any case of innuendo, supplying the unstated conclusion, and explaining why it is innuendo.

Some arguments are marked: *premise or conclusion*. Work these twice: once supply a premise, the second time a conclusion. In any argument marked: *premise and conclusion*, supply both; in any argument marked *two premises*, supply both.

1. The behavior of the active AIDS virus is not adaptive. When it multiplies and spreads, it tends to destroy the organism it depends on for support.

2. Just below the ridge they found fist-sized chunks of obsidian. This dark rock, which presents smooth, glassy surfaces when you break it open, is formed when lava cools quickly.

3. Louise's kitchen was spotless! I never would have expected that.

4. You shouldn't drive a vehicle unless you can stay awake and alert. Antihistamines, which people take for colds or allergies, often make you drowsy.

*5. Man is born free. Yet he is everywhere in chains.

Jean-Jacques Rousseau, *The Social Contract*, Book I, first sentences.

6. H. L. Mencken coined the term "booboisie" for the majority of Americans. He did not have a high opinion of their cultural or intellectual attainments. (*premise or conclusion*)

7. Friction in an automobile engine slows moving parts and reduces power output. But without the force of friction, automobile tires would not grip the road and propel the vehicle forward.

8. Virginia Beach, a resort city on the Atlantic Ocean, wants to build a pipeline to bring in water from Lake Gaston, which is 85 miles inland. (*two premises*)

9. Road sign: SLIPPERY WHEN WET (*premise and conclusion*)

10. A major earthquake was predicted for the Midwest for December 3, 1990. No such disaster was reported in the papers, news magazines, or TV news. And I got a Christmas card from Uncle John in St. Louis that did not mention any such disaster.

11. There were only two classes of women for Lennie, and Rita was most assuredly not a saint. (*premise and conclusion*)

12. People squint when they are photographed with the sun shining in their eyes. (*premise and conclusion*)

13. Road sign: DETOUR BRIDGE OUT

14. In springtime, after the thaw and run-off, you found fragments of flint arrowheads and an occasional complete arrowhead in the Nebraska cornfields.

*15. One thing you can say for sure about mom's biscuits. They really came in handy when we didn't have any rocks to throw at tin cans. (*premise or conclusion*)

16. A diet rich in fatty meat and dairy products can increase the cholesterol content of your blood. So you should eat such foods in moderation.

17. We are bound to elect a good delegate. There are three people running for the office. (*premise*)

18. Not all of the Morleys are shiftless ne'er-do-wells. You're forgetting Claudia.

19. Sign on a power relay station: DANGER

DO NOT ENTER

HIGH VOLTAGE

20. What has never been alive cannot very well go on living. So this is a book of the season only. . . . (*premise*)

From a review of F. Scott Fitzgerald's *The Great Gatsby* in the *New York Herald Tribune* of 1925.

Part B. Terse and Incomplete Arguments

Mark up, analyze, and evaluate these arguments. Supply any missing element. Identify and explain any case of innuendo. You cannot be sure that every argument has some unstated factor, so examine each one carefully.

1. Provence also has a sauce that is chiefly garlic and has been employed in this part of the country since the Middle Ages—"sauce à l'ail à la provençale." It is unusual among Provençal specialties in not employing olive oil.

Waverly Root, *The Food of France* (New York 1958), p. 337.

2. (A woman taking the prescription drug Coumadin writes "Doctor's Advice," Dr. Paul G. Donahue, *Newport News-Hampton Daily Press*, [Dec. 28, 1990], to ask whether she can get some dental work done. She gets this response.)

Coumadin is a blood thinning drug. . . . before your dental work, you have to check with the prescribing doctor, because you may have to be taken off it temporarily until the dental work (removal) is over. And you should certainly tell the dentist you are on the drug.

3. Wait! I smudged my signature on the check, so you may have trouble cashing it. Let me write you out another one.

4. It wasn't news that Ruthie and Bob got married, marriage was more or less inevitable under the circumstances; the *news* was the miracle of architecture Mrs. Mueller worked on Ruthie's dress, making it look flat in front, and then six months later, the baby boy□not *out* of wedlock, but not quite far enough *into* wedlock either.

Garrison Keillor, *Lake Wobegon Days* (New York 1985), p. 324.

5. The acting that one sees upon the stage does not show how human beings actually comport themselves in crises, but simply how actors think they ought to. It is thus, like poetry and religion, a device for gladdening the heart with what is palpably not true.

H. L. Mencken, *The Vintage Mencken*, gathered by Alistair Cooke (New York 1955), p. 188.

6. (General Mills flyer of Dec. 1990 shows two pictures of boxes of *Total Corn Flakes*. One box has the silky end of a partially husked ear of corn peeking out behind it. The other is over a bowl of *Total Corn Flakes*. This is the text.)

No other Corn Flakes can stand up to *Total*

✱ More Nutritious

✱ Better Tasting

Total Corn Flakes has twice the vitamin and mineral nutrition of *Kellogs*.

7. Most fatal home fires occur at night, while people are asleep. Poisonous gases and smoke from a fire in your home can numb the senses in a very short time.

Every home needs a device that can wake people up in time to escape from a fire. The sound of a smoke detector can do that and cut your chances of dying in a fire by 50%.

"Smoke Detectors," pamphlet of the National Fire Protection Association (Quincy, MA 1990).

8. The virtues of marriage were mostly negative virtues. . . . men had made life so intolerable for single women that most would gladly embrace even bad marriages instead. Almost anything had to be an improvement on hustling for your own keep at some low-paid job and fighting off unattractive men in your spare time while desperately trying to ferret out the attractive ones. Though . . . being single is just as lonely for a man, . . . it doesn't automatically imply poverty and the unquestioned status of a social pariah.

Erica Jong, *Fear of Flying* (New York 1973), p. 80.

9. Certain old men prefer to rise at [dawn], taking a cold bath and a long walk with an empty stomach, and otherwise mortifying the flesh. They then point with pride to these practices as the cause of their sturdy health and ripe years; the truth being that they are hearty and old, not because of their habits, but in spite of them. The reason we find only robust persons doing this thing is that it has killed all the others who have tried it.

Ambrose Bierce, *The Devil's Dictionary* (New York 1991), s.v. "Dawn."

*10. (Holly Golightly, Manhattan playgirl, speaks to bartender Bill about her brief marriage at 14 to a rural Texas veterinarian.)

Never love a wild thing, Mr. Bill. . . . A hawk with a hurt wing. One time it was a full grown bobcat with a broken leg. But you can't give your heart to a wild thing: the more you do, the stronger they get. Until they're strong enough to run into the woods. Or fly into a tree. Then a taller tree. Then the sky. That's how you'll end up, Mr. Bill. If you let yourself love a wild thing. You'll end up looking at the sky.

Truman Capote, *Breakfast At Tiffany's* (New York 1958), p. 59.

11. (In John Steinbeck's *Tortilla Flat* (Harmondsworth 1977), p. 155, several of Danny's impoverished but venturesome drinking companions live with him in his home.)

No curtains covered the windows, but a generous nature had obscured the glass with cobwebs, with dust, and with the neat marks of raindrops.

"It would be nice to clean that window with soap and water," Danny said one time.

Pilon's sharp mind leaped to the problem with energy, but it was too easy for him. It did not require a decent quota of his powers.

"More light would get in," he said. "We would not spend so much time out in the air if it were light in here. And at night, when the air is poisonous, we have no need for light."

12.. . . it's easier, I think, for musical talent to be immediately noticed in a child than it is for literary talent, in the sense that music doesn't require a great experience of life, because it's abstract and formal and emotional, and you don't have to have digested any part of your life or have arrived at a concept of yourself and the audience, or what constitutes the material for music and what doesn't.

Judith Johnson, in an interview by Susan Shafarzak,
Groundswell, Vol. II, No.1 (Winter 1986), p. 46.

*13. (In Noel Coward's farce *Blithe Spirit* (New York, n.d.), p. 70, Charles' former wife Elvira has returned as a spirit and disapproves of Ruth, the woman Charles married after her death. Charles accuses Elvira of having an affair with the man she left with when she caught the pneumonia that killed her. She denies this. State, analyze, and evaluate each argument, supplying any missing elements.)

Chas: You let him kiss you though, didn't you?

Elvr: How could I stop him. He was bigger than I was.

....

Elvr: You seem to forget *why* I went! You seem to forget that you had spent the entire evening making sheep's eyes at that overblown harridan with the false pearls.

Chas: A woman in Cynthia Cheviot's position would hardly wear false pearls.

Elvr: They were practically all she was wearing.

14. Computers are powerful and versatile and touch our lives at many points. We can easily forget that the computer is nothing but a machine. . . . the machine doesn't have reasoning power to guide it . . . It doesn't have so much as the instinctual drives of the humblest living things.

James Radlow, *Computers and the Information Society* (New York 1986), p. 104.

15. Last year handguns killed

    48 people in Japan

    8 in Great Britain

    34 in Switzerland

    52 in Canada

    58 in Israel

    21 in Sweden

    42 in West Germany

    10,728 in the United States.

Parade Magazine (Jan. 5, 1986).

16. (The author describes compulsory military training at Ohio State University during World War I.)

We drilled with old Springfield rifles and studied the tactics of the Civil War even though the World War was going on at the time. . . . It was good training for the kind of warfare that was waged at Shiloh but it had no connection with what was going on in Europe. Some people used to think there was German money behind it, but they didn't dare say so or they would have been thrown in jail as German spies. It was a period of muddy thought and marked, I believe, the decline of higher education in the Middle West.

James Thurber, "University Days,"
The Thurber Carnival, New York, p. 227.

17. (In *Words and Things* (Harmondsworth 1968), p. 68, Ernest Gellner criticizes the working method of linguistic philosophers. Their activity suggests, he urges, that since there are no genuine complexities in the world, there should be no complexities in language about the world. These philosophers are said to reject statements that are complex or paradoxical for these reasons alone.)

Academic environments are generally characterized by the presence of people who claim to understand more than in fact they do. Linguistic philosophy has produced a great revolution, generating people who claim *not* to understand when in fact they do. Some achieve great virtuosity at it. Any beginner in philosophy can manage not to understand, say, Hegel, but I have heard people who were so advanced that they knew how not to understand writers of such limpid clarity as Bertrand Russell or A. J. Ayer. But there is a serious aspect of this: by deciding what one "understands" and "does not understand," one in fact tacitly prejudges the picture of the world one is prepared to accept. Linguistic philosophers have decided in advance that they only understand established ordinary usage.

18. The notion that [corporal punishment is] degrading to boys is silly. In the main, their public opinion endorsed it as both just and humane. I went to a school where rattanning was resorted to when needed. Its effects, I am convinced, were excellent. It preserved the self-respect of the teachers, and so tended to make the boys respect them. Given command, they actually exercised it. I never heard of a boy complaining, after the smarting in his gluteus maximus had passed off, that he had been used cruelly or unjustly. He sometimes bawled during the operation, but he was content afterward. The teachers in that school were not only respected by the boys, but more or less liked. The males among them seemed to be men, not milksops.

H. L. Mencken, *The Vintage Mencken*, p. 183f.

THE CRITICAL THINKING JOURNAL

Part C. Compound Arguments and Context

10. The Terse Argument

Find in print media two terse arguments. One should have one or more unstated premises, the other an unstated conclusion. Supply the missing elements. Then diagram, analyze, and evaluate the arguments.

Further Reading

The problem of finding and formulating unstated premises of arguments has attracted much welcome attention from writers on critical thinking and informal logic. If you can only read two accounts, the following are recommended.

Robert H. Ennis, "Identifying Implicit Assumptions," *Synthese*, Vol. 51 (1982), pp. 61–86. The best article on the topic. Distinguishes background assumptions from those needed as gap fillers in arguments, and makes other valuable distinctions as well.

Michael Scriven, *Reasoning* (New York 1976), pp. 81f., 188–192. An excellent discussion of several examples showing how to formulate unstated premises to make them most useful to the argument.

The following are textbook accounts of how to deal with unstated premises for purposes of argument evaluation.

David Hitchcock, *Critical Thinking. A Guide to Evaluating Information* (Toronto 1983), pp. 73–92. Provides criteria and tests for unstated premises that are sought in order to make the original argument deductively valid.

Gerald M. Nosich, *Reasons and Arguments* (Belmont 1982), pp. 104–107, 218–222. Seeks unstated premises in order to turn informal arguments into formal deductive ones that can be tested by the standards of formal validity.

Stephen N. Thomas, *Practical Reasoning in Natural Language*, 3rd ed. (Englewood Cliffs 1986), pp. 253–264. Unstated premises are sought to bring natural-language arguments closer to deductive validity, but not to the valid forms of formal logics.

The following articles on theoretical issues take different stands on the importance, status, and acceptable treatment of unstated premises.

Michael Burke, "Unstated Premises," *Informal Logic*, Vol. VII (1984–5), pp. 107–18. We should supply an unstated premise only when we find it acceptable, when it strengthens the argument, and it agrees with the stated premises. We should not supply an unstated premise if it is the only one that will rescue the argument yet we cannot accept it (find it unsupported by evidence).

F. H. van Eemeren, and Rob Grootendorst, "Unexpressed Premises," *Journal of the American Forensic Association*, Vol. XIX (1986–87), pp. 97–106; 215–225. Draws on Grice's work on conversational implicatures to hold that we need a premise the writer is committed to, not one that he necessarily intended. In addition the unstated premise must make the argument valid and must be informative. The context should be eliminated because the same argument will be supplied with different unstated premises by different analysts who put it in different contexts.

James Gough and Christopher Tindale, "'Hidden' or 'Missing' Premises," *Informal Logic*, Vol. VII (1984–85), pp. 99–106. Advocates something like a gestalt notion of argument as a whole such that we discern and supply premises that are hidden away in it. These premises lie within the author's intention. We should not supply premises from beyond this gestalt in an effort to make the argument deductively valid.

Trudy Govier, "The Problem of Missin See Chapter Twelve, p. 414ff.g Premises," *Problems in Argument Analysis and Evaluation* (Dordrecht 1987), pp. 81–104. Generally sceptical of the search for unstated premises as a technique of argument evaluation.

David Hitchcock, "Enthymematic Arguments," *Informal Logic*, Vol. VII (1984–85), pp. 83–87. Focuses on formal aspects of the argument with unstated premises (or enthymeme). Advocates testing such arguments for validity by substituting for their exchangeable content in an effort to get the premises all true and a false conclusion.

Chapter Twelve

Relevance

[Frequently fallacies are violations of procedural rules of reasonable dialogue like] the failure to state or address an issue, failure to document a source of expertise, failure to ask reasonable questions, failure to stick to the point, use of emotions to avoid argument [or] prejudicial use of unclear terms that may be vague or ambiguous . . .
Douglas Walton

1. Evaluating Testimony

"Didn't you know that the naval shipyard was getting ready to lay off workers?" asked Pam.
"I sure didn't. Where did you hear that?" responded Michelle.
"George Coleman told me."
"And you believed him?"
"Of course I believed him," returned Pam. "After all, he does work there. And besides, what reason would he have to lie to me?"

As Pam's response suggests, we tend by and large to believe what others tell us. There would be little point to communicating if most of the information we received from others were false. In fact, there would probably be very little communication in the long run if most of what was communicated were false. A certain amount of trust may be a necessity for human survival. Some of us feel that even a bit more trust than the absolute minimum might not be such a bad thing.

Often we have little choice in the matter of trusting others. We are forced to whether we like it or not. Relative to what we need to know, the amount of information we can gather at first hand—by going and looking, or talking to someone—is often quite small. Relative to what we would *like* to know, it is often very small indeed. Limitations of time and space severely curtail our first-hand knowledge. What we know of history, for instance, depends almost wholly on the testimony of others. And much of what we know of the contemporary world depends similarly on the testimony of others, because there is so much of importance that we cannot witness directly.

But there are reasonable limits to our willingness to believe what others tell us. Some examples will allow us to explore these limits.

> "I left Rod's party and was walking home across the field," related Roger, "when I saw this bright light get bigger and come down out of the sky. When it reached the ground, a band of little green men with red lights on their foreheads came and took me up the ladder into the spaceship. They asked me some questions, then showed me on a star map where they came from. They set me down, said goodbye, and zipped off into space."
>
> "Wow! And that happened right over in old man Hawkin's field?" exclaimed Al.
>
> "Sounds to me like Roger's been smoking something you can't buy at the drugstore," commented Arthur wryly.

The degree of belief we would accord to Roger's testimony in this case would properly be influenced by our estimate of the likelihood of the event he describes. It is quite unlikely. It would also be influenced by circumstances that forced us to accept Roger's testimony as the only information we had on a matter of considerable importance to us. But in the present case we do not seem to be forced to act on the basis of Roger's information. Our degree of belief would also be influenced by the likelihood that Roger had been hallucinating. If he was returning from a party where joints were being shared or alcohol was consumed in quantity, the probability of his hallucinating seems high. As a general rule, the testimony of a witness who may have been drunk or high at the time of witnessing, or who is frequently or habitually in one of these states, should be examined quite closely.

> "How do you know it was Lois who let that bad batch slip through, and not one of the other quality-control personnel? inquired Craig.
>
> "I've known all along that she wouldn't make the grade in the end," responded Martin. "The job's just too tough for her. A woman doesn't have enough moxie to crack down on the press operators when the punch loses its sharp edges."

Suppose now you're a production executive in this firm, and customer complaints force you to tighten up on quality control. Would you act on the basis of the information supplied by Martin? If so, your decision would be unwise. On the basis of what he says, it seems likely that Martin has a prejudice or bias against women, or against women in the workplace. His identification of Lois as the culprit seems to stem more from this bias than from observation or specific pieces of information. It would be advisable to press him for specifics and then gather information from other sources before taking any steps in this matter.

If you have reason to believe that your speaker is prejudiced or biased, you must take this into account in evaluating his testimony. Evidence for bias may come from something the speaker has said or done previously, or it may emerge from his testimony as in the above case.

Now for a final example to illustrate factors to check for in evaluating testimony. This time we want to reduce our waistlines and are searching for a method to lose weight. Reading *Ms.* magazine, we encounter a full-page ad showing a man in a white medical gown extending a package of Dexatrim toward us. This is the text.

> Pharmacists' surveys reveal:
> More pharmacists recommend Dexatrim to help you lose weight.
> If you want to lose weight effectively, try Dexatrim.
> More pharmacists recommend it than any other weight loss product . . . because it works. It's proven in seven years of clinical testing conducted by doctors at leading universities and medical centers.

Is our search over? Or is there good reason to scrutinize these claims carefully? The latter is advisable. The claims may indeed be true, but we should not accept them uncritically. In this as in any other advertisement, some firm has paid for the space to tell us what it wants us to know about some product it is selling. The main purpose of an advertisement is not to tell the whole truth about a product but to sell the product. Advertisements seldom tell outright lies. But the public can be misled about a product nonetheless. For instance, an advertisement can place great stress on favorable aspects of a product and totally ignore negative aspects. It is common for an ad to provide few facts about a product, and instead place the product in surroundings likely to please potential customers.

To sum up, Dexatrim may indeed be the most effective weight loss product. But more than just the opinion of the manufacturer is needed to establish this. We might consult a physician, some of whom specialize in helping patients lose weight. We might seek the advice of friends who have successfully lost weight. But some independent evidence is needed to corroborate the manufacturer's testimony. In general, when someone provides us information with the ulterior motive of selling us something or gaining our support for some project, we should scrutinize the information carefully. The information we get from a candidate for public office also falls into this category.

We have now taken note of several points we will want to bear in mind when we are critically examining testimony for its credibility. It is time to draw these together into a list. We do not claim that this list contains all of the important points—our claim is rather that each point can be important in the right circumstances. Remember now that our starting point is the assumption that what someone is telling us is true or accurate. Then each of the following factors *can* mitigate against the truth or accuracy of the testimony, and so diminish our belief in it.

1. The events attested to are highly improbable.
2. Improbable events are not corroborated by other testimony.
3. The person attesting didn't have or couldn't have had the personal experiences on which the testimony is supposed to be based. Suppose for example that someone has just described in minute detail what daily life is like in Singapore. The credibility of her testimony is greatly diminished when we discover that she's never been to Singapore.
4. The person was or is under the influence of intoxicants or narcotics, or any substances that can severely affect perception or judgment.
5. The person has some ulterior motive such as selling us a product that might inhibit him from telling us the truth, or telling us the whole truth.
6. The person is biased or prejudiced in a way that might affect her testimony.

All of the above six factors were present in some degree and commented on in the above examples. Here now are several additional factors.

7. The person is or was mentally disturbed or unbalanced in a way that could affect his perception or report of an event. This factor must be handled with caution. Some forms of depression, for instance, are quite common and impair functioning only for short periods.
8. The person lies habitually or frequently, or tends to exaggerate grossly.
9. The person tends to make hasty or erratic judgments.

We should bear in mind that the presence of one or more of the above factors does not automatically render testimony worthless. They provide good reason for us to diminish belief, but they do not license us to abdicate judgment. Each individual case of testimony should be judged on its own merits as well as by these factors, and the degree of assent should be measured accordingly.

There are many occasions where our time is limited by circumstances, so we assent partially to testimony because it is necessary to act. We may, for instance, remain skeptical when our walking companion assures us that a rickety old wooden bridge across a steep ravine is quite safe. But if that bridge were our only escape from a rock slide menacing us on a steep slope, we would surely cross it.

2. AD HOMINEM FALLACIES

> "To deliberately take the life of a human being is murder. It is surely repulsive from a moral standpoint, and it is everywhere illegal, punishable by death or life imprisonment. Now the fetus is a human being. The science of genetics has proven conclusively that a unique human being is established by the 23 chromosome pairs constituted at conception. Why, as early as 3 to 4 weeks, a heartbeat is discernable, and at 8 weeks brain wave activity can be monitored. So abortion has got to be unthinkable. Whoever deprives this fetus of life deliberately kills a defenseless human being, and that is murder."

Bob Dolan was talking to a group of friends. The topic arose in response to news reports of a proposed amendment to the U.S. Constitution (an amendment which Bob favored) enabling states to outlaw abortion, despite the 1973 Supreme Court decision in *Roe v Wade.* Sally Clark was not at all convinced. With more than a hint of excitement in her voice, she replied:

> "Look, Bob, I'm sick of hearing men preach about the evils of abortion. And I do mean *preach.* Everyone knows you're a Catholic and that Catholics oppose abortion as a matter of religious faith. Fortunately we live in a nation that separates state and church, so that we don't have to have someone else's religious beliefs forced on us."

Is Sally's rejoinder to Bob adequate? Does it settle the issue? We would probably agree that it is not adequate. In fact, logicians analyze her reply as an *ad hominem* fallacy. Bob has advanced an argument supported by factual claims on an issue known to virtually all Americans, the abortion issue. Bob's position cannot be dealt with responsibly without taking account of these factual claims and this argument. But in directing attention to Bob and his religious faith, Sally does just that—ignores both factual claims and argument.

Sally draws attention away from the factual claims and argument to the person who has advanced them, and it is for this reason that her fallacy is called an *ad hominem* fallacy. "Ad hominem" is a Latin phrase that means "to the person." Further, this is a *circumstantial* ad hominem fallacy because Bob's being a Roman Catholic is a circumstance about him as a person.

Ad hominem fallacies are often analyzed as fallacies of relevance. We recall that premises must be probatively relevant for an argument to be strong. A fallacy of relevance is an argument that lacks probative relevance and may even lack topical relevance. An ad hominem fallacy occurs only in the context of an argument, in a situation where a speaker has advanced an argument, and someone else—an opponent—attempts to rebut the argument solely by citing information about the speaker. In those cases that we correctly clasify as ad hominem fallacies, the original argument must have some merit of its own. Suppose now that the information about the speaker is true, and that the information would tend to undercut the value of the speaker's testimony. Why would we refer to it as fallacious in the context comprising the argument? Its fallaciousness stems from the claim that information about the speaker wholly undercuts the force of his argument. In any case where an argument has merits of its own, these merits simply must be considered in any fair evaluation of the argument.

An example or two may help us appreciate the distinction of legitimate and illegitimate uses of information about a person. Suppose that instead of the above, Bob Dolan simply states:

> "Abortion is always wrong."

Or suppose he argues as follows:

> Pope Paul VI affirms in his 1968 Encyclical Humanae Vitae that even therapeutic abortion is wrong;
> So all abortion is wrong.

In either of these cases—the outright claim as well as the appeal to the authority of the Pope—Sally's information that Bob is a Catholic is not only relevant but important. For all we know, his belief that abortion is wrong is an article of his faith as a Catholic. And as an article of faith, this would have no binding force on those who like Sally were not Catholic.

But Bob doesn't make this straightforward claim, nor does he appeal to the authority of the Pope. He argues by citing information about fetuses which he claims proves they are humans, and then contends that killing humans is wrong. Any attempt to meet his argument fairly would have to deal with whether his factual claims are accurate, and if so whether they prove that fetuses are humans, and finally with whether killing humans is always wrong. Sally avoids them instead of coming to grips with them, and it is for this reason that her rebuttal fails.

A glance at the structure of Sally's rebuttal may help us understand both what it is intended to accomplish, and why it fails.

Dolan's original argument can be paraphrased like this.

① <Abortion kills the fetus.> ② <The fetus is human.> ③ <Abortion kills a human.>
④ <Killing humans is wrong.> So ⑤ <abortion is wrong.>

① + ②
↓
③ + ④
↓
⑤

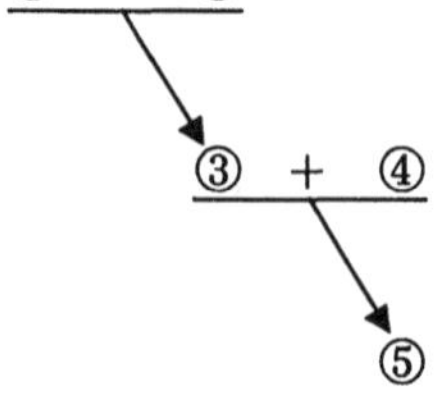

Compound Linked

In responding, Sally refuses to treat this as the argument it is. She focuses only on the conclusion, ignoring Dolan's evidence, and claims instead that it is supported by circumstances about Dolan. She then claims further to be able to undercut these supporting circumstances and show that Dolan has not established his conclusion. Here is a paraphrase of her counter-argument.

⑥ <Dolan is Roman Catholic.> ⑦ <Roman Catholics reject abortion on religious grounds.> ⑧ <This article of religious faith is not binding on non-Catholics.> ⑨ <U.S. law prohibits the state from enforcing a religion.>

[So] ⑩ <it has not been established that abortion is wrong.>

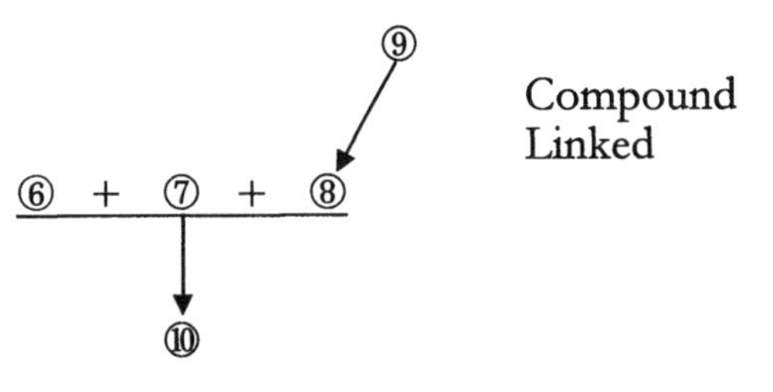

In Sally's counter-argument, ⑩ calls the conclusion of Dolan's original argument, ⑤, into question. But her entire counter-argument is a circumstantial *ad hominem* fallacy. She quite ignores the factual evidence and the inferences advanced by Dolan as supporting ⑤. This is what makes her argument fallacious.

Notice that we do not study fallacies in order to commit them. We study fallacies in order to be on guard against them. In our own thinking we do not want to be convinced by fallacies, whether the fallacy is advanced by someone else or produced by our own thought. Of course, *what* you do with your knowledge of fallacies is up to you, just like what you do with your other intellectual skills. Depending on his scruples or state of desperation, a trial lawyer may hurl at a jury an argument he knows to be fallacious. He may have no other hope of winning his case. Yet justice in America might be better served by more stress on truth in courtrooms than on winning cases. And when the people you are debating with are friends who trust you and whose trust you value, you might think twice before using fallacies on them except in jest. Their opinion of you is unlikely to be enhanced when they discover (as in time most people do) that you have duped them.

It is often the case that an ad hominem fallacy takes a nastier turn.

> "You ought to support the Equal Rights Amendment," asserted Shirley. "Statistics show that women have been discriminated against on the job by not getting promoted like men of equal ability, and by getting much less pay

for doing the same work as men. If the ERA passes, that will make it easier for women to claim their equal rights in a court of law."

"That's a lot of malarky," retorted George. "Every ERA supporter I've met so far has been a braless bubblehead."

Here George responds to an argument by directing abuse at the person who has advanced it. Unfortunately the use of such personal attacks in debating is widespread. His response is a fallacy because it ignores the argument and factual claims (statistics).

Because it is derogatory to the speaker, this fallacy is called the *abusive* ad hominem fallacy. The abusive ad hominem fallacy often cites circumstances about a person, so the two varieties of ad hominem fallacy are closely related. There may be cases where you are unsure whether you have a circumstantial or an abusive instance. Also what appears abusive to one person may not appear abusive to another. It is not essential to decide this question. What is important is to decide whether information about the person is legitimate or not in a given case.

In learning to evaluate testimony we discovered several ways in which information about a person could be helpful. Such information about a person can be legitimate when it does not ignore arguments and factual claims. There is also a smaller number of cases where information about a person is relevant or even necessary because the person *is* the issue. For instance, the issue may be who is best qualified for a certain job, or whether a specific person is qualified to fill a post. Look at this case.

The scene is a conference room of the U.S. Senate. The Foreign Relations Committee is meeting in closed session to examine the qualifications of Harold Powell, the President's nominee for Secretary of State. Senator Sharp addresses the candidate.

"Mr. Powell, though I'm a family man myself, I don't have any objection to a 49-year-old bachelor becoming our next Secretary of State. There is a very delicate matter which, with reluctance, I must probe into. The importance of the post you are nominated to fill makes it imperative for me to do so. When confronted with our evidence, you admitted to this Committee—and I commend you for your frankness—that you are a homosexual. It may be that large numbers of Americans now accept homosexuality rather than merely tolerate it. But you don't seem to think so. Otherwise you would be an overt rather than a covert homosexual, and we would have less of a problem here. My fear is that some foreign power may uncover the same evidence turned up by our investigative staff, then use it to blackmail you and influence U.S. foreign policy in its favor. Can you say anything to allay this fear?"

"Senator, I'd like to point out respectfully that you are an unwitting victim of the ad hominem fallacy. You are directing attention to the man here, to circumstances in his private life. The real issue is how our nation's foreign policy is to be conducted, and whether it will be conducted effectively."

Is Senator Sharp guilty of the ad hominem fallacy? Not in any obvious way. The issue is whether Powell is qualified to be Secretary of State. The information Sharp cites merits consideration because it bears significantly on the candidate's potential effectiveness as Secretary of State. Perhaps it should not be decisive, as the Senator seems to think. But a Committee that possessed this information yet failed to deal with it would certainly be remiss in its duty.

How do you tell in a given case whether information about a person is legitimate or illegitimate? The examples and analyses above suggest three guidelines.

1. Information about a person can be legitimate in evaluating that person's testimony.
2. Information about a person can be legitimate when that person's qualifications are the issue.
3. Information about a person can constitute an ad hominem fallacy when used to circumvent or ignore that person's argument.

There may be cases where it is not at all easy to decide whether a fallacy has been committed. Let us listen to the continuation of the above debate between Bob and Sally.

> "Oh come on, Sally, you haven't even come close to meeting my arguments. Science has indeed proved that a human being exists at conception, and it is obvious that all killing of humans is wrong. So abortion must be wrong."

At this point Rose joined the debate.

> "Bob, I don't buy your arguments at all. Science has established only that a fertilized ovum exists at conception. The question whether the fertilized ovum is a human in the sense of the homicide statutes is still an open one. Nor is it clear that all taking of human life is murder—self-defense and the enemy in wartime are obvious cases to the contrary. I too am sick of hearing men preach about the evils of abortion. But I mean *men*. Did it ever occur to you that no man ever suffered an unwanted pregnancy? A pregnancy resulting from rape and more loathed than a spreading lethal cancer? Haven't you noticed how the strongest arguments for abortion are advanced by women, the strongest against by men?"

Does Rose commit an ad hominem fallacy here? She does not ignore Bob's argument, and she also addresses his factual claims. So the question is really whether the information she cites about the speaker is relevant to the issue. What do you think?

EXERCISE 12—1: TESTIMONY AND THE AD HOMINEM

Part A. Testimony Problems

For each of the problems below consider the situation and the testimony. Decide whether the credibility of the testimony is undercut by any factors like those listed above. Be prepared to answer these questions: Would you believe the speaker? Would you act on the basis of what the speaker says?

1. Poster on outside wall of movie theater.
   "Colossal—Stupendous—Don't Miss It."

2. Confronted with massive evidence linking cigarette smoking with lung cancer and heart disease, William Toohey, spokesman for the Tobacco Institute, says,
   "We don't believe we know conclusively that smoking causes heart disease or cancer. It may or may not."
   Time, (July 18, 1983), p. 42.

3. Filling station cashier, responding to your question.
   "Lowery's restaurant? That's about half a mile down the road on your right. Big sign. You can't miss it."

*4. Texan commenting on the size of bayou mosquitoes.
   "Why those mosquitoes are so big that two of them came in and perched on the end of my bed the other night. One turned to the other and asked, 'Shall we eat him here, or carry him outside first?'"

5. Used car salesman informing a potential customer interested in an eleven-year-old vehicle.
   "It's very clean. Only 27,000 miles. It was owned by a little old lady who only used it for grocery shopping and an occasional tour in the country on weekends."

6. Motorist pulls up beside you at a signal and shouts,
   "Hey buddy, your left tail-light's out."

7. A woman suspected of being paranoid explains why she has difficulty grocery shopping.
   "Be careful. They're lurking behind every shelf, ready to lunge out and kill you."

8. Two children have raced home after dark. Very frightened and gasping for breath, they report being pursued by a huge fierce beast.
   "It was big as a house, Mommy, and it roared louder than a lion."
   "Yeah, and its breath was so hot it singed my hair."

*9. You have just purchased several cans of freon and a hose attachment for recharging auto air conditioning units in an auto parts store. The sales clerk is explaining the use of the attachment to you.
   "Remember to attach your hose to the suction intake of the compressor. This is very important. You can injure yourself seriously if you hook it up to the wrong valve."

10. A foul-smelling man in rumpled, slept-in clothes with bloodshot eyes slaps and brushes himself vigorously on his arms, shoulders, neck, and chest.
   "Hey, help me!" he shouts, reeking of whiskey. "Help me get these black spiders off me."
   No spiders can be seen on the man.

Part B. Information about the Person

In each case locate the issue and the information about a person. Decide whether the information is relevant to a person's testimony or qualifications. Identify those cases that involve arguments, and decide whether there are any ad hominem fallacies, circumstantial or abusive.

1. The time is June 1860, the place Oxford, England. The distinguished scientist, T. H. Huxley, has just finished reviewing for a scholarly audience the evidence supporting Darwin's theory of evolution. Bishop Wilberforce rises to defend the Biblical account of a divine, special creation, and begins by asking this question:
   "Will the good Mr. Huxley tell our audience whether he is descended from the ape on his mother's side or on his father's side?"

2. "Dalton says you'd better use a longer fuse when you're dynamiting a loose rock formation like that. You need time to get beyond the range of flying fragments."

   "What does Dalton know about explosives anyway. He's a farmer's son from Nebraska."
   "Yeah, but he was trained in demolitions as a Green Beret when he served his time in the military."

*3. "The poet Delmore Schwarz spoke of consciousness as a wound. That's a profound idea, calling to mind some aspects of Erich Fromm's analysis of the human situation."

"That's a crackpot idea. Schwarz battled insanity for years and finally committed suicide."

4. Senior staff of the Personnel Department are considering applicants for Chief of Research and Development.

   "I think we ought to go for Landmann. His standing in the scientific community is excellent. He has a list of publications as long as your arm. And even more to the point, he has secured an impressive number of patents."

   "I acknowledge his outstanding work, Gene. But have you noticed that none of the discoveries he's made has ever gone on to become a great market success? He's really more of a scientific visionary, with little notion of practical applications."

   "Ralph, that's not fair. You're committing the ad hominem fallacy."

5. "Green was there and saw it himself. He said that flames from the burning gas shot hundreds of feet into the air."

   "You can't believe what Green says. He's from Texas, and you know how all Texans are inclined to brag."

6. The House Judiciary Committee is holding hearings on the indictment of President Nixon. Mr. Jenner, counsel for the Committee, has just presented the evidence against the President, and sums up:

   "Gentlemen, the factors cited constitute strong evidence that President Nixon is guilty of obstructing justice."

   Representative Latta then replies in defense of the President.

   "My friends, you cannot allow any weight to the evidence supplied by Mr. Jenner. Did you know that he once served on a commission that recommended legalizing prostitution?"

7. The medium, isolated in a booth with no physical means of communication, had just written word-for-word a fourteen-word sentence a woman he didn't know had jotted down before witnesses in a city 350 miles distant. One of the scientists who had helped verify the accuracy of the medium's account then stated:

   "Despite the observers and the controlled environments, this fellow has found a way to trick us somehow. It's impossible for him to receive this message by telepathy. Mediums are notoriously unreliable and deceitful people."

8. "George Olson advised me against buying shares of the Admiralty Diversified Mutual Fund. He said it hadn't been keeping pace with the market. Instead he recommended Southern Continental Growth Fund. In fact, he said he could sell me shares in it himself."

   "You'd better get another opinion before acting on his advice. Admiralty is a no-load fund, whereas George earns a commission when he sells shares in Southern Continental. That might influence his opinion."

9. "Kant believed there was a reality independent of human perception, and he referred to it as the thing in itself. Schopenhauer argued against Kant that this was an assumption without foundation, since we could never verify that anything existed independent of human perception."
   "Schopenhauer's view must be wrong. He was a bleak pessimist who hated women and never even acknowledged his own helpless little illegitimate child."

10. "In a campaign speech last night Mr. Raleigh said he would make a good mayor. He promised to bring more city-services from downtown to the neglected north end."
    "Judging from the financial statement that appeared in the newspaper the other day, he'd have good reason to keep that promise. He owns half a million dollars worth of real estate in the north end. Whether he'd make a good mayor or not is another question. Sounds like he'd pit one end of the town against the other, which is not a very far-sighted policy."

3. Legitimate and Illegitimate Appeals

A. Appeals to Authority

In deciding questions we often appeal to authority, appeals that were called *ad verecundiam*, deferring to eminence (of authority), by writers of the early modern era. For instance, Bob *could* have appealed to the authority of the Pope in the above case, though he didn't. Part of being a Roman Catholic is acknowledging the authority of the Pope in matters of religion and morals. But appeals to authority are surprisingly common in many areas other than religion and morals. There are many cases where no better way exists to decide a question.

As we noted earlier,[1] for much of our knowledge of what is true and what false we depend on our own experience or the experience of others. In those matters where we ourselves and our friends and acquaintances have no personal experience, we frequently depend on others who have special training or ability. In some of these cases we call these people experts or authorities. It takes expertise to be able to repair an automobile whatever its defect, and it takes expertise to program a computer to handle a firm's billing operations. It is not unusual for us to confront expertise in daily life. Often we don't even think of it as expertise or authority.

[1] Above, Chapter Five, p. 93f.

"I can't hold on to that so tight. My finger is sore and infected."
"Have you done anything about it?"
"I showed it to the doctor. He told me to soak it in hot water four times a day for a couple of days. If it didn't go away, he would look at it again and probably prescribe an antibiotic."

We all acknowledge the authority of the family physician in matters of injury or illness.

When we play team sports, we acknowledge the authority of the coach. When we are driving from one city to another, we acknowledge the authority of an up-to-date road map for routes and distances. When we try out some fancy new dish in the kitchen we acknowledge the authority of Julia Child or some similar expert. When our home furnace conks out, or the air conditioner breaks down, we defer to the authority of the repairman or service representative. He can either repair the defect or tell us that our equipment is beyond repair.

So appeals to authority are part of our everyday life where they fulfill a useful function. If all appeals to authority settled their respective questions, there would be little need for us to draw attention to them here. Unfortunately they do not. So we will devote some attention to ways in which appeals to authority can mislead or go wrong. We call such cases *fallacious* appeals to authority. Here are several factors we should consider in any attempt to settle a matter by appeal to authority.

1. Is the matter one that can be settled by appeal to authority?

While there are many matters in which it makes sense to appeal to authority, there are others where expertise will not answer the important questions. Suppose for instance you decide that a certain special shade of lipstick does more for your appearance than any other. You might consult friends or even a cosmetician on this, but do any of these have an expertise that allows them to make the decision? Probably not.

On the other hand, if you want to find out whether one brand of suntan oil offers you better protection against sunburn than another, you might consult some periodical like *Consumer Reports.* This publication tests a wide variety of consumer products (including suntan oil).

Sometimes it is difficult to be sure whether an appeal to authority is appropriate, as this example illustrates.[2]

> Dear Ann Landers: Regarding the person who wanted to know if cold water boils faster than hot water and if hot water freezes faster than cold, you said you believe in going to the top and contacted Jerome Weisner, chancellor of Massachusetts Institute of Technology.

---

[2] Permission granted by Ann Landers and Creators Syndicate.

> Weisner said a problem of such extraordinary dimensions should be handled by an expert, so he turned the letter over to the dean of science, John Deutch, who said neither statement was true.
>
> Even though Deutch gave the correct answer, that procedure is called argument by authority and has absolutely no place in science.
>
> I was able to come to the same conclusion by using a pan of hot water, a thermometer, a stove, a refrigerator and a watch with a second hand.
>
> You, Ann Landers, exemplify what is wrong with our society. Too many bozos are too lazy to find the answers for themselves.
>
> It is easier to call on an "authority." How much more satisfying to rely on one's intelligence.
>
> Self-Reliant in Riverside
>
> Dear Self-Reliant: When a reader asks such a question, I am not about to tell him to do a home experiment, nor would I do one myself.
>
> I assure you Deutch didn't boil any water, either. He *knew* the answer—which is the beauty of having a battery of top consultants.

Self-Reliant makes a valid point here. Modern science grew by resisting the authority of the church on matters that the individual could test and decide for himself. Of course the tests and equipment have become increasingly sophisticated, as well as the skills required, but boiling and freezing water, and measuring temperatures, remain within the reach of most of us. And it would reassure us to know that even if Deutch didn't boil water, he was referring to the work of someone who did. But perhaps the most important thing to note here is that both experiment and authority agree, which provides powerful evidence in favor of the result.

2. Is the person whose opinion you seek really an authority?

Often authority is connected with special training of an academic or scientific kind. For instance, anyone who speaks with authority on particle physics today has had extensive academic and scientific training. Sometimes authority accrues to a person because of special talents or long years of training and practice. A good example was the American art historian and critic, Bernard Berenson. He acquired such expertise on Italian High Renaissance painting that sales of valuable works could not be consummated until he authenticated the paintings. It is proper in any case to inquire about the background and training of an authority.

3. Is the authority being consulted in the area of his or her expertise?

Authority has a tendency to carry over from its legitimate (usually limited) range and be extended questionably to a far wider area. Winning a Nobel Prize in medicine, for instance, assures us that a person can speak with confidence in her special area of medical research. But does it attest to any special acumen for deciding which of several candidates will make the best governor? Probably not. Yet people who have acquired authority in one area are continually pressed for their opinions in other areas. Often they are not too modest to favor us with their opinions on a wide variety of topics.

4. Are we dealing with a question on which there are authorities, but where the authorities differ appreciably?

Courts of law often call in expert witnesses to deal with questions which require expertise. The question of sanity is a good example. For a person to be convicted of a crime, it must be established that he had criminal intent. To have criminal intent is to know that what one is doing is illegal or wrong, and thus to be capable of distinguishing right from wrong. A person who is insane is not considered capable of distinguishing right from wrong. So if defense counsel can establish that his client is insane, this will usually allow the defendant to escape trial or avoid a guilty verdict.

Often in cases where the criminal act was witnessed by many people—as in the shooting of President Reagan—the lawyer for the accused will plead insanity. Then the defense will bring in expert psychiatric testimony that the defendant is sane. This has led one wag to assert that "For every Ph.D., there is an equal and opposite Ph.D." In those cases where authority applies but the authorities differ, we must study their opinions and make up our own minds as we would in serving on a jury. Even where we have expert opinion we must continue to think for ourselves, as the following anecdote illustrates.

> "Remember how I used to get those horrible colds, one after the other, all winter long?" asked Macnamara. "Well I read somewhere that Linus Pauling—you know, the Nobel-Prize winning biochemist—recommends massive doses of Vitamin C as a cold preventative. So last winter I tried it by taking one gram of Vitamin C every day."
>
> "How did it turn out?"
>
> "In one way it was great. I didn't catch a single cold all winter, and I felt terrific. But unfortunately that's only half the story."
>
> "What's the other half?"
>
> "Last spring I started getting attacks of sharp pain just below my ribs. When they became more frequent I had to go see a doctor. He examined me, and after studying the X-rays he recommended immediate surgery. Kidney stones. The operation was a painful and costly one, and that area is still somewhat sensitive."
>
> "What did the doctor think caused them?"
>
> "Well it's difficult to be certain. But he did tell me to lay off the Vitamin C."

B. Appeals to Pity

We appeal to authority to decide questions of knowledge. Often we appeal to pity or sympathy to get people to act. We must learn to recognize appeals to pity, called appeals *ad misericordiam* by some, because not all of them are legitimate. In a dispute or debate, one party may resort to an emotional appeal or appeal to pity because she has the weaker case. If the case is decided rationally, on its merits, she fears she will lose. So she attempts to circumvent rational scrutiny by appealing to our sympathy or pity.

> The evidence against the defendant was very strong. Several eye-witnesses, whose testimony could not be shaken, and impressive circumstantial evidence as well. Counsel for the defense rises and sums up her case.
>
> "Ladies and gentlemen of the jury. When you are deliberating the fate of this unfortunate young man, please bear in mind the following. He never had a father. His mother was a prostitute and petty thief. He was neglected, then taken from her and put in foster care. Not one foster home, but five different ones. In the last one he was beaten daily, so he ran away. Unable to find any kind of work, he lived in the streets and survived by petty theft. He never had a real chance at a decent life."

The jury is there to decide on the basis of the evidence whether the defendant is innocent or guilty. Many a jury, however, has been swayed by an emotional appeal like this to acquit a person who obviously committed the crime he was charged with. But the appeal to pity is illegitimate if it causes us to wholly overlook other important factors.

> The time: 1968. Full-page ad in a national news magazine. Photo of a pitiful, bony, sag-bellied African child. Caption to this effect: "Aid the homeless, starving children of Biafra. Send help today." The text reports atrocities carried out against the rebel Biafrans by military forces of the central Nigerian government. A cut-out coupon with mailing address is at the bottom.

Should you respond to this plea for help? One thing you would like to know is whether children were actually starving. The answer is yes. Another is whether any contribution you might make would be likely to alleviate their suffering by providing food, shelter, and medical care. This question is more difficult to answer in the affirmative. It seems that the rebel Biafrans planned a very clever media campaign to solicit funds, then used a good portion of those funds to purchase arms, ammunition, and other military supplies for their armed forces. So unless you exercise some caution here, you may end up supporting one side in a central African civil war rather than aiding needy children.

We have looked at two appeals to pity, of which one was clearly illegitimate and the other questionable. What would a legitimate appeal to sympathy or pity look like?

"Help! I'm going under."

You are at an ocean beach in the surf when you hear this cry. A strong swimmer, you turn and see a slender lad in his early teens about twenty feet distant being carried out and under by a strong current. No lifeguards or boats nearby. You are experienced at swimming in such currents. You could probably reach the youngster and bring him in or keep him afloat until help arrive, and this at small risk to yourself.

Should you respond to this appeal? Under the circumstances, probably yes. First of all, you have surveyed the situation and are aware of the important factors. A life is in danger. You can probably save it at small risk to yourself. This appeal does not distract your attention from something you should be noticing. It is not your *duty* to respond, as it might be a lifeguard's who is responsible for that stretch of beach. Yet sympathy for the plight of others and a willingness to respond are surely among man's finer qualities.

4. The Straw Man Fallacy

This fallacy is a fallacy of relevance that can be found in the context of debate or argumentation. It occurs when one party, deliberately or not, distorts the position of the other, then attacks this distorted position rather than the actual one. He wins the point only by defeating a straw man, or a sham of the true position, not the real man. It can also be viewed as a failure to assume the secondary burden of proof.

The freedom of college faculty to pursue the truth where the evidence leads them, and then to teach the best supported view to their students, is called academic freedom. In particular the defenders of academic freedom insist that faculty should not be fired or penalized for teaching a view they find best supported, even though, like Marxist economics, it may be unpopular.

John Stuart Mill puts it this way.

> On every subject on which difference of opinion is possible, the truth depends on a balance to be struck between two sets of conflicting reasons. . . . the peculiar evil of silencing the expression of an opinion is, that it is robbing the human race; posterity as well as the existing generation; those who dissent from the opinion, still more than those who hold it. If the opinion is right, they are deprived of the opportunity of exchanging truth for error: if wrong, they lose, what is almost as great a benefit, the clearer perception and livelier impression of truth, produced by its collision with error.

Against this view Dale Crowley urges that to some who demand its protection it means:

> "Unrestrained license" to teach whatever they choose, with total disregard of the basic rights of those whom they teach . . . To them it means an unhindered, unrestrained, unsupervised license to teach, as they choose, infidelity, atheism, Communism, sex perversion, intemperance, anything—even the change of our form of government from a constitutional republic to a socialist state. . . .
>
> Under this damnable cloak of so-called "academic freedom" they presume to compel the society which supports them to completely refrain from interference with their program of humanism, and to arrogantly reach their slimy hands down your pockets for the funds necessary to subvert and corrupt your children. . . . They are the biggest bunch of asinine parasites on the face of the earth.

Crowley commits the straw man fallacy here because he fails to come to grips with any of the serious reasons supporting academic freedom. You may also notice some emotive language in his comments.

Late in 1990, when U.S. armed forces were poised with those of allied nations to take the offensive against Iraqi forces occupying Kuwait, it was debated whether the President had the legal power to commit U.S. forces to battle without a supporting or authorizing resolution from the U.S. Congress. (The debate proved academic when Congress passed such a resolution.) Article I, Sect. 8, xi of the U.S. Constitution states "The Congress shall have the power to declare war . . . ," so the debate concerned whether this meant what it seemed to mean, and whether it applied to the case of Iraq. In response to this John E. Traina, Jr. wrote:

> I am ashamed of congressional members who publicly announce that our president cannot order our armed forces into battle without congressional approval. Hogwash.
>
> If this were true, we would not need a human leader and America would have to be content with a collective group of incompetent, unscrupulous, unable to perform in their elective capacity type individuals who seemingly aspire to cast doubt upon America's champion in time of crisis which, to me, is tantamount to treason.

Since he trivializes the constitutional issue of the separation of powers between the executive and legislative branches into the claim that the president is superfluous, Traina wrestles with a straw man here.

5. Thinking Critically about Advertising

As potential consumers who think critically about what we purchase, we should decide two questions about any product that interests us. Do we need it? If so, does one brand suit our needs better than others? Unfortunately in many cases those who market products do not in their advertising supply us with the kind of full and accurate information we require to answer these questions. In an advertising campaign, selling the product usually takes precedence over providing full information to the public. Advertisers feel little obligation to provide accurate information about the product, as the following comment by an insider reveals.

> Inside the agency the basic approach is hardly conducive to truth telling. The usual thinking in forming a campaign is first what can we say, true or not, that will sell the product best? The second consideration is, how can we say it effectively and get away with it so that (1) people who buy won't feel let down by too big a promise that doesn't come true, and (2) the ads will avoid quick and certain censure by the FTC.

We see that marketers and advertisers are often at cross purposes with intelligent consumers. So to help us think critically about advertising we should note important ways in which ads often fall short of providing us with full and accurate information about a product.

A. Ads seldom reveal anything negative about a product

That is, unless they are forced to by law. For years American cigarette manufacturers insisted in the face of massive evidence to the contrary that smoking cigarettes did not cause lung cancer. Now all cigarette advertising must carry a warning like this:

> Surgeon General's Warning: Smoking Causes Lung Cancer, Heart Disease, Emphysema, and May Complicate Pregnancy.

Yet the scene shown in the ad never represents a person in these circumstances. For instance, a Benson & Hedges ad pictures a healthy twentyish woman wrapped in a sheet, perched on the aquamarine tile step-up to her bathtub, drawing with deep satisfaction on her cigarette. It does not picture an emphysema victim struggling for oxygen.

An ad campaign built around a lone, rugged cowboy and his cigarette—the Marlboro man—is credited with making Marlboro the best selling cigarette in the U.S. Yet these scenes of rolling grazing land with hills or mountains in the background do not show—as does a 1976 British TV documentary entitled *Death in the West*—real cowboys who are heavy smokers dying young of lung cancer or emphysema.

> "I started smoking when I was a kid following these bronco-busters," says Julien [one of the cowboys interviewed in the film]. "I thought that to be a man you had to have a cigarette in your mouth. It took me years to discover that all I got out of it was lung cancer. I'm going to die a young man." [He lived only a few months after this interview.]

A U.S. beef industry TV spot of the mid-1980s shows James Garner, maturing macho star of *Maverick* and *The Rockford Files*, at a barbecue. Cowboy boots propped up on a table, he devours chunks of beef from a skewer while tossing the vegetables separating the chunks into a salad. As real men smoke cigarettes, so real men eat beef. Corn-fattened U.S. cattle yield steaks marbled with fat and juicy to taste. But a diet high in beef and other products rich in poly-saturated fats (those that are solid at room temperature) is linked with high cholesterol content of the blood. This in turn is linked with fatty deposits narrowing or blocking specially the coronary arteries, those that supply the heart with the blood it needs for its work. There was no corresponding beef industry TV spot of Garner being wheeled into heart surgery, of the incision from neck to navel, the cracking of the ribs, or prying them apart from the sternum so a surgeon could bypass five blocked coronary arteries. Nor was there a TV spot of his recovery from bypass surgery, a painful experience.

These are ways—there are many others—that ads do not report negative information about products. This information can be very important for your decision whether to use a product or not, so you cannot depend totally on ads for information about products.

B. Many ads use persuasive language or emotional appeals

Sometimes ads give little or no information about their product. Soft drink advertising is a good example. A soft drink can be refreshing after doing physical labor on a warm day (though most—Gatorade excepted—do not replace or claim to replace fluids lost to exertion), or during a break from office work. Soft drinks won't improve your health, but in moderate quantities they won't damage it either. They are frequently consumed on social occasions like parties or when friends drop over.

From the vantage point of the marketer, since soft drinks consist only of carbonated water and flavoring, the challenge is to convince the public to purchase one brand rather than its many competitors. Since color and flavor are the distinguishing characteristics, color gets emphasized in the ads, and claims are made for flavor. Coca-Cola, after dropping the cocaine that lent it its name, began poster, billboard, and magazine advertising in the 1910s with bottles of coke being held or drunk by young, attractive, healthy-looking, active people. Slogans were used—short, memorable phrases like "The pause that refreshes" or "Coke adds life." This is language used more for its persuasive power than its descriptive accuracy. The ads provide little information why—assuming you want a soft drink—you should choose Coca-Cola over a competitor like Pepsi-Cola. Together the images and text constitute an emotional appeal, an appeal to your desire to be young, healthy, and attractive, or to your desire to be accepted in a group of young, healthy, and attractive people.

Ads for a wide variety of products contain little or no information about the product. Instead they appeal to the fears and apprehensions of especially young people. Here are brief descriptions of a sampling of ads from *Sports Illustrated*, a periodical read mostly by men. Common to them is the suggestion that young men using certain products or services will be more attractive to women.

A. Seagram's Seven Crown whisky ad shows two men drinking whisky on a sun deck surrounded by ten females sunning themselves.

B. Man driving by in a Ford Ranger pickup gets an admiring glance from a woman in a red convertible.

C. Amtrak ad shows man seated at a dining car table with two women; text stresses "people meeting people," and how easy it is to "get connected."

D. Five women in swimsuits converge on a stack of Miller Lite six-packs.

E. Malibu cigarette ad shows couple holding hands in sunset at water's edge.

F. Cutty Sark whisky ad shows woman rested contentedly on sailing ship against arm of man who is holding glass of whisky.

G. Ad for Bushnell binoculars stresses their use for "bird" watching—woman with snorkel gear heads for water in the background.

H. Budweiser beer ad shows three women sunning themselves on a blanket-sized Bud label on a yacht deck.

Here is a similar sampling from *Seventeen*, a periodical for teenage girls. The ads suggest that users of the products become more attractive or sexually appealing.

I. OGGI Rootlift Holder (hair-care product) ad shows young woman wrapped only in long brown tresses.

J. Coppertone Sun Protectors (sunglasses) ad shows product on woman reclining on beach towel.

K. A Touch of Sun ad (bleach for hair) shows blonde in swimsuit; text: "Get a Head Start on Summer."

L. Tropical Blend Tanning Accelerator (suntan lotion) shows seated woman whose swimsuit reveals deep, even tan.

M. Vanderbilt perfume ad shows dreamy-eyed blonde in profile against dark man in tux; text: "Let it release the splendor of you."

N. Coppertone suntan lotion ad shows tanned, reclining woman in white swimsuit with square-jawed, blue-eyed man in background; text: "Summer's back."

O. Jockey for her ad shows shapely blonde construction worker Rosalyn Keathley in pink, one-piece Jockey underwear.

P. Charlie perfume ad shows from rear woman in business suit patting man striding beside her on bun; text: "She's Very Charlie."

None of these ads give us any information that would establish a rational need for the product (if we weren't inclined to use it), or reasons for preferring the advertised brand over its competitors. Each is a psychological appeal that invites us to put the reasoning portion of our mind on hold.

C. Ads are often deceptive or misleading

To the extent that the ads cited here suggest that using certain products will make us popular with our peers, or attract and charm members of the opposite sex, they are quite misleading. The case must indeed be rare of a man who is indifferent to a woman until one day she wears a scent that turns his head. Not impossible, of course, but quite unlikely. On the other hand, a carefully selected perfume can combine with other factors for a woman to become her most attractive.

Much the same holds for the case of a woman who takes no interest in a man until one day she discovers he drinks a certain brand of whisky. Quite implausible.

Today ads seldom tell outright lies. This has not always been the case. In the 19th century extravagant and utterly false claims were frequently made for products like patent medicines. A handbill for the Common Sense Electric Belt, patented in 1881 and manufactured in Chicago, makes these claims:

This Belt Cures

Paralysis	Lumbago	Malaria
Neuralgi	Dyspepsia	Lame Back
Rheumatism	Fever and Ague	Liver Complaint
Spinal Irritation	Seminal Weakness	Kidney Diseases
Nervous Exhaustion	Female Complaints	General Debility

In 1914 the Federal Trade Commission was created to combat unfair competition in interstate commerce, and it came to focus on deceptive advertising. If a firm makes a claim for a product that the FTC suspects is misleading, the firm is called to substantiate its claim. If the firm does not or cannot do so, the FTC goes to court if necessary to stop the advertising. It asked Goodyear to show that, as claimed in its TV ad, the Double-Eagle Polysteel tire could be driven over axe blades without being harmed.

The FTC has gone to court because it got no proof for claims like these for pain-relief medicine:

A. Bayer products are superior to other aspirins.

B. Bufferin or Excedrin has twice the pain-killing power of aspirin.

C. Anacin is superior to any other nonprescription pain-killer on the market.

Continental Baking Company's ad for its Profile Bread misled people into thinking that this product would help them lose weight. To avoid going to court, Continental ran a corrective ad in which it explained that its bread had seven fewer calories per slice only because it was sliced thinner than other breads.

In 1990 Volvo dramatized the stability of its automobiles in a TV ad where a large truck was lowered onto the roof of a Volvo sedan without collapsing it. The ads ceased when Volvo confessed to the public that the roof had been reinforced.

Certain words lend themselves to deceptions favored by some advertisers. For instance, the drug marketer who claims that her product "helps cure colds" wants the consumer to infer that this product cures colds. It doesn't do that, of course, because there is no cure for the common cold. If she is pressed, however, the marketer can respond she didn't claim her product would *cure* colds, only that it would *help* cure them. In this bit of ad copy "help" serves as a weasel word. It allows the ad to seem to make a claim without actually making one.

Advertisers make frequent use of such weasel words, says one insider, because "they can make you hear things that aren't being said, accept as truths things that have only been implied, and believe things that have only been suggested." Here are other words commonly used as weasel words.

"Like" as in "It's like getting a bar free." If we were really getting a bar free, Ivory would say so.

"Virtually" as in "Virtually trouble-free." Again, if the product were actually trouble-free, the marketer would certainly say so.

Any time we encounter such weasel words in an advertisement, it should set off a warning bell (if we are thinking seriously about the product). We need to ask exactly what is being claimed about it.

Another way in which ads can mislead us is with vague comparisons. One ad claims, for instance, "Today, doctors are recommending Advil more than ever." This sounds impressive. But when we stop to think about it, it doesn't mean they recommend it more than any other pain-killer. It doesn't even necessarily mean that doctors recommend Advil a lot. We must ask, more than ever but compared with when? If the comparison is to the time when Advil first came out and nobody had heard of it let alone recommended it, then doctors today could be recommending it more than ever but still not be recommending it much. But the comparison sounds impressive unless we think about it.

Another ad claims "more doctors and pharmacists recommend Robitussin." Here we must ask, more than what? If it means more than any other cough medicine, we would expect the marketer to make just this claim and back it up with reference to a survey carried out by some independent agency. Or as in the case with Advil, it could also mean that more recommend it now than when it was first introduced. The claim is so vague it could also mean more doctors and pharmacists recommend it than do stamp collectors and auto mechanics. In no case should we be impressed with claims so lacking in substance as these.

Ads can also mislead us with celebrity endorsements. The TV ad cited above with movie and TV star James Garner promoting beef is an example.[3] The celebrities in the ads may actually use and enjoy the products they endorse, as movie and TV star Michael J. Fox claims to like Pepsi-Cola. The advertisers are betting that if you're a Michael J. Fox fan, you'll be more inclined to switch to or drink even more Pepsi. But in each case we must ask whether a celebrity's endorsing a product is good reason for us to buy it. In most cases the celebrity receives a considerable sum of money for endorsing the product. So the opinion of the celebrity may be neither informed nor unbiased.

In the context of fallacious reasoning and misleading uses of language, we have focused on how ads can lead us astray. Many ads give valuable information about their products, and some groups set themselves admirably high standards. For example, notice these among the restrictions adopted in the advertising code of the California Wine Institute.

A. No wine ad shall present persons engaged in activities with appeal particularly to minors. Among those excluded: amateur or professional sports figures, celebrities, or cowboys; rock stars, race car drivers.

B. No wine ad shall exploit the human form or feature provocative or enticing poses or be demeaning to any individual.

C. No wine ad shall portray wine in a setting where food is not presented.

D. No wine ad shall present wine in quantities inappropriate to the situation.

E. No wine ad shall portray wine as similar to another type of beverage or product such as milk, soda, or candy.

F. No wine ad shall associate wine with personal performance, social attainment, achievement, wealth, or the attainment of adulthood.

G. No wine ad shall show automobiles in a way that one could construe their conjunction.

---

[3] Above, p. 379.

Finally, a suggestion about one source of worthwhile and unbiased information about consumer products, the periodical *Consumer Reports*. It accepts no advertising, so it cannot be threatened by loss of advertising revenue into adopting a favorable attitude toward a product it has found lacking. Its personnel devise ways of testing consumer products for the qualities they ought to have in order to function well, then report on these tests and rank the various brands according to how well or poorly they score.

SUMMARY

Testimony is what people relate to us of their observations and experience. We generally trust testimony, and sometimes we must depend on it. The credibility of testimony is diminished by many factors: improbability of the events, lack of corroboration in such cases, ulterior motive, bias, or prejudice, or other factors suggesting that a person's testimony might be unreliable, e.g. an habitual liar.

The ad hominem fallacy is a fallacy of relevance. It directs attention away from argument or evidence and diverts it to the person presenting the argument. It is circumstantial when attention is directed to facts or allegations about the person, and abusive when this information is derogatory. The information about the person may be accurate yet still be fallacious in the context of argument for being irrelevant. Information about the person can be relevant when the context is not that of argument but of testimony, or of someone's qualifications for a position.

Appeals to authority are legitimate when the matter is one that can be decided by authority, when you have someone who is an authority in her field of expertise, and where the authorities agree. The appeal to authority is fallacious when these conditions are not met. An appeal to pity is fallacious in cases that should be decided on the basis of reasons or evidence. In the straw man fallacy an opponent's position is distorted and weakened, then this weakened position is attacked.

We hope that advertising will help us decide whether we need a product, and whether the advertised brand is superior to others. Advertising seldom fulfills this hope. Ads are sometimes deceptive or misleading, they employ pervasive language and make emotional appeals, and they seldom reveal anything negative about a product. Usually the best we can expect is for an ad to call attention to a product in an entertaining way.

Study Questions

Section 1: Evaluating Testimony

1. What is testimony?
2. What reason do we have for thinking that much testimony is true?
3. Given that testimony might be false, why do we sometimes rely on it?
4. What factors diminish the credibility of testimony?

Section 2: Ad Hominem Fallacies

5. What is an ad hominem fallacy?
6. Why is the ad hominem a fallacy of relevance?
7. Must the information about the speaker be false for the ad hominem to be a fallacy?
8. Do we study fallacies in order to commit them?
9. What are the circumstantial and abusive ad hominems?
10. City two cases in which information about the person may not constitute a fallacy.

Section 3: Legitimate and Illegitimate Appeals

11. What is the ad verecundiam fallacy?
12. When is an appeal to authority fallacious?
13. What is the ad misericordiam fallacy?
14. When is an appeal to pity illegitimate?

Section 4: The Straw Man Fallacy

15. What is the straw man fallacy?

Section 5: Thinking Critically about Advertising

16. What two questions might a critical thinker raise about a product that interests her?
17. Does the advertising for a product typically provide the information needed to address these questions?
18. What do we find in ads instead?
19. In what ways do most ads fail to provide us with full and accurate information about a product?

Exercise 12—2: Questionable Appeals

A. Fallacies of Relevance

Decide in each case whether an appeal to authority or pity is legitimate or not. What factors do you cite as most important in support of your decision? Identify any case of straw man and explain why it is a straw man and a weak argument.

1. "Chrysler is the best buy in an automobile."
"What makes you think so?"
"Lee Iococca says so in TV ads. I admire and trust him."

2. Youngster in tears points to a frail tabby kitten stuck in a birch tree about ten feet up.
"Please lady, can you help me get my poor kitten down? She's so afraid up there."

3. "We're in the market for a new microwave oven. Our old one is too small. Gloria has a large Sharp, Model R-4A95, and is pleased with it. What do you think?"
"When *Consumer Reports* tested it, they had a problem with the one-touch popcorn control. We micro a lot of popcorn, so we'd probably look at another model or brand."

4. "There are several reasons," urged Chris, "why investing in public transportation is wise for a community of 300,000 like ours. First, it relieves congestion on our busiest streets. Second, it provides those of our citizens who don't have cars a greater range of opportunity for work, shopping, and visiting others. Finally, it is a much more efficient use of fuel, so it lessens our dependence on imported oil."
"There you go again," replied Allan, "always thinking of ways for people who work for their money to contribute to those who do not."

*5. "Your honor, if I am convicted of embezzlement as charged, my wife and two young daughters will be condemned to extreme hardship. I am their sole means of support, and my wife has never held a job. We married right out of high school. Please don't make my family suffer like that."

6. "Field reports of unacceptably high levels of the deadly chemical dioxin in the Tittabawassee River in Michigan turned out to be highly exaggerated."
"How did you find that out?"
"Dr. Hernandez of the Environmental Protection Agency sent the reports to Dow Chemical for verification. Dow found no cause for

alarm whatever. And they should know. Not only are they the manufacturer of dioxin. They're located at Midland, Michigan, right near the Tittabawassee."

7. "My gynecologist never said anything to me about the possibility of cancer or stroke. How did you find out that contraceptives like Enovid can have such serious side-effects?"

   "Simple. I looked up Enovid in the *Physicians' Desk Reference*, where they provide all that sort of information."

8. "M'am, the radar just showed you doing 52 in a 35 mph zone. Will you show me your driver's license and car registration please?"

   "Must you, officer? I just got laid off at work last week, and what with my husband in the hospital, it's wearing me to a frazzle just taking care of the kids and trying to make ends meet."

9. "We should retain the electoral college as a means of electing the president," stated Kim. "It is a venerable institution that has given us good government for nearly 200 years. It well serves its main purpose of shielding the choice of president from a mob-like majority swayed by unscrupulous demagogues. Also the winner-take-all aspect of the electoral votes of each state supports our healthy two-party system. It prevents our political energy from dissipating into the splinter parties and factional infighting that plague national politics in some other states."

   "Just because it's old doesn't mean it's good," responded Mary. "When appliances and utensils get old we throw them out and get new ones. Similarly we should get rid of the dusty old electoral college and elect our president by popular vote."

10. "Your honor, Lt. Keele is a ballistics expert with the Hampton Police Department."

    "Sir," testified Lt. Keele, "we test-fired the suspect's bolt-action .30-06 Remington on our range. We concluded that it is possible for a practiced marksman familiar with the weapon to get off three shots accurately within six seconds at a range up to 75 yards."

11. Windy, dusty inner city. Against a tall building near a corner a gaunt, unshaven man on buffered thigh stumps. Steadying himself somewhat with a palsied hand on a stick, he motions his inverted cap toward us passers-by.

    "Please sirs, a dollar for a hungry man."

12. "I'm sure that Carefree Maxi-Shields offer the most comfortable feminine protection."

    "What makes you so sure?"

    "Haven't you seen the way Cathy Rigby tumbles about while wearing one in the TV ad? She wouldn't be able to do that if they were awkward or bulky."

Part B. Advertisements

For this exercise your instructor may hand out ads in class, or ask you to find one or more ads in print media. Comment on each ad assigned. Assume first that you have no need for a product of the type advertised. Then ask whether the ad gives good reasons for your needing such a product. Then assume that you do need such a product. Decide whether the ad gives good reasons for buying its brand of the product rather than some competing one. Comment on any emotional appeals, persuasive language, omission of important information, or deception.

If you chose the ad, try to find one that illustrates as many of these techniques as possible.

THE CRITICAL THINKING JOURNAL

Part C. Compound Arguments and Context

11. Analyzing and Evaluating Advertisements

Take one full-page advertisement from a periodical. Assume first that you have no need for a product of the type advertised. Then ask whether the ad gives good reasons for your needing such a product. Then assume that you do need such a product. Decide whether the ad gives good reasons for buying its brand of the product rather than some competing one. Comment on any emotional appeals, persuasive language, omission of important information, or deception. Try to find an ad that illustrates as many of these techniques as possible.

Further Reading

The evaluation of testimony does not appear widely taught as part of critical thinking, though one wonders where there could be a better place for it.

H. H. Price, *Belief* (London 1969). Lecture 5 of Series I, "The Evidence of Testimony," pp. 112–129. A very good general account.

Factors that can influence accounts of eyewitnesses have been studied for their relevance to courtroom testimony:

E. F. Loftus, *Eyewitness Testimony* (Cambridge, MA 1979). Experiments show that eyewitness testimony is often not as reliable as it is taken to be in law courts. Memory of a witnessed event can be altered by the way questions are put as well as by other factors.

Stephen P. Norris and Ruth King, "Observational Ability: Determining and Extending Its Presence," *Informal Logic*, Vol. VI, No. 3 (1984), pp. 3–9. Testing discloses weaknesses in appraising the value of eyewitness reports. For example, jurors are influenced by how confidently a witness testifies. Develops principles for appraising observations based on facts about the observer, the conditions of observation, and the statements reporting the observations.

Historical accounts of the fallacies of relevance (except straw man) are found in:

C. L. Hamblin, *Fallacies* (Newport News 1998 reprint).

Textbook treatments of fallacies of relevance are:

Ralph H. Johnson and J. Anthony Blair, *Logical Self-Defense* (New York 1994). Presents straw man, *ad hominem*, and appeal to authority.

T. Edward Damer, *Attacking Faulty Reasoning*, 2nd ed. (Belmont 1987). Has all of the fallacies of relevance treated in this chapter.

S. Morris Engel, *With Good Reason*, 5th ed. (New York 1994). Has appeal to authority, to pity, *ad hominem*, and straw man.

Insightful discussions of the appeal to authority, to pity, and the *ad hominem* are found in:

Douglas Walton, *The Place of Emotion in Argument* (University Park 1992).

PART FIVE

CONDITIONAL AND INDUCTIVE ARGUMENTS

CHAPTER THIRTEEN

MOSTLY CONDITIONAL ARGUMENTS

1. CONDITIONS

One of the most common and important ways in which objects are linked or related to each other is as conditions. The relation is that of one object being the condition of the other, where the first object is the condition and the second is the conditioned. For instance, boiling water is a condition of making coffee. In this case one event—boiling water—is related as a condition to another—making coffee. What this means is that it is *necessary* to boil water in order to make coffee. When event A must occur before event B can occur, event A—boiling water in our present case—constitutes a *necessary condition* of event B—making coffee. Moreover, boiling water stands in a cause-effect relation to making coffee. In this sense it is a *causal* condition of making coffee. It is among the factors like fresh coffee grounds or instant coffee crystals that must be present if coffee is to be made.

Some necessary conditions are causal conditions, but others are not. For instance, one must have a piece of stationery in order to write a letter. In this sense having a piece of stationery is a necessary condition of writing a letter. But possessing the stationery does not *cause* the letter in the same sense that boiling the water causes the coffee. Having the stationery is more a prerequisite than a cause.

A necessary condition can be satisfied without its conditioned object or event coming about or taking place. For instance, we can boil water all day without making coffee. To make coffee we must percolate the boiling water through fresh coffee grounds. In those cases where we desire a specific result such as coffee we may have to satisfy several necessary conditions or prerequisites to achieve it.

There is another kind of condition, different from a necessary condition, whose satisfaction guarantees some desired result or makes some event inevitable. It is called a *sufficient condition*, because it suffices to produce the desired result or anticipated event. For example, heating water for two minutes at 150° C. is a sufficient condition of boiling the water. This means that when water is heated under normal conditions (e.g. of atmospheric pressure) at 150° C. for two minutes it will boil. It also means that it is very difficult if not impossible to heat water at this temperature for two minutes and *not* have it boil. This is why the condition is a sufficient one—the result follows on it automatically.

Many sufficient conditions relate to their conditioned object or event as cause to effect. Heating water to 150° C. for two minutes is both a sufficient and a causal condition of boiling water: it causes water to boil. Some sufficient conditions, however, are not causal conditions. Purchasing a gun, for example, is a sufficient condition for being a gun owner. But it does not cause one to be a gun owner. Instead it signals that it is correct English usage to refer to someone who has purchased a gun as "gun owner." When we ask "What causes someone to be a gun owner?" we look for a response like "He enjoys going hunting" or "She lives in a dangerous neighborhood."

In most cases sufficient conditions are not necessary conditions. For instance, though buying a gun is a sufficient condition of being a gun owner, it is not a necessary condition. One may receive a gun as a birthday present, and in this way become a gun owner without buying a gun. Similarly, even though heating water at 150° C. for two minutes is a sufficient condition of boiling water, it is not a necessary condition. We can also boil water by passing microwaves through it a short period of time. So we do not have to heat water (in the sense of applying heat to it) in order to boil it.

A *necessary* condition picks out an *indispensable* factor for a desired result or anticipated state of affairs. A *sufficient* condition picks out a factor that makes this result or state of affairs *inevitable.*

In a few cases a condition turns out to be both a necessary and sufficient one. Being the planet that lies between Venus and the sun is a necessary and sufficient condition of being Mercury. In this case we refer to one and the same object by two different descriptions. To invest at high risk in the hope of great gain is a necessary and sufficient condition of speculating. In this case we refer to the same action by two different descriptions. It is also possible for us to consider together two or more distinguishable factors as one condition. Being a slender cylinder a few inches long with a graphite core is a necessary and sufficient condition of being a pencil. Here too we pick out the same object by two different descriptions.

It is possible to ask of any two objects or events whether one is a condition of the other. In each of the above cases we encountered conditions, whether necessary, sufficient, or both. In other cases, however, it is clear that one object or event is *not* a condition of another—neither a necessary nor a sufficient condition. Being at least six feet tall is not a condition of being a good athlete. Many good athletes are less than six feet tall. Being a peanut is not a condition of being a fruit. Wielding an axe is not a condition of felling a tree. It is not necessary because a tree can be felled with a saw, and not sufficient because an axe can be wielded to split firewood. So in each such case if the question is raised whether the one is a condition of the other, we respond that it is not.

2. Conditional Statements

A conditional statement is a statement about a conditional relation. In one common form of conditional statement, two simple sentences or independent clauses are linked by "if...then...." Here is an example.

If she falls off the scaffold, then she could break a leg.

The part of the conditional statement following the "if" gives the condition, while the part following the "then" states what is conditioned.

Conditional statements need special attention because they play such a prominent role in our thinking. Their logic is complex and problematic, and they occur in deceptively different forms in natural language. We are likely to use at least some conditional statements any time we are considering possibilities. If we are thinking about what might happen in the present or future, or what might have happened in the past, chances are we'll be using some conditional statements. When a scientist formulates a hypothesis to explain some unusual phenomenon, he will probably be using some conditional statements. These are but a few of the many uses of conditional statements. Their importance and complexity are the reasons for our special interest in them.

It is helpful for us as we study the conditional statement to label its two parts. By convention the part of the statement that gives the condition—the "if" clause—is called the *antecedent.* The part giving the conditioned object or event—the "then" clause—is called the *consequent.* Here are these parts in the above example.

Antecedent:	If she falls off the scaffold
Consequent:	then she could break a leg

The consequent of a conditional statement should not be confused with the conclusion of an argument. The conclusion of an argument is a statement or thesis someone is attempting to prove. The consequent of a conditional statement presents a conditioned object or event.

Perhaps it is better to say that the consequent of a conditional statement *attempts* to present a conditioned object or event, because it actually does so only when the conditional statement is true. Some such statements are not true. A conditional statement is true when it presents a real or actual conditional relation. The object or event cited in the antecedent must be a condition of the one referred to in the consequent.

If you touch the tip of the sparkplug while the lawn-mower is running, then you'll get a shock.

In this example, touching the tip of the sparkplug is a causal condition of getting a shock.

A false conditional statement claims that a conditional relation holds between two objects or events, but the conditional relation does not in fact exist. Here is an example.

If you throw salt over your right shoulder, then you'll get rich.

There is no conditional relation between throwing salt and getting rich. The conditional statement is false because it makes a false claim. Its being false, however, does not make it cease to be a conditional statement.

The sort of condition expressed in the "if...then..." form of conditional statement is the inevitability of occurrence of the event cited in the consequent. So it is not only the case that some "if...then..." conditional statements will be false because no actual conditional relation corresponds to them. It is also the case that some "if...then..." conditional statements will be false even though they capture a conditional relation. They will be false because the conditional relation they capture is not one involving an inevitable occurrence. In particular, "if...then..." conditional statements are false when the antecedent cites *only* a necessary condition of the object or event referred to in the consequent. For example, breaking eggs is a necessary condition of making a quiche lorraine.

If you break eggs, then you are making a quiche lorraine.

But as we see, the "if...then..." conditional statement that corresponds to the conditional relation in its condition—conditioned sequence is false. We can break eggs to bake a cake instead of making a quiche, or to scramble or poach them. This conditional statement is false because the event cited in the antecedent is only a necessary condition of the one referred to in the consequent.

In every true conditional statement in "if...then..." form, the object or event mentioned in the antecedent will be a *sufficient* condition of the one given in the consequent. For example, dropping an egg on a tile floor is a sufficient condition for breaking the egg.

If you drop an egg on a tile floor, then the egg will break.

This conditional statement is true because the event referred to in the antecedent is a sufficient condition of the one cited in the consequent. The "if...then..." form of conditional statement stresses the inevitability of the event mentioned in the consequent. So it is because a sufficient condition has a conditioned object or event of certain occurrence that "if...then..." conditional statements citing sufficient conditions in their antecedents are true statements.

We have seen that when the antecedent of an "if...then..." conditional statement refers only to a necessary condition, the conditional statement itself is false. In a few cases, however, a condition is both necessary and sufficient. Flying, for instance, is both a necessary and sufficient condition of being airborne.

> If it's flying, then it's airborne.

The corresponding conditional statement is true, even though the activity referred to in the antecedent constitutes a necessary condition. The conditional statement is true, not because its antecedent cites a necessary condition, but despite its antecedent citing a necessary condition. It is true because its antecedent cites a condition that is sufficient as well as necessary. The sufficiency of the condition makes the statement true in this case.

Some conditional statements in "if...then..." form depart somewhat from the model we are using. In some cases the "then" that introduces the consequent is left understood rather than stated explicitly.

> If it's 10:00 PM, it's dark outside.

In some cases where the "then" is left implicit, the consequent is stated before the antecedent.

> Glass won't scratch it if it's a diamond.

Neither case is basically different from the full "if...then..." statement with antecedent preceding the consequent. The analysis and interpretation of truth possibilities is the same in all these cases.

We have seen how sufficient conditions are captured by "if...then..." statements. What about necessary conditions? We know that necessary conditions cannot be presented by the antecedent of the "if...then..." statement in the same way because the resulting "if...then..." statement will be false. But so far we have only explored the "if...then..." statement whose antecedent is affirmative. A necessary condition is one without which some object cannot be obtained, or some event will not occur. So if our conditional statement has a *negative* antecedent it is possible for it to present a necessary condition. By a negative antecedent we mean the antecedent is a negative rather than affirmative clause, one that has a negative predicate like "isn't," "doesn't," "can't," "won't" or something similar.

> If the concrete isn't reinforced with steel rods, the proposed structure will collapse.

This statement is true of the tall, slender structure it refers to because the antecedent presents a necessary condition, a condition that must be satisfied to prevent the collapse of the structure. What the statement stresses is the necessity of reinforcing the concrete to avoid the structure collapsing. We cannot conclude without further information that this is also a sufficient condition. Among other factors that might be relevant are the use of higher grade concrete, a more secure foundation, better design of stress-bearing joints, etc.

> If it isn't fragrant on a warm day, then it's not a Tiffany rose.

The antecedent of this conditional statement gives being fragrant on a warm day as a necessary condition of being a Tiffany rose. The antecedent does not give a sufficient condition, however, since other roses such as the Peace are fragrant on a warm day.

Another common way of introducing a necessary condition is with "only if."

> She's a senator only if she's an American citizen.

This is a true conditional statement, since being an American citizen is a necessary condition of being a senator. Being an American citizen is not a sufficient condition of being a senator. In addition to being a citizen one must be elected or appointed and take an oath of office.

Here is another example.

> It's a chili pepper only if it's a hot pepper.

It's being a hot pepper is a necessary condition of its being a chili pepper. But it isn't a sufficient condition. It could also be a jalipeño pepper.

Statements with "unless" are also conditional statements. The true "unless" statement introduces a necessary condition in the negative.

> It's not a chili pepper unless it's a hot pepper.

What this statement claims is that the object cannot be a chili pepper unless it's a hot pepper. In other words, being a hot pepper is a necessary condition of being a chili pepper.

Now we have three ways of stating necessary conditions. The following statements are equivalent.

> If it doesn't break down right after the warranty expires, then it's a bargain.
> It's a bargain only if it doesn't break down right after the warranty expires.
> It's a bargain unless it breaks down right after the warranty expires.

In each case the object's not breaking down right after expiration of the warranty is a necessary condition of it's being a bargain.

Now we can get some practice in the recognition of conditional relations and interpretation of conditional statements.

Exercise 13—1: Conditional Relations and Statements

Part A. Necessary and Sufficient Conditions

Consider the relation of the object or event in Column I to its corresponding partner in Column II. Then enter in the blank space the letter of the statement that best describes this relation.

A. I is a necessary condition of II.
B. I is a sufficient condition of II.
C. I is both necessary and sufficient condition of II.
D. I is not a condition of II.

	I	II
1.	B riding a bicycle	going somewhere
2.	__ eating vegetables	being a vegetarian
3.	__ smoking a cigar	attending a ballet
4.	__ listening to music	listening to Beethoven
5.	__ being the moon	being the earth's only natural satellite
6.	__ taking Spanish lessons	studying a foreign language
7.	__ gardening	drinking milk
8.	__ being a Cherokee	being an American Indian
9.	__ riding a motorcycle	riding a Harley-Davidson
10.	__ shaving with an electric razor	using electricity
11.	__ bowling	trying to knock down pins with a bowling ball
12.	__ buying stock	investing
13.	__ having some marbles	having some red marbles
14.	__ writing a letter	using a language

*15. __ studying hard	being a college student
16. __ eating broccoli	eating a green vegetable
17. __ fencing loot	selling stolen items
18. __ reading pages	reading a book
19. __ believing in God	being a Christian
20. __ paying back a debt	freeing oneself of a debt
21. __ operating a motor vehicle	driving on Interstate 64
*22. __ hunting fowl	hunting ducks
23. __ buying a blouse	buying wearing apparel
24. __ being angry	being livid with anger

Part B: True and False Conditional Statements

Decide which of the following conditional statements are true and which are false.

1. If you're in Nigeria, you're in Africa.
2. If the air is filled with gasoline fumes, an explosion could result.
3. Aluminum will burn if you heat it at 300 degrees Fahrenheit long enough.
4. If you mail a letter without a stamp, the U.S. Postal Service will deliver and collect the postage due from the recipient.
5. You can board a commercial flight only if you have a boarding pass.
6. There's no need to wash fresh fruit before eating it unless you're specially sensitive to pesticides.
7. If the air in the room is very dry, you can get chapped lips.

*8. You can't win consistently at poker unless you occasionally draw good cards.

9. If it's canvas, then it's duck.
10. It rains in the winter only if it's California.

3. Disjunctive Arguments

A family is sitting in the den watching a Bob Hope special on TV. Suddenly the picture and sound disappear, the lamp goes out.

> "Have we blown a fuse, or did the electricity go off?" asks Don. "Go look through the bedroom window to see whether the lights are off at our neighbors too."
> Gina hurries off and reports, "Most of the houses have lights on, and the street lights are on too."
> "It couldn't be a power outage then. I'll get the flashlight and go check the fuse box."

The reasoning used by Don and Gina to solve this problem proceeds by first setting up alternatives, then eliminating one or more of them. Logicians call this type of argument disjunctive because it turns on a disjunctive statement, one that links up independent clauses with "either...or..." Let us look at how such an argument sets out to establish its conclusion.

<Either a fuse is blown, or the electricity is off.>① But <the electricity isn't off.>② So <a fuse must be blown.>③

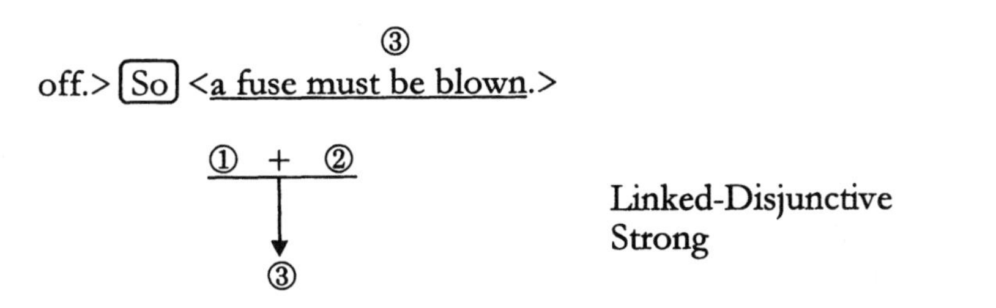

First we diagram the argument as linked. Without ①, ② has little or no tendency to establish the conclusion. But with ① and ② linked together, this could be a strong argument. In fact the disjunctive premise does list the most important alternatives. Then ② eliminates the one alternative so the other can be asserted in ③. So this is a strong argument.

In the disjunctive argument it is sometimes the inference aspect of the reasoning that is foremost. That is the case with the following example.

<Either the color of the blouse was not fast, or some other garment bled onto it in the wash.>① But <the other garments are lighter,>② and <lighter garments seldom bleed noticeably on darker>③ So <the color of the

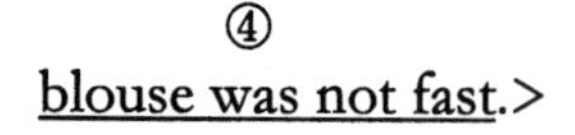
④ blouse was not fast.>

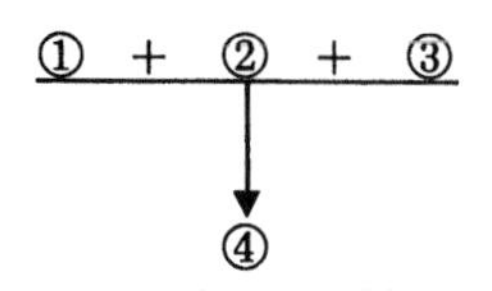

Linked-Disjunctive
Strong

Here too it appears that the disjunctive premise states the most likely alternatives. Since ② and ③ eliminate one alternative while the other is asserted in the conclusion, we have a strong inference.

> A young American couple are on their first trip to Europe, a whirlwind tour covering six countries in thirteen days. All of their travel arrangements were made beforehand, and they exchanged enough of each foreign currency to cover meals, small purchases, and incidental expenses. Having traveled and looked at sights several days, they are now finishing dinner in a small restaurant where English isn't spoken. The waiter left their check on a small tray. They are trying to figure out which of the several currencies they are carrying applies, preferring not to wave them all at the waiter if they can avoid it.
>
> "The few times I saw people buying things today, it seemed to me their currency was either red or brown."
>
> "But look at that woman putting money on a tray at the second table behind you. Those bills aren't red."
>
> "So their currency must be brown."

Again we encounter an inference that states then eliminates alternatives.

① <Their currency is either red or brown.> Yet ② <their currency isn't red.>
So ③ <their currency must be brown.>

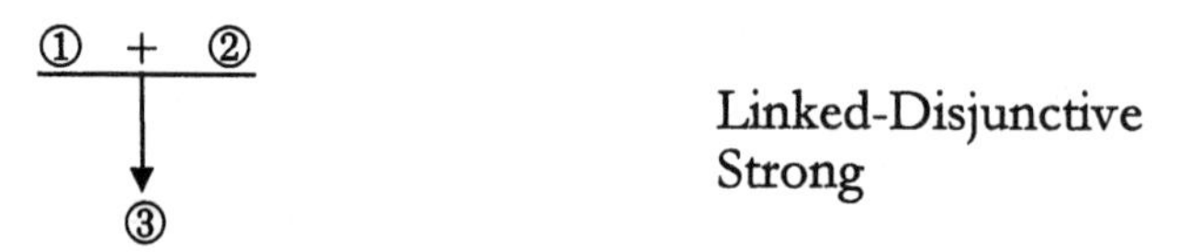

Linked-Disjunctive
Strong

Notice that when we diagram a disjunctive argument, the "either...or..." statement is never divided but is always diagramed as one statement. In the present case, the two true premises make this a strong argument.

In addition to what we know about evaluating arguments in general, two points deserve special attention in the analysis and evaluation of disjunctive arguments.

1. The first premise must list all of the important alternatives.

Suppose in the case of the above inference that it was also possible that the currency in question might be purple. In such a case, establishing that the bills weren't red would not prove that they were brown. They might also be purple.

2. In an inference with more than two alternatives, the other premise or premises must eliminate all of the alternatives not cited in the conclusion.

A disjunctive argument that has true premises and satisfies these two conditions will almost always be a strong argument.

Here is an inference that illustrates how we need to apply this second factor in our evaluations.

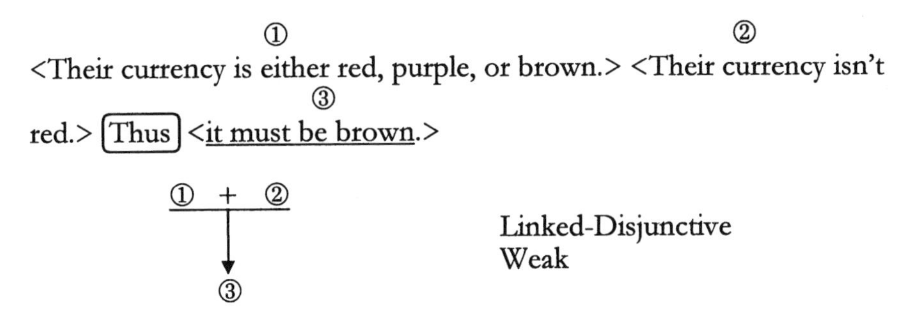
① <Their currency is either red, purple, or brown.> ② <Their currency isn't red.> Thus ③ <it must be brown.>
① + ②
③
Linked-Disjunctive
Weak

This is a weak disjunctive inference because the alternative of the currency being purple is not eliminated. But there is more than one way to change the inference to make it stronger.

① <Their currency is either red, purple, or brown.> But ② <it isn't red or purple.> Thus ③ <it must be brown>

① + ②
③
Linked-Disjunctive
Strong

Now we have a strong disjunctive inference. ② eliminates all of the alternatives except the one given in the conclusion. The inference can be strengthened in the following fashion also.

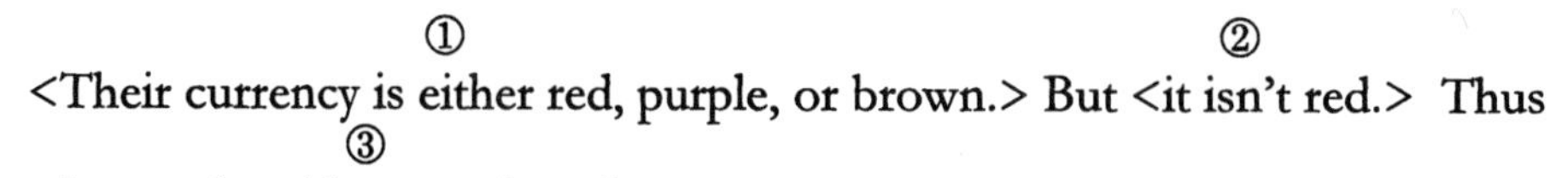
<Their currency is either red, purple, or brown.> But <it isn't red.> Thus <<u>it must be either purple or brown</u>.>

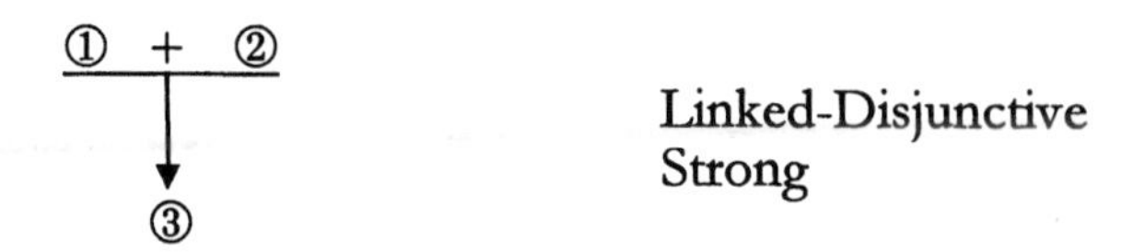

This too is a strong disjunctive inference. Again ② eliminates any alternative not stated in the conclusion. Unfortunately this conclusion is itself a disjunctive statement, so it does not satisfactorily solve the problem of the couple in the restaurant. But it does sum up logically what they do know, and also point them toward the information they have to gather to find the solution.

There is one final point we should notice about disjunctive inferences, a point that seem obvious but can cause confusion. A disjunctive inference establishes its conclusion by *eliminating* alternatives, not by *affirming* them.

① ②
<Their currency is either red or brown.> <Their currency is brown.>
③
Thus <<u>their currency is red</u>.>

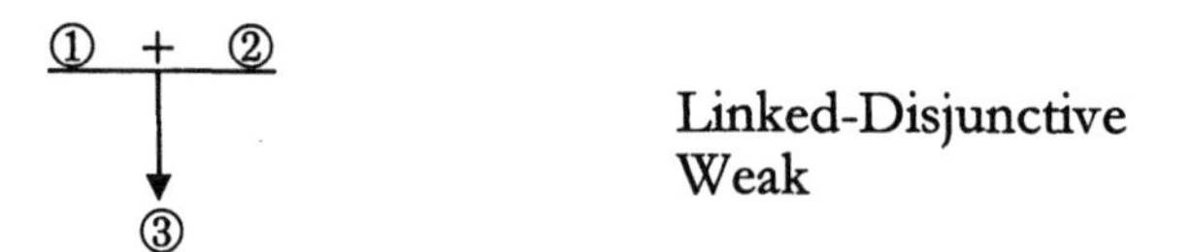

This is not only a weak inference. It scarcely makes any sense at all. If our information is good enough for us to affirm one of the alternatives, then we already have enough information to act intelligently and the inference is superfluous. When one alternative is affirmed as in ②, this is often taken as indicating that the other is negated or eliminated (rather than being affirmed). But it is best to leave this question open. In many cases affirming one alternative does not automatically eliminate another. If it is important to know the fate of other alternatives, further information about them will have to be gathered.

4. Conditional Arguments

An argument that contains a conditional statement is a conditional argument. There are several common forms of conditional argument. Some occur so frequently that they will seem familiar to you once you look at them. They can occur with a premise assumed, or with a conclusion left unstated. In many cases once you appreciate their structure, it seems intuitively obvious that they are strong arguments. Yet one of the important reasons why we study conditional arguments is that at least two relatively common forms are weak or fallacious. The terms "valid" and "invalid" are sometimes used when evaluating conditional arguments because formal or structural features of the arguments contribute to their soundness. Our first example is not obviously strong and inclines more toward inference than argument.

Contraposition

In contraposition we take a true conditional statement, change both the antecedent and the consequent into negative statements (or negate them), then change their places.

> If the antecedent is true, then the consequent is true.

When the contraposition is carried out, the following statement results.

> If the consequent is not true (is negated), then the antecedent is not true.

We can infer the new statement from the original. The inference reveals to us something already contained in our original conditional statement, but something perhaps not obvious to us until we perform the operation of contraposition. The inference is possible because in a true conditional statement, the object or event cited by the consequent gives us a necessary condition of that referred to in the antecedent. Suppose we begin with the following true conditional statement.

> If the engine turns over, the battery is charged.

Now we negate each of the clauses and change their places.

> If the battery isn't charged, the engine doesn't turn over.

The result is a different conditional statement, but one that is also true. The second statement is called the *contrapositive* of the first. The contrapositive of a true conditional statement is always true because the consequent of the true conditional statement gives a necessary condition of its antecedent. In the present case, having a charged battery is a necessary condition of the engine turning over.

We can show this as a simple argument form.

①
<If the engine turns over, the battery is charged.> <If the battery isn't
②
charged, the engine doesn't turn over.>

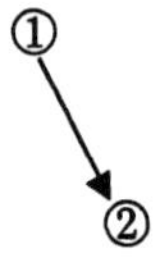

①
↓
②

Simple-Contraposition
Strong

But we do not usually diagram contraposition. Our interest is in how the two conditional statements relate, which decides whether the new can be inferred from the original.

The contrapositive of a true conditional statement will be true. We can also say that a true conditional statement implies its contrapositive.

Sometimes a conditional statement will contain one or two negative clauses. What happens when you contraposit such a conditional statement and negate an already negative dependent clause? The originally negative clause is now affirmative on the principle that two negatives add up to an affirmative. Here is an illustration.

1. If you sprain your ankle, you can't play in the big game Saturday.
2. If you play in the big game Saturday, your ankle can't be sprained.

The antecedent of (1) is negated or made negative in (2), where it functions as the consequent. The consequent of (1) is a negative statement to begin with. When we negate it the result is:

you cannot not play in the big game Saturday

The two "nots" or negatives cancel each other out, and the resulting clause is affirmative.

If you play in the big game Saturday

Modus Ponens

In one common conditional argument, one premise is a conditional statement while the second is a statement asserting or affirming the antecedent of that conditional statement. In those cases where both premises are true, this is nearly always a strong argument. Here is an example.

> You know what's going to happen if interest rates rise—there will be more bankruptcies. And interest rates are already on the rise again.

Here we have the material for a conditional argument, except that no conclusion is drawn. Let us supply the conclusion as we mark up and diagram the argument.

① ②
<You know what's going to happen> <if interest rates rise—there will be
③
more bankruptcies.> And <interest rates are already on the rise again.>
[4]
[[So] <u>there will be more bankruptcies</u>.]

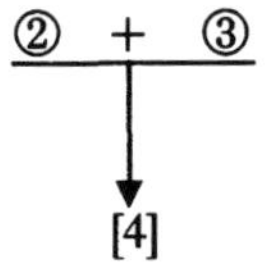

② + ③
↓
[4]

Linked-modus ponens
Strong

Logicians have traditionally labeled this form of conditional argument the *modus ponens.* This Latin phrase means "(the argument that proceeds) by way of affirming (the antecedent)."

Here is another example.

①
<If the price of oil drops, Mexico will have trouble paying its foreign
② ③
debts.> <The price of oil does drop.> [So] <<u>Mexico will have trouble</u>
<u>paying its foreign debts</u>.>

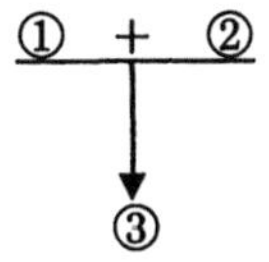

① + ②
↓
③

Linked-modus ponens
Strong

Handling negative statements in modus ponens arguments is challenging. Suppose that a conditional statement has a negative clause as its antecedent. We recall that in the true conditional statement with a negative antecedent, the antecedent presents a necessary rather than sufficient condition. Then in those cases where the second premise is similarly negative (signifying that a necessary condition has not been provided or fulfilled), the antecedent counts as affirmed and the argument will usually be strong. Here is an illustration.

① <If he doesn't use the handbrake, the car will roll back on the hill.>
② <He doesn't use the handbrake.> ③ <The car will roll back on the hill.>

① + ②
↓
③

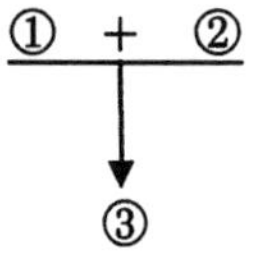

Linked-modus ponens
Strong

Modus Tollens

Another kind of conditional argument resembles modus ponens except that it proceeds by denying or negating the consequent rather than affirming the antecedent. Here is an example.

① <If Dowling buys snake oil for his gout, he'll get gypped.> ② <He doesn't get gypped.> So ③ <Dowling doesn't buy snake oil for his gout.>

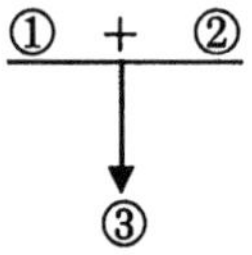

① + ②
↓
③

Linked-modus tollens
Strong

This argument is called *modus tollens* by logicians because it proceeds "by way of denying" the consequent. The consequent is denied when the second premise disputes, denies, or negates what is asserted in the consequent of the conditional statement. This argument resembles the modus ponens also in that it tends to be a strong argument when both premises are true.

Here is another example of a modus tollens argument.

① <If he gets a good lawyer, he'll be acquitted.> ② <He is convicted.>
So ③ <he didn't get a good lawyer.>

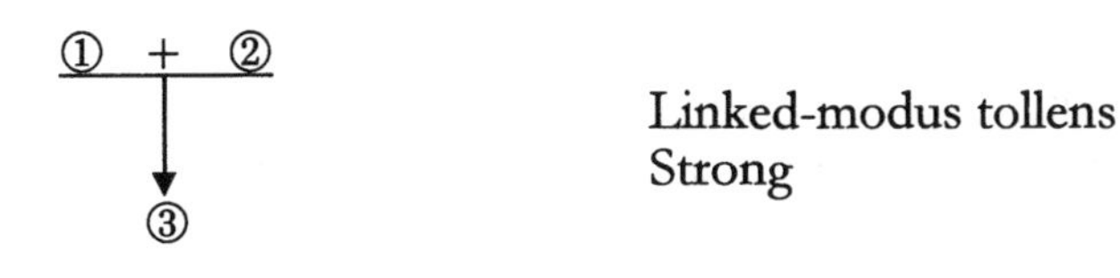

In this argument "He is convicted" negates or denies the consequent of the conditional statement "he'll be acquitted." So we have a modus tollens. When both premises are true, it is a strong argument.

Chain Argument

In a *chain argument*—sometimes called a hypothetical syllogism—two conditional statements are joined as premises to lead to a third conditional statement as conclusion. When the premises are true, those conditional arguments that are modeled on modus ponens or modus tollens are usually strong arguments. In those modeled on modus ponens, the consequent of one of the premises is the antecedent of the other. Here is an example.

① <If a spark plug wire is off, your engine is missing.> ② <If your engine is missing, the car accelerates poorly.> [So] ③ <if a spark plug wire is off, your car accelerates poorly.>

In this argument, the antecedent of ① is repeated as the antecedent of ③, the conclusion. Then the consequent of ② is repeated as the consequent of the conclusion. The antecedent and consequent are linked up (thus chain argument) by the clause "your engine is missing," which serves as the consequent of ① and the antecedent of ②. The argument is modeled on modus ponens and has true premises, so it is a strong argument.

When we were first learning to recognize arguments,[1] we discovered that a conditional statement by itself does not constitute an argument. But we also learned that conditional statements can join other statements to constitute arguments. Modus ponens and modus tollens are examples of that. Some arguments contain only conditional statements. That is the case with contraposition, and also with the chain arguments we are now studying. Here is another example.

---

[1] Above, Chapter Five, p. 104.

① <If Bailey plays well, State will have strength inside.> ② <If State has strength inside, State can win it all.> Thus ③ <if Bailey plays well, State can win it all.>

This hypothetical syllogism is like the above in proceeding by affirming the antecedent and so being close to modus ponens. In the case where ① and ② are true, that is, where they accurately describe this basketball team, it constitutes a strong argument.

Not all hypothetical syllogisms are modeled on the modus ponens, however. This example illustrates a different model.

① <If Cindy eats chocolate, she breaks out in a rash.> ② <If she breaks out in a rash, she feels miserable.> So ③ <if Cindy doesn't want to feel miserable, she shouldn't eat chocolate.>

The conclusion gives us the key to this conditional argument. The antecedent of the conclusion is the negation of the consequent of ②, while the consequent of the conclusion is the negation of the antecedent of ①. Again as above ① and ② are linked in that the consequent of ① serves as the antecedent of ②. Since this argument turns on a negated consequent based on a negated antecedent, it is modeled on modus tollens. If ① and ② are true in that their antecedents give sufficient conditions of their consequents as they appear to, it is a strong argument.

The conditional arguments we have examined so far have all had conditional statements that were true. This will not always be the case, however, as the following example illustrates.

① <If people get more freedom, they must make more choices.> ② <If people make more choices, they get more apprehensive.> So ③ <if people are to be less apprehensive, they should have less freedom.>

This argument follows the same model of the above, a chain argument modeled on modus tollens. But it isn't clear that the premises are true. In particular ②seems doubtful. Some people may indeed become apprehensive with more choices, but others relish choosing. For instance, someone who enjoys shopping for clothes or sporting goods enjoys it partly because of the choices. So making more choices is not a sufficient condition of growing more apprehensive. Since this one premise of a linked argument is doubtful, the argument itself is weak.

The types of conditional argument that we have attended to so far tend to be strong when their premises are true. We now turn to other types that tend to be weak even when they have true premises.

5. Fallacious Conditional Arguments

Illicit Conversion

It is interesting to note what happens when we take a given true conditional statement and change the places of antecedent and consequent. We start off with this statement.

> If it has been raining, the grass will be wet.

When the antecedent and the consequent exchange places, we end up with this statement.

> If the grass is wet, it has been raining.

Some writers call the second statement the *converse* of the first. If the original conditional statement is true, will the converse be true also? No, it does not have to be true, as this example shows.

Statement:	If she's a senator, then she's an American citizen.
Converse:	If she's an American citizen, then she's a senator.

The reason why in some cases the converse of a true conditional statement is not true is that the consequent gives a necessary but not a sufficient condition of the antecedent. In the present case, being an American citizen is a necessary condition of being a senator but not a sufficient one. One must in addition win an election and take an oath of office.

There are cases where the converse of a true conditional statement will be true. Here is an example.

Statement:	If it's the nearest star, then it's the sun.
Converse:	If it's the sun, then it's the nearest star.

In such cases the converse is true because the consequent of the original conditional statement gives both necessary and sufficient conditions of the antecedent. In general, however, the inference from a true conditional statement to its converse will be quite weak. This is why we call it the fallacy of illicit conversion.

Fallacy of Affirming the Consequent

In modus ponens, a valid form of conditional argument, it is the antecedent that is affirmed. The argument below resembles modus ponens but differs in one quite important respect.

① <If it's a magnolia then it doesn't shed its leaves in the fall.> ② <It doesn't shed its leaves in the fall.> [Thus] ③ <<u>it's a magnolia</u>.>

① + ②
↓
③

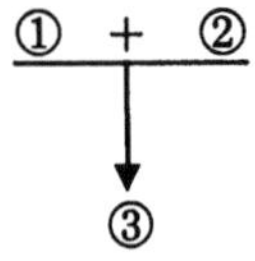

Linked-Affirms Consequent
Weak

This argument proceeds by affirming the consequent rather than the antecedent. It is fallacious because it fails to establish a conclusion even though its premises are true. Initially it points towards the conclusion that no magnolias shed leaves in the fall, which the evidence would support. What it actually ends up arguing, however, is that all trees that don't shed leaves in the fall are magnolias. This the evidence does not support. We know there are other broadleaf evergreen trees such as the yew.

Here is another example.

① <If it's a Picasso, the draftsmanship will be very skillful.> ② <The draftsmanship is indeed very skillful.> [So] ③ <it must be a Picasso.>

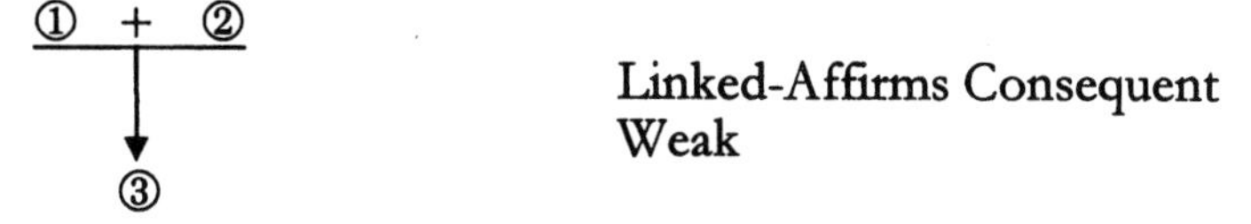

Why are conditional arguments that affirm the consequent fallacious? For basically the same reason that the conditional statement does not convert. Affirming the consequent does not allow us to infer the antecedent because the consequent gives (in most cases) a necessary rather than a sufficient condition. So the fallacy stems ultimately from the way the two conditions are linked in a true conditional statement.

Fallacy of Negating the Antecedent

In modus tollens or the valid form of conditional argument that proceeds by negating, it is the consequent that is negated. The following conditional argument resembles modus tollens in that it proceeds by negating.

① <If it's playing at the Ritz, it must be a good movie.> ② <It's not playing at the Ritz.> [So] ③ <it must be a poor movie.>

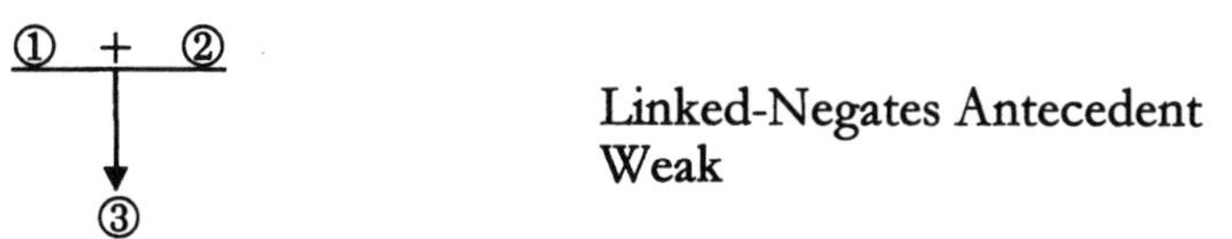

But in this argument it is the *antecedent* rather than the consequent that is negated, and the argument is fallacious. A true first premise claims that any movie playing at the Ritz is a good movie. The fallacy twists this into the quite different claim that any movie not playing at the Ritz must be a poor movie.

Why is the argument that proceeds by negating the antecedent a fallacy? Again it is because of the way the factors are combined in a true conditional statement. The antecedent gives a sufficient but not a necessary condition of the consequent.

Slippery Slope

One common use of chain arguments is to employ them against the adoption of policies or actions we deem unwise. The strategy of the argument is to show that the policy or action leads inevitably or at least strongly via one or more intermediate steps to some policy or action we clearly cannot accept. The unacceptability of this consequent policy or action indicates that we should reject the initial policy or action that leads to it. This strategy resembles that of the modus tollens, only with intermediate steps inserted between the antecedent and consequent of the original conditional statement. Here is an example.

> If you leave that drinking glass on the edge of the kitchen counter, in passing by you could easily knock it off and break it on the tile floor. Then you'd have to clean up the mess, which you don't want to do. So it's best to move the glass back from the edge of the counter.

① <If you leave that drinking glass on the edge of the kitchen counter, in passing by you could easily knock it off and break it on the tile floor.> [If you break it,] ② <Then you'd have to clean up the mess,> ③ <~~which~~ you don't want to ~~do~~. [clean up the mess.]> [So] ④ <it's best to move the glass back from the edge of the counter.>

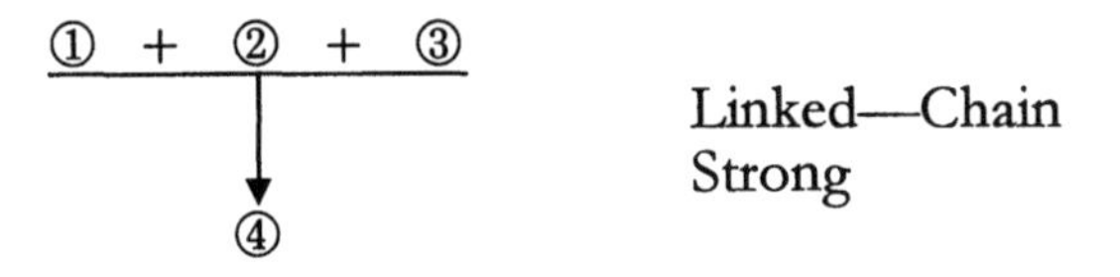

In this argument it isn't certain that the glass will break, but the argument seems fairly strong for these reasons.

1. A glass on the edge of a counter is easily knocked off, and falling from counter height to a tile floor will break most tumblers.
2. Even tiny glass slivers must be swept up for the damage they can do to feet. Nearly everyone prefers to avoid this.
3. No reason is given why it should be difficult to move the glass back from the edge, so avoiding the undesirable consequence is an option we can easily exercise.

A weak chain argument is sometimes called a *slippery slope fallacy*. This is the case specially when a link in the chain between original antecedent and final consequent is weak, or the alleged consequent is quite unlikely. Here is an illustration from a Knights of Columbus flyer picturing a robed elderly man in a wheelchair.

> If we legalize murdering the unborn, will the elderly be next?
>
> Far-fetched? Think about it a moment. If society can justify the taking of life of an unborn child whose only crime is being conceived, why not the life of a sick or elderly person who has become an unwanted burden?
>
> Once established, there is no end to the ways the principle of legalized abortion could be used to justify the taking of human life "for the good of society."

When we simplify and paraphrase this somewhat dense conditional argument we get the following:

① <If we legalize abortion, we legalize murdering the unborn.> ② <If we legalize murdering the innocent unborn, there is no end to our taking of human life "for the good of society."> ③ <In particular we will take the lives of sick or elderly who are unwanted burdens.> ④ <But we do not want the lives of sick or elderly taken in this fashion.> Thus ⑤ <we should not legalize abortion.>

① + ② + ③ + ④
↓
⑤

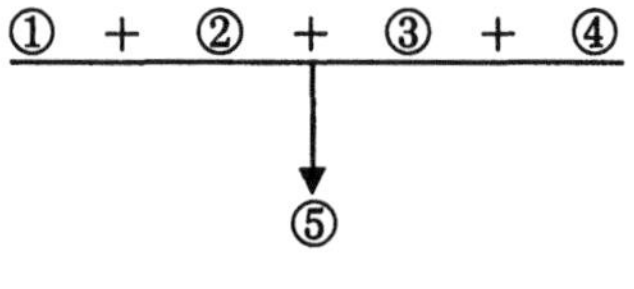

Linked—Chain
Slippery Slope
Fallacy

The argument has several important weaknesses. ① is a false conditional statement, an unsuccessful attempt to win a point by using emotive language. When we put aside that portion of the argument, there remains the claim that legalizing abortion greases the slope for other forms of taking human life. But there is no group calling for the killing of large numbers of humans in case abortion is legalized. The connection claimed between legalizing abortion and putting sick and old people to death was extremely weak before abortion was legalized in 1973. The Scandinavian nations, for example, tend to have liberal abortion laws yet are among the leading nations in providing services, care, and activities for their sick and older citizens. Now that abortion has been legalized more than 20 years, we have to concede that the claim has no validity for the US at all. The portion of the Gross National Product devoted to medical care for the sick and injured has increased faster than any other sector. Medical expenditures accounted for a little over 4% of the GNP in 1940, and was less than 6% in 1965. It is now nearing 13% of the GNP. Currently the fastest growing age groups in our country are those over 75 and those over 85. In 1984 federal per capita expenditures on those over 65 were six times greater than the same for children.

So this argument is a slippery slope fallacy. It is called slippery slope because it claims that if you put one foot on the slope (legalize abortion), you slide all the way down to something you cannot accept (killing sick and elderly). This type of argument is also sometimes called the wedge argument. Once your wedge creates an opening (legal abortion), totally unacceptable practices (killing sick and elderly) will enter. It is also referred to as the claim of a domino effect, where the reference is to dominos stood on their sides so that if the first one is knocked over, its fall knocks over its neighbor, and so on until all have fallen.

Exercise 13—2: Conditional Equivalences and Arguments

Part A. Equivalent Conditional Statements

Assume that the original conditional statement is true. Decide which of the subsequent statements are made true. Those that are implied or made true will be equivalent to the original statement. Remember that a conditional statement implies its contrapositive, but does not imply its converse.

1. If you use an aniline dye, then it won't fade.

   a.It won't fade if you use an aniline dye.

   b. It's an aniline dye only if it doesn't fade.

   c. If it doesn't fade, it must be an aniline dye.

   *d. If it fades it can't be an aniline dye.

   e. Unless it fades it's an aniline dye.

2. If it's real gold, then it's a genuine find.

   a. If it's not real gold, then it's not a real find.

   b. If it's a genuine find, then it's real gold.

c. If it's not a genuine find, then it's not real gold.

d. If it's real gold, then it's not a genuine find.

e. If it's not a genuine find, then it's real gold.

3. If the stove isn't warm, it hasn't been used.

   a. The stove can't be warm unless it has been used.

   b. The stove hasn't been used if it isn't warm.

   c. If the stove hasn't been used, it can't be warm.

   d. The stove won't be warm only if it hasn't been used.

   *e. The stove isn't warm if it hasn't been used.

4. If you want to program for business purposes, then use COBOL.

   a. Use COBOL if you want to program for business purposes.

   b. If you're not using COBOL, you're not programming for business purposes.

   c. Use COBOL unless you're programming for business purposes.

   *d. If you don't want to program for business purposes, then don't use COBOL.

   e. You are programming for business purposes only if you use COBOL.

Part B. Elementary Conditional Argument Analysis

Analyze each of the following arguments. Distinguish disjunctive arguments (arguments by eliminating alternatives) from conditional arguments. Identify any cases of modus ponens, modus tollens, or chain argument. Decide in each case whether the argument is strong or weak. Identify any fallacies of affirming the consequent or denying the antecedent.

1. The tiny blue blossoms are either bluets or forget-me-nots. But they don't have the four petals of bluets. So they must be forget-me-nots.

2. If it's genuine leather, it will be rough on the reverse side. But it's not rough on the reverse side. So it can't be genuine leather.

3. Either you have to paint that, or you have to apply varnish or shellac to it. But you don't varnish it. Hence you must apply shellac to it.

4. If the colors are matched with a deft touch, it's a genuine Matisse. The colors are matched deftly. So it is a Matisse.

5. Either Hesse wrote *Faust*, or he wrote *Steppenwolf*. Goethe, however, is the author of *Faust*. So it must have been Hesse who wrote *Steppenwolf*.

6. If Hawkins actually was with the terrorists, he's sure to plead the Fifth Amendment before the grand jury. Hawkins does plead the Fifth Amendment. So he must have been with the terrorists.

7. If you like Vivaldi you'll like Mozart, and if you like Mozart you'll like Schubert. So if you like Vivaldi, you'll like Schubert.

8. She will attend either Old Dominion, Hampton University, or Christopher Newport. She opts against Old Dominion. Thus she'll attend Hampton University.

9. If Einstein is a movie star then he's famous. Einstein isn't a movie star. So Einstein isn't famous.

*10. The accused woman is guilty unless the seamstress lied. But the seamstress didn't lie. So the accused woman must be guilty.

11. If his arm tires, his fastball fades in the late innings. If his fastball fades, hitters get to him. So if hitters get to him, his arm must have tired.

12. Unless you steam the carrots instead of boiling them, they will lose flavor. But the carrots do have a lot of flavor. So you must have steamed rather than boiled them.

13. [A TV ad for Sensodyne toothpaste in early 1991 shows first the toothpaste, then a row of dominoes. When the first domino tumbles, a chain reaction starts and all of them fall in turn. The text:]

Those with sensitive teeth may stop brushing. This can lead to gingivitis, a serious gum disease. In turn this can lead to tooth loss. Sensodyne is specially designed for sensitive teeth.

*14. [From poetry we advance to pyping,] from pyping to playing, from play to pleasure, from pleasure to slouth, from slouth to sleepe, from sleepe to sinne, from sinne to death, from death to the Divel.

Stephen Gosson, *School of Abuse* (1579); quoted in
W. K. Wimsatt, *The Verbal Icon* (London 1970), p. 87.

6. The Indirect Argument

The *indirect argument* is a more sophisticated type of conditional argument that is frequently used in the theoretical areas of logic, mathematics, and the natural sciences. It is also used in everyday arguments in natural language, and is well worth becoming acquainted with. In some ways it is an extended version of the modus tollens. The first step in an indirect argument is to state clearly what it is we seek to prove or establish. Then we assume the exact opposite of this, and attempt to show that this assumption leads to some conclusion that we simply cannot accept. The unacceptable conclusion is in some cases a self-contradictory statement, or one that cannot be true. In other cases it is an absurdity, or a statement that contradicts known facts. When two statements are exact or contradictory opposites and one of them is false, the other must be true. So the proof strategy of the indirect argument is always to show that the original assumption (the opposite of what we want to prove) is false, so that its contradictory opposite (the statement we want to prove) must be true.

Suppose for example that we want to prove in math that there is no largest integer (integers are whole numbers like 3, 111, 4,627). What we want to establish is that whatever candidate we come up with for largest integer, which we can call *n*, there is always some larger integer. We begin by assuming the opposite of what we want to prove. The opposite of "There is no largest integer" is "There is a largest integer." These two statements exhaust the possibilities. Of the largest integer, either it exists or it does not exist. There is no in-between, and there is no other possibility. Also, the statements are contradictory opposites. If one of the statements is false, like "There is a largest integer," the other must be true.

To prove: There is no largest integer.
Assume: There is a largest integer *n*.

In arithmetic there is nothing to prevent us from adding one to any integer whatever. We can have 1+1, or 452+1, or 75,401+1. Similarly we can take our largest integer *n* and add one to it.

1. We add 1 to *n*, producing *n*+1.
2. But now there is an integer, *n*+1, larger than the largest integer.
3. The statement that there is an integer larger than the largest integer is self-contradictory.
4. The original assumption, that there is a largest integer, which implies this contradiction, is false.
5. Its opposite, that there is no largest integer, is true.
6. Hence there is no largest integer.

In the sense that a contradiction or absurdity is the goal of an indirect argument, the argument is sometimes called a *reductio ad absurdum*. The idea behind this designation is that of taking an opponent's position (which is the opposite of our own) and reducing it to absurdity. The indirect argument is quite ancient. Its inventor was Zeno of Elea, who flourished around 450 B.C. Zeno really developed the first argumentative philosophical discourse, a discourse devoted to exploring and establishing or rejecting a philosophical position.

Zeno agreed with his teacher Parmenides that there existed only one substance, which they called Being, and that this Being was spread out in all directions evenly without limits. One implication of this view that affronted common sense was that there was no real motion, since there was no empty space for anything to move into. The Eleatics, as these early philosophers from Elea were called, did not question that we see what we take to be motion. This apparent motion only involved appearances, they held, not the underlying, unchanging reality. But opponents of the Eleatics had a field day ridiculing this position for denying the reality of motion.

The contribution to the Eleatics for which Zeno is best remembered is his indirect arguments against opponents. When they contended that motion was real, he argued that motion was only apparent because the very concept of it was incoherent. His best known argument involved the claim that in a race, Achilles, the fastest mortal, would not overtake the tortoise if the tortoise had a headstart. The following is an approximation of Zeno's argument for the unreality of motion.

To prove: The concept of motion is incoherent, so motion is unreal.
Assume: The concept of motion is coherent, and motion is real.

1. If motion is real, then Achilles overtakes the tortoise in a race.
3. When Achilles gets to S, the starting point of the tortoise, it has advanced to point T.
4. When Achilles reaches T, the tortoise has advanced to U.
5. In this manner the tortoise always stays ahead of Achilles.
7. So the concept of motion is incoherent.
8. Thus motion is unreal.

Another excellent example of indirect argument in physics was advanced by Galileo Galilei in his *Dialogues concerning Two New Sciences.* According to the physics accepted in his day, a heavy body falls faster than a light one. Galileo disputes this, not by performing experiments to establish the times taken by various objects to fall the same distance, but by devising an indirect argument. The argument may be summarized as follows.

To prove: The heavier body does not fall faster than the light.
Assume: The heavier body does fall faster than the light.

1. We join the heavier and the light body together in a new body.
2. The lighter body tends to retard the heavy, and the heavier to speed up the light.
3. So if the heavy falls with a speed of 8 and the light with 4, together they fall with a speed of less than 8; i.e., the new body falls slower than the heavy.
4. But joining the two together produces a body heavier than the one with a speed of 8 units.
5. So the heavy body falls slower than the light.
6. When we assume that the heavy body falls faster than the light, this implies that the heavy body falls slower than the light.

7. Since the heavy body cannot fall both faster and slower than the light, this is a contradiction.
8. Thus the heavy body does not fall faster than the light.

For an indirect argument to be strong, the internal reasoning from the assumption must be sound. The inference from one step to the next must be strong. Also the statement to be proved must be the contradictory opposite of the one assumed. Only if they are so related can the falsity of the one establish the truth of the other. Together they must exhaust the possibilities so that no third alternative can exist. The arguments from mathematics and Galileo above satisfy this condition. The one from Zeno does not, at least as it is stated here. It seems possible, for instance, for the concept of motion to be incoherent yet motion itself to be real. It also seems possible for the concept of motion to be coherent yet motion itself to be unreal.

7. More Conditional Arguments

Suppose we encounter the following conditional argument and must decide whether it is sound or unsound.

<If she likes primitive painting, she'll appreciate Grant Wood,>① and <if she's partial to aimless music, she'll enjoy John Cage.>② <She does appreciate Grant Wood,>③ but <she cannot abide John Cage's music.>④ [So] <she's not partial to aimless music.>⑤

② + ④
↓
⑤

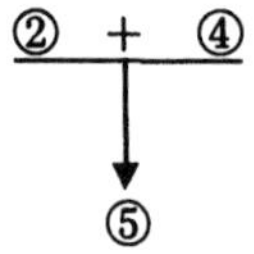

Linked—modus tollens
Strong

The conclusion cue helps us identify ⑤ as the conclusion of an argument. Statements ① and ③ don't seem relevant to it though. They may be intended to be the premises of an argument to prove "she likes primitive painting." But we will neither draw this as an implicit conclusion nor consider ① and ③ parts of an argument supporting it. It would be a fallacy of affirming the consequent. On the basis of the principle of charity we will not attribute to this writer a weak argument when she may not have intended an argument at all.

So we restrict our diagram to ②, ④, and ⑤. The first two provide linked support for ⑤. In ④ the consequent of ② is negated, and ⑤, the conclusion, gives us the negated antecedent. So this argument is a modus tollens, and a strong one, provided the conditional statement is true.

Some statements are so elliptical and allusive that we must carry out an analysis of them first of all to be sure that they are arguments, then to ascertain what they seek to establish, and finally how they attempt to establish it.

> You might ask, is any car really worth nearly $52,000 (let alone $163,000)? And the logical answer is no. A logical person would buy a $7,000 economy sedan and keep it until it wore out. But, if logic were the only thing that made automobiles appealing, we'd all be on bicycles and subway trains.

At first glance this piece of discourse little resembles an argument. It does speak of a "logical" answer to a question, and it addresses what a "logical" person would do, but "logical" in this context seems a synonym for "practical" or "economy-minded." We find no premise or conclusion cues, and there is no obvious conclusion. Further, it begins with a question, while most arguments are introduced with a premise or conclusion. It does contain a conditional statement, but without any of the accompanying statements that usually join a conditional statement in an argument. If it is an argument, it must be a terse one with important components left unstated.

It does contain two assertions, however, that may stand in some sort of support relation. The second statement, which responds in the negative to the initial question, needs paraphrasing to capture what it asserts: "Logically no car is worth $52,000." Now this might stand in some support relation to the next statement. We can spread out and mark up the text to see what we have.

①

<You might ask, is any car really worth $52,000 (let alone $163,000)?>

②

And <the logical answer is no.> [Logically no car is worth $52,000.]

③

<A logical person would buy a $7,000 economy sedan and keep it until it

④

wore out.> But, <if logic were the only thing that made automobiles

appealing, we'd all be on bicycles and subway trains.>

Now the writer may be claiming that because a logical person buys a $7,000 sedan, logically no car is worth $52,000. Or he may be claiming that because logically no car is worth $52,000, a logical person buys a $7,000 economy sedan. The third possibility, that he is advancing neither claim, still exists because each of these claims could be advanced independently on their own merits.

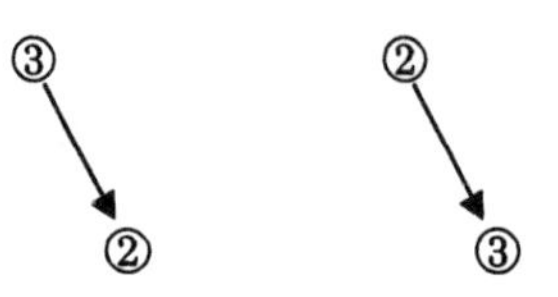

Perhaps ④ can throw some light on the question whether we have an argument or not. There are two things about this conditional statement that interest us. First, in dealing with "logic" and the worth of cars it is linked thematically with ①, ②, and ③. Secondly, the consequent of the conditional statement, if it were separated off and advanced as a claim descriptive of the world, would be false. It claims that under the condition given in the antecedent, we would all be on bicycles and subway trains. In fact, vast numbers of Americans use the auto exclusively for their transportation needs. Let us supply this relevant but unstated fact. We can consider it a suppressed premise of a conditional argument, the consequent of whose conditional statement it negates. This allows us to infer by modus tollens the negated antecedent of the same conditional statement as the unstated conclusion of this argument. We can append the unstated parts of the argument to the conditional statement.

④ <If logic were the only thing that made automobiles appealing, we'd all be on bicycles and subway trains.> [5] [We're not all on bicycles and subway trains.] [6] [So logic is not the only thing that makes automobiles appealing.]

④ + [5] → [6]   Linked—modus tollens

Before pursuing this conditional argument further we need to ask whether it links up with ② and ③ in some larger argumentative framework, or whether ② and ③ only supply information useful for understanding ④. We can set ③ in relation with ④ and [5] because of the way it links up logic with the worth of a car. This conditional statement is itself made on the basis of the claim (which it indirectly calls into question) that the logical person buys a $7,000 sedan, or in other words, that logic alone determines the worth of a car. ③ in turn receives some support from ②. It is claimed that because no car is worth $52,000, the logical person buys a $7,000 sedan. So we have ② supporting ③, and when we fit this with ④ and its now explicit further parts, the following diagram results.

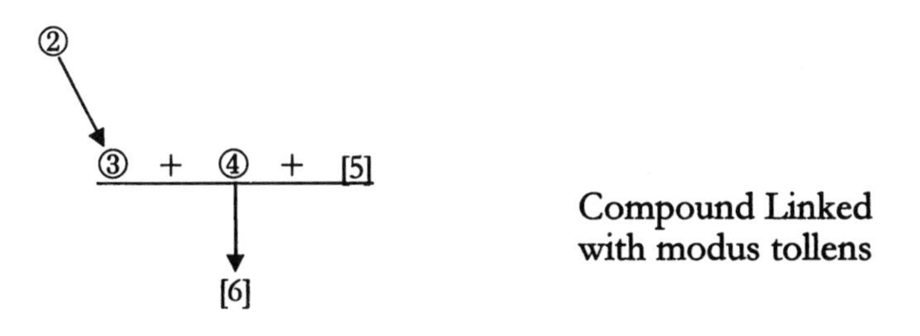

This enables us to see now that a further conclusion is implied. Down to [6] the argument has established that logic is not the only thing that determines the worth of a car. But this implies further that a car really could be worth $52,000. We can now assert this as [7], the final conclusion of this indirect argument.

① <You might ask, is any car really worth $52,000 (let alone $163,000)?> And ② <the logical answer is no.> ③ <A logical person would buy a $7,000 economy sedan and keep it until it wore out.> But ④ <if logic were the only thing that made automobiles appealing, we'd all be on bicycles and subway trains.> [5] [We're not all on bicycles and subway trains.] So [6] [logic is not the only thing that makes autos appealing.] Thus [7] [a car can be worth $52,000.]

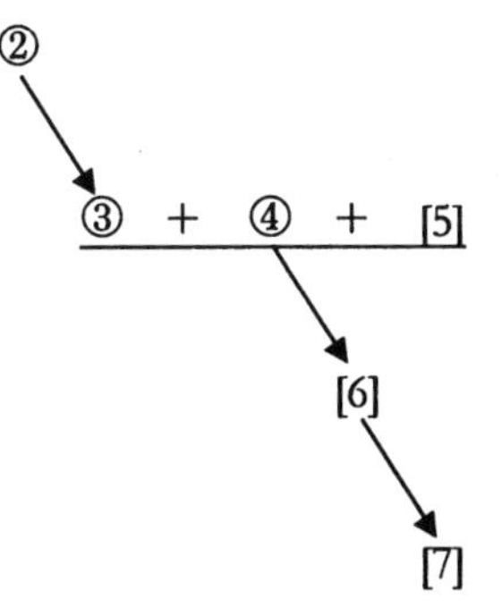

Compound Serial
with modus tollens
Weak

Now that we are more clear about what is being claimed in this terse argument, we can ask whether it is strong or weak. Recalling that we interpret "logical" to mean "practical," ③ is a sound claim. Almost any car in this price range as it ages will reach a point where repair costs and inconvenience are so great that it is more practical to buy a new car instead (or at least a newer one). But we can always say that this is the point where the car wears out.

④ is the crucial premise, and it is doubtful. When we interpret its conditional relation as a claim, it urges that the practical person interested in the most economical form of transportation will always opt for bus or subway over the automobile. In fact, bus and subway are not even options for vast numbers of Americans, who must transport themselves with their autos, their feet, or not at all. Even when these options are available, the practical person must calculate the time it takes to get from point A to point B. In almost all cases, the automobile is faster, and substantially faster, than public transportation. The rare exception is the person who lives in easy walking distance from the subway and all of the shops she needs, and also works in easy walking distance from the subway.

One can also object to this argument as a whole (not just ④) that factors other than practicality (in the sense of economy) can legitimately influence the purchase of a car. Among them are the comfort of the ride, how presentable the car is (important for the many people who use a car in their profession), the dependability of the car (will it start and get you where you need to go without breaking down), and the performance of the engine (though the type of performance that justifies the $52,000 car is more in place on the race course than a city street or highway). What social critics most frequently object to in America's auto buying habits is the amount of money spent to satisfy questionable psychological needs. There is some justice to this criticism, even though there is no consensus on what needs are legitimate. Thus an unemployed person might convince the community to help transport him to and from work by subsidizing bus or subway service if this were necessary to get him off welfare and convert him into a wage-earner. But it would probably not accept the claim that his need for self-esteem required that he be transported in an expensive automobile.

On balance, since ④ is linked with ③ and [5] and so weakens the whole of the support for [6] and [7], the argument is weak. The writer has not provided good reasons for the claim that logic is not the only thing that makes autos appealing, nor for his conclusion that a car can be worth $52,000.

Now after a summary of the chapter we will practice evaluating conditional arguments.

SUMMARY

One event is a condition of another when it is needed for the other to occur, or when it makes the other occur. A necessary condition is one that must be satisfied for some result to occur, like using coffee beans, grounds, or crystals is a necessary condition of making coffee. A sufficient condition produces or brings about some result, like striking a golf ball with the face of a wood is a sufficient condition of driving it.

Some conditions are causes of the events they condition; others are not. Some events are both necessary and sufficient conditions of others, like standing under a running shower is a necessary and sufficient condition of showering. Some events are not related to others as conditions at all, such as becoming a member of the Democratic or Republican party is not a condition of voting in a general election in the U.S.

A conditional statement relates a condition to what it conditions, frequently in "if...then..." form. The part of the conditional statement following the "if" is the antecedent: It states the condition. The part after the "then" is the consequent: It tells us what is conditioned. A conditional statement is true when the two events, states, or objects referred to are actually related as condition and conditioned. When they are not so related, the conditional statement is false.

Disjunctive arguments seek to establish their conclusions by putting forward alternatives then eliminating some of them. For a disjunctive argument to be strong, it must state all of the important alternatives, then bring sound evidence or reasoning to eliminate each of these alternatives that is not mentioned in the conclusion.

Conditional statements contraposit. When you negate both the antecedent and the consequent of a true conditional statement and exchange their places, the resulting new conditional statement will be true also. But conditional statements do not convert. We attempt to convert when we trade the places of the antecedent and the consequent of a true conditional statement. But the attempt fails, and the claim that the resulting new conditional statement is true is the fallacy of illicit conversion.

Conditional arguments are linked arguments that contain one or more conditional statements. Two common conditional arguments are usually strong when their premises are true.

> *Modus ponens*: In this argument one of the premises affirms the antecedent of the conditional statement.
> *Modus tollens*: Here one of the premises negates or denies the consequent of the conditional statement.

Two other common conditional arguments are usually weak even though their premises are true. They are the fallacy of affirming the consequent, and the fallacy of negating the antecedent.

A chain argument has only conditional statements for its premises and conclusion. Chain arguments are usually strong when their premises are true and they are modeled on modus ponens or modus tollens. Those modeled on the fallacious conditional arguments are usually weak, and are sometimes identified as slippery slope fallacies.

The indirect argument is a sophisticated argument modeled on the modus tollens. The arguer assumes the exact or contradictory opposite of what she wants to prove. Then she attempts to show that this assumption leads to a contradiction, an absurdity, or some other result that is quite unacceptable. According to modus tollens, this means that the original assumption itself is unacceptable. It must be rejected as false. This establishes that the original statement of the arguer must be true, because the contradictory opposite of a false statement must be true.

For some more challenging conditional arguments that we analyze and evaluate we may have to supply unstated premises or an unstated conclusion.

Study Questions

Section 1: Conditions

1. What is it for one object or action to be a condition of another?
2. What is a necessary condition?
3. What is a causal condition?
4. Are all necessary conditions causal conditions?
5. Does the satisfaction of a necessary condition guarantee a desired result or anticipated outcome?
6. What is a sufficient condition?
7. Are all sufficient conditions causal conditions?
8. Are sufficient conditions necessary conditions?
9. Are there conditions that are both sufficient and necessary?
10. Is any given object always related to some other given object as a condition?

Section 2: Conditional Statements

11. What is a conditional statement?
12. How is an if . . . then . . . statement a conditional statement?
13. Why are we interested in conditional statements?
14. What are the two parts of a conditional statement?
15. Is the consequent of a conditional statement the same as the conclusion of an argument?
16. When is a conditional statement true?
17. Given an affirmative antecedent, what sort of condition must it have in order for the conditional statement itself to be true?
18. What is the case with a negative antecedent?

Section 3: Disjunctive Arguments

19. What is a disjunctive statement?
20. What is a disjunctive argument?
21. How do we diagram disjunctive arguments?
22. Under which circumstances is a disjunctive argument strong?

23. What about the case of a disjunctive inference that affirms alternatives instead of eliminating them?

Section 4: Conditional Arguments

24. What is a conditional argument?
25. What is the contrapositive of a conditional statement?
26. What happens when we contraposi a true conditional statement, and why?
27. What is a modus ponens?
28. The modus tollens?
29. What do we know of the modus ponens and modus tollens?
30. What is a chain argument or hypothetical syllogism?

Section 5: Fallacious Conditional Arguments

31. What is illicit conversion?
32. Why is it illicit?
33. Why does the conditional statement not convert?
34. What is the fallacy of affirming the consequent?
35. Why is this fallacious?
36. What is the fallacy of negating the antecedent?
37. Why is it fallacious?
38. In what cases are chain arguments usually strong?
39. In what cases weak?
40. What is a slippery slope argument?
41. What is a slippery slope fallacy?

Section 6: The Indirect Argument

42. What is an indirect argument?
43. What is its strategy?
44. Why is it sometimes called a reductio ad absurdum?
45. What conditions must an indirect argument meet if it is to be strong?

Section 7: More Conditional Arguments

46. What must we do with conditional arguments composed of statements that are elliptical and/or allusive?

EXERCISE 13—3: CONDITIONAL ARGUMENTS

Analyze each of the following arguments. Distinguish disjunctive (arguments by eliminating alternatives) from conditional arguments. Identify any cases of modus ponens, modus tollens, or chain argument. Decide in each case whether the argument is strong or weak. Identify any fallacies of affirming the consequent, denying the antecedent, or slippery slope.

1. He either bought a swing and a rope, or he bought a hobby horse. He did buy a swing and a rope. So he must have bought a hobby horse.

2. The animal over there isn't a squirrel unless it has a long bushy tail. It doesn't have a long bushy tail. Thus the animal over there isn't a squirrel.

3. If the toaster works, it must be plugged in. But the toaster isn't working. So it must be unplugged.

4. If the tomato plants are wilting because of a fungus, then dusting them with an insecticide won't help. But look, a few days after we dusted them they returned to their normal healthy state. So they couldn't have been wilting from a fungus.

5. If interest rates continue to remain high, the economy will be sluggish.
But unless the economy picks up, even more people will be jobless.
So the number of unemployed will increase if interest rates remain high.

6. Anyone who believes the claim of that ad that there's an easy, legal way to make a million with a small investment is a gullible fool. And of all the things Green may be, she's certainly not a gullible fool.

7. If monopolies are always bad, then AT&T was rightly forced to divest its telephone companies. If AT&T was rightly forced to divest, the public should have benefited. But the chief results of divestment today are poorer quality service and more costly local service. So perhaps monopolies aren't always bad.

8. Dandridge can't profit from the current high interest rates unless he has money to invest. But he has no money to invest. Thus Dandridge can't profit from the current high interest rates.

*9. To judge from their neglect, people have never comprehended the power of Love. For if they had, they would have dedicated imposing temples and altars to this powerful god, and offered him solemn sacrifices, But they do not do this.

Adapted from Plato, *Symposium.*

10. Since you do not have a receipt, you can prove the bill was paid only if you have a canceled check. But you do not have a canceled check. Consequently, you cannot establish that the bill was paid.

11. Margaret: . . . so many allusions have been made to Rainbow Hill lately. You know what Rainbow Hill is? Place that is famous for treatin' alcoholics and dope fiends in the movies.

Brick: I'm not in the movies.

Margaret: No, and you don't take dope. Otherwise you're a perfect candidate for Rainbow Hill, Baby, and that's where they aim to ship you.

Tennessee Williams, *Cat on a Hot Tin Roof*, Act I.

12. If the RDA's were adequate then increased intake would not result in increased health benefits. Yet Dr. Emanuel Cheraskin and his University of Alabama colleague, Dr. W. M. Ringsdorf, have found higher intake does result in better health.

Dr. Cheraskin's group studied the number of clinical symptoms of a group of people versus their nutrient intake, and determined with every nutrient tested so far, that levels appreciably higher than the RDA resulted in the fewest symptoms, therefore, producing the best health.

The Best of Forum (1980), p. 3.

13. In his book *Witness to Power,* John Ehrlichman accuses Dan Rather of being lazy, careless in checking his facts, and calls him a reporter who lacks objectivity. How much truth is there in Ehrlichman's charge, or is it just a case of sour grapes?

Rather may have weaknesses, but laziness, carelessness and lack of objectivity aren't among them.

Adapted from Walter Scott's Personality Parade,
Parade (July 18, 1982), p. 2.

14\. . . . if Bill Clinton persists in being a president who insists on being liked by everyone, in four years he'll be neither liked nor president.

(*Supply unstated premise and conclusion.*)

Richard Cohen, "Clinton's Lack of Foreign Policy Causes Confusion," *Newport News-Hampton Daily Press*, (May 18, 1993,) p. A-8.

15. (The Lion fears the sound of a cock crowing and is ashamed of this fear. As he walks conversing with the Elephant, he notices the Elephant cock his ear as a gnat hums by. He asks why.)

"Do you see that wretched little buzzing insect? I'm terribly afraid of its getting into my ear: if it once gets in, I'm dead and done for." The Lion's spirits rose at once when he heard this: "For," he said to himself, "if the Elephant, huge as he is, is afraid of a gnat, I needn't be so much ashamed of being afraid of a cock, who is ten thousand times bigger than a gnat." [I don't want to be dead and done for.] [Therefore I needn't be ashamed of being afraid of a cock.]

"The Lion, Jupiter, and the Elephant," *Aesop's Fables*, facsimile of 1912 ed., (New York n.d.), p. 179f.

*16. (A Malthusian curve is a geometrical progression, a doubling of the earth's population every thirty years.)

If evil is a constant presence in the human soul, it is also true that there are more souls than ever, and by that logic both good and evil are rising on a Malthusian curve, or at any rate both good and evil may be said to be increasing in the world at the same rate as the population: 1.7% per annum.

Lance Morrow, "Evil," *Time* (June 10, 1991), p. 52f.

17. (Construct, analyze, and evaluate the conditional arguments implicit in this paragraph to decide the question whether Antarctica and Palestine are states.)

Take Antarctica. Is it a state? It has plenty of territory, issues postage stamps, and even has official country identification letters, AQ. Alas, it has no citizens. Palestine has lots of people, recognized diplomats, but, in practice, no land of its own.

"My Land, Your Land and Sealand," *The Economist* (Oct. 2, 1993), p. 48.

18. In his celebrated biography Boswell mentions to Johnson a person who claims there is no difference between virtue and vice. Identify both the disjunctive and the conditional aspects of the argument Johnson gives in reply.

> . . . if the fellow does not think as he speaks, he is lying; and I see not what honour he can propose to himself from having the character of a lyar. But if he does really think that there is no distinction between virtue and vice, why, Sir, when he leaves our houses, let us count our spoons.

James Boswell, *The Life of Johnson*, ed. by Christopher Hibbert (Harmondsworth 1979), p. 110.

19. (Interpret the question as rhetorical, and supply the conclusion of this conditional argument.)

The crisis that culminated in the First World War might conceivably have been resolved if some institutionalized forum for negotiations among great powers, such as that provided by . . . the Security Council of the United Nations, had existed. And certainly one of the causes of the Second World War was the failure of the major powers to support the League of Nations. Both of these assertions are, to be sure, debatable. Even the most vigorous dissenter, though, must agree that they are not entirely unreasonable. If there is a reasonable chance that an organization such as the United Nations may help the world avoid catastrophes of the magnitude of the world wars, would it not be prudent to preserve the organization?

James Lee Ray, *Global Politics*, 3rd ed. (Boston 1987), p. 377f.

20. In the spring of 1787 Dutch citizens took arms against infringements on their liberty by their ruler, Prince William V of Orange, and the aristocracy. When Prussian troops marched to support the Prince, the pro-French Dutch citizens tried to get France to intervene.

The dilemma for French policy was acute. If nothing was done to forestall a Prussian invasion, the credibility of French power and authority would suffer a disastrous humiliation virtually on France's doorstep . . . But war in behalf of a cause repudiated by the King seemed equally foolhardy. . . . The deciding factor was money. . . . Brienne worried that any kind of military action would immediately drive the state into bankruptcy. "Not one penny. . . ."

Simon Schama, *Citizens*. A Chronicle of the French Revolution (New York 1989), p. 232.

21. In the course of his third argument for the existence of God, Thomas Aquinas seeks to establish that one being exists necessarily. He starts from the premise that contingent things exist, and relies on the principle announced by the ancient Greek philosopher Parmenides that nothing comes into being from nothing (*ex nihilo nihil fit* in its Latin version).
(Display the structure of Aquinas' argument and comment on it.)

We find in nature things for which it is possible that they be or not be, since they come to be and perish, and consequently it is possible for them either to be or not to be. But it is impossible for these things to always exist, for that which can possibly perish must really not exist at some time. Therefore, if everything that now exists could possibly not exist, then at one time there was nothing in existence. Now if this were true, even now there would be nothing in existence, because that which does not exist begins to exist only through something already existing. Therefore, if at one time nothing was in existence, it would have been impossible for anything to have begun to exist; and thus even now nothing would be in existence which is absurd. Therefore not all beings are merely possible, but there must exist something the existence of which is necessary.

Summa Theologica, Part One, Question II, Third Article.

*22. Organize the following material into an indirect argument, then analyze and evaluate the argument. The argument is attributed to Xenophanes in the Pseudo-Aristotle treatise *de Melisso, Xenophane, Gorgia.*

On the supposition that God is supreme over all things Xenophanes draws the conclusion that God is one. For if there were two or more gods, each of them would be supreme, and thus in effect none of them would be supreme and best. For the very meaning of God and of divine power involves supremacy over all else. So far as he is not superior he is not God.

Philip Wheelwright, ed., *The Presocratics*
(Indianapolis 1960), p. 38.

23. (Kepler, discoverer of the laws of planetary motion, seeks in the sun the power that causes the planets to move in orbits around it. He is moving away from the view that it is something akin to soul, and considers several hypotheses to determine more closely what this power is. Remember that gravity is yet to be discovered by Newton, and that Kepler's work is a preliminary to that discovery. Construct and evaluate an indirect argument based on this quotation from Kepler's *Astronomia Nova* (Bk. III, Ch. 33), taking this as the statement to be proved: The light of the sun is not a vehicle for the moving force of the planets.)

Though the light of the sun cannot itself be the moving force . . . it may perhaps represent a kind of vehicle, or tool, that the moving force uses. But the following considerations seem to contradict this. First, the light is arrested in regions that lie in the shade. If, then, the moving force were to use light as a vehicle, darkness would bring the planets to a standstill.

Quoted in A. Koestler, *Encyclopedia of Philosophy*,
ed. by Paul Edwards (New York 1967), s.v. Kepler.

Further Reading

Stephen F. Barker, *The Elements of Logic*, 5th ed. (New York 1989), pp. 66f., 69–75. Closer to a standard treatment of disjunctive and conditional arguments, but also concerned with different ways of stating conditionals in natural language.

Alec Fisher, *The Logic of Real Arguments* (New York 1988), pp. 82–127. Develops a technique for analyzing and evaluating "suppositional" arguments, and applies it to some complex examples.

Stephen Naylor Thomas, *Practical Reasoning in Natural Language*, 3rd ed. (Englewood Cliffs 1986), pp. 191–250. Has excellent material that starts with simple conditional arguments and extends to the analysis of complex ones.

CHAPTER FOURTEEN

INDUCTIVE ARGUMENTS

To generalize is to be an idiot
William Blake

1. GENERAL STATEMENTS AND GENERALIZATIONS

What is a general statement? A general statement is one that refers to all or most members of a group or class of things.

1. All major league baseballs are made of cowhide.
2. Most hose are sheer.
3. Bald eagles are seldom seen in the forty-eight states.
4. Many inhabitants of Hampton Roads are members of the Armed Forces.
5. No BMWs are inexpensive automobiles.

All of these statements are made true or false by the way things are in the world. For instance, to decide whether (5) is true or not we must compare the prices of BMWs with those of other automobiles. Statements that are made true or false by the way things are in the world are sometimes called empirical statements. They are contrasted with analytic statements that are necessarily true or false, usually because they express our decision to use words in a certain way.

6. All deciduous trees lose their leaves in winter.
7. No wooden frame houses contain any wood.

Statement (7) is a necessarily false statement, a statement that contradicts itself, or a self-contradiction. Statement (6) is a necessarily true statement. It isn't true because we go out and examine all the deciduous trees we can find to discover whether they lose their leaves in winter. It is true because we don't call a tree deciduous unless it loses its leaves in winter. Applied to trees, "deciduous" means "loses its leaves in winter." Put another way, "loses its leaves in winter" is a defining characteristic of "deciduous tree."

Statements beginning with "all" that refer to all members of a group are for that reason sometimes called universal statements. It is important to note when a general statement is also a universal statement (though we do not have to call it "universal"). A universal statement is made false by one counter-instance (unless it is hedged), whereas other general statements beginning with "most" or "many" may have counter-instances and still remain true. For instance, statement (1) above is a universal statement. It will be false if we find one case of a horsehide baseball in the major leagues. Another way of putting this is to say that one horsehide baseball falsifies statement (1). So an argument with a universal statement as its conclusion is destroyed by a single counter-instance, no matter how weighty its evidence.

Although this is neither obvious nor commonly realized, statements beginning with "no" as a modifier of items in a group or class are not only general but also universal statements. So statement (5) above is universal because "No BMWs" refers to every BMW, thus referring to all members of a class or group.

Non-universal general statements are introduced by words like "most," "many," or phrases like "a lot of." Hedged universal statements, statements with introductory phrases like "almost all" or "practically none," are non-universal general statements.

General statements are contrasted with particular statements. Particular statements can refer to one unique individual, to one member of a group or class, or to several or some members of a group or class.[1]

There is a carved alabaster ashtray on the sideboard.

Yo-Yo-Ma is an outstanding cellist.

Some movies leave you disappointed.

There are a few chocolate-chip cookies left.

We don't construct arguments by inductive generalization to support particular statements. Such statements can refer to more than one item of a group or class. But we test their reliability in a different way. Suppose Janie asks Brett whether there are any trash bags out in the utility room. Brett looks and responds.

---

[1] In the categorical statements of syllogistic logic, particular statements are a sub-variety of general statements.

Yes, there are a few trash bags there.

This situation is typical of such statements in that we don't construct arguments to support them. They involve so few items that we simply look and decide them as empirical statements.

Some statements that look like particular statements are actually general ones in disguise.

An Infiniti is a quality automobile.

A picture is worth a thousand words.

The first of these statements refers to Infinitis in general, and the second could be paraphrased thus:

Pictures convey more information for the space than words.

Is there any difference between a generalization and a general statement? All generalizations are general statements—they couldn't be generalizations if they weren't general statements. But not all general statements are generalizations. A model generalization is a statement about all the members of a group or class based on observing only a few members of that same group or class. A general statement that is established true by direct inspection of every member of the group is not a generalization.

A. None of the apples in that bag are rotten.

In this case we established (A) by direct inspection of all the apples, so (A) is a general statement but not a generalization. We are not generalizing from inspecting a few to the whole bag-full. The following discourses contain generalizations.

"Total Raisin Bran is a great cereal."
"Why do you think so?"
"Well, I got a free sample package in our mailbox, along with a 35-cent coupon toward the purchase of a full box."
"Jamaica's a terrible place for a vacation. We went there last Christmas and it rained every day."

The generalizations are the following.

B. All Total Raisin Bran is great cereal.

C. No Jamaica vacations are good vacations.

(B) is a generalization because it refers to every box, bowl, and spoonful of Raisin Bran. (C) is a generalization because it refers to every Jamaica vacation. If a good generalization is one based on sound evidence, then neither of these is a good generalization. In (B) a cereal is judged good merely on the basis of how it is marketed, with no reference to its flavor or nutritional value. In (C) a

Caribbean island is judged unfit for vacations on the basis of several rainy days during one visit. Neither generalization is strongly supported by the evidence advanced.

Both of the above are unsound generalizations, and there are many more unsound ones we will encounter, including some we will fall victim to ourselves. Since unsound generalizations are so common, why don't we avoid them by simply not dealing in generalizations at all? Couldn't we base our beliefs (and hence our decisions and our actions) on secure knowledge based on direct observation and reliable testimony of witnesses?

Unfortunately not. We need to know things in order to function and thrive, things about which we can't get enough evidence from sense perception and testimony. We have to make generalizations to lend our experience some stability and to make reliable predictions about events that affect us. It is our generalization that highways don't end abruptly just over the crest of a hill (to leave us hurtling through space) that enables us to travel an unfamiliar highway at a high rate of speed. It is our generalization that vegetables we buy in the produce section are wholesome rather than poisonous or contaminated by pesticide residues that allows us to purchase and consume in a salad onions, tomatoes, lettuce, and radishes without worrying that we will die or become seriously ill.

On the basis of many such generalizations we form categories for the items we have experienced. Then when we encounter something new, we fit it in the closest category. This helps us form our beliefs about it, to make our decisions, and conduct ourselves accordingly. There is no question of our getting along without generalizations. Notice the quote from poet William Blake at the beginning of this chapter to the effect that to generalize is to be an idiot. Apparently he means that painting is more effective when it deals with specifics. But Blake himself fails to avoid generalizing, for his statement means:

> All generalizing is idiotic.

Not only does he generalize himself, if his statement were true, he would convict himself of idiocy. But we reject his assessment of generalizations. They are absolutely necessary for us to function. Since we must have them, it is better for us to learn to distinguish the unsound from the sound ones, and also how to form sound ones ourselves.

2. Arguments by Inductive Generalization

An inductive generalization is an inference from a (frequently small) number of items to all or most of the group or class they are members of. An argument by inductive generalization presents the evidence about the observed items and claims that this evidence supports the conclusion about all or most members of the group or class. Here is an example.

> The Datsun B210 I bought from Vaughan Motors many years ago was a good automobile. The Nissan Stanza I bought from Vaughan Motors a few years ago was a good automobile. The Nissan Sentra I bought from Vaughan Motors last year was a good automobile. So all the cars bought from Vaughan Motors are good automobiles.

We mark up inductive arguments just as we mark up other arguments in natural language. Each premise provides a measure of independent support for the conclusion, but the point of the argument is to claim that their cumulative support together with other factors establishes the conclusion. So the basic pattern of an argument by inductive generalization is convergent.

① <The Datsun B210 I bought from Vaughan Motors many years ago was a good automobile.> ② <The Nissan Stanza I bought from Vaughan Motors a few years ago was a good automobile.> ③ <The Nissan Sentra I bought from Vaughan Motors last year was a good automobile.> [So] ④ <<u>all the cars bought from Vaughan Motors are good automobiles</u>.>

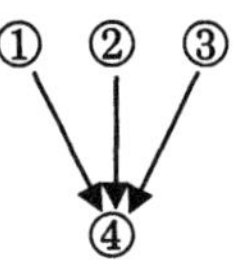

Convergent
Inductive Generalization

We must bear three factors in mind when we assess any argument by inductive generalization.

1. The size of the sample. All other factors being equal, the larger the sample, the stronger the argument.

2. The representativeness of the sample. How well are differences among items in the whole group or class represented in the sample? The more representative the sample, the stronger the argument.

3. The sweep or breadth of the conclusion. The more sweeping or broad the conclusion (the more it claims or includes), the weaker the argument.

The present argument looks weak on all three counts. First of all, the sample is too small. Simply to stay in business over many years the dealer has had to sell scores of automobiles, and he may well have sold hundreds. So a sample of three is quite small. The small size also contributes to the sample being poorly representative, even though it does contain three different models and they are from three different years. The dealer may sell other makes, and he certainly sells other models, so the sample should contain them, as well as cars from the years when I didn't buy one.

The way the conclusion is stated also contributes to the weakness of the argument. It is always a good step to examine the conclusion of an argument relative to the evidence advanced in support of it. But this is especially important with inductive generalizations. The conclusion here refers to all cars sold by Vaughan Motors, whereas the sample cites only the three cars I bought over a period of years. What exactly is meant by "all" in "All cars sold by Vaughan Motors"? Does it refer only to cars sold by Vaughan in the past? Or does it also refer to autos Vaughan is selling right now and will sell in the future? From the standpoint of the car-buying public, the latter interpretation is the more interesting, even though it makes for a more sweeping (or more broadly inclusive) generalization. To know that all of the cars sold by Vaughan in the past have been good cars is of small interest to me as a car-buyer unless it licenses the inference that cars sold by Vaughan in the future will be good ones too. What I want to know is whether any car I am likely to buy from Vaughan will be a good car.

Since my strongest interest is in the car I am likely to buy, let's rephrase the conclusion to reflect this.

All of the cars I am likely to buy from Vaughan Motors will be good cars.

This new conclusion strengthens the argument in at least two ways. First, it much reduces the sweep of the generalization. Previously (at least as we interpreted it above) it referred to all cars sold by Vaughan, past, present, or future. Now relative to the same evidence or sample it refers only to those few cars that constitute all that I am likely to buy. Secondly, the sample has been rendered more representative of all the cars cited in the conclusion in that the entire batch will have been selected by me. Without being able to pinpoint any specific feature, it could be that the way I select my cars at Vaughan Motors contributes to my purchasing good cars. If so, the factor influencing the goodness of the cars (my selecting them) is present in both the sample and the target groups.

But let us now go back to our original conclusion. Another way we can increase the strength of the argument is by increasing the size of the sample. If the sample includes 50 or 100 automobiles, we have a stronger argument. We can increase the strength much more if we increase the diversity of the sample at the same time. If Vaughan sells makes other than Datsun/Nissan we should certainly include them. We should also include any other models he sells in volume, as well as autos from those years when I purchased none. One way of getting this information would be to ask other buyers of autos at Vaughan whether they got good or bad cars. We also know that the same makes and models sold by Vaughan are also sold by other dealers nationwide. So we can get valuable information on frequencies of repairs on the makes and models that interest us from the annual *Consumer Reports Buyer's Guide*.

Of the two factors, getting a more representative sample is more important for strengthening the argument than just increasing the size of the sample. Suppose we could add to the sample information on 50 cars sold by Vaughan of the same makes, years, and models already included in the sample, or information on 25 autos representing the variety sold by Vaughan over this period. The latter information would strengthen the argument much more. So the absolute size of the sample does not affect the strength of the argument as much as its representativeness. On the other hand, it is difficult for a tiny sample to be representative. So the sample must be of a certain size in order to be representative.

Another weakness of the argument is that the term "good" as we use it here of both the sample and target automobiles is not precise. Our understanding of the argument would increase if we could determine more precisely what "good" means in this context. We should also be able to get a better estimate of the strength of the argument. It can mean several different things.

i. "Good" can refer to the car's appearance. The exterior is well designed to have aesthetic appeal, its finish is smooth and its color attractive. The interior is also well formed, with pleasant fabric and rugs.

ii. Associated with this, "good" can refer to the psychological appeal of the car. The car should impress people and make them think the owner is a fashionable or important person.

iii. "Good" can also refer to the car's performance. It accelerates from zero to 60 mph in about 6 seconds, and it can cruise on a rural interstate highway at 65 or 70 mph for days without breaking down.

iv. It can also refer to the economy of the car. The initial purchase price is low compared to that of comparable automobiles, it gets good gas mileage in both city and country driving, and it maintains a high re-sale value for many years. A car that impresses people (is "good" in sense #ii) and/or is high performance ("good" in sense #iii) will usually not be "good" in the present sense.

v. Associated with senses (iii) and (iv), "good" can also refer to the durability and dependability of the auto. We can rely on it to start in very

> cold weather, and not to boil over when we're stuck in traffic with the air-conditioner on during a summer heat wave. It breaks down on the road never or rarely. Routine maintenance is simple, infrequent, and inexpensive. Repairs are never needed.

We need to specify which of these senses of "good" we are using. In the case of incompatible senses, as of (ii) and (iii) with (iv), we need to specify which is to be given priority, or how the different senses are to be weighted. We need to draw these distinctions and make the appropriate decisions so we know what we are including as "good" automobiles in the target group. Obviously we can't get on with selecting a representative sample until we have decided what it is to be representative of.

We need now a closer look at ways in which the conclusion of an argument by inductive generalization sweeps. A conclusion sweeps always relative to the evidence advanced in support of it. Often to call a generalization "sweeping" is to imply that it goes farther beyond the evidence than it should. However, all generalizations are sweeping to a degree, since they refer to all or most members of a group or class. But we can take a specific generalization and make it more sweeping or less sweeping relative to the same body of evidence, according to how we phrase it. Assessing the sweep of a generalization is also important for assessing the strength of an argument by inductive generalization.

Suppose we are market researchers retained by the California Wine Institute, a trade association that promotes the interests of the California wine industry. They want a preliminary market survey to assess the feasibility of selling California wine in Germany. We carry out a survey of 1,703 Germans with the following results.

① <German #1 likes wine.> ② <German #2 likes wine.> ③ <German #3 likes wine.> ④ <Germans #n like wine.> ⑤ <German #1657 likes wine.> ⑥ <German #1658 doesn't like wine.> ⑦ <Germans #m don't like wine.> ⑧ <German #1703 doesn't like wine.> So ⑨ <<u>most Germans like wine</u>.>

Here Germans #n refer to Germans #4 to 1,656 who liked wine, and Germans #m to Germans #1,659 to 1,702 who didn't. The Germans who did like wine constitute evidence in support of the conclusion. Those who did not count as evidence against it. We show evidence against a conclusion with a jagged line. The argument has this diagram.

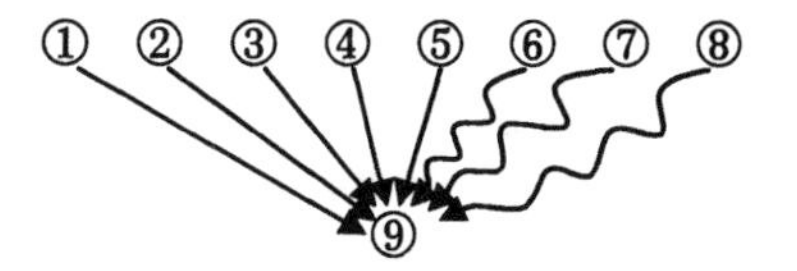

As it stands the argument is strong. We can make it stronger by making the generalization less sweeping. Relative to the same body of evidence, a less sweeping generalization as a conclusion makes a stronger argument because the evidence has less to support (a less sweeping generalization).

1. We can hedge the conclusion.

> It is probable that most Germans like wine.

Our client won't like this. He knows that such surveys can only achieve a degree of probability. He's paying us for results that he can base marketing decisions on.

2. We can make the subject narrower, so that it includes less.

> Most Rhinelanders like wine.

The generalization is now less sweeping and the argument hence stronger. But again we disappoint our client. He can't make a profit marketing in only one German province, so he needs information about the whole of Germany.

3. We can make the predicate broader, so that it includes more.

> Most Germans like alcoholic beverages.

Again the generalization is less sweeping and the argument stronger. Now we are not inquiring specifically about wine but about the entire class of alcoholic beverages that includes wine, beer, whiskey, and other alcoholic beverages among its members. But again our client is ill served by this stronger argument. He doesn't market beer or whiskey, so he needs to know specifically how things stand with Germans and wine.

4. We can both make the subject narrower or less inclusive and make the predicate broader or more inclusive.

> Most Rhinelanders like alcoholic beverages.

This conclusion gives us our strongest argument yet. But our client is even worse served. So we have explored several ways in which by stating the conclusion in different terms we can make the argument stronger using the same evidence. But in the present case none of these ways served our purpose because each such restated conclusion takes us farther from the information we need to answer the question that our survey set out to answer. It is well for us to know of these options, however. In some other case they might yield a stronger argument that does address the important question adequately.

We need also to examine the ways in which the conclusion can be restated in order to make it a more sweeping generalization, even though this yields a weaker argument. This will help us recognize more sweeping generalizations when we encounter them, and also show us what sort of evidence we would need to support a more sweeping generalization. First let us recall our original conclusion.

> Most Germans like wine.

1. We can state the conclusion in stronger terms.

> Nearly all Germans like wine.

This result would please our client, but only until he based decisions on it that went sour. If we had had the evidence to support it, this would certainly have been our original conclusion.

2. We can make our generalization more sweeping by making the subject broader, so that it includes more.

> Most Europeans like wine.

Again we have a result that would please our client until he discovered that we didn't have the evidence to support it.

3. We can make our generalization more sweeping by making the predicate narrower or more specific, so that it includes less.

> Most Germans like white wine.

Relative to the same evidence this gives us a weaker argument. Our sample includes Germans who like red wine but don't like white, and we can't be sure that we are still speaking of "most Germans" if we exclude them as we do in this new conclusion.

4. We can both make the subject broader or more inclusive and make the predicate narrower or less inclusive.

> Most Europeans like white wine.

Again we have a result that would greatly please our client, until he discovered that we didn't have the evidence to back it up.

So far we have explored how we can make our argument weaker or stronger by varying the conclusion to make it a more or less sweeping generalization. And we already know that we can make our argument stronger by increasing the size of the sample. Now let's look at how we can strengthen or weaken the argument by changing the composition of the sample rather than its size. Up to now we have said little about the 1703 Germans we included in our survey. The more these Germans resemble one another, or the more uniform the sample, the less likely it is to be representative of all Germans, and the weaker our argument is. For example, suppose our survey was carried out in wine growing and wine drinking centers like Trier and Bingen. And suppose further that we polled only those Germans we found drinking wine in wine gardens and restaurants. We might then conclude that indeed all Germans do like wine. But our argument would be very weak because the sample is seriously biased. If there are Germans who do not like wine, we're unlikely to find them in restaurants drinking wine.

So for our sample to be representative we must include Germans from all the regions of the nation, including those where much beer is consumed like Bavaria. If Germans in certain occupations are more inclined to wine than those in other occupations, then we must include Germans from all of these different occupations. The same holds for any factor that might influence whether a person likes wine or not: religion, education, socio-economic status, leisure-time activities, and the like. The more diverse our sample is in ways that make it more representative of the all or most Germans we refer to in our conclusion, the stronger our argument. But we needn't take account of all the ways in which Germans can differ. Only those that are likely to correlate with liking wine. For instance, it seems unlikely that being left- or right-handed will much influence whether a German likes wine or not.

We call a generalization for which no evidence is offered or is readily available an empty generalization.

> Acme widgets are outstanding widgets simply because they are very good.

If no further evidence is forthcoming in this case, we have an empty generalization.

But how do we classify a situation where we have counted all the members of a class? Suppose I am driving along a residential street and my auto suddenly begins to handle very sluggishly. I suspect that I have a flat tire. I pull over and inspect each tire in turn.

> Left front tire isn't flat.
> Left rear tire isn't flat.
> Right rear tire isn't flat.
> Right front tire isn't flat.
> So none of my tires are flat.

Is this a very strong argument by inductive generalization? While the evidence is indeed very strong, it doesn't really constitute an argument at all. The evidence for none of my tires being flat is my direct inspection of each tire. So the claim that none of my tires is flat is not based on argument but on direct observation of each of the tires. The purpose of an argument by inductive generalization is to bridge the gap between the items in the sample for which we have evidence and the larger number of items in the target group referred to by the "generalization." In the present case there is no such gap, since we have direct evidence for all of the items in the target group. So there is no argument by inductive generalization. This evidence by direct perception is stronger than an argument by inductive generalization and preferable to such an argument whenever it is obtainable. We construct arguments by inductive generalization when we cannot obtain such evidence for all of the items we are interested in. We cannot call such evidence of direct perception an argument by inductive generalization because that would obscure rather than clarify its nature.

Now we will get some practice in assessing the strength of inductive generalizations.

EXERCISE 14—1: INDUCTIVE GENERALIZATIONS

In I and II you find inductive generalizations. Each of the subsequent statements brings new or different information to bear on the generalization. Consider in each case whether the new or different information makes the argument weaker or stronger, and why. It may help you to distinguish information about the sample from that about the conclusion.

I. The plane you chartered as a nature photographer crash landed in an isolated stretch of New Guinean highlands, killing the pilot but miraculously allowing you to escape with only minor injuries. You walk several miles when from a hillside you peer down into a native village. You need to decide by observing the villagers and their activities whether they would be friendly and helpful to strangers. You know that there are peaceful farming tribes as well as fierce, warlike tribes in the region. After an hour of observing about 30 villagers at simple everyday activities you conclude they are all peaceful.

1. Your observations include 70 villagers.
2. The villagers you observed were all women and children.
3. Among the activities you observe is a dance where warriors brandish spears and stone clubs at each other.
4. You observe village activities over a 24-hour period.
5. Over the entrances of several huts you observe dried heads, possibly of slain enemy tribesmen, hanging by their hair.
6. The sample you observe includes villagers of all ages.

*7. You conclude there is some risk of danger.

8. You observe many villagers tending fields of yams and cassavas.

9. You observe a wooden cross before a large hut possibly used for some form of Christian worship.

10. You observe several Europeans with their wrists bound behind them who appear to be prisoners.

II. The Adler family must purchase a new washing machine. They gather information from friends and relatives, and sort it out to decide which they should buy. They want a machine that will provide superior service. For them this means at least four years of trouble-free service. The Stewarts, their neighbors, have had trouble-free service from their Whirlpool washer for five years. The Costas, also neighbors, have owned and used their Whirlpool six years without any breakdown. The Whirlpool bought by the Garcias—Mr. Garcia is Mrs. Adler's cousin—did break down and needed a belt replaced, but that was after it had given five years of trouble-free service. Aunt Stacey's Whirlpool has run for seven years without any problem. The Adlers conclude that probably all Whirlpool washers will give superior service.

1. Chip Bowen, who works with Mr. Adler, also bought a Whirlpool washer, but it broke down and needed repair the second year.

2. The Adlers conclude that all Whirlpool washers will give excellent service.

3. The Garcias have three children and the Stewarts four. But the Costas, like Aunt Stacey, have no children.

*4. The Adlers, Garcias, and Aunt Stacey all live in Oklahoma City.

5. The Adlers conclude that probably all Whirlpool washers will give better than average service—no breakdowns for three years.

*6. The Garcias and Adlers drive Nissans, while the Stewarts and Costas drive Oldsmobiles.

7. The Adlers live in Oklahoma City. But Aunt Stacey lives in Walla Walla, and the Garcias live in Minot.

8. The Adlers conclude that probably all Whirlpool appliances will give superior service.

9. The Stewarts use the soap powder recommended by the manufacturer. Aunt Stacey uses whatever soap powder is on sale when she shops. The Garcias and Costas buy inexpensive powder from a bulk merchandise store.

10. Aunt Stacey's clothes are mostly polyester. The Costas and Stewarts have quantities of cotton garments, including twills, while the Garcias have a lot of woolens.

3. Analogies and Arguments by Analogy

An analogy is a comparison, and to argue by analogy is to employ a comparison to attempt to establish a conclusion. Here is an example.

> Tom Clancy's novels *Cardinal of the Kremlin*, *Hunt for the Red October*, and *Clear and Present Danger* have good plots, are fast paced and action-packed, and are laced with interesting and accurate technical information. So his recent novel *Executive Orders* is likely to have these features also and be worth reading for those who like tales of adventure.

Since we haven't read the new novel by Clancy, we are trying to determine in this argument whether it is worth reading. What it has in common with the three novels mentioned is that it is by Tom Clancy. We are trying to determine what it will be like, and we cite features shared by the earlier novels mentioned in order to conclude that the new novel will have these features also and hence be worth reading for those who like adventure fiction.

Many analogies or comparisons are not used as arguments. So now in addition to learning to recognize analogies when we encounter them, we must also learn how to distinguish analogies used as arguments from those that are not. Some non-argumentative analogies are used for description or illustration. Good writers and poets make frequent use of analogies to convey shades and nuances of objects and feelings.

How learned is the late medieval theologian Denis the Carthusian?

> His mental range and many-sided energy are hardly conceivable. . . . His works fill forty-five quarto volumes. All medieval divinity meets in him as the rivers of a continent flow together in an estuary.

What is the poet's love like?

> O my love is like a red, red rose
> That's newly sprung in June;
> O my love is like the melody
> That's sweetly played in tune.
>
> Robert Burns

When Romeo's friend Mercutio is thrust by Tybalt's sword and Romeo allows that the wound isn't serious, Mercutio responds with this bitter analogy.

> No, 'tis not so deep as a well, nor so wide as a church door, but 'tis enough, 'twill serve.
>
> Shakespeare, *Romeo and Juliet*, Act III, Scene i.

In an analogy the object described is the *focus* and the object used for comparison is the *analogue*. In Robert Burn's poem, love is the focus and the rose and melody are the analogues. In the history, the scholarship of Denis the Carthusian is the focus, and rivers flowing into an estuary is the analogue. In Mercutio's case the wound is the focus, the well and the church door the analogues.

In other cases the analogy is used to explain something that might otherwise be unclear or puzzling to us. The descriptive use of analogy shades off into the explanatory at this point. Drawing a line between the two is difficult and in many cases unnecessary. An explanatory function is often there when a writer like the following attempts to explain something we are unfamiliar with by comparing it with something we are acquainted with.

> . . . necessity has never been the chief motivator of New York entrepreneur Ian Schraeger, who recently opened the mid-priced, much-hyped Paramount Hotel, which can best be described as a YMCA with attitude.
>
> Katherine Boo, "Wolves in Cheap Clothing."

We don't know what the new hotel is like, but many of us are familiar with the YMCA. So Boo uses the YMCA as an analogue to help us understand what the new hotel is like.

For another case, the maglev train is an experimental transportation technology. An entire train is elevated slightly above its guide rail to eliminate the drag friction of steel wheel on steel rail that gravity causes in the conventional train. This experimental train should be energy-efficient at speeds up to 250 mph. To contrast it with the conventional train, Gary Six draws this analogy.

> In some ways, it is like molding a roller coaster into a public transportation vehicle.

Here the less known focus is the maglev, and it is explained by the analogue of the roller coaster.

Some analogies are more complex and developed in more detail.

> In actual Christianity . . . there seems to have been . . . two elements, the one transient, the other permanent. The one is the thought, the folly, the uncertain wisdom, the theological notions, the impiety of man; the other, the eternal truth of God. These two bear, perhaps, the same relation to each other that the phenomena of outward nature, such as sunshine and cloud, growth, decay, and reproduction, bear to the great law of nature, which underlies and supports them all.
>
> Theodore Parker, "A Discourse of the Transient and Permanent in Christianity."

Here in a famous writing of the New England Transcendentalists Parker takes as focus the relation of the transient to the permanent in Christianity and as analogue the relation of the transient to the permanent in nature. His purpose is to explain the focus by means of the analogue. At the same time Parker may be attempting to at least partially justify the distinction of a transient from a permanent in Christianity by reference to the similar distinction in nature. But this does not yet count as argument. He does not draw a conclusion, nor does his analogy point in any obvious manner to a conclusion.

It is easiest to distinguish the argumentative from other uses of analogy when the writer draws an explicit conclusion, as in this case.

① <The consequences of bad driving may be serious accidents that destroy property, or injure, or even kill people.> [That's why] ② <everyone must pass a test on traffic laws and good driving practices, and demonstrate a command of driving skills, before they receive a license to legally operate a motor vehicle.> ③ <The consequences of bad parenting, such as neglect, brutality, or sexual abuse, can be children whose lives are ruined, or serious injury, or even death.> ④ <Yet there is no license for parenting.> [So] ⑤ <people ought to have to pass a test on their knowledge of children and command of parenting skills before they are licensed to legally have children.>

The focus here is parenting and the analogue is driving. The analogy serves as an argument with ⑤ as the explicit conclusion. The argument has the following diagram.

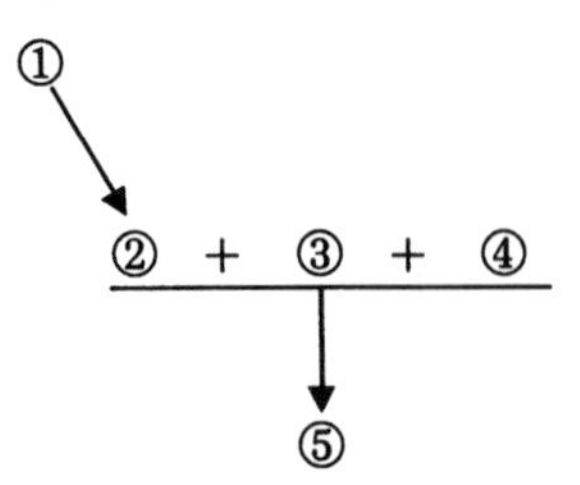

Compound Linked
Argument by Analogy

The typical argument by analogy first claims that the focus is like the analogue in some one or more (often obvious or at least unlikely to be disputed) respect or respects. The respect in which parenting and driving are claimed to be similar is that when practiced badly, each can ruin or take lives. Then the argument claims that, because of this, the two are alike or should be alike in some other respect (this respect not being as obvious or as unlikely to be undisputed). The claim here is that parenting, like driving, ought to be licensed.

4. Analyzing and Evaluating Arguments by Analogy

Once we have identified the argument by analogy, we diagram it as linked. The premises presenting the analogy need to be linked because in most cases if one is missing, the argument tends to fall apart. In the following example, there is a conclusion which makes the whole an argument, but the conclusion is unstated and must be supplied. It is frequently the case in arguments by analogy that the conclusion is left unstated. And this can present us with a problem of deciding, in the absence of an explicit conclusion, whether we have an argument, or whether the analogy serves instead the purpose of description or explanation.

> [Cockfighting is] illegal, sure. But so is everything else—smoking pot, prostitution, spitting in the streets. But these things are flourishing.

In this analogy the focus is cockfighting, and the analogue is "everything else." The reference of "everything else" cannot be wholly general, and is narrowed to the allegedly illegal acts of smoking pot, prostitution, and spitting in the streets. These analogues are claimed to be flourishing. The conclusion of the argument is "So cockfighting should flourish also." When we make it explicit, the argument scans and diagrams as follows.

① <[Cockfighting is] illegal, sure.> ② <But so is everything else—smoking pot, prostitution, spitting in the streets.> But ③ <these things are flourishing.> [4] [[So] <u>cockfighting should flourish also</u>.]

① + ② + ③
↓
[4]

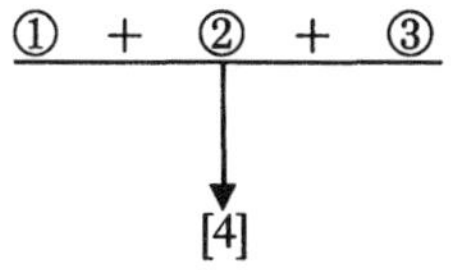

Linked
Argument by Analogy

Here ①, ②, and ③ are advanced as linked support for [4].

As with any argument we evaluate, we need to consider the soundness of the information in the premises and the relevance of the premises to the conclusion. In evaluating an argument by analogy we need to consider as many of the following points as apply.

1. In how many ways does the focus resemble the analogue? The more ways, other factors being equal, the stronger the argument.
2. How relevant are these resemblances to the conclusion? The more relevant, the stronger the argument.
3. Are there important ways in which the focus differs from the analogue? The more such ways, the weaker the argument.
4. In the case of more than one analogue, are there differences among them that are relevant to the conclusion? The more such differences, the weaker the argument.
5. How strong a claim does the conclusion make relative to the evidence? The less it claims, the stronger the argument.
6. Can the analogy be extended to cover cases we are unwilling to accept? If so, the argument is weaker.
7. Can we find a counter-analogy, one that tends to prove the opposite of the original conclusion? The more plausible a counter-analogy, the weaker the argument.

The information in ② is not accurate in a way that contributes to the strength of the argument. It is the *possession* of marijuana rather than the smoking that is illegal, but this is a minor point. Spitting by the average person (not infected with AIDS), where it is illegal at all, is at most a nuisance and not in the same category as cockfighting. The only solid point of resemblance of the focus to the analogues is their illegality. Beyond that, their differences stand out. Cockfighting also resembles forging checks, molesting children, and murder in being illegal. What distinguishes the crimes cited as analogues from these is that they are sometimes classed as victimless crimes. But since the arguer did not make this point, and since it is much disputed whether such crimes are victimless in a sense that would render them not criminal or less criminal, we will not pursue it here. Those who object to cockfighting typically cite the brutality of having animals fight bloodily to the death for sport. Dog fighting and bull fighting would be far better analogues in this important respect, and both are illegal. But neither flourishes nor is being seriously promoted in the U.S. Collectively these sports claim dead cocks, dead dogs, dead bulls, and an occasional dead human as their victims.

Lack of similarity of the focus to the analogues in a way that would support the conclusion is not the only important weakness of this argument. The claim of the unstated conclusion is quite ambiguous. Putting spitting aside as negligible, we can accept the claim in ② that smoking pot and prostitution are flourishing in the sense that they are widely practiced in the U.S. But the writer isn't attempting to demonstrate that cockfighting *is* flourishing. He doesn't cite the sort of evidence that would support this claim, e.g. the number of cockfights on given dates at towns in Arizona, Ohio, or Pennsylvania. The writer instead draws this unstated intermediate conclusion from ③.

[5]
[These practices should be allowed to flourish.]

When we add this, the argument looks like this.

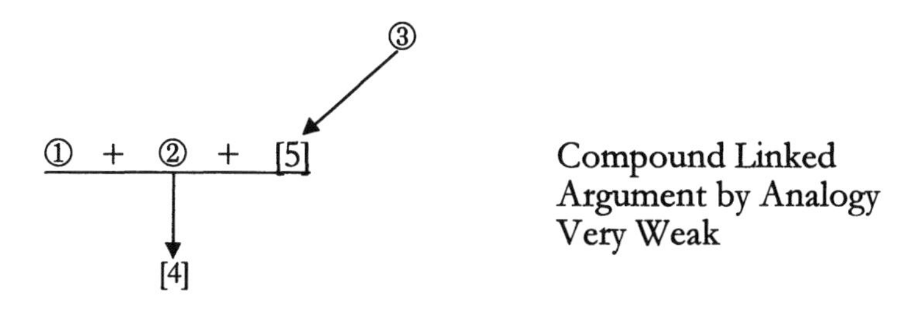

The support of ③ for [5] is very weak. Many illegal practices flourish in the U.S.—child abuse, incest, assault, rape—that most agree should not flourish. Law enforcement officials and the courts are attempting to curb them. A two-step argument is needed to establish [5] from ③. The first step would show that these practices do not harm society in the way that led to their being banned. Success here would establish that they should be legal. The second step would show that these practices make some positive contribution to society. This would show that they should be encouraged. Without this two-step argument, [5] remains a very weak link in the compound linked argument.

Overall, a very weak argument by analogy.

In assessing this argument we made use of all of the points of assessment but (7). For (1), the resemblance, we had illegality and possibly victimlessness, neither strongly relevant to the conclusion, as (2) requires. For (3), the differences, we had the brutality of the focus unmatched in the analogues, and for (4) we noted that spitting wasn't in the same category as the other analogues. For (5) we noted the ambiguity of the conclusion, and for (6) the analogy was extended to forging checks, molesting children, and murder.

Item (7) of the assessment, the use of a counter-analogy, is illustrated in an exchange on the floor of the Illinois House of Representatives in the 1838 session over public expenditure for a canal.

> In that session the *Sangamo Journal* reported that Wickliff Kitchell in effect accused Lincoln of being drunkenly extravagant in favoring a bond issue of $1,500,000 to complete the Illinois and Michigan canal. "Already prostrated by debt," said Kitchell, "that gentleman thinks it would be for the interest of the State to go still deeper." Kitchell told of a drunkard in Arkansas who "lost his reason" and lay in a dumb stupor from liquor. His wife couldn't bring him to. A neighbor came in and said "brandy toddy" might help. The drunk sat up at the word "toddy," saying "That is the stuff!" Kitchell remarked, "It is so with the gentleman from Sangamon—more debt would be for the better."
>
> Mr. Lincoln replied, "I beg leave to tell an anecdote. The gentleman's course the past winter reminds me of an eccentric old bachelor who lived in the Hoosier State. Like the gentleman from Montgomery [County], he was famous for seeing *big bugaboos* in everything. He lived with an older brother, and one day he went out hunting. His brother heard him firing back of the field, and went out to see what was the matter. He found him loading and firing into the top of a tree. Not being able to discover anything in the tree, he asked him what he was firing at. He replied a squirrel—and kept on firing. His brother believing there was some humbug about the matter, examined his person, and found on one of his eyelashes a *big louse* crawling about. It is so with the gentleman from Montgomery. He imagines he can see squirrels every day, when they are nothing but *lice*." "The House," said the *Sangamo Journal*, "was convulsed with laughter."

Kitchell uses an analogy to argue that Lincoln's support of more spending is unwise. The focus is addressing deep indebtedness by spending more, and the analogue is remedying drunkenness by more drink. Kitchell's conclusion is that as more drink is a poor remedy for drunkenness, so more spending is poor policy for one already deep in debt. Lincoln in his counter-analogy attacks Kitchell's conclusion that more spending is unwise. The focus of his analogy is Kitchell's assessment that the spending is unwise, and the analogue is the man who mistakes a louse for a squirrel and fires at a target that doesn't exist. Lincoln's conclusion is that Kitchell's assessment fails to hit its target.

Summary

General statements refer to all or most members of a group and are commonly introduced with words like "all," "most," "many," or "no." Those general statements that refer to all members of a group are sometimes called "universal." A universal statement is made false by one counter-instance, which is one member of the group that does not have the feature cited in the universal statement. Some general statements make claims about what goes on in the world, while others are more like definitions. Some general statements that make claims about the world can be supported by observation or inspection of all members of the group. But these are not generalizations. Generalizations are statements about all or most members of a group based on inspection of a few members. A sound generalization is based on good evidence, an unsound one is not.

An argument by inductive generalization claims something about all or most members of a group based on a sample. The conclusion of such an argument is always a general statement. Such arguments can be strong when the sample is large enough, particularly when the sample is representative. The more sweeping a conclusion it has, the weaker the argument. A more sweeping conclusion claims more. Conclusions become more sweeping when the group referred to by the subject becomes larger, or the features attributed to its members by the predicate become more specific. A generalization for which there is no evidence is an empty one.

An analogy is a comparison. Frequently an object or event we are interested in but relatively unknowledgeable about is compared with an object or event that is better known. The object of interest or focus is compared with its analogue for purposes of description, illustration, or explanation.

An argument by analogy advances an analogy or comparison to establish a conclusion. A typical argument by analogy states that the focus is like the analogue in several obvious respects, then concludes that it is also like the analogue in some less obvious respect. The more the focus resembles the analogue, especially in ways relevant to the conclusion, the stronger the argument. Conversely, the more focus and analogue differ, the weaker the argument. The argument is also made weaker by a conclusion that claims more relative to the same body of evidence. One way of showing weakness in an argument by analogy is by extending the analogy to cover cases it shouldn't cover. Another way is to construct a counter-analogy, an analogical argument that supports the opposite of the original conclusion.

Study Questions

Section 1: General Statements and Generalizations

1. What is a general statement?
2. What is a universal statement?
3. How are some universal statements introduced?
4. How are some non-universal general statements introduced?
5. How many counter-instances does it take to make a universal statement false?
6. What is a particular statement?
7. How are some statements introduced that fall in between general and particular?
8. What is a generalization?
9. In what case is a general statement not a generalization?

10. What is an unsound generalization?
11. Since some generalizations are unsound, why don't we just avoid generalizations altogether?

Section 2: Arguments by Inductive Generalization

12. What is an argument by inductive generalization (sometimes called an inductive generalization for short)?
13. By what diagram do we represent such an argument?
14. By what three factors do we assess such arguments?
15. How do the size and representativeness of the sample affect the strength of the argument?
16. How does the sweep of the conclusion affect the strength?
17. What makes a conclusion more sweeping?
18. In a diagram, how do we show that a statement counts *against* a conclusion?
19. What is an empty generalization?
20. How do we classify a universal statement that we arrive at by inspecting all members of a group?

Section 3: Analogies and Arguments by Analogy

21. What is an analogy?
22. What is an argument by analogy?
23. What are the two parts of an analogy?
24. How can an analogy be well used for description or explanation?

Section 4: Analyzing and Evaluating Arguments by Analogy

25. How do we diagram arguments by analogy?
26. What is the strategy of a typical argument by analogy?
27. What factors tend to make an argument by analogy strong?
28. What factors tend to make an argument by analogy weak?

EXERCISE 14—2: ARGUMENTS BY ANALOGY

In each case identify the analogy and state what the focus is and what the analogue is. Decide whether there is an argument by analogy, and if so, state its conclusion and premises. Mark up, diagram, analyze, and evaluate the argument, justifying your evaluation by reference to one or more of the above criteria. If there is no argument, decide whether the function of the analogy is more descriptive or explanatory.

1. Feeling good about government is like looking on the bright side of any catastrophe. When you quit looking at the bright side, the catastrophe is still there.

   P. J. O'Rourke, *Parliament of Whores* (New York 1992), p. 49.

2. (Pnin, the novel's main character, has just had all of his teeth pulled.)
   It surprised him to realize how fond he had been of his teeth. His tongue, a fat sleek seal, used to flop and slide so happily among the familiar rocks, checking the contours of a battered but still secure kingdom, plunging from cove to cove, climbing this jag, nuzzling that notch, finding a shred of sweet seaweed in the same old cleft; but now not a landmark remained, and all there existed was a great dark wound, a terra incognita of gums which dread and disgust forbade him to investigate.

   Vladimir Nabokov, *Nabokov's Congeries*, "Pnin" (New York 1968), p. 387.

3. (Paraphrased from Heraclitus)
   You may as well attempt to clean mud off your body by bathing in mud as to purify yourself of blood guilt by spilling the blood of a sacrificial animal.

4. Giving a boy a gun is much like striking a match over an open gasoline tank. No mishap may occur, but the chances are all in favor of a big explosion. In the case of the gasoline one explosion will occur and it will be all over. The boy with the gun may cause a number of fatal accidents; he may grow up with the love of destruction instilled in his mind. . . . Let us give our children something better to do and think about than handling toy guns or any manner of lethal weapons.

   W. A. Swallow, *Reverence for Life*, New England Anti-Vivisection Society.

*5. (Samuel Armacost was CEO of BankAmerica in the troubled years 1981–86)

   Armacost had once compared BankAmerica to an ocean liner. The captain may try to change direction, setting all the controls accordingly, but the boat has so much momentum that it travels for miles in the wrong direction before changing course. One of the jokes circulating in the bank was that Armacost had gone to the bridge, set all the levers in the right place, and now he was waiting for the ship to turn. The trouble was that none of the levers were connected.

   Gary Hector, *Breaking the Bank:The Decline of BankAmerica* (Boston 1988), p. 164.

6. If I stumbled on a watch while walking through a field I would wonder how it got there. I wouldn't assume it had always been there like a stone. Looking at it reveals that its parts were carefully made and put together to serve a purpose. It tells the time of day. The materials of the watch were carefully chosen, shaped, and fitted together to serve this purpose. So the watch must have had a maker. Yet every evidence of design in the watch is also found in the universe. Its even more complex parts fit together nicely to keep the universe functioning. So the universe too has a maker. The maker is God.

Condensed and paraphrased from William Paley, *Natural Theology*, Vol. I (London 1836), Ch. I.

7. In good years most of the young people behave well. In bad years most of them abandon themselves to evil. This is not due to any difference in the natural capacity endowed by heaven. The abandonment is due to the fact that the mind is allowed to fall into evil. Take for instance the growing of wheat. You sow the seeds and cover them with soil. The land is the same and the time of sowing is also the same. In time they all grow up luxuriantly. When the time of harvest comes, they are all ripe. Although there may be a difference between the different stalks of wheat, it is due to differences in the soil, as rich or poor, to the unequal nourishment obtained from the rain and the dew, and to differences in human effort. Therefore all things of the same kind are similar to one another. Why should there be any doubt about that?

The Book of Mencius, Book 6A:7.

8. . . . the item most frequently encountered in landfills is plain old paper—it accounts for more than 40 percent of a landfill's contents; this proportion has held steady for decades and in some landfills has actually risen. . . .

There was a lot of talk some years ago about how technology, computers in particular, would bring about a "paperless office"—a risky prediction given the already apparent increase caused by the photocopy machine. Today there are 59 million personal computers in the United States with printers attached. When the creation of paper waste is concerned, technology is proving to be not so much a contraceptive as a fertility drug.

William Rathje & Cullen Murphy, "Five Major Myths about Garbage, and Why They're Wrong," *Smithsonian* (July 1992), p. 115f.

9. "Do you think," said Candide, "that men have always massacred each other, as they do today? Have they always been liars, cheats, traitors, brigands, weak, flighty, cowardly, envious, gluttonous, drunken, grasping, and vicious, bloody, backbiting, debauched, fanatical, hypocritical and silly?"

"Do you think," said Martin, "that sparrow-hawks have always eaten the pigeons they came across?"

"Yes, of course," said Candide.

"Well," said Martin, "if sparrow-hawks have always possessed the same nature, why should you expect men to change theirs?"

Voltaire, *Candide* (New York 1929), p. 71.

10. The argument is advanced that guns cause accidental deaths and wounding in private homes. This is, of course, true.

So also do stairways, defective flooring, the edges of carpeting, power tools, lawn mowers, gas stoves, axes, heating pads, and medicine cabinets. Do you want some civil servant inspecting yours?

It seems to me that persons who wish to assume the risk of having guns in their homes ought to be permitted to do so. Else, why not ban fast cars, skiing, swimming, ocean sailing, and other activities which produce a certain amount of injury and death every year?

David B. Wilson, *The Boston Globe,* Feb. 19, 1974.

Further Reading

Robert Paul Churchill, *Logic. An Introduction*, 2nd ed. (New York 1990). Valuable perspectives are found in the material on generalization and analogy, pp. 349–379.

Trudy Govier, *A Practical Study of Argument*, 2nd ed. (Belmont 1988). An especially careful and helpful treatment of arguments by analogy is on pp. 215–243.

Kathleen Dean Moore, *Inductive Arguments. A Field Guide*, 2nd ed. (Dubuque 1989). Has excellent and accessible introductory material on hypothetical reasoning and reasoning to cause-effect relations as well as on arguments by analogy and inductive generalizations.

There is no consensus on the diagraming of arguments by inductive generalization. Nolt and Thomas diagram them as linked:

John Eric Nolt, *Informal Logic. Possible Worlds & Imagination* (New York 1984), p. 32.

Stephen N. Thomas, *Practical Reasoning in Natural Language*, 3rd ed. (New York 1986), pp. 262–264.

Stephen N. Thomas, *Argument Evaluation* (Tampa 1991), p. 103f.

Yanal has misgivings about linked representation in his 1984 article but diagrams them as linked in his 1988 textbook.

Robert J. Yanal, "'Convergent' and 'Linked' Reasons," *APA Newsletter on Teaching Philosophy*, Vol. 4, No. 4, (1984), p. 2.

Philosophy, Vol. 4, No. 4, (1984), p. 2.

Robert J. Yanal, *Basic Logic* (St. Paul 1988), p. 44f., 290–300.

Freeman diagrams them convergent and provides an extensive discussion of the question.

James B. Freeman, *Dialectics and the Macrostructure of Argument* (Berlin 1991), pp. 11f., 102f., 158–161.

PART SIX

WRITING ANALYTICAL AND ARGUMENTATIVE ESSAYS

CHAPTER FIFTEEN

LONGER ARGUMENTS

1. RECOGNIZING THE ISSUE AND THE STAND

Most of the arguments we have worked with up to now have ranged from two to six sentences in length, with some longer. Many of these were self-sufficient or independent, and others were parts of larger wholes. In the latter case we found that it was often helpful to know something of the context of the argument. In some cases the shorter individual arguments were parts of longer arguments that lent them at least some of their significance.

Such longer arguments are what we now turn our attention to. The length of written argument most practical to deal with for our purposes is that of an editorial, commentary, opinion piece, or letter to the editor of a newspaper or magazine. The same techniques we use for this are also useful with larger units like a chapter of a book or even an entire book. We consider writing "argumentative" that advances reasons, evidence, or individual arguments in support of a position, although we will use the term "argumentative" in a more special sense in the next chapter as applied to the essay we will write.

It is useful for us to be reminded at this point that much writing serves purposes other than argumentation such as description, narration, or explanation. Arguments can occur in longer pieces of writing that are primarily descriptive or explanatory. We have already learned how to identify, analyze, and evaluate such arguments. Our attention is now focused on discourse that is primarily argumentative, although such discourse may also contain parts that are descriptive or explanatory.

The first step toward understanding and evaluating a longer piece of argumentative writing is to identify the *issue*. The issue is a question that people dispute, a question that can be answered yes or no. We may recall the debate about abortion between Melanie and Glenn that we examined in connection with inconsistency.[1] The issue there is whether abortion is morally right, or stated as a question: Is abortion morally right? It is very important for us to get a clear understanding of what the issue is. Our understanding of the issue guides our understanding of the position taken on it. The issue there is not: Is the war in Vietnam morally right? Is abortion legal in the United States? Is communism the best form of government? Sometimes we get a clearer and more distinct perception of what the issue is by noting also what it is not. So our goal here is to state the issue as precisely as we can, for which we need a clear and distinct perception of that issue.

One more thing we need to bear in mind is that in formulating the issue as a question, we also aspire to be objective. We shouldn't attempt to pre-judge an answer to the question. Our goal is to state the question in such a way that a reasonable person could take a stand either for or against. Here are ways we would avoid formulating the same question as above. Isn't abortion the most disgusting thing you've ever heard of? Aren't people who oppose abortion a pack of zealots and fanatics? Two persons could debate at considerable length the first or second of these questions without ever seriously engaging the question whether abortion is morally right.

Once we have identified the issue as precisely as we can, our next step is to identify the stand taken by the writer on the issue. At this point we benefit from having the issue stated as a question, because this makes it easier to discern and state the position taken. On the issue "Is abortion morally right?" Glenn takes the stand "No, abortion is morally wrong." We suspect in their exchange that Melanie takes the stand "Yes, abortion is morally right." It is quite possible that in the overall debate she does so. But she does not defend this position in the portion of the debate presented to us. In fact, Melanie doesn't take the stand that abortion is morally wrong either. She alleges that there is an inconsistency in Glenn's position, which implies that the position is either untenable or not clearly thought out in one or more respects. So her position is best described as one of arguing that it has not been established by Glenn that abortion is morally wrong. It is not a position on the issue.

In an analysis of this piece we could state our result up to now succinctly.

> The issue is whether abortion is morally right. Glenn takes the stand that it is morally wrong.

How familiar with a piece of discourse must we be in order to state the question at issue and the stand taken on it? Typically we have an opinion on both when we start to read or listen to the piece. But this opinion can shift markedly as we become acquainted with the discourse as a whole. In the case of a piece of written discourse, we read it through once rapidly for purposes of orientation. What we should discover in this orientation is the issue and the writer's stand on it. Then we read the piece a second time, this time more slowly and carefully. As we analyze and come to understand it better, we make the

---

[1] Chapter Two, p. 11f.

adjustments needed to render our statements of issue and stand more precise.

When we are dealing with spoken discourse rather than written, like a speech or an address, it helps much to have some idea of the issue and stand in advance. This is especially the case when no recording is being made of the discourse for later study. In some cases we can form an impression of the issue from the title of the address. For instance, from the title "The Need for Gun Control Now" we can infer that the speaker will address the question whether the public should be allowed to purchase guns without restriction. We may also know something about the speaker that gives us a clue to his or her stand on the issue. If we know, for instance, that the speaker is the mother of a teenager who killed himself accidentally with a handgun kept in case of burglars, we may surmise that she supports such restrictions. If on the other hand the speaker is a prominent member of the National Rifle Association, an organization adamantly opposed to such restrictions, we expect a quite different stand. The importance of advance information in such cases is that we must refine and clarify our concepts of issue and stand as we listen to the address, since we don't have the advantage of being able to pore over it at our leisure.

Locating the issue, stating it as a question, and identifying the writer's stand on the issue can be quite challenging when we turn to complex argumentative writing. We search for all three at once in some cases, as in the following excerpt from a letter by Thomas Jefferson to Edward Carrington of Jan. 16, 1787.

> . . . the good sense of the people will always be found to be the best army. They may be led astray for a moment, but will soon correct themselves. The people are the only censors of their governors: and even their errors will tend to keep these to the true principles of their institution. To punish these errors too severely would be to suppress the only safeguard of the public liberty. The way to prevent these irregular interpositions of the people is to give them full information of their affairs thro' the channel of the public papers, and to contrive that those papers should penetrate the whole mass of the people. The basis of our governments being the opinion of the people, the very first object should be to keep that right; and were it left to me to decide whether we should have a government without newspapers or newspapers without a government, I should not hesitate a moment to prefer the latter.

Jefferson's language was not easy reading for students in his day, nor is it for students today. For a first attempt to identify the issue, we note that one thing Jefferson considers is what constitutes the best army. We may formulate this as a question then check it against the passage: Do the citizens of a nation constitute its best army? A debater taking a negative stand on this question might argue that with financial resources you could hire an army of professional soldiers or mercenaries, who would then constitute the nation's best army. Their superiority would be due to their training and martial experience. One taking an affirmative stand on the question might contend that citizens constitute the best army because they fight for the stronger motive, not pay but defending themselves from foreign conquest.

But is this the issue Jefferson is considering? His stand doesn't much resemble either of the two we identified. He seems to focus more on the relations of citizens to their own government than on their roles as defenders against foreign invaders. In gathering this letter with others under the heading "On Revolution" the editors too suggest that Jefferson is considering citizens relative to their own government. Perhaps the issue is this: Do the citizens of a nation constitute its best revolutionary soldiers? But when we reflect that a revolutionary war is one where one group or faction in a nation combats another, for any nation that has citizens (rather than subjects) a revolutionary war can only be one of some citizens against others. So the question we stated as the one at issue must be answered in the affirmative. It cannot be the issue in our sense of a contested question where a reasonable person could take either side. There is only one side to take.

Looking again at the passage, we notice that Jefferson is speaking of newspapers and information, not of weapons or tactics. Were we wrong in taking questions about soldiers to be the issue? We notice now that Jefferson speaks of the *good sense* of the people as constituting the best army, not the people themselves. Good sense cannot constitute an army in the physical sense of soldiers maneuvering on a battlefield. So Jefferson must be using "army" in a figurative sense to signify "defense" or "protection." But protection of what? And from what? And how does this link up with good sense of the people, information, and newspapers?

Jefferson does speak of a "safeguard of the public liberty." Could it be that he is considering what best preserves the freedom of a people, and that his thesis is that the good sense of the people themselves, provided adequate information by a free press, best serves this purpose? How would we state this as thesis and stand?

> Is the best defense of the freedom of a people the good sense of the people themselves? Jefferson takes the stand that it is, if a free press provides these people with sufficient information.

This way of stating the issue and stand appears to make better sense of the text than either of the earlier.

Now let us get some practice in recognizing issue and stand.

EXERCISE 15—1: ISSUE AND STAND

For each of the following, identify the issue and state it as a question on which one can take a stand for or against. Then state the stand taken by the writer. Also for each, state one or more questions which are not the issue, and tell us why they are not the issue, even though they could be mistaken for it. State a stand too that is *not* the stand taken by the writer, and tell us why it is not that stand, even though it seems close to it.

1. Discipline-based art education treats art as a subject for study, rather than as a recreational activity. Thus art content is derived from four *disciplines*: art production, art history, art criticism, and aesthetics. We believe, in other words, that art should be studied from the perspective of artist, art historian, art critic, and aesthetician.

   Dwaine Greer & Ron H. Silverman "Making Art Important for Every Child," *Educational Leadership*, Vol. 45, No.4 (Dec 87/Jan 88), p. 12f.

2. A Word of Warning. FORMAT is one of the most dangerous of all the commands in DOS because it can wipe out an entire diskette's worth of data at one go. If you format a diskette that has some valuable data on it, it is thoroughly gone and nothing will bring it back. Be very careful when you format diskettes—check that the diskette doesn't have something important on it before you wipe it off the face of the disk with FORMAT.

   Peter Norton's DOS Guide (New York 1987), p.70.

3. Most fatal fires occur between midnight and 6 am; therefore, it is very important that every house have at least one smoke detector near the bedroom area, to awaken you in the event of a fire.

   Shriners Burns Institutes, "A Home Fire Escape Plan for Survival," (Tampa 1988).

4. It is important to properly dry firewood because dry wood burns clean, creates less creosote buildup in flues and chimneys, and produces up to 30 percent more heat than green wood.

   Virginia Division of Forestry, "Firewood for Home Heating" (1979).

5. Medicine is a practical art, like technology. And in the practical arts what counts is the results. Suppose someone builds a machine that works—it does the job it is designed to do—although no one can explain why it works. That isn't science, it's technology. But the machine is no less useful for lack of a scientific explanation. Similarly, suppose the doctor knows that a certain medical treatment is generally effective but doesn't know why. She goes ahead with the treatment anyway. In a life or death

situation, she will even consider a treatment with a low or unknown success rate if there is no other alternative. It is better than doing nothing.

Daisie Radner & Michael Radner,
Science & Unreason (Belmont 1982), p. 53.

6. Health is, indeed, the first wealth. It should be nurtured. Concern for well-being is life-affirming, and thus a virtue. But within most virtues there lurks, waiting to slip its leash, a vice, in the form of excess. Any good, even the pursuit of longevity, can be pushed past its appropriate, its *natural* scope. The idealization of health is really a mere materialism, an obsession with bodily vitality and continuance.

   When Americans glimpse the skull beneath the skin of life, they wonder what something that unpleasant is doing in the midst of all the comforts of modern life. They wonder why some technology or technique cannot fix fate. But at the end of the day and the day must end—this is clear: Health, like any wealth, can be pursued too ardently and hoarded too greedily. The result is the crabbed, sad, anxious, morally unhealthy life of a miser.

   By all means jog. Just do not confuse maintenance with the conquest of mortality.

George Will, "Grandmother Was Right,"
Newsweek (Jan. 16, 1989), p. 68.

2. Arguments and Objections

What makes discourse argumentative is that in it a stand or position is taken on an issue, and reasons or evidence is advanced in support of this stand. You can take a stand on an issue yet not engage in argumentation unless you advance reasons or evidence in support of your stand. Without such reasons or evidence to support it, your discourse differs little if at all from an expression of opinion on a controversial topic.

Right now we are embarked on the analysis and evaluation of longer pieces of argumentative discourse. We have had some practice at identifying the issue and the stand taken on that issue. Our next step is to find and evaluate the reasons advanced in support of that stand. Reasons advanced in support of a stand function similarly to reasons advanced in support of a conclusion. Since we are familiar with the latter, we already have some idea of what we will be looking for. We are seeking a putative relation of logical support, where one or more statements are advanced in support of some other statement, or where it is maintained that because one or more statements are true, some other statement must be true.

Let us examine the following piece of argumentative discourse.

> You should only get admitted to a hospital when it is medically necessary. On the whole, hospitals are not very healthy places. Usually they are full of sick people whose germs could infect you. It is true that the air that circulates is often filtered, and that medical instruments are almost always sterilized. But in spite of these precautions, you are more likely to catch some infection in a hospital than in the open air outdoors.

To assess this we need to answer the following questions about it.

1. **What is the issue?**
2. **What stand does the writer take on the issue?**
3. **What argument does she advance in support of it?**
4. **Does she consider any objections to the argument?**
5. **If so, what are they?**
6. **Does she respond to the objections?**
7. **If so, what are her responses?**
8. **Does the argument survive the objections to provide strong support?**

In the present case the question is whether you should seek admission to a hospital in any circumstances other than medical necessity. This writer takes the stand that you should not. The reason she gives is that hospitals are unhealthy. She also advances an argument in support of her claim that hospitals are unhealthy. They are unhealthy, she urges, because they contain sick people whose germs might infect you.

Arguments and Reasons

We may pause a moment for orientation purposes to review the structural features of the argumentative position we have thus far uncovered.

① <You should only get admitted to a hospital when it is medically necessary.> ② <On the whole, hospitals are not very healthy places.>
③ <Usually they are full of sick people whose germs could infect you.>

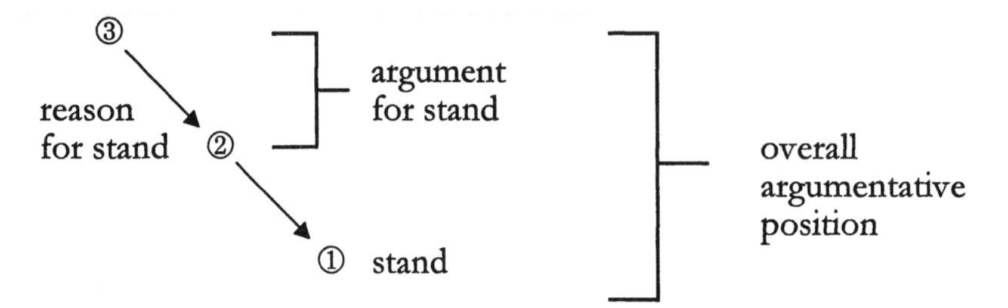

① is the stand taken on the issue. When we consider ② in relation to ①, then ② is a reason for ①. Since ② is a reason for ①, we could consider the two of them together an argument. But we won't do that. It tends to obscure rather than clarify our picture of the argument's structure.

Since ③ is advanced in support of ②, we do refer to this as an argument. This argument is advanced in support of the stand taken on the issue. Finally we may refer to the whole, where the argument:

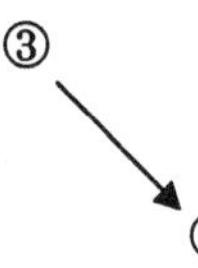

is advanced in support of ①, as the argumentative position.

So a reason by itself does not constitute an argument. It can constitute an argument, however, if it is taken together with the stand it is a reason for.

To return to our analysis of the above discourse, the writer does consider an objection to her argument, namely that hospital air is filtered and medical instruments are sterilized. Her response to this objection is that even with such precautions, you are more likely to get an infection in a hospital than in the open air outdoors.

How effective is her response to the objection? She doesn't really tell us *why* we are more likely to get an infection in the hospital, so her response is essentially a claim that is not backed up. We would have to call it inadequate. She might for instance have questioned the effectiveness of the air filtering. A filtering system could remove some of the dust particles that infectious microorganisms travel on, yet still leave enough in the air to make the hospital a more dangerous place for infections than the open air. Had she done this, the objection would perhaps not have done serious damage to her argument.

When we note the eight questions we asked of her stand, we find that the first three are a review of what we have already learned whereas the final five are about objections. Why would a writer consider an objection to her own argument? This seems almost perverse. Isn't it tantamount to weakening or destroying your own position? Shouldn't you advance the strongest arguments you can in support of your position, while letting your opponents find objections to them and thereby uncover their weaknesses?

This sounds fine and good. But a problem arises. How do you determine whether an argument is strong or weak? The very best way is to probe it for weaknesses by considering objections to it, like we did in Chapter Seven when searching for counter-arguments. So you consider and respond to objections to your own argument in order to find out whether it is indeed a strong argument, and therefore suitable to provide the support you seek for your position. And you share this process with your readers so that they can appreciate the factors you considered in deciding that a certain argument is strong and hence an appropriate support for your stand.

In an important sense good argumentative writing is an intellectual adventure. Part of this adventure is discovering or devising good arguments for taking a stand on an issue. Another part is testing these arguments by raising objections to them and responding to these objections. Suppose an objection proves decisive because you have no adequate response to it. In this case, an argument you initially thought provided strong support for your stand does not actually do so. But when you respond effectively to the most important objections that can be brought against your argument, it now becomes good or solid support for your stand.

Our focus up to now has been on the argument advanced in support of a stand, and what happens to the argument in the face of objections to it. Let us now turn to the stand you take on the issue and see how it is affected. Suppose you have advanced an argument in support of your stand and the argument falls to a serious objection. How does this affect your stand? Does it go down with its argument? No, your stand does not necessarily go down with its argument. It is suspended or in limbo, so to speak, awaiting support from some other argument. For a stand to count as reasonable, it must be supported by arguments or reasons. Without this support, your stand is no more than an expression of opinion. It is your duty to find arguments that withstand criticism and support it.

What about the opposite case? How does it affect your stand when an argument advanced in support of it survives an objection? An argument survives an objection when you respond to the objection and show that it does not weaken the argument. When an argument withstands all objections brought against it, it becomes a strong argument in support of your stand. Does this mean that your stand on the issue has been definitively established? Not necessarily. All that you have shown so far is that you have a good argument in support of it. You have not shown that there aren't any good arguments against your stand, which there may very well be. And if the arguments against it are stronger than those for it, it is not supported. Also you have not shown that there is no competing stand, supported by stronger arguments, that is incompatible with the one you take. In that case also your stand is not supported.

Now let us consider the case where you have ascertained an argument in support of a stand on an issue, but the writer takes no account of objections to his arguments. The following example provides some guidance on how to handle this case.

Should tax dollars be used to support artists working on paintings or sculptures, or writers working on fiction or poetry? No, they should not. Talented artists and writers will be able to produce works that will please the public. Their products will find buyers, and they will be able to support themselves with money from sales. As for the artists and writers who have no talent, it is best that the rejection of their works by the buying public and their ensuing inability to earn a livelihood encourage them to seek some other occupation.

Here the issue is stated clearly as a question, so we do not need to state questions that might be confused with it. The issue is whether tax dollars should go to support artists working on paintings or sculptures, or writers working on fiction or poetry. The stand taken, similarly clear, is that tax dollars should not be so used.

The writer does advance an argument in support of this stand. The argument can be treated as one disjunctive argument (based on one "either . . . or" premise), or as two separate arguments. The argument is based on a distinction made by the writer but not mentioned explicitly. The distinction is between those writers and artists with talent, and those without. The talented artists and writers, he argues, will not need the tax dollars. They will be able to support themselves by sales of their work. The talentless ones will not be able to support themselves. Economic necessity will drive them to seek their livelihood in some other area, which is what they ought to do.

The writer does not consider any objections to these arguments. Therefore we must do this for him. Generating objections to an argument, and deciding whether they are strong enough to destroy it, are an important part of evaluating that argument. This amounts to creating counter-arguments to test the strength of the original argument. To the first part of this argument it can be objected that even talented artists are frequently unable to sell their works, or to sell them for enough to support themselves. This is particularly true when their work is original and pioneering, and thus likely not to be understood by the art-buying public. Poets, for example, are almost never able to support themselves from the sale of their poetry alone. Among the better American poets from earlier in the twentieth century, for instance, Wallace Stevens was an insurance executive, and William Carlos Williams was a physician. At present most American poets support themselves with academic jobs, often as teachers.

Most painters are equally unable to support themselves from sales early in their careers. Picasso may well be the most acclaimed, talented, and financially successful twentieth-century artist, but he lived in extreme poverty for years before he could eke out a living from sales. The paintings belonging to his estate alone when he died in 1973 (as distinct from those sold during his lifetime) were valued upwards of $100 million. Occasionally the art market utterly ignores a major painter in his lifetime. Vincent Van Gogh did not sell a single painting all his life. He was supported by his brother Theo before committing suicide. At recent auctions one Van Gogh sold for $55 million dollars, and another for $83 million. There is no guarantee that the art market will recognize talent in time to benefit it. Much evidence indicates that it does not. So the first part of the argument is very weak.

If the market cannot be trusted to recognize talent, then those it ignores could just as well be talented as untalented. In this case the art market would be driving both talented and untalented artists from the field. So the second part of the argument fails also. The writer does not establish that the forces of the art market alone will further good art and discourage poor.

EXERCISE 15—2: ARGUMENT AND OBJECTIONS

Analyze in writing each of the following pieces of argumentative discourse. Be sure to answer each of the eight questions on page 483 above. Distinguish objections to an argument from objections to a position. If there are no objections, produce one or two to test the argument for strength.

1. When the federal government reaches the point where raising new revenue is of paramount importance, serious consideration should be given to a value-added tax. This is a tax the manufacturer pays on the value she adds to the product. If she buys raw materials for $35 and has manufacturing costs of $100, then sells the product for $200, she pays a tax on $65, which is the value she has added to the product. One big advantage of this is that it taxes wealth right where it is generated. Of course the manufacturer is usually able to pass the tax on to the consumer by raising the price of the product. Some say for this reason that the tax weighs more heavily on those with lower incomes. But this can be addressed by not applying the tax to necessities like food or prescription drugs.

2. Conditions are favorable for a greater use of youngsters in the U.S. labor force today. A strong economy means more working people are needed, but a decrease in the birth rate 25 years ago means fewer young people are entering the job market from high school or college. If new workers are not added to the labor pool, wages will climb higher, and American wares will become too expensive to compete with foreign ones in an open market. I favor lowering the minimum age for full-time year-round employment to 14, even to 12 if necessary. Some will charge that cur-

tailing formal education this early will rob youngsters of valuable time to learn and develop. The truth is that very little learning takes place in school anyway. Recently U.S. students tested weaker in science and math than those from twenty other industrialized and semi-industrialized nations. Allowing youngsters to enter the work force earlier might compel authorities to produce genuine teaching and learning in the fewer school years.

3. Mark Twain is the greatest American novelist. In novels like *Huckleberry Finn*, he created unforgettable characters and captured the democratic ethos of the new American society of the West. As Bernard De Voto observed, he "used local, class, and racial dialects with immeasurably greater skill than anyone before him in our literature." The use of humor and exaggeration also helped him create the first native American style of fiction, an achievement noted by Hemingway and many others. Of this prose style De Voto noted "Mark Twain wrote English of a remarkable simplicity and clarity, and of singular sensitiveness, flexibility, and beauty as well." Not all critics agreed. The Scotsman John Nichol, a contemporary of Twain's, alleges that "he has done more than any other living writer to lower the literary tone of English speaking people." Some critics were too wedded to the then fashionable stilted prose, parlour manners, and bloodless characters to appreciate the racy wit, vigor of invention, and sheer energy of Twain's writing.

4. Today's physician can get into a perplexing dilemma. Put yourself in this position: A physician, you have a patient who has just tested positive for HIV, the AIDS virus. As you know, the disease can be communicated sexually, is lethal, and has no known cure. You ask your patient whether he intends to inform his wife. He responds no. You ask his permission to inform her. He refuses. So the dilemma is: should you inform his wife anyway? I hold that you should. Her life is at stake. If she gets AIDS from her husband and conceives a child, the life of the child is at stake too. AIDS can be transmitted from a pregnant woman to her embryo. No doubt this is a breach of medical confidentiality, one that you can be held liable for in a court of law. But a human life weighs heavier in the scale than a breach of confidentiality, even one that might cost you a large sum of money. The law on this needs to be changed.

3. Alternative Positions and Assumptions

In the above section we learned to distinguish a stand or position on a controversial issue from an argument advanced in support of that stand. Now we must make the distinction between an objection to an argument and an objection to the stand or position that argument is intended to support. Often an objection to a stand or position is formulated as an alternative position, so we can choose to analyze it either as an objection to a position or as an alternative position. Analyzing and evaluating a piece of argumentative writing involves distinguishing objections to an argument (and the writer's response to them) from objections to a position, or advancing an alternative position (and the writer's response to this). An example will illustrate.

Wars of Liberation

I. A war of liberation is a civil war of one faction of a nation against its government. Some urge that we Americans should support wars of liberation around the globe. I am not convinced of that. Typically a war of liberation is little more than a grab for political and economic power by young men and women who consider themselves too clever to climb the ladder of success step by step. They employ intimidation, violence, terrorism, and armed warfare (depending on their resources) to achieve power, scattering the country with the corpses not only of those who oppose them but also of children and other innocent non-combatants. You can expect nothing but a repressive military rule from those who seize power in this ruthless, bloodthirsty fashion.

II. Some say that once such belligerents achieve power they tend to rule peacefully and grant rights to the people. They can afford to do this because they have destroyed their enemies. In fact this never happens. Winning a war of liberation typically means getting the upper hand militarily over opponents, not totally destroying them. So the government always has enemies to justify its oppressive rule.

III. Others claim that America should support these wars of liberation. They maintain that current governments are so repressive, inept, and corrupt that they must be changed by such wars, even at the cost of many lives. I dispute that this is an accurate characterization of all the governments of the world. Even if the description did fit one government or two, we should give peaceful evolution a chance to change things. That's the American way.

IV. Yet others assert that we should support some but not all such wars. In particular we should support those against governments hostile to the U.S. It is in our national interest to oppose governments that are hostile to us. My response to this is two-fold. First if we can simply be patient, peaceful evolution and a transfer of power could bring in a regime friendly to us. This would enable us to get a friendly government without bloodshed. Second, there is no guarantee that a new government formed by victorious rebels would be any less hostile to the U.S.

Analysis and Evaluation

The issue is: Should we Americans support wars of liberation around the globe? The writer takes the stand that we should not. The initial argument can be paraphrased as follows.

① <Americans should not support wars of liberation around the globe.> ② <Typically such a war is only a grab for power by impatient young people.> ③ <Terrorism and armed force are used to kill opponents and non-combatants alike.> ④ <A victory by the rebels results in a repressive military regime.>

② ③ ④

①

Each of the pieces of evidence provides separate support for the conclusion. Together they constitute a convergent argument having the writer's stand as its conclusion.

In II an objection to this argument is considered. To be more specific, the objection is directed at that part of the convergent argument where ④ is advanced in support of ①. The objection is itself an argument whose conclusion contradicts ④.

not 4 <On achieving power the rebels will rule peacefully and grant rights> because ⑤ <their enemies have been destroyed.>

In the objection we find ⑤ advanced in support of [not-4], where [not-4] contradicts ④, a premise of the original argument.

We are adopting a new convention of argument diagraming in order to be able to represent objections in our diagrams. When one statement is contradictory to another, statement X, we refer to the contradictory as not-X. One statement contradicts another, we remember,[2] when its being true makes the other false. Above we call the conclusion of the argument [not-4], because it contradicts the original statement ④. For us to so label a statement, it must deny rather neatly what the original statement affirms. If it says something else pertinent to the argument in addition, we must give it a new number.

We continue to use the technique adopted in Chapter Fourteen of representing opposed statements by drawing a jagged arrow between them. When statement X is advanced as an objection to Y, or opposes Y or is contradictory to Y, we show this by drawing a jagged arrow from X to Y.

In the above case we have identified the statement [not-4] as the contradictory of ④. So we show this relation with a jagged line.

The jagged line means that [not-4] opposes ④, or that its being true tends to make ④ false.

The writer responds to this objection to his argument with the following argument.

[not 5]
<The enemy in such wars is never really destroyed.> ⑥ <There are always enemies left to justify their oppressive rule> ④ [So] <the rule will be oppressive.>

---

[2] See the material on contradiction in Chapter Two above, p. 22.

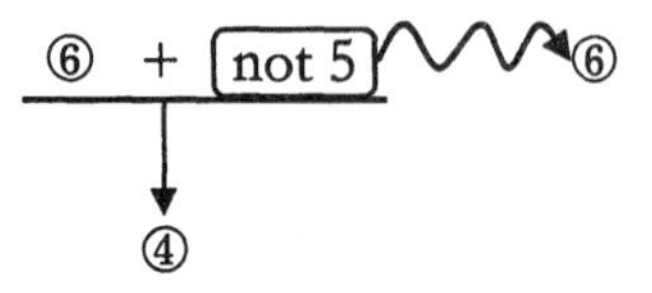

In this reply not-5 disputes ⑤ and so reaffirms ④, the piece of evidence originally advanced in support of ①.

What is the balance of this objection and defense? First we note that the objection attacks the original position indirectly by attempting to remove one of its three supporting premises. Should it succeed, this would not necessarily remove all support from the original position. There are two other premises advanced in support of it, and it would have to be shown that neither of them does actually provide any support. Does the objection succeed? Its success hinges on the claim that victors in wars of liberation totally destroy their enemies. This claim is upheld in the objection and disputed in the response. Unfortunately neither provides statistics or even one or two examples. We judge the objection unsuccessful for two reasons.

1. The person making a claim carries the burden of substantiating it. The burden of substantiation is not discharged in the objection.

2. The response to the objection that enemies are seldom totally destroyed is accurate for most wars of liberation.

So on balance the response is successful, and the objection does not diminish the strength of the original argument. What that strength is we have not yet established.

In III. the author considers an objection not to one of his arguments but to his position itself.

⑦ ⑧
<Current regimes are so repressive> that <wars of liberation to replace
not 1
them are justified.> So <such wars should be supported by the U.S.>

⑦
↓
⑧
↓
not-1

In many cases we would refer to the statement coming in the position of not-1 as an alternative position to ①. In the present case it is the contradictory opposite of ①, so we do not do so. It is better regarded as an objection to the original position than as an alternative position. As an objection to the position it does not directly attack any of the evidence or arguments for the position. Unlike the objection we just analyzed above, it leaves that part of the argumentative position untouched. It attempts to refute ① by bringing evidence directly against it.

The writer responds to this objection in the following fashion.

> [not-7] <Current regimes are not as repressive as claimed.> ⑨ <Supposing one were to be so oppressive, it would be wiser to give peaceful evolution toward less repression a chance.> [So] ① <we should not support such wars.>

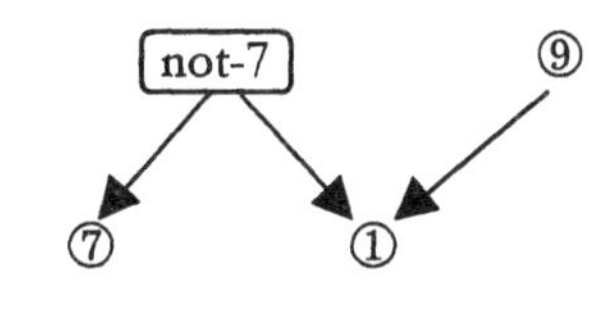

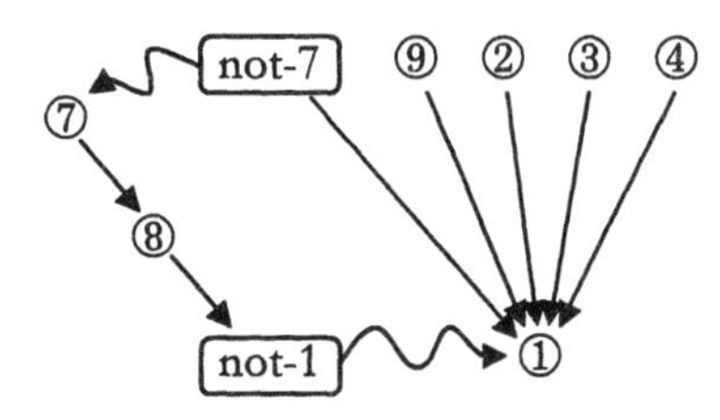

To the claim in ⑦ that current regimes are repressive the writer advances a counter-claim in [not-7] that they are not. No further evidence or reasoning is advanced to support either the claim or the counter-claim. In the absence of further support they cancel each other out. We suspect, however, that some regimes may be sufficiently repressive, a point we will recur to below. As if to allay such a suspicion, the writer advances in ⑨ new direct support for the original position ①. This new piece of evidence is intended to shore up the original position and repair any damage it may have sustained from the objection [not-1]

In IV. the writer considers an alternative position to ①. In the alternative position a distinction is drawn between wars of liberation against regimes hostile to the U.S. and such wars against any other regimes. The alternative position, that we should support wars of liberation against regimes hostile to the U.S., is supported by the claim that it is in our national interest to do so. Such an alternative position is always at least indirectly an objection to the original position. If the original position were wholly satisfactory, there would be no point to considering the alternative. We show the opposition of the alternative to the original position with a jagged arrow, because one of them being true makes the other false. It cannot be the case both that we should not support any such wars of liberation and that we should support some of them.

⑩
<We should support wars of liberation against regimes hostile to the U.S.>

⑪
<It is in our national interest to do so.>

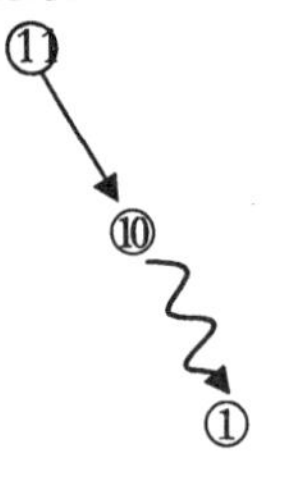

The writer responds to the alternative position by arguing against it. He denies that it is in our national interest to support such wars, and gives his evidence for doing so.

⑫
<Given some time, evolution could produce a less hostile regime.>

⑬ ⑭
<Evolution is preferable> because <it doesn't involve bloodshed.>

⑮
<Then too there is no guarantee that a regime formed by victorious rebels would be any less hostile than the original one.> So <it is not in our national interest to support such wars against regimes hostile to the U.S.> not-11

① In fact, <we should not support any such wars, whatever regimes they may be against.>

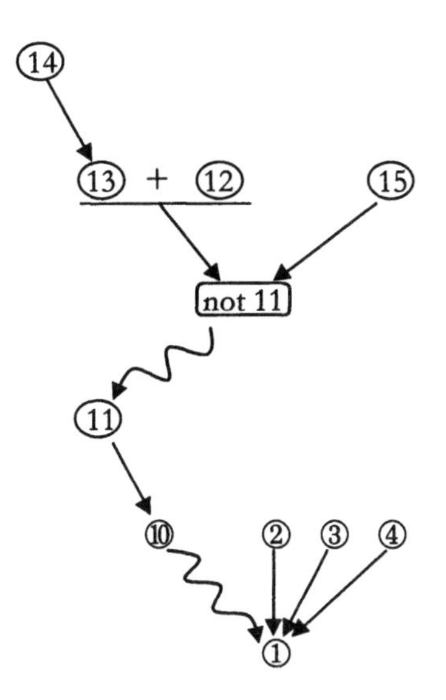

His reasons for denying in [not-11] that it is in our national interest to support such wars of liberation are twofold: evolution could produce a less hostile regime without involving us in bloodshed, and a regime formed by victorious rebels could be equally hostile. On balance, he gives two good reasons why it is not in our national interest, while the alternative position only claims that it is without advancing reasons or evidence. His defense of the original position is successful here.

We can review briefly the factors we have analyzed and evaluated so far before continuing to one more question and an evaluation of the argumentative position as a whole. We analyzed the argument as convergent, with three separate premises supporting the conclusion. An initial objection to the premise ④ is responded to successfully, so this premise retains its original force and continues along with premises ② and ③ to support the conclusion ①. Next an objection is raised to the writer's conclusion ① or stand itself. A counter-claim, not an argument, is made by the writer to reaffirm his original conclusion, and a new premise ⑨ is introduced to shore up this conclusion against the attack. For the moment we will say that the writer's position is restored to its original strength, but there is a factor here we must examine more closely below. Finally the writer considers an alternative position supported by a piece of evidence. He advances a compound convergent argument against this piece of evidence and successfully defends the original position. So on balance at this point he has successfully defended his original argumentative position.

We may now ask whether the writer makes any important assumptions that affect his position or arguments. We recall that statement B is an assumption of statement A when for A to be true B must be true also. In some cases a writer tells us when she is making an assumption. In telling us she probably calculates that the assumption is a reasonable one, and that we will accept it. Our task when confronted with such an explicit assumption is to decide whether it is a reasonable one. The present writer makes no such explicit assumptions.

The assumptions a writer tells us about are much less troublesome than the ones he makes silently. A very important silent assumption made by the present writer is that no war of liberation is ever a justified war. The closest he comes to claiming this outright is in [not-7], where he urges that current regimes are not so repressive as to justify a war of liberation. We can reasonably question the soundness of this assumption. We know from history and what goes on in the world today that a government can oppress, exploit, torture, or murder its people. This writer assumes that nothing a government can do would justify people rising up in armed rebellion against it. Where was he, we want to ask, when the Nazis murdered some six million of its own citizens and people it ruled by conquest? This is not the distant but the recent past. Can it seriously be maintained that we Americans would have been wrong to support any of the groups like the Munich White Rose that opposed Hitler? This seems wildly improbable.

The course of history would be changed dramatically if people had never risen up justly and successfully against oppressive rulers. Rome, for instance, would never have become a republic the way it did, without the people rising in revolt against Tarquin the Proud. Without this example of several hundred years of successful republican government through the Roman Senate and the persuasive oratory of those like Cicero, the modern era could be quite different. As for the modern era itself, France of course would still be ruled by Bourbon monarchs, since the French Revolution of 1789 would be an unjustified war of liberation against an oppressive regime. Also the United States of America would not exist, since the nation was founded by colonists rebelling against their country England and its King George III, declaring independence and winning a war to secure it.

There is sufficient evidence to support the claim that some wars of liberation are justified. This means that the writer's assumption that none are is unacceptable. So this unacceptable assumption greatly weakens his position, a position otherwise well defended. On balance we find his overall argument weak.

4. Case Study: Notes for an Analysis and Evaluation

Now we are going to carry out an analysis and evaluation of an editorial about liability insurance, the kind you must have to legally operate a motor vehicle. In the present section we do a step-by-step analysis and evaluation. In the next we will sum up our results in essay form.

With liability judgments soaring, who's willing to take the risk?

By David Nyhan[3]

1. Ask Maine Gov. Joseph Brennan about the biggest change in politics he's witnessed in the past 20 years, and he'll tell you it's the way people are afraid now to serve on the municipal and county boards that used to start people in political careers.

2. Why? In this suit-happy country, insurers are hiking premiums to such a level that towns and boards and skating rinks can't pay for insurance, and those who used to volunteer or run for office are afraid to take on the legal hassles.

3. Talk to Donald Rumsfeld, who's roaming the country testing the waters for a possible GOP presidential run. This former White House chief of staff is struck by the fact that everywhere he goes, schools are closing out football teams, or towns can't get insurance, or zoning boards are shying away from controversial rulings, all because of the insurance crisis.

4. In Massachusetts, 250 doctors withdraw, at least temporarily, their services in a battle over huge malpractice premiums. In New York City, the Roosevelt Island Tramway that carries thousands across the East River daily shuts down because its liability insurance is too costly.

5. All over the country, the legal system is bogged down in civil suits. In Boston, the Suffolk County Superior Court has a backlog of 20,000 civil suits. In California, the average verdict in a medical negligence suit that goes to trial exceeds $600,000. As a country, we are increasingly pricing ourselves out of the insurance market, and we now realize that means pricing ourselves out of a lot of things, like delivering babies, running high school football teams, or just getting your day in court to settle a dispute.

6. More and more organizations are having to make do without insurance. More and more institutions are cutting corners—NASA's exploding space shuttle gives us an example of corner-cutting that led to the most disastrous result. Johnson & Johnson looks at the headaches involved with Tylenol capsules and writes off $150 million in business rather than take the legal heat.

7. Juries are awarding whopping judgments, and our 600,000 lawyers—more legal beagles than the rest of the industrial world combined—provide potential litigants with an eager, highly paid, skilled cadre of professional gladiators more than willing to take on a case for contingency fees of 30 percent or even 40 percent of a potentially lucrative judgment.

8. But it's too easy just to blame ambulance-chasing lawyers. Five or six years ago, the insurance companies were in a frantic race to get business. They don't

[3] Reprinted courtesy of *The Boston Globe*

make money on premiums; they make money by amassing huge chunks of capital, then buying real estate or shopping malls or office buildings or, up till 1982, farm land. They speculated in an up market, often cutting premiums to outbid competitors and write insurance they hoped would amass them more capital to invest in other business.

9. Then the bubble burst, and insurers are now scrambling, with overbuilt office space going begging in many cities, with the oil bubble burst in the Sun Belt, with the collapse of Farm Belt real estate. Solution: jack up the premiums for those who can still afford insurance.

10. There is a larger societal problem: as people no longer take responsibility for their own actions, society turns ever-more-readily to the courts. Lifetime smokers sue tobacco companies. Suits that would have been inconceivable 20 years ago are now routine. Your daughter can't play on the Little League team? Your son can't join his sister in the Brownies? Hire a lawyer.

11. In one hard-pressed Maine school system, parents sued because their daughter was refused permission to have her school yearbook carry a particular quotation next to her picture. The school board paid $60,000 to fight the case. In medical cases, more and more doctors are sued, with the result that costs go up for everybody. Lawyers are increasingly sophisticated in persuading jurors to award big pots of money in negligence cases. Juries readily sock it to insurance companies they see as big, impersonal, profit-drenched repositories of cash. Lawyers have begun selling shares to investors in potentially rich cases, speculating in potential verdicts, driving costs ever higher.

12. Some states, such as New York, have named commissions to study skyrocketing liability insurance rates. The solution will eventually come from the states; Washington is not very good at solving problems like this. Eventually, we'll have to modify the system, and limit the types of cases that can be brought in court. The alternative: going bareback, with no insurance.

We might initially take the issue to be: What is the most significant change in politics in recent decades? The response would be that increased litigation is deterring people from serving on municipal and county boards.

But we haven't really located an argumentative issue here. One may of course debate what the most significant change is, but we have not stated it as a controversial question on which reasonable people might take a "yes" or "no" stand supported by evidence or reasons. Nyhan does bring evidence to support this response. But he doesn't consider evidence for any other candidate (for most significant change). In fact, he doesn't even mention any other candidate. So we have not stated the issue as precisely as we need to. But since Nyhan does bring evidence to support what we have identified as his response, we may be close to it.

Perhaps we can draw closer by noting the clause "we'll have to modify the system" in the next to last sentence. This sounds like a stand on a controversial issue. The content of the opinion piece suggests that "the system" refers to the purchase of liability insurance to protect us from the legal and financial consequences of our own actual or alleged carelessness. For example, most drivers carry liability insurance for driving an automobile. If we cause an accident while driving in which people are killed or injured and property is destroyed or damaged, we could be forced by a court to pay hundreds of thousands or even millions of dollars. When we carry liability insurance, the insurance company protects our interest and pays the necessary sums.

We may state the issue thus: Are the consequences of our present liability insurance system so harmful that the system needs to be changed? Nyhan's stand then is: Yes, the consequences of this system are so harmful that the system should be changed. Let us take this as our issue and stand, then see how well it helps us organize and evaluate the argumentative material.

What evidence does Nyhan advance in support of his stand? It receives direct support from the claim in {2} that liability insurance premiums are being raised beyond the ability of many to pay. The inability of town and county boards, and athletic teams to carry insurance is claimed also to have the following harmful social consequences:

1) People no longer volunteer or run for municipal or county boards because they can't cope with the legal hassles (according to Maine Gov. Joseph Brennan). {1}, {2}
2) Zoning boards shy away from controversial rulings (according to former White House chief of staff Donald Rumsfeld). {3}
3) Schools are closing out football teams (also according to Rumsfeld). {3}
4) The Roosevelt Island Tramway across the East River shuts down daily. {4}

In addition Nyhan cites the following two consequences of doctors being unable to afford premiums for malpractice insurance:

5) In Massachusetts 250 doctors temporarily withdraw their services. {4}
6) Babies will be delivered without proper medical attention. {5}

Two further disastrous consequences of corner-cutting due to the insurance system are cited by Nyhan:

7) The NASA space shuttle explodes. {6}
8) Johnson & Johnson writes off $150 million in inventory in the Tylenol capsule tampering case rather than face the legal consequences. {6}

We may pause to examine the structure and nature of Nyhan's argument thus far. His argument is essentially this:

> Because liability insurance premium hikes have unacceptable consequences 1)–8), the system should be changed.

The connection he claims between the rate hikes and the unacceptable consequences is not itself argumentative. He is not arguing "Because the rates have gone up, people should do X." His claim is that the rate hikes have *caused* the unacceptable effects (by the route of their effect e.g., on people's perceptions or attitudes, or however).

Does Nyhan consider any objections to this evidence? No, he does not. What objections might be raised? His item 7), the NASA space shuttle disaster, stands in no significant relation to the insurance situation, since NASA does not carry liability insurance. Where the connection of 7) with liability is zero, that of 8) is quite tenuous. The seven deaths and scare from cyanide-tampered Tylenol capsules occurred in 1982 because some presumably deranged person introduced the poison into capsules already on pharmacists' shelves. Johnson & Johnson's decision to pull all Tylenol from the market was a responsible corporate decision that protected the public and preserved consumer confidence.

Items 1)—6) however do provide strong support for Nyhan's stand. Items 1)—3) do not depend on the authority of their sources. The number of municipalities and counties that are struggling with the problem of liability could be multiplied manyfold. Any group up on current events can add instances to those cited by Nyhan.

Does Nyhan make any assumptions of importance here? He does assume without argument that the cases he cites are indeed harmful or damaging to society. But this is a safe assumption. We are certainly far worse off without these services and opportunities than we are with them. Nyhan also assumes we know why we have such a thing as liability insurance rather than none. Probably limitations of space prevented him from commenting on this. But comment would have proven helpful, especially relative to the second part of his thesis. We have liability insurance because people seek redress or financial compensation when they suffer or are injured through the negligence of others. The compensation sought is often enough to bankrupt an average wage-earner in the U.S., so people buy insurance to protect themselves from such potentially ruinous judgments.

The second part of Nyhan's thesis is that we will have to modify the system by limiting the types of case that can be brought in court. He does not marshal evidence in direct support of this thesis. He does, however, offer us a fairly complex explanation of how the current system has gone wrong—an explanation of why premiums for liability insurance are so high. He gives us the causes for the current system going wrong to help us get a clearer view of what we need to do to fix it.

A) Americans are less inclined to take responsibility for their actions and more inclined to sue. {11}

Nyhan supports this with further evidence of two types:

a) Courts now have more frivolous suits. {11}
  i) Lifetime smokers sue tobacco companies. {11}
  ii) Parents sue when daughter can't play Little League. {11}
  iii) Parents sue when son can't get in Brownies. {11}
  iv) Maine school board spent $60,000 when sued because child couldn't get a certain quote beside her yearbook picture. {12}

b) Courts are bogged down by absolute numbers of suits. {5}
  i) Suffolk County Superior Court in Boston has a backlog of 20,000 civil suits. {5}

B) The U.S. has more lawyers—600,000—than the rest of the industrial world combined; they eagerly take cases for 30% or 40% contingency fees, and even sell shares to investors in potentially rich cases. {7}, {12}
C) Juries award large sums of money in negligence cases, cleverly persuaded by lawyers to sock it to big, impersonal, profit-drenched insurance companies. {7}, {12}

a) The average verdict in a medical negligence suit that goes to trial in California exceeds $600,000. {5}

D) Insurance companies cut premiums to outbid competitors then speculated incautiously in real estate in the Farm Belt and oil-producing states. {9}, {10}
We note that casual factors A), B), and C) all fit together not only to explain the high premiums, but to suggest a measure like that advanced by Nyhan as part of his thesis to address them. A) shows that Americans are predisposed to sue, B) that there is a great number of lawyers eager to file for them, and C) that juries are awarding the winners vast sums of money. Premiums have shot up to cover the considerable legal expenses of the ever increasing number of suits and the vast sums awarded the litigants. The role of D) is indirect. It shows that successful real estate speculation formerly covered some of the increased costs which now due to heavy losses in such speculation must be recovered by jacking up premiums.

Nyhan does not consider objections to his thesis that we should address the problem by limiting the types of case that can be filed. He does consider an alternative, namely that we can go without insurance. But this is more part of a false dilemma than a viable alternative. To know that an individual or government could go bankrupt by losing one case and then to seriously recommend going without insurance is to advocate taking a foolish risk.

Are there genuine alternatives that address the problem as well as Nyhan's? Here are three.

I. A maximum could be set on awards, not for compensating damage or loss, but for punitive damages and perhaps for emotional loss.

II. Tort or negligence cases could be tried before judges rather than juries to avoid whopping awards.

III. A similar improvement could be wrought by lifting the exemption for well educated professionals from jury service. They are often excused from jury duty on the grounds that their services are so important to the community. But it might be much more difficult for clever lawyers to win such massive sums from juries of equally clever and highly educated doctors, engineers, and executives.

Any of I., II., or III. affords a comparable solution to this problem. Since Nyhan offers no argument for his solution being more promising than these alternatives, the second part of his thesis receives only weak support. The solution he advances could solve the problem, but we are given no reasons or arguments for preferring it to any of the alternatives.

So on balance, the first part of Nyhan's thesis, that the situation is so terrible a change is needed, receives strong support; the second part receives weak support and is not established.

5. THE ANALYTICAL ESSAY—ONE EXAMPLE

An Analysis of Nyhan on the Liability Insurance Situation

by John Hoaglund

In "With liability judgments soaring, who's willing to take the risk?" David Nyhan considers whether our present liability insurance system has such harmful results that it ought to be changed. We become legally liable to pay damages when persons or property suffer injury, or damage, or destruction due to our negligence. Liability insurance protects our interest in such situations by paying damages to the extent covered in our policy.

Nyhan takes the stand that the consequences of the present system are so harmful that it should be changed. We may call this his first thesis. From affirming the need for change, Nyhan considers the question what change would be best. On this question he takes the stand that we should modify the system by limiting the types of case that can be brought in court. We will call this Nyhan's second thesis, and now consider each thesis separately, starting with the first.

In support of his first thesis, Nyhan contends that liability insurance premiums are rising beyond the ability of many to pay. Among those unable to pay are municipal and county boards, schools, and transportation systems. As a result we have unfortunate social consequences like the following:

1. People no longer volunteer or run for municipal or county boards because they will not cope with the legal hassles.
2. Zoning boards shy away from controversial rulings.
3. Schools are closing out football teams.
4. The Roosevelt Island Tramway across the East River shuts down daily.

The following two consequences result from doctors being unable to afford premiums for malpractice insurance:

5. Two hundred and fifty Massachusetts doctors temporarily withdraw their services.
6. Babies will be delivered without proper medical attention.

Finally Nyhan cites the following devastating consequences of corner-cutting due to the insurance crisis:

7. The NASA space shuttle explodes.
8. Johnson & Johnson writes off a $150 million inventory of Tylenol capsules rather than face lawsuits for deaths and injuries due to cyanide-tainted capsules.

The type of support claimed by Nyhan can be paraphrased thus:

> Because liability insurance premium hikes have unfortunate consequences 1)—8), the system should be changed.

We should note that the relation claimed by Nyhan between premium hikes and unfortunate consequences is not itself argumentative. Nyhan does not urge "Because rates have risen, people should do X." The relation he finds is cause-effect, with the rate hikes causing the harmful social effects.

Nyhan considers no objections to this evidence. It can be objected that 7) provides no support to his assessment of the liability insurance situation, since NASA, like federal government agencies generally, carries no liability insurance. To 8) it can be objected that Johnson & Johnson's decision to pull Tylenol capsules off the market was a responsible corporate decision to protect the public and preserve consumer confidence.

When we set these two items aside, items 1)—6) still provide solid support for Nyhan's first thesis. The number of local governments and boards struggling with high rates could be multiplied manyfold. Anyone who keeps up with current events can add specific instances similar to those cited by Nyhan. He does assume that the cases he cites are harmful to society. But this is a safe assumption. The public is obviously better off with these services and opportunities than without them.

Nyhan also assumes that we know (or can infer from his information) why people buy liability insurance. The awards in many negligence cases are high enough to bankrupt even fairly wealthy individuals, who consequently buy the insurance to protect themselves from potentially ruinous judgments. We should bear this in mind in considering the second part of Nyhan's thesis, that we need to alter the system by limiting the types of case that can be brought in court.

Nyhan does not marshal evidence or argue directly for this stand, so its relation to the material he presents is unclear. He does put forward a complex explanation of how liability insurance premiums became so expensive. Apparently he assumes that if we accept his explanation of how the high rates came about, we will automatically accept his proposal as the best way to make them lower.

He identifies the following four major causes, three of them in part interlocking and themselves supported by further evidence.

A) Americans are less inclined to take responsibility for their own actions, and more inclined to sue.

This is now supported with further evidence of two types:

a) Courts now have more frivolous suits.
- i) Lifetime smokers sue tobacco companies.
- ii) Parents sue when their daughter can't play Little League.
- iii) Parents sue when their son can't get in the Brownies.
- iv) Maine school board spends $60,000 fighting suit when a child couldn't get a specific quote beside her yearbook picture.

b) Courts are bogged down by the absolute numbers of suits.
- i) Suffolk County Superior Court in Boston has a backlog of 20,000 civil suits.

B) The United States has more lawyers—600,000—than the rest of the industrial world combined; they eagerly take cases for 30% or 40% contingency fees, and even sell shares in potentially lucrative cases to investors.

C) Juries award huge sums in negligence cases, persuaded by clever lawyers to punish big, impersonal, profit-drenched insurance companies.

a) The average verdict in a medical negligence case that goes to trial in California exceeds $600,000.

D) Insurance companies cut premiums to draw business from competitors, then speculated recklessly in Farm Belt and oil related real estate.

Causal factors A), B), and C) all fit together to explain the high premiums, and also to support some measure like Nyhan's to lower them. A) shows that Americans are inclined to sue, B) that there is a huge number of lawyers eager to file for them, and C) that juries are awarding winners great sums. Premiums have rocketed to cover legal expenses in the ever-increasing number of suits and the vast sums awarded the petitioners. The role of D) is indirect. Formerly successful real estate speculation made up costs that are now recovered by increased premiums.

Nyhan does not consider objections to his thesis, but he does consider as an alternative solution that people can go without insurance. This is not a serious alternative. Few people would be motivated to work and earn if they knew that one misstep could cost them everything.

There are a number of alternatives that appear to address the problem as well as Nyhan's. Here are three of them:

I. A maximum could be set on awards, not for actual damages, but for punitive damages and perhaps emotional loss.

II. Tort or negligence cases could be tried before judges rather than juries to prevent such gigantic awards.

III. Lifting the exemption from jury duty of most well educated professionals would also decrease award amounts. They are often excused from jury duty on the grounds that their services are so important to the community. But it might be much more difficult for clever lawyers to win such massive sums from juries of equally clever and highly educated doctors, engineers, and executives.

Since Nyhan offers no evidence or reason why his solution should be preferred over any of the above, the second part of his thesis receives only weak support. His solution could address the problem, but we are not convinced that it could do so more effectively than some other.

On balance, the first part of Nyhan's thesis receives strong support and is established. The second part is not established.

SUMMARY

The first step to analyze and evaluate a longer argument is to identify the issue it is concerned with. You may need to draw on general information, or information not available in the argument itself, in order to identify the issue. This issue is best stated in form of a question that can be answered yes or no. In some cases it is helpful to state related questions that are *not* the issue, and explain why they are not. Then the stand of the writer should be stated in form of a yes or no answer to this question.

Now the piece should be examined for reasons or evidence in support of the stand. To do this we must distinguish the writer's stand from reasons or evidence she advances in support of the stand. This distinction is similar to that between conclusion and premises of an argument. We adopt it here because it is more helpful in analyzing longer arguments.

It is possible that our close examination turns up little or no evidence in support of the writer's stand. This can mean one of two things.

1. We are mistaken in interpreting the piece as argumentative. In fact it only states an opinion without marshaling evidence to support the opinion.
2. We have stated the issue or the stand incorrectly. We need to re-state one, the other, or both, to reflect the evidence our close reading has turned up.

Next we go through the piece paragraph by paragraph, noting of each one the arguments or evidence supporting the stand it contains. We also note when a paragraph contains no such reasons or evidence. We also note whether the writer considers and responds to objections to any of these arguments. The writer may also consider and respond to objections to the stand itself. Another possibility is that the writer considers alternatives to the stand, and gives reasons for rejecting them or preferring one to her original stand.

Now we categorize and organize the arguments and evidence in order to grasp more clearly how they are intended to support the writer's stand. Finally we evaluate each piece of evidence and argument, along with objections, responses, and alternative positions, for the support they provide the stand. At any point in this analysis and evaluation we may need to clarify puzzling or murky ideas, or clarify the structure of the argument.

Our result is a decision, backed up with evidence and reasoning, whether the writer has adequately supported her stand or not.

EXERCISE 15—3: THE ARGUMENT ANALYSIS ESSAY

Write an essay in analysis of a piece of argumentative discourse selected by you or your instructor from editorials, opinion pieces, or letters to the editor in a newspaper or magazine. Remember that you cannot analyze arguments in discourse that contains none, so be sure to select a piece that qualifies as argumentative writing.

You should first identify the issue and the stand, then each piece of evidence or argument advanced in support. Then identify any objection to an argument, the writer's response to the objection if any, and decide what strength the argument has in view of the objection and response. Identify and evaluate any objection to the stand and response to that objection, as well as any alternative position and response to the alternative. Finally, you should evaluate the argumentative position as a whole. Has the writer succeeded in establishing his thesis? Give reasons for your response.

It is advisable to carry out this project in two or more drafts. A first draft may be submitted to the instructor for critique and commentary. Or it may be read to the class for critique. Or the class may be split into teams of 3 to 4 students. Each team is responsible for one part of the essay, e.g. the stand. This team chooses the best statement of the stand of its members, and the writer reads it to the class. Team members comment on it first, then comment is solicited from the rest of the class. These drafts culminate in a final version with each student producing his or her own essay and submitting it to the instructor for credit.

When dealing with argumentative discourse of the length and complexity of the Nyhan piece above, it is advisable to work in steps or stages similar to the following.

1. **Identify the issue and the stand.**
2. **Examine each paragraph for whatever evidence or arguments it contains in support of the stand.**
3. **If you only find very little, reformulate the issue and stand to take account of the evidence you do find.**
4. **Prepare a draft stating the issue and stand, listing and categorizing evidence from each paragraph as it supports the stand.**
5. **After receiving feedback on this draft, proceed to lay out the argumentative structure of the piece. State the arguments in their order, consider objections to them, to the position, consider alternative positions, and finally evaluate the whole argumentative position.**
6. **Write this up as a draft.**
7. **After getting a critique of this, write your final essay paragraph by paragraph in good prose style.**

Further Reading

Alec Fisher, *The Logic of Real Arguments* (Cambridge 1988). Provides stimulating analyses of long, challenging arguments from Thomas Malthus, J. S. Mill, Karl Marx, and others.

R. H. Johnson & J. A. Blair, *Logical Self-Defense*, 2nd ed. (New York 1994). Chapter 13 on analyzing extended arguments has very helpful material.

Howard Kahane, *Logic and Contemporary Rhetoric*, 6th ed. (Belmont 1992). Kahane pioneered the analysis of extended arguments and his Chapter 6 on evaluating and constructing extended arguments is a model treatment.

Jack Meiland, *College Thinking* (New York 1981). Chapter 2 on reading with understanding has outstanding material on longer arguments.

CHAPTER SIXTEEN

WRITING THE ARGUMENTATIVE ESSAY

1. THE SHORT ARGUMENTATIVE PIECE

Our work with arguments up to this point has consisted mainly in analyzing and evaluating shorter or longer pieces of argumentative discourse. In each case we reached a decision whether the arguments or argumentative positions were strong or weak, and why. In the process we learned a considerable amount about the relation of evidence or reasons to beliefs or propositions. Now we turn to the new task of constructing our own argumentative essay. This is a rather specialized thinking and writing task that requires a few words of general guidance.

The argumentative essay we will write explores the relation of evidence to a thesis or proposition. In it we test this thesis to discover whether it receives strong or weak support, and we do so by stating the thesis and examining the arguments for and against it. Initially we may believe that the thesis is sound because there is strong evidence supporting it. Yet the question of its soundness must remain an open one for the purposes of our investigation. It must be possible for us to uncover evidence during this investigation that much weakens the thesis.

Our goal is not so much that of persuading the reader of the truth of our thesis, because at the start of our investigation our commitment to the thesis is tentative and cautious. (This holds even though we may state the thesis clearly and boldly.) Our goal is instead to establish in our own minds and for our readers to inspect whether the thesis finds strong support and is therefore one we can commit ourselves to. The relation of the argumentative essay we are writing to a persuasive essay, which is quite different, is complex and will be treated below. Nor is the format of our argumentative essay one where we first state the pros of a thesis, then the cons, and finally decide between them. Our outcome is similar to this, but the route taken is different.

We first turn our attention to the structure of a short argumentative essay. Here it is step-by-step.

A. Find the topic.

Not just any topic will serve as the subject of an argumentative essay. You must find a topic that is controversial in the sense that reasonable people can take different stands on it.

Does Wednesday follow Tuesday?

This fails as a topic for two reasons:

1. Reasonable people don't disagree on it.
2. No one is likely to be interested in it.

Better:

Is surrogate motherhood ethical?

1. Reasonable people disagree.
2. The topic is of considerable interest.

B. Locate sources for the topic.

Rarely are we so well informed on a topic that we can write a good argumentative essay right off the top of our heads. So when we choose a topic, we should bear in mind that we will need to gather information about it. Facts are the building materials of good argumentative essays. Facts alone don't make an essay, just as bricks alone don't make a building. But you can no more build without them than you can erect a building without wood, bricks, or some similar building material. One important resource for information is persons. Instructors, other faculty, fellow students, parents, friends, experts reachable by phone or mail, reference librarians and others may all be of help—depending on the topic.

We all know how to use the subject index in the card catalog or data base of the library, which can help us locate books on our topic. Indexes to newspapers like *The New York Times Index*, or to popular magazines, like the *Reader's Guide to Periodical Literature*, may also lead us to valuable sources. In fact, for a topic of current interest like the ethics of abortion, current newspapers and periodicals, and television and radio as well, are often the best sources of information. Your search can be extended beyond the print sources in your institution's library by using data bases such as *Newsbank* or *Infotrack* and working with sources on microfiche. And the Internet with search engines such as Lycos or Yahoo is an extremely valuable resource.

Sometimes you can identify an issue as belonging to a category of issues or problems that has its own specialized literature. Surrogate motherhood, for example, is a legal issue, so you may be able to find articles on it in law school reviews like the *Harvard Law Review* or *New England Law Review.* It is also an issue in medical ethics or bioethics, so another possible source of information is such specialized periodicals as *The Hastings Center Report* or the *Journal of Bioethics.*

Once you locate your sources, you must read and evaluate them for the purposes of your project. Not every article whose title promises enlightenment on the moral questions of surrogate motherhood will actually deliver on that promise. But you have to locate and read the sources to find out which are valuable. You should take notes on those that enlighten and then use this information in writing your essay.

C. Narrow the topic to manageable size.

With some topics this will not be necessary. But it is a tactic you need to be able to employ. One reason for doing it is to get a smaller, more clearly defined topic to work on from an argumentative standpoint. Also in regard to your search for information to serve in your arguments and objections, a more narrowly defined topic helps you focus and limit your search for supporting material.

> Should gambling be legalized?

The topic is too broad. The search for material could begin with the Bible or earlier sources. An entire essay - one neither argumentative nor brief - could be devoted to explaining just what counts as gambling and what doesn't.

> Should Virginia have a state lottery?

This is more narrow and focused. At the time when Virginia considered a referendum on the question, print and electronic media provided ample information and perspectives.

Many good argumentative essays grow out of false starts. Sometimes the writer starts with a topic defined very broadly, then discovers how difficult it is to construct convincing arguments for a stand on it. This then leads back to defining the topic more narrowly.

D. State the issue as a question.

> Should elected officials be members of ethnically discriminatory clubs?
>
> Is capital punishment morally acceptable?
>
> Should there be mandatory drug testing for all government employees?

In the 500 to 800-word, short essay that we are dealing with, a spare statement of the question is preferable. The question should have a "yes" or "no" answer.

E. Clearly state your position on the question.

> I take the position that Virginia should not have a state lottery.

Is it necessary for you to be strongly committed to the position you take? This cannot be a prerequisite. The question you are writing about may be one on which you have no strong conviction. Perhaps you have just confronted it and are only beginning to study it. The argumentative essay is by nature exploratory and tentative. You may decide in the course of your investigation that your initial stand is not the one that appears most reasonable.

F. State the first argument in support of your position.

> I take the position that Virginia should not have a state lottery.
>
> The Presidential Commission on Gambling in America identified a clear correlation between legal gambling and the level of illegal gambling in a community. There is more of the latter wherever citizens approve the former. . . . the cultural stigma against gambling erodes, and we find more and more people willing to take a chance. They will deal with bookies who give better odds than the state, borrow from loan sharks to make their bets, and get hurt when they cannot pay back the crime bosses. The lottery creates a whole new set of law enforcement problems that the taxpayers will have to pay for one way or another.

Notice that this is a positive argument supporting the position that Virginia should not have a state lottery.

Stating an initial argument in support of a position is a difficult step for many students, so don't be discouraged if you have to work at it. The following are two of the obstacles.

1. If you have not yet done so, it forces you to think clearly about the distinction of your position from whatever evidence or arguments you want to advance in support of this position. What happens when you fail to do this? One very common failing is to state a position, then simply give further information about the topic. Some of this information may have the potential of being arranged in the form of an argument, but it actually is not. Here is an example from a student essay on the question of surrogate motherhood:

> The issue of this paper is whether or not surrogate motherhood is ethical. The answer to this question should be no. For thousands of years there was only one way in which a couple could have a child. Now because of modern

> technology it is possible that couples who would have gone childless can now have a family. However, how far should technology go? How much are we willing to let science delve into our personal lives? The world today is well on its way to a serious over-population problem. With people (women) having children of their own and then having them for others, it's no wonder. Maybe it was meant that some people should not have children.

There is material here for two arguments against surrogate motherhood:

i) It is an unacceptable intrusion of science/technology into our private lives.

ii) It contributes to world-wide overpopulation.

But neither of these is developed clearly as an argument in support of the position. As an argumentative essay, this piece wanders without getting to the point, however informative and interesting it may be.

2. The second obstacle is a failure to appreciate that when you advance a position you shoulder the burden of proving that position. As we learned in Chapter Ten, in argumentative discourse the person who advances a thesis or position must assume the burden of proving it. Burden of proof means that she is obliged to advance positive evidence or arguments in support of it. The following illustrates what happens when a writer fails or refuses to assume the burden of proof.

> Is surrogate motherhood ethical? I take the position that it is.
>
> Has anyone ever proven that it is not ethical? No they have not. Has any important evidence been advanced to demonstrate that it is unethical? No it has not. Can you prove to me at this moment that it is unethical? No you cannot. Since it has not been proven that surrogate motherhood is unethical, it must be ethical, and I have established my position.

Instead of assuming the burden of proof - advancing reasons or evidence in support of the position - this writer attempts to shift it to her opponent. She searches for arguments against her position, and when she finds none, she challenges her opponent to prove her position false and finds no response. But she may not have looked very assiduously for opposition. She may be attempting to persuade us of something by trickery because she can think of no good arguments for her position, thus making a fallacious appeal to ignorance. But we can't accept propositions on trickery. As critical thinkers we can accept them only on the basis of adequate evidence or reasons.

G. State an objection to your argument and respond to this objection.

This may be the single most difficult step for the student to master. Possibly when you find a good argument you want to elaborate on it. Possibly you want to go directly from one argument supporting your position to the next and then to another, so that the force of the piled up arguments is felt cumulatively. But this is not the purpose of the argumentative essay as it is here conceived, nor does it serve the purpose of teaching critical thinking as well as the essay we will actually write. But more of this in a moment. First we can look at an example, obtained by rephrasing Marshall Coleman's argument against the state lottery in Virginia.

> Should Virginia have a state lottery? I take the stand that it should not.
>
> Legal gambling leads to illegal gambling, bookies, loan sharks, and new law enforcement problems. It is objected to this argument that tens of thousands of Virginians have played legal bingo at churches, but this legal form of gambling has not had the stated result. So loan sharking and organized crime are not necessary consequences of legalized gambling. To this I respond that the state lottery would be open to all citizens, not just churchgoers, and the latter may be better able to resist the temptation of betting illegally and borrowing to make their bets.

Argumentative and Persuasive Essays

At this point we must carefully distinguish the argumentative essay from the persuasive. When you write a persuasive paper, you have already made up your mind on the question and are attempting to persuade others that your position is the best one. The question is closed in the sense that you are not searching for factors that might cause you to revise your position.

The argumentative paper, on the other hand, is a form of intellectual inquiry. A reasonable position is taken, and the point of the paper is to discover what arguments count for it and what against. So it is really a scrutiny of the grounds that can be advanced for and against a position. Though we take a position initially, the purpose of our inquiry is to decide whether it is worth holding.

One possible outcome of an argumentative essay is that the position taken initially turns out to be too weak to hold and is consequently relinquished. By contrast this outcome is never possible in a persuasive essay.

There are other important ways in which the persuasive essay differs from the argumentative. The writer of the persuasive essay needs to know something about the readers he is attempting to persuade. To persuade readers of the *Richmond Times-Dispatch*, for instance, that we should mandate a one-week waiting period for the purchase of a handgun, he needs to draw on his knowledge of their present beliefs and attitudes.

The writer of the argumentative essay, on the other hand, does not have such a target readership. (As we shall see below, a conception of the reader may be useful for another purpose.) She is instead exploring the evidence for and against a position for the purpose of deciding whether the position is worth adopting or not.

The writer of the persuasive paper may employ emotive language in an effort to persuade his readers. If you consider using such emotive language yourself in your argumentative essay, recall how you felt duped when you discovered that a writer was trying to bypass your rational scrutiny by appealing to your emotions.

The writer of the argumentative essay does not employ emotive language because it is not her goal to persuade someone. She is seeking to establish what is a reasonable belief on some controversial issue. The only language use that can avail her in this quest is language chosen to fit the phenomena as accurately and precisely as possible.

A final difference is that the writer of the persuasive paper pulls his punches. Of course he presents the strongest arguments for his position he can find. But he probably presents only those objections that are easy to respond to. The writer of the argumentative paper cannot do this and still honestly probe the strengths and weaknesses of her position.

The Argumentative Essay

Returning now to the argumentative essay, it is very important for you to know at every point in your essay what you are doing. For instance, you must know whether you are stating an argument for your position or responding to an objection to an argument you stated earlier. Not only must you *know* this, you must also *articulate* it for your reader. It should be clear to the reader what you are doing at every point in your essay. A statement added to clarify what you are doing is proper even in a short essay.

This brings up the question: Who is your reader? And the question: What is your relation to her? Having just treated the contrast with the persuasive essay, we know that the reader is *not* someone you are trying to convert to your position. You really don't have a position you are trying to "sell." You do better to conceive of your reader as a person cooperating with you in this process of inquiry. But you are the leader, and the reader is your follower. So you must point out to your reader each step you are taking. This enables her to appreciate the structure of your argument and to be able to follow you.

Because of this you should not write for your teacher, even though you think the teacher may be the only one beside you who will ever read your essay. If you write for your teacher, you are likely to assume that the teacher knows so much and you want to avoid pointing out the obvious, e.g. that you are considering an objection rather than stating another argument for your position. It is better to picture your reader as a high school student, so you have to do some explaining about both the structure and the substance of your argument to get her to understand.

Here is a student essay that does not provide the reader sufficient clarity and guidance:

> The issue which this paper will look at is the question of "Is capital punishment morally justifiable?"
>
> This is a very clear cut issue for me and one which I feel very strongly about. Without question capital punishment *is* morally justifiable.
>
> Capital punishment acts as a deterrent for would-be criminals, or already criminals, from committing hideous and violent crimes against their fellow man. If a criminal knows he/she could, not only receive the death penalty, but actually have it carried out, that criminal may think twice before actually pulling the trigger or raping a defenseless victim and decide the possible end result isn't worth the moment. If capital punishment saves just one would-be victim, it's justifiable.
>
> There is no evidence to suggest capital punishment is a deterrent against violent crimes. There are no concrete statistics which show or prove that capital punishment lowers violent crimes. If a criminal intends to commit a violent crime he/she will do it and nothing can change that. Even with the institution of capital punishment, violent crimes are still on the rise. Capital punishment is a barbaric act which cannot be justified.

By and large the argumentative structure we are looking for is here in this beginning of an essay. But the reader doesn't grasp this because the writer has failed to communicate what he is doing. It seems he has started out on an essay where an argument for a position will be balanced with an argument against, and so on until the conclusion, where the result will be tallied up. At the beginning of his fourth paragraph he should have said something like "Now let me consider and respond to an objection to this argument." The final statement of that paragraph is an argument against his position, not an objection to his first argument.

That reminds us that an indicator telling your reader where you are in your argumentative essay would help at this juncture. You have been considering an objection to your argument and responding to that objection, as well as several issues that arise with this step.

You can appreciate how going from your argument to an objection to that argument helps you to articulate and keep clear the structure of your essay. Here, for example, is a condensed version of an essay beginning we looked at earlier.

> Is surrogate motherhood ethical? I take the position that it is not.
>
> It is an unacceptable intrusion of science and technology into our private lives and it contributes to world-wide overpopulation.

Now we turn to consider an objection to our argument. But which of them will we consider an objection to? For we have two arguments, and we have not distinguished them.

At this point in your essay you have options. You may want to consider a second or third objection to your argument and respond to them. Or you may want to advance a second and third argument in support of your thesis, then consider and respond to objections to each.

H. Clearly state your conclusion.

Finally you must tell your reader exactly where you stand as a result of these deliberations. Your conclusion should not leave doubt in her mind.

> I conclude that Virginia should not have a state lottery.

Now we need to draw together for convenient reference the steps of the shorter argumentative essay.

Preliminary steps:

A. Find the topic
B. Locate sources for the topic
C. Narrow the topic to manageable size

Parts of the essay (those in parentheses are optional):

1. State the issue as a question
2. Clearly state your position on the question
3. State the first argument in support of your position
4. State an objection to your argument
5. Respond to this objection
6. (Give one or two responses more to this objection)
7. State another objection to your argument
8. Respond to the second objection
9. (Give one or two responses more to this objection)
10. (State and respond to other objections to your first argument)
11. State the second argument in support of your position

12. State an objection to your second argument
13. Respond to this objection
14. (State and respond to other objections to your second argument)
15. (State other arguments for your position)
16. (State and respond to objections to these arguments)
17. Draw your conclusion

Some combination of steps like these will be present in any good argumentative essay. Aside from stating arguments for your stand, and considering and responding to objections to them, none of the steps are absolutely necessary. The ones you include as well as those you choose not to use will depend on the nature of the issue, your stand on the issue, and the evidence you have to work with.

Here is an example of a good short argumentative essay.

The Ethics of Surrogate Motherhood

by Joe Petrolia

Is surrogate motherhood unethical? I take the position that it is definitely unethical. Although this question has become controversial and complicated, my position will address just four of the contested areas: the selling of babies, the identity of the parent(s), the buying of happiness, and the question of adoption.

First of all, contract motherhood commercializes childbirth. Babies, before they are born, are purchased! One might argue that the child is not purchased, but rather the mother's services. However, if that point was acceptable, people would still be used in order to purchase other people. Many of the arguments for surrogate motherhood fail to raise the status of babies to people. Is not the selling of people unethical?

Another argument against surrogate motherhood is the fact that both the man and the woman are parents. There are those who will contest that point, saying that the only real parent is the donor, the father. An argument stated on their behalf by Sarah Ketchum is that the father is simply buying out the mother's interest in the "property" involved. However, this "property" is not land. It is living and real, and it has not consented to be sold.

The proponents to surrogate motherhood insist that it solves infertility and turns the misery of those who cannot have children into happiness. But isn't that misery transferred to those who are poor, and who initially believe that money will buy them happiness? How can a mother that conceives a child predict how she will feel about her baby when it is finally born? Will she coldly turn it over to the donor, or will she regret her contract and love this child?

Finally, advocates of contract motherhood liken it to adoption. It solves the problem of parents without children. However, adoption does two things. It gives infertile people the joy of parenthood, and it gives a homeless child the care and love of the adopting couple. The "contract baby" already has parents, and the mother who has endured the pain and labor and joy of childbirth should never be forced to sell her child.

Based on these arguments I maintain that surrogate motherhood is unethical and I conclude that it should be prohibited.

EXERCISE 16—1: WRITING THE SHORT ARGUMENTATIVE ESSAY

1. Brainstorm in class for topics for argumentative essays, bearing in mind the need for sources.
2. Write an essay of two paragraphs. State the issue and your stand in the first. In the second, state an argument for your stand, then consider an objection to your argument and respond to it.
3. Write one or more drafts of an argumentative essay for instructor's comments and class discussion.
4. Write an argumentative essay for credit.

2. THE LONGER ARGUMENTATIVE ESSAY: DELINEATING THE ISSUE

There is no difference in principle between the shorter argumentative essay and the longer one we now turn our attention to. Their goals are identical—to assess the tenability of a thesis on a controversial topic by examining the evidence for it. The longer essay is more complex, and it comprises more critical thinking techniques because it attempts to be clearer and more precise. In this longer essay there is more scope to delineate or outline the area of the controversial issue. This brings us to an aspect of the argumentative essay we have not yet considered.

A topic becomes controversial when it is a matter of importance to a number of people who hold quite different views on it. This puts an interesting perspective on our role in writing the longer argumentative essay. Our role is not one of inventing the issue—the issue is already there. Nor is our role one of initiating the controversy—it too exists already. When we start out on our essay we negotiate our way into an on-going process, much as naturalist novelists like Emile Zola or Frank Norris take us into a slice of life, or Baroque painters like Caravaggio or Rubens bring us into the scene on a diagonal. Our longer essay enables us to more fully inform the reader of this field of opposing views we are entering.

A. Why the Topic is Important.

In this longer essay we have the opportunity of explaining to our reader why the topic is important enough so that we should take a stand on it. Although it is clear to you what is controversial about your topic, it may not be equally clear to all your readers. In the longer essay you can point out briefly why the question is controversial. This is an indirect way of explaining why the question is important enough to merit the attention you are calling to it.

> Should public officials be members of private clubs that practice racial discrimination? The explicit and specific policy of the government is that of combating racial discrimination. Can an elected official who practices discrimination in his private life be expected to uphold anti-discrimination statutes vigorously as part of his job? This is a central reason why the question is important.

B. Contrast with Related Issues.

When we narrow the topic, as we learned to do in the shorter essay, we can share some of this process with our reader. We can tell her more precisely what is the issue, and contrast it with related issues that might be confused with it. We might, for example, state the issue as a broad general question at first, then narrow it down to the specific part we will deal with, and explain to our reader why we have chosen this part.

Jack Meiland makes the following sharp observation on the way in which our choice of a topic puts certain constraints on our work.

> . . . when you choose a topic, you thereby select an argumentative field to explore. This field exists independently of any particular person; these are positions, arguments, and objections which *anyone* must explore in order to understand the significance and ramifications of this particular topic. Within this argumentative field, some arguments, objections, and replies are more important than others. You are not free to choose just any set of arguments and still produce a good paper. This independently existing argumentative structure imposes constraints on you.

It is instructive to notice where a student essay goes astray in its conception of an issue and how to deal with it.

> Do women have a role in combat? As more women serve in the armed forces, this question gets more attention. The consensus now is yes, women do have a role in combat.

This appeal to a consensus reveals confusion over the aim of an argumentative essay. The aim is twofold.

1. To clarify for ourselves what evidence supports a position on a controversial issue.
2. To lay this evidence out publicly so others can examine and accept or reject it.

The argumentative essay carries out an investigation of the evidence that can be marshaled in support of a position. We assess this evidence to decide whether the position receives adequate support. If there is a sense in which this investigation is an appeal, it is an appeal to reason. More specifically, it appeals to the reasoning that evaluates the evidence relative to our position and decides whether the position is sustained.

An appeal to a consensus is something quite different. A consensus is an agreement on a controversial issue among those whose stands had previously differed. There are different ways of achieving a consensus. One party's reasoning may convince the other party. But this need not be the case. A consensus can also be reached without any reasoning if one party simply tires of the controversy and joins the other. One party may also be bribed into a consensus by concessions in some other area. Some observers claim this happens frequently in the real world of politics.

Basically what we do relative to a consensus is find out whether one exists or not, then report this fact. In many cases it is important to know whether a consensus exists or not. But finding out is essentially empirical research like polling the public. This may involve critical thinking, but not necessarily. In reporting a consensus we may also report the arguments supporting the stand. Again such reporting doesn't necessarily involve critical thinking. It is only when we *assess* the arguments to decide whether they actually support the stand that we must recur to critical thinking. Because a consensus can be reported without thinking critically, such work does not constitute a good critical thinking exercise. On the other hand, we must think critically to write a good argumentative essay, and that is why we focus on it here.

Because "Do women have a role in combat?" might also be confused with a factual question, our question might better be phrased "Should women have a role in combat?" But the question is very broad. Shall we consider the question regardless of era or society? If not, we should explain to our reader just what we will consider.

Should women have a role in combat? This question is important because of the increase in women serving in the armed forces, the tradition of keeping female personnel out of harm's way, and the importance of combat experience for a successful military career.

We are not considering the question whether women can fight. That question has been answered in the affirmative by such groups as the Amazons of antiquity and modern guerillas and terrorists. We focus on the present and inquire of women now serving in the U.S. military. Should women now serving in the U.S. military have a role in combat? Another question we are not considering is whether women should serve in the U.S. armed forces in wartime. They have done so now for many decades, and the practice is not now controversial.

One of our concerns is the amount of danger servicewomen should be exposed to in wartime. But we are not dealing with the question whether servicewomen should serve in combat zones. Some work in combat zones by medical, supply, or maintenance personnel can be distant from the front lines and so less risky. In modern warfare this risk may be only marginally greater than for someone serving in the rear but exposed to attack by aircraft or rockets. Civilians near a critical airfield hundreds of miles from the front lines may be exposed to similar or greater risk when that airfield is targeted by the enemy. In fact, the heaviest loss of life in a single incident by U.S. forces in the Gulf War of early 1991 occurred when an Iraqi Scud missile struck a barracks in Dhahran, nearly 200 miles from the front, killing 28 American reservists, including three women.

When we ask whether women should serve in combat there is an implied comparison "like men do." We can bring this out by asking whether women should serve in the infantry in combat. In combat an infantryman exchanges small arms fire with the enemy, may engage in hand-to-hand combat, and in addition to being shot or stabbed risks being captured and tortured. Let us again rephrase our question to show this. Should women now in the U.S. military serve in the infantry in combat?

C. Contrast with Other Stands.

When we state our stand, we may contrast it with other stands that either have been taken or might be taken. This allows our reader to get a more exact fix on our effort. It is often a good idea in this longer essay to explain the relation of what we are doing to what someone else has done or may do.

Should time limits be placed on welfare? I take the stand that they should.

Some who take a similar stand include the school lunch program with the welfare they want to subject to time limits. This program is supported with federal money and food from agricultural surpluses. All school lunches are subsidized for about half their cost, and the price is reduced even more or wholly eliminated for children from low income families. I do not include the school lunch program among those I propose to limit in time. I regard it as having automatic time limits. When children leave school, either by dropping out or graduating, they no longer receive this subsidy. So my stand is that time limits should be placed on welfare, excluding the school lunch program, which has a built-in time limit.

D. Overview of the Argument.

In the longer essay it is also helpful to give your reader an overview of the direction the argument will take. This can help her follow its course and discern how the different parts work together.

> Should time limits be placed on welfare? I take the stand that they should. I will examine the effect of welfare on the motivation of its recipients, the availability or lack of jobs for them, the length and effectiveness of job training programs, and the willingness or unwillingness of taxpayers to bear the burden of welfare costs.
>
> Should women now in the U.S. military serve in the infantry in combat? I take the stand that they should. In examining this question I will consider whether women are physically and psychologically prepared for this role, whether men in the infantry are psychologically prepared to have women serving alongside them in combat, whether America as a nation is prepared to accept it, and whether women have a right to such service.

3. The Longer Argumentative Essay: The Body of the Essay

E. Arguments Should Allow Objections.

How good should your first argument be? As Meiland suggests, you must find important arguments if your essay is to be a good one. But it would be a mistake to polish up a rough argument and state it so carefully that it will meet many possible objections. In this essay you must state objections, and they too should be important ones. If you so polish your first argument that it already meets many objections, then stating objections to it will be superfluous (for those it already meets) or very difficult (for those it may still be open to). But what is more important, you are carrying out silently the very process you should be sharing with your reader, namely, testing your argument for weaknesses by raising and responding to objections.

This process lies at the heart of critical thinking on the Socratic model. On that model, critical thinking is a reflective thinking activity that monitors and corrects itself. It tests its own positions and arguments by raising and responding to the same objections that a penetrating critic like Socrates would raise. Up to now we have worked mainly on learning what questions needed asking and what objections needed raising of the positions and arguments of others. It is essential for critical thinking that we now practice raising the same serious questions and objections of our own positions and arguments.

A good illustration of the Socratic method is found in Plato's dialogue *Euthyphro.* Socrates, charged with impiety, meets his friend Euthyphro, a prophet who offers to give Socrates lessons in piety, or proper behavior toward the gods. Socrates asks Euthyphro to explain what piety is in the sense of its having some one feature that makes it always identical to itself and the opposite of impiety. He seeks a definition that would include all cases of pious behavior and exclude all non-pious. Euthyphro responds that pious behavior (proper behavior to the gods) is such behavior as bringing charges for manslaughter, temple robbery, or other religious crimes. Socrates tests this and other explanation attempts of Euthyphro by raising objections to them. He objects that Euthyphro has given him many 'pieties' or examples of piety instead of the one model they agreed to seek, made identical to itself by always having some one single feature. So Euthyphro attempts again by explaining that all pious behavior pleases the gods whereas impious displeases them. But Socrates points out that the gods do not always agree, so that what pleases Zeus may not at all please Kronos. So this makes one and the same action both pious and impious for pleasing some gods and displeasing others, and piety would be not identical to itself but to its opposite. So Euthyphro concedes that this explanation of piety is inadequate also.

This brief sample of the Socratic method of questioning may yield a hint or two about how good our arguments should be and how good the objections should be that we raise against them. The following example is a question, stand, and first argument advanced by a student, to which the Socratic method is then applied.

> Do police use too much force in U.S. cities? I take the stand that they do.
>
> My first piece of evidence is the widely viewed videotape of Los Angeles police brutally beating suspect Rodney King on Mar. 3, 1991. To this it is objected that part of the job of a policeman is to use force. This includes shooting, clubbing, or striking suspects who attempt to harm them while resisting arrest. My first response to this is that the suspect in the LA videotape was not resisting arrest. My second is that he did not pose a threat to them because he was unarmed.
>
> To my responses it is further objected that King was indeed resisting arrest, since he fled officers attempting to arrest him at speeds of over 100 mph on a freeway. It is also objected that a large man like King could harm people by beating them even though he is unarmed. I concede the point that he might

> have posed a threat due to his size. But in the widely viewed videotape he did not pose a threat. He was on the ground attempting to shield himself as several officers beat on him with their clubs.
>
> A second objection to my evidence is that I have cited only one case, and so I have committed the fallacy of hasty generalization. In response I note only that there are many more cases of unnecessary police brutality as in Virginia Beach on Labor Day weekend in 1989, in New York, and in Dallas. To my response it is further objected that I am making a broad assumption of the very thesis I am attempting to prove, and thus begging the question. At most, general news accounts establish that police used force on these occasions. But I have advanced no evidence that the force amounted to brutality. Even if the force amounted to brutality, I have advanced no evidence that the force went beyond what the situation required and so was unnecessary.

After this series of objections and responses it looks as if the thesis may need to be modified if it is to be sustained by the evidence advanced. Otherwise new evidence needs to be introduced if the thesis is to be sustained as it is currently stated.

F. Clarify Obscure Points.

In the longer argumentative essay you can turn to consider a point of clarification any time it seems needed. Up to now we have clarified only the thesis at the start of the essay. But clarification can be helpful at any stage of the argument. William James reports a dispute that had reached an impasse and sorely needed clarification.

> Some years ago, being with a camping party in the mountains, I returned from a solitary ramble to find everyone engaged in a ferocious dispute. The *corpus* of the dispute was a squirrel—a live squirrel supposed to be clinging to one side of a tree-trunk; while over against the tree's opposite side a human being was imagined to stand. This human witness tries to get sight of the squirrel by moving rapidly round the tree, but no matter how fast he goes, the squirrel moves as fast in the opposite direction, and always keeps the tree between himself and the man, so that never a glimpse of him is caught. The resultant metaphysical problem is this: *Does the man go round the squirrel or not?* He goes round the tree, sure enough, and the squirrel is on the tree; but does he go round the squirrel? In the unlimited leisure of the wilderness, discussion had been worn threadbare. Every one had taken sides, and was obstinate; and the numbers on both sides were even. Each side, when I appeared, therefore appealed to me to make it a majority. Mindful of the scholastic adage that whenever you meet a contradiction you must make a distinction, I immediately sought and found one, as follows: "Which party is right," I said, "depends on what you *practically mean* by 'going round' the squirrel. If you mean passing from the north of him to the east, then to the south, then to

> the west, and then to the north of him again, obviously the man does go round him, for he occupies these successive positions. But if on the contrary you mean being first in front of him, then on the right of him, then behind him, then on his left, and finally in front again, it is quite as obvious that the man fails to go round him, for by the compensating movements the squirrel makes, he keeps his belly turned toward the man all the time, and his back turned away. Make the distinction, and there is no occasion for any further dispute. You are both right and both wrong according as you conceive the verb 'to go round' in one practical fashion or the other."
>
> Although one or two of the hotter disputants called my speech a shuffling evasion, saying they wanted no quibbling or scholastic hair-splitting, but meant just plain honest English "round," the majority seemed to think that the distinction had assuaged the dispute.

Clarification in this case is so important that it shows the original dispute to have had a strong verbal element concerning the meaning of "go around the squirrel." Let us now look at part of a student essay that can benefit from clarification.

> Should active euthanasia be legalized? I take the position that it should.
>
> First of all, euthanasia creates a solution to everlasting agony. Opponents will argue that euthanasia is murder, but would these same opponents be able to bear watching loved ones exist in constant pain and suffering while waiting to die? With the legalization of euthanasia people would have a choice of suffering while waiting for death.
>
> Another objection against legalizing euthanasia is the fact that in religion, God is the only one authorized to take a life. In the Bible it clearly states "Thou shalt not kill." If God was so against euthanasia then he wouldn't have put brains in our heads to think and make decisions.

The readers for whom this essay was written already understood the difference between passive euthanasia (where a person is allowed to die e.g. by not being hooked up to a respirator or intravenous drip) and active euthanasia (where a person is killed by a positive act, e.g. injecting poison). Even so, there are important points here that need clarifying. Paragraph two advances as an argument for the position that euthanasia should be legalized "euthanasia creates a solution to everlasting agony." Just what is this "everlasting agony" for which euthanasia is being advanced as a solution? Is it a terrible emotional anguish? If so, wouldn't we need to know that every other method of addressing it, e.g. therapy or drugs, had been tried unsuccessfully before euthanasia was being considered? Most people would flatly reject euthanasia as a solution for emotional problems altogether, no matter how severe the problems.

But perhaps we are considering the agony of someone who is in terrible physical pain? If so we need to know whether current powerful pain-killing medications have been tried unsuccessfully. Is it important (or perhaps essential) to the case that the person whose everlasting agony we are considering be a terminally ill patient? For if the person is a terminally ill patient, in great, untreatable physical pain, and suffering too the anguish of knowing that only death lies ahead, a stronger case for euthanasia as hurrying the inevitable might be made. But if these factors are indeed intended to be part of the argument, they must be spelled out explicitly.

The longer argumentative essay gives the writer the scope to do that. The reader cannot be expected to guess these important specifics when "everlasting agony" is mentioned. Nor is it wholly clear how euthanasia produces the solution. Is the physical pain so acute that death is clearly preferable? Or is it great emotional stress that would be eased by the knowledge that euthanasia was an option? Again the reader should not be left uncertain on this point. The writer has a duty to make his argument clear in this longer essay.

G. Mere Repeating the Argument Inadequate.

To simply repeat an argument is not an acceptable response to an objection. An argument can be repeated with new emphasis if it is not understood, but repeating it does not respond to any objection of substance. Paragraph two of the above sample essay gives us an example, but we must glance at another problem first. The objection "euthanasia is murder" does not directly affect the argument (as we have interpreted it) that euthanasia is an important option for the terminally ill. Instead it is directed against the position that euthanasia should be legalized.

Let us assume that the objection is directed at the argument and that it has substance. The student responds to the objection by repeating the argument with some elaboration. Why is this response lacking? To understand why we may glance at the model of disputation—similar to the Socratic model—that underlies our argumentative essay. This dispute has a proponent whose task is to defend a position and an opponent or questioner who seeks to show that the position is not established. The proponent states the thesis, the opponent calls it into question, and in response the proponent advances evidence or arguments in support of the thesis. The questioner then alleges that the evidence is unsound, or that even though it is sound it doesn't at all support the thesis. Then the proponent responds to the objection. The dispute continues until the proponent has important evidence or arguments that have withstood all challenges, or the questioner has successfully challenged all important evidence or arguments. The outcome is judged by a neutral third party, the examiner.

The goal of the dispute is for one party to win. But we employ this model here for a different purpose than to establish a winner—we employ it as a method of inquiry to increase our knowledge. Our knowledge may be increased by turning up new evidence in the course of the dispute, by rendering the support for a position (or its opposite) more subtle, or by laying out a chain of reasoning and inference that can support a position or defeat an argument. Simply repeating an argument (or an objection) cannot serve this goal and so is ruled out as a legitimate move in the dispute. Nicholas Rescher explains it thus:

> A disputation must be *progressive*: it must continually advance into new terrain. Since its aim is to deepen the grounding of contentions at issue, it must always endeavor to *improve* upon the reasoning already laid out, in the interests of achieving greater sophistication. Mere repetition would frustrate the aim of the enterprise.

In the light of this stricture against mere repetition, how might we repair paragraph two of the above essay fragment?

> My first argument is that euthanasia should be legalized because it is a much needed escape for a terminally ill patient who otherwise might suffer terribly before dying. An objection to this is that people benefit by enduring suffering rather than by avoiding it. Enduring suffering builds character in preparation for life's future challenges. My response is that such character building for future challenges has no application to the terminally ill patient, for whom there is no future in store, at least no earthly one.

H. Give Signposts.

In the longer essay it is advisable to give your reader one or more *signposts* summing up where you have taken her and pointing out where you are headed. This is particularly helpful after you have devoted space to clearing up some obscure point, or otherwise departed from the forward progress of your argument. The following example is a signpost for the essay fragment on police force.

> Now that we see that to call a police action brutal is to imply that excessive force was used, let me sum up the course of my argument thus far. In support of the thesis that police use too much force in U.S. cities, I cited the beating of Rodney King. To the objection that the police used appropriate force, I responded that he was unarmed and not resisting. After conceding that he did resist arrest, I responded to the objection that I cited only one case by urging that many more could be called in evidence. Now I will argue that in some cases police force escalates the level of violence.

I. Consider Objection to Stand.

The longer essay also provides the scope for you to consider an objection to your position as distinct from an objection to an argument supporting your position. An objection to your position is identical to an argument against your position. Your position must be carefully distinguished from any arguments advanced in support of it before you can take this step. This is the only way you can be clear about what it is you are considering an objection to. An argument against your position is sometimes called a counter-argument.

> Against my position that Virginia should not have a state lottery it is argued that the lottery would generate as much as $100 million annually for such worthy purposes as education or mental health without any additional taxes on our citizens. To this I respond that the lottery, unlike tax sources of revenue, bypasses the economy and thereby cheats Virginians of the benefits that would be derived from having this amount spent in the economy.

J. Consider Alternative to Position.

You can also consider an alternative to your position, which is an indirect form of objection to your position. In considering an alternative to your position you have several options:

1. You can reject the alternative position, giving a reason for this step.

> In my stand that welfare should have time limits, I specify welfare to include Aid to Families with Dependent Children (AFDC), food stamps, public or subsidized housing, Medicaid, Social Security, and unemployment insurance.
>
> As an alternative to this position an opponent contends that AFDC should be excluded. The argument is that, similar to the school lunch program, time limits are not needed for AFDC. By definition, a person ceases to be a child at age 18 and is at that time no longer eligible for assistance under AFDC. Since AFDC has an automatic time limit, no further time limit is needed.
>
> I reject this alternative. Eighteen years is a long time for any family to be on welfare. A much shorter time limit is needed—three years, for example—to encourage parents to become supporters of themselves and their child.

2. You can accept the alternative position. In doing this you may accede to your opponents reasons, or you may give your own reasons why the alternative is preferable to your original position.

> In my stand that welfare should have time limits, I specify welfare to include Aid to Families with Dependent Children (AFDC), food stamps, public or subsidized housing, Medicaid, Social Security, and unemployment insurance.
>
> An alternative position is advanced. Time limits should be restricted to true welfare programs, which are AFDC, food stamps, public or subsidized housing, and Medicaid. Social Security and unemployment compensation should be taken out because they are not true welfare programs. Social Security is financed by contributions from workers and employers, and unemployment compensation is financed by employers (sometimes with contributions from workers). Programs that are financed by recipients and employers

rather than tax revenues are not true welfare programs and should be excluded.

I accept this modification of my position. My stand is now that welfare is to have time limits, where welfare includes AFDC, food stamps, public or subsidized housing and Medicaid. The reasons given for this modification are good reasons. No one collects Social Security without having worked (or being a widow/widower or dependent of someone who has worked), and no one collects unemployment compensation without having worked.

3. You can accept some part of the modification and reject others, giving reasons for your choices at each point.

My opponent offers an alternative position, similar to my own but excluding Medicaid from the programs to be subjected to time limits. Medicaid is not a continuously used program like AFDC or food stamps. Recipients use Medicaid only when they have conditions that require medical attention. Since use of the program is sporadic or irregular, time limits are not needed.

I will modify my original position in the light of this alternative. I will keep time limits on Medicaid for those recipients who now also receive other welfare benefits like AFDC and food stamps, but in modified form. When the time limits for these programs are reached, the recipients will still be eligible for reduced benefits from Medicaid, based on their income. But I would not do away altogether with access to Medicaid in reduced form by those no longer receiving other welfare benefits. The opportunity of receiving occasional Medicaid benefits for costly medical services may prevent families from becoming totally prostrate financially and being forced to join the homeless.

K. State an Assumption.

You should state an *assumption* that is incorporated into your position or into your arguments. An explicit statement of the assumption helps you get a clearer, more precise view of your position, and it gives your reader a better understanding of that position.

The question is whether welfare should have time limits. I take the stand that it should. In my stand that welfare should have time limits, I specify welfare to include AFDC, food stamps, public or subsidized housing, and, under certain conditions, Medicaid.

In stating my position I assume that we are dealing with able-bodied welfare recipients. For example, I have not included Supplemental Security Income among the programs affected. It concerns people who are blind or otherwise physically hindered from seeking gainful employment.

4. The Longer Argumentative Essay: The Conclusion

L. Summarize the Argument.

Because of its scope, you need to summarize the course of the argument for the conclusion of your longer essay. You should remind your reader what your main arguments are, the objections and your responses. You should also remind the reader of any important modifications or clarification of your position.

M. Evaluate Your Position.

Your conclusion should also contain an evaluation, a summing up of what you have (and what you have not) established. You may do this in the course of your summary, or you may do it separately, following your summary. In the evaluation you need to state the fate of each of your important arguments:

> Does the argument survive the objections intact?
>
> Has the argument fallen to the objections?
>
> Does the argument survive in modified form? If so, remind your reader of that form.

You also need to weigh the impact of any argument against your position, or objection to your position.

Your assessment must state clearly the extent to which your thesis has or has not been established. The length of the essay allows you some scope to treat this. Here are some sample options.

> The arguments provide strong support for the stand.
>
> The thesis has been basically established, but important questions remain unanswered.
>
> The thesis has been modified, and the evidence for the modified version is strong.
>
> A different, alternative thesis has been adopted after the original thesis was dropped, and there is strong evidence for the alternative thesis.
>
> Careful review of the evidence reveals that it is insufficient to establish the thesis.

5. A Sample Longer Argumentative Essay

Should Time Limits Be Put On Welfare?

by Maria Whitworth

Welfare reform is a hot topic across the nation right now. Republicans and Democrats alike have used it as a rallying cry to get elected. The public at large is fed up with the current system and wants it changed. How can welfare be reformed though? One way is through the placement of time limits on the collection of welfare benefits. This issue is the one I will be considering in this paper. To the question "should time limits be put on welfare?" I respond "yes."

It is important to note that by welfare I am talking about federal programs such as Medicaid, AFDC, and Section 8 housing. Medicaid, which provides medical care to low-income people, accounts for 5.8 percent of all annual federal spending; Aid to Families with Dependent Children (AFDC), a program which gives monetary payments to low-income families with children where one or both parents is missing, accounts for one percent of the total; and Section 8 housing, a rental housing assistance program for the poor, accounts for .75 percent of the annual federal budget.[1] Another program that I am classifying as welfare is the Food Stamp program.

However, programs I am not considering include other nutritional programs which primarily benefit small children and Supplemental Security Income, a program that pays monthly stipends to low income elderly and disabled people. I have narrowed my scope on welfare to the four aforementioned programs because I am only concerned with how welfare reform via time limits can affect and motivate able bodied and able minded people who can work, and not senior citizens, small children, or the mentally or physically disabled. Thus, in considering why I believe time limits should be put on welfare-where welfare is defined as Medicaid, AFDC, Food Stamps, and Section 8 housing—I shall consider the exploitation resultant from the value of these benefits to the recipient, the burden placed on the taxpayers, and the motivation of the welfare recipients.

My first argument for the placement of time limits on the collection of welfare is that because the combined value of the welfare benefits is greater than what that same person would make from working 40 hours per week at minimum wage ($4.25 per hour), that person chooses not to work. Time limits would put an end to this kind of exploitation.

It might be objected that minimum wage work does not pay a person enough to

---

[1] Michael Dabrowa, "What's Up With Welfare Reform?" *Newport News—Hampton Daily Press*, (Feb. 19, 1995).

live on. Working 40 hours per week, a person earns $737 per month before taxes or approximately $589 per month after taxes. Using the city of Newport News as an example, the cheapest rent in a non high-crime area is $350 per month plus utilities for a one bedroom apartment. Add groceries, necessities (shampoo, soap, etc.), and gasoline for the car (or bus fare), and you are left with little or no money. Then if you have other bills such as car or health insurance, credit card payments, or medical bills (because you cannot afford health insurance), your expenses exceed income. If you have a family, these expenses will be even more. Thus, a person making minimum wage cannot subsist. Forcing them off welfare and into a minimum wage job would eventually force them out onto the streets and into homelessness.

While I agree with this objection, and without getting into a discussion of the adequacy of the minimum wage, I would argue that these people can take jobs that pay better than minimum wage. No one says they are limited to minimum wage work only.

Here, it may be countered that most people on welfare are unskilled or uneducated and, because they are, the only jobs available to them are the ones at minimum wage. Thus, welfare time limits just serve to punish them.

If this is indeed the case, I reply, then these people would be given the opportunity to complete a two-year degree program at a local community college or a job training program. Thus, these people, with their newly acquired skills and/or education will be able to find higher level and higher paying jobs thereby eliminating their need for welfare.

They may still be forced to accept minimum wage work, it may be countered, because that is all that is available due to economic conditions or such. Then, these people are stuck in the same predicament they were in before—a cycle that will eventually leave them out on the streets.

In a case such as that, I would argue that these people may be entitled to a reduced level of benefits while they are working that minimum wage job—just as long as they keep searching for a job in their skill area. The purpose of time limits on welfare here is to stop the exploitation and abuse caused by the recognition that the value of welfare benefits is greater than full-time minimum wage work which leads to the recipient not wanting to work. If this person has tried to find a good job and, in the end, can only find one that pays minimum wage, then he should not be punished for it, just as long as he keeps trying to find that better job.

A second argument in favor of the implementation of time limits on the collection of welfare benefits is that the decreased dependence on welfare would result in a decrease in the public's tax indebtedness.

When considering that only $755 of the $6,650 the average person currently pays in taxes each year, or approximately 11.5 percent of his total goes to welfare, it may be argued that welfare reform will not amount to much. Furthermore, the programs focused on in this essay (excluding Food Stamps) only account for 7.55 percent of the total [Based on Dabrowa's figures. See note 1 above]. Thus, unless reform amounts to elimination of these programs, the taxpayer will really not save very much due to reform.

To this I respond that even a miniscule saving to the taxpayer is still a saving. Therefore, his indebtedness has been decreased—even if it is small.

So far, I have examined some concrete reasons in favor of the implementation of time limits on the collection of welfare benefits. I discussed the problem of exploitation which results from the value of welfare benefits being greater than that of full-time minimum wage work. I addressed the fear that minimum wage cannot even support subsistence living by proposing job training or educational programs and amended benefits for those who still cannot find anything better after completion of these programs. I also addressed the issue of the decrease in the public's tax indebtedness. I will now look at a more abstract reason for the implementation of time limits on the collection of welfare benefits.

Noting that for most people it is easier to accept things as they are rather than change things, time limits can serve as a motivating force to get the person back into the work force and off of welfare. Time limits tell him that we (the public) understand that he is in a temporary situation due to unfortunate circumstances, but we believe things will get better and that he will be able to get back on his feet. Time limits serve to emphasize that welfare is only supposed to be a temporary stop-gap measure.

It may be countered that the argument presumes the person actually believes the situation is temporary and will get better. Perhaps the situation is so bleak to him that he sees no chance of improvement and, therefore, lacks the initiative or desire to try.

I would counter that if the person has no initiative, he'd better get it fast or he will be out on the street. However, if he has lost all hope and is really depressed—to the point of being clinically depressed—the objection becomes a moot point since I am only arguing for time limits being implemented on able-bodied and able-minded people. However, I would also argue that this person should be required to get mental health treatment so that he may eventually be able to straighten himself out and get off welfare.

Centering on time limits being a motivational force to get off welfare, I now have considered a more abstract argument in favor of time limitations, in addition to the previous, more concrete arguments. Before I continue further, however, I think it is important to clear up an assumption that I have made in my position. When talking about the implementation of time limits, I am talking about a period of four or five years. I realize that a time limit less than that may be unreasonable for many since they may be required to do remedial work or pre-training before being admitted to a college or training program. Furthermore, the scarcity of services such as childcare may force a parent into attending such programs only part-time. Thus, it would take longer to finish these programs.

Having cleared up that, I will now look at an objection to my position which says that time limits should not be implemented on the reception of welfare benefits. It is argued that since most people on welfare are single mothers, time limits end up punishing the children. To this objection I respond that the children would still be receiving benefits via programs such as free school lunches and WIC. If they are too young for school, the children would be eligible to participate in subsidized childcare. However, the parent would be forced to work.

Here, it would be countered that the working parent may still not be able to support her children. To this, I respond that, as discussed previously, the parent may still be eligible for some reduced benefits as long as she has gone through an education/training program and is still looking for a better job.

What about placing a time limit of two years on welfare benefits, someone else may ask. After all, this is what most Republicans in the United States Congress are advocating. It is argued that this is enough time to complete a degree or training program without allowing too much of an extra 'free time' cushion.

To this alternative position, I reply that such a short time period is unreasonable. As I have previously discussed, some people may need to attend some sort of remedial or pre-training program before they would be admitted into a two-year degree program or a job training program. Two-year limits would force them off welfare before they had successfully completed these programs and then they would be forced to live on minimum wage work—something that has been shown not to be possible. While welfare reform is needed, it should not be cruel to those who receive the benefits. A two-year limit would just amount to punishment of many individuals who have very low-level education or absolutely no skills.

In conclusion, the issue of welfare reform via time limits has been examined. The problem of exploitation which results from the value of welfare benefits being greater than that of full-time minimum wage work has been treated. The fear that minimum wage cannot even support subsistence living has been answered by proposing job training or educational programs and amended benefits for those who still cannot find anything better after completion of these programs. The issue of the decrease in the public's tax indebtedness was addressed. A more abstract reason which centered on time limits serving as a motivational force was also examined. Finally, an objection to the position and an alternative position were looked at. In none of the objections to either the arguments or the stand, nor in the alternative position did I find enough credible evidence to warrant the changing of my position. I, like most Americans, believe our welfare system needs reform and I agree that time limits are one way of doing so. I do believe the recipients should be given a period longer than the two years that is currently being pushed for. However, I do agree that welfare is a helping hand on the road to recovery and, as such, should not become a way of life for able-bodied and able-minded persons.

EXERCISE 16—2: THE LONGER ARGUMENTATIVE ESSAY

Expand one of your short argumentative essays into a longer one. In addition to what you have included already in the shorter essay, include the following:

Introductory section:

A. Explain why the topic is important

B. Sharpen up the issue

C. Contrast your stand with other stands

D. Give an overview

Main body of the essay:

E. Carefully choose first argument - not too difficult nor too easy

F. One or more points of clarification

G. No argument can be simply repeated in response to an objection

H. Give your reader one or more signposts on the argument's progress

I. Consider one or more objections to your position

J. Consider one or more alternate positions

K. Make an important assumption of your position explicit

Concluding section:

L. Summarize the course of your argument

M. Evaluate where you stand after the objections, responses, etc.

N. State clearly whether your thesis has been established

Further Reading

Three chapters of the following work are the best guide to the argumentative essay.

Jack Meiland, *College Thinking* (New York 1981), pp. 25–90.Ch. 3: Some Fundamental Concepts of Argumentation; Ch. 4: How to Write an Argumentative Paper; Ch. 5: Argumentative Writing. Some Concrete Examples.

Whether the goal of argument is rational persuasion or inquiry is discussed in these articles.

J. A. Blair & Ralph H. Johnson, "Argumentation as Dialectical," *Argumentation*, Vol. I (1987), pp. 41—56. The goal is rational persuasion.

Jack W. Meiland, "Argument as Inquiry and Argument as Persuasion," *Argumentation*, Vol. III (1989), pp. 185—196. The goal is inquiry.

Excellent analyses and insights bearing on the dialectical character of the argumentative essay are found in the following work.

Nicholas Rescher, *Dialectics* (Albany 1977).

SOLUTIONS TO SELECTED EXERCISES

CHAPTER TWO

Some Logical Relations of Statements

Exercise 2—1

4. Inconsistent. The presence of the hangman means that the prisoner will be hung, but the drawn sword and anticipated blow means that he will be beheaded. The prisoner will not be both hung and beheaded, so the statements cannot be true together.

Exercise 2—2: Part A

2. Consistent.
9. Contradiction.
12. Implication. Of course the photo could be taken from a satellite, but this seems oversubtle.

CHAPTER THREE

Consistency and Assumptions

Exercise 3—1

3. Suspicious statements.

   A. Maryland law requires the state to educate students age 6 to 16.

   B. . . . a 16-year-old student was expelled.

C. The strict expulsion policy of the Prince Georges County School Board prohibits teaching expelled students.

D. . . . this [expelled 16-year-old] student has received no tutoring or alternative instruction

Analysis:

A implies

E. All students 6-16 will be educated.

E contradicts D. The source is inconsistent.

Exercise 3—2: Part A

1. c. Assumed
3. d. Assumed
4. d. Assumed
5. b. Not assumed.

Exercise 3—2: Part B

7. Dinosaurs hatch from eggs.
13. The two states are Texas and Arkansas.

Statements not assumed:

7. Dinosaurs can be brought to life again by cloning.
13. Cities straddling state borders are usually named after both states.

CHAPTER FIVE

Arguments

Exercise 5—1

9. Fact
17. Opinion

Exercise 5—2: Part A

8. Not an argument. Request, statement of intent, and promise.

Exercise 5—2: Part B

16. Argument.

    Conclusion: [Ralegh] could not expect Winwood to risk becoming his advocate.

    Evidence: Ralegh . . . knew the plans for the Spanish Match had changed the king's views and altered the power and influence of his [Winwood's] faction.
    [He] knew . . . that Winwood's influence was waning.
    [He] knew . . . that his actions would have sorely tested Winwood at the least, at most have diminished his powers.
    The argument sounds impressive. But it is impossible to tell without more information than we are given whether it is strong or weak.

Exercise 5—3

7. Not argument but explanation. Piaget explains why what is taken for self-contradiction in children is actually not that. Reasonable explanation.

12. The argument here exonerates the woman of criminal charges.
    Premise: Either she committed the deed or she did not. (assumed)
    Premise: If she didn't commit the deed, she sinneth not. (assumed)
    Premise: If she committed the deed, she is mad.
    Premise: If she is mad, she sinneth not.
    Conclusion: She sinneth not.
    Strong argument.

Chapter Six

Argument Analysis by Diagraming

Exercise 6—1

3. <①<u>A home is more than a house</u>.> <②A home has to be lived in,> and <③a home is where your family is.>

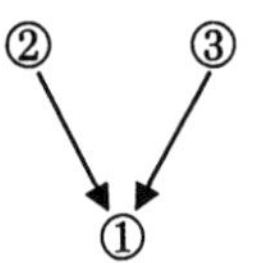

Convergent Argument
Strong

Why convergent rather than serial? Not serial because there is no tendency of ② to support ③ or vice versa. Why convergent rather than linked? ② and ③ each provide a measure of separate support for ①. ② by itself provides substantial support, as does ③. If it were linked, at least one of these would provide little or no support by itself. It would depend on the other to provide substantial support.

Why strong rather than weak? The evidence shows that we identify emotionally with "home" in ways we do not so identify with "house."

Exercise 6—2

①
4. <We totally oppose topless dancing.> [Since] <The Bible admonishes
②
that nakedness of women is very enticing to the male.>

Simple Argument
Weak

Biblical injunctions need further support to carry weight in a secular society such as ours that approves many things sexually enticing to the male, e.g., bikini beachwear. If such dancing is wrong, it is more likely to be because it degrades those who perform and watch it.

CHAPTER SEVEN

Evaluating Arguments

Exercise 7—1

①
1. <Chiffon is superior to taffeta for flounces.> <Of course it does
②
depend on the type of garment you're making.> <For a party dress it
③
is lighter in weight and livelier in appearance.>

② by itself provides no support for ①, so the argument isn't convergent. Nor does ② support ③, although both deal with restricting the claim made in ①. So the support is linked.

The argument is weak because the claim made in the conclusion is so general. It goes beyond the evidence. ② gives good reasons for chiffon being superior to taffeta for flounces in a party dress. But for the argument to be strong the conclusion would have to be qualified "on a party dress."

①
9. <The tax policy of the federal government is anti-marriage.> <A
②
spouse pays more tax on the same income than she would as a single
③
person.> <She also pays more than she would if she lived with a man

without being married to him.> <The federal government opposes
④
marriage so it will have more activities to run in the area of social

services, like food stamps.>

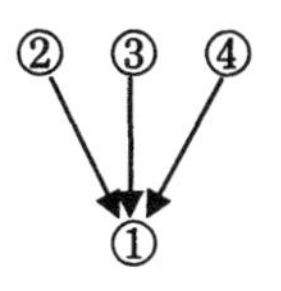

Convergent Argument
Strong

The "so" in ④ is not a conclusion cue. It introduces a purpose and is equivalent to "in order to." ④ does repeat the conclusion of the overall argument and offer new evidence. But the new evidence is weak. Unless we hold that government bureaucracy has gone completely amok, ④ is false. On the other hand ② and ③ provide sufficient support for ① to make the argument strong. We know the government uses tax policy to influence socio-economic decisions, and this counts as a specific case. This may be an inadvertent effect of a tax policy adopted for some other reason. But the evidence suffices to establish that it is anti-marriage, whether this effect was intended or not.

Exercise 7—2: Part A

4. The counter-argument appears to reduce the force of the argument considerably in this case. Rights and responsibilities are usually correlated by moral and political theorists, so that in order to have rights you must assume responsibilities that enable the rights to be realized. If a corporation avoids responsibilities on the basis of being only an artificial person, it is difficult to see how it can morally exercise the rights that are correlated with the rejected responsibilities.

Exercise 7—2: Part B

3. Counterargument: Those aren't Muslims at all. They're simply kneeling to chat and eat lunch. A weak argument, but perhaps not entirely without force. It is much in need of corroboration by other evidence like the position of the rising or setting sun, or a map of the city with an arrow indicating north.

CHAPTER EIGHT

Compound Arguments

Exercise 8—1

①
8. <The first pictures showed the bottom criss-crossed with deep gashes.>

The clear conclusion was that <the ice pack was so thick and subject
②
to such enormous pressures that "keels" of ice formed below it,

③ keels moved>
extending to the bottom.> <The ~~moving keels~~ [which] meant that
④
<oil from off-shore fields could not be brought ashore by pipelines>
⑤
since <the passing keels would cut them, sooner or later.> <Some
⑥
keels had slashed gullies in the bottom sixty miles from shore, where

the water was three hundred feet deep.>

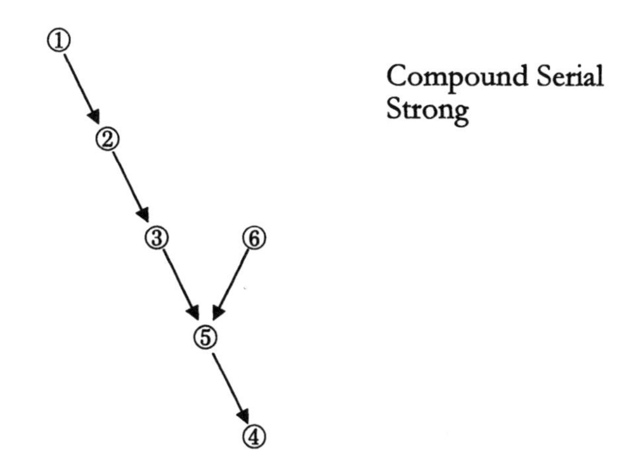

The conclusion cue shows that ① supports ②, and the premise cue that ⑤ supports ④. But why make a separate statement of ③, and let the conclusion cue show that it supports ④? Shouldn't ③ merely be a reference to ②? It adds to ② the fact that the keels moved, which is why we opt for considering it a separate statement. ④ is the final conclusion. It is what interests the writer most, and it is what the other statements can best be arranged as evidence for.

① is basic support, and ②, ③, and ⑤ are inferences from it—interpretations of the pictures. It is not clear that ⑥ is based on the same pictures, so we show it as providing separate support for ⑤. We assume it is based on similar, reliable support.

Strong argument. Given this evidence, no one would risk millions building a pipeline to test it.

①
16. <The real estate market of the Nineties is unique,> <preceded by
②
economic and demographic changes that were not present in earlier
③
cycles> and <subject to forces in the future that may prevent a

turnaround from occurring.> <In the Eighties, changes in the tax and
④
banking laws unleashed a torrent of money looking for real estate
⑤
deals.> <When the tax breaks vanished, the Japanese appeared, cash

in hand, ready to build and buy.> <Supply found demand in good form
⑥
as the baby boom filled the job market, women to the fore, and the

service economy embraced them all.> ⑦ <But these were all one-time events.>

⑧ <There are no similar demographic or economic shifts coming to refloat real estate in the Nineties.> ⑨ <The growth rate for white-collar employment is slowing,> and ⑩ <women aren't moving into the work force at the rate they once were.> . . . [Moreover] ⑪ <The recession . . . is eviscerating the very industries—financial, insurance, and retail—that drive demand for commercial space.>

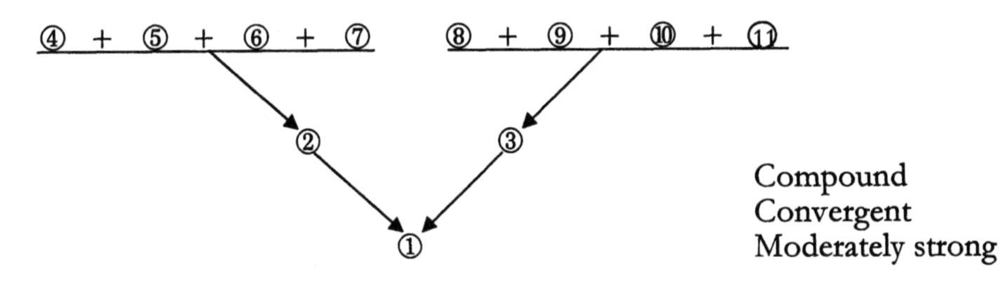

Moderately strong. Support for ② and through it for ① is strong. We can establish that the Eighties were unique in these respects by noting that no similar developments occurred in earlier decades. Support for ③ is considerably weaker. It is based on predicting what factors will most influence the commercial real estate market in the Nineties, and such predictions are notoriously difficult to make. But in a general sense it suffices to establish the uniqueness of the Eighties relative to earlier decades. If uniqueness could only be established relative to the future also, nothing would ever be established unique.

CHAPTER NINE

Clarity in Meaning

Exercise 9—1: Part B

7. Suggests that apes descended from humans; it should be the other way around. Probably means that apes and humans have a common ancestor

(in the ape family) who originated in Africa. The common ancestor of apes and humans may have originated in Africa.

13. It sounds like the diminutive police officer no longer attracts those of the opposite sex. More likely is that he lost on appeal a sex discrimination suit or sexual harassment suit. Short police officer loses the appeal of a sex discrimination case.

Exercise 9—1: Part C

10. The misused word, "appraising" means to assess the value of. The writer could mean "arresting." Closer to the misused word is "apprising," which means notifying.

Exercise 9—1: Part D

8. "Real teacher" is the source of a verbal dispute. For Linda, a real teacher encourages originality and creativity in the student. For Sandra, a real teacher enforces standards of correctness in English and other areas. A substantial dispute over what is more important for education appears to underlie the verbal dispute.

Exercise 9—2: Part B

4. Stipulative.

Exercise 9—2: Part C

10. Negative. Night is the period of darkness between sundown and sunrise.

Exercise 9—2: Part D

4. Closest to unnecessarily difficult. A person who doesn't know what a singletree is probably doesn't know what a whiffletree is either. A singletree is a pivoted swinging bar on the front of an animal-drawn vehicle that anchors the harness traces of draft animals.

12. Negative. Nitrogen is a gas without color, taste, or odor that is a chemical element, that constitutes 78% of the earth's atmosphere, and that combines to form part of all living tissue.

CHAPTER TEN

Clarity in Arguments

Exercise 10—1: Part A

3. <Every contractor is free to submit whatever bid he pleases on state construction work.>① [So] <there can be nothing wrong with contractors getting together and deciding what bid each shall submit on a state construction project.>②

① → ②

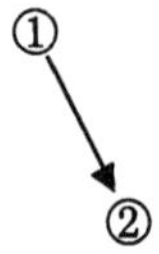

Simple—Weak Argument
Fallacy of composition

The premise ① is true. But this complete freedom to bid does not remain with the individual contractor after he has colluded with the group. The group can decide which member will submit the lowest bid, and then the lowest bid can be much higher than it would have been under the competitive conditions of each contractor bidding independently. This is called bid-rigging, which is prohibited by law.

8. <~~If we want~~ to know whether a state is brave we must look at its army,>① not [because] <the soldiers are the only brave people in the community,>② but [because] <it is only through their conduct that the courage or cowardice of the community can be manifested.>③

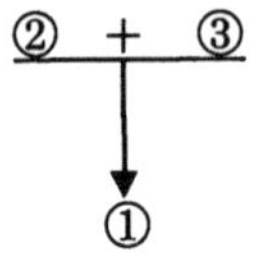

② + ③ → ①

Linked
Weak argument

③ is a false statement, and a false premise in a linked argument greatly weakens the argument. It is false that a community can manifest its courage only through the conduct of its soldiers. A community can manifest courage in the way it deals with economic hardship, an epidemic, an earthquake, or other testing circumstances.

Exercise 10—2: Part A

10. Up to this point I have tried to show clearly and convincingly how important the union is to your well-being. I have pointed out what dangers lie ahead if greed, jealousy, ambition, or deception causes it to tear apart. Now I will cite further evidence. If the path seems difficult, remember that no subject is of greater importance to a free people, that the field is large, and that sophistry has made it difficult. I will try to be brief without neglecting anything.

    I will now bring further evidence that you would be worse off without the union.

Exercise 10—2: Part B

5. ① <In communism there is no need for a state> because ② <there is no suppressed class.> ③ <Individual wrong-doers must be stopped.> ④ <But we don't need the state to do this> because ⑤ <the people themselves will do it.> ⑥ <Wrong-doing is caused by exploitation.> ⑦ <When this cause vanishes, wrong-doing will vanish also.> Since [8] [in communism exploitation, the cause of wrong-doing, vanishes,] [9] [wrong-doing vanishes too.] ⑩ <When wrong-doing vanishes, so does the state.>

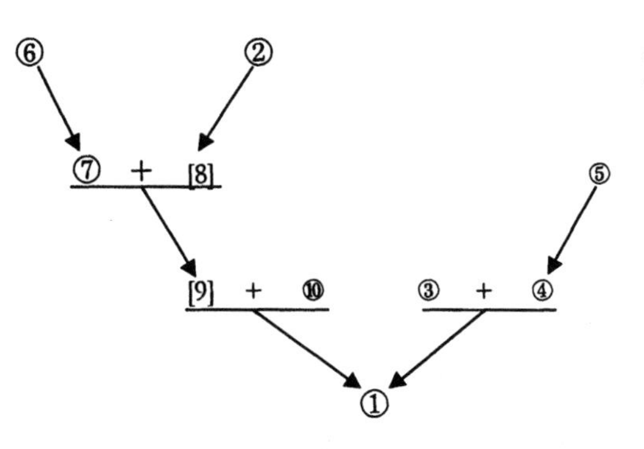

Compound Convergent
Weak

⑥ is advanced as basic support, but no evidence is put forward to substantiate that crime is due only to exploitation. Indeed this would be difficult to prove because it is so obviously false. Anger, envy, vengeance, and greed come immediately to mind as motives to commit crime, and some people commit crimes because crime yields wealth easier than honest work, and they calculate that they can get away with it.

[9] is factually inaccurate also. The Soviet Union was a communist nation for 70 years, and some Eastern European nations were communist for 40 years. Yet they all still apprehended and convicted criminals and sent them to prison.

CHAPTER ELEVEN

Context

Exercise 11—1: Part A

①   ②
5. <Man is born free.> <Yet he is everywhere in chains.>

[3]
[Therefore something happens during his life that enslaves him.]

Rousseau's thesis is that the corrupting influence of society is what enslaves men. The premises are doubtful. Infants of mothers on crack cocaine are born addicted, as infants of parents with AIDS can be born infected. Society can bind some with custom and tradition more than others, but when this is the case it is different from being in chains, even metaphorically. There is no actual paradisiacal state of nature by contrast with which society would enslave. In fact it is difficult to conceive of humans as free in a moral or political sense where society isn't the guarantor of that freedom.

①
15. <One thing you can say for sure about mom's biscuits.> <They really
②
came in handy when we didn't have any rocks to throw at tin cans.>
(premise or conclusion)

[3]
[Mom's biscuits were hard as rocks.]

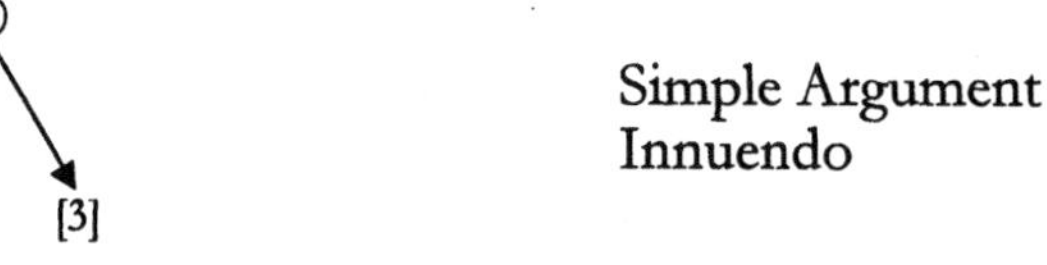

The conclusion is only hinted at, is unflattering (and quite unfilial).

Exercise 11—1: Part B

10. Never love a wild thing, Mr. Bill. . . . A hawk with a hurt wing. One time it was a full grown bobcat with a broken leg. But you can't give your heart to a wild thing: the more you do, the stronger they get. Until they're strong enough to run into the woods. Or fly into a tree. Then a taller tree. Then the sky. That's how you'll end up, Mr. Bill. If you let yourself love a wild thing. You'll end up looking at the sky. This is best paraphrased for analysis and evaluation.

① <<u>You should never love a wild thing</u>.> ② <If you love it, the wild thing gets stronger.> ③ <When it gets stronger it leaves you.> ④ <You will end up alone.> [5] [You don't want to end up alone.]

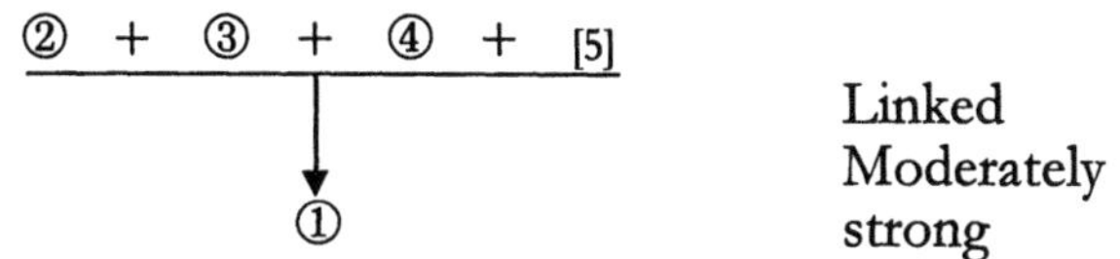

The wild creature will flee its captivity as soon as it is able. In the context of the novel this argument functions as an allegory. Holly, the wild thing, is telling her husband (Mr. Bill is a veterinarian) not to love her because she prizes her freedom.

13. (In Noel Coward's farce *Blithe Spirit* [New York, n.d.], p. 70, Charles' former wife Elvira has returned as a spirit and disapproves of Ruth, the woman Charles married after her death. Charles accuses Elvira of having an affair with the man she went with when she caught the pneumonia that killed her. She denies this. State, analyze, and evaluate each argument, supplying any missing elements.)

Chas: ① <You let him kiss you> though, didn't you?

Elvr: ② <~~How could I~~ [I couldn't] stop him.> ③ <He was bigger than I was.>

....

Elvr: ⑤ <You seem to forget *why* I went!> ⑥ <You seem to forget that you had spent the entire evening making sheep's eyes at that overblown harridan with the false pearls.>

Chas: ⑦ <A woman in Cynthia Cheviot's position would hardly wear false pearls.>

Elvr: ⑨ <They were practically all she was wearing.>

[4] [It was not my fault.] [8] [You're mistaken about sheep's eyes too.]

In this repartee or rapid, witty conversation, emphasis is on analysis and uncovering unstated material. Elvira responds initially to Charles' accusation that she let herself be kissed with the following argument.

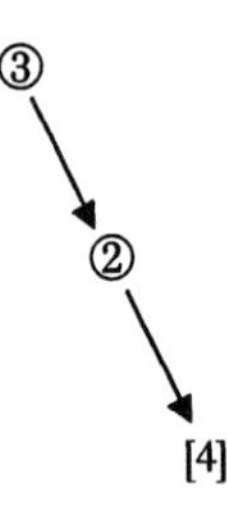

She then adds the following argument supporting the same conclusion.

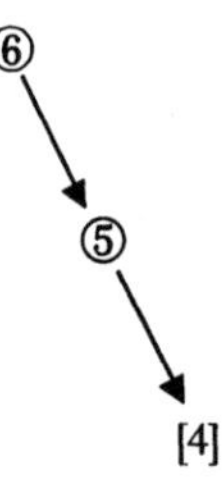

These two can be combined into the following compound convergent argument supporting Elvira's contention that getting kissed was not her fault.

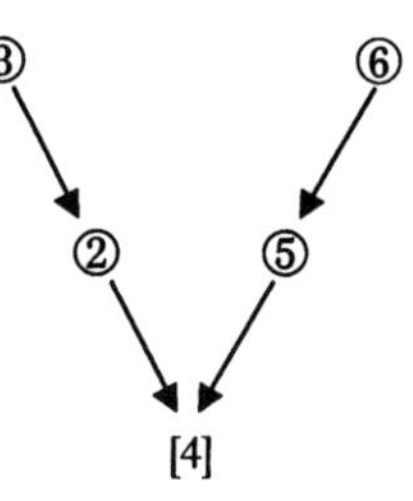

Compound Convergent

Charles now uses material from Elvira's argument to back up his initial accusation.

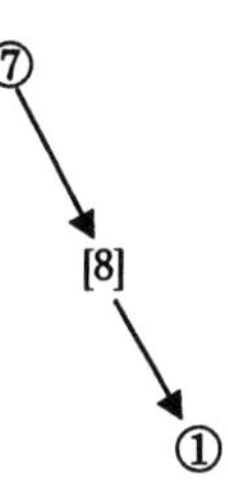

Finally Elvira rebuts and affirms with an observation statement that she wasn't at fault.

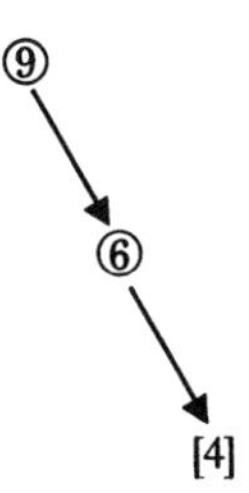

We didn't attend the party. So we need an unbiased observer to comment on Cynthia's state of dress or undress and Charles' sheep's eyes or normal eyes. Without knowing whether the basic support is sound, we can't assess these arguments.

But the compound convergent argument of Elvira is weak. Her first serial argument implies that she was forced to go along, whereas her second serial argument implies that she went along deliberately in retaliation. The two arguments are inconsistent and can yield only weak support for the conclusion.

Chapter Twelve

Relevance

Exercise 12—1: Part A

4. Not credible. The event as well as size of mosquitoes described is quite improbable, and Texans have been known to exaggerate.
9. This testimony seems trustworthy. Better follow this advice.

Exercise 12—1: Part B

3. The issue is whether Schwarz's idea of consciousness as a wound is to be taken seriously. The second speaker attacks it as testimony, citing Schwarz's bouts of insanity and suicide. But the insight—if it is one—may have come to Schwarz when he was quite sane, and it may have value as a poetic insight no matter what his mental state when it arrived. It may also be that special circumstances prevail for poets and artists—Plato contended that poetic inspiration and madness were closely related. Literature and art would be impoverished if we removed the works of those who ultimately took their own lives like Van Gogh, Hemingway, Virginia Woolf, Sylvia Plath, etc. Art, including the insights of poets, should be judged on its own merits.

Exercise 12—2: Part A

5. An illegitimate appeal to pity.

Chapter Thirteen

Mostly Conditional Arguments

Exercise 13—1: Part A

15. D
22. A

Exercise 13—1: Part B

8. true

Exercise 13—2: Part A

1.d. implied—contrapositive

3.e. not implied—converse

4.d. not implied

Exercise 13—2: Part B

10. ① <The accused woman is guilty unless the seamstress lied.> But ② <the seamstress didn't lie.> So ③ <the accused woman must be guilty.>

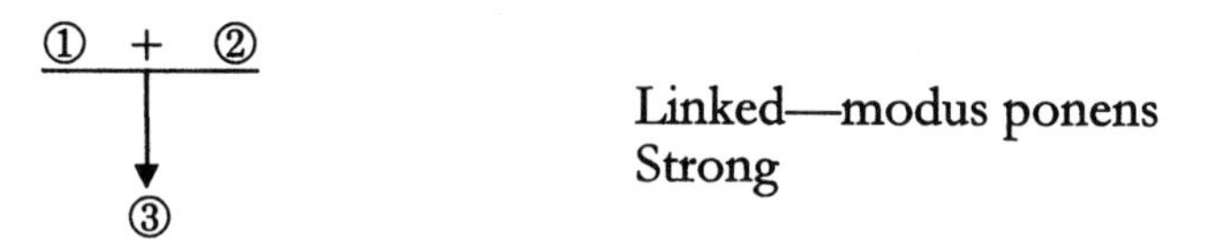

① translates into a statement beginning "if the seamstress didn't lie." ② affirms the antecedent of this statement. Strong argument, assuming the truth of the conditional statement.

14. [1] [From poetry we advance to pyping,] ② <from pyping [we advance] to playing,> ③ <from play [we advance] to pleasure,> ④ <from pleasure [we advance] to slouth,> ⑤ <from slouth [we advance] to sleepe,> ⑥ <from sleepe [we advance] to sinne,> ⑦ <from sinne [we advance] to death,> ⑧ <from death[we advance] to the Divel.> [9] [We don't want to go to the Divel.] [10] [Therefore we should not read poetry.]

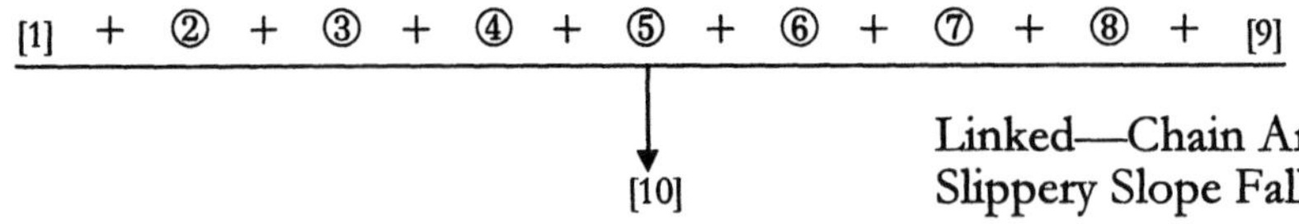

[1] + ② + ③ + ④ + ⑤ + ⑥ + ⑦ + ⑧ + [9]

↓

[10]

Linked—Chain Argument
Slippery Slope Fallacy

Weak because some of the alleged connections are dubious (e.g., how does reading poetry lead to playing music?), while others border on the unintelligible (e.g., how are sleeping and sinning necessarily connected?).

Exercise 13—3

9. ① <To judge from their neglect, people have never comprehended the power of Love.> For ② <if they had, they would have dedicated imposing temples and altars to this powerful god,> and [they would have] ③ <offered him solemn sacrifices.> ④ <But they do not do this.>

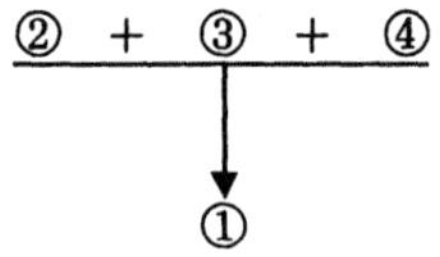

② + ③ + ④

↓

①

Linked—modus tollens
Strong

We moderns do not usually think of love as a god. So we must judge this argument on the terms of Plato's culture, where it would be strong.

16. ① <If evil is a constant presence in the human soul, it is also true that there are more souls than ever, and by that logic both good and evil are rising on a Malthusian curve, or at any rate both good and evil may be said to be increasing in the world at the same rate as the population: 1.7% per annum.> [2] [Evil is a constant presence.] [3] [There are more souls than ever.] [4] [Either both good and evil are rising on a Malthusian curve, or both are increasing in the world at the same rate as the population: 1.7% per annum.]

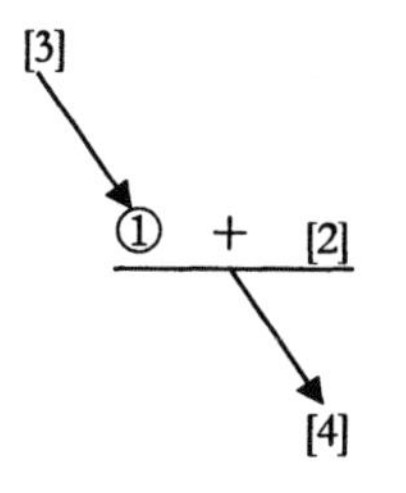

Compound linked
modus ponens
Weak

Evil, unlike energy, is not measured with the precision needed to affirm that it remains constant in some quantitative sense. So ②, which affirms the antecedent, is an unreliable claim, and the argument is weak.

①
22. On the supposition that <God is supreme over all things>
②
Xenophanes draws the conclusion that <<u>God is one</u>.> For <if there
③
were two or more gods, each of them would be supreme,> and thus
④
<in effect none of them would be supreme and best.> For <the very
⑤
meaning of God and of divine power involves supremacy over all else.>
⑥
<So far as he is not superior he is not God.>
②
To Prove: <<u>There is one god</u>.>
[7]
Assume: [There are many gods.]
[8]
[Each god is supreme.]
[9]
[To be supreme is to be not ruled by others.]
[10]
[There are not many gods.]

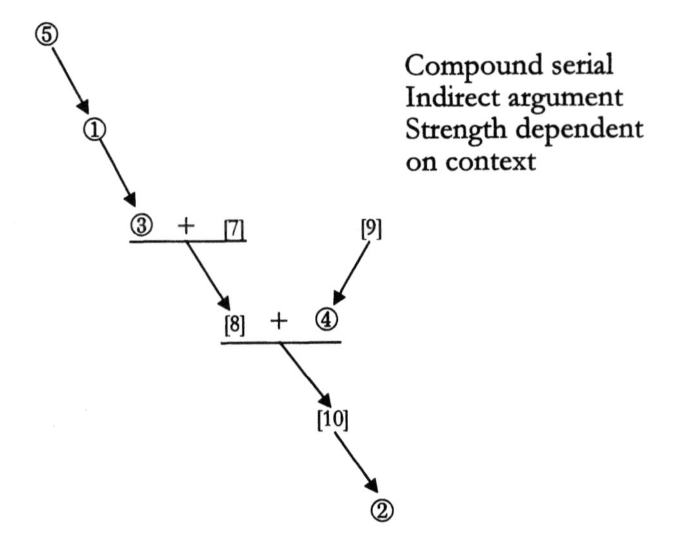

In the indirect argument the contradiction arises in the linking of [8] and ④. This supports [10], which is the negation of [7], the assumption at the basis of the indirect argument.

Structurally the argument is sound, so its strength will depend on the strength of the premises. It would probably be judged differently at the time it was advanced than it would be today. Greeks would very likely deny ⑤, a basic support statement, for it is counter to their religious beliefs. For them, gods were powerful and immortal but not supreme over all else. So the argument, which turns on this sense of "supreme," would be weak. Moderns committed to Christianity, Judaism, or Islam are more inclined to accept⑤, in which case the argument is strong.

On the historical point, how can Zeno (who flourished c. 450 B.C.) be the inventor of the indirect argument if Xenophanes (who flourished c. 540 B.C.) advanced the one we are considering here? Xenophanes is frequently cited as precursor or founder of the Eleatic school, Parmenides and Zeno being later members. Writers who hold that Xenophanes did indeed employ this indirect argument deny that Zeno invented it (e.g. Jonathan Barnes, *The Presocratic Philosophers* (London 1982), pp. 92–94, 236).

CHAPTER FOURTEEN

Inductive Arguments

Exercise 14—1

I–7. Weakens. The observations as originally described provide stronger support for the original conclusion than for this one.

II–4. Weakens. Makes the sample less diverse; the washers are now more likely all to be shipped from the same factory.

II–6. Strengthens. Adds to diversity of sample, although its contribution appears small.

Exercise 14—2

5. The analogy is of BankAmerica with an ocean liner. The focus is Armacost making changes at BankAmerica, the analogue is the captain changing the course of an ocean liner. We are not given enough information to interpret it as argument without violating the principle of charity. It is a descriptive analogy, leaning toward explanatory. More information on the trouble at BankAmerica might allow us fairly to interpret it as an explanation to justify. It would attempt to justify a slow pace of change at BankAmerica under Armacost by the analogy with the physical mass and momentum of an ocean liner. But we aren't told in this quote whether the needed changes would be short term, like increasing reserves to cover questionable loans, or long term, like becoming competitive in a new market that had been neglected.

   The joke builds on the original analogy for an opposite effect. It extends the original analogy with the focus being now the levers of a ship's steering and the analogue the personnel/policies needed for a turnaround at BankAmerica. It is a counter-analogy that affords a clever perspective on the situation. Considered as an argument it would be weak for the same reason as the original. The information provided doesn't support the conclusion.

SAMPLE STUDENT CRITICAL THINKING JOURNAL

PART A. STATEMENT RELATIONS AND INFERENCE

Section 1. Logical Relations of Statements

Student: Chris Mears
Newspaper source: *USA Today* (March 6, 1995), p. C–1.

> Swimming: Guo Qinglong, head of China's swimming association, told officials from the international governing body there will be no more illegal drug use by Chinese swimmers. Members of FINA are in China conducting an investigation prompted by positive drug tests of 11 Chinese, including two world champions, last year.

Implied statements:

A. Illegal drugs made members of China's swim team better swimmers.
B. China's swimming program is trying to clean up its act.

Contradictory statements:

A. Guo Qinglong was seen last week giving out steroids to certain members of China's swim team.
B. China's swim team was cleared by the IOC (International Olympic Committee) of any wrongdoing by tests they conducted last year.

Consistent statements:

A. The illegal drug used by the Chinese swim team was found to be steroids.
B. Drugs are becoming an increasingly bigger problem among Olympic athletes.

Student: Trista Thompson
Periodical source: *National Geographic* (May 1989), p. 571.

> Of the four known natural forces, gravity was the first seen but the least understood. The others are electromagnetism, which we know as electricity, magnetism, and light; the strong force binding atomic nuclei, and the weak force causing radioactive decay.

Implied statements:

A. Gravity's effects are the most noticeable of the four forces.
B. Electromagnetism operates in different ways.

Contradictory statements:

A. Gravity is more understood than electromagnetism.
B. Electricity was seen before gravity.

Consistent statements:

A. A falling object is a visual effect of gravity.
B. Electricity can cause light.

Section 2. Consistency Analysis

Consistent Passage

Student: Angela K. Snyder

> Say high school sports on the Peninsula and one is more likely to think of football than basketball, but high school basketball programs are slowly earning respect in the state.
>
> Kecoughtan's Warriors have already guaranteed themselves a place in the state Group AAA tournament for the third time in four years. Congratulations for a combination of talent and hard work.

Passage is consistent.

Suspicious but *Consistent* on Analysis

Student: Trista Thompson
Source: *Newport News-Hampton Daily Press* (March 2, 1995), p. A–1.

(Senate Majority Leader Bob Dole comments on the strong possibility [later a reality] that the Republicans would be unable to pass the balanced budget amendment.)

A. We may win even if we lose.
B. . . . If we lose we have the issue.

Statement A seems to be a contradiction: winning and losing are opposites. Statement B, however, explains Dole's thinking and makes the statement logically consistent.

Inconsistent on Analysis

Student: Betsey True
Source: *Newport News-Hampton Daily Press* (February 28, 1995), p. B–1.

> The fire, which investigators traced to a copying machine near the special education area of the building, damaged eight classrooms, said Rosalynne Whitaker-Heck, a spokeswoman for Newport News public schools.
> All 42 classroooms also sustained smoke damage, and some lockers were scarred by the fire, she added.

A. The fire . . . [was] traced to a copying machine . . .
B. [it] damaged eight classrooms . . .
C. All 42 classrooms also sustained smoke damage . . .
D. some lockers were scarred by the fire . . .

Statement B implies:

E. The only damage from the fire was to eight classrooms.

Statements C and D imply:

F. All the classrooms and some lockers were damaged.

The passage is inconsistent because statements E and F cannot both be true. The fire cannot have damaged only eight classrooms when it caused damage to all 42 rooms and lockers too.

Section 3. Assumptions

Student: Thanh Duong
Source: *Popular Mechanics Magazine* (February 1995), p. 17.

> After years of blueprints and blue-sky studies NASA looks ready to get serious about replacing the space shuttle. The space agency has challenged America's aerospace industry to design an experimental rocket—called the X-33—to demonstrate technologies for a next-generation commercial launch vehicle.

Assumed:

A. The space shuttle is already designed.
B. It takes time and money to replace a space shuttle.

Not assumed:

A. The space agency has canceled the project.
B. The space agency doesn't have the money to continue building the space shuttle.

Section 4. Logical Puzzles

See the logical puzzle worked in Chapter Four.

Part B. The Logic of Arguments and Inferences

Section 5. Facts and Opinions

Student: Deanna Hasenstaub
Source: *Newport News-Hampton Daily Press* (April 2, 1995).

Facts

On Sept. 1, 1939, German forces invaded Poland, setting off a conflict that, over the following six years, would visit war upon Europe, the islands of the Pacific, China, Southeast Asia, and North Africa.
Charles Leroux, "After Victory, America Changes," p. A–1.

Ricky Watters became a member of the Philadelphia Eagles on Saturday when the San Francisco 49ers refused to match a $6.9 million, three-year offer to the star running back.
"49ers let Watters go to Eagles," p. C–1.

Opinions

The only way opportunity can be equal is for two runners to start from the same spot, with the same nutrients, the same training, the same equipment.
John Young, "Equality Comes in all Shapes," p. H–1.

> Watching Phil Gramm announce for president is, for some of us, like seeing the corner hash house trying to make it as a national chain.
>
> John Young, "Phil's Place," p. H–1.

Section 6. Distinguishing Argument and Inference

Part 1. Narrative and Descriptive Writing

Student: Trista Thompson

Narrative Writing

Source: *Newport News-Hampton Daily Press* (April 19, 1995), p. C–2.

> There are days when he does not use it, but those are rare. Even then he thinks about using it, about how easy it is to buy—a telephone call and a short walk to a nearby apartment building—and how easy it is to use.

Descriptive Writing

Source: *National Geographic* (October 1987), p. 473.

> Edgerton is a small, compact man with a slight stoop. The crystal of his ancient Timex is cracked, and his serviceable suit was never fashionable. He has a shrewed glance and an abrupt way of speaking that, without his air of sunny unpretentiousness, could be brusque.

Part 2. Argument with and without cues

Student: Victoria Smith

Argument with Cues

Source: *Newport News-Hampton Daily Press* (April 9, 1995), p. I–6.

> [of architect Frank Lloyd Wright] "A lot of his work looks very familiar because so many of his designs have been studied and copied over the years," says arts center curator William Brown.

Comment: "Because" is a premise cue, so we know that what follows is the premise and what precedes is the conclusion.

Argument without Cues

Source: Mary Daniels, "New drug for pets promises help in turning back flea invasion," *Newport News-Hampton Daily Press* (April 9, 1995), p. D–3.

> "We are probably going to be inundated this year," says [Doug] Hepler [Ciba-Geigy director of research]. "Milder winters get you off to a pretty good flea season. If you have a hot, rainy summer, you are going to see a lot more fleas than if it were dry."

Comment: The last two sentences support the first. The first sentence is the conclusion and the other two are premises.

Part 3. Inference with and without cues

Student: Michael Selby

Inference with Cues

Source: "Newsbreak," *AARP Bulletin* (March 1995), p. 3.

Premise: [Labor Secretary Robert Reich] points out that while [employees] with good education and skills are doing well financially, people with poor education and skills aren't.

Premise: Moreover . . . fewer of those with poor education are getting employer-based health care and pensions.

Conclusion: Thus, education and job training matter more than ever.

Inference with No Cues

Source: *Newport News-Hampton Daily Press* (March 5, 1995), p. G–3.

Premise: I have never, ever personally known a couple to take divorce lightly.

Premise: Instead, I've seen them agonize, regret the pain it caused others, look to it as a last resort, and feel grief so tangible it twisted their insides out.

Premise: And I've never known a divorcing couple to agree on the cause in the breakdown in their marriage.

Conclusion: A failing marriage is a complex, dark place, not lending itself to legal absolutes.

Comment: Observations are usually the premises in arguments/inferences. Here that guidance seems to hold true.

Part 4. Explanation and Explanation as Justification

Student: Kathleen Wyche

Explanation

Source: *USA Today* (March 17, 1995), p. D–7.

> Fielding's Cityfax information is very well organized. It offers not only general L.A. listings, but also by neighborhood.

Comment: The first sentence tells you the information is well organized, and the second sentence explains what is meant by well organized.

Explanation as Justification

Source: *USA Today* (March 16, 1995), p. B–1.

This is being explained:
Compact pickups hold up best of all light trucks . . . according to a study by J. D. Power and Associates.

This is the explanation:
Power says small trucks probably get less abuse than big ones. Small pickups are simpler, making it less likely that something will go wrong with them.

Section 7. Diagramming and Analyzing Arguments

Simple Argument

Student: Deana Hasenstaub
Source: Thomas L. Friedman, "Keep the U.N. Strong," *New York Times*, quoted in the *Newport News-Hampton Daily Press* (March 5, 1995)

①
<The problem with the United Nations today is not that it is too strong,
②
but that it is too weak.> <It lacks the resources (and management) to do

the dirty jobs that we want done but don't want to do ourselves.>

② → ①

Simple Argument
Weak

The argument is weak because the premise doesn't justify the conclusion. It is not a sufficient explanation.

Convergent Argument

Student: Michael Selby
Source: Barrett Shaw, "The New Civil Rights," *Modern Maturity* (November–December 1994), p. 30.

(Companies are always ready to spend money on anything they think will give them a business edge: new technology, training for their employees, etc.)

Yet what many firms don't realize is that <modifying their facilities to ① serve people with disabilities is also good business:> <it opens the ② doors to a whole new contingent of dedicated and well-trained ③ employees>— and <enables a whole new contingent of paying customers to patronize their establishments.>

Premise ② and premise ③ each make good sense and offer good support to the conclusion, statement ①.

Since each premise [by itself] offers good support to the conclusion, I chose convergent.

Divergent Argument

Student: Deanna Hasenstaub
Source: "Talking too much," editorial in *Newport News-Hampton Daily Press* (March 26, 1995).

① <After Bill Clinton became president in January 1994, it didn't take long for his popularity ratings to begin to plummet.> ② <Shortly after Newt Gingrich became Speaker of the House of Representatives in January, his popularity took a dive.>

Why? ③ <Well, the one obvious thing that the two men have in common is that they are perpetual talking machines.>

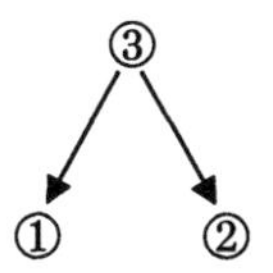

Divergent Argument
Weak

This is a weak argument because it could be made stronger with more relevant facts.

Linked Argument

Student: Betsey True
Source: *Newport News-Hampton Daily Press* (February 28, 1995), p. A–6.

① <An air bag, especially on the driver's side, is the most necessary to prevent injury.> ② <But if the bag goes off while the vehicle still has forward motion the driver cannot see where he is going, and this could be an additional hazard.> ③ <However, if the airbag were transparent, the driver could see and probably avoid further damage.>

So ④ <why not make the air bags transparent?>

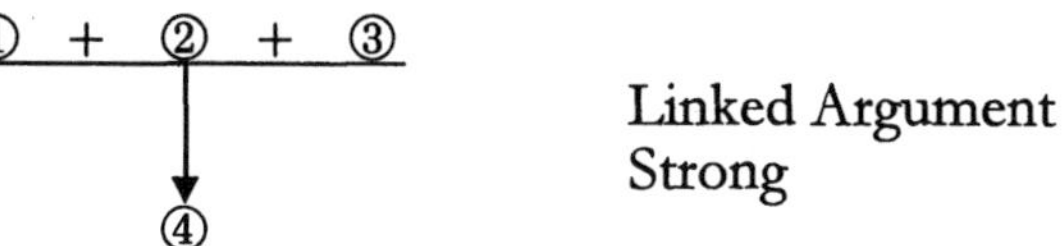

Serial Argument

Student: Victoria Smith
Source: *Newport News-Hampton Daily Press* (April 9, 1995), p. H–1.

①
<Democrats are feeling pretty good about themselves.> <The Republicans
②
have been put on the defensive in many areas.> <[One such area is] the
③
school lunch program.>

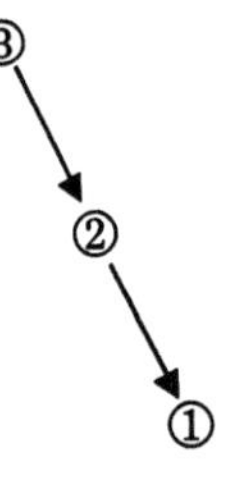

Serial Argument
Moderately Strong

The premise and intermediate sentence build a fairly strong case for the conclusion.

Part C: Compound Arguments and Context

Section 8. Assessing Compound Arguments

Compound Linked

Student: Ryder Pieratt
Source: *Mountain Bike* (July 1993), p. 57.

①
<Oakland/Berkeley area mountain bikers should consider getting active and joining BTC-East Bay.> <This bicycle access organization is well
②
connected with the East Bay Regional Park Service.> <By working within
③
the system its members have become respected players in the politics of land stewardship.> <BTC-East Bay will provide information about

④
performing trail maintenance, attending citizen advisory board meetings, and doing whatever possible to keep access legal in Sunole.>

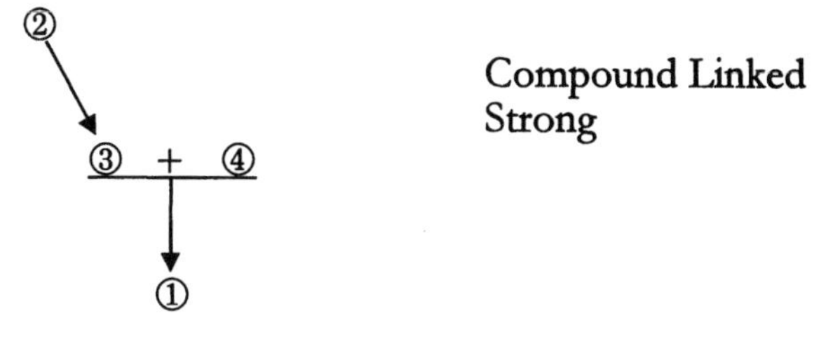

So long as the data given about this organization is true, and I assume it is, then a biker may very well want to join. In order to keep trails open, bikers should consider joining the organization in order to have place[s] to ride at all. Statements ②, ③, ④ are very good traits for a biking club to have, so the conclusion ①. ② supports ③ because by being well connected with the parks service they can more effectively work within the system.

Compound Convergent

Student: James Vance
Source: Jonathan Burgess, *The Captain's Log* (February 27, 1995), p. 3.

① <The bookstore is leeching money from the student body.> ② <The bookstore has a monopoly on books.> ③ <This means they can charge whatever they want.> ④ <If the students are "customers," then why aren't they treated as such?> ⑤ <The bookstore responds by telling the students to call the publishers and complain> and that ⑥ <they do not make much of a profit.> Is that the way ⑦ <they have made a million dollars in past years?>

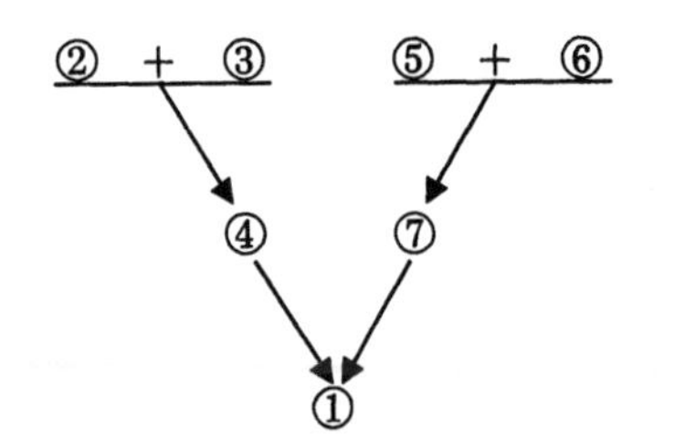

compound convergent
moderately weak

This is one of a series of arguments within a recent article in *The Captains_Log* by SGA President Jonathan Burgess. This section deals with the bookstore leeching off the student body. Linked premises ② and three advance a rhetorical question that acts as premise ④. Linked premises ⑤ and ⑥ advance ⑦ in a similar manner. These two strings converge on the conclusion, ①. The argument is moderately weak for a few reasons. The questions as support of the conclusion weakens the whole. If the information in the question was to be advanced as fact more strength would be gained. Also, premise ⑦ is somewhat ambiguous. It suggests that the bookstore has made a million dollars in past years, however, specifies neither the number of years or whether the money being made is actually profit.

Compound Serial

Student: Crystal Roberts
Source: Howard L. Nixon, II, "Reconsidering Obligatory Running and Anorexia Nervosa as Gender-Related Problems of Identity and Role Adjustment," *Journal of Sport and Social Issues*, Vol. 13 (1989).

①
The researchers also argued that <the identity crises leading to these obsessions occur earlier for females than males> because <a female's
②
self-worth is tested earlier.> <Dating, which usually begins in adolescence,
③
is a critical traditional test of a female's self-worth> because <it revolves
④ [This] ⑤
around physical appearance,> <~~which~~ is more central to a female's than to a male's self-concept.>

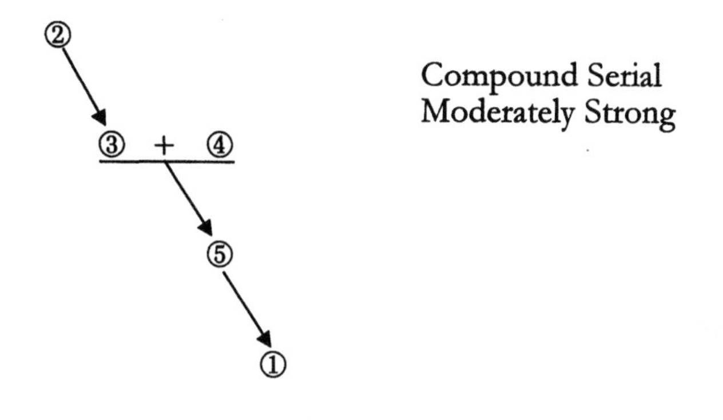

Compound Divergent

Student: Ryan Cobbins
Source: Letter to the Editor from Erik B. Pridgen, *Newport News-Hampton Daily Press* (January 22, 1995), p. H–2.

① <African Americans have been labeled as symbolic of crime, evil and death, which can corrupt the minds of our children and affect the lives of every black adult.>

<We need to address these issues more often. Neither blacks nor whites shaped this world—we're born in sin—but this world shaped the thinking of some whites.> ② <It made them believe they were superior because of the color of their skin.> ③ <It made us believe we were inferior because of the color of our skin.> ④ <They walk around with their heads poked out, we with our heads down feeling blackness is a divine curse.> ⑤

<Neither mentality is acceptable to God.> ⑥ <Both mentalities must be destroyed that life may come to both.> ⑦

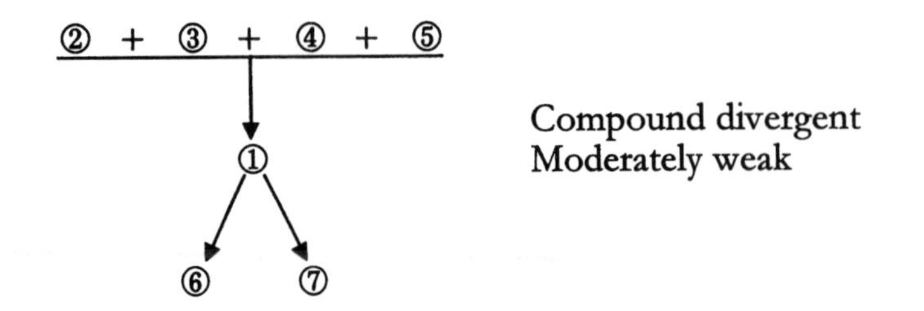

The statement, "Neither blacks nor whites shaped this world" can be argued. Some may say that whites shaped the world and produced the boundaries in which we live, making this argument moderately weak.

Section 9: Dense Arguments

Student: Jennifer Morecock
Source: Claudia Roth Pierpont, "A Critic at Large," *The New Yorker* (Aug. 31, 1992), p. 88.

The much-remarked readability of the book [*Gone With the Wind*] must have played a part in this smooth passage from the page to the screen, since "readability" has to do not only with freedom from obscurity but, paradoxically, with freedom from the actual sensation of reading—of the tug and traction of words as they move thoughts into place in the mind. Requiring, in fact, the least reading, and making the least investment in an embodying language, the most "readable" book allows its characters to slip most easily through nets of words and into other forms. Popular art has been well defined by just this effortless movement from medium to medium, which is carried out, as Leslie Fiedler observed in relation to *Uncle Tom's Cabin*, "without loss of intensity or alteration of meaning."

Paraphrase:

①
<The ease of reading the book *Gone With the Wind* played a part in

the transfer from page to screen.> <The story is enjoyable not only
②
written but seen on the screen as well.> <Its ease of reading allows
③
for its characters to slip from words to scenes very comfortably.>
④
<Popular art has been well defined by just this effortless movement

from medium to medium.> <Leslie Fiedler feels *Uncle Tom's Cabin*
⑤
moves from medium to medium without loss of intensity or meaning.>

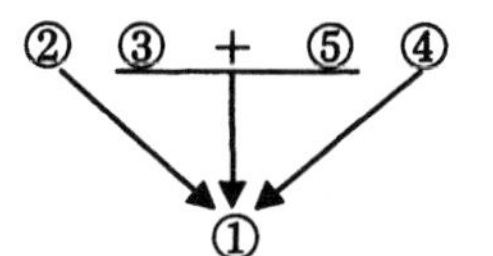

Compound Convergent
Moderately Strong

Premises seem to repeat the thesis over and over. Characters, intensity and meaning are all discussed. All these are strong elements of a book. A book that is hard to follow by reading would understandably be hard to transfer to script and screen.

Section 10. Terse Arguments—with unstated premise(s) or conclusion

Student: Ryan Cobbins

Terse Argument with Unstated Premise

Source: *Newport News-Hampton Daily Press* (January 22, 1995), p. G–3.

①
<Please remind parents to use seatbelts with preschoolers.> <Every day I see toddlers and preschool children in cars, vans and pickups who are
②
standing on the front seats or bouncing around in the back, totally without protection.> [Without the use of a seatbelt, children could
[3]
get more seriously hurt than having one on.]

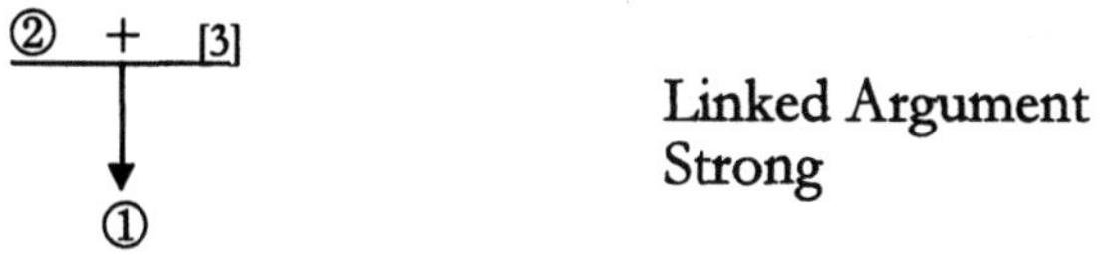

This argument is strong because it is a proven fact that seatbelts save lives.

Terse Argument with Unstated Conclusion

Student: Scott Krasche
Source: *People* (May 30, 1994), p. 47.

① <*Grace Under Fire*'s success has brought problems,> but ② <Brett Butler has seen worse.> [Therefore [3] these problems will not waylay her career.]

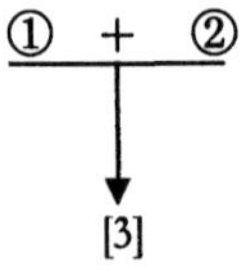

① + ②
↓
[3]

Linked Argument
Moderately Weak

This argument commits a fallacy of composition. It assumes that because a person has experienced certain hardships, they are prepared for any hardships.

Section 11. Analyzing and Evaluating Advertisements

Student Mike Anderson
Source: Full-page Hitachi TV ad from *Life* (September 1992), p. 89; caption at top: A picture so real it could fool the Audubon Society; photo of actress Jamie Lee Curtis, white cockatoo on her wrist, leaning on a Hitachi console TV; TV picture is of a white cockatoo and colored tropical birds in jungle surroundings.

① <Ultravision is an unprecedented combination of advanced technologies that create a picture so ultra clear, ultra bright and ultra sharp it looks like real life.> And since ② <a great picture deserves great sound.> ③ <Ultravision comes with 4-way Surround Sound including Dolby Pro Logic,the ultimate in audio.> [Therefore ④ <you should] Call 1-800-HITACHI for your nearest dealer> and ⑤ <[you can] see how digital convergence, fine definition and horizontal resolution up to 1,000 lines make Ultravision the ultimate home

⑥
theater.> <After all, in this case, a picture really is worth a thousand words.>

[7]
[So you should buy a Hitachi Ultravision home entertainment system.]

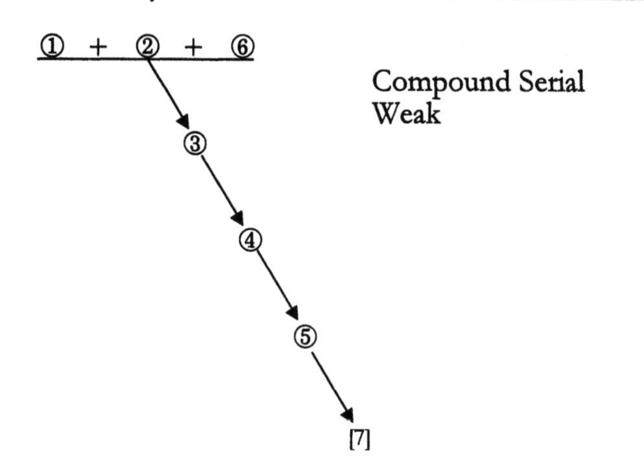

Assuming first that I do not need such a product, there does not seem to be sufficient evidence to compel me to buy this item. There is ample technical description of the Ultravision, but there is no clear explanation of what these features mean. To the uninformed, what is 4-Way Surround Sound and Dolby Pro Logic? What are the advantages of digital convergence, fine definition, and horizontal resolution up to 1,000 lines? To make this product more attractive, I think that Hitachi should use simpler language that I, the average consumer, can understand.

Supposing that I am in the market for such a product, I am still not convinced that this brand is the one that I want. How does the cost of the Hitachi Ultravision compare to a comparable product from a competing firm? With all of these advanced features, it is safe to assume that this is a rather expensive product; I will undoubtedly want to comparison shop. What proof is there that the picture of the Hitachi Ultravision is superior to that of any other comparable model? In order to further convince me that this is the brand I want, Hitachi should provide a random consumer survey that illustrates how Hitachi's Ultravision fared compared to similar products from Hitachi's competitors. If it finished at, or near the top, I would be more inclined to purchase the Ultravision.

Other questions that should be raised about the ad, whether I am in the market for such a product or not, include: How long is the warranty? In case of malfunctioning, can the console be easily serviced? If so, is there a repair center conveniently located in my area?

The validity of premise ① certainly must come into question. It is highly unlikely that any set can produce a picture that is like real life. The repetition of the adverb "ultra" in ① is an example of persuasive language, but it still does little to enhance the actual advantages of owning such a product. Therefore I believe that the ad does not supply sufficient evidence for me to purchase the Hitachi Ultravision and, hence, as an argument, the ad is relatively weak.

Glossary

Ad Hominem Ignoring the argument and instead directing attention to the person advancing it.
Affirming the Consequent, Fallacy of Fallacious argument resembling modus ponens except that the consequent rather than the antecedent of the conditional statement is affirmed.
Analogy A comparison.
Antecedent The part of an "if...then..." statement that follows the "if" and precedes the "then"; that part of a conditional statement that presents the condition.
Appeal to Authority, Fallacy of Appealing to authority in a case that should be decided by reasons or evidence.
Appeal to Pity, Fallacy of Ignoring an argument and instead appealing to sympathy.
Argument Backing up an opinion or claim with reasons or evidence; the claim that one or more statements being true makes some other statement true.
Argument Analysis Examining the premises of an argument to determine how they work together and whether they support the conclusion; (broad sense) determining whether an argument is weak or strong and for what reasons.
Argument by analogy Advancing a comparison in support of a conclusion.
Argument by inductive generalization Evidence about some members of a group advanced to support a conclusion about most or all members.
Argument Evaluation Deciding for reasons whether an argument is weak or strong.
Argument Patterns, Basic Simple, serial, divergent, convergent, and linked argument patterns.
Argumentative Essay Written inquiry into the grounds for a stand or

position on a controversial issue.
Argumentative Writing Writing in which reasons, evidence, or arguments are advanced in support of a stand on an issue.
Arrow Diagraming Drawing of arrows to display claimed support relations of an argument.
Assumption, hypothetical A statement taken for true in the absence of information or evidence to support it.
Assumption, logical A statement that must be true in order for some other statement or statements to be true.
Basic Support Premises that are not supported by any other statements in the argument.
Begging the Question, Fallacy of Assuming as a premise what the argument sets out to prove.
Burden of Proof The duty of substantiating a claim by advancing evidence in support of it.
Causal condition One event is a causal condition of another when it causes the other, or contributes to the cause of another.
Chain Argument An argument containing only conditional statements; at least one clause is common to two premises, and the conclusion contains only clauses already stated in the premises.
Complex Question, Fallacy of A question framed so that a yes or no answer elicits concessions the respondent may not want to make.
Compound Argument An argument that contains arguments of two or more basic patterns as its parts.
Conclusion That part of the argument which the premises are advanced to support; what the argument attempts to establish or prove.
Conclusion Cue A word or phrase that introduces a conclusion of an argument.
Condition One object or event is a condition of another when it causes or influences the other.
Conditional argument An argument that contains one or more conditional statements among its premises; its conclusion may also be a conditional statement.
Conditional statement A statement about a conditional relation; an "if...then..." statement.
Consequent The part of an "if...then..." statement that follows the "then"; the part of a conditional statement that presents the conditioned event.
Consistency Analysis An analysis of discourse to determine whether it is

consistent.

Consistent A relation of statements such that it is possible for all of them to be true together.

Context The situation in which an argument occurs and the discourse in which it is embedded.

Contradiction One statement making another false by virtue of its meaning.

Contraposition The operation of negating both antecedent and consequent of a conditional statement, and changing their places.

Contrapositive A conditional statement that results from contrapositing an original conditional statement; the contrapositive is true when the original statement is true.

Convergent Argument An argument with two or more premises converging on a conclusion.

Converse A conditional statement in which the subject and predicate terms have changed places.

Counter-argument An argument whose conclusion is opposed to the conclusion of another argument.

Counter-example An instance or case that is counter to a generalization and can test the strength of an argument by generalization.

Critical Thinking A practical reflective activity that has reasonable belief or action as its goal.

Cue A word or phrase used to introduce a premise or conclusion of an argument.

Dense Argument An argument in difficult prose whose meaning is tightly packed.

Dialectic A debate in which the speaker attempts to prove a proposition while a respondent argues that this proposition is not established.

Dialectical Tier The overall debate of which a stated (frequently convergent) argument is but a part; consulted for evaluating an argument and for counter-argument material.

Disjunctive argument An argument that contains a disjunctive statement as a premise.

Disjunctive statement A statement that presents alternatives; an "either...or..." statement.

Divergent Argument An argument with one premise providing direct support for two or more conclusions.

Explanation Rendering something intelligible or understandable by clarifying, simplifying, or stating the cause or function of it.

Fallacy A weak argument that can deceive some into accepting its conclusion.
Fallacy of Composition Fallacious reasoning from part to whole.
Fallacy of Division Fallacious reasoning from whole to part.
General Statement One that refers to all or most members of a group or class.
Generalization A statement about all or most members of a group based on observing only some of them.
Hypothetical Syllogism A chain argument with two premises.
Illicit Conversion The converse of a conditional statement which is not made true by that statement.
Implication One statement making another true by virtue of its meaning.
Imply (Logical sense) To make true, as in one statement implies or makes another true.
Inconsistent A relation of statements such that not all of them can be true together.
Indirect Argument A conditional argument that assumes the opposite of what it seeks to prove and tries to show that this assumption leads to a contradiction or absurdity.
Infer To draw a conclusion from given data or evidence.
Intermediate Conclusion Part of an argument receiving support from one or more premises and lending support to one or more conclusions.
Linked Argument An argument in which two or more premises are joined interdependently in support of the conclusion.
Mark Up an Argument To enclose separate statements in angle brackets, number them, encircle premise and conclusion cues, and underline final conclusions.
Modality Of an argument or of an argument conclusion: boldness or modesty of a conclusion's claim.
Modal Qualifier Word (must) or phrase (might be) that affects the modality of a conclusion.
Modus ponens A common conditional argument with one conditional statement as premise and another premise that affirms its antecedent.
Modus tollens A common conditional argument where the second premise negates the consequent of the first, which is a conditional statement.
Negating the Antecedent, Fallacy of Fallacious argument resembling modus tollens except that the antecedent rather than the consequent of the conditional statement is negated.
Necessary condition One event is a necessary condition of another when the

first must occur for the second to take place; an indispensable factor.
Only if Phrase that can introduce a necessary condition.
Paraphrase To put into other words, often in order to clarify or summarize.
Premise A statement advanced in support of the conclusion of an argument.
Premise Cue A word or phrase that introduces a premise of an argument.
Probative Relevance (Of a premise) Relates to a conclusion by tending to establish or prove it.
Reflective Thinking Thinking that observes, evaluates, and corrects itself.
Reliability Tendency of a basic support statement (premise) to be or not to be solidly based on facts or good reasons beyond the stated argument itself.
Scenario A context created for the interpretation and evaluation of an argument.
Serial Argument An argument with one premise providing basic support to an intermediate conclusion, which in turn supports a final conclusion.
Simple Argument An argument with one premise supporting a conclusion.
Slippery Slope Argument A chain argument, based on modus tollens, directed against some policy or action.
Slippery Slope Fallacy A weak slippery slope argument.
Socratic Model of Critical Thinking Critical thinking based on the method of Socrates, a 5th century B.C. Athenian philosopher who questioned theses and arguments closely.
Straw Man A fallacy where a weak position is created so that it can be defeated.
Sufficient condition One event is a sufficient condition of another when it causes or brings about the other; a sufficient condition makes what it conditions inevitable.
Support Relations Relations of premises in support of a conclusion of an argument.
Terse Argument A brief, succinct argument with one or more important factors left implicit rather than stated outright.
Unless Word that can introduce a necessary condition in the negative.
Wedge Argument A slippery slope argument.

SOURCES

Chapter One

Page 1: The Ennis quote is from "A Conception of Critical Thinking," *Conference 85 on Critical Thinking* (Newport News 1986), p. 14.

Page 3: The quote is from the *Newport News-Hampton Daily Press.* The study is by Julia H. Martin & Donna J. Tolson, published in 1986 by the Tayloe Murphy Institute in Charlottesville.

Page 4: This part of the celebrated funeral speech by Pericles is in Thucydides, *The Peloponnesian War*, Bk. II, Ch. 40 (New York 1982), p. 109f.

Page 4: G. H. Mead discusses thinking as a conversation of gestures in *Mind, Self, and Society*, ed. by Charles Morris (Chicago 1962), pp. 164–173. Socrates examines courage in Plato's dialogue *Laches.*

Page 5: Richard Paul, "Dialogical and Dialectical Thinking," in *Critical Thinking* (Rohnert Park CA 1990), pp. 245–254.

Page 5: The consensus statement is in Peter A. Facione, *Critical Thinking* (Fullerton CA 1990), p. 3.

Pages 7: The critical thinking dispositions cited are among the thirteen listed by Ennis in "A Conception," p. 35 (see note above for Page 1).

Chapter Two

Page 11: Emerson states this in "Self-Reliance," *Selected Writings of Emerson*, ed. by Donald McQuade (New York: Modern Library 1981), p. 136.

Page 13: Source for the forgery case is "Malskat and the Turkey" in Frank Arnau, *The Art of the Faker* (Boston 1961), pp. 319–335; the photo of Malskat's turkey is in Arnau, *Kunst der Fälscher der Kunst* (Düsseldorf 1960), facing p. 304.

Page 18: Problem 13 is from Crystal Snyder's Journal, Summer 2003. Problem 14 is from Jennifer Smith's Journal, Summer 2003.

Page 21: The article on species by Laura Tangley in in *US News & World Report* (Aug. 18/25, 1997), p. 79.
Page 22: The Whitman quote is from Verse 51 of "Song of Myself"; in Walt Whitman. *Poetry and Prose*, ed. by Abe Capek (Berlin 1958), p. 70.
Page 31: Bradford is in *Of Plymouth Plantation*, 1620–1647, ed. by S. E. Morison (New York 1959), p. 59.

Chapter Three
Page 37: Scriven's statement is from *Reasoning* (New York 1976), p. 31.
Page 45: Problem 1 is from Helen Dollar's Journal, Spring 2002.
Page 46: Problem 9 is from Erin Haight's Journal, Spring 2002.
Page 47: Problem 13 is from Thomas Anderson's Journal, Spring 2003.
Page 50: Problem 12 is from Kerri Glaze's Journal, Spring 2002.
Problem 13 is from Kristina Potter's Journal, Spring 2003.
Page 51: R. H. Johnson & J. A. Blair, *Logical Self-Defense*, 2nd ed. (Toronto 1983), p. 181.

Chapter Four
Page 59: C. S. Peirce, "The Fixation of Belief," Part II; in *Philosophical Writings of Peirce*, ed. by Justin Buchler (New York 1955), p. 7.
Page 63: Ennis quote same as page 1 above.
Page 67: P. F. Strawson, *Introduction to Logical Theory* (London 1963), p. 13.

Chapter Five
Page 93: *The Answer Book for Jury Service*. Prepared for Jurors in the Circuit Courts of the Commonwealth by the Judicial Council of Virginia [1989], p. 10.
Page 96: Alfred Einstein, *Mozart: His Character, His Work* (New York 1965), pp. 82, 465.
Page 98: Socrates' distinction is in Plato's dialogue *Euthyphro*, pp. 7b–7d.
Page 100: P. F. Strawson, same as p. 67 above.
Page 101f.: A. C. Doyle, *The Original Illustrated Sherlock Holmes* (Seacaucus 1983), p 63.
Page 105: John Passmore, "Explanation in Everyday Life, in Science, and in History," *History and Theory*, Vol. 2 (1962), pp. 105–123.
Page 106: The solution to this problem is in Frank Gendron, *Unexplained Patient Burns* (Brea 1985).
Eugene R. Anderson, "Lost: 75 Cents of Every Insurance Dollar," *Newport News-Hampton Daily Press* (May 9, 1986).
Page 107f.: The allergies explanation is from Amanda LaGesse's Journal, Spring 2003.
Page 110: Problem 7 is from Nicole Powell's Journal, Spring 2002.

Problem 9 is from Nicole Pace's Journal, Fall 2002.
Page 111: Problem 13 is from Jeremiah Freeman's Journal, Fall 2002.
Page 112: Howard Kahane, *Logic and Contemporary Rhetoric*, 3rd ed. (Belmont 1980), p. 3.
Page 119: Tolstoy, *The Cossacks* (Harmondsworth 1960), p. 154.

Chapter Six

Page 129f.: The collection letter example is in Stephen N. Thomas, *Practical Reasoning in Natural Language*, 3rd ed. (Englewood Cliffs 1986), p. 79.
Page 132: The KAL Flight 007 argument is in Acock, p. 90. Malcolm Acock, *Informal Logic Examples and Exercises* (Belmont, CA 1985).
Page 135: The salvage operations are described in Mel Fisher, *The Treasure of 1622* (Key West 1981).
Page 138: Thomas' proposal is on p. 61 of *Practical Reasoning in Natural Language*, 3rd ed.
Page 140f.: These examples were provided by George Teschner.
Page 153: Problem 2 is from Sharon Seltzer's Journal, Spring 1999.
The topless dancing argument is in Thomas, p. 51.
Page 154: The Hinckley argument is in Acock, p. 89.
Page 155: The Bacardi rum ad copy is in Acock, p. 73.
Page 156: This argument is in Acock, p 114.
Problem 15 is from Christin Vermiere's Journal, Spring 2003.

Chapter Seven

Page 163: The point that recognizing individual rights concerns primarily a nation's relation to its own citizens was made in class discussion by James Stevens.
Page 164f.: U.S. Department of Health and Human Services, HIV/AIDS Surveillance Report, Vol. 5, No. 2 (July 1993), p. 7.
Page 165: Figures on the poverty level are taken from the *World Book Encyclopedia* (1980 printing).
Page 167: The argument concerning Andre is in Acock, p. 74.
Jonathan Swift, *Gulliver's Travels* (New York 1958).
Page 172f.: The exchange in Ionesco, *Theatre*, Vol. I (Paris 1963), p. 24 [translation from the French by the present writer].
Page 173f.: E.C. Hammond and D. Horn, "Smoking and Death Rates," *Journal of the American Medical Association*, Vol. 166 (1958), pp. 1159–1172, 1294–1308.
Page 174: Ralph H. Johnson, *The Rise of Informal Logic* (Newport News 1996), pp. 262–266.
Page 176: *Confessions* was written about 379 A.D.; the passage is in Book VII, Chapter 6, "Refutation of Astrology." *The Confessions of St. Augustine*, trans. and annotated by J. B. Pilkington (New York 1943), pp. 141–144.

Page 182f.: The convergent argument is from Philip K. Howard, *The Death of Common Sense* (New York 1994), pp. 34-38.
Page 183f.: "Leap of support" is from Robert J. Yanal, "'Convergent' and 'Linked' Reasons," *American Philosophical Association Newsletter on Teaching Philosophy* (Summer 1984), pp. 1–3.
Page 187: Problem 3 is from Robbie Ulsh's Journal, Spring 2003.
Page 190: Problem 10 is from Lindsay Coffin's Journal, Fall 2002.
Page 191: Problem 12 is from Hope Smith's Journal, Fall 2001.

Chapter Eight

Page 193: The argument is from Emerson and Potter, *The School and Schoolmaster* (1842); quoted in Stephen N. Thomas, Practical *Reasoning in Natural Language*, 3rd ed. (Englewood Cliffs 1986), p. 80.
Page 194: *18 Best Stories by Edgar Allan Poe*, ed. by Vincent Price and Chandler Brossard (New York 1965), p. 123; used in Thomas, *Practical Reasoning*, p. 100.
Page 195f.: The rural road argument is from Gina Powell, "The Lay of the Land," *GEICO Direct* (Fall 2000), p. 9.
Page 197: The argument is adapted from Lloyd Shearer, "The Reason Why," *Parade* (Dec. 20, 1981); Quoted in Malcolm Acock, *Informal Logic Examples and Exercises* (Belmont 1985), p. 123.
Page 199: The arthroscopy argument is from *Vital Signs*, Mary Immaculate Hospital, Vol. 2, No. 1 (Newport News, Winter 1989), p. 4.
Page 216: Problem 9 is from the Journal of a student whose name was lost in copying.

Chapter Nine

Pages 233, 245f.: These captions are collected in the *Columbia Journalism Review*. Keith Johnson used them in a presentation to the Christopher Newport Philosophy Club in March 1987, taking them from a secondary source we would like to credit but have as yet been unable to trace.
Page 234: The tale of Kroesus is related in Herodotus, *The Persian Wars*, Bk. I, Chapts. 53 and 86; in the Rawlinson translation (New York 1942), pp. 27, 48.
Page 235: Richard Sheridan, *The Rivals* (Arlington Heights 1953). Mrs. Partington is quoted in Marcus Cunliffe, *The Literature of the United States*, rev. ed. (Harmondsworth 1961), p. 159f.
Page 237: Waismann, "Verifiability," in E. Nagel and R. Brandt, eds., *Meaning and Knowledge* (New York 1965), p. 40. The example is taken from this article.
Page 238: Caxton is quoted in Otto Jespersen, *Growth and Structure of the English Language*, 10th ed. (Chicago 1982), p. 63f.
Page 239: Scott, *Ivanhoe* (New York 1983), p. 35f.

Page 250: Operational definitions originated in P. W. Bridgman's scrutiny of concepts important for the special theory of relativity, in particular his attempts to link definitions of "time," "space," and "causality" to performable operations. See *The Logic of Modern Physics* (New York 1927), especially pp. 66–91.

Page 251: Aristotle, *Topics*, Bk. I, Ch. 8 (103b 14f); in *A New Aristotle Reader*, ed. by J. L. Ackrill (Oxford 1987), p. 67. This is only one aspect of Aristotle's complex account of definition.

Pages 252, 258: Wog, allibosh, pawdle, and mooble are coinages by Gelett Burgess taken from Chapter 8 on Burgessisms in Paul Dickson, *Words* (New York 1982), pp. 50–56.

Page 252: The Second College Edition of the *American Heritage Dictionary* (Boston 1991) has been consulted for this chapter and throughout. It credits the coining of "googol" to Milton Sirotto, Krasner's nephew.

Though Kaufmann's "decidophobia" is not in the dictionary cited, it is in a pamphlet *Phobias and Panic* (Rockville 1988), p. 4, prepared by the Public Health Service of the U.S. Department of Health and Human Services.

Page 252: For persuasive definitions, the pioneering work is C. L. Stevenson's *Ethics and Language* (New Haven 1944), especially pp. 206–226.

Page 254: *Dictionary of the English Language* (London: Printed by W. Strahan, 1755).

Chapter Ten

Page 263: T. E. Damer has an account of the appeal to ignorance in *Attacking Faulty Reasoning*, 2nd ed. (Belmont 1987), pp. 71–74.

Page 263: Holmes' sermon is in Paul Edwards and Arthur Pap, eds., *A Modern Introduction to Philosophy*, 3rd ed. (New York 1973), pp. 250–260; the quote is from p. 252.

Page 265: Roger Williams had been banished from the Massachusetts Bay Colony by the time he wrote *The Bloody Tenet* in 1644; *The bloudy tenent of persecution for cause of conscience discussed*, ed. by E. B. Underhill (London 1848).

Page 266: *An Enquiry Concerning Human Understanding* (1748; ed. by L .A. Selby-Bigge (Oxford 1902), p. 30. Hume's effort to justify his position is more complex and extensive than this quote suggests, occupying much of Section IV of the *Enquiry*, "Sceptical Doubts Concerning the Operations of the Understanding."

Page 266: C. L. Hamblin, *Fallacies* (Newport News 1998), p. 12.

Page 273f.: The Greenberg quote is the title of an opinion piece in the Mar. 23, 1990 *Newport News-Hampton Daily Press.*

Savage is quoted in *Newsweek* (Mar. 26, 1990), p. 13.

Page 282f.: *The Power of Words* (New York 1954), p. 259.

Page 283: "The force that drives the green fuse . . ." is from *The Collected Poems of Dylan Thomas* (New York 1957), p. 10.

The Transportation Agency is quoted in the *Newport News-Hampton Daily*

Press, Feb. 21, 1990.

Page 284: C. P. Hickman, Jr., et al., *Integrated Principles of Zoology*, 7th ed. (St. Louis 1984), p. 62; "reducing" is explained on p. 59.

Page 288: The argument is Charles Darwin's, *The Origin of the Species* (Akron n.d.), Vol. I, p. 79.

Chapter Eleven

Page 307: Nuchelmans, *Taalfilosofie: Een Inleiding* (Muiderberg 1978), p. 55; quoted in Frans H. van Eemeren and Rob Grootendorst, "[Unexpressed] Premises: Part I," *Journal of the American Forensic Association*, Vol. 19 (Fall 1982), p. 100n.

Page 309: "All Greeks are humans" is from Irving M. Copi and Carl Cohen, *Introduction to Logic*, 9th ed. (New York 1994), p. 249.

Page 309: "Beware, for I am fearless . . ." is used in Stephen N. Thomas, *Practical Reasoning in Natural Language*, 3rd ed. (Englewood Cliffs 1986), p. 77.

Page 313: The gothic horror tale is *Frankenstein* (New York 1963), the quote from p. 169.

Page 314.: "Laundromat washer" is from Margaret Atwood, *The Edible Woman* (1969), p. 94; it is used in Malcolm Acock, *Informal Logic Arguments and Exercises* (Belmont 1985), p. 89.

Page 316f.: *Newsweek* (Oct. 10, 1988), p. 73.

Page 319: From *C & P Telephone Yellow Pages* (1988), p. 416.

Page 322: Michael Scriven, *Reasoning* (New York 1976), p. 85.

Page 326: A source for the AMA Ethical Code *is Journal of the American Medical Association*, Vol. 164 (1957), p. 1119f.

Page 339: The Gatsby review is quoted from *Rotten Reviews*, ed. by Bill Henderson (New York 1988), p. 42.

Chapter Twelve

Page 359: Douglas N. Walton, "What Is a Fallacy?" *Argumentation: Across the Lines of Discipline*, ed. by F. H. van Eemeren et al. (Dordrecht 1987), p. 328.

Page 366f. The case is suggested by Alan Drury's novel, *Advise and Consent* (New York 1959).

Page 376f.: J. S. Mill, *On Liberty* in *Utilitarianism*, ed. by Mary Warnock (London 1962), pp. 163, 142f.

Crowly wrote in *The Capital Voice*, Jan. 1, 1971; his argument is quoted from Robert Baum, ed., *Ethical Arguments for Analysis*, 2nd ed. (New York 1976), p. 110.

Page 377: Traina wrote in a letter to the editor, *Newport News-Hampton Daily Press*, Jan. 19, 1991.

Page 378: The insider is Samm Sinclair Baker, *The Permissible Lie* (New York

1968), p. 16.

Page 378f.: *Death in the West* was not shown in the U.S. according to Howard Kahane. For an account of it and the source for the quote, see Kahane, *Logic and Contemporary Rhetoric.* 3rd ed. (Belmont 1980), pp. 180-182.

Page 380f.: The *Sports Illustrated* issue is Feb. 12, 1990:

A. outside back cover	B. inside back cover	C. p. 180f
D. p. 151	E. p. 145	F. p. 143
G. p. 91	H. p. 7	

The *Seventeen* issue is May 1988:

I. p. 117	J. p. 12	K. p. 101
L. p. 77	M. p. 61	N. p. 42f.
O. p. 17	P. p. 5	

Page 381: The handbill is reproduced in *Worldbook Encyclopedia*, 1979 edition, s.v. "Advertising," p. 70.

Page 382: The information on FTC activity is from Fred Luthans and Richard M. Hodgette, *Social Issues in Business*, 2nd ed. (New York 1976), p. 353f.

Page 382 For weasel words see Carl P. Wrighter, "Weasel Words," in *Speaking of English*, ed. by J. MacKillap and D. W. Cross (New York 1978), p. 216. The Advil ad is in *Newsweek*, April 16, 1990, p. 38.

Page 383: The Robitussin ad is in *For Women First*, Feb. 18, 1991, p. 38.

Chapter Thirteen

Page 399f.: This conditional statement exercise is suggested by the one in Stephen N. Thomas, *Practical Reasoning in Natural Language*, 3rd ed. (Englewood Cliffs 1986), p. 199.

Page 414f.: The Knights of Columbus source is quoted in Robert Baum, ed., *Ethical Arguments for Analysis*, 2nd ed. (New York 1976), p. 168.

Page 421f.: This indirect argument is suggested by one in Stephen F. Barker, *Elements of Logic*, 3rd ed. (New York 1980), p. 94.

Page 422f.: Zeno's four indirect arguments against motion are given in Aristotle, *Physics*, tr. H. G. Apostle (Bloomington 1969), Z9 239b5–240a18.

Page 423: Galileo, *Dialogues concerning Two New Sciences*, tr. by H. Crew and A. de Salvio (New York 1914), pp. 62–64. The sketch here is based on the account by Alec Fisher, *The Logic of Real Arguments* (New York 1988), pp. 1f., 91–98, and benefits from its sharp analysis and commentary.

Page 424 The argument about a car's worth is from P. J. O'Rourke, "How About a Dream on Wheels?" *Parade*, Oct. 5, 1986, p. 21.

Page 434: The argument about love is from the beginning of Aristophanes' speech, 189c; in Plato, *The Symposium* (Harmondsworth 1951), p. 58f.

Page 436: The RDA argument is quoted from Malcolm Acock, *Informal Logic Examples*, p. 168.

Page 445: Aquinas' Third Way, the teleological argument, is adapted from the trans. by Fathers of the English Dominican Province, Vol. I (New York 1947), p. 13; also consulted was *Basic Writings of Saint Thomas Aquinas*, ed.

by Aulin C. Pegis (New York 1945).

Chapter Fourteen

Page 449: In his *Discourses*, Joshua Reynolds speaks of generalizing as "the great glory of the human mind" (p. xcviii); Blake, whose taste in painting seems to have differed, annotated his copy: "To Generalize is to be an Idiot. To particularize is the Alone Distinction of Merit. General Knowledges are those Knowledges that Idiots possess." Blake, *Complete Writings*, ed. by Geoffrey Keynes (London 1966), p. 451.

Page 462: Denis is characterized by Johan Huizinga, *The Waning of the Middle Ages* (Harmondsworth 1968), p. 182.

Burns, *The Complete Poetical Works*, ed. by W. E. Henley & T. F. Henderson (Cambridge MA, 1897), p. 250.

Page 463: Shakespeare, *Complete Works*, ed. by Peter Alexander (London 1951), p. 920.

Boo's piece is in the *Washingtonian* (July/Aug. 1992), p. 40.

Six, "Air Train," *Scientific American* (Aug. 1992), p. 112.

Page 470: Parker's "Discourse" is reproduced *in The American Transcendentalists*, ed. by Perry Miller (Garden City 1957), pp. 106–136; the quote is from p. 110f.

Page 465: The cockfighting argument is attributed to Joe Zannino by Kathleen Maxa, writing in the *Washington Star* (Aug. 26, 1975); quoted in Robert Baum, ed., *Ethical Arguments for Analysis*, 2nd ed. (New York 1975), p. 334.

Page 467f.: The Lincoln anecdote is from Carl Sandburg, *Abraham Lincoln*, Vol. I (New York 1959), p. 121f.

Page 471: The fragment of Heraclitus is Diels-Kranz No. 5; in Charles H. Kahn, *The Art and Thought of Heraclitus* (New York 1981), p. 80f.

The boy and gun argument by Swallow is quoted in Baum, p. 142.

Page 472: Also consulted in condensing and paraphrasing Paley were the excerpt on the argument from design in *Philosophy of Religion. Selected Readings*, ed. by W. L. Rowe & W. J. Wainwright (New York 1973), pp. 149–156, and the condensed version in K. D. Moore, *Inductive Arguments. A Field Guide* (Dubuque 1986), p. 36.

Mencius is quoted in *A Source Book in Chinese Philosophy*, translated and compiled by Wing-Tsit Chan (Princeton 1963), p. 55.

Page 473: The argument about guns by Wilson is quoted from Robert P. Churchill, *Logic. An Introduction*, 2nd ed. (New York 1990), p. 377.

Chapter Fifteen

Page 479: *The Life and Selected Writings of Thomas Jefferson*, ed. by A. Koch and W. Peden (New York 1944), p. 411f.

Page 488: De Voto is quoted in his "Introduction" to *The Portable Mark Twain* (New York 1946), p. 27; Nichol in Marcus Cunliffe, *The Literature of the*

United States (Harmondsworth 1961), p. 152.
Problem 4 is adapted from Novelie Fisk, "A Modern Physician's Dilemma," senior philosophy project at Christopher Newport University presented Mar. 22, 1989.

Page 496: For an account of the White Rose by the sister of two of the resisting students who were executed, see Inge Scholl, *Die weisse Rose* (Frankfurt 1953).

Chapter Sixteen

Page 512: The argument against the lottery is quoted from Marshall Coleman, former Attorney General of Virginia, in the *Newport News-Hampton Daily Press* (May 3, 1987), Sect. I, p. 5.

Page 520: Jack W. Meiland, *College Thinking* (New York 1981), p. 78f.

Page 523: Meiland, p. 76f.

Page 525f.: This is from the beginning of James' celebrated essay "What Pragmatism Means," in *Works — Pragmatism*, ed. by F. Burkhardt (Cambridge, MA 1975), p. 27; used in Meiland, p. 27f.

Page 527f.: Nicholas Rescher, *Dialectics* (Albany 1977), p. 11.

INDEX OF NAMES

INDEX OF SUBJECTS

A

B

C

D

E

F

G

H

I

J

L

M

N

O

P

R

S

T

U

V

W